LANDMARKS OF
MODERN BRITISH DRAMA

Volume One:
The Plays of
The Sixties

ARNOLD WESKER: ROOTS

JOHN ARDEN: SERJEANT MUSGRAVE'S DANCE

HAROLD PINTER: THE CARETAKER

JOHN OSBORNE: A PATRIOT FOR ME

EDWARD BOND: SAVED

JOE ORTON: LOOT

PETER BARNES: THE RULING CLASS

in the same series

Landmarks of Modern British Drama
Volume Two: The Plays of The Seventies

LANDMARKS OF MODERN BRITISH DRAMA

VOLUME ONE:

The Plays of The Sixties

Arnold Wesker: Roots
John Arden: Serjeant Musgrave's Dance
Harold Pinter: The Caretaker
John Osborne: A Patriot For Me
Edward Bond: Saved
Joe Orton: Loot
Peter Barnes: The Ruling Class

with introductions by
Roger Cornish *and* Violet Ketels
Rutgers University   Temple University

METHUEN · LONDON and NEW YORK

This collection first published simultaneously
in hardback and as a Methuen Paperback in 1985
in Great Britain by Methuen London Ltd,
11 New Fetter Lane, London EC4P 4EE
and in the United States of America by Methuen Inc,
29 West 35th Street, New York, NY 10001.

British Library and Library of Congress Cataloging-in-Publication Data
Main entry under title:

PR

1272

.L35

1985

n.1

Landmarks of modern British drama.
Vol. 1. The plays of the sixties
1. English drama — 20th century. I. Cornish
Roger, 1934–   .   II. Ketels, Violet.
PR1272.L35 1985   822'.914'08   85–18856

ISBN 0 413 59080 1
ISBN 0 413 57260 9 (pbk.)

Printed in Great Britain
by Hazell Watson & Viney Ltd
Members of the BPCC Group
Aylesbury, Bucks

Contents

Introduction

On 8 May 1956 John Osborne's *Look Back in Anger* opened at London's Royal Court Theatre. Celebrated as 'the most vivid British play of the decade', it sparked an extraordinary renaissance in playwriting, acting, directing, and stage design. It put into the language of theatre criticism new phrases – 'kitchen sink drama' and 'angry young man'. It established a working-class milieu and made some acerbic criticism of society a dramatic staple. A generation of playwrights was emboldened by Osborne's success to write about life in the rented bed-sitters of London and the workers' cottages of grimy industrial towns across England. Gas stoves, sinks, creaking wooden chairs and bare kitchen tables replaced the earlier fashionable decors with their overstuffed comforts, velvet draperies, and stylish paintings. At last the stage was beginning to suggest the quality of life enjoyed by the majority rather than the chosen few.

Look Back in Anger reflected this majority society like a mirror, suggests Richard Courtney, with its 'drift toward anarchy, the instinctive leftishness, the automatic rejection of official attitudes, the surrealist sense of humour . . . the casual promiscuity, the sense of lacking a crusade worth fighting for'.

The play had a galvanizing effect on young writers. Arnold Wesker confides that after he saw it, he went home and wrote *Chicken Soup with Barley*. 'The extraordinary thing,' he explained,

is that we all happened round about the same time, and Osborne having Jimmy Porter say, 'There are no more brave causes left,' found a response in so many of us. Him talking about the posh Sunday papers and those bloody bells ringing on a Sunday. We were all of us somehow absorbing the same kind of atmosphere: the war had been a formative part of our lives, followed by the hope of 1945, and the general decline from then on. So that we were the generation of that decline, desperately wanting to find something, being tired of pessimism and the mediocrity, and all the energy that went into being anti-Soviet and anti-Communist.

The British theatre of the fifties was in the doldrums. It had settled into being little more than a place of fashionable diversion. The titles of American musicals regularly lit up West End marquees and guaranteed ticket sales. Drawing-room comedies and sentimental plays about the middle classes, most of them written by dramatists born before the turn of the century, dominated the nation's stages. Typical of the tone and sense of the most popular West End offerings is this brief exchange from Somerset Maugham's *The Circle:*

TEDDIE: I say, what about this tennis?
ELIZABETH: Come in. We're having a scene.
TEDDIE (*entering*): How splendid! What about?
ELIZABETH: The English language.
TEDDIE: Don't tell me you've been splitting your infinitives!

Such empty banter was commonplace in a claustrophobic theatre that created its own private and artificial world, a world of trivial pursuits, only remotely connected to the world outside the theatre.

Revivals of plays by Shaw and Galsworthy accounted for most of the weightier drama of the day, but they did not speak in the language of the day. The theatre was simply not alive. It had insulated itself against a vital part of contemporary experience, largely ignoring, for example, the post-war social revolution that was challenging traditional class barriers, especially the restless aspirations of working-class young people, enfranchised into literacy by the Education Act of 1944. The drama was backward-looking in its theatrical as well as its social forms. It had frozen into predictability. The theatres were controlled by a handful of West End impresarios, who booked plays that adhered to their model of what was commercially saleable. That model shrewdly calculated the prejudices and preferences of the middle-class, middle-aged patrons who were the typical West End audience, a segment of society allied with the ruling class, complacent about their way of life, and likely to be hostile to new ideas as unmannerly if not subversive. The drama they enjoyed was as hobbled by moral conventions and as theatrically hidebound as Victorian drama before Ibsen. Realism had displaced romantic drama as the dominant form, but it was a superficial realism trivialized by sentimentality.

Playwrights didn't think of the theatre as a social force dynamically related to the changing times. It was moribund and inert, isolated from the great drama of the past and unaffected by the adventurous drama of Western Europe, especially its lively inclination to political relevance.

Even more inhibiting was theatre censorship. Theatre managers still had to submit scripts to the Lord Chamberlain for approval. Censorship still prohibited from the stage such ordinary English words as *impotent*, *syphilis*, *abortion*, and *miscarriage*, not to mention *queer* and *fairy*.

There were a few harbingers of better things. John Whiting had won the 1951 Festival of Britain play competition with *Saint's Day*, a sober exploration of social violence. He had authored other plays exploring some of the major problems of a disintegrating society, as he saw the England of the fifties, but he had not found idioms that could catch the public ear. In 1955 the Royal Court Theatre reopened as the home of the newly formed English Stage Company. Dedicated to the discovery of new playwrights, the company advertised for new scripts and encouraged novelists to try their hand at writing for the theatre.

Such was the state of British drama when Osborne burst on the scene with *Look Back in Anger*. His brash, irreverent anti-hero sent shock waves across the establishment theatre. Endowed with his author's gift for eloquent invective, Jimmy Porter lashed out against all the social icons: authority, tradition, class distinctions, and Tory politics, among others.

Osborne's main target was the middle class, not only the proprieties of its more genteel members, but their unfeelingness. In attacking them, Osborne broke through the theatrical barriers dictated by their prejudices and smug morality. 'The theatre belongs to the middle class,' he complained. 'The middle class do not care. They must be made to care.' He would give them lessons in feeling. *Look Back in Anger* was such a lesson, and Jimmy Porter electrified audiences into feeling by the sheer energy of his language. His scornful diatribe against his wife's mother is typical:

JIMMY: There is no limit to what the middle-aged mummy will do in the holy crusade against ruffians like me. Mummy and I took one look at each other, and, from then on, the age of chivalry was dead. I knew that, to protect her innocent young, she wouldn't hesitate to cheat, lie, bully and blackmail. Threatened with me, a young man without money, background, or even looks, she'd bellow like a rhinoceros in labour – enough to make every male rhino for miles turn white, and pledge himself to celibacy. But even I under-estimated her strength. Mummy may look over-fed and flabby on the outside, but don't let that well-bred guzzler fool you. Underneath all that, she's armour plated – (*He clutches wildly for something to shock* HELENA *with.*) She's as rough as a night in a Bombay brothel and as tough as a matelot's arms.

While respectable matrons and their mates quit the theatre, offended as much by the bluntness of the language as by its sentiments, other theatre-goers, especially the young, cheered. Jimmy Porter was mean, but he was absolutely alive. And there was an audience for what he had to say. The renaissance of British theatre was on.

That renaissance is still alive and healthy, begetting new theatre voices in numbers and variety of accomplishment not matched in any other country these days. True, France produced those giant form-smashers – Beckett, Ionesco, Genet – who startled world audiences with their dread philosophies and novel dramaturgy, but, after all, Beckett is a transplanted Irishman, Ionesco an émigré Rumanian, and Genet has not produced French progeny of impressive poetic power.

Osborne, in contrast, inspired a long line of gifted English writers to choose the drama as their medium of expression. They were a new young breed, many from the working classes. Some were Oxbridge-educated, but more of them self-taught. Of the playwrights represented in Volume I of this anthology, only John Arden had a university education (at King's College, Cambridge). The others, all from working-class families, left school early, Bond at fourteen, for example, Arnold Wesker at sixteen, Peter Barnes at seventeen. They earned their living at odd jobs and drifted into playwriting by way of practical theatre work: acting, directing, stage managing. Both Joe Orton and Harold Pinter studied acting at the Royal Academy of Dramatic Arts. Wesker studied at the London School of Film Technique and wrote movie reviews. Arden aside, they were all first-generation success stories, in both professional and financial terms. They represent the breakthrough writers of the late fifties and sixties, whom John Russell Taylor called the 'first wave' of the renaissance. Osborne, Wesker, and Bond were nurtured primarily by the Royal Court Theatre. Their early plays were all produced at the Royal Court. All except Pinter were avowedly leftist. They are seven among many fine dramatists who deserve a place in this anthology. Their drama, as one critic put it, 'stunned the conditioned reflexes of centuries by which significant drama had, certainly since the seventeenth century, been associated with the upper and middle classes'.

Their central characters were like the people they had known in their childhood neighbourhoods, an underclass struggling against material and emotional deprivations, whose lives had not been regarded before as fit subject for the English stage. Such new characters and fresh themes called for fresh idioms, new patterns of stage dialogue, and new theatrical forms. The three- or four-act play structure, which for a century or more had seemed appropriate for theatre pieces, no longer seemed so. It was more and more often discarded in favour of a looser, more flexible structure of short scenes, at times interrupted by songs and poetry or other non-naturalistic devices. The changes were not merely formalistic or modish, but the consequence of a search for coherence between medium and message, new bottles for new wine. In sum, the altered perspectives of the post-World War II generation playwrights led them to reject conventional theatre forms as too closely tied to outmoded social forms. The neat patterns of the well-made play – exposition, conflict, complication, climax, and resolution, all casually connected – didn't fit the discordance, precariousness, and irrationality that the new generation saw as the underlying truth about modern life.

Like Osborne, most of the playwrights of the fifties and sixties fulminated against the British class system, entrenched authority of diverse kinds, middle-class life styles, and confirmed assumptions about everything from politics to strudel-making. They all freely borrowed, merged, or invented theatre styles and expected publicly subsidized theatres to produce their anti-establishment plays, and mass media critics to publicize them without much fault-finding comment.

Energized by their personal dissatisfaction with the capitalist system and traditional privilege, the 'first wave' playwrights were intellectually committed to the working classes, although not yet committed to doctrinaire socialism as their post-1968 successors tended to be. Nor did they sentimentalize the plight of the poor. They were far too tough-minded for that. By their uninhibited boldness and their vivid language, they recaptured for the home island some of the astonishing literary vigour of the first Elizabeth's reign. They have come to distinguish the reign of the second Elizabeth more fittingly and with greater credit than the recent skirmishes at sea in Suez ('56) and the Falklands ('83). It is surely a mark of cultural maturity when a nation esteems itself as highly for the art that crowns its science and technology as for the territory it controls. The splendour of the Elizabethan age and earlier times comes down to us more compellingly in the poetry of Shakespeare than in the chronicles of war.

Against the charge of unseemly self-trumpeting, let it be announced that the editors of these volumes are Americans with claim to the greater objectivity of family friends than family members. We especially value in the British drama of the last thirty years what seems missing from most American drama of the period: passionate concern for the quality of the national life, the energy of intelligent scepticism, and a sense of historical immediacy. The best drama represents the significant issues of life and death in its own time.

Too many contemporary American plays float adrift from the social and political realities, outside the public context against which private experience must measure itself.

For a brief time in the thirties, serious American dramatists had a strong social and political orientation that promised to revitalize American drama. They focused on some of the real and present concerns clouding the national scene, including mass unemployment and the spectre of fascism. But when the Federal Theatre Project, the first government-supported theatre in American history, ended in 1939 after only four years' existence, such themes began to disappear.

What has emerged since, of immediate relevance to the national life of America, whether in street theatre or in the special issues theatre of black identity and feminism, or in plays sparked off by the Vietnam War, has had little effect on mainstream theatre, which, like the British theatre of the early fifties, remains securely linked to the profit imperatives of commercial managers. Drama that touches a culture to the quick by exposing its painful vulnerabilities can survive only in a special nurturing climate. It must be cultivated in theatre organizations committed to artistic ideals and socially coherent purposes, to good art above good box office. Such organizations can no longer exist without the large-scale public funding traditional in Europe and inaugurated in England after the war.

Imagine English theatre without the Royal Court, the National Theatre, the Royal Shakespeare Company, and the network of regional reps! Their survival depends on the local, regional, and national arts subsidies that, instead of demanding instant financial success, permit experimentation and the possibility of excellence. There is still no comparable public subsidy or paradigmatic national theatre in the United States. American theatre remains largely one that must pay its way at the box office. Plays that are not instant hits are banished from the boards. And the theatre is doomed to follow rather than to lead public tastes.

In England the government art subsidies, established in the forties, were small at first. Nevertheless, as administered by the Arts Council, they fostered the development of non-commercial theatres across the land and proved that public support did not have to mean artistic interference.

And how serendipitous it was that Harold Wilson, leading the Labour Government in the sixties, appointed Jennie Lee Undersecretary in the Department of Education and Science, with special responsibility for the arts. Arts Council subsidies rose phenomenally. Her enlightened response to the needs of non-commercial theatre created a precedent for sizeable public funding hard to dislodge altogether even in the worst of times (as in 1985 when National Theatre director Peter Hall closed the Cottesloe Theatre because of falling subsidy). What is of primary importance is that public funding officially sealed recognition in Britain of the validity and relevance of the arts to the national purpose and image. In the decades since, Britain's theatre troupes have been venturing across seas and continents to show the colonies how it's done, in theatre at least, pridefully asserting a special eminence no competing nation has challenged. Theatre has become Britain's most exportable product, her best international emissary, and her major tourist attraction. And the envy of her American cousins!

The English Theatre of the Fifites

How did it all happen? In many ways the English theatre in the mid-fifties was unpromising. After the war many of the existing buildings were a shambles, having to be dug out of the rubble left behind by the Nazi bombings. Those buildings still standing were poorly equipped and, because of post-war fuel shortages, often very uncomfortable for actors and audiences alike. The typical theatre architecture limited staging practice to the fourth wall convention of the picture-frame stage, which had become so hospitable to the cosy intimacies of drawing-room comedy and mystery melodrama. The rigidity of the formal structures conspired with the conservative tastes of audiences to discourage change.

As this introduction has already shown, the plays that dominated the West End were substantively out of touch with the dislocations of the post-war world. They respected the taboos imposed by the Lord Chamberlain against open discussion of sex, religion, and the establishment, especially irreverent references to members of the royal family, restrictions that had been in place since the Licensing Act of 1737 established official censorship of the theatre. Of course, homosexuality, nudity, and obscenity were forbidden, but so also was much of the uninhibited language of everyday life. The frank probing of character and social environment that was liberating drama on the European continent and in America was considered bad taste, if not morbid, by the English. In his history of the English Stage Company, Terry Browne characterizes the commercial theatre of 1954-55 as 'a vast desert . . . of innocuous little plays which would provide a vehicle for a star to achieve a long and tedious run'.

Nevertheless, it is startling, from the vantage point of the eighties when British plays and playwrights dominate the American stage, to discover that Robert Warnock, editor of an anthology of modern British drama published in 1953, wrote, 'The best of England's serious dramatists in recent years have impressed American audiences as tepid and shallow, and their plays have seldom succeeded in New York.'

Something radically unexpected was stirring in England during the fifties. The country suddenly began to see its own political and cultural ferment. A novel self-awareness burst with peculiar intensity upon young writers seeking a forum for their message of dissatisfaction with things as they were. History played its role, supplying events conducive to a changing national consciousness and the new artistic vision that would express it. The demoralizing impact of the Suez fiasco had bruised the national psyche. The failures of the 1945-51 Labour government to deliver the visionary social reforms it had campaigned on helped to polarize public opinion after the bracing solidarity of the war years. In 1956 came the aborted Hungarian revolt, which foreclosed any lingering hopes for accommodation between East and West. Segments of the public traditionally at odds came together in unusual new alliances around such causes as nuclear disarmament.

The most promising developments in the post-Shavian theatre had been the poetic drama of the thirties and forties. The verse plays of W.H. Auden and Christopher Isherwood, who were frequently labelled communists and associated with the Marxist proletarian drama of the American thirties (although they were far apart in style), defended the individual against the spectre of fascist oppression and the social decadence of middle-class culture. But their disillusion with the world led them to withdraw into religious mysticism and their plays quickly faded from public notice. The expatriate American, T.S. Eliot, wrote a number of verse plays turning on crises of religious faith, *The Cocktail Party* being the most successful. The younger Christopher Fry wrote witty, poetic plays like *The Lady's Not for Burning*. Unfortunately, the verse revival proved short-lived. Audiences preferred the frothy prose of Noël Coward's *Blithe Spirit* or the cynical urbanity of Somerset Maugham's *The Constant Wife*, which mirrored the habits and morals of the English upper classes in the tradition of the comedy of manners popular since the days of Charles II.

The plays that tackled serious themes, even when they seemed critical of establishment values, did so through a rhetoric so conservative that they could be looked on as period pieces. The social reform dramas of John Galsworthy, which were occasionally revived, although they dealt with potentially inflammatory themes like labour-union strife and anti-semitism, sounded preachy. Galsworthy's naturalism was too genteel to ignite a revolution.

At the same time, several developments spurred the rejuvenation of the dramatic impulse. One was the changing relationship between the government and the arts, which had begun during the war years. After centuries of indifference, broken only by the Lord Chamberlain's occasional irritating censorship, the government launched a large-scale programme of financial aid to artistic groups. The Arts Council became a dynamic force, stimulating professional play production not only in London, but in regional and provincial companies across the land. For the first time, artistically adventurous producing groups, freed from the fear of instant bankruptcy, could experiment with plays that might not find immediate box-office success. Working committees, headed by such luminairies as Laurence Olivier, began to plan in earnest for the long-promised National Theatre. The Old Vic was to be reorganized and renovated to accommodate a permanent repertory company for the staging of the nation's classic heritage and the introduction into the mainstream of worthy new plays.

The new partnership between government and the arts was galvanizing. New theatres appeared in the provinces, among them the Belgrade, Coventry, while new companies took over older buildings, as the Bristol Old Vic took over the eighteenth-century Theatre Royal. New groups of actors and playwrights incorporated to seek funding for a variety of experimental purposes. The Royal Court, probably the theatre most responsible for the best writing in the 'first wave', was reborn as the home of the English Stage Company. The Stratford-based Royal Shakespeare Company under Peter Hall expanded into a London theatre to produce modern plays. Many of the new theatres provided alternatives to the picture-frame stage. Audiences became attuned to the excitement of theatre-in-the-round and the Elizabethan thrust stage. New plays were suddenly in demand. The climate was auspicious for Osborne and the young playwrights who rushed to follow his lead.

Joan Littlewood and the Theatre Workshop

Like the 'first wave' writers and the Royal Court theatre, yet beginning even earlier, Joan Littlewood's Theatre Workshop stimulated far-reaching changes in the British theatre after the war. Like the Royal Court, the Workshop announced objectives that sharply rejected establishment theatre standards and conventions. In the first place it was not an ad hoc producing organization putting on plays, but a collective of writers, actors, producers, technicians, and other theatre artists, guided by an aesthetic and a coherent philosophy of the relationship between theatre and society. It shared with the older Theatre Union, which it was modelled on, the conviction that drama must contribute to the struggle for peace and progress by presenting plays of social significance to the widest possible audience, especially to the theatrically starved working class.

On 8 May 1945 Joan Littlewood and a nucleus of friends, whose work in the theatre had been interrupted by the war, celebrated VE day and the forming of their Theatre Workshop. After hard weeks of training in ramshackle quarters, the company set out on a series of one-night stands and short runs in Oddfellows Halls, church basements, small theatres, and schools in the working-class sections of villages and small cities, eking out their living and production costs with their personal savings, odd jobs, and gifts. Often playing to audiences of twenty or fewer, with ticket sales rarely covering expenses, the Workshop nevertheless evolved the unique style of playing that became its trademark under the ebullient direction of Joan Littlewood.

In 1953 the Workshop moved into the Theatre Royal, Stratford, East London. Instead of taking theatre to the people, they would become part of a working-class community, in a place where they might also get the attention of the national theatre critics. Even there, however, as Harold Corbett reported, they never appealed to the working-class.

> All I could ever see were beards and duffle coats everytime I peered into the audience. It was the day of the angry young whatever. No way was there a local following, only in the sense of a few eccentrics. No solid working-class audience in any way.

The early years at the Theatre Royal were vintage years, however. Littlewood's maverick interpretations of the classics began to attract London critics. In the place of lush spectacles, which the company couldn't afford, Littlewood composed striking stage pictures and images on a more or less bare stage, ornamented only by lighting effects. She cared less for the poetry of the classics than for the meaning behind the words, as her defence of her unorthodox approach to *Henry IV* explains:

> I find the accents of Leeds, East London and Manchester as acceptable as those of St. John's Wood, Eton, or Oxford or hangovers from Edwardian dressing-rooms. It is easier to attack the Royal Family than attempt to scrape off the patina of age and the dreary respect which stifles Elizabethan verse. Shakespeare's company was made up of leary misfits, anarchists, out of work soldiers and wits who worked out their ideas in pubs and performed them as throwaways to an uninhibited pre-Puritan audience.

Her affinity with the motives and attitudes of the 'first wave' writers, especially their preference for the accents of ordinary people is clear, and many of her techniques reflected the continental influence from which mainstream British theatre seemed otherwise to be insulated.

In the same month as Osborne's *Look Back in Anger*, the Theatre

Workshop had its first landmark success with Brendan Behan's *The Quare Fellow*. Members of the cast spent weeks creating the atmosphere of prison life and exploring character relationships through improvisation before they ever saw the script. All the scripts Littlewood worked on were likely to be merely a blueprint for her own particular view of them, in any case. While the method worked admirably well with *The Quare Fellow*, its Behan successor *The Hostage*, and Shelagh Delaney's *A Taste of Honey*, which Littlewood also premiered, other kinds of plays might be damaged by it. Littlewood's refusal to consult with Brecht's assistant or to use his production notes may account for the failure of her staging of *Mother Courage*, the first major Brecht play performed in England.

Between 1959 and 1961 five Theatre Workshop productions were successfully transferred from the Theatre Royal, Stratford, to the West End. Although the financial profits were good, the ultimate consequence was the disintegration of the company, as the lure of the West End drew off many of the best players, and the continuity of the collective, its unique strength, was lost.

The last hurrah was Littlewood's return in 1963 to stage her most distinguished production, *Oh What a Lovely War*. The script was a group creation, built around songs popular during the First World War. According to Clive Barker, Littlewood rejected scripts showing what life was really like in the trenches, on the assumption that everyone already knew war is horrible. Instead she meant the piece to be 'a celebration of human resourcefulness in the face of the most appalling catastrophic conditions'. As Littlewood herself explained, 'There were no rehearsals as they are known. There was a collection of individuals, more of an anti-group than a group, working on ideas, on songs, on settings, on facts.' One of Littlewood's most striking effects was a back screen running the width of the stage, on which flashed in moving lights the terrifying statistics of the war: ten thousand men lost, a hundred yards gained. This is the production, with its episodic structure, its distancing effects, and its interfusion of songs into the action, that critics identify as an early outstanding example of the Brechtian influence on English drama.

Though Littlewood returned in 1972 for a final season, the company had long before collapsed because it never secured adequate funding. Littlewood summed up her ideal and its failure: 'I think the theatre should be as important as public libraries, art galleries and education. We are forced to export our shows to the West End and are always losing our companies. We are hamstrung by the money-grubbing commercialism of the West End.'

The story of the Theatre Workshop is familiar. The company suffered the problems of all enterprises that do not fit accepted patterns. It faced the inevitable bias against a theatre with avowedly political interests. A group theatre with a political conscience was doubly suspect. The coarse-grained, occasionally vulgar acting, the absence of standard spectacle in many of the plays, the lusty high-spiritedness of the company's approach to the classics, threatened the staid establishment, which had to be co-opted if the theatre was to survive.

At some points the legacy of the Workshop matches the influence of the English Stage Company. Both helped to increase the acceptance of a novel social and political focus on the underclass. Both subordinated individual elements of production to the meaning of the whole, although Littlewood's tampering with the playwright's text would have been anathema to the ESC, so committedly a writer's theatre. Minimal staging, whether born of economic necessity or artistic design, was an important policy for both.

Some critics attribute the singing, dancing, and use of music in 'straight plays' to Littlewood's example. Harold Hobson credits her with breaking up the focus of the British theatre by stimulating an internal revolution. Creating the text by group collaboration is commonplace now. Perhaps, too, her pioneering of theatre outside London encouraged the development of the fringe and provincial theatres that flourished in her wake.

The Royal Court Theatre and the English Stage Company

On 2 April 1956 the English Stage Company took up residence at the newly re-opened Royal Court Theatre, London, and announced itself as a writers' theatre committed to the production of new English plays. As George Devine, the ESC's first artistic director, quickly discovered, there were few interesting new English plays available. He and his young associate Tony Richardson solicited novelists for scripts, with disappointing results. Then they advertised in the *Stage* newspaper. Among the six or seven hundred scripts submitted was John Osborne's *Look Back in Anger*, which was to change theatre history.

The play had already been rejected by twenty-five managers and agents by the time George Devine rowed himself out to the barge where Osborne was living to announce that *Look Back in Anger* would be the third production at the Court.

It was not an instant success. Some reviewers were derisive. One called Osborne's Jimmy Porter a 'ruffian and an intellectual upstart who was doing the unthinkable in the drawing-room, threatening the good manners and comfortable illusions of middle-class life'. Terence Rattigan, whose establishment accents along with those of T.S. Eliot, Christopher Fry, and Somerset Maugham, were under fire, was personally affronted. He accused Osborne of yelling, 'Look, Ma, how unlike Terence Rattigan I'm being.' Laurence Olivier, later to star in Osborne's *The Entertainer*, asked why the Royal Court was doing such 'rubbish'. And Somerset Maugham announced grandly of Osborne and his play, 'They are slum'.

Nevertheless, after a twenty-minute excerpt was shown on television, audiences began to flock to it. Laudatory reviews by Harold Hobson and Kenneth Tynan helped. The play won the 1956 *Evening Standard* Award and both Osborne and the English Stage company were launched. As Richard Findlater wrote, ever since that auspicious first season, the ESC has had 'the most persistently seminal, significantly productive and stubbornly controversial place in the British, perhaps in the Western, theatre'. It has remained 'a catalyst of change, a centre of experiment, a nursery of excellence and the focus of a legend'.

Originally formed by writer Ronald Duncan and three friends as a festival service, touring non-commercial plays to the provinces, the ESC transferred to a permanent home at the Royal Court Theatre, thanks to the brokering, among others, of Albert Esdaile, his manager, Oscar Lewenstein, and a wealthy textile magnate, Neville Blond.

A mixture of public subsidy, private philanthropy and loans, supplemented by occasional box office profits, more often from revivals than new plays, kept the theatre going for its first decade. John Osborne's plays were especially lucrative. *Look Back in Anger*, revived three times in the company's second year, took in at the box office almost twice as much as its nearest competitor, William Wycherley's *The Country Wife*, an established Restoration comedy. However, consistent public subsidy, which has steadily increased, has been essential to the company's survival.

There were early skirmishes with the Lord Chamberlain. Prohibitions on political, religious, and sexual honesty were still being imposed when what Frederick Lumley called the 'Royal Court Revolution of 1956' began. The scathing frankness of Jimmy Porter's language was natural, Osborne insisted, for a character 'who speaks out of the real despair, frustrations, and sufferings of the age we are living in, now, at this moment'. The Royal Court Theatre staunchly supported his position and used the strategem of private club performances to keep Osborne's *A Patriot for Me* and other offending plays on view. In 1965 the ploy failed in the case of Edward Bond's *Saved*. The Lord Chamberlain demanded extensive cuts. The police visited the theatre, and summonses were issued against the staff and William Gaskill, who had become artistic director. Offended citizens wrote letters to the London *Times*. Most of the critics were hostile. The play, they charged, was obscene, gratuitously violent, and dangerously radical in its apparent sympathy for its homicidal and feckless characters. While the magistrate found against the company, the small fine he levied and the minor reprimand were really a moral victory that hastened the end of censorship.

The fact is that by 1966 the intellectual climate of the English theatre had changed. Osborne and the 'angry young men' in his wake had made a difference. Thanks to the ESC's persisting willingness to resist the Lord Chamberlain, Bond's *Early Morning*, banned in toto because it pictured Queen Victoria in a lesbian relationship with Florence Nightingale, was the last play in England to be censored. The Theatres Act of 1968 abolished the office of the Lord Chamberlain and ended censorship altogether. The ESC celebrated by staging a whole season of Bond plays.

The happy resolution of the censorship battles meant that public subsidy no longer implied artistic control. The shaky launching of *Look Back in Anger* contributed to wider public recognition of the fact that the best plays may not instantly draw sufficient box office to keep them running or to encourage their authors to continue writing. Plays that break new ground may need a sheltering theatre organization like the ESC and perceptive critics like Hobson and Tynan, to broker them through initial public resistance.

Look Back in Anger proved the viability of the stage as a platform for airing the new perspectives of a rising generation of writers. Suddenly, previously excluded young people discovered a ticket to the cultural mainstream. As the writers among them shifted from journalism, film, and novel into playwriting, rebellious anti-heroes in the wake of Jimmy Porter, with their boorish behaviour and demotic speech, became fashionable, dispelling the prevailing myth that the theatre had to be genteel.

This is not to suggest that writers like Arnold Wesker, John Arden, Harold Pinter, and Edward Bond simply fell to imitating Osborne. But they were emboldened by his success to use the stage to express their own artistic vision, often the fairly direct interpretation of the life they had actually lived, hearing the bombs drop on London during the blitz or trying to find a warm place in post-war society. Probably not since the medieval mystery plays had the unglamorous, the under-privileged, and the alienated, held centre-stage in such numbers. Certainly never before had so many varieties of stage language and theatrical styles assaulted the settled tastes of theatre audiences.

Many of the new playwrights first produced at the Royal Court went on to win international acclaim. Even an incomplete roster of writers who had early work staged there proves the crucial role of the Royal Court in Britain's theatre renaissance: Osborne and Bond, of course, and in addition, Arnold Wesker, John Arden, Joe Orton, David Storey, Christopher Hampton, David Hare, Howard Brenton, Brian Friel, Athol Fugard, Caryl Churchill, Howard Barker, Peter Barnes, and David Edgar. They were all viewed with alarm at first; yet most have transferred successfully to mainstream theatre and commercial success.

Perhaps the ESC's most significant contribution to English drama has been the firm belief of the artists most closely associated with it that theatre has to be about something. The liberal, humanist atmosphere the company created allowed the theatre to become 'a laboratory for expressing the connections between society and theatrical conscience'. Because it reflected the social and political contexts of its time, the Royal Court Theatre helped business men and journalists, educators, and other influential persons outside the theatre world to see the theatre as an art with a greater cultural potential than that ordinarily associated with show business. As a result, mainstream theatre in England is more substantive and adventurous than it might have been if the ESC had not existed. The company educated new audiences, and helped to broaden public tastes.

In its Sunday night productions without decor, the ESC tried out new plays and new directors. The company set up a Writers

Group and commissioned new plays, innovations copied by other groups. The theatre invited Olivier and other established stars to try new kinds of roles and acting styles there. The filmed versions of such ESC plays as *Look Back in Anger, The Entertainer, The Knack* and *The Long and the Short and the Tall* along with other films written or directed – or acted in – by people associated with the Royal Court all helped the de-gentrification of the British cinema signalled by films such as *Saturday Night and Sunday Morning*.

Another important achievement of the Royal Court was the very special and nurturing climate it offered to the artists who thronged there. Osborne fondly recalls his experience at the Royal Court as ideal for a young playwright. For ten years after the production of *Look Back in Anger*, Osborne was a member of the Royal Court 'family', housed and fed when he needed to be, employed as script reader, actor, director, and, when things got toughest, buoyed by the unflagging support of George Devine. 'You always knew he was on the writer's side', Osborne said of him. 'No one gave you that feeling before, and I've seldom had it since. It wasn't indulgent. It was inspirational support'.

The Royal Court is a continuing story of a theatre and a company that pioneered in risk-taking in order to revitalize the whole of English theatre. It has kept faith with its commitment to find and develop new English writers. The Royal Court Theatre has been, as John Russell Taylor wrote, 'as far as any one place has, the home of new drama in Britain'.

The Royal Shakespeare Company

In 1960 Peter Hall became director of the Shakespeare Memorial Theatre in Straford-upon-Avon, the little market town where Shakespeare was born and died. On his appointment, Hall immediately set out to fulfil a dream he shared with many of his predecessors: the forming of a permanent company of actors who could develop a distinctive, unified style worthy of the Shakespeare tradition, yet modern enough to awaken generations of new playgoers into enthusiasm for the greatest playwright in the language. What Hall wanted was a highly trained group of actors, regularly playing Shakespeare, but keeping their modern sensibilities acute through work on modern plays. Only so, he believed, could they express Shakespeare's meaning in terms that modern audiences could understand.

That goal, Hall announced in his first policy statement, required the immediate acquisition of a theatre in London (in addition to the one in Stratford), long-term contracts for actors, ongoing actor training classes and substantial public subsidy on a continuing basis. Hall had witnessed first-hand the value of full subsidy for theatre during his National Service stint in Germany: 'Very poor the Germans were . . . although there wasn't enough to eat and drink, they still had their theatres and opera houses!' His boldest schemes counted on the notion that 'a continual sense of drama and energy surrounding the company's activities' would attract the necessary funding. He was right. The volume and quality of RSC work, as he calculated, simply couldn't be ignored.

The choice of Peter Hall to supply vigorous entreprenurial leadership was logical. Only twenty-nine, he was already an eminent director. He had earned his credentials with the theatre work he began at Cambridge and continued with the Elizabethan Theatre Company, formed by Oxford and Cambridge students to tour Shakespeare plays. More impressive and attention-getting was his direction of the 1955 premiere at the London Arts Theatre of Samuel Beckett's *Waiting for Godot,* an event that alone would have entered Hall's name into theatre history. For, as many critics have since agreed, the London opening of *Waiting for Godot* 'was as much a theatrical revolution as the Royal Court productions of *Look Back in Anger* a year later'. All the old ideas of what theatre is about were shattered overnight. Although the opening night reviews were hostile, the Sunday columns of critics Harold Hobson and Kenneth Tynan turned public opinion around.

Hall's theatrical vision was comprehensive and daring. He wanted to create a theatre that would rank with the great theatres of the world. And he was mindful that all of them, from the Moscow Art Theatre to the Comédie Française to the Berliner Ensemble, were state-subsidized. His overall plans were very costly and the story of his tenure has in it the same frustrating struggles to become and remain solvent, notwithstanding generous public grants, that we've already traced in the Royal Court story and Joan Littlewood's Theatre Workshop.

Hall clung tenaciously to a principle theatre managers have frequently had to compromise: 'We're not running this company to make money,' he declared early on. 'We try to lose as little as possible, but we believe that the company we are trying to create is impossible to run on a commercial basis. We cannot be activated by the profit principle'. That principle, boldly professed, plunged the theatre into threatening competition with other non-commercial theatre ventures (including the National Theatre project, which had not yet come to fruition) for public funds. Actually, the precedent of Hall's success probably speeded up the formation of the National Theatre.

In 1961, prompted by Hall and his associates, Buckingham Palace announced that the Shakespeare Memorial Theatre would thenceforth be called the Royal Shakespeare Theatre and the company the Royal Shakespeare Company, a strategic name change that helped legitimize the company's claim to public subsidy as a national treasure. In the same year, however, the National Theatre project was suddenly revived. The government released funds ear-marked for a proposed merging of the Old Vic Theatre, the Stratford RSC Company, and Sadler's Wells into one national complex. Such a merger would have derailed the RSC from its ambitious course. Fortunately for Hall's grand scheme, he was able to withdraw the RSC on the persuasive argument that the Stratford tradition might be lost in such an amalgam.

In spite of bedevilment during his first two seasons by some critics, who seemed alarmed at his tampering with hallowed Stratford tradition, Hall moved swiftly ahead. Stratford was to remain the locus of the major productions of Shakespeare and his contemporaries. The Aldwych Theatre in London was leased for the presentation of modern plays and the transfer of selected Shakespeare plays. And the company would commission new plays by promising young writers.

In 1962 Hall appointed Michel St. Denis to develop the theatre's actor-training activities. A truly great theatre man with international prestige as a teacher and artistic consultant, St. Denis introduced European techniques into the company's work. His studio became a workshop for everyone at the RSC, writers, as well as actors and designers. Several months later, Hall added Peter Brook to the governing triumvirate with special responsibility for experimental work in writing and production. Brook was already celebrated as a brilliant theatre innovator for the daring theatricality that was his trademark: fiercely stark staging that was suggestive rather than realistic, and irreverently contemporary interpretations of Shakespeare texts. His approach was consistent with Hall's avowed policy: to give classic plays immediacy for a modern audience and to make Shakespeare 'an experience that reverberates with the thoughts and feelings of today'.

Hall's approach to staging had in common with the approach of the Royal Court Theatre a preference for simplicity: 'a style in which visual effects would remain secondary to the speaking actor'. As at the Royal Court, simplicity was a way to ensure the primacy of the playwright and his play in the theatre. Under John Bury, who had learned his craft as designer for Littlewood's Theatre Workshop, where constant financial stringencies required that designs be minimal and sets be improvised out of the cheapest possible materials, simplicity, then, became the hallmark. Bury's RSC designs, worked out in discussions with the director, were built around a central image. 'One can take a bit of stone in one's hand and say – this is *Hamlet* . . .,' explained Bury. Scenic elements existed for specific purposes, an austerity happily consonant with Hall's directorial style, in which each incorporated movement was chosen to serve the text.

Many of the spectacular RSC successes between 1962 and 1968 represent milestones in the theatre as well as in the history of the RSC. The 1962 production of *King Lear*, directed by Peter Brook, was the most extreme example of Shakespearean immediacy that the company achieved. Lear, played by Paul Scofield, appeared to have much more in common with the ragged derelicts of Samuel Beckett than with the kings, even the fallen ones, ordinarily encountered in Shakespeare. Moreover, the harsh and unforgiving world of the play was more pronouncedly grotesque than tragic, a world again, like Beckett's, 'in a constant state of decomposition'. At the same time, Brooks' staging showed a marked Brechtian influence, with its harsh white stage lighting and its frank exposure of the metal thunder sheets, and in its devices for abruptly shattering any sympathy or identification on the part of the audience.

In sum, the RSC contributions to the theatre renaissance include stunning experiments in staging style and interpretation that pushed back the boundaries of theatre and challenged the conventional relationship between theatre and society. Hall's *Hamlet*, for instance, with its view of Hamlet and Ophelia as beleaguered youngsters bewildered into impotent apathy by their oppressive elders, attracted a cult following of teenagers. Brooks' 1964 Theatre of Cruelty experiment, which included the staging of *Marat/Sade* by Peter Weiss, 'made rapid and varied use of every imaginable technique, dramatic device, stage picture, form of movement, speech, and song' to assault audiences emotionally so that they could not remain aloof from the play or undisturbed by its implications. The asylum world of the play represented 'the mergings of political and psychological action which derives from Europe's experience of the Nazi death camp'. *US* examined the early stages of America's role in the Vietnam War. Such plays insisted on the connections between politics and life, between art and society. More and more British playwrights felt free to use the confrontational techniques that break down audience detachment and to politicize their dramatic content.

The RSC helped to encourage new and emerging playwrights. The first new play the company commissioned was John Whiting's *The Devils*, a play of epic scale that no commercial management in 1961 would have staged. Saluted by many critics as a masterpiece, the play vindicated the commitment of the RSC and, later, the National Theatre, to the idea of a large permanent company, allowing playwrights to give full reign to their imaginations without prior considerations of staging, casting, or thematic restrictions.

While the RSC did not discover Harold Pinter, he won his mark as one of the great playwrights of the century during the decade that his plays, all directed by Peter Hall, were on view at the RSC's London theatre. Hall's willingness to innovate staging forms to fit a play's unique demands made him an ideal Pinter director. For, as Ronald Bryden observed, 'Pinter's characters have . . . an animal instinct for "territory", spatial possession of the actual area on which they battle. To have the last word coincides with dominating the stage; the actor who ends upstaging the rest has established his barnyard dominion over them like a cock on a dunghill'. Like Brooks' Theatre of Cruelty, Pinter's plays depend on body language, stage imagery, silence and non-word sounds as legitimate theatre communication.

Among the other 'first wave' playwrights whose careers were launched or bolstered by RSC productions in its first decade were David Rudkin (in a sensational production of the bizarrely violent *Afore Night Come*), David Mercer, Simon Gray, Charles Wood and Giles Cooper.

A feisty, provocative spirit animated the writers and other theatre artists in the late fifties and sixties. Peter Hall's characterization of himself applies equally well to them and their vision of the theatre: 'I am a radical,' he said. 'I could not work in the theatre if I were not. The theatre must question everything and disturb its audience'.

The National Theatre

The idea of a national theatre was first proposed in 1848. Yet not until a hundred and twenty-five years later did it actually come into being as part of the contemporary theatre renaissance. The evolution of that renaissance is largely a story of non-commercial theatres. Three of them influential in the creation and shaping of the National already existed in modest form in the 1880s. The Shakespeare Memorial Theatre had opened in 1879. In 1880 the first woman member of the London City Council turned an 'old bloodbath melodrama house' into a temperance amusement-hall. That hall became the Old Vic and, eventually, the first (and temporary) home of the National Theatre. Finally, the Royal Court Theatre, later to be the home of the English Stage Company, was built in Sloane Square in 1888.

In 1962 Sir Laurence Olivier was appointed first artistic director of the newly-formed National Theatre. An actor of surpassing gifts and accomplishments, at the peak of his career, a national hero of sorts, he had prestige enough to launch an ambitious project auspiciously. In a triumvirate with Ralph Richardson and John Burrell, Olivier had run the Old Vic company in the forties. Olivier's Richard III and Richardson's Peer Gynt are a legendary part of the boast that the Old Vic was the best acting company in the world.

More to the point, Olivier was able to bridge the gap between the traditional and the avant-garde. Although on first viewing he had disliked *Look Back in Anger,* he had been lured back to the Royal Court for a second look and had become converted to the new wave plays. Playing Archie Rice, the seedy music-hall comedian of Osborne's *The Entertainer,* he was the first major establishment star to appear with the English Stage Company. The experience was important to the development of the National because it drew Olivier into the Royal Court circle, where he absorbed some of its enthusiasm for new themes and styles. In addition, he raided the company for actors and directors to run the National.

Olivier opened the first season of the National at the Old Vic with *Hamlet* starring Peter O'Toole on 22 October 1962. But fourteen years would elapse and Olivier would step down before the National would move to its permanent home. In the meantime, the new National proclaimed a more sweeping manifesto than either the English Stage company or the Royal Shakespeare Company. 'Our aim,' said spokesman Kenneth Tynan, the theatre's first literary manager, 'is the best of everything'. Everything implied a spectrum of world drama in the tradition of such notable national theatre show-pieces as the Royal Dramatic Theatre in Stockholm and the Schiller Theatre in West Berlin.

Tynan, one of the most brilliant critics of his generation, had early championed the 'angry young men', beginning with Osborne. A theatre reviewer for the *Observer*, he had fought bourgeois morality in the theatre and crusaded fiercely against censorship. After writing an unfavourable review of an Olivier play at Chichester, he applied to Olivier for the post of literary manager and was appointed, a measure of Olivier's shrewd ability to be objective in the National's interest.

The inner core of the National Theatre, in addition to Olivier and Tynan, consisted of two directors who brought sharply contrasting sensibilities to the shaping of initial company policy: John Dexter and William Gaskill. Both were graduates of the Royal Court, the first in a series of artists who migrated to the National – and to the RSC, for that matter – after internships with the English Stage Company. Gaskill was the most 'committed' director in the narrow political sense and in his directorial views. Inspired by Brecht, he hoped to mould the National Theatre Company into a coordinated acting team without stars, working toward a better understanding of society through art.

Dexter was a practical craftsman whose reputation was founded on his productions of Wesker plays, particularly *The Kitchen* and *Chips with Everything*. It was Dexter who discovered and directed, in 1964, the first new play produced by the National – Peter Shaffer's *The Royal Hunt of the Sun*. Its success at the Old Vic, where the National Theatre was still housed, matched the success of the epic plays being staged by the RSC and led to an ongoing professional connection between Dexter and Shaffer, rather like the Hall-Pinter collaboration at the RSC.

In its first seasons, the National also produced new plays by John Arden and Tom Stoppard. Following *Hamlet*, Olivier directed and starred in *Othello*, playing the role as a quintessential symbol of blackness, 'a pompous, word-spinning, arrogant black general'. In September 1965, taking advantage of a moment when Khrushchev was thawing out international relations, Olivier took the play to Moscow for two-and-a-half weeks at the Kremlin Theatre. Russians fought for tickets, wept and cheered during the play, and hurled flowers onto the stage during certain calls. The Moscow visit, as Elsom and Tomalin report in their history of the National Theatre, 'demonstrated the value of having a company which could, in some way, represent Britain. It was breaking down international barriers of culture and thought. . . . The National was behaving like a National'.

Olivier's artistic openness coupled with Tynan's revolutionary zeal brought to public debate the issue of the changing relationship between theatre and society. The National, after all, represented the national culture. Conservative opinion on the Theatre Board was not enthusiastic about Tynan's inclination to recommend plays hostile to the government and the British establishment. Other members were prepared to support his conviction that what was happening on the stage might well be connected with what was happening in the world outside, in the great tradition, as Tynan argued, of the Greeks and Shakespeare. The question, raised with special intensity over the propriety of staging the allegedly anti-Churchill play, *Soldiers* by German writer Rolf Hochhuth, was equivocally resolved. The play went on, but not in the National, and the impression remained that the National Theatre Board and other regional and local boards might in future make more cautious appointments to the top posts of publicly subsidized theatres in order to preclude similar disagreements from arising. After all, as Elsom and Tomalin point out, what Tynan urged was dangerous to the system. Shakespeare and the Greeks had argued the great issues as defenders of their societies.

Olivier left behind a legacy of excellence, a prestigious state-supported theatre as willing to listen to new theatre voices as to pay tribute to past masters. He passed along to Peter Hall, his successor, the open issue of whether a national theatre should have social relevance. The perennial question remains: Should theatre be a library and a museum or an organic part of society, directing as well as reflecting change?

European Influences

Two signal theatrical events imported from the continent in the mid-fifties played a crucial role in the direction taken by the British theatre: the 1955 production of Samuel Beckett's *Waiting for Godot* at the Arts Theatre in London, under the direction of Peter Hall, and the 1956 visit of Bertolt Brecht's Berliner Ensemble to the Palace Theatre. The Theatre of the Absurd and the Epic Theatre had crossed the Channel.

Direct influences are hard to identify precisely, and perhaps these two events, representing the two main wings of the European avant-garde, encouraged tendencies already transforming the British theatre rather more than they instigated them.

In a 1963 *Tulane Drama Review*, Martin Esslin predicted a fusion of the twin influences of Brecht and Beckett and pointed out it was already visible in the plays of John Arden, specifically in *Serjeant Musgrave's Dance* and *The Happy Haven*, as well as in the plays of Pinter. And why not, Esslin asks, since the Brechtian epic theatre and the Beckettian theatre of the absurd spring from common roots: the general cultural and spiritual malaise of the age.

Brecht and Beckett both reject naturalist staging and its implications that literal verisimilitude in speech or setting is an authentic representation of reality. Both are anti-bourgeois in their social attitudes. Both question the validity of language itself as a reliable means of communication. For Brecht language must be interpreted situationally, which is to say politically. Capitalists and workers using the same words mean different things. For Beckett the psychological or ontological isolation of all human beings gives their language private nuances indecipherable by others.

Their disparate views of life suggest polar possibilities in a post-nuclear age. In Beckett, the universe is shrunken, claustrophobic; individuals huddle in dread inside their own skins, helpless in the face of imminent doom to do anything except go on surviving. The repetition of meaningless daily rituals depletes all their energies, yet their actions seem purposeless. They seem alone on earth, even when, as often, there is another character in the same plight. In fact, their plight is made more fearful by the presence of the other, whom they can't trust or really reach, and whom they would betray to save themselves. The interchangeability of their external realities makes communication impossible. They have no souls, no fixed identities. They're lost in an existential void without compass, centre, or orientation point.

The implied instability of character, the absence of structures, which Beckett reads negatively, are cause for optimism in Brecht. Because of them, constructive social change is possible; existing social arrangements are not final. Brecht follows Marx to the conviction that while 'philosphers have only interpreted the world in various ways, the point is to change it'.

Conceiving the drama as an agent of change, Brecht developed the epic theatre techniques so widely used in drama since. While critical response to the 1956 visit of the Berliner Ensemble to London was unenthusiastic, the impact of Brechtian dramaturgy and the company's staging methods was profound. In a 1966 article Martin Esslin wrote that 'practically all British stage design, outside the area of the most old-fashioned drawing-room comedy, today derives from the work of the main Brechtian designers . . .'. His observation still applies. Contemporary playwrights devise their own versions of the technique Brecht called *Verfremdung*, but they use it to the same purpose: a way to disrupt habitual ways of looking at things, so that audiences perceive their own life-activities as objectively as anthropologists look at the customs of aborigines, a way to reveal what is strange in the familiar.

While critics argue that the English adaptations of Brechtian devices, like the introduction of songs and music into plays, the use of harsh lighting, the frankly anti-illusionist stage designs are surface borrowings only, they concede the profound impact of such borrowings. They have contributed to the abandonment of traditional naturalist staging, with its pretense of literal verisimilitude, that still constrained the British drama of the fifties behind the fourth wall. *Look Back in Anger,* for example, in spite of its pioneering innovations in themes, characters, and language, is cast in a conventional three-act form. Osborne describes the setting in meticulously realistic detail to evoke the look and feel of a bleak room, cluttered with heavy furniture and the assorted detritus of a trio of occupants whose housekeeping standards are not very high. But already in his next play, *The Entertainer* (1957), and even more in *Luther* (1961), some critics have detected Brechtian traits. By the 1970s, the flexible staging, impressionistic settings, and the structuring of dramatic action into short scenes that Brecht introduced had become commonplace in the work of most younger British playwrights.

Beckett's bleak world turns inward to the solipsistic prison of the self. His bare and shrunken stage is a limbo inhabited by a pair or two of suvivors, representing all of humanity. They are foolish clowns, who joke inanely and fumble to keep their trousers up and their food down. They sing, sometimes, or whistle in the dark. Their lives are suspended in a life-in-death or death-in-life condition that is almost static. Their speech is laconic, except for occasional bursts into gibberish, which betray the insufficiency of their language to express their experience of life at the edge of the apocalypse.

Brecht's stage is crowded with characters from all classes and situations, clashing against history and changing it. Action alternates with polemical narration, songs, and moralizing titles or aphorisms designed to awaken audiences to constructive social action. Brecht is not naive, however. One of the stunning strengths of his playwriting is the irony he frequently juxtaposes against his visionary socialism: virtue in a bad society may be harmful! Nevertheless, the vision of a social order which distributes goods and property to those who would make the most creative human uses of them is inspiriting. For Brecht reality is socially defined. For Beckett it may be undefinable.

Brecht and Beckett echo in many concrete images in the English drama. When Peter Barnes has two Jews tell jokes as they are being gassed in *Laughter*, he is using Brechtian defamiliarization. When Jack and Harry pass the day in their mental institution by exchanging vague banalities in David Storey's *Home*, they are dancing the survival waltz of the Beckettian void. Like Brecht, Trevor Griffiths measures every act – even telling a joke – by its capacity to change society. Like Beckett, Simon Gray gives us a world peopled by isolates who, even as they inhabit the same rooms, speak past and around, but seldom to, each other.

The English drama pelts forward with the full force of its own energy, but like every art movement, it builds on the best of other times and places.

Politics in the First Wave

Since five of the playwrights in this volume are often associated with the theatrical left wing, a word about politics is appropriate. In the United States the notion of political theatre has always raised eyebrows and hackles. Whereas play-goers there think of such theatre as vaguely subversive and producers consider it 'uncommercial', in Europe drama without political resonances is rare and likely to be dismissed as naive or merely 'commercial'. Since 1956, politics in English drama has been commonplace and accounts for the rich texture much admired by American critics in their reviews of English plays. It does not necessarily mean special pleading for an orthodox Marxist position, but rather the rootedness of the dramatic action in the context of the society the characters live in. The social indictments of John Osborne and his generation are essentially non-partisan, more expressive of a general humanist concern than partisan ideology.

The definition of political theatre pertinent here is close to one used by R.G. Davis in a 1983 *Theatre Communications* article, 'Political plays are "whole plays" discussing people's problems within the fabric of society where social relations are part of everyone's psyche'.

In American plays, politics in even so general a sense is likelier to be found in 'pockets of activity, not as a nationwide phenomenon,' as James Leverett, director of literary services for Theatre Communications Group, has pointed out. American writers who supply a political context in their plays have learned to expect rejection, not only from producers, but also from critics.

In England, while left-wing playwrights are often attacked by right-wing critics, their plays have a much greater chance of being produced somewhere and given a hearing than in the United States. The fact is that ever since the premiere of *Look Back in Anger*, British playwrights have been tracking a general restlessness in the society, a developing drive toward a more egalitarian, open, and class-free society. They have moved from generalized discontent to more revolutionary sentiments.

One measure of a successful stage in a revolution may be the self-confidence of the revolutionaries about what they are doing. At Temple University in Philadelphia recently, Peter Barnes sat on the stage of a small lab theatre, facing a standing-room only crowd of theatre students. 'Why do you write?' asked one student, hoping to get credit in academic heaven, perhaps, for asking the hard, deep question. The answer shot back, 'I want to change the world'.

Peter Barnes, speaking in 1984, may well have been expressing what the 'first wave' writers of the fifties wanted, too. And the play of his included here, like the others in Volume I of this anthology, offers no neat alternative system to replace the one that needs changing. *The Ruling Class* attacks the ruling class as feelingless, sexless, lifeless, joyless. Like most of the 'first wave' plays it raises questions and disturbs assumptions without offering a programme for revolution.

John Arden, the most doggedly political playwright of the early group, hits at the moral malaise of the British nation, too 'married to its telly and its fish and chips' to monitor its national life responsibly. While *Serjeant Musgrave's Dance*, said to have been written out of Arden's white-hot anger at British violence in Cyprus, is passionately anti-war, it is not simplistically one-sided. Far from being instructed in the correct solutions to problems of war and peace, audiences are reminded how complex those issues are, given the complexities of human motives and values.

The plays in Arnold Wesker's trilogy about the life of a Jewish East End family are more emphatic about the impact of politics on family life than about the communist ideology or trade unionism which various of the family members profess.

In sum, the playwrights of the 'first wave' were more revolutionary in the degree to which they overstepped the bounds of decorum in their plays by the matter-of-factness of their themes, the frankness of their language, and their shift of focus away from the upper classes than they were in their politics, except as politics is understood as part of the social context.

Selected Bibliography

Addenbrooke, David. *The Royal Shakespeare Company: The Peter Hall Years*. London: William Kimber, 1974.

Bigsby, C. W. E. 'The Politics of Anxiety: Contemporary Socialist Theatre in England,' *Modern Drama* 24 (December 1981), pp. 393–403.

Browne, Terry W. *Playwright's Theatre: The English Stage Company at the Royal Court Theatre*. Middletown, Ct.: Wesleyan U. Press; London: Pitman, 1975.

Elsom, John and Nicholas Tomalin. *The History of the National Theatre*. London: Jonathan Cape, 1978.

Elsom, John. *Post-War British Theatre*. London: Routledge & Kegan Paul, 1976.

Esslin, Martin. 'Brecht, the Absurd, and the Future,' *Tulane Drama Review* (Summer 1963), pp. 43-54.

Findlater, Richard, ed. *At the Royal Court*. Ambergate: Amber Lane Press; N.Y.: Grove Press, 1981.

Goorney, Howard. *The Theatre Workshop Story*. London and N.Y.: Eyre Methuen, 1981.

Hall, Peter. *Diaries*, ed. John Goodwin. London: Hamish Hamilton; N.Y.: Harper & Row, 1984.

Hinchcliffe, Arnold. *British Theatre 1950–1970*. Oxford: Blackwell; Totowa, N.J.: Rowman & Littlefield, 1974.

Holland, Peter. 'Brecht, Bond, Gaskill and the Practice of Political Theatre,' *Theatre Quarterly* (Summer 1978), pp. 24–33.

Kerensky, Oleg. *The New British Drama: Fourteen Playwrights Since Osborne and Pinter*. London: Hamish Hamilton; N.Y.: Taplinger, 1977.

Leipzig, Adam. 'Political Theatre in American,' *Theatre Communications* (February 1983), pp. 2–5.

Marowitz, Charles, Tom Milne and Owen Hale (eds.). *The Encore Reader*. London: Methuen, 1965. Reprinted as: *New Theatre Voices of the Fifties and Sixties*. London and N.Y.: Eyre Methuen, 1981.

Taylor, John Russell. *Anger and After*. London: Methuen, 1962; 3rd ed. 1977. Baltimore, Md.: Penguin, 1963. Reprinted as: *The Angry Theatre*. N.Y.: Hill and Wang, 1969.

Tulane Drama Review. 'British Theatre 1955–66,' Winter 1966.

Worth, Katherine J. *Revolutions in Modern English Drama*. London: G. Bell, 1972.

Weintraub, Stanley, ed. *British Dramatists Since World War II*, 2 vols. (*Dictionary of Literary Biography*, Vol. 13, Parts I and II). Detroit: Gale, 1982.

Arnold Wesker

'I want to teach', said Wesker a few months before the premiere of *Roots*. 'I want to write my plays . . . for those to whom the phrase "form of expression" may mean nothing whatsoever'. While Wesker is never merely didactic, *Roots* reveals clearly the impulse of an artist to seize by their blue collars his least educated, least sophisticated fellows and shake them into a consciousness of the world and their places in it. It is a play about teaching and being taught.

Like Beatie Bryant, the heroine of *Roots*, Wesker was undertaught. Born in London's East End in 1932 to immigrant Jewish parents and relative poverty (his father, like Harold Pinter's, was a tailor), he left school at sixteen. Already attracted to the theatre, he auditioned for the Royal Academy, but with no way to pay the tuitition, he settled for a miscellany of jobs: cabinet-maker's apprentice, bookseller, carpenter's mate. He began to write when he joined the R.A.F. Discharged in 1952, he worked as a plumber's mate, a farm labourer, and a kitchen porter, rising eventually to pastry chef, an occupation he pursued in London and Paris. All these jobs would resurface in his drama, for, more than most playwrights, Wesker celebrates the act of labour, especially of the manual sort, and draws on his personal experiences in his plays. His wife-to-be, Doreen (Dusty) Bicker, was the model for Beatie Bryant, as Wesker bluntly acknowledges: 'Beatie Bryant is the daughter of farm labourers in Norfolk and my wife is the daughter of farm labourers in Norfolk'.

In 1955, on the money he earned in Paris, Wesker enrolled in the London School of Film Technique. He might have gone on in the film industry but for two things. First, he heard about a play competition, which prompted him to write his first play, *The Kitchen*, in 1956. He didn't win, but, in a burst of the effrontery sometimes found in neophyte artists, he collared film director Lindsay Anderson in a cinema queue and asked him to read the script. Although the startled Anderson agreed, Wesker lost his nerve and didn't send it. Second, Wesker saw *Look Back in Anger*. 'When I saw it, I just recognized that things could be done in the theatre', he explains. He immediately went home and wrote *Chicken Soup with Barley*. Courage in hand again, he sent that script to Anderson, who recommended it to the Royal Court Theatre. Unsure that it was stageworthy, the Court arranged to premiere the play at the Belgrade Theatre, Coventry. After Coventry the play transferred to the Court and director George Devine, convinced now of Wesker's talent, gave him a twenty-five pound commission to complete *Roots*, which Wesker was then working on. Wesker had become a playwright.

Like its predecessor, *Roots* opened in Coventry, then transferred to the Court and went on, briefly, to the West End.

In 1961 the Royal Court Theatre staged *The Kitchen* (also transferred from Coventry), which became the theatre's biggest money-maker that year. It had a surprising impact on the theatre world. As critic Kenneth Tynan said, the play 'achieves something that few playwrights have ever attempted; it dramatises work, the daily collision of man with economic necessity, the repetitive toil that consumes that large portion of human life which is not devoted to living'. *The Kitchen* is a complete metaphor for the world of ordinary work. In it twenty-nine actors recreate the life of a large restaurant kitchen as the staff prepares to meet the lunchtime rush. All the madness of a hot, frenzied atmosphere is in the play, as are the tensions of the frayed private lives and bristling rivalries of the staff. Chefs, waitresses, and porters execute a complex mime of their tasks. Wesker specifically stipulates that no actual food is to be used. Under the pressure of fifteen hundred unseen, detested patrons waiting to be fed, they work as frenetically as Charlie Chaplin on the speeded-up assembly line of *Modern Times*. It's 'no place for a human being', as one of the cooks puts it.

At the climax of the play, a young German chef goes berserk on learning that the waitress he's having an affair with doesn't intend to leave her husband. Instead of taking revenge on her, he seizes a meat cleaver and severs a gas main, which shuts down the kitchen completely. The physicality of *The Kitchen* dramatizes the workers' life with a vivid clarity no socialist manifesto on the hazards and burdens of manual labour could even approach. It set a standard for the new physical life of the English stage.

During the writing of *Roots*, Wesker found the idea for *I'm Talking about Jerusalem* and realized that with *Chicken Soup* and *Roots*, he would have a trilogy. The plays cover a span of twenty-three years from 1936 to 1957. They trace the impact of politics and social issues on a Jewish East End family like Wesker's own. After the Coventry premiere of *Jerusalem*, The Royal Court presented all three plays as a trilogy, performed on successive evenings. Directed by John Dexter, who staged all the early Wesker plays, the trilogy established Wesker in the critical mind. A. R. Jones wrote that 'Wesker has rewritten the myth of our time from the point of view of those who suffered and, somehow, survived the crises and disillusionments of the last twenty-five years'.

As he had used his restaurant work in *The Kitchen*, Wesker next exploited his R.A.F. service in *Chips with Everything*. In *Chips*, however, his class statement was much more explicit. Pip Thompson, son of a banker, tries to reject his upper middle-class background by refusing officer training and serving instead in the ranks. His superior officers won't accept his disloyalty to his class. They threaten and cajole him into accepting an officer's uniform. In spite of Pip's revolutionary spirit, Wesker implies, he can't hold out against the pressures of the ruling class that always manages to prevail.

In *Chips* Wesker pays careful attention to the physical details of the military life, as he had the physical side of restaurant life in *The Kitchen*. The climax of *Chips* comes in a savage scene in which Pip signifies his surrender to the officers by performing with terrifying precision and speed the bayonet drill he had resolutely refused to perform earlier.

Chips with Everything was Wesker's greatest commercial success; from the Royal Court it moved to the West End and then to Broadway. It completed a sequence of five plays, written in only five years, which earned Wesker recognition, along with Osborne, Arden, and Pinter, as one of the leaders of the new English drama. And in those five years, Wesker carved out for the working class and their left-wing aspirations a more significant niche than they had occupied before on the English stage.

Coincident with his rise in the theatre, Wesker became a political activist, as did a number of his peers in the theatre world. In 1961 he served a short jail term for civil disobedience associated with the Campaign for Nuclear Disarmament. From 1961 to 1970 he devoted much of his time to Centre 42, a trade union-inspired effort to make the arts part of working-class life, an echo of Ronnie Kahn's attempts in *Roots* to enrich Beatie Bryant's awareness of life by introducing her to culture, and her clumsy efforts to do the same for her Norfolk family. Wesker tried hard to keep the movement alive, but was forced to recognise that it had failed. The working class – or, at least, the trade unions – turned out not to be interested.

Although none of his plays since that first burst of creativity has achieved the same powerful impact, Wesker has experimented continually. In *The Four Seasons* he departed from social realism to probe an intimate male-female relationship by means of elevated language, allegory, and an atmosphere of Pinteresque mystery. Where the action of the play occurs and why it occurs there is never explained. In the middle of the play, however, in one of its few touches of realism, the male character Adam is required to make an actual apple strudel on stage. Actors are expected to learn to fence, argued Wesker, why not to cook?

In *Their Very Own and Golden City,* Wesker depicts an idealistic architect's struggle to build model cities in which a thriving working class might live humane, enlightened lives, the sort of vision he was pursuing in Centre 42. The architect's utopian ideals fail because the working class, represented by union leaders, lacks commensurate vision, a theme Wesker had first raised in the trilogy. In this play, Wesker used a 'flash forward' cinematic technique to move the action from 1926 to 1990.

During the late sixties and early seventies, Wesker seems to have been more appreciated abroad than at home. Such plays as *The Journalists*, which vividly captures the accelerating activity of getting out a weekly newspaper, *The Merchant,* and *Love Letters on Blue Paper* received their major premieres in Europe or the United States. Wesker began to feel that he didn't 'fit in anywhere at the moment – in the English theatre'. But he continued to adventure and in 1981 the National Theatre premiered *Caritas,* set, like *Roots*, in Norfolk, this time in the 1300s. A nun immured in her cell is the medium through whom we perceive that the ordinary people outside her cell are more imprisoned by their lack of knowledge or imagination than she by the walls of the convent. Her erstwhile lover Robert, like an Edward Bond character, wishes to learn to read, but is prevented by the bishop, who rightly sees literacy as the first step in rebellion against the status quo. In *Caritas*, Wesker is still sounding the call to learn that he first let loose in *Roots*.

Roots is best understood by addressing the trilogy first, for the three plays are an organic whole. On the most obvious level, they are linked by the character of Ronnie Kahn, who appears in two of the plays and is talked of constantly in *Roots*, although he does not appear in it. Ronnie is actually more important in *Roots* than in the other two plays, in both of which he is a significant but essentially passive bystander. The first play of the trilogy, *Chicken Soup with Barley*, introduces Ronnie as a fifteen-year-old London boy. It is 1946 and he is in love with the new promise of socialism: 'Nationalization! National Health! Think of it, the whole country is going to be organized to cooperate instead of tearing at each other's throats.' The play ends with Ronnie's return in 1956 from a back-breaking stint as a cook in Paris. He is dispirited and despairing, his faith in socialism and in himself quite broken. However, the play does not show what happened to Ronnie to reduce him from hopefulness to despair. He is never shown in the play as a vital adult, only as a damaged one. The same pattern recurs in the third play, *I'm Talking about Jerusalem*. The first act again shows the Ronnie of 1946, this time cheerily helping his sister and her husband launch an exhilarating utopian experiment in the Norfolk countryside. Then Ronnie disappears from the play again until the final scene, thirteen years later. Now he is 'all washed up . . . I can't keep a job and I can't keep a girl,' he says. He has lost Beatie Bryant and along with her all his hopes. As in *Chicken Soup*, Ronnie as a young man full of dynamic hope and confidence isn't shown.

In *Roots*, however, that Ronnie, although he never steps on stage, is brought vividly before us by Beatie's frequent descriptions of his efforts to awaken her to a vision of culture and social justice. Through Beatie's voice, we hear Ronnie's voice, authoritative, hopeful, visionary: " 'Christ', he says. 'Socialism isn't talking all the time, it's living, it's singing, it's dancing, it's being interested in what goes on around you, it's being concerned with people and the world.' " We see Ronnie's effect on Beatie when she brings in the paintings he encouraged her to do, and quotes his exhortations to her, 'Paint, girl. Paint.'

A letter from Ronnie is the climax of the play. He writes to sever his relationship with Beatie, out of despair of ever achieving even the small victory of bringing one other human being to the sort of light he values. Ironically, the letter does wake up Beatie into realizing she can think and speak for herself. 'God in heaven, Ronnie!' she cries out. 'It does work, it's happening to me . . . I'm beginning, on my own two feet – I'm beginning.' But her knowledge comes too late for Ronnie, who has given up on her and on himself. He is again the unreachable, beaten Ronnie of the final scenes of the other plays. Not knowing he has won with Beatie, he loses. The irony echoes in *Jerusalem* when, with Beatie gone from his life, Ronnie speculates about her. 'I don't regret it. Maybe something did happen.' And it did. In so far as it did, both *Roots* and the trilogy as a whole reaffirm Wesker's commitment to the value of teaching and the possibility of learning that can tear down the barriers of ignorance and give the working class a decent life.

The motifs of learning and resistance to learning dominate *Roots*. On fire with Ronnie's passion, Beatie hammers at her family, especially her mother, with her new knowledge – the pastry-making she learned from Ronnie, his appreciation of Bizet, and most of all, the knowledge that the mind itself has a life, 'I'll get you buggers thinking if it's the last thing I do.' But just as Beatie resisted Ronnie's teaching, her family resists hers. 'But don't you come pushin' ideas across at us –,' says Jimmy, 'we're all right as we are.' Beatie's triumphant graduation into enlightenment is hers alone. In the final stage direction of the play, Wesker notes that her family 'will continue to live as before'. For some it's too late to learn; some are impossible to teach.

Throughout the trilogy runs a connecting metaphor, electricity – modern light – as a symbol of human growth and enlightenment. In *Chicken Soup*, Sarah Kahn, Ronnie's mother, equates it with the socialism she passionately defends, even after the Soviet invasion of Hungary. She looks at that as a temporary malfunction, like a blown fuse. '. . . So I should stop having electricity?' she asks. 'I should cut off my light . . .?' In *Roots*, Beatie's family home is not equipped with electricity. Never having had it, Beatie's mother doesn't miss it, senses its usefulness scarcely better than she senses the value of Beatie's new knowledge, her light. In *I'm Talking about Jerusalem*, Ronnie's sister and her husband Dave happily give up electricity when they move to the country in quest of the simple craftsman's life their ancestors might have lived before electricity, cities, socialism, progress itself. They reject the failed socialist ideology and modernity in search of Eden. But, as it always must, Eden sours. Dave can't really turn back the clock, can't compete in an industrial society without the tools and methods of modern industry. In the final scene they return to London, seemingly defeated. But Dave twice reminds himself to call the electrician in London – he'll need power to set up shop there.

For Dave, for all the characters of the trilogy, the light is available to those who learn to know they need it. They can be taught how to seek it when they are ready and willing to learn.

Major Plays

Chicken Soup with Barley, Belgrade Theatre, Coventry, then Royal Court and Duke of Yorks, 1958.

Roots, Belgrade Theatre, Coventry, 1959.

The Kitchen, Royal Court Theatre 'production without decor', 1959; revised for Belgrade Theatre, Coventry, then Royal Court, 1961.

I'm Talking About Jerusalem, Belgrade Theatre, Coventry, then Royal Court, 1960.

Chips With Everything, Royal Court Theatre, then Vaudeville Theatre, 1962.

The Four Seasons, Belgrade Theatre, Coventry, then Saville Theatre, 1965.

Their Very Own and Golden City, Belgium National Theatre, Brussels, 1965 (in French); Royal Court Theatre, 1966.

The Friends, Stadsteater, Stockholm, 1970; Roundhouse, 1970.

The Old Ones, Royal Court Theatre, 1972.

The Merchant, Royal Dramatenteater, Stockholm, 1976; Plymouth Theatre, New York, 1977; Birmingham Repertory Theatre, 1978.

Caritas, National Theatre, 1981.

Selected Bibliography

Jones, A. R., 'The Theatre of Arnold Wesker,' *Critical Quarterly*, II, 4 (Winter 1960) 366–70.

Leeming, Glenda. *Wesker the Playwright*. London and New York: Methuen, 1983.

— (ed.). *Wesker on File*. London and New York: Methuen, 1985.

Ribalow, Harold U. *Arnold Wesker*. N.Y.: Twayne, 1965.

Wesker, Arnold. Interview with Simon Trussler in *Theatre at Work*, ed. Trussler and Marowitz. London: Methuen, 1967.

—. 'A Sense of What Should Follow,' interview with Simon Trussler reprinted from *Theatre Quarterly* in *New Theatre Voices of the Seventies*, ed. Trussler. London: Eyre Methuen, 1981.

ARNOLD WESKER

Roots

For Dusty

Note on Pronunciation

This is a play about Norfolk people; it could be a play about any country people and the moral could certainly extend to the metropolis. But as it is about Norfolk people it is important that some attempt is made to find out how they talk. A very definite accent and intonation exists and personal experience suggests that this is not difficult to know. The following may be of great help:

When the word 'won't' is used, the 'w' is left out. It sounds the same but the 'w' is lost.

Double 'ee' is pronounced 'i' as in 'it' – so that 'been' becomes 'bin', 'seen' becomes 'sin', etc.

'Have' and 'had' become 'hev' and 'hed' as in 'head'.

'Ing' loses the 'g' so that it becomes 'in'.

'Bor' is a common handle and is a contraction of neighbour.

Instead of the word 'of' they say 'on', e.g. 'I've hed enough on it' or 'What do you think on it?'

Their 'yes' is used all the time and sounds like 'year' with a 'p' – 'yearp'.

'Blast' is also common usage and is pronounced 'blust', a short sharp sound as in 'gust'.

The cockney 'ain't' becomes 'ent' – also short and sharp.

The 't' in 'that' and 'what' is left out to give 'thaas' and 'whaas', e.g. 'Whaas matter then?'

Other idiosyncrasies are indicated in the play itself.

Note to Actors and Producers

My people are not caricatures. They are real (though fiction), and if they are portrayed as caricatures the point of this play will be lost. The picture I have drawn is a harsh one, yet my tone is not of disgust – nor should it be in presentation of the play. I am at one with these people: it is only that I am annoyed, with them and myself.

Characters

BEATIE BRYANT, *a young woman aged twenty-two, a friend of Ronnie Kahn*

JENNY BEALES, *her sister*

JIMMY BEALES, *her brother-in-law*

MRS BRYANT, *her mother*

MR BRYANT, *her father*

FRANKIE BRYANT, *her brother*

PEARL BRYANT, *her sister-in-law*

STAN MANN, *a neighbour of the Bealeses*

MR HEALEY, *a manager at the farm*

ACT I: An isolated cottage in Norfolk, the house of the Bealeses

ACT II SCENE 1: Two days later at the cottage of Mr and Mrs Bryant, in the kitchen

SCENE 2: The same a couple of hours later

ACT III: Two weeks later in the front room of the Bryants'

Time: The Present

Roots was first presented at the Belgrade Theatre, Coventry, on 25 May 1959, with the following cast:

JENNY BEALES	Patsy Byrne
JIMMY BEALES	Charles Kay
BEATIE BRYANT	Joan Plowright
STAN MANN	Patrick O'Connell
MRS BRYANT	Gwen Nelson
MR BRYANT	Jack Rodney
MR HEALEY	Richard Martin
FRANKIE BRYANT	Alan Howard
PEARL BRYANT	Brenda Peters

Directed by JOHN DEXTER
Designed by JOCELYN HERBERT

The play was transferred to the Royal Court Theatre, London, on 30 June 1959, and subsequently to the Duke of York's on 30 July 1959. At the Duke of York's the part of MR HEALEY was played by Barry Wilsher.

Act One

A rather ramshackle house in Norfolk where there is no water laid on, nor electricity, nor gas. Everything rambles and the furniture is cheap and old. If it is untidy it is because there is a child in the house and there are few amenities, so that the mother is too overworked to take much care.

An assortment of clobber lies around: papers and washing, coats and basins, a tin wash-tub with shirts and underwear to be cleaned, Tilley lamps and Primus stoves. Washing hangs on a line in the room. It is September.

JENNY BEALES is by the sink washing up. She is singing a recent pop song. She is short, fat and friendly, and wears glasses. A child's voice is heard from the bedroom crying 'Sweet, Mamma, sweet.'

JENNY (*good-naturedly*). Shut you up Daphne and get you to sleep now. (*Moves to get a dishcloth.*)

CHILD'S VOICE. Daphy wan' sweet, sweet, sweet.

JENNY (*going to cupboard to get sweet*). My word child, Father come home and find you awake he'll be after you. (*Disappears to bedroom with sweet.*) There – now sleep, gal, don't wan' you grumpy wi' me in mornin'.

Enter JIMMY BEALES. Also short, chubby, blond though hardly any hair left, ruddy complexion. He is a garage mechanic. Wears blue dungarees and an army pack slung over his shoulder. He wheels his bike in and lays it by the wall. Seems to be in some sort of pain – around his back. JENNY returns.

Waas matter wi' you then?

JIMMY. I don' know gal. There's a pain in my guts and one

a'tween my shoulder blades I can hardly stand up.

JENNY. Sit you down then an' I'll git you your supper on the table.

JIMMY. Blust gal! I can't eat yit.

JIMMY *picks up a pillow from somewhere and lies down on the sofa holding pillow to stomach.* JENNY *watches him a while.*

JENNY. Don't you know what 'tis yit?

JIMMY. Well, how should *I* know what 'tis.

JENNY. I told Mother about the pain and she says it's indigestion.

JIMMY. What the hell's indigestion doin' a'tween my shoulder blades then?

JENNY. She say some people get indigestion so bad it go right through their stomach to the back.

JIMMY. Don't be daft.

JENNY. That's what I say. Blust Mother, I say, you don't git indigestion in the back. Don't you tell me, she say, I hed it!

JIMMY. What hevn't she hed.

JENNY *returns to washing up while* JIMMY *struggles a while on the sofa.* JENNY *hums. No word. Then—*

JENNY. Who d'you see today?

JIMMY. Only Doctor Gallagher.

JENNY (*wheeling round*). You see who?

JIMMY. Gallagher. His wife driv him up in the ole Armstrong.

JENNY. Well I go t'hell if that ent a rum thing.

JIMMY (*rising and going to table; pain has eased*). What's that then?

JENNY (*moving to get him supper from oven*). We was down at the whist drive in the village and that Judy Maitland say he were dead. 'Cos you know he've hed a cancer this last year and they don't give him no longer'n three weeks don't you?

JIMMY. Ole crows. They don' wan' nothing less than a death to wake them up.

JENNY. No. No longer'n three weeks.

GIRL'S VOICE (*off*). Yoo-hoo! Yoo-hoo!

JIMMY. There's your sister.

JENNY. That's her.

GIRL'S VOICE (*off*). Yoo-hoo! Anyone home?

JENNY (*calling*). Come you on in gal, don't you worry about yoo-hoo.

Enter BEATIE BRYANT, *an ample, blond, healthy-faced young woman of twenty-two years. She is carrying a case.*

JIMMY. Here she is.

JENNY (*with reserve, but pleased*). Hello, Beatrice – how are you?

BEATIE (*with reserve, but pleased*). Hello, Jenny – how are you? What's that lovely smell I smell?

JENNY. Onions for supper and bread for the harvest festival.

BEATIE. Whatcha Jimmy Beales, ho you doin' bor?

JIMMY. Not so bad gal, how's yourself?

BEATIE. All right you know. When you comin' to London again for a football match?

JIMMY. O blust gal, I don' wanna go to any more o' those things. Ole father Bryant was there in the middle of that crowd and he turn around an' he say (*imitating*), Stop you a-pushin' there, he say, stop you a-pushin'.

JENNY. Where's Ronnie?

BEATIE. He's comin' down at the end of two weeks.

JIMMY. Ent you married yit?

BEATIE. No.

JIMMY. You wanna hurry then gal, a long engagement don't do the ole legs any good.

JENNY. Now shut you up Jimmy Beales and get that food down you. Every time you talk, look, you miss a mouthful! That's why you complain of pain in your shoulder blades.

BEATIE. You bin hevin' pains then Jimmy?

JIMMY. Blust yes! Right a'tween my shoulder blades.

JENNY. Mother says it's indigestion.

BEATIE. What the hell's indigestion doin' a'tween his shoulder blades?

JENNY. Mother reckon some people get indigestion so bad it go right through their stomach to the back.

BEATIE. Don't talk daft!

JENNY. That's what I say. Blust Mother, I say, you don't git indigestion in the back. Don't you tell me, she say, I hed it!

BEATIE. What hevn't she hed. How is she?

JENNY. Still the same you know. How long you staying this time?

BEATIE. Two days here – two weeks at home.

JENNY. Hungry gal?

BEATIE. Whatcha got?

JENNY. Whatcha see.

BEATIE. Liver? I'll hev it!

BEATIE *makes herself at home. Near by is a pile of comics. She picks one up and reads.*

JENNY. We got some ice-cream after.

BEATIE (*absorbed*). Yearp.

JENNY. Look at her. No sooner she's in than she's at them ole comics. You still read them ole things?

JIMMY. She don't change much do she?

BEATIE. Funny that! Soon ever I'm home again I'm like I always was – it don' even seem I bin away. I do the same lazy things an' I talk the same. Funny that!

JENNY. What do Ronnie say to it?

BEATIE. He don't mind. He don't even know though. He ent never bin here. Not in the three years I known him. But I'll tell you (*she jumps up and moves around as she talks*) I used to read the comics he bought for his nephews and he used to get riled –

Now BEATIE *begins to quote Ronnie, and when she does she imitates him so well in both manner and intonation that in fact as the play progresses we see a picture of him through her.*

'Christ, woman, what can they give you that you can *be* so absorbed?' So you know what I used to do? I used to get a copy of the *Manchester Guardian* and sit with that wide open – and a comic behind!

JIMMY. *Manchester Guardian*? Blimey Joe – he don't believe in hevin' much fun then?

BEATIE. That's what I used to tell him. 'Fun?' he say, 'fun? Playing an instrument is fun, painting is fun, reading a book is fun, talking with friends is fun – but a comic? A comic? for a young woman of twenty-two?

JENNY (*handing out meal and sitting down herself*). He sound a queer bor to me. Sit you down and eat gal.

BEATIE (*enthusiastically*). He's alive though.

JIMMY. Alive? Alive you say? What's alive about someone who can't read a comic? What's alive about a person that reads books and looks at paintings and listens to classical music?

There is a silence at this, as though the question answers itself – reluctantly.

JIMMY. Well, it's all right for some I suppose.

BEATIE. And then he'd sneak the comic away from me and read it his-self!

JENNY. Oh, he didn't really mind then?

BEATIE. No – 'cos sometimes I read books as well. 'There's nothing wrong with comics,' he'd cry – he stand up on a chair when he want to preach but don't wanna sound too dramatic.

JIMMY. Eh?

BEATIE. Like this, look. (*Stands on a chair.*) 'There's nothing wrong with comics only there's something wrong with comics all the time. There's nothing wrong with football, only there's something wrong with *only* football. There's nothing wrong with rock 'n' rolling, only God preserve me from the girl that can do nothing else!' (*She sits down and then stands up again, remembering something else.*) Oh yes, 'and there's nothing wrong with talking about the weather, only don't talk to me about it!' (*Sits down.*)

JIMMY *and* JENNY *look at each other as though she, and no doubt*

Ronnie, is a little barmy. JIMMY *rises and begins to strap on boots and gaiters ready for going out to an allotment.*

JENNY. He never really row with you then?

BEATIE. We used to. There was a time when he handled all official things for me you know. Once I was in between jobs and I didn't think to ask for my unemployment benefit. *He* told me to. But when I asked they told me I was short on stamps and so I wasn't entitled to benefit. *I* didn't know what to say but he did. He went up and argued for me – he's just like his mother, she argues with everyone – and I got it. I didn't know how to talk see, it was all foreign to me. Think of it! An English girl born and bred and I couldn't talk the language – except for to buy food and clothes. And so sometimes when he were in a black mood he'd start on me. 'What can you talk of?' he'd ask. 'Go on, pick a subject. Talk. Use the language. Do you know what language is?' Well, I'd never thought before – hev you? – it's automatic to you isn't it, like walking? 'Well, language is words,' he'd say, as though he were telling me a secret. 'It's bridges, so that you can get safely from one place to another. And the more bridges you know about the more places you can see!' (*To* JIMMY.) And do *you* know what happens when you can see a place but you don't know where the bridge is?

JIMMY (*angrily*). Blust gal, what the hell are you on about.

BEATIE. Exactly! You see, you hev a row! Still, rows is all right. I like a row. So then he'd say: 'Bridges! bridges! bridges! Use your bridges woman. It took thousands of years to build them, use them!' And that riled me. 'Blust your bridges,' I'd say. 'Blust you and your bridges – I want a row.' Then he'd grin at me. 'You want a row?' he'd ask. 'No bridges this time?' 'No bridges,' I'd say – and we'd row. Sometimes he hurt me but then, slowly he'd build the bridges up *for* me – and then we'd make love! (*Innocently continues her meal.*)

JENNY. You'd what, did you say?

BEATIE. Make love. Love in the afternoon gal. Ever had it? It's
the only time *for it*. Go out or entertain in the evenings; sleep
at night, study, work and chores in the mornings; but the love
– alert and fresh, when you got most energy – love in the
afternoon.

JIMMY. I suppose you take time off from work every afternoon
to do it?

BEATIE. I'm talking about week-ends and holidays – daft.

JENNY. Oh, Beatie, go on wi' you!

BEATIE. Well, go t'hell Jenny Beales, you're blushin'. Ent you
never had love in the afternoon? Ask Jimmy then.

JENNY (*rising to get sweet*). Shut you up gal and get on wi' your
ice-cream. It's strawberry flavour. Want some more James?

JIMMY (*taking it in the middle of lacing up boots*). Yes please,
vanilla please. (*Eating*) Good cream ent it? Made from the
white milk of a Jersey cow.

BEATIE. This is good too – made from pink milk ent it?

Pause.

JIMMY. Yearp! (*Pause.*) Come from a pink cow!

Pause. They are all enjoying the cream.

JENNY (*eating*). You remember Dickie Smart, Beatie?

BEATIE (*eating*). Who?

JENNY (*eating*). We had a drink wi' him in the Storks when you
was down last.

BEATIE (*eating*). Yearp.

JENNY (*eating*). Well, he got gored by a bull last Thursday. His
left ear was nearly off, his knee were gored, his ribs bruised
and the ligaments of his legs torn.

Pause as they finish eating.

BEATIE (*euphemistically*). He had a rough time then!

JENNY. Yearp. (*To* JIMMY.) You off now?

JIMMY. Mm.

JENNY *collects dishes.*

BEATIE. Still got your allotment Jimmy?

JIMMY. Yearp.

BEATIE. Bit heavy going this weather.

JIMMY. That ent too bad just yit – few more weeks an' the old mowld'll cling.

BEATIE. Whatcha got this year?

JIMMY. Had spuds, carrots, cabbages you know. Beetroot, lettuces, onions, and peas. But me runners let me down this year though.

JENNY. I don't got much on them old things.

BEATIE. You got a fair owle turn then?

JIMMY. Yearp.

JIMMY *starts to sharpen a reap hook.*

BEATIE (*jumping up*). I'll help you wash.

JENNY. That's all right gal.

BEATIE. Where's the cloth?

JENNY. Here 'tis.

BEATIE *helps collect dishes from table and proceeds to help wash up. This is a silence that needs organizing. Throughout the play there is no sign of intense living from any of the characters – BEATIE's bursts are the exception. They continue in a routine rural manner. The day comes, one sleeps at night, there is always the winter, the spring, the autumn, and the summer – little amazes them. They talk in fits and starts mainly as a sort of gossip, and they talk quickly too, enacting as though for an audience what they say. Their sense of humour is keen and dry. They show no affection for each other – though this does not mean they would not be upset were one of them to die. The silences are important – as important as the way they speak, if we are to know them.*

JENNY. What about that strike in London? Waas London like wi'out the buses?

BEATIE. Lovely! No noise – and the streets, you should see the streets, flowing with people – the city looks human.

JIMMY. They wanna call us Territorials out – we'd soon break the strike.

BEATIE. That's a soft thing for a worker to say for his mates.

JIMMY. Soft be buggered, soft you say? What they earnin' those busmen, what they earnin'? And what's the farm worker's wage? Do you know it gal?

BEATIE. Well, let the farm workers go on strike too then! It don't help a farm labourer if a busman don't go on strike do it now?

JENNY. You know they've got a rise though. Father Bryant's go up by six and six a week as a pigman, and Frank goes up seven 'n' six a week for driving a tractor.

JIMMY. But you watch the Hall sack some on 'em.

JENNY. Thaas true Beatie. They're such sods, honest to God they are. Every time there's bin a rise someone get sacked. Without fail. You watch it – you ask father Bryant when you get home, ask him who's bin sacked since the rise.

BEATIE. One person they 'ont sack is him though. They 'ont find many men'd tend to pigs seven days a week and stay up the hours he do.

JENNY. Bloody fool! (*Pause.*) Did Jimmy tell you he've bin chosen for the Territorials' Jubilee in London this year?

BEATIE. What's this then? What'll you do there?

JIMMY. Demonstrate and parade wi' arms and such like.

BEATIE. Won't do you any good.

JIMMY. Don't you reckon? Gotta show we can defend the country you know. Demonstrate arms and you prevent war.

BEATIE (*she has finished wiping up*). Won't demonstrate anything bor. (*Goes to undo her case.*) Present for the house! Have a hydrogen bomb fall on you and you'll find them things silly in your hands. (*Searches for other parcels.*)

JIMMY. So you say gal? So you say? That'll frighten them other buggers though.

BEATIE. Frighten yourself y'mean. (*Finds parcels.*) Presents for the kid.

JIMMY. And what do you know about this all of a sudden?

JENNY (*revealing a table-cloth*). Thank you very much Beatie. Just what I need.

BEATIE. You're not interested in defending your country Jimmy, you just enjoy playing soldiers.

JIMMY. What did I do in the last war then – *sing* in the trenches?

BEATIE (*explaining – not trying to get one over on him*). Ever heard of Chaucer, Jimmy?

JIMMY. No.

BEATIE. Do you know the M.P. for this constituency?

JIMMY. What you drivin' at gal – don't give me no riddles.

BEATIE. Do you know how the British Trade Union Movement started? And do you believe in strike action?

JIMMY. No to both those.

BEATIE. What you goin' to war to defend then?

JIMMY (*he is annoyed now*). Beatie – you bin away from us a long time now – you got a boy who's educated an' that and he's taught you a lot maybe. But don't you come pushin' ideas across at us – we're all right as we are. You can come when you like an' welcome but don't bring no discussion of politics in the house wi' you 'cos that'll only cause trouble. I'm telling you. (*He goes off.*)

JENNY. Blust gal, if you hevn't touched him on a sore spot. He live for them Territorials he do – that's half his life.

BEATIE (*she is upset now*). What's he afraid of talking for?

JENNY. He ent afraid of talking Beatie – blust he can do that, gal.

BEATIE. But not talk, not really talk, not use bridges. I sit with Ronnie and his friends sometimes and I listen to them talk about things and you know I've never heard half of the words before.

JENNY. Don't he tell you what they mean?

BEATIE. I get annoyed when he keep tellin' me – and he want me to ask. (*Imitates him half-heartedly now*) 'Always ask, people love to tell you what they know, always ask and people will respect you.'

JENNY. And you do?

BEATIE. No! I don't! An' you know why? Because I'm stubborn, I'm like Mother, I'm stubborn. Somehow I just can't bring myself to ask, and you know what? I go mad when I listen to them. As soon as they start to talk about things I don't know about or I can't understand I get mad. They sit there, casually talking, and suddenly they turn on you, abrupt. 'Don't you think?' they say. Like at school, pick on you and ask a question you ent ready for. Sometimes I don't say anything, sometimes I go to bed or leave the room. Like Jimmy – just like Jimmy.

JENNY. And what do Ronnie say to that then?

BEATIE. He get mad too. 'Why don't you ask me woman, for God's sake why don't you ask me? Aren't I dying to tell you about things? Only ask!'

JENNY. And he's goin' to marry you?

BEATIE. Why not?

JENNY. Well I'm sorry gal, you mustn't mind me saying this, but it don't seem to me like you two got much in common.

BEATIE (*loudly*). It's not true! We're in love!

JENNY. Well, you know.

BEATIE (*softly*). No, I don't know. I won't know till he come here. From the first day I went to work as waitress in the Dell Hotel and saw him working in the kitchen I fell in love – and I thought it was easy. I thought everything was easy. I chased him for three months with compliments and presents until I finally give myself to him. He never said he love me nor I didn't care but once he had taken me he seemed to think he was responsible for me and I told him no different. I'd *make* him love me I thought. I didn't know much about him except he was different and used to write most of the time. And then he went back to London and I followed him there. I've never moved far from home but I did for him and he felt all the time he couldn't leave me and I didn't tell him no different. And then I got to know more about him. He was interested in all the things I never even thought about. About politics and art and all that, and he tried to teach me. He's a socialist and he used to say you couldn't bring socialism to a country by making speeches, but perhaps you could pass it on to someone who was near you. So I pretended I was interested – but I didn't understand much. All the time he's trying to teach me but I can't take it Jenny. And yet, at the same time, I want to show I'm willing. I'm not used to learning. Learning was at school and that's finished with.

JENNY. Blust gal, you don't seem like you're going to be happy then. Like I said.

BEATIE. But I love him.

JENNY. Then you're not right in the head then.

BEATIE. I couldn't have any other life now.

JENNY. Well, I don't know and that's a fact.

BEATIE (*playfully mocking her*). Well I don't know and that's a fact! (*Suddenly*) Come on gal, I'll teach you how to bake some pastries.

JENNY. Pastries?

BEATIE. Ronnie taught me.

JENNY. Oh, you learnt that much then?

BEATIE. But he don't know. I always got annoyed when he tried to teach me to cook as well – Christ! I had to know something – but it sank in all the same.

By this time it has become quite dark and JENNY *proceeds to light a Tilley lamp.*

JENNY. You didn't make it easy then?

BEATIE. Oh don't you worry gal, it'll be all right once we're married. Once we're married and I got babies I won't need to be interested in half the things I got to be interested in now.

JENNY. No you won't will you! Don't need no education for babies.

BEATIE. Nope. Babies is babies – you just have 'em.

JENNY. Little sods!

BEATIE. You gonna hev another Jenny?

JENNY. Well, course I am. What you on about? Think Jimmy

don't want none of his own?

BEATIE. He's a good man Jenny.

JENNY. Yearp.

BEATIE. Not many men'd marry you after you had a baby.

JENNY. No.

BEATIE. He didn't ask you any questions? Who was the father? Nor nothing?

JENNY. No.

BEATIE. You hevn't told no one hev you Jenny?

JENNY. No, that I hevn't.

BEATIE. Well, that's it gal, don't you tell me then!

By this time the methylated spirit torch has burned out and JENNY *has finished pumping the Tilley lamp and we are in brightness.*

JENNY (*severely*). Now Beatie, stop it. Every time you come home you ask me that question and I hed enough. It's finished with and over. No one don't say nothing and no one know. You hear me?

BEATIE. Are you in love with Jimmy?

JENNY. Love? I don't believe in any of that squit – we just got married, an' that's that.

BEATIE (*suddenly looking around the room at the general chaos*). Jenny Beales, just look at this house. Look at it!

JENNY. I'm looking. What's wrong?

BEATIE. Let's clean it up.

JENNY. Clean what up?

BEATIE. Are you going to live in this house all your life?

JENNY. You gonna buy us another?

BEATIE. Stuck out here in the wilds with only ole Stan Mann and his missus as a neighbour and sand pits all around. Every time it rain look you're stranded.

JENNY. Jimmy don't earn enough for much more 'n we got.

BEATIE. But it's so untidy.

JENNY. You don' wan' me bein' like sister Susan do you? 'Cos you know how clean she is don' you – she's so bloody fussy she's gotten to polishing the brass overflow pipe what leads out from the lavatory.

BEATIE. Come on gal, let's make some order anyway – I love tidying up.

JENNY. What about the pastries? Pastries? Oh my sainted aunt, the bread? (*Dashes to the oven and brings out a most beautiful-looking plaited loaf of bread. Admiring it.*) Well, no one wanna complain after that. Isn't that beautiful Beatie?

BEATIE. I could eat it now.

JENNY. You hungry again?

BEATIE (*making an attack upon the clothes that are lying around*). I'm always hungry again. Ronnie say I eat more'n I need. 'If you get fat woman I'll leave you – without even a discussion!'

JENNY (*placing bread on large oval plate to put away*). Well, there ent nothin' wrong in bein' fat.

BEATIE. You ent got no choice gal. (*Seeing bike*) A bike! What's a bike doin' in a livin' room – I'm putting it outside.

JENNY. Jimmy 'ont know where it is.

BEATIE. Don't be daft, you can't miss a bike. (*Wheels it outside and calls from there*) Jenny! Start puttin' the clothes away.

JENNY. Blust gal, I ent got nowhere to put them.

BEATIE (*from outside*). You got drawers – you got cupboards.

JENNY. They're full already.

BEATIE (*entering – energy sparks from her*). Come here – let's look. (*Looks.*). Oh, go away – you got enough room for ten families. You just bung it all in with no order, that's why. Here – help me.

They drag out all manner of clothes from the cupboard and begin to fold them up.

BEATIE. How's my Frankie and Pearl?

JENNY. They're all right. You know she and Mother don't talk to each other?

BEATIE. What, again? Who's fault is it this time?

JENNY. Well, Mother say it's Pearl's fault and Pearl she say it's

Mother.

BEATIE. Well, they wanna get together quick and find whose fault it is 'cos I'm going to call the whole family together for tea to meet Ronnie.

JENNY. Well, Susan and Mother don't talk neither so you got a lot of peace-making to do.

BEATIE. Well go t'hell, what's broken them two up?

JENNY. Susan hev never bin struck on her mother, you know that don't you – well, it seems that Susan bought something off the club from Pearl and Pearl give it to Mother and Mother sent it to Susan through the fishmonger what live next door her in the council houses. And of course Susan were riled 'cos she didn't want her neighbours to know that she bought anything off the club. So they don't speak.

BEATIE. Kids! It makes me mad.

JENNY. And you know what 'tis with Pearl don't you – it's 'cos Mother hev never thought she was good enough for her son Frankie.

BEATIE. No more she wasn't neither!

JENNY. What's wrong wi' her then? I get on all right.

BEATIE. Nothing's wrong wi' her, she just wasn't good enough for our Frankie, that's all.

JENNY. Who's being small-minded now?

BEATIE. Always wantin' more'n he can give her.

JENNY. An' I know someone else who always wanted more'n she got.

BEATIE (sulkily). It's not the same thing.

JENNY. Oh yes 'tis.

BEATIE. 'Tent.

JENNY. 'Tis my gal. (Mimicking the child BEATIE) I wan' a 'nana, a 'nana, a 'nana. Frankie's got my 'nana, 'nana, 'nana.

BEATIE. Well, I liked bananas.

JENNY. You liked everything you could get your hands on and Mother used to give in to you 'cos you were the youngest. Me and Susan and Frankie never got nothing 'cos o' you – 'cept a clout round the ear.

BEATIE. 'Tent so likely. You got everything and I got nothing.

JENNY. All we got was what we pinched out the larder and then you used to go and tell tales to Mother.

BEATIE. I never did.

JENNY. Oh, didn't you my gal? Many's the time I'd've willingly strangled you – with no prayers – there you are, no prayers whatsoever. Strangled you till you was dead.

BEATIE. Oh go on wi' you Jenny Beales.

By now they have finished folding the clothes and have put away most of the laundry and garments that have till this moment cluttered up the room. BEATIE *says* 'There', *stands up and looks around, finds some coats sprawled helter-skelter, and hangs them up behind the door.*

BEATIE. I'll buy you some coat hangers.

JENNY. You get me a couple o' coats to hang on 'em first please.

BEATIE (*looking around*). What next. Bottles, jars, nicknacks, saucepans, cups, papers – everything anywhere. Look at it! Come on!

BEATIE *attempts to get these things either into their proper places or out of sight.*

JENNY. You hit this place like a bloody whirlwind you do, like a bloody whirlwind. Jimmy'll think he've come into the wrong house and I shan't be able to find a thing.

BEATIE. Here, grab a broom. (*She is now gurgling with sort of animal noises signifying excitement. Her joy is childlike.*) How's Poppy?

JENNY. Tight as ever.

BEATIE. What won't he give you now?

JENNY. 'Tent nothing wi' me gal. Nothing he do don't affect me. It's Mother I'm referring to.

BEATIE. Don't he still give her much money?

JENNY. Money? She hev to struggle and skint all the time – *all* the time. Well it ent never bin no different from when we was kids, hev it?

BEATIE. No.

JENNY. I tell you what. It wouldn't surprise me if Mother were in debt all the time, that it wouldn't. No. It wouldn't surprise me at all.

BEATIE. Oh, never.

JENNY. Well, what do you say that for Beatie – do you know how much he allow her a week look?

BEATIE. Six pounds?

JENNY. Six pounds be buggered. Four pounds ten! An' she hev to keep house *an'* buy her own clothes out of that.

BEATIE. Still, there's only two on 'em.

JENNY. You try keepin' two people in food for four pound ten. She pay seven an' six a week into Pearl's club for clothes, two and six she hev on the pools, and a shilling a week on the Labour Tote. (*Suddenly*) Blust! I forgot to say. Pearl won the Tote last week.

BEATIE. A hundred pounds?

JENNY. A hundred pounds! An' ole Mrs Dyson what used to live Startson way, she come up second wi' five pounds and seventy.

BEATIE. Well no one wrote me about it.

JENNY. 'Cos you never wrote no one else.

BEATIE. What she gonna do wi' it – buy a TV?

JENNY. TV? Blust no. You know she hevn't got electricity in that house. No, she says she's gonna get some clothes for the kids.

There is a sound now of a drunk old man approaching, and alongside of it the voice of JIMMY. *The drunk is singing:* 'I come from Bungay Town, I calls I Bungay Johnnie.'

Well I go t'hell if that ent Stan Mann drunk again. And is that Jimmy wi' him? (*Listens.*).

BEATIE. But I thought Stan Mann was paralysed.

JENNY. That don't stop him getting paralytic drunk. (*Listens*

again.) That's Jimmy taking him into the house I bet. A
fortune that man hev drunk away – a whole bleedin' fortune.
Remember the fleet of cars he used to run and all that land
he owned, and all them cattle he had and them fowl? Well,
he've only got a few acres of land and a few ole chickens. He
drink it all away. Two strokes he've had from drinking and
now he's paralysed down one side. But that don't stop him
getting drunk – no it don't.

JIMMY *enters and throws his jacket on the couch, takes off his boots
and gaiters, and smiles meanwhile*.

JIMMY. Silly ole bugger.

JENNY. I was just telling Beatie how he've drunk a fortune away
hevn't he?

JIMMY. He wanna drink a little more often and he'll be finished
for good.

JENNY. Didn't he hev all them cows and cars and land Jimmy?
And didn't he drink it all away bit by bit?

JIMMY. Silly ole sod don't know when to stop.

JENNY. I wished I had half the money he drink.

JIMMY. He messed his pants.

JENNY. He what? Well where was this then?

JIMMY. By the allotment.

JENNY. Well, what did *you* do then?

JIMMY. He come up to me – 'course I knowed he were drunk the
way he walk – he come up to me an' he say, "Evenin' Jimmy
Beales, thaas a fine turnover you got there.' An' I say, 'Yearp
'tis.' An' then he bend down to pick a carrot from the ground
an' then he cry, 'Oops, I done it again!' An' 'course, soon ever
he say 'done it again' I knowed what'd happened. So I took
his trousers down and ran the ole hose over him.

BEATIE. Oh, Jimmy, you never did.

JIMMY. I did gal. I put the ole hose over him and brought him
home along the fields with an ole sack around his waist.

BEATIE. He'll catch his death.

JIMMY. Never – he's strong as an ox.

JENNY. What'd you do with his trousers and things?

JIMMY. Put it on the compost heap – good for the land!

Now STAN MANN *enters. He's not all that drunk. The cold water has sobered him a little. He is old – about seventy-five – and despite his light stoop one can see he was a very strong upright man. He probably looks like everyman's idea of a farmer – except that he wears no socks or boots at this moment and he hobbles on a stick.*

STAN. Sorry about that ole son.

JIMMY. Don't you go worrying about that my manny – get you along to bed.

JENNY. Get some shoes on you too Stan, or you'll die of cold *and* booze.

STAN (*screwing up his eyes across the room*). Is that you Jenny? Hello ole gal. How are you?

JENNY. It's you you wanna worry about now ole matey. I'm well enough.

STAN (*screwing his eyes still more*). Who's that next to you?

JENNY. Don't you recognize her? It's our Beatie, Stan.

STAN. Is that you Beatie? Well blust gal, you gotten fatter since I seen you last. You gonna be fat as Jenny here? Come on over an' let's look at you.

BEATIE (*approaching*). Hello Stan Mann, how are you?

STAN (*looking her up and down*). Well enough gal, well enough. You married yit?

BEATIE. No.

STAN. You bin courtin' three years. Why ent you married yit?

BEATIE (*slightly embarrassed*). We ent sure yit.

STAN. You ent sure you say? What ent you sure of? You know how to do it don't you?

JENNY. Go on wi' you to bed Stan Mann.

STAN. Tell your boy he don't wanna waste too much time or I'll be hevin' yer myself for breakfast – on a plate.

JENNY. Stan Mann, I'm sendin' you to your bed – go on now,

off wi' you, you can see Beatie in the mornin'.

STAN (*as he is ushered out – to Beatie*). She's fat ent she? I'm not sayin' she won't do mind, but she's fat. (*As he goes out*) All right ole sweetheart, I'm goin'. I'm just right for bed. Did you see the new bridge they're building? It's a rum ole thing isn't it . . . (*Out of sound*.)

JIMMY. Well, I'm ready for bed.

BEATIE. I can't bear sick men. They smell.

JIMMY. Ole Stan's all right – do anything for you.

BEATIE. I couldn't look after one you know.

JIMMY. Case of hevin' to sometimes.

BEATIE. Ronnie's father's paralysed like that. I can't touch him.

JIMMY. Who see to him then?

BEATIE. His mother. She wash him, change him, feed him. Ronnie help sometimes. I couldn't though. Ronnie say, 'Christ, woman, I hope you aren't around when I'm ill.' (*Shudders*.) Ole age terrify me.

JIMMY. Where you sleepin' tonight gal?

BEATIE. On the couch in the front room I suppose.

JIMMY. You comfortable sleepin' on that ole thing? You wanna sleep with Jenny while you're here?

BEATIE. No thanks, Jimmy. (*She is quite subdued now*.) I'm all right on there.

JIMMY. Right, then I'm off. (*Looking around*) Where's the *Evening News* I brought in?

JENNY (*entering*). You off to bed?

JIMMY. Yearp. Reckon I've had 'nough of this ole day. Where's my *News*?

JENNY. Where did you put it Beatie?

JIMMY (*suddenly seeing the room*). Blust, you movin' out?

BEATIE. Here you are Jimmy Beales. (*Hands him paper*.) It's all tidy now.

JIMMY. So I see. Won't last long though will it? Night. (*Goes to bed*.)

JENNY. Well I'm ready for my bed too – how about you Beatie?

BEATIE. Yearp.

JENNY (*taking a candle in a stick and lighting it*). Here, take this with you. Your bed's made. Want a drink before you turn in?

BEATIE. No thanks gal.

JENNY (*picking up Tilley lamp and making towards one door*). Right then. Sleep well gal.

BEATIE (*going to other door with candle*). Good night Jenny. (*She pauses at her door. Loud whispers from now on.*) Hey Jenny.

JENNY. What is it?

BEATIE. I'll bake you some pastries when I get to Mother's.

JENNY. Father won't let you use his electricity for me, don't talk daft.

BEATIE. I'll get Mother on to him. It'll be all right. Your ole ovens weren't big 'nough anyways. Good night.

JENNY. Good night.

BEATIE (*an afterthought*). Hey Jenny.

JENNY. What now?

BEATIE. Did I tell you I took up painting?

JENNY. Painting?

BEATIE. Yes – on cardboard and canvases with brushes.

JENNY. What kind of painting?

BEATIE. Abstract painting – designs and patterns and such like. I can't do nothing else. I sent two on 'em home. Show you when you come round – if Mother hevn't thrown them out.

JENNY. You're an artist then?

BEATIE. Yes. Good night.

JENNY. Good night.

They enter their bedrooms, leaving the room in darkness.★ Perhaps we see only the faint glow of moonlight from outside and then:
the curtain falls.

★It might be better for Jenny to have previously made up Beatie's bed in the couch on the set. Then Beatie would not have to leave the stage at all.

Act Two

SCENE ONE

Two days have passed. BEATIE *will arrive at her own home, the home of her parents. This is a tied cottage on a main road between two large villages. It is neat and ordinary inside. We can see a large kitchen – where most of the living is done – and attached to it is a large larder; also part of the front room and a piece of the garden where some washing is hanging.*

MRS BRYANT *is a short, stout woman of fifty. She spends most of the day on her own, and consequently when she has a chance to speak to anybody she says as much as she can as fast as she can. The only people she sees are the tradesmen, her husband, the family when they pop in occasionally. She speaks very loudly all the time so that her friendliest tone sounds aggressive, and she manages to dramatize the smallest piece of gossip into something significant. Each piece of gossip is a little act done with little looking at the person to whom it is addressed. At the moment she is at the door leading to the garden, looking for the cat.*

MRS BRYANT. Cossie, Cossie, Cossie, Cossie, Cossie, Cossie! Here Cossie! Food Cossie! Cossie, Cossie, Cossie! Blust you cat, where the hell are you. Oh hell on you then, I ent wastin' my time wi' you now.

She returns to the kitchen and thence the larder, from which she emerges with some potatoes. These she starts peeling. STAN MANN *appears round the back door. He has a handkerchief to his nose and is blowing vigorously, as vigorously as his paralysis will allow.* MRS BRYANT *looks up, but continues her peeling.*

STAN. Rum thing to git a cold in summer, what you say Daphne?

MRS BRYANT. What'd you have me say my manny. Sit you down
   bor and rest a bit. Shouldn't wear such daf' clothes.

STAN. Daf' clothes? Blust woman! I got on half a cow's hide,
   what you sayin'! Where's the gal?

MRS BRYANT. Beatie? She 'ent come yit. Didn't *you* see her?

STAN. Hell, I was up too early for her. She always stay the week-
   end wi' Jenny 'fore comin' home?

MRS BRYANT. Most times.

STAN *sneezes*.

What you doin' up this way wi' a cold like that then? Get you
home to bed.

STAN. Just come this way to look at the vicarage. Stuff's comin'
   up for sale soon.

MRS BRYANT. You still visit them things then?

STAN. Yearp. Pass the ole time away. Pass the ole time.

MRS BRYANT. Time drag heavy then?

STAN. Yearp. Time drag heavy. She do that. Time drags so slow,
   I get to thinkin' it's Monday when it's still Sunday. Still, I had
   my day gal I say. Yearp. I had that all right.

MRS BRYANT. Yearp. You had that an' a bit more ole son. I shant
   grumble if I last as long as you.

STAN. Yearp. I hed my day. An' I'd do it all the same again, you
   know that? Do it all the same I would.

MRS BRYANT. Blust! All your drinkin' an' that?

STAN. Hell! Thaas what kep' me goin' look. Almost anyways.
   None o' them young' uns'll do it, hell if they will. There ent
   much life in the young 'uns. Bunch o' weak-kneed ruffians.
   None on 'em like livin' look, non on 'em! You read in them
   ole papers what go on look, an' you wonder if they can see.
   You do! Wonder if they got eyes to look around them. Think
   they know where they live? 'Course they don't, they don't you
   know, not one. Blust! the winter go an' the spring come on
   after an' they don't see buds an' they don't smell no breeze
   an' they don't see gals, an' when they see gals they don't know

whatta do wi' 'em. They don't!

MRS BRYANT. Oh hell, they know *that* all right.

STAN. Gimme my young days an' I'd show 'em. Public
demonstrations I'd give!

MRS BRYANT. Oh shut you up Stan Mann.

STAN. Just gimme young days again Daphne Bryant an' I'd
mount you. But they 'ont come again will they gal?

MRS BRYANT. That they 'ont. My ole days working in the fields
with them other gals, thems 'ont come again, either.

STAN. No, they 'ont that! Rum ole things the years ent they?
(*Pause.*) Them young 'uns is all right though. Long as they
don't let no one fool them, long as they think it out theirselves.
(*Sneezes and coughs.*)

MRS BRYANT (*moving to help him up*). Now get you back home
Stan Mann. (*Good-naturedly.*) Blust, I aren't hevin' no dead
'uns on me look. Take a rum bor, take a rum an' a drop o'
hot milk and get to bed. What's Mrs Mann thinking of lettin'
you out like this.

*She pulls the coat round the old man and pushes him off. He goes
off mumbling and she returns, also mumbling, to her peeling.*

STAN. She's a good gal, she's right 'nough, she don't think I got
it this bad. I'll pull this ole scarf round me. Hed this scarf a
long time, hed it since I started wi' me cars. *She* bought it me.
Lasted a long time. Shouldn't need it this weather though
. . . (*Exits.*)

MRS BRYANT (*mumbling same time as Stan*). Go on, off you go.
Silly ole bugger, runnin' round with a cold like that. Don't
know what 'e's doin' half the time. Poor ole man. Cossie?
Cossie? That you Cossie? (*Looks through door into front room
and out of window at Stan.*) Poor ole man.

*After peeling some seconds she turns the radio on, turning the dial
knob through all manner of stations and back again until she finds
some very loud music which she leaves blaring on. Audible to us,
but not to* MRS BRYANT, *is the call of* 'Yoo-hoo Mother, yoo-

hoo'. BEATIE *appears round the garden and peers into the kitchen.*
MRS BRYANT *jumps.*

MRS BRYANT. Blust, you made me jump.

BEATIE (*toning radio down*). Can't you hear it? Hello, Mother.
(*Kisses her.*)

MRS BRYANT. Well, you've arrived then.

BEATIE. Didn't you get my card?

MRS BRYANT. Came this morning.

BEATIE. Then you knew I'd arrive.

MRS BRYANT. 'Course I did.

BEATIE. My things come?

MRS BRYANT. One suitcase, one parcel in brown paper –

BEATIE. My paintings.

MRS BRYANT. And one other case.

BEATIE. My pick-up. D'you see it?

MRS BRYANT. I hevn't touched a thing.

BEATIE. Bought myself a pick-up on the H.P.

MRS BRYANT. Don't you go telling that to Pearl.

BEATIE. Why not?

MRS BRYANT. She'll wanna know why you didn't buy off her on
the club.

BEATIE. Well, hell, Mother, I weren't gonna hev an ole pick-up
sent me from up north somewhere when we lived next door
to a gramophone shop.

MRS BRYANT. No. Well, what bus you come on – the half-past-
ten one?

BEATIE. Yearp. Picked it up on the ole bridge near Jenny's.

MRS BRYANT. Well I looked for you on the half-past-nine bus and
you weren't on that so I thought to myself I bet she come on
the half-past-ten and you did. You see ole Stan Mann?

BEATIE. Was that him just going up the road?

MRS BRYANT. Wearin' an ole brown scarf, that was him.

BEATIE. I see him! Just as I were comin' off the bus. Blust!
Jimmy Beales give him a real dowsin' down on his allotment

'cos he had an accident.

MRS BRYANT. What, another?

BEATIE. Yearp.

MRS BRYANT. Poor ole man. Thaas what give him the cold then. He come in here sneezin' fit to knock himself down.

BEATIE. Poor ole bugger. Got any tea Ma? I'm gonna unpack.

BEATIE *goes into front room with case. We see her take out frocks, which she puts on hangers, and underwear and blouses, which she puts on couch.*

MRS BRYANT. Did you see my flowers as you come in? Got some of my hollyhocks still flowering. Creeping up the wall they are – did you catch a glimpse on 'em? And my asters and geraniums? Poor ole Joe Simonds gimme those afore he died. Lovely geraniums they are.

BEATIE. Yearp.

MRS BRYANT. When's Ronnie coming?

BEATIE. Saturday week – an' Mother, I'm heving all the family along to meet him when he arrive so you patch your rows wi' them.

MRS BRYANT. What you on about gal? What rows wi' them?

BEATIE. You know full well what rows I mean – them ones you hev wi' Pearl and Susan.

MRS BRYANT. 'Tent so likely. They hev a row wi' me gal but I give 'em no heed, that I don't. (*Hears van pass on road.*) There go Sam Martin's fish van. He'll be calling along here in an hour.

BEATIE (*entering with very smart dress*). Like it Mother?

MRS BRYANT. Blust gal, that's a good 'un ent it! Where d'you buy that then?

BEATIE. Swan and Edgar's.

MRS BRYANT. Did Ronnie choose it?

BEATIE. Yearp.

MRS BRYANT. He've got good taste then.

BEATIE. Yearp. Now listen Mother, I don't want any on you to let me down. When Ronnie come I want him to see we're proper. I'll buy you another bowl so's you don't wash up in the same one as you wash your hands in and I'll get some more tea cloths so's you 'ont use the towels. And no swearin'.

MRS BRYANT. Don't he swear then?

BEATIE. He swear all right, only I don't want him to hear *you* swear.

MRS BRYANT. Hev you given it up then?

BEATIE. Mother, I've never swore.

MRS BRYANT. Go to hell, listen to her!

BEATIE. I never did, now! Mother, I'm *telling* you, listen to me. Ronnie's the best thing I've ever had and I've tried hard for three years to keep hold of him. I don't care what you do when he's gone but don't show me up when he's here.

MRS BRYANT. Speak to your father gal.

BEATIE. Father too. I don't want Ronnie to think I come from a small-minded family. 'I can't bear mean people,' he say. 'I don't care about their education, I don't care about their past as long as their minds are large and inquisitive, as long as they're generous.'

MRS BRYANT. Who say that?

BEATIE. Ronnie.

MRS BRYANT. He *talk* like that?

BEATIE. Yearp.

MRS BRYANT. Sounds like a preacher.

BEATIE (*standing on a chair*). 'I don't care if you call me a preacher, I've got something to say and I'm going to say it. I don't care if you don't like being told things – we've come to a time when you've got to say this is right and this is wrong. God in heaven, have we got to be wet all the time? Well, have we?' Christ, Mother, you've got them ole wasps still flying around. (*She waves her arms in the air flaying the wasps.*) September and you've still got wasps. Owee! shoo-hoo! (*In the voice of her childhood*) Mammy, Mammy, take them ole things away. I doesn't like the – ooh! Nasty things.

BEATIE *jumps off chair and picks up a coat hanger. Now both she and her mother move stealthily around the room 'hunting' wasps. Occasionally* MRS BRYANT *strikes one dead or* BEATIE *spears one against the wall.* MRS BRYANT *conducts herself matter-of-fact-like but* BEATIE *makes a fiendish game of it.*

MRS BRYANT. They're after them apples on that tree outside. Go on! Off wi' you! Outside now! There – that's got 'em out, but I bet the buggers'll be back in a jiffy look.

BEATIE. Oh yes, an' I want to have a bath.

MRS BRYANT. When d'you want that then?

BEATIE. This morning.

MRS BRYANT. You can't hev no bath this morning, that copper won't heat up till after lunch.

BEATIE. Then I'll bake the pastries for Jenny this morning and you can put me water on now. (*She returns to sort her clothes.*)

MRS BRYANT. I'll do that now then. I'll get you the soft water from the tank.

MRS BRYANT *now proceeds to collect bucket and move back and forth between the garden out of view and the copper in the kitchen. She fills the copper with about three buckets of water and then lights the fire underneath it. In between buckets she chats.*

(*Off – as she hears lorry go by*) There go Danny Oakley to market. (*She returns with first bucket.*)

BEATIE. Mother! I dreamt I died last night and heaven were at the bottom of a pond. You had to jump in and sink and you know how afeared I am of water. It was full of film stars and soldiers and there were two rooms. In one room they was playing skiffle and – and – I can't remember what were goin' on in the other. Now who was God? I can't remember. It was someone we knew, a she. (*Returns to unpacking.*)

MRS BRYANT (*entering with second bucket; automatically*). Yearp. (*Pause.*) You hear what happened to the headache doctor's patient? You know what they say about him – if you've got a headache you're all right but if you've got something more you've had it! Well he told a woman not to worry about a lump she complained of under her breast and you know what that were? That turned out to be thrombosis! There! Thrombosis! She had that breast off. Yes, she did. Had to hev it cut off. (*Goes for next bucket.*)

BEATIE (*automatically*). Yearp. (*She appears from front room with two framed paintings. She sets them up and admires them. They are primitive designs in bold masses, rather well-balanced shapes and bright poster colours – red, black, and yellow – see Dusty Bicker's work.*) Mother! Did I write and tell you I've took up painting? I started five months ago. Working in gouache. Ronnie says I'm good. Says I should carry on and maybe I can sell them for curtain designs. 'Paint girl,' he say. 'Paint! The world is full of people who don't do the things they want so you paint and give us all hope!'

MRS BRYANT *enters.*

BEATIE. Like 'em?

MRS BRYANT (*looks at them a second*). Good colours ent they. (*She is unmoved and continues to empty a third bucket while BEATIE returns paintings to other room.*) Yes gal, I ent got no row wi' Pearl but I ask her to change my Labour Tote man 'cos I wanted to give the commission to Charlie Gorleston and she didn't do it. Well, if she can be like that I can be like that too. You gonna do some baking you say?

BEATIE (*enters from front room putting on a pinafore and carrying a parcel*). Right now. Here y'are Daphne Bryant, present for you. I want eggs, flour, sugar, and marg. I'm gonna bake a sponge and give it frilling. (*Goes to larder to collect things.*)

MRS BRYANT (*unpacking parcel; it is a pinafore*). We both got one now.

MRS BRYANT *continues to peel potatoes as* BEATIE *proceeds to separate four eggs, the yolks of which she starts whipping with sugar. She sings meanwhile a ringing folk song.*

BEATIE.

    Oh a dialogue I'll sing you as true as me life.

    Between a coal owner and poor pitman's wife

    As she was a-walking along the highway

    She met a coal owner and to him did say

        Derry down, down, down Derry down.

    Whip the eggs till they're light yellow he says.

MRS BRYANT. Who says?

BEATIE. Ronnie.

    Good morning Lord Firedamp the good woman said

    I'll do you no harm sir so don't be afraid

    If you'd been where I'd been for most of my life

    You wouldn't turn pale at a poor pitman's wife

        Singing down, down, down Derry down.

MRS BRYANT. What song's that?

BEATIE. A coalmining song.

MRS BRYANT. I tell you what I reckon's a good song, that 'I'll wait for you in the heavens blue'. I reckon that's a lovely song I do. Jimmy Samson he sing that.

BEATIE. It's like twenty other songs, it don't mean anything and it's sloshy and sickly.

MRS BRYANT. Yes, I reckon that's a good song that.

BEATIE (*suddenly*). Listen Mother, let me see if I can explain something to you. Ronnie always say that's the point of knowing people. 'It's no good having friends who scratch each other's back,' he say. 'The excitement in knowing people is to hand on what you know and to learn what you don't know. Learn from me,' he say, 'I don't know much but learn what I know.' So let me try and explain to you what he explain to me.

MRS BRYANT (*on hearing a bus*). There go the half-past-eleven bus to Diss – blust that's early. (*Puts spuds in saucepan on oven and goes to collect runner beans, which she prepares.*)

BEATIE. Mother, I'm *talking* to you. Blust woman it's not often we get together and really talk, it's nearly always me listening to you telling who's dead. Just listen a second.

MRS BRYANT. Well go on gal, but you always take so long to say it.

BEATIE. What are the words of that song?

MRS BRYANT. I don't know all the words.

BEATIE. I'll tell you.

Recites them.

I'll wait for you in the heavens blue
As my arms are waiting now.
Please come to me and I'll be true
My love shall not turn sour.
I hunger, I hunger, I cannot wait longer,
My love shall not turn sour.
There! Now what do that mean?

MRS BRYANT (*surprised*). Well, don't you know what that mean?

BEATIE. I mean what do they do to you? How do the words affect you? Are you moved? Do you find them beautiful?

MRS BRYANT. Them's as good words as any.

BEATIE. But do they make you feel better?

MRS BRYANT. Blust gal! That ent meant to be a laxative!

BEATIE. I must be mad to talk with you.

MRS BRYANT. Besides it's the tune I like. Words never mean anything.

BEATIE. All right, the tune then! What does *that* do to you? Make your belly go gooey, your heart throb, make your head spin with passion? Yes, passion, Mother, know what it is? Because you won't find passion in that third-rate song, no you won't!

MRS BRYANT. Well all right gal, so it's third-rate you say. Can you say why? What make that third-rate and them frilly bits of opera and concert first-rate? 'Sides, did I write that song? Beatie Bryant, you do go up and down in your spirits, and I don't know what's gotten into you gal, no I don't.

BEATIE. I don't know either, Mother. I'm worried about Ronnie

I suppose. I have that same row with him. I ask him exactly
the same questions – what make a pop song third-rate. And
he answer and I don't know what he talk about. Something
about registers, something about commercial world blunting
our responses. 'Give yourself time woman,' he say. 'Time!
You can't learn how to live overnight. *I* don't even know,' he
say, 'and half the world don't know but we got to try. Try,'
he say, "cos we're still suffering from the shock of two world
wars and we don't know it. Talk,' he say 'and look and listen
and think and ask questions.' But Jesus! I don't know what
questions to ask or *how* to talk. And he gets so riled – and yet
sometimes so nice. 'It's all going up in flames,' he say, 'but
I'm going to make bloody sure I save someone from the fire.'

MRS BRYANT. Well I'm sure *I* don't know what he's on about.
Turn to your baking gal look and get you done, Father'll be
home for his lunch in an hour.

A faint sound of an ambulance is heard. MRS BRYANT *looks up but
says nothing.* BEATIE *turns to whipping the eggs again and* MRS
BRYANT *to cleaning up the runner beans. Out of this pause* MRS
BRYANT *begins to sing 'I'll wait for you in the heavens blue', but
on the second line she hums the tune incorrectly.*

BEATIE (*laughs*). No, no, hell Mother, it don't go like that. It's –

BEATIE *corrects her and in helping her mother she ends by singing
the song, with some enthusiasm, to the end.*

MRS BRYANT. Thank God you come home sometimes gal – you
do bring a little life with you anyway.

BEATIE. Mother, I ent never heard you express a feeling like that.

MRS BRYANT (*she is embarrassed*). The world don't want no
feelings gal. (*Footsteps are heard.*) Is that your father home
already?

MR BRYANT *appears at the back door and lays a bicycle against
the wall. He is a small shrivelled man wearing denims, a peaked*

cap, boots, and gaiters. He appears to be in some pain.

BEATIE. Hello poppy Bryant.

MR BRYANT. Hello Beatie. You're here then.

MRS BRYANT. What are you home so early for?

MR BRYANT. The ole guts ache again. (*Sits in armchair and grimaces.*)

MRS BRYANT. Well, what is it?

MR BRYANT. Blust woman, I don't know what 'tis n'more'n you, do I?

MRS BRYANT. Go to the doctor man I keep telling you.

BEATIE. What is it father Bryant?

MRS BRYANT. He got guts ache.

BEATIE. But what's it from?

MR BRYANT. I've just said I don't know.

MRS BRYANT. Get you to a doctor man, don't be so soft. You don't want to be kept from work do you?

MR BRYANT. That I don't, no I don't. Hell, I just see ole Stan Mann picked up an' thaas upset me enough.

MRS BRYANT. Picked up you say?

MR BRYANT. Well, didn't you hear the ambulance?

MRS BRYANT. There! I hear it but I didn't say narthin'. Was that for Stan Mann then?

MR BRYANT. I was cycling along wi' Jack Stones and we see this here figure on the side o' the road there an' I say, thaas a rum shape in the road Jack, and he say, blust, that's ole Stan Mann from Heybrid, an' 'twere. 'Course soon ever he see what 'twere, he rushed off for 'n ambulance and I waited alongside Stan.

BEATIE. But he just left here.

MRS BRYANT. I see it comin'. He come in here an' I shoved him off home. Get you to bed and take some rum an' a drop o' hot milk, I tell him.

BEATIE. Is he gonna die?

MR BRYANT. Wouldn't surprise me that it wouldn't. Blust, he

look done in.

MRS BRYANT. Poor ole fellah. Shame though ent it?

MR BRYANT. When d'you arrive Beatie?

MRS BRYANT. She come in the half-past-ten bus. I looked for her on the nine-thirty bus and she weren't on that, so I thought to myself I bet she come on the half-past-ten. She did.

BEATIE. Yearp.

MRS BRYANT. You gonna stay away all day?

MR BRYANT. No I aren't. I gotta go back 'cos one of the ole sows is piggin'. 'Spect she'll be hevin' them in a couple of hours. (*To Beatie*) Got a sow had a litter o' twenty-two. (*Picks up paper to read.*)

BEATIE. Twenty-two? Oh Pop, can I come see this afternoon?

MR BRYANT. Yearp.

MRS BRYANT. Thought you was hevin' a bath.

BEATIE. Oh yes, I forgot. I'll come tomorrow then.

MR BRYANT. They'll be there. What you doin' gal?

MRS BRYANT. She's baking a sponge, now leave her be.

MR BRYANT. Oh, you learnt something in London then.

BEATIE. Ronnie taught me.

MR BRYANT. Well where *is* Ronnie then?

MRS BRYANT. He's comin' on Saturday a week an' the family's goin' to be here to greet him.

MR BRYANT. All on 'em?

MRS BRYANT *and* BEATIE. All on 'em!

MR BRYANT. Well that'll be a rum gatherin' then.

MRS BRYANT. And we've to be on our best behaviour.

MR BRYANT. No cussin' and swearin'?

MRS BRYANT *and* BEATIE. No.

MR BRYANT. Blust, I shan't talk then.

A young man, MR HEALEY, *appears round the garden – he is the farmer's son, and manager of the estate Bryant works for.*

MRS BRYANT (*seeing him first*). Oh, Mr Healey, yes. Jack! It's Mr Healey.

MR BRYANT rises and goes to the door. HEALEY speaks in a firm, not unkind, but business-is-business voice. There is that apologetic threat even in his politeness.

MR HEALEY. You were taken ill.

MR BRYANT. It's all right, sir, only guts ache, won't be long goin'. The pigs is all seen to, just waiting for the ole sow to start.

MR HEALEY. What time you expecting it?

MR BRYANT. Oh, she 'ont come afore two this afternoon, no she 'ont be much afore that.

MR HEALEY. You're sure you're well, Jack? I've been thinking that it's too much for you carting those pails round the yard.

MR BRYANT. No, that ent too heavy, sir, 'course 'tent. You don't wanna worry, I'll be along after lunch. Just an ole guts ache that's all – seein' the doctor tonight – eat too fast probably.

MR HEALEY. If you're sure you're all right, then I'll put young Daniels off. You can manage without him now we've fixed the new pump in.

MR BRYANT. I can manage, sir – 'course I can.

MR HEALEY (*moving off outside*). All right then, Jack, I'll be with you around two o'clock. I want to take the old one out of number three and stick her with the others in seventeen. The little ones won't need her, will they? Then we'll have them sorted out tomorrow.

MR BRYANT. That's right, sir, they *can* go on their own now, they can. I'll see to it tomorrow.

MR HEALEY. Right then, Jack. Oh – you hear Stan Mann died?

MR BRYANT. He died already? But I saw him off in the ambulance no more'n half-hour ago.

MR HEALEY. Died on the way to hospital. Jack Stones told me. Lived in Heybrid, didn't he?

MR BRYANT. Alongside my daughter.

MR BRYANT (*calling*). Well, good morning, Mrs Bryant.

MRS BRYANT (*calling*). Good morning, Mr Healey.

The two men nod to each other, MR HEALEY *goes off.* MR BRYANT *lingers a second.*

MRS BRYANT (*to Beatie*). That was Mr Healey, the new young manager.

BEATIE. I know it Mother.

MR BRYANT (*turning slowly*). He's dead then.

MRS BRYANT. Who? Not Stan Mann!

MR BRYANT. Young Healey just tell me.

MRS BRYANT. Well I go t'hell. An' he were just here look, just here alongside o' me not more'n hour past.

MR BRYANT. Rum ent it?

BEATIE (*weakly*). Oh hell, I hate dying.

MRS BRYANT. He were a good ole bor though. Yes he was. A good ole stick. There!

BEATIE. Used to ride me round on his horse, always full o' life an' jokes. 'Tell your boy he wanna hurry up and marry you,' he say to me, 'or I'll hev you meself on a plate.'

MRS BRYANT. He were a one for smut though.

BEATIE. I was talkin' with him last night. Only last night he was tellin' me how he caught me pinchin' some gooseberries off his patch an' how he gimme a whole apron full and I went into one o' his fields near by an' ate the lot. 'Blust,' he say, 'you had the ole guts ache,' an' he laugh, sat there laughin' away to hisself.

MRS BRYANT. I can remember that. Hell, Jenny'll miss him – used always to pop in an' out o' theirs.

MRS BRYANT. Seem like the whole world gone suddenly dead don' it?

MR BRYANT. Rum ent it?

Silence.

MRS BRYANT. You say young Healey tell you that? *He's* a nice man Mr Healey is, yes he is, a good sort, I like him.

BEATIE. Sound like he were threatening to sack Father; don't know about being nice.

MR BRYANT. That's what I say see, get a rise and they start

cutting down the men or the overtime.

MRS BRYANT. The Union magazine's come.

MR BRYANT. I don't want that ole thing.

BEATIE. Why can't you do something to stop the sackings?

MR BRYANT. You can't, you can't – that's what I say, you can't. Sharp as a pig's scream they are – you just *can't* do nothin'.

BEATIE. Mother, where's the bakin' tin?

MR BRYANT. When we gonna eat that?

BEATIE. You ent! It's for Jenny Beales.

MR BRYANT. You aren't making that for Jenny are you?

BEATIE. I promised her.

MR BRYANT. Not with my electricity you aren't.

BEATIE. But I promised, Poppy.

MR BRYANT. That's no matters. I aren't spendin' money on electricity bills so's you can make every Tom, Dick 'n' Harry a sponge cake, that I aren't.

MRS BRYANT. Well, don't be so soft man, it won't take more'n half-hour's bakin'.

MR BRYANT. I don't care what it'll take I say. I aren't lettin' her. Jenny wants cakes, she can make 'em herself. so put that away Beatie and use it for something else.

MRS BRYANT. You wanna watch what you're sayin' of 'cos I live here too.

MR BRYANT. I know all about that but I pay the electricity bill and I say she isn't bakin'.

BEATIE. But Poppy, one cake.

MR BRYANT. No I say.

BEATIE. Well, Mummy, do something – how can he be so mean.

MRS BRYANT. Blust me if you ent the meanest ole sod that walks this earth. Your own daughter and you won't let her use your oven. You bloody ole hypercrite.

MR BRYANT. You pay the bills and then you call names.

MRS BRYANT. What I ever seen in you God only knows. Yes! an' he never warn me. Bloody ole hypercrite!

MR BRYANT. You pay the bills and then you call names I say.

MRS BRYANT. On four pounds ten a week? You want me to keep
you *and* pay bills? Four pound ten he give me. God knows
what he do wi' the rest. I don't know how much he've got.
I don't, no I don't. Bloody ole hypercrite.

MR BRYANT. Let's hev grub and not so much o' the lip woman.

BEATIE *begins to put the things away. She is on the verge of the
tears she will soon let fall.*

MRS BRYANT. That's how he talk to me – when he do talk. 'Cos
you know he don't ever talk more'n he hev to, and when he
do say something it's either 'how much this cost' or 'lend us
couple o'bob'. He've got the money but sooner than break
into that he borrow off me. Bloody old miser. (*To Beatie*)
What you wanna cry for gal? 'Tent worth it. Blust, you don't
wanna let an ole hypercrite like him upset you, no you don't.
I'll get my back on you my manny, see if I don't. You won't
get away with no tricks on me.

BEATIE *has gone into the other room and returned with a small
packet.*

BEATIE (*throwing parcel in father's lap*). Present for you.

MRS BRYANT. I'd give him presents that I would! I'd walk out
and disown him! Beatie, now stop you a-cryin' gal – blust, he
ent worth cryin' for, that he ent. Stop it I say and we'll have
lunch. Or you lost your appetite gal?

BEATIE *sniffs a few tears back, pauses, and –*

BEATIE. No – no, that I ent. Hell, I can eat all right!

Curtain.

SCENE TWO

Lunch has been eaten. MR BRYANT *is sitting at the table rolling himself a cigarette.* MRS BRYANT *is collecting the dishes and taking them to a sink to wash up.* BEATIE *is taking things off the table and putting them into the larder – jars of sauce, plates of sliced bread and cakes, butter, sugar, condiments, and bowl of tinned fruit.*

MRS BRYANT (*to Beatie*). Ask him what he want for his tea.

MR BRYANT. She don't ever ask me before, what she wanna ask me now for?

MRS BRYANT. Tell him it's his stomach I'm thinking about – I don't want him complaining to me about the food I cook.

MR BRYANT. Tell her it's no matters to me – I ent got no pain now besides.

BEATIE. Mother, is that water ready for my bath?

MRS BRYANT. Where you hevin' it?

BEATIE. In the kitchen of course.

MRS BRYANT. Blust gal, you can't bath in this kitchen during the day, what if someone call at the door?

BEATIE. Put up the curtain then, I shant be no more'n ten minutes.

MR BRYANT. 'Sides, who want to see her in her dickey suit.

BEATIE. I know men as 'ould pay to see me in my dickey suit. (*Posing her plump outline.*) Don't you think I got a nice dickey suit?

MR BRYANT *makes a dive and pinches her bottom.*

Ow! Stoppit Bryants, stoppit!

He persists.

Daddy, stop it now!

MRS BRYANT. Tell him he can go as soon as he like, I want your bath over and done with.

BEATIE. Oh Mother, stop this nonsense do. If you want to tell him something tell him – not me.

MRS BRYANT. *I* don't want to speak to him, hell if I do.

BEATIE. Father, get the bath in for me please. Mother, where's them curtains.

> MR BRYANT *goes off to fetch a long tin bath – wide at one end, narrow at the other – while* MRS BRYANT *leaves washing up to fish out some curtains which she hangs from one wall to another concealing thus a corner of the kitchen. Anything that is in the way is removed.* BEATIE *meanwhile brings out a change of underwear, her dressing-gown, the new frock, some soap, powder, and towel. These she lays within easy reach of the curtain.*

BEATIE. I'm gonna wear my new dress and go across the fields to see Frankie and Pearl.

MRS BRYANT. Frankie won't be there, what you on about? He'll be gettin' the harvest in.

BEATIE. You makin' anything for the harvest festival?

MR BRYANT (*entering with bath, places it behind curtain*). Your mother don't ever do anything for the harvest festival – don't you know that by now.

BEATIE. Get you to work father Bryant, I'm gonna plunge in water and I'll make a splash.

MRS BRYANT. Tell him we've got kippers for tea and if he don' want none let him say now.

BEATIE. She says it's kippers for tea.

MR BRYANT. Tell her I'll eat kippers. (*Goes off, collecting bike on the way.*)

BEATIE. He says he'll eat kippers. Right now, Mother, you get cold water an' I'll pour the hot.

> *Each now picks up a bucket.* MRS BRYANT *goes off out to collect the cold water and* BEATIE *plunges bucket into boiler to retrieve hot water. The bath is prepared with much childlike glee.* BEATIE *loves her creature comforts and does with unabashed, almost animal, enthusiasm that which she enjoys. When the bath is prepared,* BEATIE *slips behind the curtain to undress and enter.*

MRS BRYANT. You hear about Jimmy Skelton? They say he've bin arrested for accosting some man in the village.

BEATIE. Jimmy Skelton what own the pub?

MRS BRYANT. That's him. I know all about Jimmy Skelton though. He were a young boy when I were a young girl. I always partner him at whist drives. He's been to law before you know. Yes! An' he won the day too! Won the day he did. I don't take notice though, him and me gets on all right. What do Ronnie's mother do with her time?

BEATIE. She've got a sick husband to look after.

MRS BRYANT. She an educated woman?

BEATIE. Educated? No. She's a foreigner. Nor ent Ronnie educated neither. He's an intellectual, failed all his exams. They read and things.

MRS BRYANT. Oh, they don't do nothing then?

BEATIE. Do nothing? I'll tell you what Ronnie do, he work till all hours in a hot ole kitchen. An' he teach kids in a club to act and jive and such. And he don't stop at week-ends either 'cos then there's political meetings and such and I get breathless trying to keep up wi' him. OOOhh, Mother it's hot . . .

MRS BRYANT. I'll get you some cold then.

BEATIE. No – ooh – it's lovely. The water's so soft Mother.

MRS BRYANT. Yearp.

BEATIE. It's so soft and smooth. I'm in.

MRS BRYANT. Don't you stay in too long gal. There go the twenty-minutes-past-one bus.

BEATIE. Oh Mother, me bath cubes. I forgot me bath cubes. In the little case by me pick-up.

MRS BRYANT *finds bath cubes and hands them to Beatie.*

MRS BRYANT (*continuing her work*). I shall never forget when I furse heard on it. I was in the village and I was talking to Reggie Fowler. I say to him, there've bin a lot o'talk about Jimmy ent there? Disgustin', I say. Still, there's somebody wanna make some easy money, you'd expect that in a village wouldn't you? Yes, I say to him, a lot of talk. An' he stood there, an' he were a-looking' at me an' a-looking' as I were a-

talking' and then he say, missus, he say, I were one o' the
victims! Well, you could've hit me over the head wi' a
hammer. I was one o' the victims, he say.

BEATIE. Mother, these bath cubes smell beautiful. I could stay
here all day.

MRS BRYANT. Still, Jimmy's a good fellow with it all – do
anything for you. I partner him at whist drives; he bin had
up scores o' times though.

BEATIE. Mother, what we gonna make Ronnie when he come?

MRS BRYANT. Well, what do he like?

BEATIE He like trifle and he like steak and kidney pie.

MRS BRYANT. We'll make that then. So long as he don't complain
o' the guts ache. Frankie hev it too much you know.

BEATIE. Know why? You all eat too much. The Londoners think
we live a healthy life but they don't know we stuff ourselves
silly till our guts ache.

MRS BRYANT. But you know what's wrong wi' Jimmy Beales? It's
indigestion. He eat too fast.

BEATIE. What the hell's indigestion doin' a'tween his shoulder
blades?

MRS BRYANT. 'Cos some people get it so bad it go right through
their stomach to the back.

BEATIE. You don't get indigestion in the back Mother, what you
on about?

MRS BRYANT. Don't you tell me gal, I hed it!

BEATIE. Oweee! The soap's in me eyes – Mother, towel, the
towel, quickly the towel!

MRS BRYANT *hands in towel to Beatie. The washing up is probably
done by now, so* MRS BRYANT *sits in a chair, legs apart and arms
folded, thinking what else to say.*

MRS BRYANT. You heard that Ma Buckley hev been taken to
Mental Hospital in Norwich? Poor ole dear. If there's one
thing I can't abide that's mental cases. They frighten me –
they do. Can't face 'em. I'd sooner follow a man to a

churchyard than the mental hospital. That's a terrible thing to see a person lose their reason – that 'tis. Well, I tell you what, down where I used to live, down the other side of the Hall, years ago we moved in next to an old woman. I only had Jenny and Frank then – an' this woman she were the sweetest of people. We used to talk and do errands for each other – Oh she was a sweet ole dear. And then one afternoon I was going out to get my washin' in and I saw her. She was standin' in a tub o' water up to her neck. She was! Up to her neck. An' her eyes had that glazed, wonderin' look and she stared straight at me she did. Well, do you know what? I was struck *dumb*. I was *struck* dumb wi' shock. What wi' her being so nice all this while, the sudden comin' on her like that in the tub fair upset me. It did! And people tell me afterwards that she's bin goin' in an'out o' hospital for years. Blust, that scare me. That scare me so much that she nearly took me round the bend wi' her.

BEATIE *appears from behind the curtain in her dressing-gown, a towel round her head.*

BEATIE. There! I'm gonna hev a bath every day when I'm married.

BEATIE *starts rubbing her hair with towel and fiddles with radio. She finds a programme playing Mendelssohn's Fourth Symphony, the slow movement, and stands before the mirror, listening and rubbing.*

BEATIE (*looking at her reflection*). Isn't your nose a funny thing, and your ears. And your arms and your legs, aren't they funny things – sticking out of a lump.

MRS BRYANT (*switching off radio*). Turn that squit off!

BEATIE (*turning to her mother violently*). *Mother!* I could kill you when you do that. No wonder I don't know anything about anything. I never heard nothing but dance music because you always turned off the classics. I never knowed anything about the news because you always switched off after the headlines. I never read any good books 'cos there was never any in the house.

MRS BRYANT. What's gotten into you now gal?

BEATIE. God in heaven Mother, you live in the country but you got no – no – no majesty. You spend your time among green fields, you grow flowers and you breathe fresh air and you got no majesty. Your mind's cluttered up with nothing and you shut out the world. What kind of a life did you give me?

MRS BRYANT. Blust gal, I weren't no teacher.

BEATIE. But you hindered. You didn't open one door for me. Even his mother cared more for me than what you did. Beatie, she say, Beatie, why don't you take up evening classes and learn something other than waitressing. Yes, she say, you won't ever regret learnin' things. But did you care what job I took up or whether I learned things? You didn't even think it was necessary.

MRS BRYANT. I fed you. I clothed you. I took you out to the sea. What more d'you want. We're only country folk you know. We ent got no big things here you know.

BEATIE. Squit! Squit! It makes no difference country or town. *All* the town girls I ever worked with were just like me. It makes no difference country or town – that's squit. Do you know when I used to work at the holiday camp and I sat down with the other girls to write a letter we used to sit and discuss what we wrote about. An' we all agreed, all on us, that we started: 'Just a few lines to let you know', and then we get on to the weather and then we get stuck so we write about ecah other and after a page an' half of big scrawl end up: 'Hoping this finds you well as it leaves me.' There! We couldn't say any more. Thousands of things happening at this holiday camp and we couldn't find words for them. All of us the same. Hundreds of girls and one day we're gonna be mothers, and you *still* talk to me of Jimmy Skelton and the ole woman in the tub. Do you know I've heard that story a dozen times. A dozen times. Can't you hear yourself Mother? Jesus, how can I bring Ronnie to this house.

MRS BRYANT. Blust gal, if Ronnie don't like us then he –

BEATIE. Oh, he'll like you all right. He like people. He'd've loved ole Stan Mann. Ole Stan Mann would've understood everything Ronnie talk about. Blust! That man liked livin'. Besides, Ronnie say it's too late for the old 'uns to learn. But he says it's up to us young 'uns. And them of us that know hev got to teach them of us as don't know.

MRS BRYANT. I bet he hev a hard time trying to change you gal!

BEATIE. He's *not* trying to change me Mother. You can't change people, he say, you can only give them some love and hope they'll take it. And he's tryin' to teach me and I'm tryin' to understand – do you see that Mother?

MRS BRYANT. I don't see what that's got to do with music though.

BEATIE. Oh my God! (*Suddenly*) I'll show you. (*Goes off to front room to collect pick-up and a record.*). Now sit you down gal and I'll show you. Don't start ironing or reading or nothing, just sit there and be prepared to learn something. (*Appears with pick-up and switches on.*) You aren't too old, just you sit and listen. That's the trouble you see, we ent ever prepared to learn anything, we close our minds the minute anything unfamiliar appear. *I* could never listen to music. I used to like some on it but then I'd lose patience, I'd go to bed in the middle of a symphony, or my mind would wonder 'cos the music didn't mean anything to me so I'd go to bed or start talking. 'Sit back woman,' he'd say, 'listen to it. Let it happen to you and you'll grow as big as the music itself.'

MRS BRYANT. Blust he talk like a book.

BEATIE. An' sometimes he talk as though you didn't know where the moon or the stars was. (BEATIE *puts on record of Bizet's* L'Arlésienne *Suite*.) Now listen. This is a simple piece of music, it's not highbrow but it's full of living. And that's what he say socialism is. 'Christ,' he say. 'Socialism isn't talking all the time, it's living, it's singing, it's dancing, it's being interested in what go on around you, it's being concerned about people and the world.' Listen Mother. (*She becomes breathless and excited*). Listen to it. It's simple isn't it? Can you call that squit?

MRS BRYANT. I don't say it's all squit.

BEATIE. You don't have to frown because it's alive.

MRS BRYANT. No, not all on it's squit.

BEATIE. See the way the other tune comes in? Hear it? Two simple tunes, one after the other.

MRS BRYANT. I aren't saying it's all squit.

BEATIE. And now listen, listen, it goes together, the two tunes together, they knit, they're perfect. Don't it make you want to dance? (*She begins to dance a mixture of a cossack dance and a sailor's hornpipe.*)

The music becomes fast and her spirits are young and high.

Listen to that Mother. Is it difficult? Is it squit? It's light. It makes me feel light and confident and happy. God, Mother, we could all be so much more happy and alive. Wheeeee . . .

BEATIE *claps her hands and dances on and her* MOTHER *smiles and claps her hands and* —

the curtain falls.

Act Three

Two weeks have passed. It is Saturday, the day Ronnie is to arrive. One of the walls of the kitchen is now pushed aside and the front room is revealed. It is low-ceilinged, and has dark brown wooden beams. The furniture is not typical country farmhouse type. There may be one or two windsor-type straight-back chairs, but for the rest it is cheap utility stuff. Two armchairs, a table, a small bamboo table, wooden chairs, a small sofa, and a swivel bookcase. There are a lot of flowers around – in pots in the window ledge and in vases on the bamboo table and swivel case.

It is three in the afternoon, the weather is cloudy – it has been raining and is likely to start again. On the table is a spread of food (none of this will be eaten). There are cakes and biscuits on plates and glass stands. Bread and butter, butter in a dish, tomatoes, cheese, jars of pickled onions, sausage rolls, dishes of tinned fruit – it is a spread! Round the table are eight chairs. Beatie's paintings are hanging on the wall. The room is empty because BEATIE *is upstairs changing and* MRS BRYANT *is in the kitchen.* BEATIE – *until she descends – conducts all her conversation shouting from upstairs.*

BEATIE. Mother! What you on at now?

MRS BRYANT (*from kitchen*). I'm just puttin' these glass cherries on the trifle.

BEATIE. Well come on look, he'll be here at four thirty.

MRS BRYANT (*from kitchen*). Don't you fret gal, it's another hour 'n' half yet, the postman hevn't gone by. (*Enters with an enormous bowl of trifle.*) There! He like trifle you say?

BEATIE. He love it.

MRS BRYANT. Well he need to 'cos there's plenty on it. (*To herself, surveying the table*) Yes, there is, there's plenty on it. (*It starts to rain.*) Blust, listen to that weather.

BEATIE. Rainin' again!

MRS BRYANT (*looking out of window*). Raining? It's rainin' fit to drowned you. (*Sound of bus.*) There go the three o'clock.

BEATIE. Mother you get changed, come on, I want us ready in time.

MRS BRYANT. Blust you'd think it were the bloody Prince of Egypt comin'. (*Goes upstairs.*)

The stage is empty again for a few seconds. People are heard taking off their macs and exclaiming at the weather from the kitchen. Enter FRANK *and* PEARL BRYANT. *He is pleasant and dressed in a blue pin-striped suit, is ruddy-faced and blond-haired. An odd sort of shyness makes him treat everything as a joke. His wife is a pretty brunette, young, and ordinarily dressed in plain, flowered frock.*

FRANK (*calling*). Well, where are you all? Come on – I'm hungry.

PEARL. Shut you up bor, you only just had lunch.

FRANK. Well I'm hungry again. (*Calling*) Well, where is this article we come to see?

BEATIE. He ent arrived.

FRANK. Well, he want to hurry, 'cos I'm hungry.

BEATIE. You're always hungry.

FRANK. What do you say he is – a strong socialist?

BEATIE. Yes.

FRANK. And a Jew boy?

BEATIE. Yes.

FRANK (*to himself*). Well, that's a queer mixture then.

PEARL (*calling*). I hope he don't talk politics all the time.

FRANK. Have you had a letter from him yet?

PEARL. Stop it Frank, you know she hevn't heard.

FRANK. Well that's a rum boy friend what don't write. (*Looks at paintings, pauses before one of them and growls.*)

PEARL. Watch out or it'll bite you back.

BEATIE *comes down from upstairs. She is dressed in her new frock and looks happy, healthy, and radiant.*

FRANK. Hail there, sister! I was then contemplating your masterpiece.

BEATIE. Well don't contemplate too long 'cos you aren't hevin' it.

FRANK. Blust! I'd set my ole heart on it.

PEARL. That's a nice frock Beatie.

FRANK. Where's the rest of our mighty clan?

BEATIE. Jenny and Jimmy should be here soon and Susie and Stan mightn't come.

FRANK. What's wrong wi' them?

BEATIE. Don't talk to me about it 'cos I hed enough! Susie won't talk to Mother.

PEARL. That make nearly eighteen months she hevn't spoke.

BEATIE. Why ever did *you* and Mother fall out Pearl?

FRANK. 'Cos Mother's so bloody stubborn that's why.

PEARL. Because one day she said she wanted to change her Labour Tote man, that's why, and she asked me to do it for her. So I said all right, but it'll take a couple of weeks; and then she get riled because she said I didn't want to change it for her. And then I ask her why didn't she change him herself and she say because she was too ill to go all the way to see John Clayton to tell him, and then she say to me, why, don't you think I'm ill? And I say – I know this were tactless o' me – but I say, no Mother, you don't look ill to me. And she didn't speak to me since. I only hope she don't snub me this afternoon.

BEATIE. Well, she tell me a different story.

FRANK. Mother's always quarrelling.

PEARL. Well I reckon there ent much else she *can* do stuck in this ole house on her own all day. And father Bryant he don't say too much when he's home you know.

FRANK. Well blust, she hevn't spoke to her own mother for three years, not since Granny Dykes took Jenny in when she had that illegitimate gal Daphne.

BEATIE. Hell! What a bloody family!

FRANK. A mighty clan I say.

JIMMY *and* JENNY BEALES *now enter.*

JIMMY. Hello Frankie, hello Pearl, hellow Beatie.

FRANK. And more of the mighty clan.

JENNY. Mighty clan you say? Mighty bloody daft you mean. Well, where is he?

FRANK. The mysterious stranger has not yet come – we await.

JENNY. Well, I aren't waitin' long 'cos I'm hungry.

PEARL. That's all this family of Bryants ever do is think o' their guts.

FRANK (*to Jimmy*). Have you formed your association yit?

JENNY. What association is this?

FRANK. What! Hevn't he told you?

JIMMY. Shut you up Frank Bryant or you'll get me hung.

FRANK. Oh, a mighty association – a mighty one! I'll tell ye. One day you see we was all sittin' round in the pub – Jimmy, me, Starkie, Johnny Oats, and Bonky Dawson – we'd hed a few drinks and Jimmy was feelin' – well, he was feelin' – you know what, the itch! He hed the itch! He started complaining about ham, ham, ham all the time. So then Bonky Dawson say, blust, he say, there must be women about who feel the same. And Starkie he say, well 'course they are, only how do you tell? And then we was all quiet a while thinkin' on it when suddenly Jimmy says, we ought to start an association of them as need a bit now and then and we all ought to wear a badge he say, and when you see a woman wearin' a badge you know she need a bit too.

JIMMY. Now that's enough Frank or I'll hit you over the skull.

FRANK. Now, not content wi' just that, ole Jimmy then say, and we ought to have a password to indicate how bad off you are.

So listen what he suggest. He suggest you go up to any one o' these women what's wearin' a badge and you say, how many lumps of sugar do you take in your tea? And if she say 'two' then you know she ent too badly off, but she's willin'. But if she say 'four' then you know she's in as bad a state as what you are, see?

Long pause.

JENNY. He'd hev a fit if she said she took sixteen lumps though wouldn't he?

Pause.

PEARL. Where's mother Bryant?

BEATIE. Upstairs changin'.

PEARL. Where's father Bryant?

BEATIE. Tendin' the pigs.

FRANK. You're lucky to hev my presence you know.

BEATIE. Oh?

FRANK. A little more sun and I'd've bin gettin' in the harvest.

PEARL. Well, what did you think of that storm last night? All that thunder'n'lightnin' and it didn't stop once.

BEATIE. Ronnie love it you know. He sit and watch it for bloody hours.

FRANK. He's a queer article then.

JENNY. He do sound a rum 'un don't he?

BEATIE. Well you'll soon see.

JIMMY. Hev he got any sisters?

BEATIE. One married and she live not far from here.

PEARL. She live in the country? A town girl? Whatever for?

BEATIE. Her husband make furniture by hand.

PEARL. Can't he do that in London?

BEATIE. Ronnie say they think London's an inhuman place.

JIMMY. So 'tis, so 'tis.

BEATIE. Here come father Bryant.

MR BRYANT *enters. He is in denims and raincoat, tired, and stooped slightly.*

FRANK. And this must be the male head of the mighty Bryant clan!

MR BRYANT. Blust, you're all here soon then.

BEATIE. Get you changed quick Father – he'll be along any minute look.

MR BRYANT. Shut you up gal, I'll go when I'm ready, I don't want you pushin' me.

MRS BRYANT *comes from upstairs. She looks neat and also wears a flowered frock.*

FRANK. And this be the female head o' the mighty Bryant clan!

MRS BRYANT. Come on Bryant, get you changed – we're all ready look.

MR BRYANT. Blust, there go the other one. Who is he this boy, that's what I wanna know.

MRS BRYANT. He's upset! I can see it! I can tell it in his voice. Come on Bryants, what's the matters.

MR BRYANT. There ent much up wi' me, what you on about woman. (*Makes to go.*) Now leave me be, you want me changed look.

MRS BRYANT. If there ent much up wi' you, I'll marry some other.

FRANK. Healy bin at you Pop?

BEATIE. The pigs dyin'?

MRS BRYANT. It's something serious or he wouldn't be so happy lookin'.

MR BRYANT. I bin put on casual labour.

JENNY. Well isn't that a sod now.

MRS BRYANT. Your guts I suppose.

MR BRYANT. I tell him it's no odds, that there's no pain. That don't matters Jack, he says, I aren't hevin' you break up completely on me. You go on casual, he say, and if you gets better you can come on to the pigs again.

MRS BRYANT. That's half pay then?

BEATIE. Can't you get another job?

FRANK. He've bin wi' them for eighteen years.

BEATIE. But you must be able to do something else – what about cowman again?

MR BRYANT. Bill Waddington do that see. He've bin at it this last six 'n' half years.

JENNY. It's no good upsettin' yourself Beatie. It happen all the time gal.

JIMMY. Well, we told her when she was at ours didn't we.

MRS BRYANT (*to Mr Bryant*). All right, get you on up, there ent nothin' we can do. We'll worry on it later. We always manage. It's gettin' late look.

MR BRYANT. Can he swim? 'Cos he bloody need to. It's rainin' fit to drowned you. (*Goes off upstairs.*)

MRS BRYANT. Well, shall we have a little cup o' tea while we're waitin'? I'll go put the kettle on. (*Goes to kitchen*).

Everyone sits around now. JENNY *takes out some knitting and* JIMMY *picks up a paper to read. There is a silence. It is not an awkward silence, just a conversationless room.*

PEARL (*to Jenny*). Who's lookin' after your children?

JENNY. Ole mother Mann next door.

PEARL. Poor ole dear. How's she feelin' now?

JENNY. She took it bad. (*Nodding at Jimmy.*) Him too. He think he were to blame.

PEARL. Blust that weren't his fault. Don't be so daft Jimmy Beales. Don't you go fretting yourself or you'll make us all feel queer look. You done nothin' wrong bor – he weren't far off dying 'sides.

FRANK. They weren't even married were they?

JENNY. No, they never were – she started lookin' after him when he had that first stroke and she just stayed.

JIMMY. Lost her job 'cos of it too.

FRANK. Well, yes, she would, wouldn't she – she was a State Registered Nurse or something weren't she? (*To Beatie*) Soon

even the authorities got to hear o' that they told her to pack
up livin' wi' him or quit her job, see?

JENNY. Bloody daft I reckon. What difference it make whether
she married him or not.

PEARL. I reckon you miss him Jenny?

JENNY. Hell yes – that I do. he were a good ole bor – always
joking and buying the kid sweets. Well, do you know I cry
when I heard it? I did. Blust, that fair shook me – that it did,
there!

JIMMY. Who's lookin' after *your* kid then, Pearl?

PEARL. Father.

Pause.

JIMMY (*to Frank*). Who do you think'll win today?

FRANK. Well Norwich won't.

JIMMY. No.

Pause. MRS BRYANT *enters and sits down.*

MRS BRYANT. Well the kettle's on.

PEARL (*To Beatie*). Hev his sister got any children?

BEATIE. Two boys.

JIMMY. She wanna get on top one night then they'll hev girls.

JENNY. Oh shut you up Jimmy Beales.

MRS BRYANT. Hed another little win last night.

JENNY. When was this?

MRS BRYANT. The fireman's whist drive. Won seven 'n' six in the
knockout.

JENNY. Yearp.

FRANK (*reading the paper*). I see that boy what assaulted the ole
woman in London got six years.

MRS BRYANT. Blust! He need to! I'd've given him six years and
a bit more. Bloody ole hooligans. Do you give me a chance
to pass sentence and I'd soon clear the streets of crime, that
I would. Yes, that I would.

BEATIE (*springing into activity*). All right Mother – we'll give you a chance. (*Grabs Jimmy's hat and umbrella. Places hat on mother's head and umbrella in her arms*.) There you are, you're a judge. Now sum up and pass judgement.

MRS BRYANT. I'd put him in prison for life.

FRANK. You gotta sum up though. Blust, you just can't stick a man in prison and say nothing.

MRS BRYANT. Good-bye, I'd say.

BEATIE. Come on Mother, speak up. Anybody can say 'go to prison', but *you* want to be a judge. Well, you show a judge's understanding. Talk! Come on Mother, talk!

Everyone leans forward eagerly to hear Mother talk. She looks startled and speechless.

MRS BRYANT. Well I – I – yes I – well I – Oh, don't be so soft.

FRANK. The mighty head is silent.

BEATIE. Well yes, she would be wouldn't she.

MRS BRYANT. What do you mean, I would be? You don't expect me to know what they say in courts do you? I aren't no judge.

BEATIE. Then why do you sit and pass judgement on people? If someone do something wrong and you don't stop and think why. No discussin', no questions, just (*snap of fingers*) – off with his head. I mean look at Father getting less money. I don't see the family sittin' together and discussin' it. It's a problem! But which of you said it concerns you?

MRS BRYANT. Nor don't it concern them. I aren't hevin' people mix in my matters.

BEATIE. But they aren't just people – they're your family for hell's sake!

MRS BRYANT. No matters, I aren't hevin' it!

BEATIE. But Mother I –

MRS BRYANT. Now shut you up Beatie Bryant and leave it alone. I shall talk when I hev to and I never shall do, so there!

BEATIE. You're so stubborn.

MRS BRYANT. So you keep saying.

MR BRYANT *enters, he is clean and dressed in blue pin-striped suit.*

MR BRYANT. You brewed up yit?

MRS BRYANT (*jumping and going to kitchen*). Oh hell, yes – I forgot the tea look.

MR BRYANT. Well, now we're all waitin' on him.

JENNY. Don't look as if Susie's comin'.

BEATIE. Stubborn cow!

Silence.

JENNY. Hev you seen Susie's television set yit?

BEATIE. I seen it.

FRANK. Did you know also that when they fist hed it they took it up to bed wi' them and lay in bed wi' a dish of chocolate biscuits?

PEARL. But now they don't bother – they say they've had it a year now and all the old programmes they saw in the beginning they're seein' again.

MRS BRYANT (*entering wih tea*). Brew's up!

BEATIE. Oh, for Christ's sake let's stop gossiping.

PEARL. I aren't gossiping. I'm making an intelligent observation about the state of television, now then.

MR BRYANT. What's up wi' you now?

BEATIE. You weren't doin' nothin' o' the sort – you was gossiping.

PEARL. Well that's a heap sight better'n quotin' all the time.

BEATIE. I don't quote all the time, I just tell you what Ronnie say.

FRANK. Take it easy gal – he's comin' soon – don't need to go all jumpin' an' frantic.

BEATIE. Listen! Let me set you a problem.

JIMMY. Here we go.

BEATIE. While we're waitin' for him I'll set you a moral problem. You know what a moral problem is? It's a problem about right and wrong. I'll get you buggers thinking if it's the last thing I do. Now listen. There are four huts –

FRANK. What?

BEATIE. Huts. You know – them little things you live in. Now there are two huts on one side of a stream and two huts on the other side. One one side live a girl in one hut and a wise man in the other. On the other side live Tom in one hut and Archie in the other. Also there's a ferryman what run a boat across the river. Now – listen, concentrate – the girl loves Archie but Archie don't love the girl. And Tom love the girl but the girl don't go much on Tom.

JIMMY. Poor bugger.

BEATIE. One day the girl hears that Archie – who don't love her, remember – is going to America, so she decides to try once more to persuade him to take her with him. So listen what she do. She go to the ferryman and ask him to take her across. The ferryman say, I will, but you must take off all your clothes.

MRS BRYANT. Well, whatever do he wanna ask that for?

BEATIE. It don't matters why – he do! Now the girl doesn't know what to do so she ask the wise man for advice, and he say, you must do what you think best.

FRANK. Well that weren't much advice was it!

BEATIE. No matters – he give it. So the girl thinks about it and being so in love she decides to strip.

PEARL. Oh I say!

MR BRYANT. Well, this is a rum ole story ent it?

BEATIE. Shut up Father and listen. Now, er – where was I?

MR BRYANT. She was strippin'.

BEATIE. Oh yes! So, the girl strips and the ferryman takes her over – he don't touch her or nothing – just takes her over and she rushes to Archie's hut to implore him to take her with him and to declare her love again. Now Archie promises to take her with him and so she sleeps with him the night. But when she wake up in the morning he've gone. She's left alone. So she go across to Tom and explain her plight and ask for help. But soon ever he knowed what she've done, he chuck her out see? So there she is. Poor little gal. Left alone with no clothes and no friends and no hope of staying alive. Now – this is the question, think about it, don't answer quick – who is the person most responsible for her plight?

JIMMY. Well, can't she get back?

BEATIE. No, she can't do anything. She's finished. She've hed it! Now, who's to blame?

There is a general air of thought for the moment and BEATIE *looks triumphant and pleased with herself.*

MRS BRYANT. Be you a-drinkin' on your tea look. Don't you worry about no naked gals. The gal won't get cold but the tea will.

PEARL. Well I say the girl's most responsible.

BEATIE. Why?

PEARL. Well, she made the choice didn't she?

FRANK. Yes, but the old ferryman made her take off her clothes.

PEARL. But she didn't hev to.

FRANK. Blust woman, she were in love!

BEATIE. Good ole Frank.

JENNY. Hell if I know.

BEATIE. Jimmy?

JIMMY. Don't ask me gal – I follow decisions, I aren't makin' none.

BEATIE. Father?

MR BRYANT. I don't know what you're on about.

BEATIE. Mother?

MRS BRYANT. Drink your tea gal – never you mind what I think.

This is what they're waiting for.

PEARL. Well – what do Ronnie say?

BEATIE. He say the girl is responsible only for makin' the decision to strip off and go across and that she do that because she's in love. After that she's the victim of two phoney men – one who don't love her but take advantage of her and one who say he love her but don't love her enough to help her, and that the man who say he love her but don't do nothin' to help her is most responsible because he were the last one she could turn to.

JENNY. He've got it all worked out then!

BEATIE (*jumping on a chair thrusting her fist into the air like Ronnie, and glorying in what is the beginning of a hysteric outburst of his quotes*). 'No one do that bad that you can't forgive them.'

PEARL. He's sure of himself then?

BEATIE. 'We can't be sure of everything but certain basic things we must be sure about or we'll die.'

FRANK. He think everyone is gonna listen then?

BEATIE. 'People *must* listen. It's no good talking to the converted. *Everyone* must argue and think or they will stagnate and rot and the rot will spread.'

JENNY. Hark at that then.

BEATIE (*her strange excitement growing; she has a quote for everything*). 'If wanting the best things in life means being a snob then glory hallelujah I'm a snob. But I'm not a snob Beatie, I just believe in human dignity and tolerance and cooperation and equality and –'

JIMMY (*jumping up in terror*). He's a communist!

BEATIE. I'm a socialist!'

There is a knock on the front door.

BEATIE (*jumping down joyously as though her excited quotes have been leading to this one moment*). He's here, he's here! (*But at the door it is the* POSTMAN, *from whom she takes a letter and a parcel.*) Oh, the silly fool, the fool. Trust him to write a letter on the day he's coming. Parcel for you Mother.

PEARL. Oh, that'll be your dress from the club.

MRS BRYANT. What dress is this then? I didn't ask for no dress from the club.

PEARL. Yes you did, you did ask me, didn't she ask me Frank? Why, we were looking through the book together Mother.

MRS BRYANT. No matters what we was doin' together I aren't hevin' it.

PEARL. But Mother you distinctly –

MRS BRYANT. I aren't hevin' it so there now!

> BEATIE *has read the letter – the contents stun her. She cannot move. She stares around speechlessly at everyone.*

MRS BRYANT. Well, what's the matter wi' you gal? Let's have a read. (*Takes the letter and reads contents in a dead flat but loud voice – as though it were a proclamation*) 'My dear Beatie. It wouldn't really work would it? My ideas about handing on a new kind of life are quite useless and romantic if I'm really honest. If I were a healthy human being it might have been all right but most of us intellectuals are pretty sick and neurotic – as you have often observed – and we couldn't build a world even if we were given the reins of government – not yet any-rate. I don't blame you for being stubborn, I don't blame you for ignoring every suggestion I ever made – I only blame myself for encouraging you to believe we could make a go of it and now two weeks of your not being here has given me the cowardly chance to think about it and decide and I –'

BEATIE (*snatching letter*). Shut up!

MRS BRYANT. Oh – so we know now do we?

MR BRYANT. What's this then – ent he comin'?

MRS BRYANT. Yes, we know now.

MR BRYANT. Ent he comin' I ask?

BEATIE. *No he ent comin'.*

> *An awful silence ensues. Everyone looks uncomfortable.*

JENNY (*softly*). Well blust gal, didn't you know this was going to happen?

> BEATIE *shakes her head.*

MRS BRYANT. So *we're* stubborn are we?

JENNY. Shut up you Mother, the girl's upset.

MRS BRYANT. Well I can see that, I can see that, he ent coming, I can see that, and we're here like bloody fools, I can see that.

PEARL. Well did you quarrel all that much Beatie?

BEATIE (*as if discovering this for the first time*). He always wanted me to help him but I never could. Once he tried to teach me to type but soon ever I made a mistake I'd give up. I'd give up every time! I couldn't bear making mistakes. I don't know why, but I couldn't bear making mistakes.

MRS BRYANT. Oh – so we're hearing' the other side o' the story now are we?

BEATIE. He used to suggest I start to copy real objects on to my paintings instead of only abstracts and I never took heed.

MRS BRYANT. Oh, so you never took heed.

JENNY. Shut you up I say.

BEATIE. He gimme a book sometimes and I never bothered to read it.

FRANK (*not maliciously*). What about all this discussion we heard of?

BEATIE. I *never* discussed things. He used to beg me to discuss things but I never saw the point on it.

PEARL. And he got riled because o' that?

BEATIE (*trying to understand*). I didn't have any patience.

MRS BRYANT. Now it's coming out.

BEATIE. I couldn't help him – I never knew patience. Once he looked at me with terrified eyes and said, 'We'e been together for three years but you don't know who I am or what I'm trying to say – and you don't care do you?'

MRS BRYANT. And there she was tellin' me.

BEATIE. I never knew what he wanted – I didn't think it mattered.

MR BRYANT. And there she were gettin' us to solve the moral problem and now we know she didn't even do it herself. That's a rum 'un, ent it?

MRS BRYANT. The apple don't fall far from the tree – that it don't.

BEATIE (*wearily*). So you're proud on it? You sit there smug and you're proud that a daughter of yours wasn't able to help her boy friend? Look at you. All of you. You can't say anything. You can't even help your own flesh and blood. Your daughter's bin ditched. It's your problem as well isn't it? I'm part of your family aren't I? Well, help me then! Give me words of comfort! Talk to me – for God's sake, someone talk to me. (*She cries at last.*)

MR BRYANT. Well, what do we do now?

MRS BRYANT. We sit down and eat that's what we do now.

JENNY. Don't be soft Mother, we can't leave the girl crying like that.

MRS BRYANT. Well, blust, 'tent my fault she's cryin'. I did what I could – I prepared all this food, I'd've treated him as my own son if he'd come but he hevn't! We got a whole family gathering specially to greet him, all on us look, but he hevn't come. So what am I supposed to do?

BEATIE. My God, Mother, I hate you – the only thing I ever wanted and I weren't able to keep him, I didn't know how. I hate you, I hate . . .

MRS BRYANT *slaps Beatie's face. Everyone is a little shocked at this harsh treatment.*

MRS BRYANT. There! I hed enough!

MR BRYANT. Well what d'you wanna do that for?

MRS BRYANT. I hed enough. All this time she've bin home she've bin tellin' me I didn't do this and I didn't do that and I hevn't understood half what she've said and I've hed enough. She talk about bein' part o' the family but she've never lived at home since she've left school look. Then she go away from here and fill her head wi' high-class squit and then it turn out she don't understand any on it herself. It turns out she do just the same things she say I do (*Into Beatie's face.*) Well, am I right gal? I'm right ent I? When you tell me I was stubborn, what you mean was that *he* told you *you* was stubborn – eh? When you tell me I don't understand you mean *you* don't understand isn't it? When you tell me I don't make no effort you mean *you* don't make no effort. Well, what you blaming me for? Blaming me all the time! I haven't bin responsible for you since you left home – you bin on your own. She think I like it, she do! Thinks I like it being cooped up in this house all day. Well I'm telling you my gal – I don't! There! And if I had a chance to be away working somewhere the whole lot on you's could go to hell – the lot on you's. All right so I am a bloody fool – all right! So I know it! A whole two weeks I've bin told it. Well, so then I can't help you my gal, no that I can't, and you get used to that once and for all.

BEATIE. No you can't Mother, I know you can't.

MRS BRYANT. I suppose doin' all those things for him weren't enough. I suppose he weren't satisifed wi' goodness only.

BEATIE. Oh, what's the use.

MRS BRYANT. Well, don't you sit there an' sigh gal like you was Lady Nevershit. I ask you something. Answer me. You do the talking then. Go on – you say you know something we don't so *you* do the talking. Talk – go on, talk gal.

BEATIE (*despairingly*). I can't Mother, you're right – the apple don't fall far from the tree do it? You're right, I'm like you. Stubborn, empty, wi' no tools for livin'. I got no roots in nothing. I come from a family o' farm labourers yet I ent got no roots – just like town people – just a mass o' nothin'.

FRANK. Roots, gal? What do you mean, roots?

BEATIE (*impatiently*). Roots, roots, roots! Christ, Frankie, you're in the fields all day, you should know about growing things. Roots! The things you come from, the things that feed you. The things that make you proud of yourself – roots!

MR BRYANT. You got a family ent you?

BEATIE. I am not talking about family roots – I mean – the – I mean – Look! Ever since it begun the world's bin growin' hasn't it? Things hev happened, things have bin discovered, people have bin thinking and improving and inventing but what do we know about it all?

JIMMY. What is she on about?

BEATIE (*various interjections*). What do you mean, what am I on about? I'm talking! Listen to me! I'm tellin' you that the world's bin growing for two thousand years and we hevn't noticed it. I'm telling you that we don't know what we are or where we come from. I'm telling you something's cut us off from the beginning. I'm telling you we've got no roots. Blimey Joe! We've all got large allotments, we all grow things around us so we should know about roots. You know how to keep your flowers alive don't you Mother? Jimmy – you know how to keep the roots of your veges strong and healthy. It's not only the corn that need strong roots, you know, it's us too. But what've we got? Go on, tell me, what've we got? We don't know where we push up from and we don't bother neither.

PEARL. Well, I aren't grumbling.

BEATIE. You say you aren't – oh yes, you say so, but look at you. What've you done since you come in? Hev you said anythin'? I mean really said or done anything to show what it mean? Any of you? Shall I tell you what Susie said when I went and saw her? She say she don't care if that ole atom bomb drop and she die – that's what she say. And you know why she say it? I'll tell you why, because if she had to care she'd have to do something about it and she find *that* too much effort. Yes she do. She can't be bothered – we're all too bored.

MRS BRYANT. Blust woman – bored you say, bored? You say Susie's bored, with a radio and television an' that? I go t'hell if she's bored!

BEATIE. Oh yes, we turn on a radio or a TV set maybe, or we go to the pictures – if them's love stories or gangsters – but isn't that the easiest way out? Anything so long as we don't have to make an effort. Well, am I right? You know I'm right. Education ent only books and music – it's asking questions, all the time. There are millions of us, all over the country, and no one, not one of us, is asking questions, we're all taking the easiest way out. We don't fight for anything, we're so mentally lazy we might as well be dead. Blust, we are dead! And you know what Ronnie say sometimes? He say it serves us right! That's what he say – it's our own bloody fault!

JIMMY. So that's us summed up then – so we know where *we* are then!

MRS BRYANT. Well if he don't reckon we count nor nothin', then it's as well he didn't come. There! It's as well he didn't come.

BEATIE. Oh, *he* thinks we count all right – living in mystic communion with nature. Living in mystic bloody communion with nature (indeed). But us count? Count Mother? I wonder. Do we? Do you think we really count? You don' wanna take any notice of what them ole papers say about the workers bein' all-important these days – that's all squit! 'Cos we aren't. Do you think when the really talented people in the country get to work they get to work for us? Hell if they do! Do you think they don't know we 'ont make the effort? The writers don't write thinkin' we can understand, nor the painters don't paint expecting us to be interested – that they don't, nor don't the composers give out music thinking we can appreciate it. 'Blust,' they say, 'the masses is too stupid for us to come down to them. Blust,' they say, 'if they don't make no effort why should we bother?' So you know who come along? The slop singers and the pop writers and the film makers and women's magazines and the Sunday papers and the picture strip love stories – that's who come along, and you don't have to make no effort for them, it come easy. 'We know where the money lie,' they say, 'hell we do! The workers've got it so let's give them what they want. If they want slop songs and film idols we'll give 'em that then. If they want the third-rate, *blust!* We'll give 'em *that* then. Anything's good enough for them 'cos they don't ask for no more!' The whole stinkin' commercial world insults us and we don't care a damn. Well, Ronnie's right – it's our own bloody fault. We want the third-rate – we got it! We got it! We got it! We . . .

Suddenly BEATIE *stops as if listening to herself. She pauses, turns with an ecstatic smile on her face –*

D'you hear that? D'you hear it? Did you listen to me? I'm
talking. Jenny, Frankie, Mother – I'm not quoting no more.

MRS BRYANT (*getting up to sit at table*). Oh hell, I hed enough of
her – let her talk a while she'll soon get fed up.

The others join her at the table and proceed to eat and murmur.

BEATIE. Listen to me someone. (*As though a vision were revealed
to her*) God in heaven, *Ronnie!* It does work, it's happening
to me, I can feel it's happened, I'm beginning, on my own two
feet – I'm beginning . . .

The murmur of the family sitting down to eat grows as BEATIE's
*last cry is heard. Whatever she will do they will continue to live
as before. As* BEATIE *stands alone, articulate at last –*

the curtain falls.

'I'LL WAIT FOR YOU
IN THE HEAVENS BLUE'

John Arden

When *Serjeant Musgrave's Dance* opened at the Royal Court in 1959, *Manchester Guardian* critic Philip Hope-Wallace wrote, 'I think it is something just short of a great play.' Unfortunately, Hope-Wallace was in a small minority; most reviewers were very hard on Arden. Their derisive rejection of *Musgrave*, like the initial rejections of early Osborne, Pinter, and Bond plays, suggests again that the critics, like most of us, often fail to grasp a genuinely fresh piece of theatre on first viewing. For Arden 'is one of our few complete originals,' as John Russell Taylor has said of him.

Aided by the 1965 Royal Court revival, *Serjeant Musgrave's Dance* gradually gained acceptance, a process formally ratified when the play was designated as required text for English advanced-level school candidates, which gave it the status of a national cultural treasure by government fiat. Even today, however, the respect accorded the play is usually tempered by some cavil or other – the slow pace of the first two acts, implausible character behaviour, or overblown language. The respect is grudging, like that paid a great footballer who always manages to score, but never shows flashes of classic style.

Fortunately, John Arden does not pin his hopes on the praise of the crowd. His theatrical way marks him a rebel, an innovator, an independent. Born in Yorkshire in 1930, Arden, alone among the 'first wave' playwrights, enjoyed the advantage of higher education. He took a Cambridge degree in 1953 and in 1955 added to it a diploma in architecture from the College of Art in Edinburgh, where he began writing plays. A radio drama prize brought him to the Royal Court, where after a trial production of *The Waters of Babylon* (1957), they staged *Live Like Pigs*, a tough account of the social war between two kinds of council housing have-nots, the conventional Jacksons with their pretensions to middle-class gentility and the disreputable Sawneys forced by the authorities to move into the local housing project. The Sawneys' neighbours, scandalized by what they see as their disruptive vulgarity, turn into a mob and attack the Sawney family with fists and bricks. When the police intervene, instead of quelling the violence, they aggravate it. Arden does not stack the cards simplistically against authority, however. The Sawneys are an unappealing bunch, petty and cruel to each other as well as destructively indifferent to community standards. In the preface to his play, Arden noted that it was 'a study of different ways of life brought sharply into conflict and both losing their particular virtues under the stress of indolence and misunderstanding'. His even-handedness irritated critics and audiences who wanted him to take sides. But that even-handedness, Arden's unwillingness to distort the facts even in a good cause (in this case, protection of the beleaguered and vulnerable under-dog Sawneys) is a constant in his work. To some extent, it continues to impede warm critical reception. Audiences prefer clear-cut value judgments and Arden refuses to assign all the virtue to any one side.

By the late sixties *Serjeant Musgrave's Dance* had had several productions (student and professional) in Britain and the United States. However, of the four dramatists commonly credited with launching the drama renaissance in England, Pinter, Osborne, Wesker, and himself, Arden has had the least success in terms of major stagings and box office takings. Nevertheless, Arden has pursued his political and artistic course with firm commitment. During the sixties, he gradually developed a collaborative artistic and political relationship with actress Margaretta D'Arcy, an Irish patriot and fervent socialist, whom he had married in 1957. Together the Ardens developed numerous projects designed to make audiences and fellow-artists co-workers in the exploring of social or political questions. In 1967, for example, they led theatre students at New York University in the creation of a 'War Carnival' – a day-long event focusing on United States' involvement in Vietnam and consisting of theatre games, speeches, improvisations, and satirical sketches.

In 1969, Arden and D'Arcy visited India. The exposure there to primitive performance modes radicalized their notions of dramatic structure by suggesting alternatives to the techniques of social realism. In addition, the experience profoundly affected their political perspective. Arden writes about it in *To Present the Pretence*, in an essay which describes his growing awareness that third world nations suffer from all sorts of cultural and economic exploitation that the rich powers (among whom he includes England, the United States, and the USSR) have disguised as aid.

Using India as an example, he declares, 'The rich half of the world has drained that country dry and is now dumping rubbish therein.'

In the years since, the Ardens have applied this deepened understanding of the nature of imperialism in a series of plays on the English/Irish troubles. They collaborated on the writing of *Vandaleur's Folly* and *The Ballygombeen Bequest* (later reworked as *The Little Gray Home in the West*), which examine imperialism as it affects the individual lives, especially the moral decisions, of people living under it. Baker-Fortesque, the English landlord of *Vandaleur's Folly*, set in the pre-independence Ireland of the 1830s, is imbued with the imperialist spirit. He engages in slave trading and subverts an attempt to reform the exploitation of Irish farm workers. His descendant, a central character in *The Little Gray Home in the West*, set in the independent Ireland of the post-World War II years, inherits the imperialist motives. An absentee landlord, he makes his money by fleecing his tenants out of their land rights and turning the estate into a tourist resort. The point the Ardens make, of course, is that, when great powers grant formal political independence, they do not necessarily relinquish their capacity nor lose their will to continue economic exploitation. As in other Arden plays the moral lines are not simplistically drawn. The idealistic landowner in *Vandaleur's Folly* who wants to reform the system fails because he is an obsessive gambler. An Irish contractor cooperates with the British landlowner for his own profit. Many of the Irish are willing to conspire with the English in the slave trade. The Irish capitalists make common cause with the 'foreign' English capitalists rather than with the Irish socialists, who appear to be the best hope for Ireland in the struggle against England.

The Island of the Mighty studies the fall of King Arthur in terms of the Marxist class struggle. When the play, a trilogy picturing the Arthurian knights and the common workers united against exploiters, went into rehearsal for a production by the Royal Shakespeare Company, Arden and D'Arcy became alarmed at the cuts made by the director. True to their own political commitment and the sense of fairness that tripped up Arden early in his career, they believed that the director's interpretation tended to turn Arthur into a cardboard hero and to reduce the complexities of their political theme. When their objections did not prevail, they picketed their own play. At a preview performance some of their supporters demanded the authors be permitted to speak. When

Arden tried, the audience shouted him down, rather as the audience shouts down Dr. Stockman in Ibsen's *Enemy of the People*, when he tries to deliver his message about the contaminated springs of his town. The incident prompted Arden, like Stockman, to sever his connections with the establishment. He vowed never to write again for the establishment theatre of England, in which he now included the Royal Shakespeare Company and the Royal Court. Since then all of his stage plays have been premiered in Ireland, and co-authored with D'Arcy.

Serjeant Musgrave's Dance, written before Arden's collaborations with D'Arcy, remains, however, the best known and most admired of his plays. His major themes are present in it and much of his best theatricality. Like the intrusive Sawneys of *Live Like Pigs*, Musgrave and his band of fellow-deserters disrupt the peaceful life of the community to which they have come, apparently, to recruit soldiers for the army. Actually, their motive is to protest against war in general. In the passion of his crusade, Musgrave becomes as violent and as careless of human life as the most rapid warmonger. Once again Arden denies audiences the reassurance of simplistic morality. Musgrave's horrifying singlemindedness entraps him in the false notion that his ends justify his means. His vaguely worthy idealism makes him dangerous when it is combined with his insensitivity to pain in others. Inspired by an actual incident of atrocity in Cyprus, Arden is certainly sympathetic to the cause of pacifism, but his dramatic instincts are so sure that he cannot refrain from picturing all sides of the issue fairly. He is interested in the impact of social and political events on individuals as individuals, as real human beings, not as symbols.

Critics complain about Arden's cumbersome exposition. Since, when the play opens, Musgrave and his men are already on the run and fearful of being hunted down before they accomplish their mission, Arden must explain through exposition the complicated series of events that got them there: how Billy Hicks, whose body they carry in a heavy wooden box, died; how they became enmeshed in a horrible atrocity; how and why Musgrave took on his deadly mission. Since Arden does not show in action the transformation of Musgrave into a crusader for peace, the audience is struggling for much of the play to understand his motives. The mystery supplies suspense, of course, but tends to blur the moral issue.

In spite of the fact that the need for so much exposition slows the opening, Arden's play has a stunning theatrical impact. Like the plays of the other 'first wave' dramatists, Arden tackles a weighty issue in *Serjeant Musgrave's Dance*. Like them, too, he breaks out of the conventionality of the prevailing realist mode. And he goes even further than many of them in confounding audience expectations. The plays of Osborne, Wesker, and Pinter that were staged in the fifties shattered conventions of form, style, and theme, but at first glance at least, their plays looked familiar. People sat in ordinary rooms and talked recognizable, if ungrammatical, English. When songs and music were introduced into their plays, as they occasionally were, they were realistically motivated. Arden is far less conventional. He anticipates the mimetic uses of music, gesture, and dance commonly associated with the Theatre of Cruelty, a form borrowed from Artaud, and not then known in England. Like Artaud, Arden discards logical verbal language for an instinctive pre-logical language of sound and gesture whenever conventional theatre dialogue seems too constricting to catch the cruel truth of natural life. A good example is Musgrave's macabre dance to Billy Hick's bones with its strange song – 'Up she goes and no one knows,' to the accompaniment of Hurst's demonic drumming. The image is a sensory metaphor for the madness made in the crucible of war that rages within Musgrave. Realistic English dialogue could not convey that madness with half the force.

Arden also experiments uniquely with the word — 'our white shining word,' as Musgrave calls it. He moves freely between prose and verse, ordinarily using prose to convey plot, character, and relationships and verse to comment on them or to express emotional highpoints. He is especially fond of ballads because their rhythms underlie the greatness of English literature from Chaucer to Joyce and still have the capacity to 'reach to the heart of the people'. He uses ballads in a variety of ways. The opening ballad in *Serjeant Musgrave's Dance* characterizes Sparky, who sings it, as the most light-hearted soldier of the group, and also links him to the dead Billy Hicks, whose girl and fate he will share. Mrs. Hitchcock's brief ballad, 'Into the river, out of the river,' introduces important information about the cold, strike-torn mining town in which the action of the play occurs. Later, her little song about the 'yellow-haired boy' leads into the passage of exposition about Billy's desertion of the pregnant Annie. At other times, a ballad motivates melodramatic physical action. For example, when the Slow Collier sings 'Thirteen fourteen fifteen sixteen/Into the bed and there we'll fix him,' the Pugnacious Collier, thinking the song a slur on his wife's fidelity, punches him in the belly. A ballad sums up the thematic core of the play when Attercliffe sings of the withered blood-red rose, the symbol of death, and the greengrocer's apple in which lies the seeds of life.

Arden's characters speak a dialect that is not simply a naturalistic recreation of regional speech but a language full of imagery, often rich colour imagery: the greengrocer 'sold good green apples . . . I'm a dirty old bastard in a red coat and blue britches . . . Blood y'see: killing,' says Attercliffe.

Arden's willingness to make free with the accepted styles of the English theatre matches the challenge to all forms of authority that runs through his work as a recurring theme. Albert Hunt calls Arden 'a revolutionary who instinctively and intellectually rejects authority'. In every play he asks audiences to examine their assumption that men must be told how they ought to live and, if they fail to obey, be forced into submission. Alan Brien summed up the theme of *Serjeant Musgrave's Dance* as 'You cannot order men to be free, you cannot teach pacifism with a gun.' He added, in defence of Arden, that if *Serjeant Musgrave's Dance* had been written in German or signed by Brecht or Ibsen, it would have been hailed immediately as a masterpiece.

Musgrave tries to enforce pacifism by violent authoritarian means. He rules absolutely, even resorting to blackmail as a way of controlling the toughest of his soldiers, Private Hurst. He uses the Bible like an army rule book, demands that his men take him as God's surrogate, flays Annie for her natural sexuality, and fianlly delivers his sermon to the townspeople from the barrel of a Gatling gun. All in the name of peace! Driven by his mad logic of death, Musgrave and his soldiers have already killed five men in retaliation for the death of their comrade, Billy Hicks. Now in his home town they intend to kill twenty-five more in order to ram down the throats of the townspeople the horrors of violence. What is achieved by this geometric progression of deaths is a plague as awful as the plague of imperialist war that he fights.

Yet the play is a moving argument for pacifism. The final scene is an epiphany to peace. Attercliffe, the oldest, mellowest of the soldiers, reckons up his life as he contemplates the gallows: 'Holy God save us,' he says, 'Why warn't I a greengrocer, then I'd never ha' been cuckolded, never gone for no soldier, never no dead Sparky, and never none of this.' Musgrave was wrong to demand peace with a gun, but not wrong to demand peace.

Major Plays

Live Like Pigs, Royal Court Theatre, 1958.

Serjeant Musgrave's Dance, Royal Court Theatre, 1959.

The Happy Haven (with D'Arcy), Drama Studio, Bristol University, 1960; Royal Court Theatre, 1960.

The Workhouse Donkey, Festival Theatre, Chichester, 1963.

Armstrong's Last Goodnight, Citizen's Theatre, Glasgow, 1964; Festival Theatre, Chichester, then National Theatre at the Old Vic, 1965.

Left Handed Liberty, Mermaid Theatre, 1965.

The Royal Pardon (with D'Arcy), Beaford Arts Centre, Devon, 1966.

The Ballygombeen Bequest (with D'Arcy), St. Mary's College, Belfast, 1972; on tour by 7:84 Theatre Company, 1972.

The Island of the Mighty (with D'Arcy), RSC at the Aldwych Theatre, 1972.

The Non-Stop Connolly Show (with D'Arcy), Liberty Hall, Dublin, 1975; Almost Free Theatre, 1976.

Vandaleur's Folly (with D'Arcy), on tour by 7:84 Theatre Company, 1978.

Selected Bibliography

Arden, John. *To Present the Pretence: Essays on the Theatre and Its Public*. London: Eyre Methuen, 1977.

—. 'Telling a True Tale.' *The Encore Reader*, ed. Marowitz et al. London: Methuen, 1965, pp. 125-9.

Brien, Alan. 'Disease of Violence.' *The Spectator*, 30 October 1959, p. 594.

Brown, John Russell. *Theatre Language: A Study of Arden, Osborne, Pinter, Wesker*. London: Allen Lane; New York: Taplinger Pub. Co., 1972.

Gray, Frances. *John Arden*. London: Macmillan; New York: Grove Press, 1983.

Hope-Wallace, Philip. 'Something just short of a great play.' *Manchester Guardian*, 23 October 1959, p. 9.

Hunt, Albert. *Arden: A Study of His Plays*. London: Eyre Methuen, 1974.

Page, Malcolm (ed.). *Arden on File*. London and New York: Methuen, 1985.

JOHN ARDEN

Serjeant Musgrave's Dance
AN UN-HISTORICAL PARABLE

To Margaret

INTRODUCTION

This is a realistic, but not a naturalistic, play. Therefore the design of the scenes and costumes must be in some sense stylised. The paintings of L. S. Lowry might suggest a suitable mood. Scenery must be sparing – only those pieces of architecture, furniture, and properties actually used in the action need be present: and they should be thoroughly realistic, so that the audience sees a selection from the details of everyday life rather than a generalised impression of the whole of it. A similar rule should also govern the direction and the acting. If this is done, the obvious difficulties, caused by the mixture of verse, prose, and song in the play, will be considerably lessened.

The exact date of the play is deliberately not given. In the London production, the details of costume covered approximately the years between 1860 and 1880. For instance, the soldiers wore the scarlet tunics and spiked helmets characteristic of the later (or 'Kipling') epoch, while the Constable was dressed in tall hat and tail coat as an early Peeler – his role in the play suggesting a rather primitive type of police organisation.

The songs should be sung to folk-song airs. There are many available tunes which equally well suit the various songs – perhaps these are as good as any:

Sparky's song (Act One, Scene 1): 'Six Jolly Wee Miners' – Scottish.

Sparky's song and chorus (Act Two, Scene 2): 'Blow away the Morning Dew' – English.

Sparky's song (Act Two, Scene 3): 'The Black Horse' – Irish.

Attercliffe's song (Act Three, Scene 2): First three stanzas – 'John Barleycorn' – English Air. Final stanza – 'John Barleycorn' – Irish Air.

Musgrave's song (Act Three, Scene 1) proved in production to be more satisfactory if the words were spoken against a background of drum rolls and recorded music.

The characters perhaps need a few notes of description:

The Soldiers: these are regulars and seasoned men. They should all have moustaches and an ingrained sense of discipline. Musgrave is aged between thirty and forty, tall, swart, commanding, sardonic but never humorous; he could well have served under Cromwell. Attercliffe is aged about fifty, grey-haired, melancholy, a little embittered. He is the senior O.R. of the party and conscious of his responsibility. Hurst, in his twenties, is bloody-minded, quick-tempered, handsome, cynical, tough, but not quite as intelligent as he thinks he is. Sparky, also in his twenties, is easily led, easily driven, inclined to hide from himself behind a screen of silly stories and irritating clownishness. The Dragoon Officer is little more than the deus-ex-machina at the end of the play. All he needs to be is tall, calm, cold, and commanding. His Trooper is a tough, reliable soldier.

The Townsmen: The Mayor is a bustling, shrewd, superficially jovial man with a coarse accent and an underlying inclination to bully. The Parson is very much a gentleman: he is conscious of the ungentlemanly nature of the community in which he lives. He must have the accent and manners of a balked aristocrat rather than a stage-clergyman. He too has some inclination to bully. The Constable has a continual inclination to bully, except when in the presence of his superiors. He is as inefficient as he is noisy. The Colliers are all embittered but not so as to make them unpleasant. Walsh is a strong man, physically and morally. He knows what he wants and is entirely impatient with those who are not so single-minded. The Slow Collier is not particularly intelligent but has a vacuous good humour. The Pugnacious Collier is pugnacious, and very quick to show it. The Bargee is something of a grotesque, a hunchback (though this should not be over-emphasised), very rapid in his movements, with a natural urge towards intrigue and mischief.

The Women: The Landlady is a large, immobile widow of about fifty. She sits behind her bar and watches everything that happens. She is clearly a woman of deep sympathies and intelligence, which she disguises with the normal north-country sombre pessimism. Annie is a big-boned girl, not particularly attractive, but in an aggressive sort of way she provokes the men. Her emotional confusion expresses itself in a deliberately enigmatic style of speech and behaviour. Her voice is harsh.

As for the 'Meaning of the Play': I do not think that an introductory note is a suitable place for a lengthy analysis of the work, but in view of the obvious puzzlement with which it was greeted by the critics, perhaps a few points may be made. This is not a nihilistic play. This is not (except perhaps unconsciously) a symbolist play. Nor does it advocate bloody revolution. I have endeavoured to write about the violence that is so evident in the world, and to do so through a story that is partly one of wish-fulfilment. I think that many of us must at some time have felt an overpowering urge to match some particularly outrageous piece of violence with an even greater and more outrageous retaliation. Musgrave tries to do this: and the fact that the sympathies of the play are clearly with him in his original horror, and then turn against him and his intended remedy, seems to have bewildered many people. I would suggest, however, that a study of the roles of the women, and of Private Attercliffe, should be sufficient to remove any doubts as to where the 'moral' of the play lies. Accusations of nihilism seem to derive from the scene where the Colliers turn away from Musgrave and join in the general dance around the beer barrel. Again, I would suggest, that an unwillingness to dwell upon unpleasant situations that do not immediately concern us is a general human trait, and recognition of it need imply neither cynicism nor despair. Complete pacifism is a very hard doctrine: and if this play appears to advocate it with perhaps some timidity, it is probably because I am naturally a timid man – and also because I know that if I am hit I very easily hit back: and I do not care to preach too confidently what I am not sure I can practise.

J.A.

Serjeant Musgrave's Dance was first performed at the Royal Court Theatre on 22 October 1959, with the following cast:

PRIVATE SPARKY	Donal Donnelly
PRIVATE HURST	Alan Dobie
PRIVATE ATTERCLIFFE	Frank Finlay
BLUDGEON, *a bargee*	James Bree
SERJEANT MUSGRAVE	Ian Bannen
THE PARSON	Richard Caldicot
MRS. HITCHCOCK	Freda Jackson
ANNIE	Patsy Byrne
THE CONSTABLE	Michael Hunt
THE MAYOR	Stratford Johns
A SLOW COLLIER	Jack Smethurst
A PUGNACIOUS COLLIER	Colin Blakely
WALSH, *an earnest collier*	Harry Gwynn Davies
A TROOPER OF DRAGOONS	Barry Wilsher
AN OFFICER OF DRAGOONS	Clinton Greyn

Produced by LINDSAY ANDERSON
Music by DUDLEY MOORE
Decor by JOCELYN HERBERT

The play is set in a mining town in the north of England eighty years ago. It is winter.

Act One

A canal wharf. Evening.

HURST *and* ATTERCLIFFE *are playing cards on the top of a side-drum. A few yards away* SPARKY *stands, as though on guard, clapping himself to keep warm. There is a pile of three or four heavy wooden boxes with the WD broad arrow stencilled on them, and a lantern set on top.*

SPARKY. Brr, oh a cold winter, snow, dark. We wait too long, that's the trouble. Once you've started, keep on travelling. No good sitting to wait in the middle of it. Only makes the cold night colder. (*He sings*):

> One day I was drunk, boys, on the Queen's Highway
> When a recruiting party come beating that way.
> I was enlisted and attested before I did know
> And to the Royal Barracks they forced me to go.

Brr! And they talk of the Crimea! Did I ever tell you that one about the field kitchens at Sebastopol? Well, there was this red-haired provost-sarnt, y'see . . . and then the corporal-cook – now *he'd* got no hair at all . . . now the Commissary in that Regiment was – oh . . . (*He finds no one paying attention.*) Who's winning?

HURST. I'm winning.

ATTERCLIFFE. Oho, no you're not. The black spades carry the day. Jack, King and Ace. *We* throw the red Queen over. That's another shilling, you know. Let's have it.

HURST. All right. Deal agen, boy. Or no, no, *my* deal, this game. Now let's see if I can't turn some good cards on to my side for a difference. Here: one, two, three, four . . . (*He deals the cards.*)

SPARKY. How much longer we got to wait, I'd like to know. I want to be off aboard that damned barge and away. What's happened to our Black Jack Musgrave, eh? Why don't he come and give us the word to get going?

ATTERCLIFFE. He'll come on the stroke, as he said. He works his life to bugle and drum, this serjeant. You ever seen him late?

SPARKY. No. (*He sings*):

> When first I deserted I thought myself free
> Till my cruel sweetheart informed upon me –

ATTERCLIFFE (*sharpl*). I don't think you ought to sing *that* one.

SPARKY. Why not? It's true, isn't it? (*He sings*):

> Court martial, court martial, they held upon me
> And the sentence they passed was the high gallows tree.

HURST (*dropping cards and springing up in a rage*). Now shut it, will you! God-damned devil of a song to sing on this sort of a journey! He said you didn't ought to, so don't! (*He glances nervously around.*)

SPARKY. Ha, there's nobody to hear us. You're safe as a bloody blockhouse out here – I'm on the sentry, boy, *I'm* your protection.

ATTERCLIFFE (*irritably*). You make sure you are then. Go on: keep watching.

SPARKY (*returns to his guard*). Ah. Ha-ha . . . Or did you think *he* could hear you? (*He gestures towards the boxes.*) Maybe, maybe . . . *I* thought I heard him laugh.

ATTERCLIFFE. Steady, boy.

SPARKY (*a little wildly*). Steady yourself, you crumbling old cuckold. He might laugh, who knows? Well, make a rattling any road. Mightn't he, soldier boy?

HURST. Are you coming funny wi' me –

SPARKY. Funny? About *him*? You don't tell me he don't know what we're at. Why shouldn't he have a laugh at it, if that's how he feels?

HURST. Arrh, you're talking daft.

SPARKY. Now don't you be nervous, boy: not for *you* to be nervous. You're a man and a soldier! Or an old red rag stretched over four pair o' bones – well, what's the odds? Eh?

HURST (*after glaring angrily, sits down again*). *All right . . .* All right, play.

They play in silence. SPARKY *hums and blows his knuckles. Then he starts.*

SPARKY. Who goes there!

The BARGEE *enters with a lantern, whistling 'Michael Finnegan'.*

BARGEE. Hooroar, my jolly buckos! It's only old Joe Bludgeon, the Captain of the Lugger. Crooked old Joe. Heh heh. And what's the news with you? Are we ready yet, are we?

SPARKY. Ready for what?

BARGEE. Ready for off, of course, what do you think? Are we?

ATTERCLIFFE. No.

BARGEE. Why not, then?

ATTERCLIFFE. 'Cos it's not time, that's why not. Half-past seven, you was told.

BARGEE. Oh, it's as near as –

ATTERCLIFFE. No begod it's not, and he won't be here till it is.

BARGEE. Ah, the serjeant, eh?

ATTERCLIFFE. Aye, the serjeant. Is your barge up yet?

BARGEE. It's up. And the old horse waiting.

ATTERCLIFFE. Then we'll start to load.

HURST. Hey, we've not finished the game.

ATTERCLIFFE. Save it, mucker. You heard what Black Jack said.

HURST. All right. All right.

BARGEE. You can load these smaller cases 'side of the cabin. What you got in 'em, for Godsake? Ten ton and a half here.

SPARKY (*kicking one of them*). There's a Gatling gun in that one. You know what a Gatling gun is, friend?

BARGEE. I don't, and I don't care neither, tell you truth of it. By Lordy, what a life, the bloody Army. Do they still tie you fellers up and stripe you across with the cat-o'-nine-tails, eh?

HURST. No they don't.

ATTERCLIFFE *and* HURST *start carrying the cases out.*

BARGEE (*gloating*). Heheh, when I wor a young lad they told me, they did. Whack, whack, whack. Ooh, cruel it was. You know what they used to call 'em in them days – soldiers, I mean? Eh?

SPARKY. I know a lot o' names for calling soldiers.

BARGEE. I'll bet you don't know this one, though. Heh. Bloodred roses, that was it. What d'you think o' that, eh? Whack, whack, whack. Bloodred roses, eh? (*He calls off-stage.*) Not there, don't put it there, give me some room to swing me tiller, can't you! Soldiers. Get 'em aboard a barge, you'd be as well off wi' a row of deaf niggers from Peru. That's right, now leave it where you've dropped it, and come ashore before you capsize her—you bloodred bloody roses, you!

HURST *re-enters.*

HURST. That's enough of that, matey. Watch it.

MUSGRAVE *enters.*

MUSGRAVE (*to the* BARGEE). Aye, you watch it. Now I'll tell you just once, old man, and that's all. We travel on your barge, passengers: we pay our fare. So don't you talk to my men like they're deck-hands. Clear?

BARGEE. Oh it's clear, serjeant, I only wanted a little joke.

MUSGRAVE. Aye. And now you've had one. So be thankful.

ATTERCLIFFE *re-enters.*

ATTERCLIFFE (*as he and* HURST *pick up the remaining smaller boxes*). We got the Gatling loaded on serjeant, and we're fetching the rest of it. Then there's just the drum and the other box left. Any news?

MUSGRAVE (*quietly to him*). We're all all right. Don't worry.

ATTERCLIFFE *and* HURST *go out with their load.* MUSGRAVE *taps the drum meditatively and turns to the* BARGEE.

I say, you, bargee. Is it going to snow again before to-morrow?

BARGEE. Likely. There's ice coming on the water too. Give her another day and this canal'll be closed. They say the road over the moors is fast already with the drifts. You've chose a merry time o' year beating up for recruities, haven't you? What you got in here? Another Gatling gun? (*He smacks the last box.*)

MUSGRAVE. Why not? Show 'em all the best equipment, glamourise 'em, man, fetch 'em in like conies . . . Now get this last box loaded, and be careful. And then we're all ready. You can start.

ATTERCLIFFE *and* HURST, *having returned, pick up the box and carry it out,* SPARKY *going with them, the drum slung on his shoulder.* MUSGRAVE *takes the soldiers' lantern and makes a rapid circuit of the stage to see if anything is left. He stands for a moment looking out in the direction from which he has come in.*

BARGEE (*waiting for him*). This your first trip to the coal-mining towns, serjeant?

MUSGRAVE. It is.

BARGEE. Ooh, brr, bitter and bleak: hungry men for the Queen. If you're used to a full belly, you'll want it when you get there.

MUSGRAVE (*curtly*). It's not material. We have our duty. A soldier's duty is a soldier's life.

BARGEE. Ah, duty.

> The Empire wars are far away
> For duty's sake we sail away
> Me arms and legs is shot away
> And all for the wink of a shilling and a drink . . .

Come on, me cheery serjeant, you've not left nowt behind.

They go out after the soldiers.

SCENE TWO

The bar of a public house.

MRS. HITCHCOCK *is sitting in the body of the room, talking to the* PARSON, *who is very much at his ease, with a glass of brandy in his hand.* ANNIE *is polishing glasses etc. behind the bar.*

PARSON. No. No, madam, no. I cannot be seen to countenance idleness, pauperism, beggary. If no one comes to buy your drink, I am sorry for you. But the fact is, madam, a little less drunkenness and disorder will do this town no harm. The Church is not a speculative bank, you know, to subsidise pot-houses.

MRS. HITCHCOCK (*sulkily*). Always a respectable house.

PARSON. What?

MRS. HITCHCOCK. Always a respectable house, reverend. Aye. If not, why renew the licence? You're a magistrate, you know. You could have spoke agen me on me application. But you didn't.

PARSON. That is not to the purpose, Mrs. Hitchcock. The Bench allows that there have to be public houses to permit an outlet for the poorer sort of people, but in times of regrettable industrial conflict it is better that as many of them as possible remain empty. If the colliers cannot afford drink because of the strike – because of their own stupidity – then there is the less likelihood of their being inflamed to acts of violence. I am not at all certain that the Bench ought not to withdraw all licences altogether until the pits are working.

MRS. HITCHCOCK. That'd be grand. See half a dozen publicans going on the parish – beer-dregs from the workhouse served to the Trade – ooh, talk of arsy-versy! (*She laughs throatily.*)

PARSON. I'm quite sure that would not be necessary.

MRS. HITCHCOCK (*reasonably*). Now, look, reverend, you've been taking me crossroads since the minute I began. All I asked you in to say is this: this strike is bad for the town. Well, I mean, of course, that means me. But it means you too. *And* it means His Worship the Mayor: oh aye, aye:

> I am a proud coalowner
> And in scarlet here I stand.
> Who shall come or who shall go
> Through all my coal-black land?

(*She laughs again.*) Eh, if we can't have a laugh, we'll starve!

PARSON. You are impertinent. I have nothing more to say.

MRS. HITCHCOCK. Ah, but I come to you because you're Church, you're charity. Go on, reverend, you tell the Mayor to agree with his men and give them a good price, then they'll buy and sell in the town and they'll drink in this taproom, and – ho-hoo – who knows, they might even come to church! That'll be the day.

The PARSON *turns irritably from her and goes to the door.*
The BARGEE *enters and confronts him.*

BARGEE (*touching his cap mockingly*). Parson.

PARSON (*coldly*). Good afternoon.

BARGEE. Cold enough for you, eh?

PARSON (*trying to pass*). It is cold, yes.

BARGEE. How's the strike?

PARSON. It is not yet settled.

BARGEE. No, I bet it's not, and all. Hey missus!

MRS. HITCHCOCK. Hello.

BARGEE. A quart o' taddy. Best!

MRS. HITCHCOCK (*impassive*). Can you pay for it?

BARGEE. 'Course I can pay – wait a minute, Parson, just a
minute, all under control – I'm not one of your colliery
agitators, you know. *I'm* still in work. I've news for you.

MRS. HITCHCOCK (*to* ANNIE). He says he can pay. Draw him
his quart.

BARGEE (*to the* PARSON). I didn't think, like, to find you here,
but, eh, well, seeing as how here you are – canal's froze up,
you know.

PARSON. Well?

BARGEE. Well. Last barge come in this morning. *My* barge.
There was passengers.

PARSON. I am not really interested.

BARGEE (*significantly*). Four on 'em, Parson. Soldiers.

ANNIE *hands the* BARGEE *his tankard.*

PARSON (*in some alarm*). Soldiers! Already? Who sent for
them? Why was I not told? This could be very dangerous –

BARGEE. They're not here for what you think, you know. Not
yet, any road. You see, they've come recruiting.

PARSON (*relieved, but vexed*). Oh . . . Well, what if they have?
Why bother me with it? You're just wasting time, man.
Come on, get out of my way . . .

BARGEE (*still detaining him*). Eh, but, Parson, you're a magistrate.

PARSON. Of course I'm a magistrate.

BARGEE. You're a power, you are: in a town of trouble, in a place of danger. Yes. You're the word and the book, aren't you? Well then: soldiers. Recruiting. Useful?

PARSON (*beginning to follow his drift*). H'm. I do not think the Bench is in any real need of *your* suggestions. But I am obliged to you for the news. Thank you.

He gives the BARGEE *a coin and leaves.*

BARGEE (*flipping the coin*). Heh, heh, I said I could pay.

He gives it to ANNIE *and starts whistling 'Michael Finnegan'.* ANNIE *goes back to the bar.* MRS. HITCHCOCK *takes the coin from her and tests it between her teeth.*

MRS. HITCHCOCK. Soldiers. Annie, love, you could tell us what soldiers is good for.

ANNIE (*sullen*). Why should I tell you?

BARGEE (*gleefully*). Go on, go on, lassie, tell us about the soldiers. She knows the good redcoat button-to-back, I'll bet. Go on, it's a cold day, warm it up for us. Heh, heh, our strong Annie's the champion, eh?

He smacks her on the bottom. She swerves angrily.

ANNIE. *When* I've given you leave: and not afore. You bloody dog, sit down.

BARGEE (*subsiding in mock terror*). Ooh, sharp, sharp.

MRS. HITCHCOCK. Aye, so sit down . . . Go on, Annie, tell us.

ANNIE. I'll tell you for what a soldier's good:

> To march behind his roaring drum,
> Shout to us all: 'Here I come
> I've killed as many as I could –
> I'm stamping into your fat town

> From the war and to the war
> And every girl can be my whore
> Just watch me lay them squealing down.
> And that's what he does and so do we.
> Because we know he'll soon be dead
> We strap our arms round the scarlet red
> Then send him weeping over the sea.
> Oh he will go and a long long way.
> Before he goes we'll make him pay
> Between the night and the next cold day –
> By God there's a whole lot more I could say –

What good's a bloody soldier 'cept to be dropped into a slit in the ground like a letter in a box. How many did you bring with you – is it four?

BARGEE. Aye. Four.

ANNIE. That's four beds in this house?

MRS. HITCHCOCK. I should hope it's in this house. It's the best house in town.

ANNIE (*in a sudden outburst*). Then you'd do well to see they stay four nights because I'll not go with more nor one in one night, no, not for you nor for all of Egypt!

She lets out a howl and rushes out of the door behind the bar, clattering a tin tray full of tankards on to the floor.

BARGEE. Ooh, Lordy! Champion, strong, and sharp. Annie! Tell us some more!

MRS. HITCHCOCK (*crossly*). Let her alone. She's said enough for you, hasn't she? It's not right to set her off . . . I suppose they *are* coming to this house?

BARGEE. Oh surely, aye, surely. *I* told 'em: *I* took care.

A rat-tat-tat on the drum heard, off.

There, you see, they're coming.

SPARKY *enters magnificently, beating the drum.*

SPARKY. Ho-ho, atten-tion! Stand by your beds! Name of the Queen, missus – has he told you – there's four on us: we three, we'll settle for palliasses in the loft, but the serjeant he wants a big brass bed with knobs on, that's his fancy! Can you do it?

MRS. HITCHCOCK. So here they are, the gay recruiters. Aye, I can do it, young man. I've only one room in the house. The serjeant can have that. The three of you'll have to doss down in me old stable, out back, but there's a good stove, you'll be warm. Now, who's going to pay? You or the Queen?

SPARKY. Oh, Queen at end of it all, I suppose.

MRS. HITCHCOCK. But you at beginning, eh?

SPARKY. Oh-oh, chalk it up, you know . . . we've brought some gear with us too.

BARGEE. Ten and a half ton. Nigh foundered the old barge, it did, I can tell you.

SPARKY. But we got here, friend, didn't we? Like we get ourselves to everywhere we go, we do. No question o' that, y'see.

BARGEE. Heh, heh, none.

SPARKY (*calls to offstage*). Serjeant! We're fixed!

MUSGRAVE (*off*). And the equipment?

SPARKY. And the equipment, missus?

MRS. HITCHCOCK. There's a coach-house across the yard.

SPARKY (*calls to offstage*). Coach-house across the yard, serjeant! . . . While they're taking it round there, missus, let's have a pint apiece drawn ready. Like what *he* drinks, eh? Recommend it, friend?

BARGEE. You could stand your bayonet up in this, you could.

SPARKY. Right, then. And we'll give you another while we're at it. That's five on 'em, pints, unless *you're* drinking with us, too, are you?

MRS. HITCHCOCK. Why not, soldier? Queen as pays . . . Annie! Hey Annie!

As there is no reply, she goes herself behind the bar and starts filling the tankards. MUSGRAVE *enters.*

MUSGRAVE. Is the padlock on your coach-house door a strong one, ma'am?

MRS. HITCHCOCK. Likely so.

MUSGRAVE. Valuable equipment, y'see. Your window in there's barred, I notice.

MRS. HITCHCOCK. That's right.

MUSGRAVE (*picking up a tankard*). Good . . . This for me?

MRS. HITCHCOCK. If you want it.

The other two soldiers enter.

ATTERCLIFFE. The cases are all locked up and safe, serjeant.

MUSGRAVE (*indicates drinks*). Very good. Here you are.

HURST and ATTERCLIFFE. Thank you, serjeant.

BARGEE (*raising his drink*). Good health to Her Majesty; to Her Majesty's wars; to the girls we leave behind us. Drink!

They all drink.

MRS. HITCHCOCK (*raising her drink*):

> Into the river, out of the river
> Once I was dry, now I am wet
> But hunger and cold they hold me yet.

They drink again, with a certain puzzlement at the toast.

MRS. HITCHCOCK. They hold this town today, any road, serjeant; or had you been told?

MUSGRAVE. What's the matter?

MRS. HITCHCOCK. No work in the colliery. The owner calls it a strike, the men call it a lock-out, we call it starvation.

The CONSTABLE *enters violently.*

CONSTABLE. His Worship the Mayor.

MRS. HITCHCOCK. Eh?

CONSTABLE. I said, His Worship the Mayor!

BARGEE. Oho, *now*, me jolly buckos, give attention, stand-to, to the present!

CONSTABLE (*to the* BARGEE]. Ssssh – ssh –

BARGEE. Heh, heh, heh –

The MAYOR *enters at speed, wearing his gold chain. After him comes the* PARSON. MUSGRAVE *calls his men to attention.*

MAYOR. Mrs. Hitchcock, I'm seeking the soldiers. Ah, here they are! Well, I'm the Mayor of this town, I own the colliery, I'm a worried man. So I come seeking you when I could send for you, what do you think to that? Let's have a look at you . . . Ah. Haha . . . Clear the snug a minute, missus. I want a private word with the Parson. Serjeant, be ready outside when I send for you.

MUSGRAVE. At your service, sir . . . Come on.

Beckoned by MRS. HITCHCOCK, *he leads his party out behind the bar.*

CONSTABLE (*propelling the* BARGEE *to the street door*). Go on, you, out this road.

BARGEE (*dodging him*). Oo-er –

> Constable Constable alive or dead
> His head is of leather and his belly's of lead.

Go – whoops . . . How are you, Parson?

He ducks out, whistling 'Michael Finnegan'.

MRS. HITCHCOCK (*sourly, to the* MAYOR). Do you want a drink?

MAYOR. No.

MRS. HITCHCOCK. *At* your service, when you do.

She curtsies and goes out behind the bar.

MAYOR. What do you think to 'em, Parson?

PARSON. Fine strong men. They make me proud of my country. Mr. Mayor, Britain depends upon these spirits. It is a great pity that their courage is betrayed at home by skulkers and shirkers. What do *you* think?

MAYOR (*looking at him sideways*). *I* think we'll use 'em, Parson. Temporary expedient, but it'll do. The price of coal has fell, I've had to cut me wages, I've had to turn men off. They say they'll strike, so I close me gates. We can't live like that for ever. There's two ways to solve this colliery – one is build the railway here and cut me costs of haulage, *that* takes two years and an Act of Parliament, though God knows I want to do it. The other is clear out half the population, stir up a diversion, turn their minds to summat else. The Queen's got wars, she's got rebellions. Over the sea. All right. Beat these fellers' drums high around the town, I'll put one pound down for every Royal Shilling the serjeant pays. Red coats and flags. Get rid o' the trouble-makers. Drums and fifes and glory.

PARSON (*severely*). The soldier's calling is one of honour.

MAYOR. It's more than that. It's bloody convenient. Town Constable, fetch that serjeant in!

CONSTABLE (*nervously*). Er, excuse me, Your Worship. A point. Soldiers, you see. Now, I've got a very small force in this town. Only one other regular officer, you know: the rest is them deputy-specials – I can't trust *that* lot to stand fast and fear nowt when the time comes.

PARSON. What time?

CONSTABLE. There's been stone-throwing this morning. Two of my office windows is broke. And I'm nervous—that's frank, you know – I *am*.

MAYOR. Well?

CONSTABLE. Your Worship. I want these soldiers added to my force. It's all right recruiting. But what we need's patrols.

MAYOR. Not yet.

CONSTABLE. Your Worship. I'm asking you formal. You've got agitators here, and they won't stop at throwing stones: that's frank.

MAYOR (*angrily*). I said not yet. We'll try it my road first. Godsake, man, what's four soldiers agen the lot of 'em? This town's wintered up, you'll get no more help till there's a thaw. So work on that. Call in the serjeant.

CONSTABLE. Right, Your Worship. Serjeant! Come in here!

MUSGRAVE re-enters.

MUSGRAVE. Sir?

MAYOR. Serjeant, we're very glad to have you. I speak for the Council, I speak for the magistrates. Now listen: there's loyal hearts and true here, and we're every man-jack of us keen to see our best lads flock to the colours. Isn't that so, Parson?

PARSON (*taken a little by surprise*). Ha-h'm – with great pride, yes.

MAYOR. Right. For every Queen's Shilling you give out, I give out a golden sovereign – no, two. One for the recruit, and one to be divided among you and your three good lads. What do you say to that?

MUSGRAVE. That's most handsome, sir.

MAYOR. I should damn well think it is. How do you propose to work?

MUSGRAVE. Sir?

MAYOR. Aye, I mean, d'you tramp around the streets drumming, or set on your fannies in a pub—or what?

MUSGRAVE. Depends what's most appropriate, sir, according to the type of town. I've not had time for a look at yours yet. But the pubs seem pretty empty, if this one's owt to go by.

PARSON. They *are* empty.

MUSGRAVE. Aye. Well, in that case, I'll have to make a reconnaissance, won't I? When I'm decided, I'll let you know.

CONSTABLE. And let me know, serjeant. I'll see you get facilities.

MUSGRAVE. Thank you, mister.

MAYOR. And while you're on about them facilities, constable, perhaps you might let in the serjeant on a few likely names for his list, eh? Could you pick him some passable strong-set men, could you?

CONSTABLE (*significantly*). I could have a try, Your Worship.

MAYOR. Right. Then if that's settled, I'll be off back to town hall. I've not got time to waste wi' nattering, snug and all though it is in here. Come along, Constable. I want a little word wi' you about them stones.

MAYOR *and* CONSTABLE *go out.*

PARSON (*severely*). I think I ought to make one thing clear, serjeant. I know that it is customary for recruiting-parties to impress themselves upon the young men of the district as dashingly as possible, and no doubt upon the young women also. Now I am not having any of that. There's enough trouble in the place as it is. So remember.

MUSGRAVE. Yes, sir. I'll remember.

PARSON. I want no drunkenness, and no fornication, from your soldiers. Need I speak plainer?

MUSGRAVE. No, sir. There will be none. I am a religious man.

PARSON. Very well. Good day to you.

MUSGRAVE. Good day, sir.

The PARSON *goes.* MUSGRAVE *sits down, takes out a small pocket bible and reads.* MRS. HITCHCOCK *enters.*

MRS. HITCHCOCK. What, they've not all gone, already?

MUSGRAVE. They have, ma'am.

MRS. HITCHCOCK. Just like, isn't it? Use my bar for a council-parlour, leave nowt behind 'em but bad breath and a shiny bench – *they* take care. I'm giving your three their dinners in back. You eating with 'em?

MUSGRAVE (*of-handed*). No. I'll have a hand of bread and cheese and eat it here.

MRS. HITCHCOCK. Drink with it?

MUSGRAVE (*still at his book*). No . . . Thanks, no. Just the cheese.

MRS. HITCHCOCK (*sourly*). H'm, another on 'em . . . Hey, Annie! Slice o' bread and a piece o' cheese in here for this one! Pickles?

MUSGRAVE. Eh?

MRS. HITCHCOCK (*annoyed*). Pickles!

MUSGRAVE. No . . . (*He looks up suddenly.*) Tell me, ma'am, is there many from this town lately have gone for a soldier?

MRS. HITCHCOCK. Some. It's not a common pleasure here – not as long as the coal wor right to sell, any road. But there was some. You'll know the sort o' reasons, I daresay?

> The yellow-haired boy lay in my bed
> A-kissing me up from me toes to me head.
> But when my apron it did grow too short
> He thought it good time to leave his sport.

Enter ANNIE *with the bread and cheese. She gives it to* MUSGRAVE.

MUSGRAVE. Thank you.

ANNIE (*confronting him*). Serjeant you are.

MUSGRAVE. That's right.

ANNIE. You seem a piece stronger than the rest of 'em.

He nods.

And they call you Black Jack Musgrave?

He looks at her.

Well, I'm looking at your face, mister serjeant. Now do you know what I'd say?

MUSGRAVE. What?

ANNIE.   The North Wind in a pair of millstones
          Was your father and your mother
          They got you in a cold grinding.
          God help us all if they get you a brother.

She looks at him another minute, then nods her head and goes out.

MUSGRAVE (*wryly*). She talks a kind of truth, that lassie. Is she daft?

MRS. HITCHCOCK. No, no, no, I wouldn't say daft. But there's not many would let her bide in their house.

MUSGRAVE. Tell me, ma'am. It sticks on my mind that I once had a sort of a comrade came from this town. . . Long, yellow-haired lad, like in your little verse. Name of, oh, Hickson, was it, Hickman?

MRS. HITCHCOCK (*astonished and disturbed*). Ey, ey –

MUSGRAVE. What was it now, his name – Billy – Billy –

MRS. HITCHCOCK (*very upset*). Billy Hicks. Hicks. Aye, oh, strange, serjeant, strange roads bringing you along, I'd not wonder.

MUSGRAVE. What do you mean? . . . It *was* Hicks – I remember.

MRS. HITCHCOCK (*reminiscently*). Not what you'd call a bad young feller, you know – but he weren't no good neither. He'd come in here pissed of a Sat'dy night – I'd tell him straight out, 'You needn't reckon on to get any more here.' But he'd lean on this bar and he'd look at me, and he'd sing. You know – *hymns* – 'Uplift your heads, you gates of brass' – church hymns, he'd sing. Like he'd say to me, 'I'll sing for me drinking, missus' . . . hymns . . .

She hums the tune of 'Uplift your heads' and breaks off sharply.

He gave her a baby, and he went straight off to the war. Or the rebellions, they called it. They told us he was killed.

MUSGRAVE (*without emotion*). Aye, he was killed. He was shot
   dead last year . . . Gave a baby to who?

MRS. HITCHCOCK (*jerks her thumb to door behind bar*). Her.

MUSGRAVE (*truly surprised*). Go on?

MRS. HITCHCOCK. True. But when it wor born, it came a
   kind of bad shape, pale, sick: it wor dead and in the ground
   in no more nor two month. About the time they called
   him dead, y'see. What d'you reckon to that?

MUSGRAVE (*carelessly*). It's not material. He was no great
   friend to me. But maybe, as you said, strange. He did use
   to sing. And yellow hair he had, didn't he? (*He goes to the
   door behind the bar and calls.*) Have ye finished your dinners?
   Because we'll take a look at the town before it gets dark.
   (*Confidently to* MRS. HITCHCOCK) What you've just
   been telling me, don't tell it to these. Dead men and dead
   children should bide where they're put and not be rose up
   to the thoughts of the living. It's bad for discipline . . . (*He
   calls again.*) Come on, let's be having you!

The SOLDIERS *come in.* MUSGRAVE *points to each one as they
enter.*

East; south; west; I'll go north; I'm told it suits my nature.
Then meet at the churchyard rail and tell me what you've
seen. Let's make it sharp.

They go out.

SCENE THREE

The churchyard.

Sunset. HURST *enters and walks about, whistling nervously. The*
SLOW COLLIER *enters and looks at him. They pass each other,
giving each other good hard stares. The* SLOW COLLIER *is about
to leave the stage when he turns round and calls.*

SLOW COLLIER. Hey! Soldier!

HURST. Aye?

SLOW COLLIER. How many on you is there?

HURST. Four.

SLOW COLLIER. Four . . . Four dead red rooks and be damned.

HURST. What? What's that?

SLOW COLLIER (*contemptuously*). Arrh . . .

He slouches out.

HURST *makes to follow, but decides not to, and continues walking about.*

MUSGRAVE *enters.*

MUSGRAVE. Coldest town I ever was in. What did you see?

HURST. Hardly a thing. Street empty, windows shut, two old wives on a doorstep go indoors the minute I come. Three men on one corner, two men on another, dirty looks and no words from any on 'em. There's one man swears a curse at me just now. That's all.

MUSGRAVE. H'm . . .

He calls to offstage.

Hello! We're over here!

ATTERCLIFFE *enters.*

What did you see?

ATTERCLIFFE. Hardly a thing. Street empty, doors locked, windows blind, shops cold and empty. A young lass calls her kids in from playing in the dirt—she sees me coming, so she calls 'em. There's someone throws a stone –

MUSGRAVE. A stone?

ATTERCLIFFE. Aye. I don't know who did it and it didn't hit me, but it was thrown.

HURST. It's a cold poor town, I'm telling you, serjeant.

MUSGRAVE. Coldest town I ever was in. And here's the fourth of us.

Enter SPARKY.

What did you see?

SPARKY. Hardly a thing. Street empty, no chimneys smoking, no horses, yesterday's horsedung frozen on the road. Three men at a corner-post, four men leaning on a wall. No words: but some chalked up on a closed door – they said: 'Soldiers go home'.

HURST. Go home?

SPARKY. That's it, boy: home. It's a place they think we have somewhere. And what did *you* see, serjeant?

MUSGRAVE. Nothing different from you . . . So, here is our town and here are we. All fit and appropriate.

HURST (*breaking out suddenly*). Appropriate? Serjeant, now we've come with you so far. And every day we're in great danger. We're on the run, in red uniforms, in a black-and-white coalfield; and it's cold; and the money's running out that you stole from the Company office; and we don't know who's heard of us or how much they've heard. Isn't it time you brought out clear just what you've got in mind?

MUSGRAVE (*ominously*). Aye? Is it? And any man else care to tell me what the time is?

ATTERCLIFFE (*reasonably*). Now serjeant, please, easy—we're all your men, and we agreed –

HURST. All right: if we *are* your men, we've rights.

MUSGRAVE (*savagely*). The only right *you* have is a rope around your throat and six foot six to drop from. On the run? Stolen money? I'm talking of a murdered officer, shot down in a street fight, shot down in one night's work. They put that to the rebels, but *I* know *you* were the man. We deserted, but you killed.

HURST. I'd a good reason . . .

MUSGRAVE. I know you had reason, else I'd not have left you alive to come with us. All I'm concerned about this minute is to tell you how you stand. And you stand in my power. But there's more to it than a bodily blackmail – isn't there? – because my power's the power of God, and that's what's brought me here and all three of you with me. You know my words and purposes – it's not just authority of the orderly room, it's not just three stripes, it's not just given to me by the reckoning of my mortal brain – well, *where* does it come from?

He flings this question fiercely at HURST.

HURST (*trying to avoid it*). All right, I'm not arguing –
MUSGRAVE. *Where!*
HURST (*frantically defensive*). I don't believe in God!
MUSGRAVE. You don't? Then what's this!

He jabs his thumb into HURST'S *cheek and appears to scrape something off it.*

HURST. Sweat.
MUSGRAVE. The coldest winter for I should think it's ten years, and the man sweats like a bird-bath!
HURST (*driven in a moral corner*). Well, why not, because –
MUSGRAVE (*relentless*). Go on – because?
HURST (*browbeaten into incoherence*). All right, because I'm afraid. 'Cos I thought when I met you, I thought we'd got the same motives. To get out, get shut o' the Army – with its 'treat-you-like-dirt-but-you-do-the-dirty-work' – 'kill *him*, kill *them*, they're all bloody rebels, State of Emergency, high standard of turnout, military bearin' – so *I* thought up some killing, I said I'll get me own in. I thought o' the Rights of Man. Rights o' the Rebels: that's *me*! Then I *went*. And here's a serjeant on the road, he's took two men, he's deserted same as me, he's got money, he can bribe a civvy skipper to carry us to England . . . It's nowt to do wi' God. I don't understand all that about God, why d'you bring God into it! You've come here to tell the people and then there'd be no more war –

MUSGRAVE (*taking him up with passionate affirmation*). Which
is the word of God! Our message without God is a bad belch
and a hiccup. You three of you, without me, are a bad belch
and a hiccup. How d'you think you'd do it, if I wasn't here?
Tell me, go on, tell me!

HURST (*still in his corner*). Why then I'd – I'd – I'd tell 'em,
Sarnt Musgrave, I'd bloody stand, and tell 'em, and –

MUSGRAVE. Tell 'em *what*!

HURST (*made to appear more stupid than he really is*). All right:
like, the war, the Army, colonial wars, we're treated like
dirt, out there, and for to do the dirty work, and –

MUSGRAVE (*with withering scorn*). And they'd run you in and
run you up afore the clock struck five! You don't understand about God! But you think, yourself, you, alone,
stupid, without a gill of discipline, illiterate, ignorant of the
Scriptures – you think you can make a whole town, a whole
nation, understand the cruelty and greed of armies, what it
means, and how to punish it! You hadn't even took the pre-
caution to find the cash for your travel. I paid your fare!

HURST (*knuckling under*). All right. You paid . . . You're the
Serjeant . . . All right. Tell us what to do.

MUSGRAVE (*the tension eased*). Then we'll sit down, and we'll
be easy. It's cold atween these tombs, but its private. Sit
down. Now: you can consider, and you can open your lugs
and you can listen – ssh! Wait a minute . . .

The SLOW COLLIER *enters at one side, the* PUGNACIOUS
and EARNEST COLLIERS *at the other. All three carry pick-hefts
as clubs.*

SLOW COLLIER (*calls to the other two*). Four on 'em, you see.
They're all here together.

PUGNACIOUS COLLIER. Setting in the graveyard, eh, like a
coffin-load o' sick spooks.

EARNEST COLLIER (*coming towards the soldiers*). Which one's
the Serjeant?

MUSGRAVE (*standing up*). Talk to me.

EARNEST COLLIER. Aye and I will too. There's a Union made at this colliery, and we're strong. When we say strike, we strike, all ends of us : that's fists, and it's pick-hefts and it's stones and it's feet. If you work in the coal-seam you carry iron on your clogs – see!

He thrusts up his foot menacingly.

PUGNACIOUS COLLIER. And you fight for your life when it's needed.

MUSGRAVE. So do some others of us.

EARNEST COLLIER. Ah, no, lobster, *you* fight for pay. You go sailing on what they call punitive expeditions, against what you call rebels, and you shoot men down in streets. But not here. These streets is *our* streets.

MUSGRAVE. Anything else?

EARNEST COLLIER. No. Not this evening. Just so as you know, that's all.

PUGNACIOUS COLLIER. Setting in the graveyard. Look at 'em, for Godsake. Waiting for a riot and then they'll have a murder. Why don't *we* have one *now* : it's dark enough, ent it?

EARNEST COLLIER. Shut up. It'll do when it's time. Just so as they know, that's all.

The COLLIERS *turn to go.*

MUSGRAVE. Wait a minute.

They pause.

Who told you we'd come to break the strike?

EARNEST COLLIER. Eh?

MUSGRAVE. Who told you?

EARNEST COLLIER. Nobody told us. We don't need to be told. You see a strike : you see soldiers : there's only one reason.

MUSGRAVE. Not this time there isn't. We haven't been sent
for –

PUGNACIOUS COLLIER. Get away wi' that –

MUSGRAVE. And all soldiers aren't alike, you know. Some of
us is human.

SLOW COLLIER   } Arrh –
PUGNACIOUS COLLIER } *(laughs)*

MUSGRAVE. Now I'm in Mrs. Hitchcock's bar tonight until
such time as she closes it. There'll be my money on the
counter, and if you want to find what I'm doing here you
can come along and see. I speak fair; you take it fair. Right?

EARNEST COLLIER. No it's not right, Johnny Clever. These
streets is our streets, so you learn a warning . . . Come on,
leave 'em be, *we* know what they're after. Come on . . .

The COLLIERS *go, growling threateningly.*

ATTERCLIFFE. They hate us, Serjeant, don't they? Wouldn't
you say that's good?

MUSGRAVE. Because of the bad coal-trade they hate us; the
rest just follows. True, there's one man talks of shooting
rebels down in streets, but the others only think of bayonets
turned on pitmen, and that's no good. At the present, they
believe we've come to kill them. Soon they'll find we
haven't, so they'll stop hating. Maybe even some o' them'll
come and sign on. You'll see: His Worship's sovereigns –
they'll fall too damned heavy into these boys' pockets. But
we'll watch and take count, till we know the depth of the
corruption. 'Cos all that we know now is that we've had to
leave behind us a colonial war that is a war of sin and
unjust blood.

ATTERCLIFFE *(sharply)*. All wars is sin, serjeant . . .

MUSGRAVE *(impatient)*. I'm not discussing that. Single purpose at a single time: your generalities aren't material: this
is particular – one night's work in the streets of one city, and
it damned all four of us and the war it was part of. We're

each one guilty of particular blood. We've come to this town to work that guilt back to where it began.

He turns to SPARKY.

Why to this town? Say it, say it!

SPARKY (*as with a conditioned reflex*). Billy. Billy's dead. He wor my mucker, back end of the rear rank. He wor killed dead. He came from this town.

MUSGRAVE (*relentless*). Go on.

SPARKY (*appealing*). Serjeant –

MUSGRAVE. Use your clear brain, man, and tell me what you're doing here! Go on.

SPARKY (*incoherent with recollecting what he wants to forget*). I'm doing here? I'm doing . . . Serjeant, you know it. 'Cos he died. That wor Billy. I got drunk. Four days and four nights. After work of one night. Absent. Not sober. Improperly dressed.

He tries to turn it into one of his jokes.

> Stick me in a cell, boys,
> Pull the prison bell
> Black Jack Musgrave
> To call the prison roll –

Sarnt, no offence – 'First ye'll serve your punishment' he says. 'Then I'll show you how,' he says, the Serjeant. I says, 'You'll show me what?' He says, 'I'll show you how your Billy can be paid for.' . . . I didn't want to pay for him – what had I to care for a colonial war? . . .

He meets MUSGRAVE'S *eye and takes a grip on his motives.*

But I *did* want to pay for him, didn't I?' Cos that's why I'm here. 'You go down, I'll follow' . . . You, Serjeant, ent it?

> Black Jack Musgrave
> He always calls the roll.

He says:

> Go down to Billy's town
> Tell 'em how he died.

And that's what I'm doing here. The Serjeant pays the fare. Here I am, I'm paid for. Next turn's for Billy. Or all that's left of Billy. Who'll give me an offer for his bones? Sixpence for a bone, for a bone of my dead mucker ...

He again avoids emotion by turning on HURST, *jeeringly.*

You didn't even know him when he lived, you weren't in his squad, what do *you* care that he's dead? To you he's like God, ent that the truth, you don't care and you're not bothered!

HURST (*angrily*). Hold your noise, you dirty turd! Who are you telling!

SPARKY. You. Oh you, me boy, you. A man and a soldier –

He meets MUSGRAVE'S *eye again, and his voice trails away.*

– a man and a soldier ...

MUSGRAVE (*emphatically*). Aye. And *you're* a soldier. Don't forget that. You're my man and you'll hear me. You're not on any drunk now. Now you've got discipline. You've got grief, but good order, and its turned to the works of God!

SPARKY (*submissively*). Yes, Sarnt.

MUSGRAVE (*to* HURST). Turned to the works of God!

HURST (*submissively*). Yes, Sarnt.

MUSGRAVE (*in a more encouraging voice*). There was talk about danger. Well, I never heard of no danger yet that wasn't comparative. Compare it against your purposes. And compare it against my strategy. Remember: the roads are closed, the water's frozen, the telegraph wires are weighted down with snow, they haven't *built* the railway. We came here safe, and here we are, safe here. The winter's giving us one day, two days, three days even – that's clear safe for us to hold our time, take count of the corruption, then stand before this people with our white shining word, and let it dance! It's a hot coal, this town, despite that it's freezing – choose your minute and blow: and whoosh, she's flamed your roof off! They're trembling already into the strikers' riots. Well, their riots and our war are the same one corruption. This town is ours, it's ready for us: and its people, when they've heard us, and the Word of God, crying the murders that we've done – I'll tell you they'll turn to us, and they'll turn against that war!

ATTERCLIFFE (*gravely*). All wars, Serjeant Musgrave. They've got to turn against all wars. Colonial war, do we say, no war of honour? I'm a private soldier, I never had no honour, I went killing for the Queen, I did it for me wages, that wor my life. But I've got a new life. There was one night's work, and I said: no more killing.

HURST (*with excitement*). It's time we did our *own* killing.

ATTERCLIFFE. No, boy, it isn't.

HURST. Aye, and I mean it. We're all on the run, and we're all of us deserters. We're wild-wood mad and raging. We caught it overseas and now we've got to run around the English streets biting every leg to give it *them* – that can't be done without –

MUSGRAVE (*interrupting*). Listen to me!

HURST (*subsiding*). Serjeant.

MUSGRAVE (*with angry articulation*). We are here with a word. That's all. That's particular. Let the word dance. That's all that's material, this day and for the next. What happens afterwards, the Lord God will provide. I am with you, He said. Abide with Me in Power. A Pillar of Flame before the people. What we show here'll lead forward forever, against dishonour, and greed, and murder-for-greed! There is our duty, the new, deserter's duty: God's dance on this earth: and all that we are is His four strong legs to dance it . . . Very well. That'll do. It's dark. We'll go in. Now we'll be likely buying drinks around and so on, in the public tonight.

I don't want to see any o' you with more nor you can hold.
When there's danger, there's temptation. So keep it gay, but
that's all. Off you go now! Take 'em in.

ATTERCLIFFE (*as the senior*). All right then, smartly now,
walking up the street. Remember, we're recruiting. I'll give
you the time – left right left right.

They walk out briskly, leaving MUSGRAVE *alone. As they go,
the* BARGEE *enters, and gives them a parody salute in passing.*
MUSGRAVE *doesn't see him, walks downstage, crosses his hands
on his chest and stands to pray. The* BARGEE *parodies his
attitude behind his back.*

MUSGRAVE. God, my Lord God. Have You or have You not
delivered this town into my hands? All my life a soldier I've
made You prayers and made them straight, I've reared my
one true axe against the timber and I've launched it true.
My regiment was my duty, and I called Death honest,
killing by the book – but it all got scrawled and mucked
about and I could not think clear . . . Now I have my duties
different. I'm in this town to change all soldiers' duties. My
prayer is: keep my mind clear so I can weigh Judgement
against the Mercy and Judgement against the Blood, and
make this Dance as terrible as You have put it into my brain.
The Word alone is terrible: the Deed must be worse. But I
know it is Your Logic, and You will provide.

*He pauses for a moment, then turns sharply on his heel and
strides away after the soldiers. He still fails to see the* BARGEE.
The latter has whipped off his hat at the conclusion of MUS-
GRAVE'S *prayer, and now he stands looking solemnly up to
Heaven. He gives a sanctimonious smirk and breathes: 'Amen'.*

Act Two

The bar of the public house.

A scene of noise and conviviality, crowded confusion. MRS. HITCHCOCK *is seated behind the bar, drinking tea with brandy in it.* ANNIE *is going backwards and forwards in the room carrying drinks and empties.* MUSGRAVE *is sitting with a tankard, calmly watching.* SPARKY *is wearing his drum and alternately beating it and drinking and singing. The* SLOW *and* PUGNACIOUS COLLIERS, *well-oiled, are drinking and dancing. The* BARGEE *is drinking and dancing and playing a mouth-organ and beating time to the singing.* ATTERCLIFFE *is drinking and dancing and pinning cockades to the hats of the* COLLIERS. *At intervals one of the dancers grabs hold of* ANNIE *and swirls her around, but she retains a contemptuous aloofness and carries on with her work. As the scene opens the men (save* MUSGRAVE) *are all joining in the chorus:*

CHORUS. Blow your morning bugles
           Blow your calls ey-ho
           Form platoon and dress the ranks
           And blow, boys blow!

This chorus is sung (with progressively less correctness) by most of the men at the end of each verse of the song.

SPARKY (*singing*).

           When first I came to the barracks
           My heart it grieved full sore
           For leaving of my old true love
           That I would see no more.

chorus

SLOW COLLIER (*to* MUSGRAVE, *who is studying a notebook*).
I'm not signing nowt. Provisional, I said, provisional.
MUSGRAVE. Aye, aye, provisional. No one makes it different.
SPARKY (*sings*).

> They made us drill and muster
> And stand our sentries round
> And I never thought I'd lay again
> A girl upon the ground.

chorus

PUGNACIOUS COLLIER (*to* ATTERCLIFFE). That's *my* point,
my point, too . . . all right enlisting, aye . . . but I'm a
married man –
SPARKY (*sings*).

> But soon we were paraded
> And marching to the war
> And in every town the girls lay down
> And cried out loud for more.

chorus

PUGNACIOUS COLLIER (*to* ATTERCLIFFE). I'm not so sure I
like your looks, aye, *you*!
SPARKY. Me?
PUGNACIOUS COLLIER (*pointing to* ATTERCLIFFE). You!
SPARKY (*sings*).

> And when we'd lodge in billets
> We'd beer in every can
> And the landlord's wife and daughters learnt
> Just how to love a man.

chorus

PUGNACIOUS COLLIER (*going at* SPARKY). I'm a married
man, bedamn, I've got a wife, I've got a wife, a wife . . .

SPARKY. No one's taking her from you.

PUGNACIOUS COLLIER. Not you?

SPARKY. No.

MUSGRAVE (*interrupting*). All right, steady, friend, *no one*.

SLOW COLLIER. *I'll* take her from you when you go to the war, I'll take her –

PUGNACIOUS COLLIER. You?

SLOW COLLIER. Me! Or no, no, no: I'll make do with our Annie!

He makes a drunken lurch at her which she more or less evades.

Come on then, mucker!

Foiled by ANNIE, *he seizes the* PUGNACIOUS COLLIER *and they do a clog dance together while the* BARGEE *plays. Chorus while they dance, and general cheer.*

BARGEE. Bring 'em in some more, Annie, it's all on the Queen tonight – how many have you listed, serjeant!

MUSGRAVE. I'm not listing no one tonight. (*He bangs with his tankard for silence*). Now then, boys, everybody –

BARGEE (*officiously*). Everybody listen!

A roll on the drum.

BARGEE. Listen!

MUSGRAVE (*expansively*). This is Her Majesty's hospitality – that's *all* that it is, boys, on a soldier's honour, so! Any man that drinks tonight –

BARGEE. Any man that drinks tonight –

MUSGRAVE. He drinks at the Queen's pleasure, and none of you need fear to find a shilling in your mug at end of it – that like o' lark's finished and gone with the old days – the Army only wants good men, that's free men, of your own true will for the Empire – so drink and welcome: and all men in this town –

BARGEE. All men in this town –

MUSGRAVE. When we hold our meeting and the drum beats and we bring out our colours, then you can make your return in the signing of your names – but only those men willing! That's all : drink and away!

A roll on the drum.

BARGEE. Drink and away, me boys, hurray!

PUGNACIOUS COLLIER. Serjeant, you're a bleeding lobster, but you're a man! Shake me by the hand!

The BARGEE *gives a whoop and starts to dance, playing a mouth-organ. He stumbles, and everybody laughs.*

ANNIE (*scornfully*). And what regiment's *that* one, serjeant? The Backwards-Mounted-Foot?

BARGEE. I'll tell you, me lovely, why not? The Queen's Own Randy Chancers : or the Royal Facing-Both-Ways – hey, me clever monkeys :

> Old Joe looks out for Joe
> Plots and plans and who lies low?
> But the Lord provides, says Crooked Old Joe.

MUSGRAVE (*looking sharply at him*). Eh?

The BARGEE *shrugs and grins.* MUSGRAVE *dismisses the question.*

BARGEE. Just a little joke . . . little joke : little dog, I'll be with you . . .

He whistles 'Michael Finnegan' and ducks out of the pub. Meanwhile SPARKY *has taken off his drum and come downstage to intercept* ANNIE. ATTERCLIFFE *is drinking with the* COLLIERS *and one or other of these plays the drum at intervals. The going of the* BARGEE *has made the room somewhat quieter for a while.*

SPARKY (*to* ANNIE). Little dog – bow-wow, *I'm* a little dog, any trick for a bit of biscuit, Annie, bit o' meat – look :

He takes a pack of cards out of his pocket and presents it.

Take one, go on, take one.

She obeys.

Well?

ANNIE. Queen o' Spades.

SPARKY (*laughing*). That's a hell of a card to take: I think there's treacle on it, sticks to all fingers out o' this pack, I call her Grandma, makes her gentle, y'see – hope she'll kiss me whiskers and leave it at that.

He has replaced the card and shuffles.

Now then, take first four cards on top. Tell me what they are.

ANNIE (*obeying*). Eight Nine Ten Jack, all spades.

SPARKY (*triumphantly*). Right, right, calls the roll straight up to the one you took, the Queen, and where's the one you took? On the bottom – take it!

ANNIE (*obeying*). It is the Queen and all!

SPARKY. 'Course it is: I *told* you. That's what I call life – it all turns up in the expected order, but not when you expect it. And that's what sets your two teeth laughing, click-clack, doesn't it, ha ha ha! Oh I'm a clever lad, you see, they call me Sparky, lots o' games, lots o' jokes . . .

ANNIE (*not impressed*). Lots of liquor too. Now get out of me road while I fetch some more – *I've* got *work*, you know.

SPARKY (*going after her and again intercepting her*). Hey, but lovey, listen: there was an Englishman, a Welshman and a bloody great Irish – all three of 'em on Defaulters, y'see, for drunk. Now the Orderly Sarnt, he says, 'One, Two, Three, all we want's a Scotchman.' And a voice in the guardroom-yard says: 'Hoots awa', man, I'm taking back the empties fairst.'

She avoids him and goes away to the bar, thus ruining the

climax of his tale. He tries to follow her up, but this time he is intercepted by MUSGRAVE. HURST *appears in the doorway.* ANNIE *looks up at him and follows him with her eyes for the rest of this dialogue.*

MUSGRAVE (*to* SPARKY). You've had enough.

SPARKY. I'm not drunk.

MUSGRAVE. No and you won't be neither. This is no time.

SPARKY (*pointing to* HURST). No – and *here* he comes, look at him.

MUSGRAVE (*striding angrily over to* HURST). Where have you been?

HURST (*surlily*). Down by the canal.

MUSGRAVE. Why?

HURST. All right, I'd got things on my mind. And I'll tell you this, Serjeant, it isn't enough.

MUSGRAVE. What isn't enough?

HURST. What you and that old cuckold are reckoning to do. It's all soft, it's all flat, it's all – God and the Word! Tchah! What good's a word, what good's a bloody word, they can *all* talk bloody words – it isn't enough: we've got to be strong!

MUSGRAVE. Leave it alone, boy. *I* hold the logic. *You* hold some beer and get on with your work.

MUSGRAVE *walks away from* HURST.

HURST (*shouts after him*). It isn't enough!

He turns to find ANNIE *standing at his elbow, looking into his face and handing him a tankard of beer. He takes it and drinks it rapidly, without looking at her.*

MRS. HITCHCOCK (*calling from the bar*). The Queen's in debt, Serjeant!

MUSGRAVE. Hello, ma'am?

MRS. HITCHCOCK. I said the Queen's in debt!

MUSGRAVE. Chalk it up Ma'am, and another round for us all.

MRS. HITCHCOCK. No more chalk.

MUSGRAVE. Easily found though.

He plunges his hand in his pocket and pulls out a quantity of money. He does a rapid count, whistles in consternation, and selects a few coins.

ATTERCLIFFE (*watching him*). Not so much of it left, is there?

MUSGRAVE. Easy, easy.

He goes over to the bar and pays. SPARKY *is now showing his card tricks to the* COLLIERS. ANNIE *plucks at the sleeve of the pensive* HURST.

ANNIE (*simply*). You're the best to look at of all the four, aren't you?

HURST. Eh? What's that?

ANNIE. Tell you again? Why? You know it, don't you?

HURST (*preoccupied*). I'd forgot it. I'd other matter beyond wondering what you'd think to our looks.

He studies her closer, and snaps out of his gloomy mood into an attitude of lady-killing arrogance.

Why, I don't need to think o' women. I let them think of *me*. I've knocked greasier ones than you between me porridge and me bacon. Don't flatter yourself.

ANNIE. I'm not, soldier: I'm flattering you. I'll come to you tonight.

HURST (*pleased, though trying not to show it*). Will you? That's a good choice, you've got sense.

ANNIE (*meaningly*). But you forget them other matters, eh?

HURST (*decidedly warming to her*). I'll try . . . I'd rather. I hope I can . . . Stand straight: let's see . . . Gay and greasy, like I like 'em! You're big, and you're bonny. A good shape, I'd call it. And you've got good hair, but wants a comb in it. You ought to wash your face. And your neck smells of soot, don't it?

ANNIE (*accepting this in the spirit in which it's meant*). I've been blowing up the fire.

HURST (*boastfully*). Ah, the last I had was a major's daughter. I've got standards. Lovely.

ATTERCLIFFE *comes across to them.*

ATTERCLIFFE. You said he was the best looker. I heard you. But it's not true.

ANNIE. Then who is? You?

ATTERCLIFFE. I'll tell you a tale about that. That pitman over there – he said to me he thought I'd steal his wife. By God, I'd sooner steal his nightsoil . . . I've got a wife. Ask me to tell you one o' these days.– Sparky'd make a joke of it – wouldn't you, Sparky!

The last phrases are shouted across the room.

SPARKY (*shouts back*). Not any more – we're all going too fast.

He turns back to the COLLIERS

Down, down – any card, any card, mate – tell me its name – down.

PUGNACIOUS COLLIER. Six o' Hearts!

SPARKY. Right, right – *and* we shuffle and cut –

Enter the BARGEE.

BARGEE (*shouts*). Time, gennelmen please, everybody time, last orders everybody!

MRS. HITCHCOCK (*angrily*). Who's given *you* leave to do the calling here!

BARGEE (*singing*).

> Blow your morning bugles
> Blow your calls ey-ho –

If it's not me and it's not you, there'll be somebody else – *look*!

Enter CONSTABLE.

CONSTABLE. All right, Mrs. Hitchcock, it's time you closed your bar.

MRS. HITCHCOCK. What are you talking about!

CONSTABLE. Magistrates' orders, missus. All public houses to close at nine o'clock sharp, pending settlement of colliery dispute.

MRS. HITCHCOCK. It's the first I've heard of it.

SLOW COLLIER (*to the* CONSTABLE). Get out of it.

PUGNACIOUS COLLIER (*ditto*). Go home, you closhy bluebottle, and sweep your bloody chimney.

CONSTABLE. That'll do there.

MUSGRAVE. That'll do, lads, keep it easy.

PUGNACIOUS COLLIER (*to* MUSGRAVE). We're not in the Army yet, y'know!

ATTERCLIFFE. Steady, matey, steady. All friends, y'know: married men together.

PUGNACIOUS COLLIER. But, Serjeant, you're a man, and I'll *shake* you by the hand.

CONSTABLE (*now things seem quiet again.*). Magistrates issued the order only this evening, missus. I've let you stay open a lot longer than the others – it's nigh on a quarter to ten already – and I'm in my rights to allow an exception for this house, on account of the Army. Question of facilities. I trust you've made good use of the extra time, Sarnt Musgrave?

MUSGRAVE. H'm.

PUGNACIOUS COLLIER (*with great friendliness*). Have the last drink on me, bluebottle!

CONSTABLE (*curtly*). The last drink's been had already. Close your bar, please, missus.

PUGNACIOUS COLLIER (*an angry idea occurring to him*). Wait a minute . . . Suppose I join your Army. Suppose I bloody 'list. What does my wife do?

BARGEE. Cock-a-doodle-do!

PUGNACIOUS COLLIER (*finding his own answer*). She goes to bed with the Peeler! I'll break his wooden head off.

He goes for the CONSTABLE *with a tankard, the* CONSTABLE *staggers backwards and falls, the* COLLIER *raises his tankard to smash it into his face.* ATTERCLIFFE *and* MUSGRAVE, *being nearest, jump to prevent him.*

ATTERCLIFFE (*pulling the* COLLIER *fiercely back*). Hey, ey, ey, ey-ey, hold it there, boy, hold it there! My God, you might ha' killed him. No...

ATTERCLIFFE *is trembling all over.*

SLOW COLLIER. Why shouldn't he if he wants to?

ATTERCLIFFE (*with great passion*). We've had enough o' that already – no more, no more, no more of it.

MUSGRAVE (*holding* ATTERCLIFFE *to quiet him*). Stop it there!

CONSTABLE (*getting up slowly*). Stand back, stand back. By God, it's *time* this place was closed. Turn out into the street, go on with you, get home. D'ye want me to whistle up me specials? Go on.

He hurls the COLLIERS *and* BARGEE *out of the pub.*

ATTERCLIFFE. He was going to, Serjeant. He would have, he'd have killed him. It's always here. Kill him. Kill.

MUSGRAVE (*roughly*). That'll do... We've all had enough, Mr. Constable. I'll get this lot to bed.

CONSTABLE. All right then. And try and keep folk quiet. I know you've got to buy 'em drink and that – but ... *you* know – easy?

MUSGRAVE. Aye aye, easy. We know the trends. Don't you worry: *we* stand for law-and-order too, don't we?

CONSTABLE. Well, I hope so –

He goes to the door and calls into the street.

I said home, no loitering, go on, go on, or I'll run you in!

He comes back to MUSGRAVE *in a confidential conspiratorial sort of way.*

It's a sort of curfew, you see. I told His Worship: 'If there's trouble at night, you can't hold *me* responsible. I've done my best,' I said – I told him frank . . . Oh, and while we're on about His Worship, Serjeant, I might as well take occasion to discuss some names with you. There's a few like I could tell you as'd look very convenient on a regimental muster.

MUSGRAVE (*coldly*). I'm here for volunteers only, you know.

CONSTABLE (*insinuatingly*). Ah well, what's a volunteer? You, you, and you – the old Army custom – eh, Serjeant? Mrs. Hitchcock! A couple o' pints o' taddy for me and the Serjeant.

MRS. HITCHCOCK. We're closed.

CONSTABLE (*broad-mindedly*). That's all right, missus. Serve to the Serjeant: hotel-resident. All above the board.

MRS. HITCHCOCK (*to* ANNIE). So take 'em their drinks. Queen as pays.

She pours herself out another cup of tea. ANNIE *prepares the drinks and brings them to* MUSGRAVE *and the* CONSTABLE, *who gets into a huddle over a list the latter produces.*

SPARKY (*to the other two* SOLDIERS). Very commodious Queen. I say, a very commodious Queen, ha ha, if she'd drank all she paid for tonight, heh, Sponge By Appointment, they could swab out the Windsor Castle Guardhouse, ha ha, who'd be a Coldstream! I say, they could swab out –

ATTERCLIFFE. Oh shut up, man, for God's sake. We've had all we can take of your stinking patter.

SPARKY (*aggrieved*). Ey-ey, matey – ey-ey.

He withdraws, hurt.

HURST (*to* ATTERCLIFFE). Shut up yourself – what's got into you?

ATTERCLIFFE. Why, *you* were making enough carry-on earlier, weren't you? Are you so daft or so drunk you didn't see what just happened?

HURST. There was nowt happened. Couple o' pitmen three parts pissed? What's the matter wi' that? You were near as bad yourself – don't tell *me*. *You* were on about your *wife!*

ATTERCLIFFE. There was all but a man killed. We've come to stop it, not to start it – go on, sing to us.

He sings, with savage emphasis.

> Who'll give a penny to the poor blind man
> Holds out his hand with an old tin can.

– 'Cos that's all you are and it curdles up my bowels. I'm going to the coach-house.

HURST. The coach-house! What for?

ATTERCLIFFE. Where there's a man to talk to who don't talk like a fool.

He goes out of the door behind the bar.

SPARKY. Here, what d'you think to *him*? What sort o' talk does he reckon he'll get.

HURST. Keep your mind off that!

SPARKY (*wildly*). Rattling, clattering, old bones in a box? Billy used to sing, d'you think he'll have a sing-song?

HURST. I don't understand you. This don't make *me* laugh. It fair makes me sick.

SPARKY (*jeeringly*). Sick and bloody scared. Hey-ey, that's you, that's you truly.

HURST. Well, I've got things on my mind. If you can call it scared –

SPARKY. You and me, we're a pair, boy.

HURST (*savagely*). All right. But you'll learn. All *right*.

He turns abruptly away, and broods.

SPARKY (*beckoning* ANNIE, *who comes unenthusiastically*). I say, Annie – oh I'll tell you what, Annie, I don't know what I'm doing here.

She looks at him questioningly; he waves the point aside.

Aha, for that . . . Look, we've made us our beds up in the stables – ha, loose-box for every man, but the serjeant in the house.

ANNIE. Aye, I know.

SPARKY. We call it the Discipline, y'see. Yes-sarnt-no-sarnt, three-bags-full-sarnt – that's our merry lives. Ha ha. Third box from the end tonight, the fastest racehorse of 'em all. Oaks, Derby, I carry 'em away, boy: but I'm best at a steeple-chase – *hup* and *hover*, hedge and ditch, dear, and not by soldiers' numbers neither . . . Come for a gallop.

It is clear from the tone of the last phrase he is not joking.

ANNIE (*unemotionally*). Not tonight.

SPARKY. Oh . . . Go on, tonight.

ANNIE (*with something of a sneer*). Maybe next I will. I can't tell from day to day.

SPARKY. No more can I. You know, you've not yet give me one little laugh . . . But I'll contrive it: now y'see, there was a butcher, a baker, and a cats'-meat-man, all on the edge of the river. And down this river comes this dead dog, floating.

HURST (*whose head has dropped, suddenly jerks himself up again*). God, I was near asleep! I started a bad dream and it woke me.

MUSGRAVE (*to the* CONSTABLE). No, mister, it won't wash. We can't play pressgangs these days. If a man gets drunk and then signs, all right: but otherwise –

CONSTABLE (*vexed*). You're not over-co-operative, are you?

MUSGRAVE. I'm sorry. Oh, I'll see what I can do: but I won't promise more. Besides, agitators is agitators, in or out the Army. I'm not sure we want 'em. But I'll think. Good night.

He goes with the CONSTABLE *to the street door.*

CONSTABLE. Good night. Good night, missus.

Exit the CONSTABLE. MUSGRAVE *comes down to the* SOLDIERS.

MUSGRAVE (*calling* ANNIE). Lassie.

ANNIE. Hello.

MUSGRAVE. These are my men. They're here with their work to do. You will not distract them.

ANNIE. I won't?

MUSGRAVE. No. Because *they* know, whether you know it or not, that there's work is for women and there's work is for men : and let the two get mixed, you've anarchy.

ANNIE (*rather taken aback*). Oh? And what's anarchy? You, you clever grinder – words and three stripes –

MUSGRAVE. Look, lassie, anarchy : now, we're soldiers. Our work isn't easy, no and it's not soft : it's got a strong name – duty. And it's drawn out straight and black for us, a clear plan. But if you come to us with what you call your life or love – *I'd* call it your indulgence – and you scribble all over that plan, you make it crooked, dirty, idle, untidy, *bad* – there's anarchy. I'm a religious man. I know words, and I know deeds, and I know how to be strong. So do these men. You will not stand between them and their strength! Go on now : take yourself off.

ANNIE. A little bit of wind and a little bit of water –

MRS. HITCHCOCK. Annie –

ANNIE. But it drowned three score of sailors, and the King of Norway's daughter. (*She smiles for the first time in the play.*)

She sings:

> O mother O mother
> It hurts me so sore
> Sing dody-eye-dodo
> Then ye daft little bitch

Ye should do it no more
For you've never left off
Since we sailed from the shore.

MRS. HITCHCOCK (*sharply*). Annie, get to bed.

MUSGRAVE (*to the* SOLDIERS). You two, get to bed. And pay
heed to what I say.

ANNIE *goes out behind the bar, with a satirical curtsy.*
MUSGRAVE *goes out by the street door.* HURST *makes a move
as though to speak to him, but is too late. He stands reflective.*

SPARKY.

To bed to bed says Sleepy-head
Tarry a while says Slow
Open the book, says the wise old Rook
We'll have prayers before we go.

He sways a little tipsily, and laughs.

SCENE TWO

A street. Night.

The PUGNACIOUS *and* SLOW COLLIERS *enter, drunk and
marching, the* BARGEE *drilling them.* (*This is a kind of 'Fred
Karno' sequence which must be kept completely under control. At
each command each of the three carries out, smartly, a drill-
movement; but each drill movement is different for each man, and
none of them performs the movement shouted. They must not be
so drunk that they cannot appear erect and alertly jerking. The
effect should be, not so much of three incompetents pretending to be
soldiers, but of three trained soldiers gone mad.*) *The* COLLIERS
carry pickhefts as rifles, and the BARGEE *an oar.*
MUSGRAVE *enters, and stands quietly watching.*

BARGEE. Right turn. Forward march. Left right left right left
right left.

PUGNACIOUS COLLIER. To the front present. Halt.

BARGEE. About turn.

SLOW COLLIER. One two three four.

BARGEE. Order arms.

PUGNACIOUS COLLIER. Present and correct. By the right, number.

SLOW COLLIER. One two three four.

They are now at attention, together.

PUGNACIOUS COLLIER. Present and correct.

BARGEE (*this order is properly obeyed*). Stand-at-ease. Easy . . .

PUGNACIOUS COLLIER (*breaking the spell*). I'll tell you what, we're bloody good.

BARGEE (*with enthusiasm*). Eh. Lordy, mucker – good! By, I've never seen the like – y'know, if you signed on they'd excuse you three weeks' drill on the spot. You make that serjeant look like Old-Mother-Bunch-in-the-Popshop, alongside o' you – love you, mucker, you're *born* to it!

PUGNACIOUS COLLIER. Well, why didn't I think on it afore?

SLOW COLLIER (*still on parade*). One two three four.

PUGNACIOUS COLLIER. I'd not ha' got wed if I'd known!

SLOW COLLIER (*suddenly coming to attention and starting off*).
Quick march. One two three –

He bumps against WALSH, *who has just entered.*

Arh and be damned.

WALSH. Where the hell are you going to?

MUSGRAVE *starts to go out. He passes* WALSH, *who stops him with a hand on his chest.*

WALSH. So we was mistook, eh? You're not here for no riots after all, but catching up men: that's it, in'it? Guineas?

MUSGRAVE. Sovereigns.

PUGNACIOUS COLLIER (*suddenly indicating* MUSGRAVE *to* WALSH). Here. This one: three stripes, but he's a man.

WALSH. Aye? And what are you? Drunk on *his* money: marching and drilling like a pack o' nit-headed kids at a barrack-gate!

PUGNACIOUS COLLIER. Better nor bloody starve for no coal-owners, any road!

WALSH (*with passion*). I'll tell you, I'm that ashamed, I could spew.

MUSGRAVE (*gripping* WALSH *by the lapel and drawing him away*). Now listen here. I can see you, and see *you* what you are. I wasn't given these – (*he touches his stripes*) – for not knowing men from ninepins. Now I'm telling you one word and I'm telling you two, and that's all. (*He lowers his voice.*) You and me is brothers –

WALSH (*in high irony*). Eh begod! A Radical Socialist! Careful, soldier, careful. D'ye want to be hanged?

MUSGRAVE (*very seriously*). No jokes. I mean this. I mean it. Brothers in God –

WALSH (*even more scornful*). Oh, hoho, *that* –

MUSGRAVE. – And brothers in truth. So watch. And wait. I said, *wait.*

WALSH (*jeering*). Brothers in God.

> Gentle Jesus send us rest
> Surely the bosses knows what's best!

Get along with yer –

MUSGRAVE (*calmly*). Well: I said, wait. You'll see.

Exit MUSGRAVE.

SLOW COLLIER (*who has been marking time since his collision, now mutters*).

> One two three four
> Where's the man as lives next door?
> Five six seven eight
> Come on in, he's working late.

WALSH (*looking at him in disgust*). Holy God, I'd never ha'
dreamt it.

SLOW COLLIER (*his muttering rising in volume*).

> Nine ten eleven twelve
> Take his place and help yourself,
> Thirteen fourteen fifteen sixteen –

PUGNACIOUS COLLIER (*with a stupid laugh*). He's talking
about my wife.

SLOW COLLIER (*annoyed at being interrupted*).

> Thirteen fourteen fifteen sixteen
> Into the bed and there we'll fix him!

PUGNACIOUS COLLIER (*in rising rage*). I couldn't do it to the
soldiers, I couldn't do it to the Peeler, but by, I'll do it to
you! I'll break your bloody head.

He goes for SLOW COLLIER, *who hits him in the belly, lets off
a yell and runs out.* PUGNACIOUS COLLIER *follows with a
roar.*

BARGEE (*calling after them in glee*). Watch out for the Constable! Heh heh heh.

WALSH. Holy God! My mates! My brothers!

BARGEE (*kindly*). Ah well, they're drunk.

WALSH. I know they're drunk, and I know who's helped 'em
to it.

BARGEE. I could help *you* to summat, and all.

WALSH. What's that?

BARGEE. They won't stay drunk all week. Oh the soldiers gives
'em sport, they *need* a bit o' sport, cold, hungry . . . When
you want 'em, they'll be there. Crooked Joe, he's *here*.

WALSH. Aye?

BARGEE. Could you shoot a Gatling gun?

WALSH (*looking at him sideways*). I don't know.

BARGEE. If you really want a riot, why don't you go at it

proper? Come on, I'll tell you . . . (*He hops out, whistling 'Michael Finnegan' and looking back invitingly.*)

WALSH (*considering*). Aye, aye? Crooked, clever, keelman, eh? . . . Well – all right – then *tell* me!

He hurries after him.

SCENE THREE

Interior of the pub (stable and bedroom).

Night. The stage is divided into two distinct acting-areas. The downstage area represents the stable, and is supposed to be divided into three loose boxes. If it is not practicable for the partitions between these to be built, it should be sufficient to suggest them by the three mattresses which are laid parallel, feet to the audience. The actors must not appear to be able to see each other from box to box. The forestage represents the central passage of the stable and is the only access to the boxes. Entry to the forestage can be from both wings (one side leads to the house, the other to the yard and coach-house).

The upstage area, raised up at least a couple of feet, represents a bedroom in the house. It is only large enough to contain a brass-knobbed bedstead with a small table or other support for a candle. The two areas must be treated as completely separate. Access to the bedroom area should be from the rear, and the audience must not be allowed to think that the actors can see from one area to the other (except as regards the light in the window, which is supposed to be seen as if from across the yard).

MUSGRAVE, *in shirt and trousers, is sitting on the bed, reading by candlelight. His tunic etc. lies folded beside the bed.*

HURST *and* SPARKY *come into the stable from the house carrying palliasses and blankets. They proceed to make up their beds (in the two end boxes, leaving the middle one empty.* SPARKY *is at the house end,* HURST *next to the yard). They also undress to their shirts (of grey flannel) and their (long woollen) underpants and socks. Their clothes are laid out neatly beside the beds.*

SPARKY (*as he prepares for bed*). I say . . . I say, can you hear me?

HURST (*uninterested*). I can.

SPARKY. You know, I'll tell you: I'm a bit pissed tonight.

HURST. Uh. What of it?

SPARKY. What's that?

HURST. I said what of it? We all are, aren't we? *I* want an hour or two's sleep, I don't know about *you*, so let's have less o' your gab.

SPARKY. I say, there's a light on still in Black Jack's window.

HURST grunts.

MUSGRAVE *has now lain down on top of his blanket, but has not taken off his trousers, or put out his candle.*

SPARKY. Aye, aye. God's awake. Ha, Ha! Not only God neither. Y'know, I think there might be some of us mortal, even yet . . . I said God's awake!

HURST. I *heard* you, and be damned.

A pause.

SPARKY. Hour or two's sleep . . . What do you want to *sleep* for, and a fine fat tart all promised and ready!

HURST (*who has got undressed and under his blanket*). That'll do. Now shut your row, can't ye, when you're asked! I said I wanted to sleep, so let me.

SPARKY. Why, it's you she's promised, y'see – *you*, not me – wake up, mucker, wake up. She'll soon be here, y'see. She'll soon be here! (*He blows 'reveille' with his lips, then gets under his blanket.*) You, boy, *you*, not me! . . . Shall I sing you a song?

HURST (*almost asleep, and woken again*). Eh, what? Are you going to shut up, or aren't you!

SPARKY. Well, are *you* going to shut up or aren't you, when she comes? It's all right the best-looker loving the girl, but his two mates along the row wi' nowt but a bit o' wainscot atween – hey-ey-ey, it'll be agony for *us* tonight, y'know – so keep it quiet.

A pause.

(*He starts to sing, softly*).

> She came to me at midnight
> With the moonshine on her arms
> And I told her not to make no noise
> Nor cause no wild alarms.
> But her savage husband he awoke
> And up the stairs did climb
> To catch her in her very deed:
> So fell my fatal crime . . .

While he is singing, ANNIE *enters from the house, carrying a candle. She goes gently to* HURST'S *box and stands looking down at him. When she speaks, he sticks his head out of the bedclothes and looks at her.*
In the bedroom, MUSGRAVE *sits up, blows out his light, and goes to sleep.*

ANNIE (*with tender humour*). Here I come. Hello. I'm cold. I'm a blue ghost come to haunt you. Brr. Come on, boy, warm me up. You'll not catch cold off *me*.
HURST (*getting up*). No . . . I daresay not . . .

They put their arms round each other.

But what about the morning?
ANNIE. Ah, the morning's different, ent it? I'll not say nowt about mornings, 'cos then we'll *all* be cold. Cold and alone. Like, stand in a crowd but every one alone. One thousand men makes a regiment, you'd say?
HURST. Near enough.

ANNIE. But for all that, when you're with them, you're still alone. Ent that right? So huggle me into the warm, boy, now. Keep out the wind. It's late. Dark.

HURST (*suddenly breaking away from her*). No, I won't. I don't care what I said afore, it's all done, ended, capped – get away. Go on. Leave me be.

ANNIE (*astonished and hurt*). What is it? What's the matter? Lovey –

HURST (*with violence*). Go on. As far as *my* mind goes, it's morning already. Every one alone – that's all. You want me to lose my life inside of you –

ANNIE. No. No. But just for five hours, boy, six –

HURST. You heard Black Jack say what's right. Straight, clear, dark strokes, no scrawling, I was wrong afore, I didn't trust him. He talked about God, so I thought he wor just nowt. But what he said about *you*: there, that was truth. He's going to be *strong!*

ANNIE (*scornfully*). So *you* take note of Black Jack, do you?

HURST. Aye, and I do. It's too late tonight for anything else. He's got to be trusted, got to be strong, we've got no alternative!

ANNIE (*standing a little away from him*). My Christ then, they *have* found him a brother! It was only this evening, warn't it, *I* saw you, down by the canal, all alone and wretched –

She sings with fierce emphasis:

All round his hat he wore the green willow – !

HURST. All right.

ANNIE (*not letting him off*). But it can't have been you, can it? 'Cos now you're just the same as the rest of 'em – the Hungry Army! You eat and you drink and you go. Though *you* won't even eat when it's offered, will you? So *sprawl* yourself on the straw without me, get up to your work tomorrow, drum 'em in and write 'em down, infect 'em all and bury 'em! I don't care.

HURST. What are you on about, what's the matter, why don't you go when you're told? Godsake, Godsake, leave a man to his sleep!

ANNIE. You know what they call me?

HURST. I'd call you a bloody whoor –

ANNIE (*savagely ironical*). Oh, not just a whoor – *I'm* a whoor-to-the-soldiers – it's a class by itself.

ATTERCLIFFE *has entered from the yard with his bedding. They do not notice him yet.* ANNIE *turns to pleading again.*

ANNIE. Christ, let me stay with you. He called me life and love, boy, just you think on *that* a little.

HURST *pushes her away with a cry. She falls against* ATTERCLIFFE.

ATTERCLIFFE (*holding her up*). Life and love, is it? I'm an old soldier, girly, a dirty old bastard, me, and *I've* seen it all. Here.

He grips her and kisses her violently all over face and neck. He sneers at HURST.

Hey-up there, son, get in your manger and sleep, and leave this to the men.

HURST. All right . . . and you're welcome.

He goes to his box and lies down again, huffily, trying to sleep.

ATTERCLIFFE (*still holding* ANNIE, *with a sort of tenderness*). Now then, what'll I do to you, eh? How d'you reckon you're going to quench *me*? Good strong girly with a heart like a horsecollar, open it up and let 'em all in. And it still wouldn't do no good.

ANNIE (*hard and hostile*). Wouldn't it? Try.

ATTERCLIFFE. Ah, no. Not tonight. What would *you* know of soldiers?

ANNIE. More'n you'd think I'd know, maybe.

ATTERCLIFFE. I doubt it. Our Black Jack'd say it's not material. He'd say there's blood on these two hands. (*He looks at his hands with distaste.*) You can wipe 'em as often as you want on a bit o' yellow hair, but it still comes blood the next time so why bother, *he'd* say. And *I'd* say it too. Here. (*He kisses her again and lets her go.*) There you are, girly: I've given you all you should get from a soldier. Say 'Thank you, boy', and that's that.

ANNIE (*still hard*). Thank you boy . . . You know it, don't you? All I should get. All I ever have got. Why should I want more? You stand up honest, you do, and it's a good thing too, 'cos you're old enough.

ATTERCLIFFE (*with a wry smile*). H'm. I am and all. Good night.

He starts making up his bed and undressing. SPARKY *has sat up and is listening. As* ANNIE *is standing still,* ATTERCLIFFE *starts talking to her again.*

ATTERCLIFFE. Girly. When I was a young lad I got married to a wife. And she slept with a greengrocer. He was the best looker (like *he's* the best looker) – (*he points towards* HURST'S *box*) – or any road that's what *she* said. *I* saw him four foot ten inch tall and he looked like a rat grinning through a brush; but he sold good green apples and he fed the people and he fed my wife. I didn't do neither. So now I'm a dirty old bastard in a red coat and blue breeches and that's all about it. Blood, y'see: killing. Good night.

He has now undressed and lies down to sleep immediately.
ANNIE *stands for a minute, then subsides to a crouching position, in tears.*
SPARKY *creeps out of his box.*

SPARKY. Tst tst tst, Annie. Stop crying: come here.

ANNIE. Don't talk to me, go to bed, I can't bear wi' no more of you.

SPARKY. Annie, Annie, look now, I want to talk. I'm not deaf, y'know, and I'm not that drunk, I mean I've been drunker, I mean I can stand, ha ha, one foot and all, I'm a stork, look at me – (*He tries to balance on one foot*). Him at the far end – don't you worry for *him*, Annie – why, he's not mortal any more, he's like God, ent he? And God – (*He looks towards* MUSGRAVE'S *light*) – hello, God's asleep.

ANNIE. God?

SPARKY. He's put his light out. Look,

ANNIE. That's where the serjeant is.

SPARKY. That's right. I never thought he'd sleep. *I* can't sleep . . . what have you got against me?

ANNIE (*surprised*). Nowt that I know.

SPARKY. But you didn't come to me, did you? I mean, you asked *him* and he said no, I asked *you* and you said no. That's all wrong. I mean, you know what the Black Musgrave'd call that, don't you – *he'd* say anarchy!

ANNIE. *He'd say*? He?

MUSGRAVE *groans in his bed.*

Every one of you swaggering lobsters, that serjeant squats in your gobs like an old wife stuck in a fireplace. What's the matter with you all!

SPARKY. Ssh ssh, keep it quiet. Come down here . . .

He leads her as far as possible from the other two.

Listen.

ANNIE. What for?

SPARKY. Snoring. Him? Him? Good, two snorings. They're asleep . . . I told you in the bar, y'know, they call me Sparky – name and nature – Sparky has his laugh. . . . A man can laugh, because or else he might well howl – and howling's not for men but for dogs, wolves, seagulls – like o' that, ent it?

ANNIE. You mean that you're frightened?

SPARKY (*with a sort of nervous self-realisation*). Aye, begod,

d'you know: I am. God's not here, he's put his light out:
so I can tell you, love: I *am*. Hey, not of the war, bullets in
the far Empire, that's not the reason, don't think it. They
even give me a medal, silver, to prove so. But I'll tell you,
I'm – here, kiss me, will you, quickly, I oughtn't to be talking . . . I think I've gone daft.

ANNIE (*who is looking at him curiously but fascinated*). All
right, I will . . .

She kisses him, and he holds her.

MUSGRAVE (*in clear categorical tones, though in his sleep*).
Twenty-five men. Nine women. Twenty-five men. No
children. No.

ANNIE (*in a sudden uprush*). Look, boy, there was a time *I* had
a soldier, he made jokes, he sang songs and all – ah, *he* lived
yes-sarnt no-sarnt three-bags-full-serjeant, but he called it
one damned joke. God damn you, he was killed! Aye, and
in your desert Empire – so what did *that* make?

SPARKY. I don't know . . .

ANNIE. It made a twisted little thing dead that nobody laughed
at. A little withered clover – three in one it made. There was
me, and there was him: and a baby in the ground. Bad shape.
Dead.

*She can say nothing more and he comforts her silently a
moment.*

SPARKY (*his mind working*). Why, Annie . . . Annie . . . you as
well: another one not paid for . . . O, I wish *I* could pay.
Say, suppose I paid for yours; why, maybe you could pay
for mine.

ANNIE. I don't understand.

SPARKY (*following his thought in great disturbance of mind*). It
wouldn't be anarchy, you know; he can't be right there! All
it would be, is: *you* live and *I* live – we don't need his duty,
we don't need his Word – a dead man's a dead man! We

could call it *all* paid for! Your life and my life – make our *own* road, we don't follow nobody.

ANNIE. What are you talking about?

SPARKY (*relapsing into his despair again*). Oh God, I don't know. God's gone to sleep, but when he wakes up again –

ANNIE (*bewildered but compassionate*). Oh quiet, boy, be quiet, easy, easy.

She stoops over him, where he has crumpled into a corner, and they embrace again with passion.

MUSGRAVE (*now shouting in his sleep*). Fire, fire! Fire, fire, London's burning, London's burning!

MRS. HITCHCOCK, *in a nightdress and robe, and carrying a tumbler, hurries into his bedroom.*

MRS. HITCHCOCK. What's the matter?

She lights his candle.

MUSGRAVE (*sitting up and talking very clearly as if it made sense*). Burning. Burning. One minute from now, and you carry out your orders – get *that* one! *Get* her! Who says she's a child! We've got her in the book, she's old enough to kill! You will carry out your orders. Thirty seconds. Count the time. (*He is looking at his watch.*) Twenty-six . . . twenty-three . . .

MRS. HITCHCOCK (*very alarmed*). Serjeant – Serjeant –

MUSGRAVE. Be quiet. Twenty . . . Eighteen . . . I'm on duty, woman. I'm timing the end of the world. Ten more seconds, sir . . . Five . . . three . . . two . . . one.

He lets out a great cry of agony and falls back on the bed.
All in the stable hear and take notice. ATTERCLIFFE *turns over again to sleep.* HURST *sits up in alarm.* ANNIE *and* SPARKY *stand apart from each other in surprise.*

ANNIE. Sparky, it's your God. He's hurt.

SPARKY *sits staring and gasping, till* ANNIE *pulls him to her again.*

MRS. HITCHCOCK. What are you playing at – you'll wake up the town!

MUSGRAVE *shivers and moans.*

MRS. HITCHCOCK (*shaking him gently*). Come on – it's a nightmare. Wake up and let's get rid of it. Come on, come on.

MUSGRAVE. Leave me alone. I wasn't asleep.

MRS. HITCHCOCK. You warn't awake, any road.

MUSGRAVE. Mind your own business.

MRS. HITCHCOCK. I thought you might be poorly.

MUSGRAVE. No . . . No . . . (*Suddenly*) But it *will* come, won't it?

MRS. HITCHCOCK. What will?

MUSGRAVE. The end of the world? You'll tell me it's not material, but if you could come to it, in control; I mean, numbers and order, like so many ranks this side, so many that, properly dressed, steadiness on parade, so that whether you knew you was right, or you knew you was wrong – you'd know it, and you'd stand. (*He shivers.*) Get me summat to eat.

MRS. HITCHCOCK. I got you a hot grog. Here. (*She gives him a tumbler.*)

MUSGRAVE. What – what . . .?

MRS. HITCHCOCK. I take it at nights for me bad back. I heard you calling so I brought it in. Have a biscuit.

She gives him a biscuit from her dressing gown pocket.

MUSGRAVE. Aye, I will . . . (*He eats and drinks.*) That's better . . . You *do* understand me, don't you? Look, if you're the right-marker to the Company and you're marching to the right, you can't see the others, so you follow the orders you can hear and hope you hear them true. When I was a recruit

I found myself once half across the square alone – *they'd* marched the other way and I'd never heard the word!

MRS. HITCHCOCK. You ought to lie down. You *are* poorly, I can tell. Easy, Serjeant, easy.

MUSGRAVE (*relaxing again*). Easy . . . easy . . .

She draws the blanket over him and sits soothing him to sleep.

SPARKY (*with a sudden access of resolution*). Annie, I don't care. Let him wake when he wants to. All I'll do this time is to stand and *really* laugh. Listen to this one, because here's what I'll be laughing at. There was these four lads, y'see, and they made it out they'd have a strong night all night in the town, each boozer in turn, pay-day. And the first one in the first boozer, he says: 'Each man drinks my choice,' he says. 'One sup of arsenic to every man's glass' – and *that's* what they've to drink. Well, one of them, he drinks and he dies, next man drinks and *he* dies, what about the third? Has he to drink to that rule? 'Cos they'd *made* it a rule – each man to the first man's choice.

HURST *has left his box and crept up and is now listening to this.*

ANNIE. I don't know –

SPARKY. Neither do I. But I can tell you what *I'd* do.

ANNIE. What?

SPARKY (*with a switch to hard seriousness*). I'd get out of it, quick. Aye, and with you. Look, love, its snowing, we can't leave the town now. But you could bed me down somewheres, I mean, like, hide; bide *with* me while it's all over, and then get me some clothes and we'd go – I mean, like, go to London? What about London? You've never been to London?

ANNIE. Bide hid while *what's* all over? What's going to happen?

SPARKY. Eh, that's the question. I wish I could tell you. It's Black Jack's work, not mine.

ANNIE. Bad work, likely?

SPARKY. Likely . . . I don't know. D'you know, I never *asked!* You see, he's like God, and it's as if *we* were like angels — *angels*, ha, ha! But that's no joke no more for me. This is funnier nor *I* can laugh at, Annie, and if I bide longer here, I'm *really* wild-wood mad. So get me out of it, quick!

ANNIE (*decisively*). I will. I'm frightened. Pull your clothes on, Sparky. I'll hide you.

SPARKY. Good love, good —

ANNIE. But you'll not leave me behind?

He has started dressing, very confusedly, putting his tunic on first.

SPARKY. No.

ANNIE. Swear it.

He has his trousers ready to step into. He lets them fall while he takes her for a moment in his arms:

SPARKY. Sworn.

HURST *nips in and seizes the trousers.*

(*Releasing* ANNIE) Now then, sharp. Hey, where's me trousers?

HURST. Here!

SPARKY. What's the goddamn — give 'em back, you dirty —

HURST (*triumphantly*). Come and get 'em, Sparky! Heh, you'll be the grand deserter, won't you, running bare-arsed over the moor in six-foot drifts of snow!

SPARKY. Give me them!

He grabs one end of the trousers and a farcical tug-o'-war begins.

HURST (*in high malice*). A man and a soldier! Jump, natter, twitch, like a clockwork puppet for three parts of the night, but the last night of all, you *run*! You little closhy coward.

ATTERCLIFFE *has woken and tries to intervene.*

ATTERCLIFFE. What the hell's the row – easy, easy, *hold* it!
SPARKY. He's got my bloody trousers!

He gives a great tug on the trousers and pulls them away,
HURST *falling down.*

HURST. I'm going to *do* you, Sparky.

His hand falls on SPARKY'S *belt, with bayonet scabbard
attached, which is lying on the floor. He gets up, drawing the
bayonet.*

ANNIE. No, no, stop him!
ATTERCLIFFE. Drop that bayonet!

ANNIE *mixes in, seizing* HURST'S *wrist and biting it. The
bayonet drops to the floor.* ATTERCLIFFE *snatches it and*
HURST *jumps upon him. Together they fall against* SPARKY
and all three crash to the floor. SPARKY *gives a terrifying,
choking cry.*
MUSGRAVE *leaps up in the bedroom. Those on the forestage
all draw back, appalled, from* SPARKY'S *dead body.*

MUSGRAVE (*to* MRS. HITCHCOCK). Stay where you are.

He leaves the bedroom.

HURST. He's dead. He's dead. *I* didn't do it. Not me. No.
ATTERCLIFFE. Dead?
HURST. Of course he's dead. He's stuck in the gut. That's you.
  Your hand. You killed him.
ATTERCLIFFE. I can't have.
HURST. You did.
ATTERCLIFFE (*stupidly*). I've got the bayonet.
HURST. Aye, and you've killed him.
ATTERCLIFFE. O Holy God!

MUSGRAVE *enters from the house.* MRS. HITCHCOCK *has left the bedroom.*

MUSGRAVE. What going on?

HURST. Sparky's been killed.

MUSGRAVE. *What!* How?

HURST. His own bayonet. He was deserting. I tried to stop him. Then *he* –

He points to ATTERCLIFFE.

MUSGRAVE (*to* ATTERCLIFFE). Well?

ATTERCLIFFE (*hopelessly*). Here's the bayonet. I got holding it, Serjeant. I did. It's always me. You can call it an accident. But *I* know what that means, it means that it –

MUSGRAVE. Shut up. You said deserting?

HURST *nods.*

What's *she* doing here? Was she with him?

HURST *nods.*

Aye, aye . . . Desertion. Fornication. It's not material. He's dead. Hide him away.

HURST. Where?

MUSGRAVE. In the midden at back of the yard. And don't show no lights while you're doing it. Hurry.

HURST (*to* ATTERCLIFFE). Come on.

ATTERCLIFFE. Holy God, Holy God!

They carry the body out.

MUSGRAVE (*to* ANNIE, *unpleasantly*). Oh, you can shake, you can quiver, you can open your mouth like a quicksand and all – blubbering and trouble – but *I've* got to think, and *I've* got to do.

MRS. HITCHCOCK *enters from the house. She is carrying* MUSGRAVE'S *tunic, hat, and boots, which she puts down.*

Missus, come here. There's things going wrong, but don't ask me what. Will you trust me?

She looks at him searchingly and gives a short nod.

Get hold of this lassie, take her upstairs, lock her in a cupboard, and keep quiet about it. I've got a right reason : you'll know it in good time. Do as I tell you and you won't take no harm.

MRS. HITCHCOCK. The end of the world, already.

MUSGRAVE. What's that? D'ye hear what I say?

MRS. HITCHCOCK. Oh aye, I heard you.

She takes the shuddering ANNIE *by the hand, and then looks sharply at her fingers.*

Hey-ey-ey, this here, it's blood.

MUSGRAVE. I know. I repeat it : don't ask me.

ANNIE *looks at* MUSGRAVE *and at* MRS. HITCHCOCK, *then licks her hand, laughing in a childish fashion.*

MRS. HITCHCOCK. Come away in, Annie . . . Aye, I'll go and lock her up . . . It might be the best thing. I've got to trust you, haven't I? I've always praised religion.

She takes ANNIE *away, into the house.* MUSGRAVE *sits down suddenly, with his head in his hands. The* BARGEE *creeps in from the yard and sits beside him, in a similar attitude.*

BARGEE (*singing softly*).

> Here we set like birds in the wilderness,
>   birds in the –

MUSGRAVE *sits up, looks at him, realises who it is, and grabs him by the throat.*

BARGEE (*struggling free*). It's all right, bully, it's only Old Joe.

MUSGRAVE (*relaxing, but still menacing*). Oh it is, is it? Well?

BARGEE (*significantly*). I was thinking, like, if I wor you, *I* wouldn't just set down in a stable, not now I wouldn't, no.

MUSGRAVE. Why not?

BARGEE. *I* see your jolly muckers, over there, mucking in the muck-pile, eh? But if they turned theirselves around and looked at the coach-house –

MUSGRAVE *leaps up in alarm.*

MUSGRAVE. What about the coach-house?

BARGEE. There's bars at its windows : and there's a crowbar at the bars – listen!

A crash of glass offstage from the yard.

That's the glass gone now! If you're quick, you can catch 'em!

MUSGRAVE *has run to the yard side of the stage.*

MUSGRAVE (*calling to offstage*). Get to the coach-house, get round the back! Quick! Quick!

He runs off in great excitement.
More crashes of glass, shouting and banging.
The BARGEE *watches what is happening in the yard, leaping up and down in high delight.*

BARGEE. Go on, catch 'em, two to the back and the serjeant to the door, open the padlock, swing back the wicket – one little laddie, he's trapped in the window – head in, feet out – pull him down, Serjeant, pull him down, soldiers – boot up, fist down, tie him in a bundle – oh me pretty roses, oh me blood-red flowers o' beauty!

The two SOLDIERS *hurry back, with* WALSH *frogmarched between them, his hands bunched up and tied behind his back.* MUSGRAVE *follows. All are panting. They throw* WALSH *down.*

MUSGRAVE. What about the others?

HURST. Run away, Serjeant.

ATTERCLIFFE. Nigh on a dozen of 'em.

HURST. Ran down the alley.

MUSGRAVE. Let's have a look at this one! Oho, so it's *you!* What were you after?

WALSH (*grinning*). What d'you think, lobster?

MUSGRAVE. Our little Gatling? Isn't that right?

WALSH. That's right, boy, you're sharp.

MUSGRAVE (*quieter*). But *you're* not sharp, brother, and I'm going to tell you why.

Shouting and shrill whistles, off.

HURST. It's that Constable's out, and his Specials and all – listen! Hey, we'd better get dressed.

He starts huddling on his tunic and trousers.

MUSGRAVE (*to* WALSH). Chasing your friends. He'll be coming here, shortly.

Whistles again.

CONSTABLE (*offstage, in the house*). Open up, Mrs. Hitchcock, open up – name of the Law!

MUSGRAVE. Ah, here he is. Now he asked me this evening to kidnap you for the Army. But *I* told you we was brothers, didn't I? So watch while I prove it. (*To* HURST.) Take him out and hide him.

HURST (*taken aback*). Him in the midden too?

MUSGRAVE. Don't be a fool. Do as you're told.

WALSH. Wait – wait a minute.

MUSGRAVE (*furiously*). Go with him, you damned nignog. Would ye rather trust the Constable?

WALSH (*very puzzled*). What are you on, for God's sake?

MUSGRAVE. Don't waste time! (*He pushes* WALSH *and barks*

at HURST.) Get him in that woodshed. God, what a shower o' tortoises!

HURST *hustles* WALSH *out to the yard.* MUSGRAVE *turns on* ATTERCLIFFE.

You get your trousers on.

ATTERCLIFFE *obeys.* MRS. HITCHCOCK *comes in, very agitated.*

MRS. HITCHCOCK. The Constable's here, he's running through the house.

MUSGRAVE. Then send him to me! It's in control, in control, woman. I *know* all about it!

MRS. HITCHCOCK *goes back into the house.*

ATTERCLIFFE. Musgrave, what are you doing?

MUSGRAVE. I'm doing what comes next and that's all I've got time for.

ATTERCLIFFE (*in a gush of despair*). But he was killed, you see, killed. Musgrave, don't you see, that wipes the whole thing out, wiped out, washed out, finished.

MUSGRAVE. *No!*

MRS. HITCHCOCK *and the* CONSTABLE *hurry in from the house.*

CONSTABLE. Ah, Serjeant, what's happened? Saw a gang breaking in at the back of this coach-house. What's kept in the coach-house? (*To* MRS. HITCHCOCK.)

MRS. HITCHCOCK. The Serjeant's got his –

MUSGRAVE. I've got my gear.

MRS. HITCHCOCK. Hello, here's the Parson.

The PARSON *hurries in from the house.*

PARSON. Constable, what's going on?

CONSTABLE. I think it's beginning, sir. I think it's the riots.

at HURST.) Get him in that woodshed. God, what a shower o' tortoises!

HURST *hustles* WALSH *out to the yard.* MUSGRAVE *turns on* ATTERCLIFFE.

You get your trousers on.

ATTERCLIFFE *obeys.* MRS. HITCHCOCK *comes in, very agitated.*

MRS. HITCHCOCK. The Constable's here, he's running through the house.
MUSGRAVE. Then send him to me! It's in control, in control, woman. I *know* all about it!

MRS. HITCHCOCK *goes back into the house.*

ATTERCLIFFE. Musgrave, what are you doing?
MUSGRAVE. I'm doing what comes next and that's all I've got time for.
ATTERCLIFFE (*in a gush of despair*). But he was killed, you see, killed. Musgrave, don't you see, that wipes the whole thing out, wiped out, washed out, finished.
MUSGRAVE. *No!*

MRS. HITCHCOCK *and the* CONSTABLE *hurry in from the house.*

CONSTABLE. Ah, Serjeant, what's happened? Saw a gang breaking in at the back of this coach-house. What's kept in the coach-house? (*To* MRS. HITCHCOCK.)
MRS. HITCHCOCK. The Serjeant's got his –
MUSGRAVE. I've got my gear.
MRS. HITCHCOCK. Hello, here's the Parson.

The PARSON *hurries in from the house.*

PARSON. Constable, what's going on?
CONSTABLE. I think it's beginning, sir. I think it's the riots.

MUSGRAVE. You! You, Parson, too. Mrs. Hitchcock, free beer to the crowd!

PARSON. No!

MAYOR (*catching the idea*). *Aye*, missus, bring it! *I'll* pay for it and all!

MUSGRAVE (*to the* BARGEE). *You*, if you want to help, you can carry a flag. (*To* ATTERCLIFFE.) Get him a flag!

Exit ATTERCLIFFE. *Enter* HURST, *drumming furiously.*

We'll *all* carry flags. Fetch me me tunic.

MRS. HITCHCOCK. Here it is, I brought it.

MUSGRAVE (*quite wild with excitement*). Flags, ribbons, bunches o' ribbons, glamourise 'em, glory!

ATTERCLIFFE *hurries in from the yard, with his arms full of colours. He hands these out all round.*

BARGEE. Rosebuds of Old England!

MAYOR. Loyal hearts and true!

PARSON. The Lord mighty in battle!

MUSGRAVE. GOD SAVE THE QUEEN!

General noise, bustle and confusion.

Act Three

SCENE ONE

The market-place.

*Early morning. In the centre of the stage is a practicable feature –
the centre-piece of the market-place. It is a sort of Victorian
clock-tower-cum-lamppost-cum-market-cross, and stands on a
raised plinth. There is a ladder leaning against it. On the plinth
are the soldiers' boxes and a coil of rope. The front of the plinth is
draped with bunting, and other colours are leaning against the
centre-piece in an impressive disposition.*

*When the scene opens, the stage is filled with noise and movement
HURST is beating his drum, the MAYOR, the PARSON and
MUSGRAVE are mounting the plinth, and ATTERCLIFFE is up
already, making the last arrangements. The CONSTABLE takes
up his stand beside the centre-piece, as does HURST. The BARGEE
is hopping about on the forestage.*

*The SOLDIERS are all now properly dressed, the MAYOR has put
on his cocked hat and red robe and chain, and the PARSON his
gown and bands, and carries a Bible. They are all wearing bright
cockades.*

*The role of the BARGEE in this scene is important. As there is no
crowd, the speeches are delivered straight out to the audience, and
the BARGEE acts as a kind of fugleman to create the crowd-
reactions. Noises-off indicated in the dialogue are rather unrealistic
– as it were, token-noises only.*

At one side of the stage there is an upper-storey window.

BARGEE (*casting his cap*).

> Hip hip hooroar
> Hark hark the drums do bark
> The Hungry Army's coming to town
> Lead 'em in with a Holy Book
> A golden chain and a scarlet gown.

Here they are on a winter's morning, you've got six kids at home crying out for bread, you've got a sour cold wife and no fire and no breakfast: and you're too damn miserable even to fight – if there's owt else at all to take your mind off it – so here you are, you lucky people, in your own old market-place, a real live lovely circus, with real live golden sovereigns in somebody's pocket and real live taddy ale to be doled out to the bunch of you!

MRS. HITCHCOCK *enters, trundling a beer-barrel.*

Oh, it's for free, you can be certain o' that, there's no strings to this packet – let's lend you a hand wi' that, missus!

He helps her roll the barrel to one side of the centre-piece, where she chocks it level and sits down on it. She also has a hand-basket full of tankards. The BARGEE *comes back downstage.*

There we are, then. And here *you* are, the streets is filling, roll up, roll up, and wallow in the lot! I'll tell you the word when to cheer.

The platform party is now all in place. The drum gives a final roll. The MAYOR *steps forward.*

CONSTABLE. Silence for the Mayor!

BARGEE. Long live His Worship, who gives us food and clothing and never spares to meet the people with a smile! Hooroar!

Three boos, off.

Boo, boo, boo? Don't be so previous, now; he'll surprise us

all yet, boys. Benevolence and responsibility. Silence for the Mayor!

MAYOR. All right. Now then. It's been a hard winter. I know there's a bit of a thaw this morning, but it's not over yet, there may be worse to come. Although you might not think it, I'm as keen and eager as any o' you to get the pits working again, so we can all settle down in peace to a good roast and baked 'taters and a good pudding and the rest of it. But I'm not here to talk strikes today.

A noise off.

BARGEE (*interpreting*). He says : 'Who says strikes, it's a bloody lockout.'

CONSTABLE. Silence for the Mayor!

BARGEE. Silence for His Worship!

MAYOR. I said I'm not up here to talk on that today. Serjeant Musgrave, on my right, has come to town to find men for the Queen. Now that's a good opportunity – it's a *grand* opportunity. It's up to you to take it. By God, if I was a young lad in a town without work, you'd not catch me thinking twice –

BARGEE. He says: 'There's only one man drives the work away in this town.'

The CONSTABLE *steps forward, but the* BARGEE *forestalls him.*

Silence for the Mayor!

MAYOR. All right. You think I'm playing it crooked all the time – *I* know.

A cheer off.

But listen to this : (*He holds up a jingling money-bag.*) Here's real gold. It rings true to me, it rings true to you, and there's one o' these for every lad as volunteers. That's straight. It's from the shoulder. It pulls no punches. Take it or throw it away – I'm set up here and waiting. (Parson, tell 'em *your* piece now.) And keep quiet while the Rector's at you : he talks good sense and you need it. If you can't give *me* credit, at least you can give *him* some, for considering what's best for the community. Go on, Parson : tell 'em.

He retires and the PARSON *steps forward.*

PARSON. 'And Jesus said, I come not to bring peace but a sword.' I know very well that the times are difficult. As your minister of religion, and as a magistrate, it is my business to be aware of these matters. But we must remember that this town is only one very small locality in our great country.

BARGEE. Very true, very true.

Two cheers, off.

PARSON. And if our country is great, and I for one am sure that it *is* great, it is great because of the greatness of its responsibilities. They are world wide. They are noble. They are the responsibilities of a first-class power.

BARGEE. Keep 'em there, Reverend! First-class for ever! Give a cheer, you boys!

Three cheers, very perfunctory.

And the crowd roars! Every hat in the air, you've struck 'em in the running nerve, hooroar!

PARSON. Therefore, I say, therefore : when called to shoulder our country's burdens we should do it with a glancing eye and a leaping heart, to draw the sword with gladness, thinking nothing of our petty differences and grievances – but all united under one brave flag, going forth in Christian resolution, and showing a manly spirit! The Empire calls! Greatness is at hand! Serjeant Musgrave will take down the names of any men willing, if you'll file on to the platform in an orderly fashion, in the name of the Father, the Son and mumble mumble mumble . . .

He retires. There is a pause.

MUSGRAVE. Perhaps, Mr. Mayor, before we start enrolling names, it might be as well if I was to say a few words first, like, outlining the type of service the lads is likely to find, overseas, and so forth?

The SLOW COLLIER *slouches in, and up to the base of the plinth.*

SLOW COLLIER. Have you got my name down?

MUSGRAVE. No. Not yet.

SLOW COLLIER. Are you sure of that?

MUSGRAVE. Aye, I'm sure. D'you want me to take it?

SLOW COLLIER. Some of us was a bit full, like, last night in the boozer.

MUSGRAVE. A man's pleasuring, friend, that's all. No harm in that?

SLOW COLLIER (*thrusting forward his hat with the cockade in it*). Then what's this? Eh? Someone gave me this.

MUSGRAVE (*laughs*). Oh I'll tell you what that means: you drank along of me – that's all that it means – and you promised you'd come and hear me this morning. Well, here you are.

SLOW COLLIER. Ah. Provisional. Aye. I thought that's what it was. Provisional.

The PUGNACIOUS COLLIER *slouchse in.*

PUGNACIOUS COLLIER. Provisional or not, we're not signing nowt without we've heard more. So go on then, soldier, tell us. Prove it's better to be shot nor starve, *we'll* listen to you, man, 'cos we're ready to believe. And more of us and all.

CRIES OFF. Aye. Aye. Aye. Tell us.

BARGEE. Go on, Serjeant, tell us. It's a long strong tale, quiet while he tells it – quiet!

MUSGRAVE. Now there's more tales than one about the Army,

and a lot of funny jokers to run around and spread 'em, too. Aye, aye, we've all heard of 'em, we know all about 'em, and it's not my job this morning to swear to you what's true and what's not true. O' *course* you'll find there's an RSM here or a Provost-sarnt there what makes you cut the grass wi' nail-scissors, or dust the parade-ground with a toothbrush. It's all the bull, it's all in the game – but it's not what sends me here and it's not what put *these* on my arm, and it's nowt at all to do with *my* life, or these two with me, or any o' yours. So easy, me boys, don't think it. (*To the* COLLIERS.) There was another lad wi' *you*, in and out last night. He ought to be here. (*To the* BARGEE.) Go and fetch him, will you? You know where he is.

BARGEE (*finger to nose*). Ah. Ha ha. Aye aye.

He slips out conspiratorily.

MUSGRAVE (*continues his speech*). I said, easy me boys, and don't think it. Because there's *work* in the Army, and bull's not right work, you can believe me on that – it's just foolery – any smart squaddy can carry it away like a tuppenny-ha'penny jam jar. So I'll tell you what the *work* is – open it up!

ATTERCLIFFE *flings open one of the boxes. It is packed with rifles. He takes one out and tosses it to* MUSGRAVE.

MUSGRAVE. Now this is the rifle. This is what we term the butt of the rifle. This is the barrel. This here's the magazine. And this – (*he indicates the trigger*) – you should know what *this is*, you should know what it does . . . Well, the rifle's a good weapon, it's new, quick, accurate. This is the bayonet – (*he fixes his bayonet*) – it kills men smart, it's good and it's beautiful. But I've more to show than a rifle. Open it up!

ATTERCLIFFE *opens a second case. It contains a Gatling gun and tripod mounting.*

This is the newest, this is the smartest, call it the most beautiful. It's a Gatling gun, this. Watch how it works!

ATTERCLIFFE *secures the gun to its mounting.*

ATTERCLIFFE. The rounds are fed to the chambers, which are arranged in a radial fashion, by means of a hopper-shaped aperture, *here.* Now pay attention while I go through the preliminary process of loading.

He goes through the preliminary process of loading.

MUSGRAVE (*his urgency increasing all the time*). The point being that here we've got a gun that doesn't shoot like: *Bang,* rattle-click-up-the-spout-what're-we-waiting-for, *bang!* But: Bang-bang-bang-bang-bang-bang-bang-bang-*bang* – and there's not a man alive in the whole of this market-place. Modern times. Progress. Three hundred and fifty rounds in one minute – *flat!*

The BARGEE *re-enters, soft-footed.*

MUSGRAVE (*quickly to him*). Is he coming?

The BARGEE *nods, finger to lips.*

ATTERCLIFFE. Now then, you see, the gun's loaded.
MUSGRAVE. It didn't take long, you see.
ATTERCLIFFE. No.

HURST *gives a roll on the drums.*
ATTERCLIFFE *swivels the gun to face out into the audience.*
MUSGRAVE *loads his rifle with a clip of cartridges.*

MUSGRAVE (*his voice very taut and hard*). The question remains as to the *use* of these weapons! (*He pushes his rifle-bolt home.*) You'll ask me: what's their purpose? Seeing we've beat the Russians in the Crimea, there's no war with France (there *may* be, but there isn't yet), and Germany's our friend, who do we have to fight? *Well,* the Reverend answered *that* for you, in his good short words. Me and my three lads – two lads, I'd say rather – we belong to a regiment is a few thousand miles from here, in a little country without much importance except from the point of view that there's a Union Jack flies over it and the people of that country can write British Subject after their names. And that makes us proud!

ATTERCLIFFE. I tell you it makes us proud!

HURST. We live in tattered tents in the rain, we eat rotten food, there's knives in the dark streets and blood on the floors of the hospitals, but we stand tall and proud : because of why we are there.

ATTERCLIFFE. Because we're there to serve our duty.

MUSGRAVE. A soldier's duty is a soldier's life.

WALSH enters at the extreme rear of the stage and walks slowly up behind the others and listens.
A roll on the drum.

MUSGRAVE. A soldier's life is to lay it down, against the enemies of his Queen,

A roll on the drum.

against the invaders of his home,

A roll on the drum.

against slavery, cruelty, tyrants.

A roll on the drum.

HURST. You put on the uniform and you give your life away, and who do you give it to?

ATTERCLIFFE. You give it to your duty.

MUSGRAVE. And you give it to your people, for peace, and for honesty.

A roll on the drum.

MUSGRAVE. That's *my* book. (*He turns on the* MAYOR.) What's *yours?*

MAYOR (*very taken aback*). Eh? What? I'm not a reading man, but it *sounds* all right . . . strong. Strong . . .

MUSGRAVE (*to the* PARSON). What about *yours?*

PARSON (*dubiously*). You speak with enthusiasm, yes. I hope you'll be listened to.

MUSGRAVE (*at the top of his passion*). By God, I hope I am! D'ye hear me, d'ye hear me, d'ye hear me – I'm the Queen of England's man, and I'm wearing her coat and I know her Book backwards. I'm Black Jack Musgrave, me, the hardest serjeant of the line – I work my life to bugle and drum, for eighteen years I fought for one flag only, salute it in the morning, can you haul it down at dark? The Last Post of a living life? Look – I'll show it to you all. And I'll *dance* for you beneath it – hoist up the flag, boy – up, up, *up!*

ATTERCLIFFE *has nipped up the ladder, holding the rope. He loops the rope over the cross-bar of the lamp-bracket, drops to the plinth again, flings open the lid of the big box, and hauls on the rope.*

HURST *beats frantically on his drum. The rope is attached to the contents of the box, and these are jerked up to the cross-bar and reveal themselves as an articulated skeleton dressed in a soldier's tunic and trousers, the rope noosed round the neck. The* PEOPLE *draw back in horror.* MUSGRAVE *begins to dance, waving his rifle, his face contorted with demoniac fury.*

MUSGRAVE (*as he dances, sings, with mounting emphasis*).

> Up he goes and no one knows
> How to bring him downwards
> Dead man's feet
> Over the street
> Riding the roofs
> And crying down your chimneys

> Up he goes and no one knows
> Who it was that rose him
> But white and red
> He waves his head
> He sits on your back
> And you'll never never lose him
> Up he goes and no one knows
> How to bring him downwards.

He breaks off at the climax of the song, and stands panting. The drum stops.

That'll do. That'll do for *that*. (*He beckons gently to the* PEOPLE.) You can come back. Come back. Come back. We're all quiet now. But nobody move out of this market-place. You saw the gun loaded. Well, it's on a very quick swivel and the man behind it's well trained. (*He gestures with his rifle towards the platform party*.) And *I've* won a regimental cup four year running for small-arms marksmanship. So be good, and be gentle, *all* of you.

That checks the BARGEE, *who made a move. The* MAYOR *seems to be about to speak.*

Right, Mr. Mayor – I'll explain the whole business.

PARSON (*in a smaller voice than usual*). Business? What business, sir? Do you intend to imply you are *threatening* us with these weapons?

MAYOR. The man's gone balmy. Constable, do summat, grab him, quick!

The CONSTABLE *makes an indecisive move.*

MUSGRAVE. Be *quiet*. I shan't warn agen. (*To the* MAYOR *and the* PARSON.) You two. Get down there! Constable, *there!*

He gestures peremptorily and the three of them obey him, moving downstage to stand facing the platform and covered by the gun.

Now I said I'll explain. So listen. (*He points to the skeleton.*) This, up here, was a comrade of mine – of ours. At least, he was till a few months since. He was killed, being there for his duty, in the country I was telling you about, where the regiment is stationed. It's not right a colony, you know, it's a sort of Protectorate, but British, y'know, British. This, up here, he was walking down a street latish at night, he'd been to the opera – *you've* got a choral society in this town, I daresay – well, he was only a soldier, but North Country, he was full of music, so he goes to the opera. And on his way again to camp he was shot in the back. And it's not surprising, neither: there was patriots abroad, anti-British, subversive; like they didn't dare to shoot him to his face. He was daft to be out alone, wasn't he? Out of bounds, after curfew.

ATTERCLIFFE (*with suppressed frenzy*). Get on to the words as matter, serjeant!

MUSGRAVE (*turning on him fiercely*). *I'm* talking now; you wait your turn! . . . So we *come* to the words as matter. He was the third to be shot that week. He was the fifteenth that month. In the back and all. Add to which he was young, he was liked, he sang songs, they say, and he joked and he laughed – he was a good soldier, too, else *I'd* not have bothered (we'll leave out his sliding off to the opera WOL, but by and large good, and I've got standards). So at twelve o'clock at night they beat up the drums and sounded the calls and called out the guard and the guard calls us *all* out, and the road is red and slippery, and every soldier in the camp no longer in the camp but in the streets of that city, rifle-butts, bayonets, every street cut off for eight blocks north and west the opera-house. And that's how it began.

HURST (*the frenzy rising*). The streets is empty, but the houses is full. He says, 'no undue measures, minimum violence', he says. 'But bring in the killers.'

ATTERCLIFFE. The killers are gone, they've gone miles off in that time – *sporting* away, right up in the mountains, I told you at the time.

MUSGRAVE. That's not material, there's one man is dead, but there's *everyone's* responsible.

HURST. So bring the *lot* in! It's easy, they're all in bed, kick the front doors down, knock 'em on the head, boys, chuck 'em in the wagons.

ATTERCLIFFE. I didn't know she was only a little kid, there was scores of 'em on that staircase, pitch-dark, trampling, screaming, they're all of 'em screaming, what are we to do?

HURST. Knock 'em on the head, boy, chuck 'em in the wagons.

ATTERCLIFFE. How was I to tell she was only a little kid?

MUSGRAVE (*bringing it to an end*). THAT'S NOT MATERIAL! You were told to bring 'em in. If you killed her, you killed her! She was just one, and who cares a damn for that! Stay in your place and keep your hands on that Gatling. We've got to have order here, whatever there was *there;* and I can tell you it wasn't order . . . (*To* HURST.) You, take a rifle. Leave your drum down.

HURST *jumps on the plinth, takes a rifle and loads.*

We've *got* to have order. So I'll just tell you quietly how many there were was put down as injured – that's badly hurt, hospital, we don't count knocks and bruises, any o' that. Twenty-five men. Nine women. *No* children, whatever *he* says. She was a fully grown girl, and she had a known record as an associate of terrorists. That was her. Then four men, one of them elderly, turned out to have died too. Making five. Not so very many. Dark streets. Natural surge of rage.

HURST. We didn't find the killers.

MUSGRAVE. Of course we didn't find 'em. Not *then* we didn't, any road. We didn't even know 'em. But *I* know 'em, now.

(*He turns on* WALSH.) So what's *your* opinion?

MAYOR. He's not balmy, he's mad, he's stark off his nut.

PARSON. Why doesn't somebody do something, Constable?

Noises off.

MUSGRAVE (*indicates* WALSH). I'm talking to *him*.

CONSTABLE (*very shakily*). I shall have to ask you to – to come down off this platform, Sarnt Musgrave. It looks to me like your – your meeting's got out of hand.

HURST (*covering the* CONSTABLE). Aye, it has.

MUSGRAVE (*to* WALSH). Go on, brother. Tell us.

WALSH *climbs up at the back of the plinth.*

WALSH (*with a certain levity*). *My* opinion, eh? I don't know why you need it. You've got *him*, haven't you? (*He waggles the skeleton's foot familiarly*.) What more d'you want? (*He comes forward and sits on the front of the plinth, looking at the other two* COLLIERS.) Aye, or you too, with your natty little nosegays dandled in your hatbands. Take 'em out, sharp! He's learnt you the truth, hasn't he?

They remove their cockades, shamefacedly.

PUGNACIOUS COLLIER. All right, *that'll* do.

WALSH. Will it, matey, will it? If it helps you to remember what we've been fighting for, I daresay it will. Trade Unions aren't formed, you know, so we can all have beer-ups on the Army.

SLOW COLLIER. He said that'll do. I'm sick and bloody tired – I don't know *what* it's all about.

WALSH (*drops down to the forestage*). Come home and I'll tell you. The circus is over. Come on.

MUSGRAVE. Oh no it's not. Just bide still a while. There's more to be said yet. When I asked you your opinion I meant about them we was talking about – them as did *this*, up here.

WALSH. Well, *what* about them – brother? Clear enough to me. You go for a soldier, you find yourself in someone else's country, you deserve all you get. *I'd* say it stands to reason.

MUSGRAVE. And that's *all* you would say? I'd thought better of you.

WALSH (*irritated*). Now look, look here, what *are* you trying to get? You come to this place all hollering for sympathy, oh you've been beating and murdering and following your trade boo-hoo: but we're not bloody interested! You mend your own heartache and leave us to sort with ours – we've enough and to spare!

MUSGRAVE (*very intensely*). This *is* for your heart. Take another look at *him*. (*Points to skeleton.*) Go on, man, both eyes, and carefully. Because you all used to know him: or most of you did. Private Billy Hicks, late of this parish, welcome him back from the wars, he's bronzed and he's fit, with many a tall tale of distant campaigning to spin round the fireside – ah, *you* used to know him, *didn't* you, Mrs. Hitchcock!

MRS. HITCHCOCK *has risen in great alarm.*

SLOW COLLIER. That's never Billy Hicks, ye dirty liar.

PUGNACIOUS COLLIER. He wor my putter for two year, when I hewed coal in number five – he hewed there hisself for nigh on a year alongside o' my brother.

SLOW COLLIER. He left his clogs to me when he went to join up – that's never our Billy.

NOISES OFF. Never Billy. Never Billy.

BARGEE. 'Never Billy Hicks' – 'Never Billy Hicks' – they don't dare believe it. You've knocked 'em to the root, boy. Oh the white faces!

MRS. HITCHCOCK. She ought to be told. She's got a right to know.

MUSGRAVE. Go along then and tell her.

HURST (*to* MUSGRAVE). You letting her go?

MUSGRAVE. Yes.

HURST. But –

MUSGRAVE (*curtly*). Attend to your orders.

MRS. HITCHCOCK *goes out.*

When I say it's Billy Hicks, you can believe me it's true.

WALSH. Aye, I'll believe you. And you know what I think – it's downright indecent!

MUSGRAVE. Aye, aye? But wait. Because here is the reason. I'm a religious man, and I see the causes of the Almighty in every human work.

PARSON. That is absolute blasphemy!

MAYOR. This won't do you a pennorth o' good, you know.

MUSGRAVE. Not to me, no. But maybe to you? Now as I understand the workings of God, through greed and the world, this man didn't die because he went alone to the opera, he was killed because he had to be – it being decided; that now the people in that city was worked right up to killing soldiers, then more and more soldiers should be sent for them to kill, and the soldiers in turn should kill the people in that city, more and more, always – that's what I said to you: four men, one girl, then the twenty-five and the nine – *and* it'll go on, there or elsewhere, and it can't be stopped neither, except there's someone finds out Logic and brings the wheel round. You see, the Queen's Book, which eighteen years I've lived, it's turned inside out for *me*. There used to be my duty: now there's a disease –

HURST. Wild-wood mad.

MUSGRAVE. Wild-wood mad we are; and so we've fetched it home. You've had Moses and the Prophets – that's *him* – (*He points at* WALSH.) – 'cos he told you. But you were all for enlisting, it'd still have gone on. Moses and the Prophets, what good did they do?

He sits down and broods. There is a pause.

WALSH (*awkwardly*). There's no one from this town be over

keen to join up now. You've preached your little gospel: I
daresay we can go home?

MUSGRAVE *makes no reply. The* SOLDIERS *look at one another
doubtfully.*

HURST. What do we do now?
ATTERCLIFFE. Wait.
HURST. Serjeant –
ATTERCLIFFE (*shushing him*). Ssh-ssh!

A pause. Restive noises, off.

HURST. Serjeant –
ATTERCLIFFE. Serjeant – they've heard your message, they'll
none of them forget it. Haven't we done what we came for?
HURST (*astonished, to* ATTERCLIFFE). Done what we came
for?

ATTERCLIFFE *shushes him again as* MUSGRAVE *stirs.*

MUSGRAVE (*as though to himself*). One man, and for him five.
Therefore, for five of them we multiply out, *and* we find it
five-and-twenty. . . . So, as I understand Logic and Logic to
me is the mechanism of God – that means that today there's
twenty-five persons will have to be –

ATTERCLIFFE *jumps up in horror.* ANNIE *and* MRS. HITCH-
COCK *appear at the upper window. When she sees the skeleton*
ANNIE *gasps and seems about to scream.*

MUSGRAVE (*cutting her short*). It's true. It's him. You don't
need to cry out; you knew it when he left you.
ANNIE. Take him down. Let me have him. I'll come down for
him now.
BARGEE. Away down, me strong Annie. I'll carry you a golden
staircase – aha, she's the royal champion, stand by as she
comes down.
*As he speaks he jumps on to the plinth, takes away the ladder,
nips across the stage and props it under the window.*

MUSGRAVE. No! Let her wait up there. I said: wait! . . . Now
then, who's with me! Twenty-five to die and the Logic is
worked out. Who'll help me? You? (*He points to* WALSH.)
I made sure that you would: you're a man like the Black
Musgrave, you: you have purposes, and you can lead. Join
along with my madness, friend. I brought it back to England
but I've brought the cure too – to turn it on to them that
sent it out of this country – way-out-ay they sent it, where
they hoped that only soldiers could catch it and rave! Well
here's three redcoat ravers on their own kitchen hearthstone!
Who do we start with? These? (*He turns on the* MAYOR.)
'Loyal hearts and true, every man jack of us.' (*To the*
PARSON.) 'Draw the sword with gladness.' Why, *swords* is
for honour, carry 'em on church parade, a *sword'll* never
offer you three hundred and fifty bullets in a minute – and it
was no bright sword neither finished *his* life in a back street!
(*He points to* BILLY, *and then at the* CONSTABLE.) Or what
about the Peeler? If we'd left it to *him, you'd* ha' been boxed
away to barracks six or eight hours ago! Come on now, let's
have you, you know I'm telling you truth!

WALSH. Nay: it won't do.

HURST. It won't do? Why not?

WALSH. I'm not over clear why not. Last night there was
me and some others tried to whip away that Gatling. And
we'd ha' used it and all: by God, there was need. But that's
one thing, y'see, and this is another – ent it, you tell me?

He appeals to the COLLIERS.

PUGNACIOUS COLLIER. Nay, I don't know.

SLOW COLLIER. I think they're all balmy, the whole damn
capful's arse-over-tip –

WALSH. No it's not. *I'm* not. And it comes to this wi' me: *he's*
still in uniform, and he's still got his Book. He's doing his
duty. Well, I take no duties from no bloody lobsters. This
town lives by collieries. That's coal-owners and it's pitmen

– aye, and they battle, and the pitmen'll win. But not wi' no soldier-boys to order our fight for us. Remember their trade: you give 'em one smell of a broken town, you'll never get 'em out!

MUSGRAVE (*with growing desperation*). But you don't understand me – all of you, listen! I told you we could *cure* –

ATTERCLIFFE. I don't think you can.

MUSGRAVE (*flabbergasted*). Eh? What's that? Stay by your weapon!

ATTERCLIFFE. No. (*He stands away from the gun.*)

HURST *rapidly takes his place.*

HURST (*to the crowd*). Keep still, the lot of you!

ATTERCLIFFE. It won't do, Black Jack. You swore there'd be no killing.

MUSGRAVE. No I did not.

ATTERCLIFFE. You gave us to believe. We've done what we came for, and it's there we should have ended. *I've* ended. No killing.

He deliberately gets down from the platform, and squats on the ground. MUSGRAVE *looks around him, appealing and appalled.*

BARGEE. I'm with you, general!

MUSGRAVE. You?

BARGEE. Nobody else! I'll serve you a lovely gun! Rapine and riot! (*He scrambles on to the plinth, picks up a rifle from the box and loads it.*) When do we start breaking open the boozers? Or the pawnshops and all – who's for a loot?

MUSGRAVE. None of you at all? Come on, come on, why, he was your Billy, wasn't he? That you knew and you worked with – don't you want to revenge him?

ANNIE. Somebody hold the ladder. I'm going to come down.

The SLOW COLLIER *does so.*

MUSGRAVE (*urgently, to her*). Billy Hicks, lassie: here: he used to be yours! Tell them what they've got to do : tell them the truth!

ANNIE has started to come down the ladder. When she is down, the COLLIER *lowers it to the ground.*

HURST. Wait a minute, serjeant, leave me to talk to them! We've not got time bothering wi' no squalling tarts.

MUSGRAVE. Keep you your place.

HURST (*furiously*). I'm in my bloody place! And I'll tell you this straight, if we lose this crowd now, we've lost all the work, for ever! And remember summat else. There's Dragoons on the road!

General sensation. Shouts off: 'Dragoons'.

HURST (*to the crowd*). So you've just got five minutes to make up your minds.

He grabs his rifle up, and motions the BARGEE *violently to the Gatling. The* BARGEE *takes over, and* HURST *leaps off the plinth and talks straight into the* COLLIERS' *faces and at the audience.*

We've earned our living by beating and killing folk like yourselves in the streets of their own city. Well, it's drove us mad – and so we come back here to tell you how and to show you what it's like. The ones we want to deal with aren't, for a change, you and your mates, but a bit higher up. The ones as never get hurt. (*He points at the* MAYOR, PARSON *and* CONSTABLE.) Him. Him. Him. You hurt them hard, and they'll not hurt you again. And they'll not send *us* to hurt you neither. But if you let 'em be, then us three'll be killed – aye and worse, we'll be forgotten – and the whole bloody lot'll start all over again!

He climbs back and takes over the gun.

MUSGRAVE. For God's sake stand with us. We've *got* to be remembered!

SLOW COLLIER. We ought to, you know. He might be right.

WALSH. I don't know. I don't trust it.

PUGNACIOUS COLLIER. Ahr and be damned, these are just like the same as us. Why don't we stand with 'em?

WALSH (*obstinately*). I've not yet got this clear.

ANNIE. To me it's quite clear. He asked me to tell you the truth. My truth's an easy tale, it's old true-love gone twisted, like they called it 'malformed'– they put part in the ground, and hang the rest on a pillar here, and expect me to sit under it making up song-ballads. All right.

> My true love is a scarecrow
> Of rotted rag and bone
> Ask him : where are the birds, Billy?
> Where have they all gone?

He says: Unbutton my jacket, and they'll all fly out of the ribs – oh, oh, I'm not mad, though you told us that *you* were – let's have that bundle!

MRS. HITCHCOCK *throws down a bundle.* ANNIE *shakes it out, revealing* SPARKY'S *tunic.*

Take a sight o' this, you hearty colliers : see what they've brought you. You can match it up with Billy's. Last night there were four o' these walking, weren't there? Well, this morning there's three. They buried the other one in Ma Hitchcock's midden. Go on, ask 'em why!

HURST. He's a deserter, is why!

ANNIE (*holding up the tunic*). Hey, here's the little hole where they let in the bayonet. Eee, aie, easily in. His blood's on my tongue, so hear what it says. A bayonet is a raven's beak. This tunic's a collier's jacket. That scarecrow's a birdcage. What more do you want!

WALSH. Is this what she says true? Where *is* he, the fourth of you?

MUSGRAVE. He was killed, and that's all. By an accident killed. It's barely materi –

ATTERCLIFFE. Oh, it's material. And no goddamned accident. I said it to you, Musgrave, it washes it all out.

WALSH. It bloody does and all, as far as I go. (*He turns to the other* COLLIERS.) If you want to stand by 'em when they've done for their own mucker and not one of the bastards can tell ye the same tale, well, you're at your damned liberty and take it and go!

The COLLIERS *murmur dubiously.*

HURST (*frantic*). I'm going to start shooting!

General reaction of fear: he clearly means it. He spits at MUSGRAVE.

You and your everlasting Word – you've pulled your own roof down! But *I'll* prop your timber for you – I'll give a One, Two, and a Three : and I'm opening fire!

ATTERCLIFFE. No.

He jumps up and stands on the step of the plinth, below the gun and facing it, with his arms spread out so that the muzzle is against his breast.

HURST (*distorted with rage*). Get down! Get down off it, you old cuckold, I don't care who you are. I'll put the first one *through* you! I *swear* it, I will! One! Two! . . .

MAYOR (*to the* CONSTABLE). Go for that gun.

The CONSTABLE *is making a cautious move towards the gun, but he is forestalled by* MUSGRAVE, *who flings himself at* HURST *and knocks him away from the breach. There is a moment's tense struggle behind the gun.*

MUSGRAVE (*as he struggles*). The wrong way. The wrong way. You're trying to do it without Logic.

Then HURST *gives way and falls back down the steps of the plinth. He recovers himself.*

HURST (*panting with excitement*). All right then, Black Jack. All right, it's finished. The lot. You've lost it. I'm off!

MUSGRAVE (*stunned*). Come back here. You'll come back, you'll obey orders.

HURST *makes a grab forward, snatches his rifle from the platform and jumps back clear.*

HURST (*to the crowd*). Get out o' my road!

At the very instant he turns towards the wings to run away, a shot is fired offstage. His quick turn changes into a grotesque leap as the bullet hits him, and he collapses on the stage. A bugle blares from offstage.

VOICES OFF. Dragoons!

Orders shouted and general noise of cavalry coming to a halt and dismounting.

MAYOR   ⎫ (*one after another, rapidly.*)
CONSTABLE ⎬ The Dragoons! The Dragoons!
PARSON   ⎭ Saved! Saved! Saved!
VOICES OFF. Saved! Saved! Saved!

MUSGRAVE *is standing beside the gun, temporarily at a loss.* ATTERCLIFFE *has jumped down beside* HURST *and lifted his head. Everyone else stands amazed.*
Suddenly MUSGRAVE *swings the gun to point toward the Dragoons. The* BARGEE *ups with his rifle and sticks it into* MUSGRAVE'S *back.*

BARGEE. Serjeant, put your hands up!

MUSGRAVE *is pushed forward by the rifle, but he does not obey. The* TROOPER *enters, clicking the bolt of his smoking carbine, and shouting.*

TROOPER. Everybody stand where you are! You, put your hands up!

MUSGRAVE *does so.*

BARGEE. I've got him, soldier! I've got him! Crooked Joe's got him, Mr. Mayor.

The OFFICER *strides in, drawing his sabre.*

Give a cheer – hooroar!

Cheers off.
The OFFICER *comes to attention before the* MAYOR *and salutes with his sabre.*

OFFICER. Mr. Mayor, are we in time?

MAYOR. Aye, you're in time. You're *just* in bloody time.

OFFICER (*seeing* MUSGRAVE). 22128480 Serjeant Musgrave, J.?

MUSGRAVE. My name.

OFFICER. We heard word you'd come here. You are under arrest. Robbery and desertion. There were *three* who came with you.

ATTERCLIFFE (*getting up from* HURST, *whose head falls back.*) You can count me for one of them. One other's dead already. Here's the third.

OFFICER. You're under arrest.

CONSTABLE. Hold out your hands.

He takes out two pairs of handcuffs and fetters them.

OFFICER. Mr. Mayor, my troopers are at your disposal. What do you require of us?

MAYOR. Well, I'd say it was about all over by now, young man – wouldn't you?

OFFICER. Law and order is established?

PARSON. Wiser counsels have prevailed, Captain.

BARGEE. *I* caught him, *I* caught him, *I* used me strategy!

OFFICER. My congratulations, all.

WALSH (*with great bitterness*). The community's been saved. Peace and prosperity rules. We're all friends and neighbours for the rest of today. We're all sorted out. We're back where we were. So what do we do?

BARGEE.

> Free beer. It's still here.
> No more thinking. Easy drinking.
> End of a bad bad dream. Gush forth the foaming stream.

He takes the bung out of the barrel and starts filling tankards.

OFFICER. The winter's broken up. Let normal life begin again.

BARGEE. Aye, aye, *begin* again!

He is handing the mugs to the people. He starts singing, and they all join in, by degrees.

> There was an old man called Michael Finnegan
> He had whiskers on his chin-egan
> The wind came out and blew them in agen
> Poor old Michael Finnegan –
> Begin agen –
>
> There was an old man etcetera . . .

He gives out mugs in the following order: the MAYOR, *the* PARSON, *the* SLOW COLLIER, *the* PUGNACIOUS COLLIER, *the* CONSTABLE. *Each man takes his drink, swigs a large gulp, then links wrists with the previous one, until all are dancing round the centre-piece in a chain, singing.*

ANNIE *has climbed the plinth and lowers the skeleton. She sits with it on her knees. The* DRAGOONS *remain standing at the side of the stage.* MUSGRAVE *and* ATTERCLIFFE *come slowly downstage. The* BARGEE *fills the last two tankards and hands one to* WALSH, *who turns his back angrily. The* BARGEE *empties one mug, and joins the tail of the dance, still holding the other. After one more round he again beckons* WALSH. *This time the latter thinks for a moment, then bitterly throws his hat on the ground, snarls into the impassive face of the* DRAGOON, *and joins in the dance, taking the beer.*

The scene closes, leaving MUSGRAVE *and* ATTERCLIFFE *on the forestage.* MRS. HITCHCOCK *retires from the window.*

SCENE TWO

A prison cell.

This scene is achieved by a barred wall descending in front of the dancers of the previous scene. After a while the sound dies away, and the lights change so that we can no longer see past the bars.

MUSGRAVE *remains standing, looking into the distance with his back to the audience.* ATTERCLIFFE *sighs and sits down gingerly on the floor.*

ATTERCLIFFE. Sit down and rest yourself, serjeant. That's all there is left . . . Go on, man, sit down . . . Then stand and the devil take you! It's *your* legs, not mine. It's my *hands* is what matters. They finished Sparky and that finished me, and Sparky finished you. Holy God save us, why warn't I a greengrocer, then I'd never ha' been cuckolded, never gone for no soldier, never no dead Sparky, and never none of this. Go on, serjeant, talk to me. I'm an old old stupid bastard and I've nowt to do now but fret out the runs of the consequence; and the whole croaking work it's finished and done. Go on, serjeant, talk.

MUSGRAVE *does not move.*
A pause.
MRS. HITCHCOCK *enters, carrying a glass.*

MRS. HITCHCOCK (*to* MUSGRAVE). It's port with a bit o'

lemon. I often take it of a morning; like it settles me stummick for the day. The officer said I could see you, if I warn't no more nor five minutes. Sit down and I'll give it to your mouth – them wrist-irons makes it difficult, I daresay.

MUSGRAVE (*without looking at her*). Give it to him. I don't want it.

MRS. HITCHCOCK. He can have half of it. You take a sup first.

MUSGRAVE *shakes his head.*

All right. How you like.

She goes to ATTERCLIFFE *and puts the glass to his mouth.*

ATTERCLIFFE. I'm obliged to you, missus.

MRS. HITCHCOCK. It's on the house, this one. Change from the Queen, ent it?

MUSGRAVE. Numbers and order. According to Logic. I had worked it out for months.

He swings round to MRS. HITCHCOCK.

What made it break down!

MRS. HITCHCOCK. Ah, there's the moral of it. You ask our Annie.

MUSGRAVE (*furiously*). He was killed by pure accident! It had nothing to do –

ATTERCLIFFE. Oh by God, it had.

MRS. HITCHCOCK. The noisy one, warn't he? Pack o' cards and all the patter. You asked me to trust you – (*her voice rises with rage and emotion*) – he was only a young lad, for gracious goodness Christ, he'd a voice like a sawmill – what did you want to do it for, you gormless great gawk!

ATTERCLIFFE. *He* didn't do it.

MRS. HITCHCOCK. He did, oh he did! And he broke his own neck.

MUSGRAVE. What's the matter with you, woman!

MRS. HITCHCOCK. All wrong, you poured it out all wrong! I

could ha' told you last night if only I'd known – the end of the world and you thought you could call a parade. In control – *you!*

MUSGRAVE (*very agitated*). Don't talk like that. You're talking about my duty. Good order and the discipline: it's the only road I know. Why can't you see it?

MRS. HITCHCOCK. All I can see is Crooked Joe Bludgeon having his dance out in the middle of fifty Dragoons! It's time you learnt your life, you big proud serjeant. Listen: last evening you told all about this anarchy and where it came from – like, scribble all over with life or love, and that makes anarchy. Right?

MUSGRAVE. Go on.

MRS. HITCHCOCK. Then *use* your Logic – if you can. Look at it this road: here we are, and we'd got life and love. Then *you* came in and you did your scribbling where nobody asked you. Aye, it's arsy-versey to what you said, but it's still an anarchy, isn't it? And it's all your work.

MUSGRAVE. Don't tell me there was life or love in this town.

MRS. HITCHCOCK. There was. There was hungry men, too – fighting for their food. But *you* brought in a different war.

MUSGRAVE. I brought it in to end it.

ATTERCLIFFE. To end it by its own rules: no bloody good. She's right, you're wrong. You can't cure the pox by further whoring. Sparky died of those damned rules. And so did the other one.

MUSGRAVE. That's not the truth. (*He looks at them both in appeal, but they nod.*) That's not the truth. God was with me . . . God . . . (*He makes a strange animal noise of despair, a sort of sob that is choked off suddenly, before it can develop into a full howl.*) – and all they dancing – all of them – there.

MRS. HITCHCOCK. Ah, not for long. And it's not a dance of joy. Those men are hungry, so they've got no time for *you*. One day they'll be full, though, and the Dragoons'll be gone, and then they'll remember.

MUSGRAVE (*shaking his head*). No.

MRS. HITCHCOCK. Let's hope it, any road, Eh?

She presents the glass to his lips. This time he accepts it and drinks, and remains silent.

ATTERCLIFFE (*melancholy but quiet*). That running tyke of a Sparky, he reckoned he wor the only bastard in the barracks had a voice. Well, he warn't. There's other men can sing when he's not here. So listen at this.

He sings.

>   I plucked a blood-red rose-flower down
>   And gave it to my dear.
>   I set my foot out across the sea
>   And she never wept a tear.
>
>   I came back home as gay as a bird
>   I sought her out and in:
>   And I found her at last in a little attic room
>   With a napkin round her chin.

At her dinner, you see. Very neat and convenient.

He sings.

>   Oh are you eating meat, I said,
>   Or are you eating fish?
>   I'm eating an apple was given me today,
>   The sweetest I could wish.

So I asked her where she got it, and by God the tune changed then. Listen at what she told me.

He sings to a more heavily accented version of the tune.

>   Your blood-red rose is withered and gone
>   And fallen on the floor:
>   And he who brought the apple down
>   Shall be my darling dear.

For the apple holds a seed will grow
In live and lengthy joy
To raise a flourishing tree of fruit
For ever and a day.
With fal-la-la-the-dee, toor-a-ley,
For ever and a day.

They're going to hang us up a length higher nor most apple-trees grow, Serjeant. D'you reckon we can start an orchard?

Harold Pinter

'My aim is stringency, shading, accuracy,' said Harold Pinter of his own writing in a letter to a friend when he was only twenty-four. Several decades later, in a penetrating appraisal of Pinter's plays, Martin Esslin pays tribute to the 'economy, subtlety and density of subtext beneath the spareness of the text itself'. By the eighties, in Pinter's three-play triptych, *Other Places*, the writing is leaner than ever, more condensed and elliptical, the nuances and shadings subtler. Pinter's dialogue is rooted in the banal reality of the every day, yet it is so uncommonly precise that single lines seem fraught with disturbing implications.

In *The Room*, Pinter's first play, Rose muses as she sits with her silent husband, 'No, this room's all right for me. You know where you are. When it's cold for instance.' The series of ordinary remarks ends in a sudden revelation of some unexplained inner thought. Pinter uses the same device in *A Kind of Alaska*, one of the 'other places'. A middle-aged woman waking after thirty years in a coma gropes for her past. 'You shouldn't have touched me like that. I shan't tell my mother. I shouldn't have touched you like that.' In both cases, the subtle unexpected turn breaking the surface is mysterious and unsettling. Such little shifts are part of the compulsive power that accumulates in Pinter and intensifies the central conceit in many of his plays: a nameless uncertainty that keeps his characters in a constantly fearful state of disequilibrium.

There is a prodigious Pinter industry in criticism: new books, articles, profiles, dissertations, and speculations appear regularly. But there is little consensus about what his plays mean or what dramatic pigeon-hole to put them in.

Most scholars and critics look for the secret of Pinter's dramatic mastery in the clever manipulation of language and the silence that punctuates it. He creates a world that is absurd in the existential sense of being emptied of meaning, a world where horror lurks at the root of human actions, however harmless they may seem, yet a world eerily familiar. His characters are pathetically funny in their obtuseness and their circumscribed preoccupations; they are frightening in their elemental helplessness. And they are incessantly struggling, vainly – for safety, power, territory, relationships, their very identities. They are usually stripped-down losers, denied nobility or even the aspiration to nobility of traditional dramatic characters. 'They're exactly like animals!' fumed the indignant woman fleeing a provincial production of *The Homecoming* in 1965. Exactly! Like human animals. And they act out of instinctual acquisitiveness, primal drives, and terrors. Like most of us.

Hoping to pin him down, critics have dutifully traced the influences in Pinter's work: Kafka in the ambiguous terror that stalks characters, especially in the early plays, so that they crouch in their rooms in fear of the knock at the door, in *The Birthday Party*, *The Dumb Waiter*, *A Silent Ache*, for example; Chekhov for the extraordinary intensity of the characters' inner insecurity, which erupts out of appalling silence into non-sequitur speech, and also for the tyranny of objects as threat, weapon, security blanket – Ruth in *The Homecoming* seduces Lenny with an ordinary water glass and Stanley in *The Birthday Party* is terrorized by the sight of a van; the naturalists of the Osborne-Wesker school, of course, who proved the theatrical vitality of the working-class idiom, for which Pinter has a marvelously acute and cruel ear; Pirandello for the shifting identities of characters who tell conflicting accounts of what they are and want; Beckett for the anguish at the core of Pinter's characters, isolated in a no-man's land, like Beckett's, ringed round with nameless malevolence; and even Noël Coward, especially in the later plays like *Betrayal* and *Old Times*, for the caustic repartee that exposes Pinter's characters as babbling poseurs, desperate lest they reveal themselves and lose place and power.

However such tracings may help to illumine Pinter's dramatic method or simply prove he's well-read, they do not catch the riveting uniqueness of a Pinter evening in the theatre. Somehow the play exists in what happens between the performers and the audience: what evocations are summoned, what resonances stirred. The plays are eerie and funny and grotesquely familiar. While they remain theatrically elusive, they connect with the dreads and longings buried in the human psyche. The 'thrill of recognition' that audiences conventionally enjoy becomes a shudder as they seek to evade the most unsettling recognition Pinter forces on them: the absolute ambiguity of everything.

Naturalistic on the surface – most of them call for box sets and curtain lines – the plays quickly subvert naturalistic structure. Exposition is absent, as in *The Dumb Waiter*. Or it is unreliable, as in *The Homecoming*: Teddy and Ruth may or may not live in America with their two children; she may or may not have been 'a model for the body'. In place of conflict sharply defined there is indeterminacy. Characters have no reliable histories or predictable futures. They exist moment to moment, improvising their guarded actions in bewildered response to whatever happens next. The plays, even those set at the seaside, have a hermetically urban atmosphere. There is no consoling nature in Pinter. What is outside the walls of a room always threatens.

What is clear, after thirty years in the theatre, is Pinter's undisputed place in the forefront of contemporary dramatists. Critics, among them the American Robert Brustein, mention Edward Bond alone as Pinter's peer among British playwrights. His reputation seems impervious to dissenters like the American John Simon who called Pinter the 'Grand Poseur' and a 'linguistically nouveau-riche' writer of 'fear-jerkers'.

At every stage, experimenting with new techniques and modifying his Pinteresquerie without ever spelling out his intentions, Pinter has puzzled and irritated critics into rancour. The reviewers of the 1958 London opening of *The Birthday Party*, Pinter's first full-length play, unanimously panned it. They chided the upstart author for baffling them with the 'half-gibberish and lunatic ravings' of characters who can't explain their actions, thoughts, or feelings. *Punch* called the play a 'masterpiece of meaninglessness'. Even Kenneth Tynan, usually eager to champion innovation, had a dismissive tone, as he granted some 'effective and witty non-sequiturs,' in a play about 'a fat, torrid young man oppressed by his maternal landlady, and visited by a beaming Jew and a snickering Irishman who nudge him into a game of blindman's bluff, break his spectacles and lead him off their captive'.

Only Harold Hobson appreciated Pinter at first. Writing a few days after *The Birthday Party* had prematurely closed at the end of its first week, he called Pinter 'the most original, disturbing and arresting talent in theatrical London'. He found the characters in the play fascinating, the plot with its 'verbal arabesques and echoing explorations of memory and fancy' first rate. He considered its frightening vagueness about who the two intruders are and what they have to do with the helpless Stanley among the play's greatest merits, part of its spine-chilling power.

Like other outstanding dramatists of the British renaissance, Pinter has been very successful in radio, film and television. Although it has not yet been filmed, his brilliant screen adaptation of Proust's *Remembrance of Things Past* has won him considerable literary approbation. His screen versions of John Fowles' *The French Lieutenant's Woman*, L. P. Hartley's *The Go-Between*, Penelope Mortimer's *The Pumpkin Eater*, as well as several of his own plays, including *Betrayal*, gained him new audiences. He is a more than competent director, especially of the plays of Simon Gray. His poetry is published and his personal life tracked by journalists. His one-acts and black-out sketches are staples for university, amateur and community theatre.

Two short radio plays, *A Slight Ache* and *A Night Out*, broadcast by the BBC Third Programme in 1960, are credited with creating the favourable critical climate for Pinter's first major stage success, *The Caretaker*, which opened on 27 April 1960. Critics wrote of the 'pleasurable confusion' of Pinter's fine play, acknowledging him as a 'genuine original,' herald of a 'New Movement' in the theatre, a fascinating tour guide into 'the shut-off mind'. The volubility of Osborne's characters suddenly seemed old-fashioned. Pinter made the fraughtness of understatement thrilling. Minimalist art became a viable alternative to the conventional realism of mainstream British theatre.

As Martin Esslin observed, naturalistic life-likeness in Pinter is suffused with poetic imagery to become 'a metaphor for a greater or more general truth, the powerful universal archetype'. *The Caretaker*, in particular, is grounded in the solid reality of a meticulously observed environment – as so often in Pinter, a room – which expands to become a portent of terror, not only for its occupants, but vicariously for the onlooker.

The Caretaker opens on a room ominously cluttered with derelict things – a kitchen sink, a gas stove, a very old electric toaster, old newspapers piled under old beds, a vacuum-cleaner, a bucket hung from the ceiling to catch rain, a Buddha, other bric-à-brac, debris. Mick, a young man wearing a leather jacket, is sitting on a bed, staring expressionless, silent, for thirty seconds, the stage directions indicate. A door bangs and the young man swiftly, softly exists. Aston, shabbily dressed, shuffles in, followed by a scabrous old tramp in shapeless trousers. Aston has rescued Davies from some sort of bar fight, it turns out, and offered him temporary shelter. The rest of the play concerns the hostility that breaks into a kind of jungle warfare between Mick, probably a small-time crook, and the old man as the lobotomized Aston, who may or may not be the pawn in their power struggle, dully watches.

The seediness of the setting and the characters seems to place the play squarely in the naturalist tradition in its most sordid mode. But the meticulous opening stage directions, faithfully performed, create a supra-natural atmosphere of eeriness. They take time, insist on a rhythm that is non-naturalistic. Three times in half a page Pinter specifies silence, as if to bracket the spelled-out studied gestures and movements of Mick before he slips furtively out of the room. The objects in the room, which he slowly fixes his gaze upon, one by one, take on malevolence. The audience is unsettled by this disquieting rhythm of silence before a line is spoken.

The dialogue works in the same way. Its hesitancies, incoherencies, banalities, non-sequiturs, its trick of verbalizing the self-evident, strike first as the profoundly authentic speech of lower class characters. Gradually, however, the speech, like the room's physical objects and the quirky silent movement the stage directions describe, takes on a supra life. It always seems to mean more or other or disappointingly less than it says. In its rhythms, resonances, and repetitions, in its precision and allusiveness, it functions like poetry: pared down, weighted with the significance of poetic truth which lifts the particular to the universal.

As Esslin explains, 'The spectator's sense of reality gets sharpened to the point when he suddenly perceives ordinary and everyday events with such intensity of insight that they transcend themselves and become symbolic of a whole category of experience.'

For example, the struggle of the two young men with old Davies can be read as the archetypal yearning for a loving father figure, who then is displaced by the son figures, as all human fathers are displaced by their sons. The shamefully degraded Davies himself may embody the tragic guilt of the parent, who always must be inadequate to the unrealistic wishes of the child. At the same time, the shifting allegiances among the trio parody the permutations of the eternal triangle, three's a crowd. Aston and Davies are briefly allied against Mick, who resents Davies' intrusion into the cluttered domain he provides for his brother. Then, once he thinks the power lies there, Davies tries to insinuate himself into Mick's orbit. He sees in the vulnerability of the brain-damaged Aston the chance to wrest some security for himself. But in the end the brothers re-establish their bond, more out of conspiratorial cruelty than the loyalty of blood ties. Among other implications that easily translate into universal metaphor is the strategy of their tilting for territory. Who sleeps where and whether the window should be opened at night are tactical decisions based on the balance of power.

The characters quiz each other as they jockey for position. Answers are never full or clear. They prattle tediously or fall into stuporous silences. Their language, usually wary, more like boxing feints than conversation, can suddenly become body blows. Mick batters the old derelict with verbal insults, accusations, and innuendoes that reduce Davies to the whimperings of a whipped puppy. Similar in their deadly impact are the McCann-Goldberg verbal assaults on Stanley in *The Birthday Party*. The technique of language as evasion and weapon rather than communication in the ordinary sense is effective in all of Pinter's plays. Pinter uses it to create the threat of physical violence among the down-and-outs of the early plays. It becomes even more lethal among the more sophisticated, upper-class characters of later plays, such as *Old Times* and *Betrayal*.

Pinter's view of life as incomprehensible and non-rational, which is always part of the dramatic structure of his plays, is very strong in *Betrayal*. As if in answer to his early critics or to any who might still be clamouring for rational casuality in human motivation and behaviour, Pinter runs the action of *Betrayal* backwards. The dispirited end of a love affair is traced, scene by scene, to its beginnings years earlier. Yet nothing in the flashback scenes necessarily points to the subsequent action they should presumably explain. Life remains mysterious, inexplicable.

In a number of his plays, Pinter explores the instability of memory and time. For example, the three characters in *Old Times*, as the balance of power shifts among them, offer conflicting impressions of shared experience to corroborate or undermine each other's recollections, or because their own are faulty. Time present coexists with the past in some unnerving way, blurring perceptions so that past and present are not easily distinguishable. The gestures, inflections and reactions of the characters lack spontaneity. They seem to be evoked by the pressures exerted on each from moment to moment by the words and glances of the others. In *The Homecoming*, *The Birthday Party*, and *The Caretaker*, characters tell contradictory stories of their own pasts out of fear, defence, ignorance, malice, or weak memories. In *A Kind of Alaska*, praised as a masterpiece of miniaturist art by Esslin, Pinter explores the daunting universal experience of life's transiency: lost youth, lost, irretrievable time.

Until his short play about torture, *One for the Road* (1984), which was taken into the *Other Places* trilogy, revealed the extent of his political commitment, Pinter's plays were not thought of as overtly political in the way Arden's or Bond's are. Nevertheless he evokes through his victim-characters the nightmare of the knock in the night which came for millions of bewildered victims of Hitler's holocaust. In the aggressions of his character, Pinter exposes the innate cruelty and violence that lurk in humankind like a reflex, readily triggered by appropriate pressures or criminal persuasion.

Born in 1930 to Jewish working-class parents, Pinter grew up in Hackney. He remembers the unpleasant smells from a neighbourhood soap factory (later he suspected he had exaggerated), and the anti-semitism of the time that made him the potential victim of roaming street gangs. Pinter recalls holding off a group of bottle-wielding youths once by turning upon them the kind of opaque dialogue his characters speak: 'Are you all right?' he asked. 'Yes, I'm all right,' came the answer. 'Well, that's all right then, isn't it?' he said as he walked on past them. Pinter saw German bombs fall on London. The nameless fear that haunts the routines of his very ordinary characters, then, is not the abstraction of a literary imagination, but – oddly, in a playwright who refuses to verify anything – a verifiable fact of his own contemporary existence, and of ours.

Major Plays

The Birthday Party, Arts Theatre, Cambridge; then Lyric Theatre, Hammersmith, London, 1958
The Caretaker, Arts Theatre Club, then Duchess Theatre, 1960
The Homecoming, RSC of the Aldwych, 1965
Old Times, RSC at the Aldwych, 1971

No Man's Land, National Theatre at the Old Vic, 1975
Betrayal, National Theatre, 1980
Other Places, National Theatre, 1982; revised for Duchess
Theatre, 1985

Selected Bibliography

Dukore, Bernard. *Harold Pinter*. London: Macmillan; N.Y.:
Grove Press, 1982.
— 'Pinter's Staged Monologue.' *Theatre Journal* (4 December
1980), pp. 499-50.
Esslin, Martin. *The Peopled Wound*. London: Methuen 1970;
Garden City: Doubleday, 1970. Revised as *Pinter: A Study of
His Plays*. London: Eyre Methuen, 1973. Further revised as
Pinter the Playwright. London and N.Y.: Methuen, 1982.
— 'Other Places'. *Plays and Players* (December 1982), pp. 20–
21.
Scruton, Roger. 'Pinter's Progress,' *Encounter* (January 1983),
pp. 37-40.

HAROLD PINTER

The Caretaker

This play was first presented by the Arts Theatre Club in association with Michael Codron and David Hall at the Arts Theatre, London, WC2, on 27th April, 1960.

On 30th May, 1960, the play was presented by Michael Codron and David Hall at the Duchess Theatre, London, with the following cast:

MICK, *a man in his late twenties*	Alan Bates
ASTON, *a man in his early thirties*	Peter Woodthorpe
DAVIES, *an old man*	Donald Pleasence

The play was directed by Donald McWhinnie

On 2nd March, 1972, a revival of the play directed by Christopher Morahan was presented at the Mermaid Theatre, London, with the following cast:

MICK	John Hurt
ASTON	Jeremy Kemp
DAVIES	Leonard Rossiter

The action of the play takes place in a house in west London

ACT I A night in winter
ACT II A few seconds later
ACT III A fortnight later

A room. A window in the back wall, the bottom half covered by a sack. An iron bed along the left wall. Above it a small cupboard, paint buckets, boxes containing nuts, screws, etc. More boxes, vases, by the side of the bed. A door, up right. To the right of the window, a mound: a kitchen sink, a step-ladder, a coal bucket, a lawn-mower, a shopping trolley, boxes, sideboard drawers. Under this mound an iron bed. In front of it a gas stove. On the gas stove a statue of Buddha. Down right, a fireplace. Around it a couple of suitcases, a rolled carpet, a blow-lamp, a wooden chair on its side, boxes, a number of ornaments, a clothes horse, a few short planks of wood, a small electric fire and a very old electric toaster. Below this a pile of old newspapers. Under ASTON'S *bed by the left wall, is an electrolux, which is not seen till used. A bucket hangs from the ceiling.*

Act One

MICK *is alone in the room, sitting on the bed. He wears a leather jacket.*

Silence.

He slowly looks about the room looking at each object in turn. He looks up at the ceiling, and stares at the bucket. Ceasing, he sits quite still, expressionless, looking out front.

Silence for thirty seconds.

A door bangs. Muffled voices are heard.

MICK *turns his head. He stands, moves silently to the door, goes out, and closes the door quietly.*

Silence.

Voices are heard again. They draw nearer, and stop. The door opens. ASTON *and* DAVIES *enter,* ASTON *first,* DAVIES *following, shambling, breathing heavily.*

ASTON *wears an old tweed overcoat, and under it a thin shabby dark-blue pinstripe suit, single-breasted, with a pullover and faded shirt and tie.* DAVIES *wears a worn brown overcoat, shapeless trousers, a waistcoat, vest, no shirt, and sandals.* ASTON *puts the key in his pocket and closes the door.* DAVIES *looks about the room.*

ASTON. Sit down.
DAVIES. Thanks. (*Looking about.*) Uuh. . . .
ASTON. Just a minute.

> ASTON *looks around for a chair, sees one lying on its side by the rolled carpet at the fireplace, and starts to get it out.*

DAVIES. Sit down? Huh . . . I haven't had a good · sit down . . . I haven't had a proper sit down . . . well, I couldn't tell you. . . .

ASTON (*placing the chair*). Here you are.

DAVIES. Ten minutes off for a tea-break in the middle of the night in that place and I couldn't find a seat, not one. All them Greeks had it, Poles, Greeks, Blacks, the lot of them, all them aliens had it. And they had me working there . . . they had me working. . . .

> ASTON *sits on the bed, takes out a tobacco tin and papers, and begins to roll himself a cigarette.* DAVIES *watches him.*

All them Blacks had it, Blacks, Greeks, Poles, the lot of them, that's what, doing me out of a seat, treating me like dirt. When he come at me tonight I told him.

> *Pause.*

ASTON. Take a seat.

DAVIES. Yes, but what I got to do first, you see, what I got to do, I got to loosen myself up, you see what I mean? I could have got done in down there.

> DAVIES *exclaims loudly, punches downward with closed fist, turns his back to* ASTON *and stares at the wall.*
> *Pause.* ASTON *lights a cigarette.*

ASTON. You want to roll yourself one of these?

DAVIES (*turning*). What? No, no, I never smoke a cigarette. (*Pause. He comes forward.*) I'll tell you what, though. I'll have a bit of that tobacco there for my pipe, if you like.

ASTON (*handing him the tin*). Yes. Go on. Take some out of that.

DAVIES. That's kind of you, mister. Just enough to fill my pipe, that's all. (*He takes a pipe from his pocket and fills it.*) I had a tin, only . . . only a while ago. But it was knocked off. It was knocked off on the Great West Road. (*He holds out the tin*). Where shall I put it?

ASTON. I'll take it.

DAVIES (*handing the tin*). When he come at me tonight I told him. Didn't I? You heard me tell him, didn't you?

ASTON. I saw him have a go at you.

DAVIES. Go at me? You wouldn't grumble. The filthy skate, an old man like me, I've had dinner with the best.

Pause.

ASTON. Yes, I saw him have a go at you.

DAVIES. All them toe-rags, mate, got the manners of pigs. I might have been on the road a few years but you can take it from me I'm clean. I keep myself up. That's why I left my wife. Fortnight after I married her, no, not so much as that, no more than a week, I took the lid off a saucepan, you know what was in it? A pile of her underclothing, unwashed. The pan for vegetables, it was. The vegetable pan. That's when I left her and I haven't seen her since.

> DAVIES *turns, shambles across the room, comes face to face with a statue of Buddha standing on the gas stove, looks at it and turns.*

I've eaten my dinner off the best of plates. But I'm not young any more. I remember the days I was as handy as any of them. They didn't take any liberties with me. But I haven't been so well lately. I've had a few attacks.

Pause.

(*Coming closer.*) Did you see what happened with that one?

ASTON. I only got the end of it.

DAVIES. Comes up to me, parks a bucket of rubbish at me tells me to take it out the back. It's not my job to take out the bucket! They got a boy there for taking out the bucket. I wasn't engaged to take out buckets! My job's cleaning the floor, clearing up the tables, doing a bit of washing-up, nothing to do with taking out buckets!

ASTON. Uh.

> *He crosses down right, to get the electric toaster.*

DAVIES (*following*). Yes, well say I had! Even if I had! Even if I was supposed to take out the bucket, who was this git to

come up and give me orders? We got the same standing.
He's not my boss. He's nothing superior to me.

ASTON. What was he, a Greek?

DAVIES. Not him, he was a Scotch. He was a Scotchman.
(ASTON *goes back to his bed with the toaster and starts to
unscrew the plug.* DAVIES *follows him*). You got an eye of him,
did you?

ASTON. Yes.

DAVIES. I told him what to do with his bucket. Didn't I? You
heard. Look here, I said, I'm an old man, I said, where I was
brought up we had some idea how to talk to old people with
the proper respect, we was brought up with the right ideas,
if I had a few years off me I'd . . . I'd break you in half.
That was after the guvnor give me the bullet. Making too
much commotion, he says. Commotion, me! Look here, I
said to him, I got my rights. I told him that. I might have
been on the road but nobody's got more rights than I have.
Let's have a bit of fair play, I said. Anyway, he give me the
bullet. (*He sits in the chair*). That's the sort of place.
    Pause.
If you hadn't come out and stopped that Scotch git I'd be
inside the hospital now. I'd have cracked my head on that
pavement if he'd have landed. I'll get him. One night I'll get
him. When I find myself around that direction.

    ASTON *crosses to the plug box to get another plug.*
I wouldn't mind so much but I left all my belongings in that
place, in the back room there. All of them, the lot there was,
you see, in this bag. Every lousy blasted bit of all my bleeding belongings I left down there now. In the rush of it. I bet
he's having a poke around in it now this very moment.

ASTON. I'll pop down sometime and pick them up for you.

    ASTON *goes back to his bed and starts to fix the plug on the
    toaster.*

DAVIES. Anyway, I'm obliged to you, letting me . . . letting me have a bit of a rest, like . . . for a few minutes. (*He looks about.*) This your room?

ASTON. Yes.

DAVIES. You got a good bit of stuff here.

ASTON. Yes.

DAVIES. Must be worth a few bob, this . . . put it all together.

> *Pause.*

There's enough of it.

ASTON. There's a good bit of it, all right.

DAVIES. You sleep here, do you?

ASTON. Yes.

DAVIES. What, in that?

ASTON. Yes.

DAVIES. Yes, well, you'd be well out of the draught there.

ASTON. You don't get much wind.

DAVIES. You'd be well out of it. It's different when you're kipping out.

ASTON. Would be.

DAVIES. Nothing but wind then.

> *Pause.*

ASTON. Yes, when the wind gets up it. . . .

> *Pause.*

DAVIES. Yes. . . .

ASTON. Mmnn. . . .

> *Pause.*

DAVIES. Gets very draughty.

ASTON. Ah.

DAVIES. I'm very sensitive to it.

ASTON. Are you?

DAVIES. Always have been.

> *Pause.*

You got any more rooms then, have you?

ASTON. Where?

DAVIES. I mean, along the landing here . . . up the landing there.

ASTON. They're out of commission.

DAVIES. Get away.

ASTON. They need a lot of doing to.

Slight pause.

DAVIES. What about downstairs?

ASTON. That's closed up. Needs seeing to. . . . The floors. . . .

Pause.

DAVIES. I was lucky you come into that caff. I might have been done by that Scotch git. I been left for dead more than once.

Pause.

I noticed that there was someone was living in the house next door.

ASTON. What?

DAVIES. (*gesturing*). I noticed. . . .

ASTON. Yes. There's people living all along the road.

DAVIES. Yes, I noticed the curtains pulled down there next door as we came along.

ASTON. They're neighbours.

Pause.

DAVIES. This your house then, is it?

Pause.

ASTON. I'm in charge.

DAVIES. You the landlord, are you?

He puts a pipe in his mouth and puffs without lighting it.

Yes, I noticed them heavy curtains pulled across next door

as we came along. I noticed them heavy big curtains right across the window down there. I thought there must be someone living there.

ASTON. Family of Indians live there.

DAVIES. Blacks?

ASTON. I don't see much of them.

DAVIES. Blacks, eh? (DAVIES *stands and moves about.*) Well you've got some knick-knacks here all right, I'll say that. I don't like a bare room. (ASTON *joins* DAVIES *upstage centre*). I'll tell you what, mate, you haven't got a spare pair of shoes?

ASTON. Shoes?

ASTON *moves downstage right.*

DAVIES. Them bastards at the monastery let me down again.

ASTON. (*going to his bed.*) Where?

DAVIES. Down in Luton. Monastery down at Luton. . . . I got a mate at Shepherd's Bush, you see. . . .

ASTON (*looking under his bed*). I might have a pair.

DAVIES. I got this mate at Shepherd's Bush. In the convenience. Well, he was in the convenience. Run about the best convenience they had. (*He watches* ASTON.) Run about the best one. Always slipped me a bit of soap, any time I went in there. Very good soap. They have to have the best soap. I was never without a piece of soap, whenever I happened to be knocking about the Shepherd's Bush area.

ASTON (*emerging from under the bed with shoes*). Pair of brown.

DAVIES. He's gone now. Went. He was the one who put me on to this monastery. Just the other side of Luton. He'd heard they give away shoes.

ASTON. You've got to have a good pair of shoes.

DAVIES. Shoes? It's life and death to me. I had to go all the way to Luton in these.

ASTON. What happened when you got there, then?

    Pause.

DAVIES. I used to know a bootmaker in Acton. He was a good
mate to me.
    Pause.
You know what that bastard monk said to me?
    Pause.
How many more Blacks you got around here then?

ASTON. What?

DAVIES. You got any more Blacks around here?

ASTON (*holding out the shoes*). See if these are any good.

DAVIES. You know what that bastard monk said to me? (*He
looks over to the shoes.*) I think those'd be a bit small.

ASTON. Would they?

DAVIES. No, don't look the right size.

ASTON. Not bad trim.

DAVIES. Can't wear shoes that don't fit. Nothing worse. I said
to this monk, here, I said, look here, mister, he opened the
door, big door, he opened it, look here, mister, I said, I
come all the way down here, look, I said, I showed him these,
I said, you haven't got a pair of shoes, have you, a pair of
shoes, I said, enough to keep me on my way. Look at these,
they're nearly out, I said, they're no good to me. I heard you
got a stock of shoes here. Piss off, he said to me. Now look
here, I said, I'm an old man, you can't talk to me like that, I
don't care who you are. If you don't piss off, he says, I'll
kick you all the way to the gate. Now look here, I said, now
wait a minute, all I'm asking for is a pair of shoes, you don't
want to start taking liberties with me, it's taken me three
days to get here, I said to him, three days without a bite,
I'm worth a bite to eat, en I? Get out round the corner to
the kitchen, he says, get out round the corner, and when
you've had your meal, piss off out of it. I went round to this
kitchen, see? Meal they give me! A bird, I tell you, a little

bird, a little tiny bird, he could have ate it in under two minutes. Right, they said to me, you've had your meal, get off out of it. Meal? I said, what do you think I am, a dog? Nothing better than a dog. What do you think I am, a wild animal? What about them shoes I come all the way here to get I heard you was giving away? I've a good mind to report you to your mother superior. One of them, an Irish hooligan, come at me. I cleared out. I took a short cut to Watford and picked up a pair there. Got onto the North Circular, just past Hendon, the sole come off, right where I was walking. Lucky I had my old ones wrapped up, still carrying them, otherwise I'd have been finished, man. So I've had to stay with these, you see, they're gone, they're no good, all the good's gone out of them.

ASTON. Try these.

DAVIES *takes the shoes, takes off his sandals and tries them on.*

DAVIES. Not a bad pair of shoes. (*He trudges round the room.*) They're strong, all right. Yes. Not a bad shape of shoe. This leather's hardy, en't? Very hardy. Some bloke tried to flog me some suede the other day. I wouldn't wear them. Can't beat leather, for wear. Suede goes off, it creases, it stains for life in five minutes. You can't beat leather. Yes. Good shoe this.

ASTON. Good.

DAVIES *waggles his feet.*

DAVIES. Don't fit though.

ASTON. Oh?

DAVIES. No. I got a very broad foot.

ASTON. Mmnn.

DAVIES. These are too pointed, you see.

ASTON. Ah.

DAVIES. They'd cripple me in a week. I mean these ones I got on, they're no good but at least they're comfortable. Not much cop, but I mean they don't hurt. (*He takes them off and gives them back*). Thanks anyway, mister.

ASTON. I'll see what I can look out for you.

DAVIES. Good luck. I can't go on like this. Can't get from one place to another. And I'll have to be moving about, you see, try to get fixed up.

ASTON. Where you going to go?

DAVIES. Oh, I got one or two things in mind. I'm waiting for the weather to break.

   Pause.

ASTON (*attending to the toaster*). Would . . . would you like to sleep here?

DAVIES. Here?

ASTON. You can sleep here if you like.

DAVIES. Here? Oh, I don't know about that.

   Pause.

How long for?

ASTON. Till you . . . get yourself fixed up.

DAVIES (*sitting*). Ay well, that. . . .

ASTON. Get yourself sorted out. . . .

DAVIES. Oh, I'll be fixed up . . . pretty soon now. . . .

   Pause.

Where would I sleep?

ASTON. Here. The other rooms would . . . would be no good to you.

DAVIES (*rising, looking about*). Here? Where?

ASTON (*rising, pointing upstage right*). There's a bed behind all that.

DAVIES. Oh, I see. Well, that's handy. Well, that's . . . I tell you what, I might do that . . . just till I get myself sorted out. You got enough furniture here.

ASTON. I picked it up. Just keeping it here for the time being. Thought it might come in handy.

DAVIES. This gas stove work, do it?

ASTON. No.

DAVIES. What do you do for a cup of tea?

ASTON. Nothing.

DAVIES. That's a bit rough. (DAVIES *observes the planks*.) You building something?

ASTON. I might build a shed out the back.

DAVIES. Carpenter, eh? (*He turns to the lawn-mower*.) Got a lawn.

ASTON. Have a look.

   ASTON *lifts the sack at the window. They look out.*

DAVIES. Looks a bit thick.

ASTON. Overgrown.

DAVIES. What's that, a pond?

ASTON. Yes.

DAVIES. What you got, fish?

ASTON. No. There isn't anything in there.

   Pause.

DAVIES. Where you going to put your shed?

ASTON (*turning*). I'll have to clear the garden first.

DAVIES. You'd need a tractor, man.

ASTON. I'll get it done.

DAVIES. Carpentry, eh?

ASTON (*standing still*). I like . . . working with my hands.

   DAVIES *picks up the statue of Buddha.*

DAVIES. What's this?

ASTON (*taking and studying it*). That's a Buddha.

DAVIES. Get on.

ASTON. Yes. I quite like it. Picked it up in a . . . in a shop. Looked quite nice to me. Don't know why. What do you think of these Buddhas?

DAVIES. Oh, they're . . . they're all right, en't they?

ASTON. Yes, I was pleased when I got hold of this one. It's very well made.

>   DAVIES *turns and peers under the sink.*

DAVIES. This the bed here, is it?

ASTON (*moving to the bed*). We'll get rid of all that. The ladder'll fit under the bed. (*They put the ladder under the bed.*)

DAVIES (*indicating the sink*). What about this?

ASTON. I think that'll fit in under here as well.

DAVIES. I'll give you a hand. (*They lift it.*) It's a ton weight, en't?

ASTON. Under here.

DAVIES. This in use at all, then?

ASTON. No. I'll be getting rid of it. Here.
>   *They place the sink under the bed.*
There's a lavatory down the landing. It's got a sink in there. We can put this stuff over there.

>   *They begin to move the coal bucket, shopping trolley, lawn-mower and sideboard drawers to the right wall.*

DAVIES (*stopping*). You don't share it, do you?

ASTON. What?

DAVIES. I mean you don't share the toilet with them Blacks, do you?

ASTON. They live next door.

DAVIES. They don't come in?
>   ASTON *puts a drawer against the wall.*
Because, you know . . . I mean . . . fair's fair. . . .

>   ASTON *goes to the bed, blows dust and shakes a blanket.*

ASTON. You see a blue case?

DAVIES. Blue case? Down here. Look. By the carpet.
>   ASTON *goes to the case, opens it, takes out a sheet and pillow and puts them on the bed.*
That's a nice sheet.

ASTON. The blanket'll be a bit dusty.

DAVIES. Don't you worry about that.

> ASTON *stands upright, takes out his tobacco and begins to roll a cigarette. He goes to his bed and sits.*

ASTON. How are you off for money?

DAVIES. Oh well . . . now, mister, if you want the truth . . I'm a bit short.

> ASTON *takes some coins from his pocket, sorts them, and holds out five shillings.*

ASTON. Here's a few bob.

DAVIES (*taking the coins*). Thank you, thank you, good luck. I just happen to find myself a bit short. You see, I got nothing for all that week's work I did last week. That's the position, that's what it is.

> *Pause.*

ASTON. I went into a pub the other day. Ordered a Guinness. They gave it to me in a thick mug. I sat down but I couldn't drink it. I can't drink Guinness from a thick mug. I only like it out of a thin glass. I had a few sips but I couldn't finish it.

> ASTON *picks up a screwdriver and plug from the bed and begins to poke the plug.*

DAVIES (*with great feeling*). If only the weather would break! Then I'd be able to get down to Sidcup!

ASTON. Sidcup?

DAVIES. The weather's so blasted bloody awful, how can I get down to Sidcup in these shoes?

ASTON. Why do you want to get down to Sidcup?

DAVIES. I got my papers there!

> *Pause.*

ASTON. Your what?

DAVIES. I got my papers there!

> *Pause.*

ASTON. What are they doing at Sidcup?

DAVIES. A man I know has got them. I left them with him. You see? They prove who I am! I can't move without them papers. They tell you who I am. You see! I'm stuck without them.

ASTON. Why's that?

DAVIES. You see, what it is, you see, I changed my name! Years ago. I been going around under an assumed name! That's not my real name.

ASTON. What name you been going under?

DAVIES. Jenkins. Bernard Jenkins. That's my name. That's the name I'm known, anyway. But it's no good me going on with that name. I got no rights. I got an insurance card here. (*He takes a card from his pocket.*) Under the name of Jenkins. See? Bernard Jenkins. Look. It's got four stamps on it. Four of them. But I can't go along with these. That's not my real name, they'd find out, they'd have me in the nick. Four stamps. I haven't paid out pennies. I've paid out pounds. I've paid out pounds, not pennies. There's been other stamps, plenty, but they haven't put them on, the nigs, I never had enough time to go into it.

ASTON. They should have stamped your card.

DAVIES. It would have done no good! I'd have got nothing anyway. That's not my real name. If I take that card along I go in the nick.

ASTON. What's your real name, then?

DAVIES. Davies. Mac Davies. That was before I changed my name.

Pause.

ASTON. It looks as though you want to sort all that out.

DAVIES. If only I could get down to Sidcup! I've been waiting for the weather to break. He's got my papers, this man I left them with, it's got it all down there, I could prove everything.

ASTON. How long's he had them?

DAVIES. What?

ASTON. How long's he had them?

DAVIES. Oh, must be . . . it was in the war . . . must be . . . about near on fifteen year ago.

He suddenly becomes aware of the bucket and looks up.

ASTON. Any time you want to . . . get into bed, just get in. Don't worry about me.

DAVIES (*taking off his overcoat*). Eh, well, I think I will. I'm a bit . . . a bit done in. (*He steps out of his trousers, and holds them out*). Shall I put these on here?

ASTON. Yes.

DAVIES *puts the coat and trousers on the clothes horse.*

DAVIES. I see you got a bucket up here.

ASTON. Leak.

DAVIES *looks up.*

DAVIES. Well, I'll try your bed then. You getting in?

ASTON. I'm mending this plug.

DAVIES *looks at him and then at the gas stove.*

DAVIES. You . . . you can't move this, eh?

ASTON. Bit heavy.

DAVIES. Yes.

DAVIES *gets into bed. He tests his weight and length.*

Not bad. Not bad. A fair bed. I think I'll sleep in this.

ASTON. I'll have to fix a proper shade on that bulb. The light's a bit glaring.

DAVIES. Don't you worry about that, mister, don't you worry about that. (*He turns and puts the cover up*).

ASTON *sits, poking his plug.*
The LIGHTS FADE OUT. *Darkness.*
LIGHTS UP. *Morning.*
ASTON *is fastening his trousers, standing by the bed. He straightens his bed. He turns, goes to the centre of the room*

and looks at DAVIES. *He turns, puts his jacket on, turns, goes towards* DAVIES *and looks down on him.*
He coughs. DAVIES *sits up abruptly.*

DAVIES. What? What's this? What's this?

ASTON. It's all right.

DAVIES (*staring*). What's this?

ASTON. It's all right.

DAVIES *looks about.*

DAVIES. Oh, yes.

ASTON *goes to his bed, picks up the plug and shakes it.*

ASTON. Sleep well?

DAVIES. Yes. Dead out. Must have been dead out.

ASTON *goes downstage right, collects the toaster and examines it.*

ASTON. You . . . er. . . .

DAVIES. Eh?

ASTON. Were you dreaming or something?

DAVIES. Dreaming?

ASTON. Yes.

DAVIES. I don't dream. I've never dreamed.

ASTON. No, nor have I.

DAVIES. Nor me.

   Pause.

 Why you ask me that, then?

ASTON. You were making noises.

DAVIES. Who was?

ASTON. You were.

DAVIES *gets out of bed. He wears long underpants.*

DAVIES. Now, wait a minute. Wait a minute, what do you mean? What kind of noises?

ASTON. You were making groans. You were jabbering.

DAVIES. Jabbering? Me?

ASTON. Yes.

DAVIES. I don't jabber, man. Nobody ever told me that before.

Pause.

What would I be jabbering about?

ASTON. I don't know.

DAVIES. I mean, where's the sense in it?

Pause.

Nobody ever told me that before.

Pause.

You got hold of the wrong bloke, mate.

ASTON (*crossing to the bed with the toaster*). No. You woke me up. I thought you might have been dreaming.

DAVIES. I wasn't dreaming. I never had a dream in my life.

Pause.

ASTON. Maybe it was the bed.

DAVIES. Nothing wrong with this bed.

ASTON. Might be a bit unfamiliar.

DAVIES. There's nothing unfamiliar about me with beds. I slept in beds. I don't make noises just because I sleep in a bed. I slept in plenty of beds.

Pause.

I tell you what, maybe it were them Blacks.

ASTON. What?

DAVIES. Them noises.

ASTON. What Blacks?

DAVIES. Them you got. Next door. Maybe it were them Blacks making noises, coming up through the walls.

ASTON. Hmmnn.

DAVIES. That's my opinion.

ASTON *puts down the plug and moves to the door.*

Where you going, you going out?

ASTON. Yes.

DAVIES (*seizing the sandals*). Wait a minute then, just a minute.

ASTON. What you doing?

DAVIES (*putting on the sandals*). I better come with you.

ASTON. Why?

DAVIES. I mean, I better come out with you, anyway.

ASTON. Why?

DAVIES. Well . . . don't you want me to go out?

ASTON. What for?

DAVIES. I mean . . . when you're out. Don't you want me to get out . . . when you're out?

ASTON. You don't have to go out.

DAVIES. You mean . . . I can stay here?

ASTON. Do what you like. You don't have to come out just because I go out.

DAVIES. You don't mind me staying here?

ASTON. I've got a couple of keys. (*He goes to a box by his bed and finds them.*) This door and the front door. (*He hands them to* DAVIES.)

DAVIES. Thanks very much, the best of luck.

Pause. ASTON *stands.*

ASTON. I think I'll take a stroll down the road. A little . . . kind of a shop. Man there'd got a jig saw the other day. I quite liked the look of it.

DAVIES. A jig saw, mate?

ASTON. Yes. Could be very useful.

DAVIES. Yes.

Slight pause.

What's that then, exactly, then?

ASTON *walks up to the window and looks out.*

ASTON. A jig saw? Well, it comes from the same family as the fret saw. But it's an appliance, you see. You have to fix it on to a portable drill.

DAVIES. Ah, that's right. They're very handy.

ASTON. They are, yes.

Pause.

You know, I was sitting in a café the other day. I happened to be sitting at the same table as this woman. Well, we started to . . . we started to pick up a bit of a conversation. I don't know . . . about her holiday, it was, where she'd been. She'd been down to the south coast. I can't remember where though. Anyway, we were just sitting there, having this bit of a conversation . . . then suddenly she put her hand over to mine . . . and she said, how would you like me to have a look at your body?

DAVIES. Get out of it.

Pause.

ASTON. Yes. To come out with it just like that, in the middle of this conversation. Struck me as a bit odd.

DAVIES. They've said the same thing to me.

ASTON. Have they?

DAVIES. Women? There's many a time they've come up to me and asked me more or less the same question.

Pause.

ASTON. What did you say your name was?

DAVIES. Bernard Jenkins is my assumed one.

ASTON. No, your other one?

DAVIES. Davies. Mac Davies.

ASTON. Welsh, are you?

DAVIES. Eh?

ASTON. You Welsh?

Pause.

DAVIES. Well, I been around, you know . . . what I mean . . . I been about. . . .

ASTON. Where were you born then?

DAVIES. (*darkly*). What do you mean?

ASTON. Where were you born?

DAVIES. I was . . . uh . . . oh, it's a bit hard, like, to set your mind back . . . see what I mean . . . going back . . . . a good way . . . lose a bit of track, like . . . you know. . . .

ASTON (*going to below the fireplace*). See this plug? Switch it on here, if you like. This little fire.

DAVIES. Right, mister.

ASTON. Just plug in here.

DAVIES. Right, mister.

  ASTON *goes towards the door*.

  (*Anxiously*). What do I do?

ASTON. Just switch it on, that's all. The fire'll come on.

DAVIES. I tell you what. I won't bother about it.

ASTON. No trouble.

DAVIES. No, I don't go in for them things much.

ASTON. Should work. (*Turning*). Right.

DAVIES. Eh, I was going to ask you, mister, what about this stove? I mean, do you think it's going to be letting out any . . . what do you think?

ASTON. It's not connected.

DAVIES. You see, the trouble is, it's right on top of my bed, you see? What I got to watch is nudging . . . one of them gas taps with my elbow when I get up, you get my meaning?

He goes round to the other side of stove and examines it.

ASTON. There's nothing to worry about.

DAVIES. Now look here, don't you worry about it. All I'll do, I'll keep an eye on these taps every now and again, like, you see. See they're switched off. You leave it to me.

ASTON. I don't think . . . .

DAVIES (*coming round*). Eh, mister, just one thing . . . eh . . . . you couldn't slip me a couple of bob, for a cup of tea, just, you know?

ASTON. I gave you a few bob last night.

DAVIES. Eh, so you did. So you did. I forgot. Went clean out of my mind. That's right. Thank you, mister. Listen. You're sure now, you're sure you don't mind me staying here? I mean, I'm not the sort of man who wants to take any liberties.

ASTON. No, that's all right.

DAVIES. I might get down to Wembley later on in the day.

ASTON. Uh-uh.

DAVIES. There's a caff down there, you see, might be able to get fixed up there. I was there, see? I know they were a bit short-handed. They might be in the need of a bit of staff.

ASTON. When was that?

DAVIES. Eh? Oh, well, that was . . . near on . . . that'll be . . . that'll be a little while ago now. But of course what it is, they can't find the right kind of people in these places. What they want to do, they're trying to do away with these foreigners, you see, in catering. They want an Englishman to pour their tea, that's what they want, that's what they're crying out for. It's only common sense, en't? Oh, I got all that under way . . . that's . . . uh . . . that's . . . what I'll be doing.

Pause.

If only I could get down there.

ASTON. Mmnn. (ASTON *moves to the door.*) Well, I'll be seeing you then.

DAVIES. Yes. Right.

ASTON *goes out and closes the door.*

DAVIES *stands still. He waits a few seconds, then goes to the door, opens it, looks out, closes it, stands with his back to it, turns swiftly, opens it, looks out, comes back, closes the door, finds the keys in his pocket, tries one, tries the other, locks the door. He looks about the room. He then goes quickly to* ASTON'S *bed, bends, brings out the pair of shoes and examines them.*

Not a bad pair of shoes. Bit pointed.

He puts them back under the bed. He examines the area by ASTON'S *bed, picks up a vase and looks into it, then picks up a box and shakes it.*

Screws!

He sees paint buckets at the top of the bed, goes to them, and examines them.

Paint. What's he going to paint?

He puts the bucket down, comes to the centre of the room, looks up at bucket, and grimaces.

I'll have to find out about that. (*He crosses right, and picks up a blow-lamp.*) He's got some stuff in here. (*He picks up the Buddha and looks at it.*) Full of stuff. Look at all this. (*His eye falls on the piles of papers.*) What's he got all those papers for? Damn pile of papers.

He goes to a pile and touches it. The pile wobbles. He steadies it.

Hold it, hold it!

He holds the pile and pushes the papers back into place.
The door opens.
MICK *comes in, puts the key in his pocket, and closes the door silently. He stands at the door and watches* DAVIES.

What's he got all these papers for? (DAVIES *climbs over the rolled carpet to the blue case.*) Had a sheet and pillow ready in here. (*He opens the case.*) Nothing. (*He shuts the case.*) Still, I had a sleep though. I don't make no noises. (*He looks at the window.*) What's this?

He picks up another case and tries to open it. MICK *moves up-stage, silently.*

Locked. (*He puts it down and moves downstage.*) Must be something in it. (*He picks up a sideboard drawer, rummages in the contents, then puts it down.*)

MICK *slides across the room.*
DAVIES *half turns,* MICK *seizes his arm and forces it up his back.* DAVIES *screams.*

Uuuuuuuhhh! Uuuuuuuhhh! What! What! What! Uuuuuuuhhh!

MICK *swiftly forces him to the floor, with* DAVIES *struggling, grimacing, whimpering and staring.*

MICK *holds his arm, puts his other hand to his lips, then puts his hand to* DAVIES' *lips.* DAVIES *quietens.* MICK *lets him go.* DAVIES *writhes.* MICK *holds out a warning finger. He then squats down to regard* DAVIES. *He regards him, then stands looking down on him.* DAVIES *massages his arm, watching* MICK. MICK *turns slowly to look at the room. He goes to* DAVIES' *bed and uncovers it. He turns, goes to the clothes horse and picks up* DAVIES' *trousers.* DAVIES *starts to rise.* MICK *presses him down with his foot and stands over him. Finally he removes his foot. He examines the trousers and throws them back.* DAVIES *remains on the floor, crouched.* MICK *slowly goes to the chair, sits, and watches* DAVIES, *expressionless.*

Silence.

MICK. What's the game?

Curtain.

Act Two

A few seconds later.

> MICK *is seated,* DAVIES *on the floor, half seated, crouched.*
> *Silence.*

MICK. Well?

DAVIES. Nothing, nothing. Nothing.

> *A drip sounds in the bucket overhead. They look up.* MICK
> *looks back to* DAVIES.

MICK. What's your name?

DAVIES. I don't know you. I don't know who you are.

> *Pause.*

MICK. Eh?

DAVIES. Jenkins.

MICK. Jenkins?

DAVIES. Yes.

MICK. Jen . . . kins.

> *Pause.*

You sleep here last night?

DAVIES. Yes.

MICK. Sleep well?

DAVIES. Yes.

MICK. I'm awfully glad. It's awfully nice to meet you.

> *Pause.*

What did you say your name was?

DAVIES. Jenkins.

MICK. I beg your pardon?

DAVIES. Jenkins!

> *Pause.*

MICK. Jen . . . kins.

A drip sounds in the bucket. DAVIES *looks up.*

You remind me of my uncle's brother. He was always on the move, that man. Never without his passport. Had an eye for the girls. Very much your build. Bit of an athlete. Long-jump specialist. He had a habit of demonstrating different run-ups in the drawing-room round about Christmas time. Had a penchant for nuts. That's what it was. Nothing else but a penchant. Couldn't eat enough of them. Peanuts, walnuts, brazil nuts, monkey nuts, wouldn't touch a piece of fruit cake. Had a marvellous stop-watch. Picked it up in Hong Kong. The day after they chucked him out of the Salvation Army. Used to go in number four for Beckenham Reserves. That was before he got his Gold Medal. Had a funny habit of carrying his fiddle on his back. Like a papoose. I think there was a bit of the Red Indian in him. To be honest, I've never made out how he came to be my uncle's brother. I've often thought that maybe it was the other way round. I mean that my uncle was his brother and he was my uncle. But I never called him uncle. As a matter of fact I called him Sid. My mother called him Sid too. It was a funny business. Your spitting image he was. Married a Chinaman and went to Jamaica.

Pause.

I hope you slept well last night.

DAVIES. Listen! I don't know who you are!

MICK. What bed you sleep in?

DAVIES. Now look here—

MICK. Eh?

DAVIES. That one.

MICK. Not the other one?

DAVIES. No.

MICK. Choosy.

Pause.

How do you like my room?

DAVIES. Your room?

MICK. Yes.

DAVIES. This ain't your room. I don't know who you are. I ain't never seen you before.

MICK. You know, believe it or not, you've got a funny kind of resemblance to a bloke I once knew in Shoreditch. Actually he lived in Aldgate. I was staying with a cousin in Camden Town. This chap, he used to have a pitch in Finsbury Park, just by the bus depot. When I got to know him I found out he was brought up in Putney. That didn't make any difference to me. I know quite a few people who were born in Putney. Even if they weren't born in Putney they were born in Fulham. The only trouble was, he wasn't born in Putney, he was only brought up in Putney. It turned out he was born in the Caledonian Road, just before you get to the Nag's Head. His old mum was still living at the Angel. All the buses passed right by the door. She could get a 38, 581, 30 or 38A, take her down the Essex Road to Dalston Junction in next to no time. Well, of course, if she got the 30 he'd take her up Upper Street way, round by Highbury Corner and down to St. Paul's Church, but she'd get to Dalston Junction just the same in the end. I used to leave my bike in her garden on my way to work. Yes, it was a curious affair. Dead spit of you he was. Bit bigger round the nose but there was nothing in it.

   Pause.

Did you sleep here last night?

DAVIES. Yes.

MICK. Sleep well?

DAVIES. Yes!

MICK. Did you have to get up in the night?

DAVIES. No!

   Pause.

MICK. What's your name?

DAVIES (*shifting, about to rise*). Now look here!

MICK. What?

DAVIES. Jenkins!

MICK. Jen . . . kins.

>   DAVIES *makes a sudden move to rise. A violent bellow*
>   *from* MICK *sends him back.*

(*A shout.*) Sleep here last night?

DAVIES. Yes. . . .

MICK (*continuing at great pace*). How'd you sleep?

DAVIES. I slept—

MICK. Sleep well?

DAVIES. Now look—

MICK. What bed?

DAVIES. That—

MICK. Not the other?

DAVIES. No!

MICK. Choosy.

>   Pause.

(*Quietly.*) Choosy.

>   Pause.

(*Again amiable.*) What sort of sleep did you have in that bed?

DAVIES (*banging on floor*). All right!

MICK. You weren't uncomfortable?

DAVIES (*groaning*). All right!

>   MICK *stands, and moves to him.*

MICK. You a foreigner?

DAVIES. No.

MICK. Born and bred in the British Isles?

DAVIES. I was!

MICK. What did they teach you?

>   Pause.

How did you like my bed?

>   Pause.

That's my bed. You want to mind you don't catch a draught.

DAVIES. From the bed?

MICK. No, now, up your arse.

> DAVIES *stares warily at* MICK, *who turns.* DAVIES *scrambles to the clothes horse and seizes his trousers.* MICK *turns swiftly and grabs them.* DAVIES *lunges for them.* MICK *holds out a hand warningly.*

You intending to settle down here?

DAVIES. Give me my trousers then.

MICK. You settling down for a long stay?

DAVIES. Give me my bloody trousers!

MICK. Why, where you going?

DAVIES. Give me and I'm going, I'm going to Sidcup!

> MICK *flicks the trousers in* DAVIES' *face several times.* DAVIES *retreats.*
>
> *Pause.*

MICK. You know, you remind me of a bloke I bumped into once, just the other side of the Guildford by-pass—

DAVIES. I was brought here!

> *Pause.*

MICK. Pardon?

DAVIES. I was brought here! I was brought here!

MICK. Brought here? Who brought you here?

DAVIES. Man who lives here . . . he. . . .

> *Pause.*

MICK. Fibber.

DAVIES. I was brought here, last night . . . met him in a caff . . . I was working . . . I got the bullet . . . I was working there . . . bloke saved me from a punch up, brought me here, brought me right here.

> *Pause.*

MICK. I'm afraid you're a born fibber, en't you? You're speaking to the owner. This is my room. You're standing in my house.

DAVIES. It's his . . . he seen me all right . . . he. . . .

MICK (*pointing to* DAVIES' *bed*). That's my bed.

DAVIES. What about that, then?

MICK. That's my mother's bed.

DAVIES. Well she wasn't in it last night!

MICK (*moving to him*). Now don't get perky, son, don't get perky. Keep your hands off my old mum.

DAVIES. I ain't . . . I haven't. . . .

MICK. Don't get out of your depth, friend, don't start taking liberties with my old mother, let's have a bit of respect.

DAVIES. I got respect, you won't find anyone with more respect.

MICK. Well, sto elling me all these fibs.

DAVIES. Now listen to me, I never seen you before, have I?

MICK. Never seen my mother before either, I suppose?

Pause.

I think I'm coming to the conclusion that you're an old rogue. You're nothing but an old scoundrel.

DAVIES. Now wait—

MICK. Listen, son. Listen, sonny. You stink.

DAVIES. You ain't got no right to—

MICK. You're stinking the place out. You're an old robber, there's no getting away from it. You're an old skate. You don't belong in a nice place like this. You're an old barbarian. Honest. You got no business wandering about in an unfurnished flat. I could charge seven quid a week for this if I wanted to. Get a taker tomorrow. Three hundred and fifty a year exclusive. No argument. I mean, if that sort of money's in your range don't be afraid to say so. Here you are. Furniture and fittings, I'll take four hundred or the nearest offer. Rateable value ninety quid for the annum. You can reckon water, heating and lighting at close on fifty. That'll cost you eight hundred and ninety if you're all that keen. Say the word and I'll have my solicitors draft you out a contract. Otherwise I've got the van outside, I can run you

to the police station in five minutes, have you in for tres-
passing, loitering with intent, daylight robbery, filching,
thieving and stinking the place out. What do you say?
Unless you're really keen on a straightforward purchase. Of
course, I'll get my brother to decorate it up for you first. I've
got a brother who's a number one decorator. He'll decorate
it up for you. If you want more space, there's four more
rooms along the landing ready to go. Bathroom, living-
room, bedroom and nursery. You can have this as your
study. This brother I mentioned, he's just about to start on
the other rooms. Yes, just about to start. So what do you
say? Eight hundred odd for this room or three thousand
down for the whole upper storey. On the other hand, if you
prefer to approach it in the long-term way I know an
insurance firm in West Ham'll be pleased to handle the
deal for you. No strings attached, open and above board,
untarnished record; twenty per cent interest, fifty per cent
deposit; down payments, back payments, family allowances,
bonus schemes, remission of term for good behaviour, six
months lease, yearly examination of the relevant archives,
tea laid on, disposal of shares, benefit extension, compen-
sation on cessation, comprehensive indemnity against Riot,
Civil Commotion, Labour Disturbances, Storm, Tempest,
Thunderbolt, Larceny or Cattle all subject to a daily check
and double check. Of course we'd need a signed declaration
from your personal medical attendant as assurance that you
possess the requisite fitness to carry the can, won't we?
Who do you bank with?

Pause.

Who do you bank with?

The door opens. ASTON *comes in.* MICK *turns and drops the
trousers.* DAVIES *picks them up and puts them on.* ASTON,
*after a glance at the other two, goes to his bed, places a bag
which he is carrying on it, sits down and resumes fixing the
toaster.* DAVIES *retreats to his corner.* MICK *sits in the chair.*

Silence.
A drip sounds in the bucket. They all look up.
Silence.

You still got that leak.

ASTON. Yes.

Pause.

It's coming from the roof.

MICK. From the roof, eh?

ASTON. Yes.

Pause.

I'll have to tar it over.

MICK. You're going to tar it over?

ASTON. Yes.

MICK. What?

ASTON. The cracks.

Pause.

MICK. You'll be tarring over the cracks on the roof.

ASTON. Yes.

Pause.

MICK. Think that'll do it?

ASTON. It'll do it, for the time being.

MICK. Uh.

Pause.

DAVIES (*abruptly*). What do you do—?
   They both look at him.
What do you do . . . when that bucket's full?

Pause.

ASTON. Empty it.

Pause.

MICK. I was telling my friend you were about to start decorating the other rooms.

ASTON. Yes.

    Pause.

    (*To* DAVIES.) I got your bag.

DAVIES. Oh. (*Crossing to him and taking it*). Oh thanks, mister, thanks. Give it to you, did they?

> DAVIES *crosses back with the bag.*
> MICK *rises and snatches it.*

MICK. What's this?

DAVIES. Give us it, that's my bag!

MICK (*warding him off*). I've seen this bag before.

DAVIES. That's my bag!

MICK (*eluding him*). This bag's very familiar.

DAVIES. What do you mean?

MICK. Where'd you get it?

ASTON (*rising, to them*). Scrub it.

DAVIES. That's mine.

MICK. Whose?

DAVIES. It's mine! Tell him it's mine!

MICK. This your bag?

DAVIES. Give me it!

ASTON. Give it to him.

MICK. What? Give him what?

DAVIES. That bloody bag!

MICK (*slipping it behind the gas stove*). What bag? (*To* DAVIES.) What bag?

DAVIES (*moving*). Look here!

MICK (*facing him*). Where you going?

DAVIES. I'm going to get . . . my old . . .

MICK. Watch your step, sonny! You're knocking at the door when no one's at home. Don't push it too hard. You come busting into a private house, laying your hands on anything you can lay your hands on. Don't overstep the mark, son.

> ASTON *picks up the bag.*

DAVIES. You thieving bastard ... you thieving skate ... let me get my—

ASTON. Here you are. (ASTON *offers the bag to* DAVIES.)

> MICK *grabs it.* ASTON *takes it.*
> MICK *grabs it.* DAVIES *reaches for it.*
> ASTON *takes it.* MICK *reaches for it.*
> ASTON *gives it to* DAVIES. MICK *grabs it.*
> *Pause.*
> ASTON *takes it.* DAVIES *takes it.* MICK *takes it.* DAVIES *reaches for it.* ASTON *takes it.*
> *Pause.*
> ASTON *gives it to* MICK. MICK *gives it to* DAVIES. DAVIES *grasps it to him.*
> *Pause.*
> MICK *looks at* ASTON. DAVIES *moves away with the bag. He drops it.*
> *Pause.*
> *They watch him. He picks it up. Goes to his bed, and sits.* ASTON *goes to his bed, sits, and begins to roll a cigarette.* MICK *stands still.*
> *Pause.*
> *A drip sounds in the bucket. They all look up.*
> *Pause.*

How did you get on at Wembley?

DAVIES. Well, I didn't get down there.

> *Pause.*

No. I couldn't make it.

> MICK *goes to the door and exits.*

ASTON. I had a bit of bad luck with that jig saw. When I got there it had gone.

> *Pause.*

DAVIES. Who was that feller?

ASTON. He's my brother.

DAVIES. Is he? He's a bit of a joker, en'he?

ASTON. Uh.

DAVIES. Yes . . . he's a real joker.

ASTON. He's got a sense of humour.

DAVIES. Yes, I noticed.

Pause.

He's a real joker, that lad, you can see that.

Pause.

ASTON. Yes, he tends . . . he tends to see the funny side of things.

DAVIES. Well, he's got a sense of humour, en' he?

ASTON. Yes.

DAVIES. Yes, you could tell that.

Pause.

I could tell the first time I saw him he had his own way of looking at things.

ASTON *stands, goes to the sideboard drawer, right, picks up the statue of Buddha, and puts it on the gas stove.*

ASTON. I'm supposed to be doing up the upper part of the house for him.

DAVIES. What . . . you mean . . . you mean it's his house?

ASTON. Yes. I'm supposed to be decorating this landing for him. Make a flat out of it.

DAVIES. What does he do, then?

ASTON. He's in the building trade. He's got his own van.

DAVIES. He don't live here, do he?

ASTON. Once I get that shed up outside . . . I'll be able to give a bit more thought to the flat, you see. Perhaps I can knock up one or two things for it. (*He walks to the window.*) I can work with my hands, you see. That's one thing I can do. I never knew I could. But I can do all sorts of things now, with my hands. You know, manual things. When I get that shed up out there . . . I'll have a workshop, you see. I . . . could do a bit of woodwork. Simple woodwork, to start. Working with . . . good wood.

Pause.

Of course, there's a lot to be done to this place. What I think, though, I think I'll put in a partition ... in one of the rooms along the landing. I think it'll take it. You know ... they've got these screens ... you know ... Oriental. They break up a room with them. Make it into two parts. I could either do that or I could have a partition. I could knock them up, you see, if I had a workshop.

Pause.

Anyway, I think I've decided on the partition.

Pause.

DAVIES. Eh, look here, I been thinking. This ain't my bag.

ASTON. Oh. No.

DAVIES. No, this ain't my bag. My bag, it was another kind of bag altogether, you see. I know what they've done. What they done, they kept my bag, and they given you another one altogether.

ASTON. No ... what happened was, someone had gone off with your bag.

DAVIES (*rising*). That's what I said!

ASTON. Anyway, I picked that bag up somewhere else. It's got a few ... pieces of clothes in it too. He let me have the whole lot cheap.

DAVIES (*opening the bag*). Any shoes?

    DAVIES *takes two check shirts, bright red and bright green, from the bag. He holds them up.*

Check.

ASTON. Yes.

DAVIES. Yes ... well, I know about these sort of shirts, you see. Shirts like these, they don't go far in the winter-time. I mean, that's one thing I know for a fact. No, what I need, is a kind of a shirt with stripes, a good solid shirt, with stripes going down. That's what I want. (*He takes from the bag a deep-red velvet smoking-jacket.*) What's this?

ASTON. It's a smoking-jacket.

DAVIES. A smoking-jacket? (*He feels it.*) This ain't a bad piece of cloth. I'll see how it fits.

He tries it on.

You ain't got a mirror here, have you?

ASTON. I don't think I have.

DAVIES. Well, it don't fit too bad. How do you think it looks?

ASTON. Looks all right.

DAVIES. Well, I won't say no to this, then.

ASTON *picks up the plug and examines it.*

No, I wouldn't say no to this.

Pause.

ASTON. You could be . . . caretaker here, if you liked.

DAVIES. What?

ASTON. You could . . . look after the place, if you liked . . . you know, the stairs and the landing, the front steps, keep an eye on it. Polish the bells.

DAVIES. Bells?

ASTON. I'll be fixing a few, down by the front door. Brass.

DAVIES. Caretaking, eh?

ASTON. Yes.

DAVIES. Well, I . . . I never done caretaking before, you know . . . I mean to say . . . I never . . . what I mean to say is . . . I never been a caretaker before.

Pause.

ASTON. How do you feel about being one, then?

DAVIES. Well, I reckon . . . Well, I'd have to know . . . you know. . . .

ASTON. What sort of. . . .

DAVIES. Yes, what sort of . . . you know. . . .

Pause.

ASTON. Well, I mean. . . .

DAVIES. I mean, I'd have to . . . I'd have to. . . .

ASTON. Well, I could tell you. . . .

DAVIES. That's . . . that's it . . . you see . . . you get my meaning?

ASTON. When the time comes. . . .

DAVIES. I mean, that's what I'm getting at, you see. . . .

ASTON. More or less exactly what you. . . .

DAVIES. You see, what I mean to say . . . what I'm getting at is . . . I mean, what sort of jobs. . . .

   Pause.

ASTON. Well, there's things like the stairs . . . and the . . . the bells. . . .

DAVIES. But it'd be a matter . . . wouldn't it . . . it'd be a matter of a broom . . . isn't it?

ASTON. Yes, and of course, you'd need a few brushes.

DAVIES. You'd need implements . . . you see . . . you'd need a good few implements. . . .

   ASTON *takes a white overall from a nail over his bed, and shows it to* DAVIES.

ASTON. You could wear this, if you liked.

DAVIES. Well . . . that's nice, en't?

ASTON. It'd keep the dust off.

DAVIES (*putting it on*). Yes, this'd keep the dust off, all right. Well off. Thanks very much, mister.

ASTON. You see, what we could do, we could . . . I could fit a bell at the bottom, outside the front door, with "Caretaker" on it. And you could answer any queries.

DAVIES. Oh, I don't know about that.

ASTON. Why not?

DAVIES. Well, I mean, you don't know who might come up them front steps, do you? I got to be a bit careful.

ASTON. Why, someone after you?

DAVIES. After me? Well, I could have that Scotch git coming looking after me, couldn't I? All I'd do, I'd hear the bell, I'd go down there, open the door, who might be there, any Harry might be there. I could be buggered as easy as that, man. They might be there after my card, I mean look at it, here I am, I only got four stamps, on this card, here it is, look, four stamps, that's all I got, I ain't got any more, that's all I got, they ring the bell called Caretaker, they'd have me in, that's what they'd do, I wouldn't stand a chance. Of course I got plenty of other cards lying about, but they don't know that, and I can't tell them, can I, because then they'd find out I was going about under an assumed name. You see, the name I call myself now, that's not my real name. My real name's not the one I'm using, you see. It's different. You see, the name I go under now ain't my real one. It's assumed.

> *Silence.*
> THE LIGHTS FADE TO BLACKOUT.
> THEN UP TO DIM LIGHT THROUGH THE WINDOW.
> *A door bangs.*
> *Sound of a key in the door of the room.*
> DAVIES *enters, closes the door, and tries the light switch, on, off, on, off.*

DAVIES (*muttering*). What's this? (*He switches on and off.*) What's the matter with this damn light? (*He switches on and off.*) Aaah. Don't tell me the damn light's gone now.
> *Pause.*
What'll I do? Damn light's gone now. Can't see a thing.
> *Pause.*
What'll I do now? (*He moves, stumbles.*) Ah God, what's that? Give me a light. Wait a minute.
> *He feels for matches in his pocket, takes out a box and lights one. The match goes out. The box falls.*
Aah! Where is it? (*Stooping.*) Where's the bloody box?
> *The box is kicked.*
What's that? What? Who's that? What's that?
> *Pause. He moves.*

Where's my box? It was down here. Who's this? Who's moving it?

Silence.

Come on. Who's this? Who's this got my box?

Pause.

Who's in here!

Pause.

I got a knife here. I'm ready. Come on then, who are you?

He moves, stumbles, falls and cries out.

Silence.

A faint whimper from DAVIES. *He gets up.*

All right!

He stands. Heavy breathing.

Suddenly the electrolux starts to hum. A figure moves with it, guiding it. The nozzle moves along the floor after DAVIES, *who skips, dives away from it and falls, breathlessly.*

Ah, ah, ah, ah, ah, ah! Get away-y-y-y-y!

The electrolux stops. The figure jumps on ASTON'S *bed.*

I'm ready for you! I'm . . . I'm . . . I'm here!

The figure takes out the electrolux plug from the light socket and fits the bulb. The light goes on. DAVIES *flattens himself against right wall, knife in hand.* MICK *stands on the bed, holding the plug.*

MICK. I was just doing some spring cleaning. (*He gets down.*) There used to be a wall plug for this electrolux. But it doesn't work. I had to fit it in the light socket. (*He puts the electrolux under* ASTON'S *bed.*) How do you think the place is looking? I gave it a good going over.

Pause.

We take it in turns, once a fortnight, my brother and me, to give the place a thorough going over. I was working late tonight, I only just got here. But I thought I better get on with it, as it's my turn.

Pause.

It's not that I actually live here. I don't. As a matter of fact I live somewhere else. But after all, I'm responsible for the upkeep of the premises, en' I? Can't help being house-proud.

He moves towards DAVIES *and indicates the knife.*

What are you waving that about for?

DAVIES. You come near me. . . .

MICK. I'm sorry if I gave you a start. But I had you in mind too, you know. I mean, my brother's guest. We got to think of your comfort, en't we? Don't want the dust to get up your nose. How long you thinking of staying here, by the way? As a matter of fact, I was going to suggest that we'd lower your rent, make it just a nominal sum, I mean until you get fixed up. Just nominal, that's all.

Pause.

Still, if you're going to be spiky, I'll have to reconsider the whole proposition.

Pause.

Eh, you're not thinking of doing any violence on me, are you? You're not the violent sort, are you?

DAVIES (*vehemently*). I keep myself to myself, mate. But if anyone starts with me though, they know what they got coming.

MICK. I can believe that.

DAVIES. You do. I been all over, see? You understand my meaning? I don't mind a bit of a joke now and then, but anyone'll tell you . . . that no one starts anything with me.

MICK. I get what you mean, yes.

DAVIES. I can be pushed so far . . . but. . . .

MICK. No further.

DAVIES. That's it.

MICK sits on junk down right.

What you doing?

MICK. No, I just want to say that . . . I'm very impressed
by that.

DAVIES. Eh?

MICK. I'm very impressed by what you've just said.

Pause.

Yes, that's impressive, that is.

Pause.

I'm impressed, anyway.

DAVIES. You know what I'm talking about then?

MICK. Yes, I know. I think we understand one another.

DAVIES. Uh? Well . . . I'll tell you . . . I'd . . . I'd like
to think that. You been playing me about, you know. I don't
know why. I never done you no harm.

MICK. No, you know what it was? We just got off on the wrong
foot. That's all it was.

DAVIES. Ay, we did.

DAVIES *joins* MICK *in junk.*

MICK. Like a sandwich?

DAVIES. What?

MICK (*taking a sandwich from his pocket*). Have one of these.

DAVIES. Don't you pull anything.

MICK. No, you're still not understanding me. I can't help
being interested in any friend of my brother's. I mean,
you're my brother's friend, aren't you?

DAVIES. Well, I . . . I wouldn't put it as far as that.

MICK. Don't you find him friendly, then?

DAVIES. Well, I wouldn't say we was all that friends. I mean,
he done me no harm, but I wouldn't say he was any particular friend of mine. What's in that sandwich, then?

MICK. Cheese.

DAVIES. That'll do me.

MICK. Take one.

DAVIES. Thank you, mister.

MICK. I'm sorry to hear my brother's not very friendly.

DAVIES. He's friendly, he's friendly, I didn't say he wasn't. . . .

MICK (*taking a salt-cellar from his pocket*). Salt?

DAVIES. No thanks. (*He munches the sandwich.*) I just can't exactly . . . make him out.

MICK (*feeling in his pocket*). I forgot the pepper.

DAVIES. Just can't get the hang of him, that's all.

MICK. I had a bit of beetroot somewhere. Must have mislaid it.

   Pause.

   DAVIES *chews the sandwich.* MICK *watches him eat. He then rises and strolls downstage.*

Uuh . . . listen . . . can I ask your advice? I mean, you're a man of the world. Can I ask your advice about something?

DAVIES. You go right ahead.

MICK. Well, what it is, you see, I'm . . . I'm a bit worried about my brother.

DAVIES. Your brother?

MICK. Yes . . . you see, his trouble is. . . .

DAVIES. What?

MICK. Well, it's not a very nice thing to say. . . .

DAVIES (*rising, coming downstage*). Go on now, you say it.

   MICK *looks at him.*

MICK. He doesn't like work.

   Pause.

DAVIES. Go on!

MICK. No, he just doesn't like work, that's his trouble.

DAVIES. Is that a fact?

MICK. It's a terrible thing to have to say about your own brother.

DAVIES. Ay.

MICK. He's just shy of it. Very shy of it.

DAVIES. I know that sort.

MICK. You know the type?

DAVIES. I've met them.

MICK. I mean, I want to get him going in the world.

DAVIES. Stands to reason, man.

MICK. If you got an older brother you want to push him on, you want to see him make his way. Can't have him idle, he's only doing himself harm. That's what I say.

DAVIES. Yes.

MICK. But he won't buckle down to the job.

DAVIES. He don't like work.

MICK. Work shy.

DAVIES. Sounds like it to me.

MICK. You've met the type, have you?

DAVIES. Me? I know that sort.

MICK. Yes.

DAVIES. I know that sort. I've met them.

MICK. Causing me great anxiety. You see, I'm a working man: I'm a tradesman. I've got my own van.

DAVIES. Is that a fact?

MICK. He's supposed to be doing a little job for me . . . I keep him here to do a little job . . . but I don't know . . . I'm coming to the conclusion he's a slow worker.

Pause.

What would your advice be?

DAVIES. Well . . . he's a funny bloke, your brother.

MICK. What?

DAVIES. I was saying, he's . . . he's a bit of a funny bloke, your brother.

MICK *stares at him.*

MICK. Funny? Why?

DAVIES. Well . . . he's funny. . . .

MICK. What's funny about him?

Pause.

DAVIES. Not liking work.

MICK. What's funny about that?

DAVIES. Nothing.

Pause.

MICK. I don't call it funny.

DAVIES. Nor me.

MICK. You don't want to start getting hypercritical.

DAVIES. No, no, I wasn't that, I wasn't . . . I was only saying. . . .

MICK. Don't get too glib.

DAVIES. Look, all I meant was—

MICK. Cut it! (*Briskly.*) Look! I got a proposition to make to you. I'm thinking of taking over the running of this place, you see? I think it could be run a bit more efficiently. I got a lot of ideas, a lot of plans. (*He eyes* DAVIES.) How would you like to stay on here, as caretaker?

DAVIES. What?

MICK. I'll be quite open with you. I could rely on a man like you around the place, keeping an eye on things.

DAVIES. Well now . . . wait a minute . . . I . . . I ain't never done no caretaking before, you know. . . .

MICK. Doesn't matter about that. It's just that you look a capable sort of man to me.

DAVIES. I am a capable sort of man. I mean to say, I've had plenty offers in my time, you know, there's no getting away from that.

MICK. Well, I could see before, when you took out that knife, that you wouldn't let anyone mess you about.

DAVIES. No one messes me about, man.

MICK. I mean, you've been in the services, haven't you?

DAVIES. The what?

MICK. You been in the services. You can tell by your stance.

DAVIES. Oh . . . yes. Spent half my life there, man. Overseas . . . like . . . serving . . . I was.

MICK. In the colonies, weren't you?

DAVIES. I was over there. I was one of the first over there.

MICK. That's it. You're just the man I been looking for.

DAVIES. What for?

MICK. Caretaker.

DAVIES. Yes, well . . . look . . . listen . . . who's the landlord here, him or you?

MICK. Me. I am. I got deeds to prove it.

DAVIES. Ah . . . (*Decisively.*) Well listen, I don't mind doing a bit of caretaking, I wouldn't mind looking after the place for you.

MICK. Of course, we'd come to a small financial agreement, mutually beneficial.

DAVIES. I leave you to reckon that out, like.

MICK. Thanks. There's only one thing.

DAVIES. What's that?

MICK. Can you give me any references?

DAVIES. Eh?

MICK. Just to satisfy my solicitor.

DAVIES. I got plenty of references. All I got to do is to go down to Sidcup tomorrow. I got all the references I want down there.

MICK. Where's that?

DAVIES. Sidcup. He ain't only got my references down there, he got all my papers down there. I know that place like the back of my hand. I'm going down there anyway, see what I mean, I got to get down there, or I'm done.

MICK. So we can always get hold of these references if we want them.

DAVIES. I'll be down there any day, I tell you. I was going down today, but I'm . . . I'm waiting for the weather to break.

MICK. Ah.

DAVIES. Listen. You can't pick me up a pair of good shoes, can you? I got a bad need for a good pair of shoes. I can't get anywhere without a pair of good shoes, see? Do you think there's any chance of you being able to pick me up a pair?

THE LIGHTS FADE TO BLACKOUT.

LIGHTS UP. *Morning.*

ASTON *is pulling on his trousers over long underwear. A slight grimace. He looks around at the head of his bed, takes a towel from the rail and waves it about. He pulls it down, goes to* DAVIES *and wakes him.* DAVIES *sits up abruptly.*

ASTON. You said you wanted me to get you up.

DAVIES. What for?

ASTON. You said you were thinking of going to Sidcup.

DAVIES. Ay, that'd be a good thing, if I got there.

ASTON. Doesn't look much of a day.

DAVIES. Ay, well, that's shot it, en't it?

ASTON. I . . . I didn't have a very good night again.

DAVIES. I slept terrible.

Pause.

ASTON. You were making. . . .

DAVIES. Terrible. Had a bit of rain in the night, didn't it?

ASTON. Just a bit.

He goes to his bed, picks up a small plank and begins to sand- paper it.

DAVIES. Thought so. Come in on my head.

Pause.

Draught's blowing right in on my head, anyway.

Pause.

Can't you close that window behind that sack?

ASTON. You could.

DAVIES. Well then, what about it, then? The rain's coming right in on my head.

ASTON. Got to have a bit of air.

DAVIES *gets out of bed. He is wearing his trousers, waistcoat* and vest.

DAVIES (*putting on his sandals*). Listen. I've lived all my life in the air, boy. You don't have to tell me about air. What I'm saying is, there's too much air coming in that window when I'm asleep.

ASTON. Gets very stuffy in here without that window open.

ASTON *crosses to the chair, puts the plank on it, and continues sandpapering.*

DAVIES. Yes, but listen, you don't know what I'm telling you. That bloody rain, man, come right in on my head. Spoils my sleep. I could catch my death of cold with it, with that draught. That's all I'm saying. Just shut that window and no one's going to catch any colds, that's all I'm saying.

Pause.

ASTON. I couldn't sleep in here without that window open.

DAVIES. Yes, but what about me? What . . . what you got to say about my position?

ASTON. Why don't you sleep the other way round?

DAVIES. What do you mean?

ASTON. Sleep with your feet to the window.

DAVIES. What good would that do?

ASTON. The rain wouldn't come in on your head.

DAVIES. No, I couldn't do that. I couldn't do that.

Pause.

I mean, I got used to sleeping this way. It isn't me has to change, it's that window. You see, it's raining now. Look at it. It's coming down now.

Pause.

ASTON. I think I'll have a walk down to Goldhawk Road. I got talking to a man there. He had a saw bench. It looked in pretty good condition to me. Don't think it's much good to him.

Pause.

Have a walk down there, I think.

DAVIES. Listen to that. That's done my trip to Sidcup. Eh, what about closing that window now? It'll be coming in here.

ASTON. Close it for the time being.

DAVIES *closes the window and looks out.*

DAVIES. What's all that under that tarpaulin out there?

ASTON. Wood.

DAVIES. What for?

ASTON. To build my shed.

DAVIES *sits on his bed.*

DAVIES. You haven't come across that pair of shoes you was going to look out for me, have you?

ASTON. Oh. No. I'll see if I can pick some up today.

DAVIES. I can't go out in this with these, can I? I can't even go out and get a cup of tea.

ASTON. There's a café just along the road.

DAVIES. There may be, mate.

During ASTON'S *speech the room grows darker.*
By the close of the speech only ASTON *can be seen clearly.*
DAVIES *and all the other objects are in the shadow. The fade-down of the light must be as gradual, as protracted and as unobtrusive as possible.*

ASTON. I used to go there quite a bit. Oh, years ago now. But I stopped. I used to like that place. Spent quite a bit of time in there. That was before I went away. Just before. I think that . . . place had a lot to do with it. They were all . . . a good bit older than me. But they always used to listen. I thought . . . they understood what I said. I mean I used to talk to them. I talked too much. That was my mistake. The same in the factory. Standing there, or in the breaks, I used to . . . talk about things. And these men, they used to listen, whenever I . . . had anything to say. It was all right. The trouble was, I used to have kind of hallucinations.

They weren't hallucinations, they . . . I used to get the feeling I could see things . . . very clearly . . . everything . . . was so clear . . . everything used . . . everything used to get very quiet . . . everything got very quiet . . . all this . . . quiet . . . and . . . this clear sight . . . it was . . . but maybe I was wrong. Anyway, someone must have said something. I didn't know anything about it. And . . . some kind of lie must have got around. And this lie went round. I thought people started being funny. In that café. The factory. I couldn't understand it. Then one day they took me to a hospital, right outside London. They . . . got me there. I didn't want to go. Anyway . . . I tried to get out, quite a few times. But . . . it wasn't very easy. They asked me questions, in there. Got me in and asked me all sorts of questions. Well, I told them . . . when they wanted to know . . . what my thoughts were. Hmmnn. Then one day . . . this man . . . doctor, I suppose . . . the head one . . . he was quite a man of . . . distinction . . . although I wasn't so sure about that. He called me in. He said . . . he told me I had something. He said they'd concluded their examination. That's what he said. And he showed me a pile of papers and he said that I'd got some-thing, some complaint. He said . . . he just said that, you see. You've got . . . this thing. That's your complaint. And we've decided, he said, that in your interests there's only one course we can take. He said . . . but I can't . . . exactly remember . . . how he put it . . . he said, we're going to do something to your brain. He said . . . if we don't, you'll be in here for the rest of your life, but if we do, you stand a chance. You can go out, he said, and live like the others. What do you want to do to my brain, I said to him. But he just repeated what he'd said. Well, I wasn't a fool. I knew I was a minor. I knew he couldn't do anything to me without getting permission. I knew he had to get permission from my mother. So I wrote to her and told her what they were trying to do. But she signed their form, you see, giving them permission. I know that because he showed me her signature when I brought it up. Well, that night I tried to escape, that night. I spent five hours sawing at one of the bars on the window in this ward. Right throughout the dark. They used to shine a torch over the beds every half hour. So I timed it just right. And then it was nearly done, and a man had a ... he had a fit, right next to me. And they caught me, anyway. About a week later they started to come round and do this thing to the brain. We were all supposed to have it done, in this ward. And they came round and did it one at a time. One a night. I was one of the last. And I could see quite clearly what they did to the others. They used to come round with these ... I don't know what they were ... they looked like big pincers, with wires on, the wires were attached to a little machine. It was electric. They used to hold the man down, and this chief ... the chief doctor, used to fit the pincers, something like earphones, he used to fit them on either side of the man's skull. There was a man holding the machine, you see, and he'd ... turn it on, and the chief would just press these pincers on either side of the skull and keep them there. Then he'd take them off. They'd cover the man up ... and they wouldn't touch him again until later on. Some used to put up a fight, but most of them didn't. They just lay there. Well, they were coming round to me, and the night they came I got up and stood against the wall. They told me to get on the bed, and I knew they had to get me on the bed because if they did it while I was standing up they might break my spine. So I stood up and then one or two of them came for me, well, I was younger then, I was much stronger than I am now, I was quite strong then, I laid one of them out and I had another one round the throat, and then suddenly this chief had these pincers on my skull and I knew he wasn't supposed to do it while I was standing up, that's why I . . . . . anyway, he did it. So I did get out. I got out of the place . . . but I couldn't walk very well. I don't think my spine was damaged. That was perfectly all right. The trouble was . . . my thoughts . . . had become very slow . . . I couldn't think at all . . . I couldn't . . . get . . . my thoughts . . . together . . . uuuhh . . . I could . . . never quite get it . . . together. The trouble was, I couldn't hear what people were saying. I couldn't look to the right or the left, I had to look straight in front of me, because if I turned my head round . . . I couldn't keep . . . upright. And I had these headaches. I used to sit in my room. That was when I lived with my mother. And my brother. He was younger than me. And I laid everything out, in order, in my room, all the things I knew were mine, but I didn't die. The thing is, I should have been dead. I should have died. Anyway, I feel much better now. But I don't talk to people now. I steer clear of places like that café. I never go into them now. I don't talk to anyone . . . like that. I've often thought of going back and trying to find the man who did that to me. But I want to do something first. I want to build that shed out in the garden.

Curtain

Act Three

Two weeks later.
   MICK is lying on the floor, down left, his head resting on the
   rolled carpet, looking up at the ceiling.
   DAVIES is sitting in the chair, holding his pipe. He is wearing
   the smoking jacket. It is afternoon.
   Silence.

DAVIES. I got a feeling he's done something to them cracks.
   Pause.
   See, there's been plenty of rain in the last week, but it ain't
   been dripping into the bucket.
   Pause.
   He must have tarred it over up there.
   Pause.
   There was someone walking about on the roof the other
   night. It must have been him.
   Pause.
   But I got a feeling he's tarred it over on the roof up there.
   Ain't said a word to me about it. Don't say a word to me.
   Pause.
   He don't answer me when I talk to him.
   He lights a match, holds it to his pipe, and blows it.
   He don't give me no knife!
   Pause.
   He don't give me no knife to cut my bread.
   Pause.
   How can I cut a loaf of bread without no knife?
   Pause.
   It's an impossibility.

Pause.

MICK. You've got a knife.

DAVIES. What?

MICK. You've got a knife.

DAVIES. I got a knife, sure I got a knife, but how do you expect me to cut a good loaf of bread with that? That's not a bread-knife. It's nothing to do with cutting bread. I picked it up somewhere. I don't know where it's been, do I? No, what I want—

MICK. I know what you want.

Pause. DAVIES *rises and goes to the gas stove.*

DAVIES. What about this gas stove? He tells me it's not connected. How do I know it's not connected? Here I am, I'm sleeping right with it, I wake up in the middle of the night, I'm looking right into the oven, man! It's right next to my face, how do I know, I could be lying there in bed, it might blow up, it might do me harm!

Pause.

But he don't seem to take any notice of what I say to him. I told him the other day, see, I told him about them Blacks, about them Blacks coming up from next door, and using the lavatory. I told him, it was all dirty in there, all the banisters were dirty, they were black, all the lavatory was black. But what did he do? He's supposed to be in charge of it here, he had nothing to say, he hadn't got a word to say.

Pause.

Couple of weeks ago . . . he sat there, he give me a long chat . . . about a couple of weeks ago. A long chat he give me. Since then he ain't said hardly a word. He went on talking there . . . I don't know what he was . . . he wasn't looking at me, he wasn't talking to me, he don't care about me. He was talking to himself! That's all he worries about. I mean, you come up to me, you ask my advice, he wouldn't never do a thing like that. I mean, we don't have any conversation, you see? You can't live in the same room with someone who . . . who don't have any conversation with you.

Pause.

I just can't get the hang of him.

Pause.

You and me, we could get this place going.

MICK (*ruminatively*). Yes, you're quite right. Look what I could do with this place.

Pause.

I could turn this place into a penthouse. For instance . . . this room. This room you could have as the kitchen. Right size, nice window, sun comes in. I'd have . . . I'd have teal-blue, copper and parchment linoleum squares. I'd have those colours re-echoed in the walls. I'd offset the kitchen units with charcoal-grey worktops. Plenty of room for cupboards for the crockery. We'd have a small wall cupboard, a large wall cupboard, a corner wall cupboard with revolving shelves. You wouldn't be short of cupboards. You could put the dining-room across the landing, see? Yes. Venetian blinds on the window, cork floor, cork tiles. You could have an off-white pile linen rug, a table in . . . in afromosia teak veneer, sideboard with matt black drawers, curved chairs with cushioned seats, armchairs in oatmeal tweed, a beech frame settee with a woven sea-grass seat, white-topped heat-resistant coffee table, white tile surround. Yes. Then the bedroom. What's a bedroom? It's a retreat. It's a place to go for rest and peace. So you want quiet decoration. The lighting functional. Furniture . . . mahogany and rosewood. Deep azure-blue carpet, unglazed blue and white curtains, a bedspread with a pattern of small blue roses on a white ground, dressing-table with a lift-up top containing a plastic tray, table lamp of white raffia . . . (MICK *sits up.*) it wouldn't be a flat it'd be a palace.

DAVIES. I'd say it would, man.

MICK. A palace.

DAVIES. Who would live there?

MICK. I would. My brother and me.

Pause.

DAVIES. What about me?

MICK (*quietly*). All this junk here, it's no good to anyone. It's just a lot of old iron, that's all. Clobber. You couldn't make a home out of this. There's no way you could arrange it. It's junk. He could never sell it, either, he wouldn't get tuppence for it.

Pause.

Junk.

Pause.

But he doesn't seem to be interested in what I got in mind, that's the trouble. Why don't you have a chat with him, see if he's interested?

DAVIES. Me?

MICK. Yes. You're a friend of his.

DAVIES. He's no friend of mine.

MICK. You're living in the same room with him, en't you?

DAVIES. He's no friend of mine. You don't know where you are with him. I mean, with a bloke like you, you know where you are.

MICK *looks at him.*

I mean, you got your own ways, I'm not saying you ain't got your own ways, anyone can see that. You may have some funny ways, but that's the same with all of us, but with him it's different, see? I mean at least with you, the thing with you is you're . . .

MICK. Straightforward.

DAVIES. That's it, you're straightforward.

MICK. Yes.

DAVIES. But with him, you don't know what he's up to half the time!

MICK. Uh.

DAVIES. He's got no feelings!

Pause.

See, what I need is a clock! I need a clock to tell the time! How can I tell the time without a clock? I can't do it! I said to him, I said, look here, what about getting in a clock, so's I can tell what time it is? I mean, if you can't tell what time you're at you don't know where you are, you understand my meaning? See, what I got to do now, if I'm walking about outside, I got to get my eye on a clock, and keep the time in my head for when I come in. But that's no good, I mean I'm not in here five minutes and I forgotten it. I forgotten what time it was!

DAVIES *walks up and down the room.*

Look at it this way. If I don't feel well I have a bit of a lay down, then, when I wake up, I don't know what time it is to go and have a cup of tea! You see, it's not so bad when I'm coming in. I can see the clock on the corner, the moment I'm stepping into the house I know what the time is, but when I'm *in*! It's when I'm *in* . . . that I haven't the foggiest idea what time it is!

Pause.

No, what I need is a clock in here, in this room, and then I stand a bit of a chance. But he don't give me one.

DAVIES *sits in the chair.*

He wakes me up! He wakes me up in the middle of the night! Tells me I'm making noises! I tell you I've half a mind to give him a mouthful one of these days.

MICK. He don't let you sleep?

DAVIES. He don't let me sleep! He wakes me up!

MICK. That's terrible.

DAVIES. I been plenty of other places. They always let

me sleep. It's the same the whole world over. Except here.

MICK. Sleep's essential. I've always said that.

DAVIES. You're right, it's essential. I get up in the morning, I'm worn out! I got business to see to. I got to move myself, I got to sort myself out, I got to get fixed up. But when I wake up in the morning, I ain't got no energy in me. And on top of that I ain't got no clock.

MICK. Yes.

DAVIES (*standing, moving*). He goes out, I don't know where he goes to, where's he go, he never tells me. We used to have a bit of a chat, not any more. I never see him, he goes out, he comes in late, next thing I know he's shoving me about in the middle of the night.

Pause.

Listen! I wake up in the morning . . . I wake up in the morning and he's smiling at me! He's standing there, looking at me, smiling! I can see him, you see, I can see him through the blanket. He puts on his coat, he turns himself round, he looks down at my bed, there's a smile on his face! What the hell's he smiling at? What he don't know is that I'm watching him through that blanket. He don't know that! He don't know I can see him, he thinks I'm asleep, but I got my eye on him all the time through the blanket, see? But he don't know that! He just looks at me and he smiles, but he don't know that I can see him doing it!

Pause.

(*Bending, close to* MICK.) No, what you want to do, you want to speak to him, see? I got . . . I got that worked out. You want to tell him . . . that we got ideas for this place, we could build it up, we could get it started. You see, I could decorate it out for you, I could give you a hand in doing it . . . between us.

Pause.

Where do you live now, then?

MICK. Me? Oh, I've got a little place. Not bad. Everything

laid on. You must come up and have a drink some time. Listen to some Tchaikovsky.

DAVIES. No, you see, you're the bloke who wants to talk to him. I mean, you're his brother.

Pause.

MICK. Yes . . . maybe I will.

A door bangs.

MICK *rises, goes to the door and exits.*

DAVIES. Where you going? This is him!

Silence.

DAVIES *stands, then goes to the window and looks out.*

ASTON *enters. He is carrying a paper bag. He takes off his overcoat, opens the bag and takes out a pair of shoes.*

ASTON. Pair of shoes.

DAVIES (*turning*). What?

ASTON. I picked them up. Try them.

DAVIES. Shoes? What sort?

ASTON. They might do you.

DAVIES *comes down stage, takes off his sandals and tries the shoes on. He walks about, waggling his feet, bends, and presses the leather.*

DAVIES. No, they're not right.

ASTON. Aren't they?

DAVIES. No, they don't fit.

ASTON. Mmnn.

Pause.

DAVIES. Well, I'll tell you what, they might do . . . until I get another pair.

Pause.

Where's the laces?

ASTON. No laces.

DAVIES. I can't wear them without laces.

ASTON. I just got the shoes.

DAVIES. Well now, look that puts the lid on it, don't it? I mean, you couldn't keep these shoes on right without a pair of laces. The only way to keep a pair of shoes on, if you haven't got no laces, is to tighten the foot, see? Walk about with a tight foot, see? Well, that's no good for the foot. Puts a bad strain on the foot. If you can do the shoes up proper there's less chance of you getting a strain.

ASTON *goes round to the top of his bed.*

ASTON. I might have some somewhere.

DAVIES. You see what I'm getting at?

Pause.

ASTON. Here's some. (*He hands them to* DAVIES.)

DAVIES. These are brown.

ASTON. That's all I got.

DAVIES. These shoes are black.

ASTON *does not answer.*

Well, they can do, anyway, until I get another pair.

DAVIES *sits in the chair and begins to lace his shoes.*

Maybe they'll get me down to Sidcup tomorrow. If I get down there I'll be able to sort myself out.

Pause.

I've been offered a good job. Man has offered it to me, he's ... he's got plenty of ideas. He's got a bit of a future. But they want my papers, you see, they want my references. I'd have to get down to Sidcup before I could get hold of them. That's where they are, see. Trouble is, getting there. That's my problem. The weather's dead against it.

ASTON *quietly exits, unnoticed.*

Don't know as these shoes'll be much good. It's a hard road, I been down there before. Coming the other way, like. Last time I left there, it was ... last time ... getting on a while back ... the road was bad, the rain was coming down, lucky I didn't die there on the road, but I got here, I kept going, all along . . . yes . . . I kept going all along. But all the same, I can't go on like this, what I got to do, I got to get back there, find this man—

He turns and looks about the room.

Christ! That bastard, he ain't even listening to me!

BLACKOUT.
DIM LIGHT THROUGH THE WINDOW.
It is night. ASTON *and* DAVIES *are in bed,* DAVIES *groaning.* ASTON *sits up, gets out of bed, switches on the light, goes over to* DAVIES *and shakes him.*

ASTON. Hey, stop it, will you? I can't sleep.

DAVIES. What? What? What's going on?

ASTON. You're making noises.

DAVIES. I'm an old man, what do you expect me to do, stop breathing?

ASTON. You're making noises.

DAVIES. What do you expect me to do, stop breathing?

ASTON *goes to his bed, and puts on his trousers.*

ASTON. I'll get a bit of air.

DAVIES. What do you expect me to do? I tell you, mate, I'm not surprised they took you in. Waking an old man up in the middle of the night, you must be off your nut! Giving me bad dreams, who's responsible, then, for me having bad dreams? If you wouldn't keep mucking me about I wouldn't make no noises! How do you expect me to sleep peaceful when you keep poking me all the time? What do you want me to do, stop breathing?

He throws the cover off and gets out of bed, wearing his vest, waistcoat and trousers.

It's getting so freezing in here I have to keep my trousers on to go to bed. I never done that before in my life. But that's what I got to do here. Just because you won't put in any bleeding heating! I've had just about enough with you mucking me about. I've seen better days than you have, man. Nobody ever got me inside one of them places, anyway. I'm a sane man! So don't you start mucking me about. I'll be all right as long as you keep your place. Just you keep your place, that's all. Because I can tell you, your brother's got his eye on you. He knows all about you. I got a friend there, don't you worry about that. I got a true pal there. Treating me like dirt! Why'd you invite me in here in the first place if you was going to treat me like this? You think you're better than me you got another think coming. I know enough. They had you inside one of them places before, they can have you inside again. Your brother's got his eye on you! They can put the pincers on your head again, man! They can have them on again! Any time. All they got to do is get the word. They'd carry you in there, boy. They'd come here and pick you up and carry you in! They'd keep you fixed! They'd put them pincers on your head, they'd have you fixed! They'd take one look at all this junk I got to sleep with they'd know you were a creamer. That was the greatest mistake they made, you take my tip, letting you get out of that place. Nobody knows what you're at, you go out you come in, nobody knows what you're at! Well, nobody messes me about for long. You think I'm going to do your dirty work? Haaaaahhhhh! You better think again! You want me to do all the dirty work all up and down them stairs just so I can sleep in this lousy filthy hole every night? Not me, boy. Not for you boy. You don't know what you're doing half the time. You're up the creek! You're half off! You can tell it by looking at you. Who ever saw you slip me a few bob? Treating me like a bloody animal! I never been inside a nuthouse!

ASTON *makes a slight move towards him.* DAVIES *takes his knife from his back pocket.*

Don't come nothing with me, mate. I got this here. I used it. I used it. Don't come it with me.

A pause. They stare at each other.

Mind what you do now.

Pause.

Don't you try anything with me.

Pause.

ASTON. I . . . I think it's about time you found somewhere else. I don't think we're hitting it off.

DAVIES. Find somewhere else?

ASTON. Yes.

DAVIES. Me? You talking to me? Not me, man! You!

ASTON. What?

DAVIES. You! You better find somewhere else!

ASTON. I live here. You don't.

DAVIES. Don't I? Well, I live here. I been offered a job here.

ASTON. Yes . . . well, I don't think you're really suitable.

DAVIES. Not suitable? Well, I can tell you, there's someone here thinks I am suitable. And I'll tell you. I'm staying on here as caretaker! Get it! Your brother, he's told me, see, he's told me the job is mine. Mine! So that's where I am. I'm going to be his caretaker.

ASTON. My brother?

DAVIES. He's staying, he's going to run this place, and I'm staying with him.

ASTON. Look. If I give you . . . a few bob you can get down to Sidcup.

DAVIES. You build your shed first! A few bob! When I can earn a steady wage here! You build your stinking shed first! That's what!

ASTON stares at him.

ASTON. That's not a stinking shed.

Silence.

ASTON moves to him.

It's clean. It's all good wood. I'll get it up. No trouble.

DAVIES. Don't come too near!

ASTON. You've no reason to call that shed stinking.

    DAVIES *points the knife.*

You stink.

DAVIES. What!

ASTON. You've been stinking the place out.

DAVIES. Christ, you say that to me!

ASTON. For days. That's one reason I can't sleep.

DAVIES. You call me that! You call me stinking!

ASTON. You better go.

DAVIES. I'LL STINK YOU!

    He thrusts his arm out, the arm trembling, the knife pointing
    at ASTON'S *stomach.* ASTON *does not move. Silence.*
    DAVIES' *arm moves no further. They stand.*

I'll stink you. . . .

    Pause.

ASTON. Get your stuff.

    DAVIES *draws the knife in to his chest, breathing heavily.*
    ASTON *goes to* DAVIES' *bed, collects his bag and puts a few*
    of DAVIES' *things into it.*

DAVIES. You ain't . . . you ain't got the right . . . Leave
that alone, that's mine!

    DAVIES *takes the bag and presses the contents down.*

All right . . . I been offered a job here . . . you wait . . .
(*He puts on his smoking-jacket.*) . . you wait . . . your
brother . . . he'll sort you out . . . you call me that . . .
you call me that . . . no one's ever called me that ·. .
(*He puts on his overcoat.*) You'll be sorry you called me that
. . . . you ain't heard the last of this . . . (*He picks up his*
bag and goes to the door.) You'll be sorry you called me
that. . . .

    He opens the door, ASTON *watching him.*

Now I know who I can trust.

DAVIES *goes out.* ASTON *stands.*

BLACKOUT.

LIGHTS UP. *Early evening.*

Voices on the stairs.

MICK *and* DAVIES *enter.*

DAVIES. Stink! You hear that! Me! I told you what he said, didn't I? Stink! You hear that? That's what he said to me!

MICK. Tch, tch, tch.

DAVIES. That's what he said to me.

MICK. You don't stink.

DAVIES. No, sir!

MICK. If you stank I'd be the first one to tell you.

DAVIES. I told him, I told him he . . . I said to him, you ain't heard the last of this man! I said, don't you forget your brother. I told him you'd be coming along to sort him out. He don't know what he's started, doing that. Doing that to me. I said to him, I said to him, he'll be along, your brother'll be along, he's got sense, not like you—

MICK. What do you mean?

DAVIES. Eh?

MICK. You saying my brother hasn't got any sense?

DAVIES. What? What I'm saying is, you got ideas for this place, all this . . . all this decorating, see? I mean, he's got no right to order me about. I take orders from you, I do my caretaking for you, I mean, you look upon me . . . you don't treat me like a lump of dirt . . . we can both . . . we can both see him for what he is.

Pause.

MICK. What did he say then, when you told him I'd offered you the job as caretaker?

DAVIES. He . . . he said . . . he said . . . something about. . . he lived here.

MICK. Yes, he's got a point, en he?

DAVIES. A point! This is your house, en't? You let him live here!

MICK. I could tell him to go, I suppose.

DAVIES. That's what I'm saying.

MICK. Yes. I could tell him to go. I mean, I'm the landlord. On the other hand, he's the sitting tenant. Giving him notice, you see, what it is, it's a technical matter, that's what it is. It depends how you regard this room. I mean it depends whether you regard this room as furnished or unfurnished. See what I mean?

DAVIES. No, I don't.

MICK. All this furniture, you see, in here, it's all his, except the beds, of course. So what it is, it's a fine legal point, that's what it is.

Pause.

DAVIES. I tell you he should go back where he come from!

MICK (*turning to look at him*). Come from?

DAVIES. Yes.

MICK. Where did he come from?

DAVIES. Well . . . he . . . he. . . .

MICK. You get a bit out of your depth sometimes, don't you?
Pause.
(*Rising, briskly.*) Well, anyway, as things stand, I don't mind having a go at doing up the place. . . .

DAVIES. That's what I wanted to hear!

MICK. No, I don't mind.
He turns to face DAVIES.
But you better be as good as you say you are.

DAVIES. What do you mean?

MICK. Well, you say you're an interior decorator, you'd better be a good one.

DAVIES. A what?

MICK. What do you mean, a what? A decorator. An interior decorator.

DAVIES. Me? What do you mean? I never touched that. I never been that.

MICK. You've never what?

DAVIES. No, no, not me, man. I'm not an interior decorator. I been too busy. Too many other things to do, you see. But I . . . but I could always turn my hand to most things . . . give me . . . give me a bit of time to pick it up.

MICK. I don't want you to pick it up. I want a first-class experienced interior decorator. I thought you were one.

DAVIES. Me? Now wait a minute— wait a minute—you got the wrong man.

MICK. How could I have the wrong man? You're the only man I've spoken to. You're the only man I've told, about my dreams, about my deepest wishes, you're the only one I've told, and I only told you because I understood you were an experienced first-class professional interior and exterior decorator.

DAVIES. Now look here—

MICK. You mean you wouldn't know how to fit teal-blue, copper and parchment linoleum squares and have those colours re-echoed in the walls?

DAVIES. Now, look here, where'd you get—?

MICK. You wouldn't be able to decorate out a table in afro-mosia teak veneer, an armchair in oatmeal tweed and a beech frame settee with a woven sea-grass seat?

DAVIES. I never said that!

MICK. Christ! I must have been under a false impression!

DAVIES. I never said it!

MICK. You're a bloody impostor, mate!

DAVIES. Now you don't want to say that sort of thing to me. You took me on here as caretaker. I was going to give you a helping hand, that's all, for a small . . for a small wage, I never said nothing about that . . . you start calling me names—

MICK. What is your name?

DAVIES. Don't start that—

MICK. No, what's your real name?

DAVIES. My real name's Davies.

MICK. What's the name you go under?

DAVIES. Jenkins!

MICK. You got two names. What about the rest? Eh? Now come on, why did you tell me all this dirt about you being an interior decorator?

DAVIES. I didn't tell you nothing! Won't you listen to what I'm saying?

Pause.

It was him who told you. It was your brother who must have told you. He's nutty! He'd tell you anything, out of spite, he's nutty, he's half way gone, it was him who told you.

MICK walks slowly to him.

MICK. What did you call my brother?

DAVIES. When?

MICK. He's what?

DAVIES. I . . . now get this straight. . . .

MICK. Nutty? Who's nutty?

Pause.

Did you call my brother nutty? My brother. That's a bit of . . . . that's a bit of an impertinent thing to say, isn't it?

DAVIES. But he says so himself!

MICK walks slowly round DAVIES' figure, regarding him, once. He circles him, once.

MICK. What a strange man you are. Aren't you? You're really strange. Ever since you come into this house there's been nothing but trouble. Honest. I can take nothing you say at face value. Every word you speak is open to any number of different interpretations. Most of what you say is lies. You're violent, you're erratic, you're just completely unpredictable. You're nothing else but a wild animal, when you come down to it. You're a barbarian. And to put the old tin lid on it, you stink from arse-hole to breakfast time. Look at it. You come here recommending yourself as an interior decorator, where-upon I take you on, and what happens? You make a long speech about all the references you've got down at Sidcup, and what happens? I haven't noticed you go down to Sidcup to obtain them. It's all most regrettable but it looks as though I'm compelled to pay you off for your caretaking work. Here's half a dollar.

He feels in his pocket, takes out a half-crown and tosses it at DAVIES' *feet.* DAVIES *stands still.* MICK *walks to the gas stove and picks up the Buddha.*

DAVIES (*slowly*). All right then . . . you do that . . . you do it . . . if that's what you want. . . .
MICK. THAT'S WHAT I WANT!
He hurls the Buddha against the gas stove. It breaks.
(*Passionately.*) Anyone would think this house was all I got to worry about. I got plenty of other things I can worry about. I've got other things. I've got plenty of other interests. I've got my own business to build up, haven't I? I got to think about expanding . . . in all directions. I don't stand still. I'm moving about, all the time. I'm moving . . . all the time. I've got to think about the future. I'm not worried about this house. I'm not interested. My brother can worry about it. He can do it up, he can decorate it, he can do what he likes with it. I'm not bothered. I thought I was doing him a favour, letting him live here. He's got his own ideas. Let him have them. I'm going to chuck it in.

Pause.

DAVIES. What about me?

Silence. MICK *does not look at him.*
A door bangs.

Silence. They do not move.

ASTON *comes in. He closes the door, moves into the room and faces* MICK. *They look at each other. Both are smiling, faintly.*

MICK (*beginning to speak to* ASTON). Look. . . uh . . .
He stops, goes to the door and exits. ASTON *leaves the door open, crosses behind* DAVIES, *sees the broken Buddha, and looks at the pieces for a moment. He then goes to his bed, takes off his overcoat, sits, takes the screwdriver and plug and pokes the plug.*

DAVIES. I just come back for my pipe.

ASTON. Oh yes.

DAVIES. I got out and . . . half way down I . . . I suddenly . . . found out . . . you see . . . that I hadn't got my pipe. So I come back to get it. . . .
Pause. He moves to ASTON.
That ain't the same plug, is it, you been . . .?
Pause.
Still can't get anywhere with it, eh?
Pause.
Well, if you . . . persevere, in my opinion, you'll probably . . .
Pause.
Listen. . . .
Pause.
You didn't mean that, did you, about me stinking, did you?
Pause.
Did you? You been a good friend to me. You took me in. You took me in, you didn't ask me no questions, you give me a bed, you been a mate to me. Listen. I been thinking, why I made all them noises, it was because of the draught, see, that draught was on me as I was sleeping, made me make noises without me knowing it, so I been thinking, what I mean to say, if you was to give me your bed, and you have

my bed, there's not all that difference between them, they're the same sort of bed, if I was to have yourn, you sleep, wherever bed you're in, so you have mine, I have yourn, and that'll be all right, I'll be out of the draught, see, I mean, you don't mind a bit of wind, you need a bit of air, I can understand that, you being in that place that time, with all them doctors and all they done, closed up, I know them places, too hot, you see, they're always too hot, I had a peep in one once, nearly suffocated me, so I reckon that'd be the best way out of it, we swap beds, and then we could get down to what we was saying, I'd look after the place for you, I'd keep an eye on it for you, for you, like, not for the other . . . not for . . . for your brother, you see, not for him, for you, I'll be your man, you say the word, just say the word. . . .

    Pause.

What do you think of this I'm saying?

    Pause.

ASTON. No, I like sleeping in this bed.

DAVIES. But you don't understand my meaning!

ASTON. Anyway, that one's my brother's bed.

DAVIES. Your brother?

ASTON. Any time he stays here. This is my bed. It's the only bed I can sleep in.

DAVIES. But your brother's gone! He's gone!

    Pause.

ASTON. No. I couldn't change beds.

DAVIES. But you don't understand my meaning!

ASTON. Anyway, I'm going to be busy. I've got that shed to get up. If I don't get it up now it'll never go up. Until it's up I can't get started.

DAVIES. I'll give you a hand to put up your shed, that's what I'll do!

    Pause.

I'll give you a hand! We'll both put up that shed together! See? Get it done in next to no time! Do you see what I'm saying?

Pause.

ASTON. No. I can get it up myself.
DAVIES. But listen. I'm with you, I'll be here, I'll do it for you!

Pause.

We'll do it together!

Pause.

Christ, we'll change beds!

   ASTON *moves to the window and stands with his back to* DAVIES.

You mean you're throwing me out? You can't do that. Listen man, listen man, I don't mind, you see, I don't mind, I'll stay, I don't mind, I'll tell you what, if you don't want to change beds, we'll keep it as it is, I'll stay in the same bed, maybe if I can get a stronger piece of sacking, like, to go over the window, keep out the draught, that'll do it, what do you say, we'll keep it as it is?

Pause.

ASTON. No.
DAVIES. Why . . . not?

   ASTON *turns to look at him.*

ASTON. You make too much noise.
DAVIES. But . . . but . . . look . . . listen . . . listen here . . . I mean. . . .

   ASTON *turns back to the window.*

What am I going to do?

Pause.

What shall I do?

Pause.

Where am I going to go?
Pause.
If you want me to go . . . I'll go. You just say the word.
Pause.
I'll tell you what though . . . them shoes . . . them shoes
you give me . . . they're working out all right . . . they're
all right. Maybe I could . . . get down. . . .
ASTON *remains still, his back to him, at the window.*
Listen . . . if I . . . got down . . . if I was to . . . get
my papers . . . would you . . . would you let . . . would
you . . . if I got down . . . and got my. . . .

Long silence.

Curtain.

John Osborne

'The birth of the modern British theatre has an actual date, a genuine birthday,' wrote the *New York Post* critic in a review of the 1980 revival of *Look Back in Anger*. That date is 8 May 1956, the premiere performance of the play that launched the Royal Court Theatre and became the dramatic triumph of the decade. *Look Back in Anger* liberated the stage from its preoccupation with the privileged classes and inspired writers to explore social and political issues, including the smouldering resentments of the working class. It symbolized the need for change. Tom Stoppard spoke for a generation of writers who took fire from the exitement it stirred, 'Everybody my age who wanted to write wanted to write plays.' Arnold Wesker turned from film to the theatre because he wanted to address 'the bus driver, the housewife, the miner and the Teddy Boy'.

Osborne's play lashed out against the establishment with such compelling energy that not only fellow writers, but also audiences and critics had to take note. Artistic forms, like entrenched societies, do not yield easily to displacement, yet *Look Back in Anger* seemed to revolutionize the British theatre overnight. Minority quibbles outside, *revolutionize* may not be too strong a word. For Osborne attacked theatrical and social conventions at the same time and managed to shake up both artists and audiences. Unsavoury subjects and gutter language became permissible. Questions that might have seemed closed were really open; attitudes hardened by decades of acceptance could be challenged.

At first, reviewers found Jimmy Porter, Osborne's angry young anti-hero, baffling and sadistic. While they praised the extraordinary vitality of his language and the stunning impact of his seething energies, they couldn't figure out what he was angry about. While the *Evening Standard* critic dismissively concluded that *Look Back in Anger* 'sets up a wailing wall for the latest post-war generation of under-thirties' and achieves 'only the stature of a self-pitying snivel,' Kenneth Tynan saw Jimmy as the compelling voice of a whole lost generation who felt betrayed by their elders.

As early as 1959, however, A.E. Dyson suggested that what Osborne called the 'posh papers' created a myth about Jimmy Porter as an admirable hero taking dead aim against the corruption and hypocrisy of British society in the mid-fifties. But the myth obscures Osborne's profounder irony. For Jimmy Porter is not only 'a warm-hearted idealist raging against the evils of man and the universe, he is also a cruel and even morbid misfit in a group of reasonably normal and well-disposed people'. It is that ironical paradox that gives the play continuing interest.

In fact, by the 1980s, many critics were writing more sweepingly and confidently of the play as a powerful study of the collapse of a whole way of life, as much a frightening and prophetic indictment of the 'psychic and social paralysis' of the rising generation as a denunciation of the status quo. Many critics began to see in Jimmy's respect for his wife's kindly, conservative father a wistfulness for the very values the play seems to attack. *Look Back in Anger* had become 'a classic play' in its 'crystalline, crystallized view of its own special historical moment', reinterpretable, of course, in the light of new insights, like all classic plays.

While the play is caustic about the frustrating social conditions in the England of the fifties, its anti-establishment assaults are generalized and its central character incapable of action. Later playwrights would empower their angry young men to active, often violent, rebellion.

For anyone who has neither seen nor read *Look Back in Anger*, a word about the plot of the play may be helpful. Jimmy Porter, a working-class, university-educated (as Osborne was not) malcontent lives in an odd *ménage à trois* with his wife Alison, daughter of a rich middle-class family, and his amiable friend Cliff, who proclaims with true lower-class bravado, 'Where I come from, we're used to brawling and excitement. Perhaps I enjoy being in it.' Alison, of course, doesn't. And her reaction to the squalid disorder of their dreary bed-sitter and Jimmy's non-stop bullying is the well-bred response of avoidance. She pretends not to notice. Their marriage is a form of class warfare, with Alison the stand-in for everything Jimmy loathes. Eventually, worn down by his insults, she goes home to have her baby. But she comes crawling back to him, apparently willing to grovel for the sake of his vitality. He takes her back with a rare show of tenderness. In the final image of the play they huddle together in a squirrel-and-bear fantasy as if, by hiding in each other, they can escape the ravages of the world outside. For all their childish playacting, they are old, never having been young. Their world's been out of joint all the days of their lives.

It is easy to see why Jimmy quickly became a symbol of the post-World War II youth, who regarded all authority and institutions with suspicion. Like his real life peers, Jimmy discovers his education liberated him into nothing more life-fulfilling than alienation from his roots – he has only a callous contempt for his own past – and an even acuter sense of deprivation than he had as a child pressing his nose longingly against the window of a sweet-shop. The prizes promised by a newly mobile post-war society are still on the other side of the glass. Worse, his idealism, kindled by the philosophy and literature he debated in the ivied halls of Oxbridge, has no focus. Jimmy, in a characteristic diatribe, speaks for the disillusion of his peers:

> There aren't any good, brave causes left. If the big bang does come, and we all get killed off, it won't be in aid of the old-fashioned, grand design. It'll just be for the Brave-new-nothing-very-much-thank-you. About as pointless and inglorious as stepping in front of a bus.

The nostalgia implied in the play's title, the looking back, recurs in Osborne's work. In Jimmy Porter's anger against his parents' generation, the Labour Government they installed, the social order they tolerated, there is a painful sense of loss. Alison's father, who represents the older values, is a kindly decent person whom Jimmy admires in spite of himself. He is secure in his values as Jimmy and Alison never can be, yet clear-eyed enough to see that his daughter's moral ambiguity plays a negative role in her marriage.

Look Back in Anger reasserted the power of passionate speech to energize drama, and showed that an unsympathetic character could compel audience attention; moreover, its depiction of the effects of class conditioning and stunted ambitions on personal relationships foreshadowed themes brilliantly explored further in the plays of Edward Bond. At the same time, the play implied the futility of the moral permissiveness, which succeeded the collapse of traditional values in England and the United States.

The same combination of unheroic characters who have lost their grounding in a relativistic society and a lament for some of the healthy certainties of the past pervades *The Entertainer*, Osborne's requiem for England's former spiritual and political pre-eminence, its death symbolized by the passing of the music-hall tradition.

Archie Rice, a third-rate song-and-dance-man, who tells crude jokes between burleseque numbers in a tawdry music hall, is attractive, like Jimmy Porter, because of the gutsy vitality of his complaints against the world. His father, Billy, an old music-hall entertainer of the World War I era, also brings an engaging energy to life, unlike the younger generation, represented by Archie's passive daughter Jean, who is trapped in a swamp of confusion: 'Why do people like us sit here and just lap it all up, why do boys die or stoke boilers . . . . What's it all in aid of – is it really just for the sake of a gloved hand waving at you from a golden coach?'

That sense of empty geatures, of attitudes and actions drained not only of vitality, but of purpose, is as pervasive in Osborne as despair. It makes his plays melancholic under their corrosive wit and rich theatricality.

Like many of the 'first wave' playwrights, Osborne writes out of the personal experience of emotional as well as material poverty. His father died of tuberculosis when Osborne was still a child. His mother was a pub-keeper from a family of pub-keepers, and reared him in an atmosphere of brawling, rough jokes, and drinking. Osborne was disgusted by the pretensions to lace curtain gentility of both his parents. He was expelled from school at sixteen for slapping the headmaster, then worked at odd jobs before he drifted into the theatre, first as an assistant stage manager, then as actor.

For Osborne's reputation, *Look Back in Anger* has perhaps been too successful. Annointed by critics and theatre historians as a pivotal event in theatre history, it overshadows the more complex and more spectacularly theatrical later plays, among them *A Patriot for Me*.

Osborne is a prolific, multi-talented writer, not a one-play wonder. He has written at least twenty-two plays, a number of television and film scripts, including the Oscar-winning *Tom Jones*. He is a political activist, who crusades for his causes and fulminates against public policy in frequent letters to the *Times*. More flamboyant than many of his peers who share his dislike of critics, he launched a formal campaign against them for treating serious plays trivially. His tirades are as scathing as the vituperations of his characters.

His dramatic style is versatile and inventive. He moved from the essentially conventional naturalism of *Look Back in Anger* to the loosely episodic structure of *The Entertainer*, in which he alternates family scenes with song and dance sequences. *Inadmissible Evidence*, which takes place largely in Bill Maitland's head, has a suffocatingly claustrophobic atmosphere. *Luther* and *A Patriot for Me* have the sweep and pageantry of epic theatre, while the fantasy of his *Plays for England* anticipates Bond's satirical *Early Morning*.

Even though the focus in Osborne's plays sometimes shifts from dislocations in the working class to those in the professional class, the plays remain emotionally powerful lessons in the virtue of feeling. They all cry out against the cool psychic state of the disengaged who are 'dead behind the eyes', unreachable, incapable of connecting with other people, the failed inheritors of a failed world.

Osborne explores the desolation and defeats of such characters in both private and public contexts. The psychic disintegration of Bill Maitland in *Inadmissible Evidence* is intensely private. Like a middle-aged Jimmy Porter, Maitland craves relationships and tries forcibly to elicit the loving responses he is himself incapable of. Of course he fails. His intense narcissism, his terrified self-loathing, explode like Jimmy Porter's into harsh harangues, alienating one by one all those around him, wife, mistress, daughter, co-workers. The play is almost a monodrama, the secondary characters drifting in and out, their dramatic function to occasion the stunning invective which marks the stages in Maitland's mental collapse and makes the play an actor's tour de force. Maitland's growing inability to distinguish between hallucination and reality plunges him into a Kafkesque hell he must ultimately inhabit alone. His contempt for the world shrivels into bewildered despair at his own terrible isolation just at the moment when his nerves seem to come alive to his own and other people's needs – the inadmissible evidence, come too late to save him.

By contrast, the disintegration of army officer Albert Redl in *A Patriot for Me* unfolds in a more public arena. Based on a real life story of a young man of modest origins who worked his way up into the top ranks of the Imperial Austrian Army during the waning days of the Hapsburg Empire, the play traces the private and professional consequences of Redl's insufficiency of character. As in the stories of Jimmy Porter, Bill Maitland and Archie Rice, Osborne here is perversely merciless in his exposure of Redl's weaknesses and follies. He dares audiences not to empathize.

In the very opening scenes, designed to show the young officer's courage and human sympathies, Osborne also carefully plants clues to the psychological vulnerabilities that become the downfall of his protagonist. Redl consents to be the second in a duel, on the side of an unpopular fellow-officer smarting under racial and sexual slurs. But Redl's motives may include a lurking homosexual attraction to his young colleague and conceal a self-serving anti-semitism: attributes likely to antagonize or baffle typical middle-class audiences.

During an interview with his battalion commander, who praises Redl's acceptance into the War College, despite his 'unremarkable background', Redl allows a lie to stand about his racial background. The erosion of his integrity thus set in motion early ends in his vulnerability to blackmail.

In the drag ball sequence, a stunning theatrical scene central to the play, Osborne again risks distancing his audience by showing Redl as a giggling drunk telling silly homosexual in-jokes. By the end of the play, the audience knows him as a politically inadequate traitor, a loser in his personal relationships, reduced to the degradation of lies and strategems, prey to violent impulses that prompt him in the ball scene to strike one of the drag queens and to come close to throttling the waiter who spots him as a homosexual. Nevertheless, Redl engages and sustains audience sympathy. Perhaps that is because the violent gestures seem directed against himself: they express a rage against his inability to control his own nature or to remake the world so he can be himself in it.

The play is not about homosexuality, although that theme, along with Jewishness, is a powerful symbol for the outsider Osborne is studying.

A Patriot for Me is fascinating as a spy thriller, but it is more profoundly a study of homelessness, the homelessness of human beings in a world where society requires conformity to roles that often go against the natural grain of sensitive human creatures who are inadequately adaptive.

The unique strengths of Obsorne as a dramatist begin, of course, with the unique articulacy of his central characters, their resort to insolence as part of their eloquence. The splendid rhetoric of the title character in *Luther*, Osborne's Brechtian epic, develops considerable theatrical power. Even Redl, unusually taciturn through much of *A Patriot for Me*, has several bravura arias that recall the withering scorn of Jimmy Porter. During one of them he hauls his faithless young lover out of bed, thumping his naked body to the floor, and screaming vituperations. He pauses, exhausted. Then, as in the beautiful early duelling scene when he cradles the young officer's dead body in his arms, he embraces the boy tenderly, whispering, 'It's not true . . .'.

Redl's emotional flip-flop is an example of an arresting paradox in Osborne's most memorable characters: that the intransigent verbal eloquence they use to intimidate and bully arises out of the throttled compassion and stifled humaneness of characters who are "queer" in the sense of being always out of their element.

Equally impressive is Osborne's theatricality, the stage imagery that is often as powerful as his language. The pageantry of the ecclesiastical scenes in *Luther* intensifies the bleakness of the scenes in a monastic cell where Luther fights his spiritual battles. In *A Patriot for Me*, the stuffy establishment ball with its bemedalled officers, their bejewelled ladies on their arms, its atmosphere of *ennui* and *noblesse oblige* ironically counterpoints the grotesque drag ball with its garishly masked transvestites in their gaudy costumes rubbing elbows with some of the same military officers so hypocritically correct at the earlier ball. But then almost every scene in the play has a thrilling theatricality: from the duelling scene, which in itself is a fine one-act play in character and emotional power, to the intimate bedroom scenes contrasting Redl's debauchery with his decorous bearing in the public scenes.

The point in *A Patriot for Me* is not the obvious one that homosexuality makes men corruptible, but the far subtler and more universal one that prevailing social attitudes require hypocritical adjustments that undermine psychic stability and threaten selfhood. Those who are good at hypocrisy and evasion may win worldly success, but the price is the self, human-ness, which depends on honest communication with others. The duplicity Redl is forced into costs him his integrity, and eventually his life.

In sum: on the thematic level Osborne paints an alarming picture of a world in which the social order in its political and economic realities, its establishment assumptions and mores, almost inevitably destroys what is alive and humane in people. It is an order in which people cannot find the strength or wisdom necessary to remake it so that it might encourage what is best in human potential or even allow what is natural and healthy. Those within the system lose their souls and their goods, but so do the rebellious deviants. You can't beat this life, according to Osborne. Putting up a good fight is the closest human beings can come to being constructive.

Major Plays

Look Back in Anger, Royal Court Theatre, 1956
The Entertainer, Royal Court Theatre, 1957
Luther, Royal Court Theatre, 1961
Plays for England, Royal Court Theatre, 1962
Inadmissible Evidence, Royal Court Theatre, 1964
A Patriot for Me, Royal Court Theatre, 1965
A Sense of Detachment, Royal Court Theatre, 1972

Selected Bibliography

Allsop, Kenneth. *The Angry Decade*. London: Peter Owen, 1958.

Brown, John R. *Theatre Language: A Study of Arden, Osborne, Pinter, and Wesker*. London: Allen Lane; N.Y.: Taplinger, 1972.

Evans, Gareth Lloyd. *The Language of Modern Drama*. London: Dent; Totowa, N.J.: Rowman and Littlefield, 1977.

Ferrar, Harold, ed. *John Osborne*. N.Y. and London: Columbia University Press, 1973.

Lumley, Frederick. *New Trends in Twentieth Century Drama*. London: Barrie and Rockliffe; N.Y.: Oxford U. Press, 1967.

Nathan, David. 'John Osborne – Is His Anger Simmering?' in *The Curtain Rises*, compiled by David Richards. London: Trewin, 1966.

Osborne, John. *A Better Class of Person, An Autobiography 1929–56*. London: Faber & Faber; N.Y.: Dutton, 1981

Rigg, Diana. *No Turn Unstoned*. London: Elm Tree Books, 1982; Garden City, N.Y.: Doubleday, 1983.

Tynan, Kenneth. *Tynan Right and Left*. London: Longman; N.Y.: Atheneum, 1967.

JOHN OSBORNE

A Patriot for Me

All applications for professional and amateur rights should be addressed to Robin Dalton Associates, c/o Fraser & Dunlop Scripts Ltd, 91 Regent Street, London W1R 8RU.

Characters

ALFRED REDL
AUGUST SICZYNSKI
STEINBAUER
LUDWIG MAX VON KUPFER
LT.-COL. LUDWIG VON MÖHL
ADJUTANT
MAXIMILIAN VON TAUSSIG
ALBRECHT
ANNA
HILDE
STANITSIN
COL. MISCHA OBLENSKY
GEN. CONRAD VON HÖTZENDORF
COUNTESS SOPHIA DELYANOFF
JUDGE ADVOCATE JAROSLAV KUNZ
YOUNG MAN IN CAFÉ
PAUL
BARON VON EPP
FERDY
FIGARO
LT. STEFAN KOVACS
MARIE-ANTOINETTE
TSARINA
LADY GODIVA
DR SCHOEPFER
2ND LT. VIKTOR JERZABEK
ORDERLY
MISCHA LIPSCHUTZ
MITZI HEIGEL
MINISTER
KUPFER'S SECONDS, PRIVATES, WAITERS AT ANNA'S, OFFICERS, WHORES, FLUNKEYS, HOFBURG GUESTS, CAFÉ WAITERS, GROUP AT TABLE, BALL GUESTS, SHEPHERDESSES, BOY, HOTEL WAITERS

A Patriot for Me was first performed at the Royal Court Theatre, Sloane Square, London, on 30 June 1965, by the English Stage Society, by arrangement with the English Stage Company. The cast was as follows:

ALFRED REDL	Maximilian Schell
AUGUST SICZYNSKI	John Castle
STEINBAUER	Rio Fanning
LUDWIG MAX VON KUPFER	Frederick Jaeger
KUPFER'S SECONDS	Lew Luton, Richard Morgan
PRIVATES	Tim Pearce, David Schurmann, Thick Wilson
LT.-COL. LUDWIG VON MÖHL	Clive Morton
ADJUTANT	Timothy Carlton
MAXIMILIAN VON TAUSSIG	Edward Fox
ALBRECHT	Sandor Eles
WAITERS AT ANNA'S	Peter John, Domy Reiter
OFFICERS	Timothy Carlton, Lew Luton, Hal Hamilton, Richard Morgan
WHORES	Dona Martyn, Virginia Wetherell, Jackie Daryl, Sandra Hampton
ANNA	Laurel Mather
HILDE	Jennifer Jayne
STANITSIN	Desmond Perry
COL. MISCHA OBLENSKY	George Murcell
GEN. CONRAD VON HÖTZENDORF	Sebastian Shaw
COUNTESS SOPHIA DELYANOFF	Jill Bennett
JUDGE ADVOCATE JAROSLAV KUNZ	Ferdy Mayne
FLUNKEYS	Jim Forbes, Richard Morgan, Peter John, Timothy Carlton
HOFBURG GUESTS	Cyril Wheeler, Douglas Sheldon, Bryn Bartlett, Dona Martyn, Virginia Wetherell, Jackie Daryl, Sandra Hampton, Laurel Mather
CAFÉ WAITERS	Anthony Roye, Domy Reiter, Bryn Bartlett, Cyril Wheeler
GROUP AT TABLE	Dona Martyn, Laurel Mather,

	Bryn Bartlett, Cyril Wheeler
YOUNG MAN IN CAFÉ	Paul Robert
PAUL	Douglas Sheldon
PRIVATES	Richard Morgan, David Schurmann, Tim Pearce, Thick Wilson
BARON VON EPP	George Devine
FERDY	John Forbes
FIGARO	Thick Wilson
LT. STEFAN KOVACS	Hal Hamilton
MARIE-ANTIONETTE	Lew Luton
TSARINA	Domy Reiter
LADY GODIVA	Peter John
BALL GUESTS	Cyril Wheeler, Richard Morgan, Timothy Carlton, John Castle, Edward Fox, Paul Robert, Douglas Sheldon, Tim Pearce
FLUNKEY	David Schurmann
SHEPHERDESSES	Franco Derosa, Robert Kidd
DR. SHOEPFER	Vernon Dobtcheff
BOY	Franco Derosa
2ND. LT. VIKTOR JERZABEK	Tim Pearce
HOTEL WAITERS	Bryn Bartlett, Lew Luton
ORDERLY	Richard Morgan
MISCHA LIPSCHUTZ	David Schurmann
MITZI HEIGEL	Virginia Wetherell
MINISTER	Anthony Roye
VOICES OF DEPUTIES	Clive Morton, Sebastian Shaw, George Devine, Vernon Dobtcheff, Cyril Wheeler
MUSICAL DIRECTOR	Tibor Kunstler
MUSICIANS	Reg Richman (Bass), Michael Zborowski (Piano), Ray Webb (Guitar)

Directed by ANTHONY PAGE
Décor by JOCELYN HERBERT
Musical adviser JOHN ADDISON

Act One

SCENE ONE

A Gymnasium. Of the Seventh Galician Infantry Regiment at Lemburg, Galicia, 1890. It appears to be empty. From the high windows on one side, the earliest morning light shows up the climbing bars that run from floor to ceiling. From this, a long, thick rope hangs. Silhouetted is a vaulting horse. The lonely, slow tread of one man's boots is heard presently on the harsh floor. A figure appears. At this stage, his features can barely be made out. It is ALFRED REDL, *at this time Lieutenant. He has close cropped hair, a taut, compact body, a moustache. In most scenes he smokes long black cheroots, like Toscanas. On this occasion, he takes out a shabby cigarette case, an elegant amber holder, inserts a cigarette and lights it thoughtfully. He looks up at the window, takes out his watch and waits. It is obvious he imagines himself alone. He settles down in the half light. A shadow crosses his vision.*

REDL. Who's there? (*Pause.*) Who is it? Come on! Hey!

VOICE. Redl?

REDL. Who is it?

VOICE. Yes. I see you now.

REDL. Siczynski? Is it? Siczynski?

A figure appears, PAUL SICZYNSKI. *He is a strong, very handsome young man about the same age as* REDL, *but much more boyish looking.* REDL *already has the stamp of an older man.*

SICZYNSKI. Sorry.

REDL. Not at all.

SICZYNSKI. I startled you.

REDL. Well: we're both early.

SICZYNSKI. Yes.

REDL. Still. Not all that much. Cigarette?

SICZYNSKI *takes one*. REDL *lights it for him*.

Almost light. I couldn't sleep anyway. Could you?

SICZYNSKI (*smiles*). I haven't the style for that. Von Kupfer has though. Expect he's snoozing away now. (*Looks at his watch.*) Being wakened by his servant.

Um?

REDL. He gave a champagne supper at Anna's.

SICZYNSKI. Who was invited?

REDL. Half the garrison, I imagine.

SICZYNSKI. Did you go?

REDL. I'm your second . . .

SICZYNSKI. Is that what prevented you being asked?

REDL. It would have stopped me going.

SICZYNSKI. Well then, he'll have stayed there till the last moment, I should think. Perhaps he'll have been worn down to nothing by one of those strapping Turkish whores.

REDL. I doubt it.

SICZYNSKI. His spine cracked in between those thighs. Snapped. . . . All the way up. No, you're most likely right. *You're* right.

REDL. He's popular: I suppose.

SICZYNSKI. Yes. Unlikeable too.

REDL. Yes. He's a good, what's he, he's a good officer.

SICZYNSKI. He's a gentleman. And adjutant, adjutant mark you, of a field battery at the ripe old age of twenty-one. He's not half the soldier you are.

REDL. Well . . .

SICZYNSKI. And now he's on his way to the War College.

REDL (*quick interest*). Oh?

SICZYNSKI. Of course. If you'd been in his boots, you'd have been in there and out again by this time, you'd be a major at least, by now (*Pause.*) Sorry – didn't mean to rub it in.

REDL. Kupfer. Ludwig Max Von Kupfer . . . it's cold.

SICZYNSKI. Cigarette smoke's warm.

Pause.

REDL. How are you?

SICZYNSKI. Cold.

REDL. Here

SICZYNSKI. Cognac? Your health. Here's to the War College. And you.

REDL. Thank you.

SICZYNSKI. Oh, you will. Get in, I mean. *You* just have to pack in all the effort, while the Kupfers make none at all. He'll be sobering up by now. Putting his aristocratic head under the cold tap and shouting in that authentic Viennese drawl at whoever's picking up after him. You'd better, make it, I mean. Or you'll spend the rest of it in some defeated frontier town with debts. And more debts to look forward to as you go on. Probably the gout.

Pause.

I just hope there isn't ever a war.

They smoke in silence. Slightly shy, tense. SICZYNSKI *leans against the vaulting horse.*

REDL. You may underestimate Kupfer.

SICZYNSKI. Maybe. But then he overestimates himself. *You*'ve tremendous resources, reserves, energy. You won't let any old waters close over your head without a struggle first.

REDL. What about you?

SICZYNSKI (*smiles*). I'm easily disheartened.

REDL. He's destructive, *very* destructive.

SICZYNSKI. Who?

REDL. Kupfer.

SICZYNSKI. Yes, yes. And wilful. Coldly, not too cold, not disinterested.

REDL. That's why I think you underestimate him.

SICZYNSKI. But more vicious than most. you're right there. He's a killer all right.

REDL. Someone'll chalk him up . . . sometime.

SICZYNSKI. What about me?

REDL. That would be very good. Very good.

SICZYNSKI. Just not very likely . . .

REDL. Have you done this before?

SICZYNSKI (*smiles*). No, never. Have you?

REDL. Only as a bystander.

SICZYNSKI. Well, this time you're a participant . . . I'd always expected to *be* challenged a hundred times. I never thought *I'd* do it. Well, picked the right man. Only the wrong swordsman. May I?

He indicates Cognac. REDL *nods.*

Have you seen him?

REDL. Seen? Oh, with a sabre. No. Have you?

SICZYNSKI. No. Have you seen *me*?

REDL. Often.

SICZYNSKI. Well, there it is.

REDL (*softly*). More times than I can think of.

SICZYNSKI. They say only true illiterate minds are obdurate. Well, that's me and Kupfer.

REDL. Why do you feel like this about him? He's not exactly untypical.

SICZYNSKI. Not by any means. For me, well, perhaps he just plays the part better. He makes me want to be sick. Over *him* preferably.

REDL. I don't understand you. You're more than a match for his sort.

SICZYNSKI. I just chose the wrong ground to prove it, here.

Pause.

REDL. Look, Siczynski, why don't I, I'm quite plausible and not half a bad actor, for one . . . reason and another, why don't you let me, sort of . . .

SICZYNSKI. Thank you Redl. You can't do anything now.

REDL. Very well.

SICZYNSKI. Don't be offended.

REDL. Why should I?

SICZYNSKI (*wry*). Someone who looks as good as me ought to be able to handle himself a bit better, don't you agree?

REDL. Yes.

SICZYNSKI. At least – physically. . . . A *little* better don't you think? Why did you agree to be my second?

REDL. Why did you ask me?

SICZYNSKI. I thought you'd agree to. Did you get anyone else?

REDL. Steinbauer.

SICZYNSKI. As a favour to you? No, I didn't think you'd have to be persuaded.

REDL. No.

SICZYNSKI. Mine's gone out.

REDL *offers him a cigarette, from which he takes a light.*

I thought you always smoked those long Italian cigars.

REDL *nods.*

Expensive taste. What is it?

REDL. I was only going to ask you: *are* you a Jew?

SICZYNSKI (*smiles*). Grandmother. Maternal Grandmother. Quite enough though, don't you think? Oh, she became Catholic when she married my Grandfather. Not that she ever took it seriously, any more than him. She'd a good sense of fun, not like the rest of my family. You think it doesn't matter about Kupfer's insult, don't you? Well of course you're right. I don't think it would have mattered *what* he said. Oh, I quite enjoyed his jokes about calling me Rothschild. What *I* objected to, from him, – in the circumstances, was being called Fräulein Rothschild. . . .

REDL. You shouldn't gamble.

SICZYNSKI. I don't.

REDL. On people's goodwill.

SICZYNSKI. I don't. *You* do.

REDL. I do? No, I don't . . . I try not to.

He is confused for a moment. SICZYNSKI *watches him thoughtfully, through his cigarette smoke. It is getting lighter, colder.*

SICZYNSKI. You smell of peppermints.

REDL. Nearly time (*He stands.*)

SICZYNSKI. Kupfer's breath stinks.

REDL. I hadn't noticed.

SICZYNSKI. You mean you haven't got near enough? You don't need to. *He* should chew peppermints.

Pause.

Have some of your brandy.

REDL. Thanks.

SICZYNSKI. It's a cold time to be up, to be up at all.

REDL. I've hardly ever had warm feet. Not since I went to Cadet School.

SICZYNSKI. You work too hard.

REDL. What else can I do?

SICZYNSKI. Sorry. Of course, you're right. I'm just waiting. Can't think much any more.

REDL *would like to help if there were some means. But he can't.*

Go on. If you can, I mean. Don't if you can't . . . Won't be long, now . . .

REDL. We've never talked together much, have we? We must have both been here? What? Two years?

SICZYNSKI. Why couldn't you sleep?

REDL. Don't know. Oh yes, I had a dream . . .

SICZYNSKI. But then you're not what they call sociable, are you?

REDL. Aren't I?

SICZYNSKI. Well! Asking for extra duties, poring over all those manuals.

REDL. You don't make it sound very likeable.

SICZYNSKI. It isn't – much.

REDL *takes out his watch*.

REDL. I told Steinbauer two minutes before. He's pretty reliable.

SICZYNSKI. Anyway, you're taking a risk doing *this*. But I suppose Kupfer will draw the fire.

REDL. And you. You specially.

SICZYNSKI. The Galician Jew, you mean? Yes. But that's only if I win.

REDL. It needn't come to that.

SICZYNSKI. It will.

REDL. I'll see it doesn't.

SICZYNSKI. No, you won't. You can't . . . What, what does one, do you suppose, well, look for in anyone, anyone else, I mean?

REDL. For?

SICZYNSKI. Elsewhere.

REDL. I haven't tried. Or thought about it. At least . . .

SICZYNSKI. I mean: That isn't clearly, really, clearly, already in oneself?

REDL. Nothing, I expect.

Pause.

SICZYNSKI. Tell me about your dream.

REDL. Do you believe in dreams?

SICZYNSKI. Not specially. They're true while they last, I suppose.

REDL. Well, it wasn't –

There is the sound of boots. Walking swiftly, confidently, this time. The two men look at each other.

Steinbauer. On the dot.

STEINBAUER *enters*.

Morning, Steinbauer.

STEINBAUER *nods, slightly embarrassed. Clicks his heels at* SICZYNSKI.

Cold.

STEINBAUER. Yes.

SICZYNSKI. Got the cutlery? Oh, yes I see.

STEINBAUER. All here.

SICZYNSKI. Redl was telling me his dream. Go on.

REDL. It's nothing.

SICZYNSKI. That hardly matters, does it?

REDL. Not really time.

SICZYNSKI. Please.

STEINBAUER *takes out his watch.*

REDL. Just, oh, I was, well later, I was, I won't tell you the first—

SICZYNSKI. Why not?

REDL. It's too dull. So is *this* too. Anyway: I was attending a court martial. Not mine. Someone else's. I don't quite know whose. But a friend of some sort, someone I liked. Someone upright, frank, respected, but upright. It was quite clear from the start what the outcome would be, and I was immediately worrying about having to go and visit him in gaol. And it wasn't just because I knew I would be arrested myself as soon as I got in there. It wasn't for that. Anyhow, there I was, and I went and started to talk to him. He didn't say anything. There was just the wire netting between us . . . and then of course, they arrested *me*. I couldn't tell whether he was pleased or not. They touched me on the shoulder and told me to stand up, which I did. And by that time he'd gone. Somehow.

Sound of several pairs of boots clattering on the unyielding floor into the Gymnasium. REDL *frowns anxiously at* SICZYNSKI, *who smiles at him. As soon as* KUPFER *and his seconds arrive, they get to their feet. Both sides salute each other and prepare for the duel in silence. Sabres are selected. Tunics discarded, etc. All brisk. The duel begins. The four men watch almost indifferently at first. But the spectacle soon strips away this. Blood is drawn, sweat runs, breathing tightens. At one point* REDL *steps forward.* KUPFER *orders him back curtly. All settle down for the end. It comes fairly soon.*

SICZYNSKI *cries out and falls to the ground.* KUPFER *begins dressing almost immediately. He goes out with his companions, who are trying to be composed.*

STEINBAUER. Shall I? Yes, I'd better get the doctor.

REDL. Yes, I suppose so.

STEINBAUER *follows the others out.* REDL *wipes the blood from* SICZYNSKI'S *mouth, cradling him in his arms. He is clearly dead.*

Fade.

SCENE TWO

Office of the Commandant, Seventh Galician Infantry Regiment. The Commandant, LIEUTENANT-COLONEL VON MÖHL, *is seated at his desk. A sharp rap at the door.* VON MÖHL *grunts. The door is opened smartly by the* ADJUTANT.

ADJUTANT. Lieutenant Redl, sir.

REDL *enters, salutes, etc.*

MÖHL. Is Taussig there?

ADJUTANT. Yes, sir.

MÖHL. Good. All right.

ADJUTANT *goes out.*

Redl, Redl, Redl: yes. (*He looks up.*) Sit down, please.

REDL *sits.* MÖHL *scrutinises him.*

Well, Redl. You've quite a good deal of news to come it seems to me. Yes.

REDL. Yes, sir?

MÖHL. You may think that a young officer gets lost among all the others, that he isn't observed, constantly, critically and sympathetically. You might think that an officer with an unremarkable background, or without rather dazzling connections of one sort or another would go unnoticed. Do you think that, Redl?

REDL. Sir, my own experience is that genuine merit rarely goes unnoticed or unrewarded. Even, particularly in the army.

MÖHL. Good. And quite correct, Redl, and for a very obvious reason. The future of the Empire depends on the Army, probably the future of Europe, on an alert, swift machine that can meet instant crisis from whatever quarter it may come. It's taken us a long time to learn our lesson, lessons like Solferino. Expensive, humiliating and inglorious, but worth it now. Only the very best kind of men can be entrusted in the modern army.

He waves at the map of pre-1914 Europe, with Austria-Hungary in the middle, behind him.

No one's going to be passed over, every man'll have his chance to prove himself, show what he could do, given half the chance. I don't say there still aren't short cuts for people who don't apparently deserve it, but that's not for you or me to argue. What we *can* do is make sure the way's made to virgin merit, someone with nothing else. What do you say?

REDL. I'm sure you're right, sir.

MÖHL. Oh?

REDL. It always seems quite clear to me, sir, the officers who complain about privilege are invariably inferior or mediocre.

REDL speaks coolly and carefully. He is anxious to be courteous and respectful without seeming unctuous, or sound a false, fawning note. He succeeds.

MÖHL. Exactly. The real good 'uns don't ever really get left out, that's why so much nonsense is talked, especially about the Army. You can't *afford* to ignore a good man. He's too valuable. A good soldier always knows another one. That's what comradeship is. It's not an empty thing, not an empty thing at all. It's knowing the *value* of other men. And cherishing it. Now: Redl. Two reasons I sent for you. I'll, yes, we'll, I think we'll deal with the best first.

He pauses. REDL *waits.*

As you know, as Commander, it's my duty to recommend officers for War College examination. This year I only felt able to recommend Von Taussig, Von Kupfer, and yourself. The result I can now tell you, after the final examination and interview, is that you have all three been granted admission, a very fine achievement for us all. Four hundred and eighteen candidates for thirty-nine places. Well, Von Taussig has been admitted number twenty-eight, yourself twenty-six and Von Kupfer seventeen. Congratulations.

REDL. Thank you, sir.

MÖHL. Well, I'm very pleased indeed myself, with the result. All three accepted. It's quite something for me too, you know, especially over you. I was pretty sure about the other two, well, of course. . . . But you, well, I knew you had the education, enough . . . There it is. Now you've done it.

REDL. I'm very grateful, sir.

MÖHL. By yourself. You. Number twenty-six! Please. Smoke, if you wish. Here – one of these.

Offers him a cigar. Takes one himself. REDL *lights both of them.*

So: How do you feel?

REDL. Very proud – and grateful, sir.

MÖHL. I don't think you realize, you've made quite an impression. Here, listen to this. Arithmetic, algebra, geometry, trigonometry – all excellent. Elementary engineering, construction, fortification, geography and international law, all eighty-five per cent, all first class. Riding – required standard. That's the only begrudging remark on any of your reports, required standard. Anyway, get that horse out in the school a bit. Yes?

REDL. Yes, sir.

MÖHL. Let's see now, what does it say, do you speak Russian?

REDL. No, sir.

MÖHL. No matter. You will. Native language?

REDL. Ruthenian.

MÖHL. German – excellent. Polish, French – fair. Punctilious knowledge military and international matters. Seems to know Franco-Prussian campaign better than anyone who actually took part. Learned. All the qualities of first-class field officer and an unmistakable flair for intelligence. No. Wait a minute, there's more yet. Upright, discreet, frank and open, painstaking, marked ability to anticipate, as well as initiate instructions, without being reckless, keen judgement, cool under pressure – *that's* Erdmannsdorfer, so that's good, very good indeed – Yes, cool, fine interpreter of the finest modern military thinking. Personality: friendly but unassertive, dignified and strikes everyone as the type of a gentleman and distinguished officer of the Royal and Imperial Army. Well, what do you say?

REDL. I'm overwhelmed, sir.

MÖHL. Well, I like to see this sort of thing happen. Kupfer and Taussig are one thing, and I'm proud of them. But you're another. . . . Yours is effort, effort, concerted, sustained, intelligent effort. Which: brings me to the Siczynski affair. Of course, you realize that if your part in that incident had been made properly known, it would almost certainly have prejudiced your application?

REDL. Yes, sir.

MÖHL. However, we chose to be discreet.

REDL. I'm more grateful than I can tell you, sir.

MÖHL. Well, of course, with Kupfer, it was more difficult.

However, he has been in trouble of this kind before, and, let's be honest about it, he does have advantages. He is able to get away with incidents like Siczynski occasionally, though even he can't do it too often. Of course, he was a principal in this case and you weren't, but I must tell you it was a grave error on your part ever to have consented to become involved in an affair which ends in a brother officer's death. I'm saying this to you as a warning for the future. *Don't* get involved.

REDL. Yes, sir. May I ask where is Lieutenant Von Kupfer, sir?

MÖHL. Temporarily transferred to Wiener Neustadt. . . . Was Siczynski a friend of yours?

REDL. No, sir.

MÖHL. What was your opinion of him?

REDL. I hardly knew him, sir. (*Realizes quickly he needs to provide more than this.*) He struck me as being hyper-critical, over-sceptical about things.

MÖHL. What things?

REDL. Army life and traditions, esprit—

MÖHL. Religion?

REDL. We never discussed it. But – yes, I suspect so, I should think . . .

MÖHL. Jewish . . . ?

REDL. Yes, sir. I believe.

MÖHL. Galician, like yourself.

REDL. Yes.

MÖHL. You're yes, Catholic, of course.

REDL. Yes, sir.

MÖHL. What about women?

REDL. Siczynski?

Nod from MÖHL.

As I say, I didn't know him well.

MÖHL. But?

REDL. I never thought of him, no one seemed to, as a ladies' man.

MÖHL. Precisely. Yet he was very attractive, physically, wouldn't you say?

REDL. That's a hard question for another man to answer –

MÖHL. Oh, come, Redl, you know what women are attracted –

REDL. Yes. Of course, I should say he was, quite certainly.

MÖHL. But you never heard of any particular girl or girls?

REDL. No. But then, we weren't exactly, and I don't –

MÖHL. You are a popular officer – Redl – Siczynski wasn't. He had debts, too. And quite hefty ones. Oh, one expects all young officers to have debts. It's always been so, and always will, till they pay soldiers properly. Every other week, a fund has to be raised for this one or that. Fine. But this officer had, or so it seems, and frankly it doesn't surprise me, no friends, was in the hands of moneylenders, of his own race, naturally, and why? Women? Of course, one asks. But who? No one knows. No family. Who was worth nine thousand kronen in debts.

REDL. Nine . . .

MÖHL. Do you think I can find out? It *is* odd, after all. Young officer, apparently attractive in many ways, work excellent, intelligence exceptional, diligent, manly disposition and all the rest of it. Then: where are you?

REDL. Perhaps? – I don't think he was ever in his right element.

MÖHL. Well. There it is. Incident closed now, including your part in it.

REDL. Thank you, sir.

MÖHL. Only remember. Involvement. Debts – well, you'll be all right. Also, you have friends, and *will* have. As for women, I think you know what you're doing.

REDL. I hope so, sir.

MÖHL. What about marriage?

REDL. I'm not contemplating it, not for quite some time, that is.

MÖHL. Good. You've got ideals and courage and fortitude, and I'm proud and delighted you'll be going from this regiment to War College. You're on your way, Redl. Taussig!

ADJUTANT *enters.*

Send in Taussig.

ADJUTANT *clicks heels. Enter* TAUSSIG *presently.*

Ah, Taussig. Come in. You know Redl. You two should have something to celebrate together tonight.

Fade.

SCENE THREE

ANNA'S. *A private cubicle. In the background a gipsy orchestra, and flash young officers eating, drinking, swearing, singing, entertaining* ANNA'S *young ladies.* REDL *is alone in the cubicle. He leans forward, scoops a champagne bottle from its bucket to pour himself another glass. It is empty. He draws the curtain aside and bawls into the smoke and noise.*

REDL. Anna! Anna! Hey! You! What's your name?! Max! Leo! Anna! Damn!

He gives up. Looks in his tunic for his cigar case. Takes one out, a long black Italian cheroot. A YOUNG WAITER *enters.*

Ah, there you are. Thank God. Another – please. Oh – you've got it. That's clever.

WAITER. I guessed you'd be wanting another, sir.

REDL. Good fellow. Open it, would you?

WAITER. At once, sir.

REDL. Which one are you then?

WAITER. Which one, sir?

REDL. You're not Leo or that other stumpy creature, what's his name –

WAITER. I am Albrecht, sir.

REDL. You're new then.

WAITER. Seven months, sir.

REDL. Oh. I didn't notice you.

WAITER. You don't often do us the honour, sir.

REDL. Light this for me.

> WAITER *does so*.

I can't afford time for this sort of caper very often.

WAITER. What a magnificent cigar case, sir.

REDL. What? Oh. Yes. Present. From my uncle.

WAITER. Very fine indeed. Shall I pour it now?

REDL. Yes.

WAITER. Pol Roger eighty-one, sir.

REDL (*shortly*). Fine.

WAITER. Would that be crocodile, sir?

REDL. Eh? Oh. Yes. Have you seen my guest anywhere among that mob?

WAITER. Lieutenant Taussig, sir?

REDL. Well, who else?

WAITER. He is talking with Madame Anna.

> REDL *sips his champagne. The* WAITER *has increased his restless, uneasy mood. He can't bring himself to dismiss him yet.*

REDL. Rowdy, roaring mob you've got in here.

WAITER. Yes, sir.

REDL. Why do they have to make such a damned show? Howling and vomiting or whoring.

> *They listen.*

Drunk. . . . Why do they need to get so drunk?

WAITER. End of the summer manoeuvres they tell me, sir. Always the same then.

REDL. This place'll get put out of bounds one day. Someone should warn Anna.

WAITER. I think she just does her best to please the young officers, sir. Giving them what they ask for.

REDL. They'll get it too, and no mistake. What's that young officer's name?

WAITER. Which one, sir? Oh, with the red-haired girl, Hilde – yes, Lieutenant Steinbauer, sir.

REDL. So it is.

WAITER. Very beautiful girl, sir.

REDL. Yes.

WAITER. Very popular, that one.

REDL. Garbage often is.

WAITER. That's true too, of course, sir.

Pause.

REDL. Taussig! Where the hell is he?

WAITER. Shall I tell him you want him, sir?

REDL. No. Better not. I'm getting bored sitting here on my own.

WAITER. Can I do anything else, sir?

REDL. No. (*Detaining him.*) Do you remember Kupfer?

WAITER. Lieutenant Kupfer? Oh yes, he used to be in here nearly every night, sometimes when he shouldn't have been. We were sorry when he was re-posted.

REDL. And Lieutenant Sicynski? Do you remember him?

WAITER. No, sir, I don't.

REDL. You don't come from Lemberg?

WAITER. No, sir. From Vienna. Oh, you mean the one who was killed in the duel? He used to come in sometimes, usually on his own. But no one seemed to take much notice of him. He didn't exactly avail himself of the place. Like Lieutenant Kupfer. *He* used to have this cubicle regularly.

REDL. You must miss Vienna.

WAITER. I do, sir. There are always so many different things to do *there*. In Lemberg everybody knows who you are and everything about you. . . . Well, no doubt you'll be in Vienna yourself before long. May I congratulate you, sir?

REDL. Thank you.

WAITER. On the General Staff, I've no doubt, sir.

REDL. We'll see.

A roar and banging of tables.

What the devil's going on?

WAITER. Lieutenant Steinbauer has passed out, sir. They're passing him over their heads . . . One by one . . . Now he's being sick. I'd better go.

REDL. Well, he's better off: see someone takes him home, if you can.

WAITER. I'll do my best, sir. So, as I say, you'll soon be seeing for yourself.

REDL. What?

WAITER. Why, Vienna.

REDL. Oh. All I'll see is work. Maps, tactical field work, riding drill, Russian language, maps.

WAITER. Oh, of course.

REDL. That'll be enough for me.

WAITER. Yes, sir.

Pause. Enter TAUSSIG.

TAUSSIG. Well, I've fixed us up.

REDL. What?

TAUSSIG. Girls. One each. I've been arguing ten minutes with Anna, and she insisted she'd only got one spare, that lovely great black gipsy with the mole on her cheek. There.

WAITER. Zoe.

TAUSSIG. That's the one. So I said to her, I know she's a big girl, but I know my friend Lieutenant Redl won't go much on sharing, especially on an occasion like this evening.

REDL. Please forget it. I'm bored with the place.

TAUSSIG. So am I. We'll take another, oh, you've got another, we'll take some more champagne upstairs with us and be entertained properly, me by big black Zoe, and you, you my friend by Hilde. And very lucky you are, double lucky, because she was tied up by young Steinbauer until a few moments ago, but he's now safely on his face in the cellar, he won't be capable of fulfilling his little engagement tonight, he'll be lucky to stand up on parade in the morning, and Hilde, . ., pale, vacant and booked this moment by me is all yours.

REDL. It doesn't matter.

TAUSSIG. Of course, it doesn't. It's all fixed. Fixed by me and paid for.

REDL. Taussig, I can't allow it.

TAUSSIG. Nonsense. It's done.

WAITER *pours champagne.* TAUSSIG *drinks.*

You insisted on buying the dinner and champagne. And now, *more* champagne. Now, *I* insist on treating you. Your health.

He glances quickly at the WAITER.

To black Zoe and her gipsy mole. And Hilde and her red whatever special she's got in there. Drink up.

REDL *drinks.*

(*To* WAITER.) What are *you* standing about for?

REDL. He was opening the champagne.

TAUSSIG. Well, take another one up. On *my* bill.

REDL. Are you sure?

TAUSSIG. Of course I'm sure. We're going to need it. Come on, I'm glad to see you smoking a cigar again. Can't stand the smell of those peppermints. I've always wanted to tell you. I say, that's a pretty classy case.

REDL. My uncle.

TAUSSIG. I didn't know you had rich relatives.

REDL. Only him.

TAUSSIG. Perhaps I should have let you pay for Hilde yourself.

REDL. Of course. Please.

TAUSSIG. Unless you *would* have preferred Zoe. Sharing, I mean.

REDL. Hilde sounds just the thing.

TAUSSIG. I think she's more your type. Bit on the skinny side.

No bottom, little tiny bottom, not a real roly-poly. And breasts made like our friend here. Go on, go and get that other bottle!

REDL (*to* WAITER). Just a moment.

TAUSSIG. I'll round them up.

Pause.

Don't be all night then.

REDL. Just coming.

He goes to his wallet, trying not to be awkward. He hands a note to the WAITER.

WAITER. Thank you, sir.

He lights a match for REDL, *who looks up. Then notices his cigar is out.*

REDL. Oh, yes.

WAITER. Shall I take this bottle up then, sir?

REDL. Yes. Wait a minute.

WAITER *pauses.*

Pour me another glass.

He does so. Picks up bucket.

WAITER. Good night, sir.

REDL. Good night.

The WAITER *goes out.* REDL *stares into his glass, then drains it, fastens his tunic smartly and steps through the curtain into the tumult.*

Fade.

SCENE FOUR

ANNA'S. *An upstairs room. Bare save for a bed. Lying on it are*

HILDE *and* REDL. *Only the outline of their bodies is visible. In the darkness* REDL's *cigar glows. Silence. Then there is an occasional noise from one of the other rooms.*

HILDE (*whispers*). Hullo. (*Pause.*) Hullo.

REDL. Yes.

HILDE. Alfred! Can't you sleep?

REDL. No. I'm not tired.

HILDE. You slept a little. Oh, not for long. Can I get you anything?

REDL. No thank you.

HILDE. You clench your teeth. Did you know that?

REDL. No.

HILDE. When you're asleep. It makes quite a noise. Scraping together.

REDL. I'm sorry.

HILDE. Oh, please. I didn't mean that. But it'll wear your teeth down. And you've got such nice teeth. You smell of peppermints. Can I put the light on?

REDL. It's your room.

HILDE. It's yours tonight.

She lights the lamp.

Some men's mouths are disgusting.

REDL. I'm sure.

HILDE. You look better. You almost fainted. Can't I get you anything? (*Pause.*) Is there any champagne left?

He pours her some from beside the bed.

Don't often get champagne brought me. Well, here's to Vienna. Wish I was going.

REDL. Why don't you?

HILDE. I shall, I'm saving up.

REDL. What will you do—the same thing—when you get there?

HILDE. I suppose so. Do you know, your eyes are like mine?

REDL. Are they?

HILDE. I've never seen a man faint before.

REDL. You should be in the army. Do you want to get married?

HILDE (*softly*). Yes. Of course. Why? Are you proposing?

REDL. I've seen what you've got to offer.

HILDE. Only just. I'm sorry.

REDL. What about?

HILDE. You don't like me.

REDL. What *are* you on about?

HILDE. Never mind. More warm champagne, please.

He pours.

REDL. What do you mean? Eh?

HILDE. Nothing. Thank you. God bless. And I hope you'll, you'll be happy in Vienna.

REDL. I'm sorry. Those exams and things have taken it out of me. Perhaps I'll come back tomorrow.

HILDE. Was Lietenant Siczynski a friend of yours?

REDL. No. Why, did you know him?

HILDE. I used to see him.

REDL. Did he –

HILDE. No. Not with anyone. He usually sat on his own in a corner, reading the foreign papers or just drinking. I used to look at his eyes. But he never looked at me.

REDL *leans over the bed and kisses her lingeringly. She returns the embrace abstractedly. He looks down at her.*

Peppermints!

REDL. Damn it! I apologized, didn't I?

HILDE. *And* cigars. That's what you smell of, and horses and saddles. What could be nicer, and more manly?

REDL. You're very, very pretty, Hilde. I love your red hair.

HILDE. You don't have to make love to me, Alfred. I'm only a whore.

REDL. But I mean it.

HILDE. Hired by your friend.

REDL. Pretty little, brittle bones.

REDL. Lieutenant Taussig.

REDL. Is that him, next door?

HILDE (*listens*). At this moment, I should say.

They listen.

Is he a good friend of yours?

REDL. I can't say I'd call anyone I know a good friend.

HILDE. Are you sure you can't sleep?

REDL. Yes . . . But why don't you?

HILDE. May I put my head on your arm?

REDL. If you wish . . .

HILDE. No, I'll finish my champagne. Do you like children?

REDL. Yes. Why?

HILDE. Would you like some of your own?

REDL. Very much. Wouldn't you?

HILDE. Yes, I would.

REDL. Then what's stopping you?

HILDE. One would like to be loved, if it's possible.

REDL. Love's hardly ever possible.

HILDE. Do you believe that?

REDL. Yes. Anyway, there are always too many babies being born. So –

HILDE. You may be right. Perhaps that's why you're in the army.

REDL. What's the matter with you? I'm in the army because it suits *me* and I'm suited to *it*. I can make my own future. I can style it my own way.

HILDE. What about Siczynski?

REDL. He wasn't suited to it. Who's in that other room, there?

HILDE. Albrecht . . . Would you like to go?

REDL. No. I just asked a question, that's all. Albrecht who?

HILDE. The waiter you were talking to while I was with the young lieutenant.

Pause.

REDL. He's a noisy fellow.

HILDE. Or whoever's with him.

They listen. She watches REDL'*s face.*

Your cigar's gone out. Here. He always gets the pick, Albrecht. Anything he wants. Anyone.

She moves over to the wall and pulls back a flap and looks through.

Come here.

REDL. What for?

But he joins her.

HILDE. Do you want to look?

He hesitates, then does so. She returns to the bed, empties the champagne into her glass, and watches him. Presently, he turns away and sits on the bed. She puts her arm round his shoulder. Offers him drink.

Have some?

He shakes his head.

Sad?

REDL. No. Not sad. One always just wishes that a congenial evening had been – even more congenial.

HILDE. Think I'll go to bed. It's made me sleepy again.

REDL *listens.*

Shall I turn the light out?

He nods. She does so. He goes to the window and looks out. Presently –

Good night, Alfred.

REDL. Good night, Hilde.

HILDE. Sorry. I can't keep awake. But you don't mind . . .

He looks across at her, puts on his tunic, takes out a bank note, picks up his cap.

REDL. Good night, Hilde. Thank you.

He presses the note into her hand.

HILDE. I'll tell your friend you left in time for reveille.

He turns.

Alfred –

She sits up and kisses him lightly.

You have the most beautiful mouth that ever, ever kissed me. Good night, Lieutenant.

REDL. Good night.

HILDE (*sleepily*). You'll be a colonel one day. On the General Staff. Or even a general.

He gazes down at her, re-lights his cigar. The noise from the adjoining room has subsided. He slips out.

Fade.

SCENE FIVE

Warsaw. A darkened office. The light from a magic lantern shines white on a blank screen which faces the audience. A figure is seen to be operating it. Another, seated in front of it, is watching the screen. The first figure is LIEUTENANT STANITSIN. *The second* COLONEL OBLENSKY.

OBLENSKY. Next!

STANITSIN. Redl.

REDL's photograph in uniform on the screen.

Alfred Von Redl. Captain. Seventh Galician Infantry Regiment. Lemberg. Born Lemberg March 4th, 1864. Family background: parents Leopold and Marthe Redl. Eighth of eleven children. Father ex-horse trooper, now second-grade clerical worker Royal and Imperial Railway. Religion: Catholic. Education: Cadet School, passed out with honours. Equitation school.

OBLENSKY. Oh, do get to the meat, Stanitsin. I want my dinner.

STANITSIN (*flustered slightly*). Oh – just –

OBLENSKY. If there is any. They're not a very promising lot this time, are they?

STANITSIN. Passed out of War College May of last year, number twenty-three of his entry, recommended particularly, on pink paper, recommended.

OBLENSKY (*turns head*). So it is. Meticulous.

STANITSIN. For appointment on General Staff.

OBLENSKY. Yes.

STANITSIN. Health: periodic asthma while at Cadet School, twice almost leading to his discharge. However, in the past ten years, this complaint seems to have been almost completely overcome. Contracted syphilis two and a half years ago, underwent treatment and discharged Lemberg Military Hospital. One serious breach of discipline, involved in duel when fellow officer was killed. Acted as one of the officer's seconds. Affair hushed up and Redl reprimanded. Otherwise unblemished record sheet. Present duty: shortly returned from nine months on staff of Military Attaché in St. Petersburg, ostensibly learning Russian language.

OBLENSKY. Probably all he did do. That's all *ours* do in Vienna. Pick up German in that atrocious, affected accent. I don't know why either of us bothers to observe – just young officers going to diplomatic functions, learning the language painstakingly, like an English governess, and about as well, and not a secret in sight. Most of them just came back like Redl, with the clap at least, or someone else's crabs. Well?

STANITSIN. Waiting for new posting. Financial affairs: No source of income apart from army pay. Although he seems to have invented a fond uncle who occasionally gives him fancy presents or gratuities, of whom there is no trace. Debts, not exactly serious, are considerable. They include: tailor, the biggest trade debt, outstanding accounts at various cafés, restaurants, bootmakers, livery, wine merchants and cigar –

OBLENSKY. Oh, come along, friend. What else?

STANITSIN. Not much. Two moneylenders, small, Fink, Miklas also.

OBLENSKY. Oh – Miklas. I know him. How much?

STANITSIN. Together, some twenty-two hundred kronen.

OBLENSKY. Yes?

STANITSIN. He is also negotiating the lease of a thirdfloor apartment in the Eighth District.

OBLENSKY. Yes?

STANITSIN. That's about it.

OBLENSKY. Personal?

STANITSIN. Studious. Popular with fellow officers.

OBLENSKY. Oh, come along: women?

STANITSIN. Occasionally. Nothing sustained.

OBLENSKY. Spare time?

STANITSIN. Work mostly. Otherwise cafés, reading foreign newspapers, drinking with friends.

OBLENSKY. All army?

STANITSIN. Mostly.

OBLENSKY. Languages?

STANITSIN. Ruthenian native. Polish, German, some French.

OBLENSKY. And Russian. Some. Yes?

STANITSIN. I'm sorry?

OBLENSKY. What else? If anything?

STANITSIN. That's all, sir.

OBLENSKY. All right. Clever, brilliant officer, unpromising background. Ambitious. Bit extravagant . Popular. Diligent. What do you want to do?

STANITSIN. Continue surveillance, sir?

OBLENSKY. Unpromising lot. Very well. Get me a drink. Ah – good. Redl. Yes. All right. Background: nil. Prospects of brilliant military career exceptional. What he needs now, at this exact stage, is a good, advantageous marriage. An heiress is the ideal. But a rich widow would do even better. He probably needs someone specially adroit socially, a good listener, sympathetic, a woman other men are pleased to call a friend and mean it. Experienced. He knows what he wants, I dare say. He just needs someone to unobtrusively provide the right elements . . . Perhaps we should think about it . . . Anyway, remind me – sometime next week. Right. Come on then. Next!

STANITSIN. Kupfer.

REDL's *photograph is switched abruptly from the screen and replaced by* KUPFER's.

Kupfer. Ludwig Max Von Kupfer. Major.

Fade.

SCENE SIX

A terrace in the Hofburg, the Emperor's residence in Vienna. Through the french windows, naturally, is where the court ball is going on, with the aristocracy, diplomatic corps, officers of the Royal and Imperial Army, flunkeys, etc. Talking to VON MÖHL *is the Chief of the General staff, General* CONRAD VON HÖTZENDORF.

MÖHL. Haven't been here for years.
HÖTZENDORF. Oh?
MÖHL. It's good to be back.
HÖTZENDORF. I'm sure.
MÖHL. There's nowhere quite like it, really, is there?
HÖTZENDORF. No. There's not.
MÖHL. Not where I've been, anyway. What about you, General?
HÖTZENDORF. No, no I don't think so.
MÖHL. I haven't been here since, oh, well, when was it, well I

was a young captain, and I was in the Railway Bureau.

HÖTZENDORF. Were you?

MÖHL. Wiry. I could bend, do anything. Like a willow. Where's your wife, General? Would you like me –

HÖTZENDORF. No. She's all right. She's somewhere . . . Paris, that's the nearest to it, I suppose.

MÖHL. Yes.

HÖTZENDORF. But really, altogether different.

MÖHL. Entirely.

HÖTZENDORF. In Vienna, well, everyone is bourgeois, or whatever it is, and a good thing too, everyone, the beggars in the street, kitchen maids, the aristocracy and, let's be honest, the Emperor.

MÖHL. Yes.

HÖTZENDORF. And they all of them enjoy themselves. In Paris, well, in my experience, they're all pretending to be bohemians, from top to bottom, and all the time, every one of them are tradesmen. Well, I don't think you're a real bohemian if you've one eye – or *both* eyes in the case of Paris – on the cash box.

MÖHL. Quite.

HÖTZENDORF. Yes. That's Paris. That's the French. Trouble with Vienna: seems to have old age built into it.

MÖHL. Still that's better than moving on to God knows what, *and* in such an ugly way, like Prussia, for instance.

HÖTZENDORF. Yes. Or England. Even more. They'll soon wreck it. Prussians *are* efficient. English wilful. There *is* a difference. Still, all *we* do is celebrate and congratulate ourselves on saving Europe from the infidel.

MÖHL. I know . . . There's little credit for it.

HÖTZENDORF. Still. It *was* a long time ago.

MÖHL. Redl!

He hails REDL *from the ballroom, who appears.*

Redl, my dear boy! What a pleasant surprise. General, may

I? Captain Alfred Redl: General Von Hötzendorf.

They acknowledge.

Since I last saw you, Redl, I now have the honour of working on the General's staff.

REDL. Indeed, sir. Congratulations.

MÖHL. Redl was just about the finest young officer, all round, when I was commandant in Lemberg, for eleven years.

HÖTZENDORF. So you told me. Who was the very pretty young lady you were dancing with?

REDL. I'm sorry, sir, which one?

MÖHL. Hah! Which *one*!

HÖTZENDORF. Small-boned, dark, brown eyes.

REDL. Miss Ursula Kunz, sir.

HÖTZENDORF. Kunz?

MÖHL. Ah, Kunz. Miss Kunz, youngest daughter of Judge Advocate Jaroslaw Kunz.

HÖTZENDORF. Ah.

MÖHL. Good man. Very.

HÖTZENDORF. Is he?

MÖHL. Seems to be.

HÖTZENDORF. Would you agree, Redl?

REDL. I, sir? From the little I know, and have been able to observe reliably, he is very competent indeed.

HÖTZENDORF. No more?

REDL. Accomplished, too . . . Unpopular.

HÖTZENDORF. Why?

REDL. I don't know, sir.

HÖTZENDORF. I believe it. Something odd, don't know what.

MÖHL. Well – yes . . . But how useful.

HÖTZENDORF. Oh, yes. Useful. Remember what Radetsky said about General Haynau? He said about Haynau, let's see: 'He's my best general all right, but he's like a razor. When you've used him, put him back in his case'.

MÖHL. The General was talking about Vienna, Redl. Well –

How are *you* enjoying it?

REDL. Very much, sir.

MÖHL. Better than St. Petersburg?

REDL. The Russians find it very difficult to enjoy life. Although they *do* manage occasionally.

HÖTZENDORF. Yes. Yes, but, you know, this is a great place to do *nothing*, sit in a café, and dream, listen to the city, *do nothing* and not even anticipate regretting it.

MÖHL. Ah, there's friend Kunz.

HÖTZENDORF. Who? Where?

MÖHL. With the Countess Delyanoff.

HÖTZENDORF. So he is.

MÖHL. You know her?

HÖTZENDORF. Just.

MÖHL. I think they're coming out here.

HÖTZENDORF (*to* REDL). . . . . Sort of woman, know her – ?

REDL *shakes his head*.

Well, the sort of woman who looks at you for five minutes without a word and then says 'what do you think about Shakespeare?' Or, something like that. Unbelievable.

MÖHL. Ah, Kunz! Countess.

Enter MAJOR JAROSLAW KUNZ *and the* COUNTESS SOPHIA DELYANOFF.

We were just watching you.

MÖHL *makes the introductions, leaving* REDL *till last*.

COUNTESS. We've met before.

REDL. Forgive me –

COUNTESS. Oh, yes. Not once, but at least three times. You were on General Hauser's staff in St. Petersburg, and a short spell in Prague, were you not?

REDL. I'm sorry.

COUNTESS. Please. I'm sure you had no eye –

MÖHL. Oh, come, Countess, I can't think of anyone more likely to get his eye fixed on someone like you. You're being unfair.

COUNTESS. No. I think not. But I forgive him.

A FLUNKEY *presents glasses of champagne.*

MÖHL. The General and I were just talking about Vienna.

KUNZ. Yes.

MÖHL. We were just saying – there's nowhere quite like it.

KUNZ. No. You've been away some time, I believe, Colonel. Where was it?

MÖHL. Przemysl.

KUNZ. Przemysl. Ah yes, with all the fortifications.

MÖHL. Four twelve-inch howitzers, some nine- and some six-inch, forty battalions, four squadrons, forty-three artillery companies, eight sapper companies – oh, please forgive me.

KUNZ. Yes. Nowhere quite like Przemysl, in fact.

COUNTESS. I'm afraid I simply can't understand the army, or why any man is ever in it.

HÖTZENDORF. Nor should you. The army's like nothing else. It goes beyond religion. It serves everyone and everyone serves it, even Hungarians and Jews. It conscripts, but it calls the best men out, men who'd never otherwise have been called on.

KUNZ. I think perhaps it's a little like living in the eighteenth century; the army. Apart from Przemysl, that is. Still that *is* a Viennese speciality? Don't you think, General?

HÖTZENDORF. I see nothing about the eighteenth century that makes me believe the nineteenth was any better. And what makes *you* think that the twentieth will be an improvement?

KUNZ. But why do you assume *I* should think it would be?

COUNTESS. I don't think I could ever have been a soldier. I'd want to be a stranger in a street, a key on a concierge's board, inaccessable if I wanted.

MÖHL. But that's what a *soldier* is.

COUNTESS. Only at the cost of his identity. Wouldn't you say, Captain? (*To* REDL.)

REDL. I think the General's right. The army creates an élite.

COUNTESS. No. I believe *it* is created. The army. It can't change. And it is changed from outside.

MÖHL. Nothing else trains a man –

KUNZ. Aptitudes, aptitudes at the expense of character.

COUNTESS. But it can, in its own way, provide a context of expression for people, who wouldn't otherwise have it.

KUNZ. I can only say, Countess, you can have met very few soldiers.

COUNTESS. You're quite wrong, Major. Why, look at me now. Several hundred guests and who am I with? The Chief of the General Staff himself, a distinguished Colonel from Przemysl, a Judge Advocate Major from Vienna and a splendid young Captain. And how different you all are, each one of you. I must say: I can't think of anything more admirable than not having to play a part.

KUNZ. I'm sorry, Countess, but nonsense! We all play parts, *are* doing so now, *will* continue to do so, and as long as we are playing at being Austrian, Viennese, or whatever we think we are, cosmopolitan and nondescript, a position palmed on us by history, by the accident of having held back the Muslim horde at the gates of Europe. For which no one is grateful, after all, it was two centuries ago, and we resent it, feel ill-used and pretend we're something we're not, instead of recognizing that we're the provincial droppings of Europe. The army, all of *us*, and the Church, sustain the empire, which is what, a convenience to other nations, an international utility for the use of whoever, Russia, England or Francis Joseph, which again, is what? Crown Imperial of non-intellect. Which is why, for the moment, it survives. Like this evening, the Hofball, perspiring gaiety and pointlessness.

Pause.

HÖTZENDORF. Countess, please excuse me.

KUNZ. Plus a rather heavy odour of charm.

HÖTZENDORF *clicks his heels and goes out.*

COUNTESS (*to* MÖHL). I'm sorry if I've offended the General.

KUNZ. *I* offended, not you, Countess.

MÖHL. Correct. He's not accustomed to your kind of young banter, Kunz.

KUNZ. I didn't expect him to take me so seriously.

COUNTESS (*smiles*). Of course you did.

MÖHL. He is still the finest officer in the Royal and Imperial Army.

KUNZ. Very probably.

MÖHL. He is an old friend. He may not be as clever as you, Major, but his heart is in the right place.

KUNZ. Where it can be seen by everyone.

MÖHL. And I will not stand by and allow him to be sneered at and insulted.

KUNZ. I quite agree. Please excuse me, Countess. Gentlemen.

COUNTESS. Well. What tempers you men do have! What about you, Captain, we've not heard much out of you yet? I've a feeling you're full of shocking things.

REDL. What about?

COUNTESS. Why, what we've been talking about.

REDL. Like the army, you mean? I'm afraid I don't agree with the Major.

COUNTESS. No?

REDL. No. I mean, for myself, I didn't want to be, or mean to be: rigid or fixed.

COUNTESS. But you're not.

REDL. No. At the same time, there must be bonds, some bonds that have more meaning than others.

COUNTESS. I don't follow.

MÖHL. Now you're baiting, Countess. Of course he's right. No officer should be allowed to speak in the way of Major Kunz.

COUNTESS. He offends against blood. He –

MÖHL. Against himself; it's like being a Pole or a Slovak or a Jew, I suppose. All these things have more meaning than being, say, a civil servant, or a watchmaker. And all these things are brought together in the army like nowhere else. It's the same experience as friendship or loving a woman, speaking the same tongue, that is a *proper* bond, it's *human*, you can see it and experience it, more than 'all men are brothers' or some such nonsense.

COUNTESS. And do *you* agree with that, Captain Redl?

REDL. I don't agree that all men are brothers, like Colonel Möhl. We are clearly not. Nor should be, or ever want to be.

COUNTESS. Spoken like a true aristocrat.

REDL. Which, as you must know, I am not –

COUNTESS. Oh, but I believe you are. Don't you, Colonel?

REDL. We're meant to clash. And often and violently. I am proud to be despised by some men, no perhaps most men. Others are to be tolerated or ignored. And if they do the same for me, I am gratified, or, at least relieved.

MÖHL. I agree with the Countess about you, Redl. He has style, always had it, must have had it as a tiny boy.

COUNTESS. Your pride in the Captain is quite fierce, Colonel. It's quite touching.

MÖHL. I don't know about touching, as you call it . . . it's *real*, anyhow.

COUNTESS. But that's only too clear, and why not? It's quite obviously justified.

MÖHL. Some men have a style of living like bad skins. Coarse grained, erupting, spotty. Let me put it this way: I don't have to tell you that, even in this modern age of what they call democracy, the army is still a place of privilege. Redl is the rare type that redeems that privilege. And why? Because he overpowers it, overpowers it by force, not mob-trained force, but natural, disciplined character, ability and honour. And that's all I've got to say on the subject.

COUNTESS. My dear Colonel, I don't know who is the most

embarrassed – you or Captain Redl.

REDL. Myself, Countess. A truly honest man is never embarrassed.

COUNTESS. You mean: *you* are not honest?

MÖHL. The boy's an open book. He should be in Intelligence. No one would believe him!

COUNTESS. But not tolerant.

REDL. I don't think so.

COUNTESS. Oh, indeed, I think you ignore what doesn't interest you. Which is why you didn't remember me in spite of the fact of our having met on three separate occasions.

REDL. Pardon me, Countess. I remembered immediately after.

COUNTESS. You think I am a snob because I accused you of trumpeting like an aristocrat just now. *You* are the snob, Captain Redl, not I. As Colonel Von Möhl here will tell you, my husband was a petty landowner from Cracow and *I* am the daughter of a veterinary surgeon.

MÖHL (*laughs*). Well, don't take that too seriously, Redl.

COUNTESS. Colonel: I appeal to you!

MÖHL. Well, let me say you would say there was only *some* truth in it.

He chuckles again. A FLUNKEY *approaches* REDL *with a salver with a card on it.*

FLUNKEY. Captain Redl, sir?

REDL. Please excuse me.

He takes the card out of the envelope, reads it, hands it to MÖHL.

MÖHL. Archduke Ferdinand . . . Ah, well, you'd better get along! Quickly. Here, you! ·

Grabs more champagne glasses from passing FLUNKEY.

Get this down you first. Very beautiful, if I may say so. Redl! Countess, your health. The Archduke's the man now. Ferdinand's the one to watch, and I think he's probably all right. Knows what he's doing. Knows what's going on in the

Empire, Hungary, for instance, Serbia. You see, the Belvedere, that's going to be the centre of things, not the Hofburg any more. Pity that, about all that, what do you call it, morganatic marriage business.

COUNTESS. Yes, indeed. Poor woman. Having to trail behind countesses, a hundred yards behind him.

MÖHL. Why do you think he married her?

COUNTESS. Why does any man get married?

REDL. Children, property.

COUNTESS. But one sees all that, but it couldn't have operated in this case. He could have had her as his mistress like his uncle. But then, when you think of the men one knows who *are* married, and who they're married *to*, and what their real, snotty little longings are underneath their proud watch and chains, their constant broken, sidelong glances. Oh, I know all about it, even if it's difficult to understand sometimes. Captain, you mustn't keep His Imperial Highness waiting. Not while *I* lecture you on marriage.

REDL *clicks his heels and leaves them.*

MÖHL. Well!

COUNTESS. Yes, Colonel.

MÖHL. I was just thinking, what you were saying about marriage then.

COUNTESS. And – ?

MÖHL. It really is the most *lamentable* thing for most of us, isn't it? I mean, as you say, it doesn't work really. Only the appearances function. Eh? Everyone knows the *feelings*, but what's the answer, what's the answer do you think?

COUNTESS. The only answer is not to be drawn into it, like the Captain.

MÖHL. No, I think you're wrong there. Redl would make a first-class husband.

COUNTESS. You think so?

MÖHL. Absolutely. He's steadfast, sober, industrious, orderly, he likes orderly things, hates chaos. That's why marriage would suit him so well. That's what marriage represents, I suppose. I say, I *am* enjoying talking to you.

COUNTESS. And I am enjoying talking to you. Do you think Captain Redl will come back to us?

MÖHL. Oh, I should think so. Order out of chaos. I know, we'll keep an eye out for him, learn what the Archduke had to say to him. You wouldn't care to dance with such an old man, would you?

COUNTESS. But, of course, delighted. Major Kunz is a very uninspired dancer.

MÖHL. That's because he doesn't like it. Now *I* love it. I'm so glad Redl got that invitation. Good boy! Oh, I say, I *am* having a good time.

He beams boyishly, offers his arm to her, and they leave the terrace to join the dancers in the ballroom.

Fade.

SCENE SEVEN

One drawing room of COUNTESS DELYANOFF's *house. One oil lamp burns on a desk. On a chair are* REDL's *tunic, sword, and cap and gloves. A sharp, clear, moaning cry is heard. Once, quickly. Then again, longer, more violent. Then silence. Fumbling footsteps outside the door.* REDL *enters in his breeches, putting on his vest, carrying his boots. He slumps into a chair, dropping the boots beside him. A voice outside calls softly: 'Alfred, Alfred!'*

The COUNTESS *enters swiftly, anxious, her hair down to her waist, very beautiful in her nightgown. She looks across at* REDL *as if this had happened before, goes to a decanter and pours a brandy. With it, she crosses to* REDL's *armchair and looks down at him.*

REDL. Sophia?

COUNTESS. My dear?

REDL. Sorry I woke you.

COUNTESS. I should think you woke the entire street.

REDL. Sorry. So sorry.

COUNTESS. Don't be silly. Here.

She hands him the brandy. He takes some. Stares at his boots.

REDL. I think I'd better go.

COUNTESS. It's early yet. Why, it's only, I can't see, look, it's only half-past one.

REDL. Still . . .

COUNTESS. You left me *last* night at three. And when you're gone I can't sleep. I wake the moment you've gone. All I can do is think about you.

REDL. I know. Please forgive me . . . Better put these on.

Takes one of his boots.

COUNTESS. Alfred. Please come back to bed . . . I know you hate me asking you, but I do beg you . . . Just for an hour. You *can't* go out now.

REDL. I need some air.

COUNTESS (*softly*) Darling —

REDL. Need my orderly on these occasions. Can't get my boots on.

She grasps his knee and kneels.

COUNTESS. Why did you wake?

REDL. Oh: Usual.

COUNTESS. And you're crying again.

REDL. I know . . . (*His face is stony. His voice firm.*) Why do you always have to look at me?

COUNTESS. Because I love you.

REDL. You'd look away . . .

COUNTESS. That's why. What can I do, my darling?

REDL. Nothing . . . I must get these damned things . . . (*Struggles with boots.*) I'd love another brandy.

She rises and gets it.

It's like a disease.

COUNTESS. What is?

REDL. Oh, all this incessant, *silly* weeping. It only happens, it creeps up on me, when I'm asleep. No one else has ever noticed it . . . Why do you have to wake up?

COUNTESS. Here. Alfred: don't turn away from me.

REDL. My mouth tastes sour.

COUNTESS. I didn't mean that. Anyway, what if it is? Don't turn your head away.

She grasps his head and kisses him. He submits for a moment, then thrusts her away.

REDL. Please!

COUNTESS. What is it? Me?

REDL. No. You're – you're easily the most beautiful . . . desirable woman I've ever . . . There couldn't be . . .

COUNTESS. It's not easy to believe.

REDL. Sophia: it's *me*. It's like a disease.

COUNTESSS. You must feel deeply. So do I. Why do you think you've got *me* crying as well. No one's done that to me for years!

REDL. It's like, I can't . . .

COUNTESS (*impatient*). But it *isn't* like the clap you got off some garrison whore. That's all over. You know it, you were cured, cured, you've got a paper to say so, and even if you weren't do you think I would care?

REDL. It isn't that.

COUNTESS. Then what is it? Why do you dream? Why do you sweat and cry out and *leave* me in the middle of the night? Oh God!

She recovers.

REDL. Here, have some of this. I'll get some more.

COUNTESS. No, that's fine.

REDL. Why don't you commit yourself?

COUNTESS. Why don't *you*? My darling, try not to drink so much.

REDL. I've told you. I drink. I drink, heavily sometimes, I don't get *drunk*.

COUNTESS. Yes. So you say.

REDL. It's the truth.

COUNTESS. What are you saying? No, forget I asked. Don't take any of this as *true*, Alfred, I beg of you. It's early in the morning, everything's asleep and indifferent now – *threatening to us*, both of us, *you're* in tears, you wake up in a depression, in a panic, you're dangerous and frightened again and I'm in tears. Please, don't, please, stay, stay with me, I'll look after you, I'll make up . . . at least for something. I'll protect you, protect you . . . and love you.

REDL. I can protect myself.

COUNTESS. But you can't. Not *always*. Can you? What is it?

REDL. I must go. I can't sit here.

COUNTESS. Why can't you trust me?

REDL. I've told you . . . I *don't* mean to hurt you.

COUNTESS. And I believe you.

REDL. I just can't.

Pause.

COUNTESS. Have you never confided in anyone?

REDL. No.

COUNTESS. Hasn't there ever been anyone? (*Pause.*) What about another man? I know friendship means a lot to you . . . What about Taussig?

REDL. No. At least . . . Only a very, a very little. I did try one evening. But he doesn't welcome confidences. He doesn't know what to do with them . . . or where to put them.

COUNTESS. You mean nobody else, not *one*, your mother, your grandfather, no one?

REDL. They might have been; –

COUNTESS. Um?

REDL. But I never did.

COUNTESS. Why?

REDL. I suppose I . . . they, *I* waited too long, and then . . . they were killed. An accident. You're shivering.

COUNTESS. Please try. Everyone owes something to someone. You *are* in love with me, Alfred, I know you are, and you've told me yourself. That must be something.

REDL. Put this on.

He places his tunic round her shoulders.

COUNTESS. What about you?

He shrugs.

You look better. *Are* you?

REDL. Yes. At least they go quickly. Just at a bad time. In the night. Or when I'm having to force myself to do something as an exercise, or a duty, like working late.

COUNTESS. I tell you: you work too hard.

REDL. Or sometimes I get caught in some relaxation. Sitting in a café, listening to gossip, and I enjoy that after a long day, and I'm curious. But if I listen to a conversation that's got serious, say, about politics, the Magyars or merging with Germany, or something like that, I feel myself, almost as if I were falling away and disappearing. I want to run. . . . But, I've felt I should take a serious, applied interest in this sort, in, ours is a complicated age, and I'm some small part of it, and I should devote as much attention and interest to it as I can muster. I should be giving up time –

COUNTESS. What time, for heaven's sake? You already –

REDL. Much more than I do, *much* more. I used not even to try.

COUNTESS. You mean *I* waste it?

REDL. But I can't relax or be at ease.

COUNTESS. Why are you so watchful? You always seem to be at the ready in some way, listening for something . . . some stray chance thing.

REDL. I don't know what that means.

He goes to the decanter.

COUNTESS. Please, Alfred. You've an early train in the morning . . .

REDL. Do you know: the only time I drink heavily is when I'm with you? No, I didn't mean that. But when you're badgering me and sitting on my head and, and I can't breathe.

COUNTESS. Why do you always have to make love to me with the —

REDL. There you go!

COUNTESS. Why? Why do you insist? Before we even begin?

REDL. I might ask you why *you* insist on turning the light on.

COUNTESS. Because I want to look at your face. Is that so strange?

REDL. You must know, *you* must know, we're not all the same.

COUNTESS. Why do you never kiss me?

REDL. But I do.

COUNTESS. But never in bed.

REDL. Oh, let's go back. We're tired.

COUNTESS. And turn your head away?

REDL. Damn your eyes, I *won't* be catechized!

COUNTESS. Why do you never speak?

REDL. What do you want out of me? Well, I tell you, whatever it is, I *can't* give it. Can't and won't.

Pause.

COUNTESS. I thought it was only whores you didn't kiss or speak to.

REDL. You would know more about that.

She looks up at him miserably, shivering. He feels outmanoeuvred. Takes his tunic from her and puts it on.

Excuse me.

COUNTESS. If you leave me, you'll be alone.

REDL. That's what I want, to be left alone.

COUNTESS. You'll always be alone.

REDL. Good. Splendid.

COUNTESS. No it isn't. You know it isn't. That's why you're so frightened. You'll fall alone.

REDL. So does everyone. Even if they don't know it.

COUNTESS. You can't be *saved* alone.

REDL. I don't expect to be saved, as you put it. Not by you.

COUNTESS. Or any other woman?

REDL. Or anyone at all.

He picks up his cap and gloves.

COUNTESS. What have I done?

REDL. *I* am the guilty one. Not you. Please forgive me.

COUNTESS. Don't, don't go. (*Pause.*) One feels very old at this time of night.

She goes to the window. He watches her, distressed.

It's the time of night when people die. People give up.

He goes behind her, hesitates, puts his head against hers for comfort. Pause.

You can't have your kind of competitive success *and* seclusion.

He sighs, draws away and goes to the door.

REDL. Good night, Sophia.

COUNTESS. Good night.

Pause.

REDL. Would you like to have tea?

COUNTESS. When?

REDL. Tuesday?

COUNTESS. I can't.

REDL. Wednesday?

COUNTESS. Please.

He turns.

Yes, please.

He goes out.

Fade.

SCENE EIGHT

OBLENSKY's *office. He is reading a letter to* STANITSIN.

OBLENSKY. 'In haste. Enroute for Prague. Wherever I am, my dearest, you will trouble my heart. I can say no more, I cannot think. The work here will do me good I expect. Try to do something yourself. This is a difficult time. I seem to: seem to –' can't read it – 'speak . . . speak out of nowhere. You deserve only the best, not the worst. Forgive me: Alfred'. Where's hers? Ah: 'My dearest love, why are you writing to me like this? You seem to have forgotten everything. It was not all like those short times during the night. The rest *was* different' – underlined. 'Don't, I beg you, *don't* deceive yourself. Why don't you answer my letters? I wait for them. Give me a word, or something that will do. At least something I can go over. I can do nothing. Now *I* am helpless. Loved one, don't something this. Forever, your Sophia. P.S. Did you never intend coming that Wednesday? I can't believe it.' Hum. What do you suppose he means, where is it – 'this is a difficult time'?

STANITSIN. Well, the moneylenders are pressing pretty hard. He's sold his gold cigarette case and fancy watch.

OBLENSKY. Has he? 'You deserve only the best, not the worst.' Odd sentiment for a distinguished officer, don't you think? He can't feel *that* sensitive about his extravagance, he's too reckless. Besides, as far as *he* knows, she's quite rich.

STANITSIN. Maybe he's just bored with her.

OBLENSKY. I don't think so, I'd say he's a passionate man, a bit callous too, and selfish, very, but there's something *in* all this.

STANITSIN. Come to that, the Countess sounds pretty convincing.

OBLENSKY. I hope not. All right.

He nods to STANITSIN, *who opens the office door, and admits the* COUNTESS.

Sit down. You seem to have lost your man.

COUNTESS. For the moment.

OBLENSKY. You mean you think you can get him back?

COUNTESS. Possibly.

OBLENSKY. Do you want to?

COUNTESS. What do you mean? I do what you tell me.

OBLENSKY. What's your assessment of Redl?

COUNTESS. Ambitious. Secretive. Violent. Vain. Extravagant. I expect you know as much as I do. You don't have to sleep with him to find that out.

OBLENSKY. Precisely. It doesn't seem to have added much to our total knowledge. However, patience. We're in no hurry. Captain Redl will be with us for a long time yet. Years and years. He'll probably improve with keeping. What's he doing with himself?

STANITSIN. What he says, working. Of course, he's hard up for the moment, but he'll —

OBLENSKY. Have you offered him money?

COUNTESS. Twice. He refused.

OBLENSKY. Won't take money from a woman. And I suppose you told him it didn't count between lovers?

COUNTESS. Naturally.

OBLENSKY. And there's no woman in Prague, nowhere, anyone? No one-night stands or twopenny standups?

STANITSIN. Nothing. He leaves his office in the War Building every day at 4.15, goes down to the café, has a coffee or two, reads all the foreign newspapers, has an early dinner, then goes back to his office and works till about ten, even eleven or twelve sometimes.

OBLENSKY. He *is* telling the truth.

STANITSIN. Occasionally he'll drop in for a drink somewhere on his way home or meet his friend Taussig for half an hour. More often than not he just sits alone.

OBLENSKY. Doing nothing?

STANITSIN. Just sitting. Looking.

OBLENSKY. Looking at what?

STANITSIN. I don't know. What *can* you look at from a café window? Other people, I suppose. Watch.

OBLENSKY. The Passing Show.

COUNTESS. Is there anything else?

OBLENSKY. No, my dear. Stanitsin will brief you.

She rises.

COUNTESS. Is it – may I have my letter?

OBLENSKY. I don't see why not.

Hands one to her.

COUNTESS. No, I meant his, to me.

OBLENSKY. I'm afraid that's for the File. Sorry. I can send you a copy. I wonder if he *will* write again. Don't forget to report, will you?

STANITSIN *sees her out.* OBLENSKY *lights a cigarette.*

Fade.

SCENE NINE

A café. REDL *sits alone at a table. Sitting a few tables away is a young man.* REDL *reads the paper. Throws away his cigar butt. Enter* TAUSSIG.

TAUSSIG. Ah, Redl, there you are. Sorry I'm late.

REDL. What will you have?

TAUSSIG. Don't think I'll bother. I promised to meet someone in ten minutes.

REDL. The one in the chorus at the Opera House?

TAUSSIG. That's the one.

REDL. Where?

TAUSSIG. She's taking me to her lodgings.

REDL. Before the performance? I hope it doesn't affect her voice. What's she like?

TAUSSIG. She rattles. Nice big girl.

REDL. They always are.

TAUSSIG. She's got a girl friend.

REDL. Thank you, no.

TAUSSIG. You seem awfully snobbish sometimes, Alfred.

REDL. Do I? I'm sorry. It's just that I'm not too keen on the opera. Are you going – afterwards?

TAUSSIG. What?

REDL. To the performance?

TAUSSIG. Oh, yes, I suppose so. Your head must be hardened by all those ciphers. *Löhengrin*, I think. What's it like?

REDL. Boring.

TAUSSIG. So I believe. Oh, well. Sure you won't have supper after? She really is quite nice. They both are.

REDL. No, thank you, really.

TAUSSIG. Not going to Madam Heyse's do are you?

REDL. No. (*Pause.*)

TAUSSIG. Does that young man over there know you?

REDL. What young man?

TAUSSIG. Well, there's only one.

REDL. No. Why?

TAUSSIG. He's done nothing but stare at you. Oh, he's turned away now. Knows we're talking about him.

REDL. Prague's as bad as Vienna.

TAUSSIG. Keeps giggling to himself, as far as I can see.

REDL. Probably a cretin. Or a Czech who hates Austrian Army Officers. I can't face another of those evenings or dinners, here or anywhere. They all talk about each other. They're all clever and they're afraid of each other's cleverness. They're like beautiful, schooled performing dogs. Scrutinizing and listening for an unsteady foot. It's like hunting without the pig. Everyone sweats and whoops and rides together, and, at any time, any moment, the pig may turn out to be *you*. Stick!

TAUSSIG. Well, if I can't tempt you . . . Can I have one of your cigarettes? I say, the old case back, eh?

REDL. And the watch. Everything in fact.

TAUSSIG. Good for you. Make a killing?

REDL. I tipped my mare against Steinbauer's new gelding. Want a loan?

TAUSSIG. No thanks. The Countess isn't bothering you, is she?

REDL. I told you – no. We never got on. She was prickly and we were always awkward together. It was like talking to my sister. Who died, last week incidentally, consumption, and I can't say I thought about it more than ten minutes.

TAUSSIG. What will you do?

REDL. Now? Oh, have a quiet dinner. Go for a walk.

TAUSSIG. A walk? I don't know – well, if I can't persuade you. 'Bye.

REDL *nods.* TAUSSIG *strides off. He picks up a paper, lights a new cigar. Presently the* YOUNG MAN *comes up to him.*

YOUNG MAN. Excuse me, sir.

REDL. Well?

YOUNG MAN. May I glance at your paper?

REDL. If you wish. (*Irritated.*) The waiter will bring you one if you ask.

YOUNG MAN. I only want to see what's on at the Opera.

REDL. *Löhengrin.*

YOUNG MAN. Oh, thank you. No. I don't think I like Wagner

much. Do you?

REDL. No. Now please go away.

The YOUNG MAN *grins at him, and leans across to him, saying softly.*

YOUNG MAN. I know what *you're* looking for.

REDL *looks stricken. The* YOUNG MAN *walks away. He is almost out of sight when* REDL *runs after him.*

REDL. You!

REDL *grabs him with ferocious power by the neck.*

What do you mean?

YOUNG MAN. Nothing! Let me go!

REDL. You pig, you little upstart pig. What did you mean?

YOUNG MAN (*yells*). Let me go!

Heads turn. REDL'S *anger subsides into embarrassment. The* YOUNG MAN *walks away.* REDL *returns to his seat, lights his cigar, orders a drink from the* WAITER. *A Gipsy Band strikes up.*

Fade.

SCENE TEN

A bare, darkened room. In it is a bed. On it two figures, not yet identifiable. A light is struck. A cigar end glows.

REDL'S VOICE. Why wouldn't you keep the light on?

A figure leaves the bed and goes to a wash basin. Sound of water.

Um? Oh! Why did I wait – so long.

REDL *lights a lamp beside the bed. By the washstand is the handsome form of a young* PRIVATE SOLDIER.

Paul?

PAUL. Yes?

REDL. Why?

PAUL. I don't know. I just prefer the dark.

REDL. But why? My darling. You're so exquisite to look on –
You mean it's me?

PAUL. No. You look all right.

REDL. What is it, then? What are you dressing for?

PAUL. Got to get back to barracks, haven't I?

REDL. What's your unit?

PAUL. That'd be telling, wouldn't it?

REDL. Oh, come on, I can find out.

PAUL. Yes. General Staff and all that, isn't it?

REDL. Paul. What is it? What have I done? What are you
opening the door for?

PAUL has opened the door. Four young SOLDIERS *come in. They
look at* REDL, *who knows instantly what will happen. He struggles
violently at first, and for a while it looks as if they might have
taken on too much. The young* SOLDIERS *in turn become amazed
by* REDL's *vicious defence of himself, which is like an attack. All
the while* PAUL *dresses, pockets* REDL's *gold cigarette case, cigar
case, watch and chain, gold crucifix, notes and change.* REDL
becomes a kicked, bloody heap on the floor. The SOLDIERS *leave.*
PAUL, *having dressed fully by now, helps* REDL *sit up against the
bed, looks down at his bloody face.*

PAUL. Don't be too upset, love. You'll get used to it.

Exit.

Curtain.

Act Two

A Ballroom, Vienna. A winter evening in 1902. In the background a small, eccentrically dressed ORCHESTRA *plays. The light is not bright when the curtain goes up, except on the* SINGERS. *Concentrated silently, at first anyway, are the* GUESTS, *among whom is* REDL, *one of the few not in fancy dress of some kind. However, he looks magnificent in his uniform and has put on his few decorations. He sprawls, listening thoughtfully to the* SINGER, *smoking one of his long black cigars. The* SINGER *is dressed in an eighteenth century dress which might allow the wearer to play Susanna in 'Figaro' or one of Mozart's ladies like* ZERLINA. *The* ORCHESTRA *plays very softly, the* SINGER *is restrained at this time, which is as well, because the voice is not adequate. However, it has enough sweetness in feeling to immediately invoke the pang of Mozart. Perhaps 'Vedrai Carino' or 'Batti, Batti' from 'Don Giovanni'. It ends quickly. Applause. Then a* MAN *dressed to play 'Figaro' appears, the lights become brighter, and the two go into the duet in the first scene of 'Figaro'. This should take no more than three minutes. It should be accepted at the beginning as the indifferent effort of a court opera house cast with amateurs, but not without charm and aplomb.*

The 'Figaro' in this case is a straight man. Presently, the 'Susanna' begins straight, then gradually cavorting, camping, and sending up the character, the audience, and Mozart as only someone in drag has the licence. The ballroom audience has been waiting for this, and is in ecstasy by the time it is over. Some call out 'do the Mad Scene'. Or 'Come Scoglio'. The 'Susanna', egged on, does a short parody of something like 'Come Scoglio', or 'Lucia' done in the headlong, take-it-on-the-chin manner.

This only takes a couple of minutes and should be quite funny. Anyhow, the ballroom audience apparently think so. Obviously, most of them have seen the performance before. There is a lot of giggling and even one scream during the ARIA, *which 'Susanna-Lucia' freezes with mock fury, and ends to great applause. 'Susanna' curtsies graciously. The lights in the room come up, the* ORCHESTRA *strikes up and most of the guests dance. It is essential that it should only gradually be revealed to the audience that all the dancers and guests are men. The costumes, from all periods, should be in exquisite taste, both men's and women's, and those wearing them should look exotic and reasonably attractive, apart from an occasional grotesque. The music is gay, everyone chatters happily like a lot of birds and the atmosphere is generally relaxed and informal, in contrast to the somewhat stiff atmosphere of the ball in Act One. Among those dancing at present are* KUPFER, *dressed rather dashingly as* SCARAMOUCHE. KUNZ, *dancing one handed, with* MARIE ANTOINETTE, *looks rather good as* LORD NELSON. *The* WAITER ALBRECHT *from Act One Scene Three, dressed as* COLUMBINE *with* KUPFER. FIGARO *dances with a* LADY BARON VON EPP. *He is an imposing man with a rich flexible voice which he uses to effect. At present, he looks astonishingly striking with upswept hair, ospreys in pompadour feathers, a pearl and diamond dog collar at his neck, and a beautiful fan, as* QUEEN ALEXANDRA. *Again, it is essential that the costume should be in meticulous taste and worn elegantly and with natural confidence. Sitting beside him is someone dressed as a wimpled medieval lady, to be identified as* STEINBAUER. *Like* REDL *now, some years older.* REDL *is accompanied by* LIEUTENANT STEFAN KOVACS, *who is fixed in a mixture of amusement and embarrassment.* REDL *himself is quite cool, looking extremely dashing in his Colonel's uniform and decorations and close-cropped hair, staring very carefully around at all the guests, his eyes missing no one. He lights one of his long black cigars and joins the* BARON's *group, which includes* STEINBAUER, SUSANNA *and a ravishing* TSARINA.

NOTE: *At any drag ball as stylish and private as this one the guests* can be seen to belong to entirely different and very distinct categories.

1. *The paid bum boys whose annual occasion it is – they wait for it from one year to the next and spend between 3 and 6 months preparing an elaborate and possibly bizarre costume. This is the market place where in all probability they will manage to acquire a meal ticket for months ahead. They tend to either tremendously careful, totally feminine clothes – or the ultimate in revelation – e.g. Lady Godiva, except that he/she might think, instead of a gold lamé jockstrap, that a gold chastity belt with a large and obvious gold key on a chain round her/his neck, be better.*

2. *The discreet drag queens. Like the Baron/Queen Alexandra, and the Tsarina – their clothes, specially made for the occasion by a trusted dressmaker, as the night becomes wilder are usually found to have a removable skirt revealing stockings, suspenders, jewelled garters and diamond buckles on their shoes. But even despite this mild strip tease, they still remain in absolutely perfect taste.*

3. *The more self-conscious rich queens, who, though in drag, tend to masculine drag, and end up looking like lesbians. Someone tells me they saw one once in marvellously cut black riding habit – frilled white jabot and cuffs – long skirt and boots – top hat with veil. Also in this category are the ones who go out of their way to turn themselves into absolute grotesques, and quite often arrive in a gaggle. They make a regal entry enjoying having their disguise penetrated or not as the case may be. If, for instance, the theme of the ball were theatrical they would probably choose to come as the witches from Macbeth. But marvellously theatrically thought out in every detail.*

4. *Another category of rich, discreet queens, who don't want to offend their host by making no effort at all but who baulk at dressing up; for them full and impeccable evening dress with sash orders and neck decorations and elaborately over made-up faces. They usually look more frightening than any of the others – with middle-aged decadent faces, painted like whores.*

5. *There are the men who positively dislike women and only put on drag in order to traduce them and make them appear as odious, immoral and unattractive as possible.*

6. *Finally, the ones who don't even make that effort but wear, like Redl, full-dress uniform and decorations – or evening dress.*

It is not inconceivable that some of the bum boys would dress as pampered children.

Remember when they dance you don't find the male ones only dancing with the female ones – but possibly a hussar with a man in evening dress – or two men in evening dress together – or two shepherdesses together.

In category 4 you would also be likely to find the made-up face – the impeccable tails and white tie plus ropes of pearls and blazing diamonds.

BARON. Ah, Redl! How good to see you. Where have you been? You're always so busy. Everyone says you're in Counter Intelligence or something and you're frightfully grand now. I hope you're not spying on anyone here, Colonel. You know I won't have that sort of thing. I only give this ball once a year, and everyone invited is under the obligation of strictest confidence. No gossiping after. Otherwise you can all do as you like. Who's this?

REDL. May I introduce Lieutenant Stefan Kovacs – Baron Von Epp.

BARON. Very nice. Why are you both in mufti? You know my rule.

REDL. I wouldn't call the dress uniform of the Royal Imperial Army exactly mufti.

BARON. I'm surprised they let you in. I expect you know everyone, or will do.

REDL. It's rather astonishing. Almost everyone.

BARON. It's not astonishing at all. Colonel Redl, this is Captain Steinbauer – aren't you? Yes. She is.

REDL (*to* STEINBAUER). Lemberg. Seventh Galician.

STEINBAUER. That's right. Siczynski.

REDL. Yes.

They look at each other. Sudden gratitude for the remembrance.

And weariness, sadness. The BARON *quickly dismisses the cloud.*

BARON. And that's the Tsarina there. I don't know *who* she is exactly. A Russian spy I should think. Watch yourself, my dear, the Colonel eats a spy in bed every morning, don't you, Alfred? That's what they all tell me. It's even in the papers. And this is Ferdy.

He indicates SUSANNA.

REDL. Superb.

STEFAN. He really has a fine voice. I thought he was a real soprano at first.

They all look at him with some suspicion.

SUSANNA. What do you mean? I *am* a real soprano?

They all laugh. STEFAN *feels he has blundered more than he has in fact.* REDL *chips in.*

REDL. Isn't that Major Advocate Kunz?

BARON. Where? Oh, yes I see. Nelson, you mean. Doesn't he look marvellous. One arm and all! Wonder where he keeps it? He's my insurance.

REDL. What?

BARON. If there's ever any trouble, Kunz is my legal insurance. *Very* influential that one! She'll deal with anything that ever came up – Secret Police, anything, spies. No, spies is you, isn't it, Alfred, *you're* the spy-catcher, we'll leave any lovely little spies to you.

(*To* TSARINA.) Wait till he catches *you*. I daren't think *what* he'll do to you!

The TSARINA *giggles.*

Eh. Alfred? What do you do to naughty little spies?

REDL (*bends down and grasps the* TSARINA'S *ear lobe*). I tie them over the back of my mare, Kristina, on a leading rein, and beat them with my crop at a slow canter.

BARON. How delicious! Now, her earring's fallen off, you've

excited her so!

The TSARINA *retrieves her earring and smiles up in a sweet, friendly curious way at* REDL, *who smiles back, touched by an instant, simple, affectionate spirit. He turns to* STEFAN, *who has looked away. Quickly noted by the* BARON.

BARON. I haven't seen your Lieutenant Kovacs before, Alfred.

REDL. He's only just graduated from War School.

BARON. All that studying and hardening the body and noontide heat and sweating and horses! You all look quite beautiful, well, some of you, but I hate to think of you in a war. A real war.

A SHEPHERDESS *serves champagne.*

Oh, come along, come along. No one's drinking half enough yet. Alfred!

REDL *downs a glass. He looks flushed and suddenly relaxed.*

And another! You're behind the rest of us. And a good place for you, said someone.

REDL *takes another. Hands one to* STEFAN.

And Ferdy, you have some more. Good for the voice. Bit strained tonight, dear. I want you to do 'Una Donna A Quindici Anni'.

FERDY. Don't think I can.

BARON. You can do *anything*. Practically. (*To* REDL.) He has hair on his instep – like a goat. Show them. Oh, well . . . Where have you two come from? The Lieutenant looks rather glum.

REDL. We were at the Hofburg for an hour or two.

BARON. No wonder he looks glum. Come along! Drink up, Lieutenant. I can't have anyone sober at my party. (*To* REDL.) I suppose you *had* to go, being so powerful now and impressive.

REDL. Oh, come along.

BARON. No, I hear it's quite true. (*To* STEINBAUER.) You

remember the Colonel then?

STEINBAUER. Years ago. I always knew he'd make a brilliant officer. We all did. Congratulations, Colonel! (*Raises glass – talks to* TSARINA.)

BARON. Mind your wimple. She gets drunk too easily, that one. Which is probably why she's still only a humble captain in number seventy-seven. (*Out of* STEFAN'S *hearing.*) Are you sure your friend wouldn't rather be back at the Hofburg?

REDL. He'll be all right. Try and leave him alone.

BARON. I can't leave anyone *that* pretty alone. Do you want the Tsarina? She's Kunz's really, but she's pretty available. (*Pause.* REDL *considers.*) And Kunz isn't the kind who makes scenes. He doesn't care . . . He's a bit cold too.

STEFAN *hears the last of this.*

STEFAN. Did you say Kunz? Isn't a man like that taking a bit of a risk?

BARON. Aren't we all?

STEFAN. Yes. But for someone . . .

BARON. We are none of us safe. This –

He sweeps his fan round the ballroom.

is the celebration of the individual against the rest, the us's and the them's, the free and the constricted, the gay and the dreary, the lonely and the mob, the little Tsarina there and the Emperor Francis Joseph.

They laugh.

Tell your friend it's so, Alfred.

REDL. Oh, I agree.

STEFAN (*to* REDL). Forgive me, I feel I'm unwanted.

BARON. Nonsense. You're *wanted*. Tell him not to be a silly, solemn boy, Alfred.

REDL *squeezes the boy's arm and laughs. The* BARON *refills* STEFAN'S *glass.*

Actually, Kunz is an odd one. He seems to take appalling

risks, but he knows the right people everywhere and anywhere, and he's sell anyone, and I know him. He's my first cousin. He'd do it to me.

STEFAN. Blood not thicker than water?

BARON. His blood is thinner than anything, my dear.

FERDY. Darling! She wants to know —

BARON. What is it? I'm talking.

FERDY. Are you really a Baron?

The TSARINA *giggles.*

BARON. Tell her she'll find out if she's not careful.

TSARINA (*to* FERDY). Are you the Baroness then?

FERDY (*nods*). Oh I let him. He fancies himself chasing the ladies, but he's just the same as I am. Nothing more at all.

TSARINA. What about the Lieutenant?

FERDY. Oh, I should think so. Either too stupid to know it, or hasn't woken up to it yet.

TSARINA. Or doesn't want to wake up to it. Looks a bit dreary.

FERDY. Do you fancy him? You'll have the Colonel after you. You'll be shot down.

While this duet has gone on, the BARON, STEFAN *and* REDL *have drawn away from the* GIRLS *into their own conversation. Some class division here too.*

BARON. Vienna is so dull! All that Spanish gloom at the Hofburg gets in everywhere, like the month.

FERDY (*calls out*). *You* need moth balls! (*Collapse.*)

BARON. The Viennese gull themselves they're gay, but they're just stiff-jointed aristocrats like puppets, grubbing little tradesmen or Jews and chambermaids, making a lot of one-two-three noises all the time. Secretly, they're feeling utterly thwarted and empty. The bourgeoisie daren't enjoy themselves except at someone else's expense or misfortune. And all those cavorting, clever Jews are even more depressing, pretending to be generous — and *entirely* unspontaneous. Hungarians, they're gay, perhaps that's because they're quite selfish and pig-headed. Kovacs: oh, dear, are you Hungarian? Well, never mind, that's me again I'm afraid, speak first, think afterwards –

REDL. No, Baron, you're ahead of everyone.

BARON. Only wish I were. Poles are fairly gay. You're Polish or something, aren't you, Alfred? And somehow they're less *common* than Russians. Serbs are impossible, of course, savage, untrustworthy, worse than Hungarians, infidels in every sense. I think your friend despises me because I'm such a snob. What is your father, Lieutenant?

STEFAN. A chef at the Volksgarten Restaurant.

BARON. And do you think I'm a snob?

STEFAN. You appear to be.

BARON. Well, of course, I am. Alfred will tell you how much. However, I'm also a gentleman, which is preferable to being one of our dear Burgomaster Lueger's mob. Taste, a silk shirt, a perfumed hand, an ancient Greek ring are things that come from a way not only of thinking but of being. They can add up to a man. (*To* STEFAN.) Would you like to walk on the terrace? The view is rather remarkable on an evening like this.

STEFAN. Alfred?

BARON. We'll join you. Or come back soon. I want to ask the Colonel's advice. About some espionage.

STEFAN *bows and leaves through the high central glass doors.*

Well, my dear friend. And how are you? You're prosperous I hear.

REDL. I had a small legacy.

BARON. Good. A man like you knows what money's for. And you *look* so well. Forgive me for sending the boy away for a moment.

REDL. That's all right. He'll find something to amuse him.

BARON. Would it be impertinent to ask: you're not wasting your time there are you?

REDL. It would.

BARON. What? Oh, I see. Quite right. Only I admire you, Redl. So does everyone else. You're a credit to – everyone. I just want you to succeed in everything you undertake.

REDL. Thank you.

KUNZ comes over with his partner, MARIE ANTOINETTE.

BARON. Jaroslaw! Have some champagne.

KUNZ. Thank you.

BARON. And let me introduce Colonel Redl – Major Advocate Kunz.

They salute each other appropriately.

FERDY. Colonel! Would you come over here a minute. The Tsarina wants to give herself up.

TSARINA screams.

She says, she says she wants to confess!

The TSARINA pulls off FERDY's wig and smacks him with it. REDL smiles and excuses himself to KUNZ.

BARON. Ferdy! That's naughty! The Colonel was talking to Major Kunz.

FERDY. No, he wasn't. Here!

He places REDL beside him and the TSARINA.

We've been talking to you. (*To BARON.*) *You* don't listen! It's secret.

The BARON smiles happily.

BARON. Alfred *knows* all the secrets. It's his job.

FERDY and the TSARINA conduct a whispered conversation with REDL for a while. He is drinking freely now, and is excited and enjoying himself. The BARON turns to KUNZ.

Don't you think my little Ferdy's brilliant? He'd make an adorable 'Cherubino'.

KUNZ. I think he's prettier as 'Susanna'.

BARON. Perhaps. He made that costume himself. Up half the night.

KUNZ. Did you see who I came with?

BARON. No. Why?

KUNZ. Good. I thought I'd spice your party a bit this year.

BARON. What have you done?

KUNZ. I brought a woman.

The BARON *looks astonished. Then yelps with laughter.*

BARON. Oh, *what* a good idea! What a *stroke*! Where is she?

He looks around.

KUNZ. That's the point. Later on, we'll all have to guess.

BARON. And find out! Marvellous! We'll unmask her. I'll offer a prize to the man who strips her.

KUNZ. And, I think, a punishment for anyone who is mistaken.

BARON. Exactly. What fun! I do enjoy these things. I wish we could have one every month. I'm so glad you liked Ferdy.

KUNZ. How long is it now?

BARON. Three years.

KUNZ. Long time.

BARON. For me. Let's be honest, for nearly all of us. *And* women. No, three years is a big bite out of a lifetime when you never know when it may come to an end, or what you may have missed. But he's very kind. He's still young. But his growing old gnaws at me a bit, you know. Not that he still doesn't look pretty good in the raw. Oh, he does. But about me, he doesn't mind at all.

KUNZ. Who's the little flower with Redl?

BARON. No idea. *Something's* made her wilt. They've both just come from the Hofball.

KUNZ. So have I.

BARON. Of course. Poor you. And with your lady escort. I wonder if I'll spot her.

He stares around.

That's her!

KUNZ. That is the doorman at the Klomser Hotel.

BARON. Oh! I see I'm not going to. What on earth made you go to the Hofball?

KUNZ. I thought it might be amusing to go there first.

KUNZ nods at REDL, *who is being captivated by* FERDY, *and starting to get recurring fits of giggles.*

Look at the Colonel.

BARON (*pleased*). He's enjoying himself.

KUNZ. I've never seem him like that before.

BARON. How many people have seen *you*? He's letting his hair down. What's left of it. It's starting to go. I noticed just now. He's a handsome devil.

KUNZ. Very.

BARON. And a brilliant officer, they say. Suppose you should be if you're at the top in counter espionage.

KUNZ. Preferably. He works morning and night.

BARON. He's only a railway clerk's son, did you know? So I suppose he's had to. Work, I mean. But he plays too. Look at him.

REDL and FERDY *are swopping stories and giggling intermittently and furiously.* REDL *tries to light another cigar, but he can scarcely get it going. The* TSARINA *watches blankly and happily.*

He told me once how hard he'd tried to change.

KUNZ. Hey, you! Little Shepherdess!

He takes a drink from a blushing SHEPHERDESS.

Beautiful. Yes?

BARON. Tried everything, apparently. Resolutions, vows, religion, medical advice, self-exhaustion. Used to flog a dozen horses into the ground in a day. And then gardening, if you please, fencing and all those studies they do, you do, of course

– military history, ciphers, telegraphy, campaigns, he knows, hundreds of them, by heart. He knows his German literature, speaks superb French and Russian, Italian, Polish, Czech *and* Turkish if you please.

KUNZ. Not bad for a Ruthenian railway clerk.

BARON. As you say. Oh, take your eye off Redl. He's not after the Tsarina. Or Ferdy. Is he? No, I don't think so. He's just being himself for once. Don't you think we should all form an Empire of our own?

KUNZ. What's that?

BARON. Well, instead of all joining together, you know, one Empire of sixty million Germans, like they're always going on about. What about an Empire of *us*. Ex million queens.

KUNZ. Who would there be?

BARON. Well, you and me for a start. I'd be Minister of Culture, I think. Redl could catch any spies, *women* spies. And you could do what you liked.

KUNZ. And who else?

BARON. Not Jews I think. They're the least queer in my opinion. Their mothers won't let them. Germans, Prussians, they're *very* queer. All that duelling. Poles, not so much.

KUNZ. Italians?

BARON. No, they're like women, only better, women *con brio*. Hungarians are just goats, of course, but some are quite nice. French: too spry to let life play a trick on *them*.

KUNZ. What about the English?

BARON. Next, after the Germans.

KUNZ. I agree with that. Queen Victoria was quite clearly a man.

BARON. But *she* was a German, wasn't she?

KUNZ. Ah, yes. Still, you're right about the English.

BARON. I believe Redl has an Eton straw boater hanging over his bed as a trophy. They say it belongs to the younger son of the British Ambassador.

Pause.

How's that son of yours?

KUNZ *looks immediately on guard.*

I was only asking.

KUNZ. He's well.

BARON. I'm sorry. It must be difficult. If people *will* get married.

KUNZ. Well, *I* did.

BARON. The boy knows nothing?

KUNZ. Nothing.

BARON. His mother hasn't –

KUNZ. No. And she won't.

BARON. Why not? Doesn't she –

KUNZ. She pretends.

BARON. Ah! They *do*. And the boy?

KUNZ. *He's* all right, if that's what you mean.

BARON. You mean you're *not* all right?

KUNZ. Who knows? Is this Redl's flower?

STEFAN *approaches.*

BARON. Yes. My dear boy, you must meet the Major Advocate
Kunz. Lieutenant – I'm sorry – ?

STEFAN. Kovacs.

They salute.

BARON. Hungarian. Did you enjoy the terrace? I knew you
would. Oh, thank heavens the music's stopped. Alfred's been
having the giggles with little Ferdy while you've been away.
Do have another glass, dear boy.

REDL *and* FERDY *stand up, giggling helplessly. The others listen.*

FERDY. And the manager, said, he said to me: we don't allow
ladies in here, in here without male escorts.

REDL *doubles up.*

And, so I pointed at the Baron and said, what do you think
he is!

REDL *falls on the* TSARINA *who squeals.*

KUNZ (*to* STEFAN). Is this your first visit to this kind of thing?

STEFAN. Yes, sir.

BARON. Oh, don't call him sir. Just because he's dressed as Nelson. He's only an old army lawyer. I must say you look very fine with that black patch. We must find a Lady Hamilton for him before the evening's out, mustn't we? I was saying, where do you keep your arm?

KUNZ *leaves it out of his tunic, and stretches it.*

Ah, there it is, you see?

KUNZ. That's better.

BARON. You danced very well, all the same.

KUNZ (*to* STEFAN). Would you care to?

STEFAN *is slightly confused for a moment.*

STEFAN. Thank you, I'm a bit hot.

BARON. Must be cold on that terrace.

KUNZ. You see, this is a place for people to come together. People who are very often in their everyday lives, rather lonely and even miserable and feel hunted. As if they had a spy catcher like the Colonel on their heels.

STEFAN. Of course. I understand that.

KUNZ. And, because of the Baron's panache and generosity – and, let's be frank, recklessness –

BARON. Look's who's talking –

KUNZ. They come together and become something else. Like sinners in a church.

FERDY *stands up.*

LADY GODIVA. Two monks in the street.

TSARINA. I *like* monks.

LADY GODIVA. Two monks. Walking in the street. One's saying his rosary to himself. The other passes by as he's saying 'Hail Mary'. And the other stops and says: 'Hullo, Ursula.'

REDL *collapses. So does* FERDY. *Then recovers professionally. The others watch, and some of the dancers too, including* KUPFER *and* ALBRECHT-COLUMBINE, *and* FIGARO *and* LADY GODIVA. *General laughter. The* BARON *is pleased.* FERDY *sits back next to* REDL *and they both drink and giggle together, mostly at nothing, until later in the scene when* REDL *takes in* KUPFER *and becomes hostile: to* KUPFER, *drunkenness and himself.*

KUNZ. You're not enjoying yourself much. (*Small pause.*) Are you?

STEFAN *blushes.*

STEFAN. Not at all.

KUNZ. You mustn't judge the world at carnival time. There is such a thing, such a contract, such a bond as marriage –

BARON. You should know, poor soul.

KUNZ. And there is friendship, comradeship. In the midst of all this, I ask you not to sneer, or I will beat your sanctimonious head in –

BARON. Jaroslaw –

KUNZ. Aristotle, if you've heard of him.

STEFAN. I have –

BARON. Please; take no notice . . .

KUNZ. I'm glad to hear it. Says it can be either good, or pleasant or useful. Which is true, but not always. But he also says it lasts in such men only, only as long as they keep their goodness. And goodness, unfortunately, Lieutenant, does not last.

STEFAN. No?

KUNZ. No. And don't be insolent.

STEFAN. Then don't be offensive.

BARON. Tempers, darling, tempers!

KUNZ. It seldom lasts shall we say? But then such men are rare, anyway.

The other guests gather round, and listen, and begin to take part.

During this sequence, REDL *sobers up and stiffens.*

KUPFER. Good evening, Colonel Redl.

REDL. I don't . . .

KUPFER. *Now* you do . . .

BARON. *Everyone!* Met *everyone* before. (*To* ALBRECHT.)

KUPFER. Kupfer. Major Kupfer, sir. General Staff. Ninth Corps. Prague.

REDL. Prague, Prague . . . This is Vienna. What are you doing here?

KUPFER. Same as you, sir. On leave.

REDL. *I'm* not on leave.

KUPFER. I didn't necessarily mean literally –

REDL. You'll remember Steinbauer then?

KUPFER. Of course.

He greets the wimpled STEINBAUER *casually.*

It was a blow about Siczynski. (*Pause.*) Wasn't it?

REDL. Was it?

KUPFER. Wasn't he a particular friend of yours?

REDL. I scarcely knew him. We neither of us did . . .

KUPFER. Why did you agree to be his second? It wasn't a very correct thing for such a correct officer as you to be doing.

REDL. I thought he should have support . . . No one liked him.

KUPFER. But *you've* always been popular, Colonel.

REDL. Are you being . . . because if so . . .

KUPFER. You only have my admiration, Colonel. With all the advantages I was born with, I only wish I – could – ever go – so far. You seemed to be having an entertaining time just there, Colonel. Please don't let me –

FERDY. Don't you think he's beautiful? I adore it when he screws his monocle in his eye.

REDL *doesn't think this at all funny, though the* BARON *and* KUNZ *are pleased, and, of course,* KUPFER. REDL *stands more erect than ever, and lights up a fresh cigar, grabbing a glass from the passing* SHEPHERDESS.

REDL. Hey, you! Fräulein!

FERDY. Have you heard about that extraordinary Dr. Schoepfer?

KUPFER. No. Who is he?

FERDY. Don't you know? My dear, he sounds divine! The Tsarina went there last night.

STEINBAUER. What does he do?

FERDY. Just talks, my dear, for *hours*. Not a smile. Medical do's and all that, but, if you say you're a student, you can get in.

KUPFER. What's he talk about?

FERDY. Why, *us*. He sounds an absolute scream. Can't stop talking about it.

REDL. Us? Speak for yourself.

BARON. What's he say then, Ferdy?

FERDY. Oh, that we're all demented something, something cox on the end, darling.

Laughter.

LADY GODIVA. Well, he's right, of course.

FERDY. That we're all potential criminals, and some of us should even be castrated.

Screams.

And that we're a warning symptom of the crisis in, oh, civilization, and the decline in Christian whatnots.

BARON. Oh, and he goes on about marriage and the family being the basis of the Empire, and *we* must be rooted out. *She* says he's a scream.

They look at the TSARINA, *who nods, giggles and goes crimson.*

MARIE ANTOINETTE. Is he a Jew?

FERDY. But, of course, darling! She says he looks like Shylock's mother.

KUPFER. But who is he?

KUNZ. A neurologist, I believe. Nerves.

BARON. Well, I'm sure he'd get on mine.

KUNZ. I think he's one of those people who insist they can penetrate the inner secrets of your own nature.

BARON. I understand the inner secrets of my nature perfectly well. I don't admire them, but I do know them, anyway better than this Dr. Schoepfer.

FERDY. Silly mare!

BARON. And I'm quite happy as I am, I'm no criminal, thank you, and I don't corrupt anything that isn't already quite clearly corrupt, like this ghastly city. On the contrary, I bring style, wit, pleasure, energy and good humour to it that I wouldn't otherwise have.

KUPFER. Well said, Baron.

BARON. More drinks, everyone! And music! (*To* MUSICIANS.)

ALBRECHT. I went to a doctor once, and he just said 'pull your socks up'. Do you know what he told me to do? Go into the army! (*Shrieks.*) And find yourself a nice girl. Get married. So: naturally, I went into the army. Artillery. In the second week I'd been seduced by the Corporal of Horse *and* a sub-lieutenant.

BARON. Oh, I went to a doctor like a silly thing when I was a student. He just looked very agitated and told me there was nothing he could do and to go away. A few years later I heard he'd cut his throat . . .

MARIE ANTOINETTE. I plucked up courage to tell *our* family doctor, and I said I'd like to be sent away to some special clinic in Vienna . . . Well, I thought he was going to go raving mad. Vienna, he said, Vienna, *you* want to go to Vienna. I'll send you to hell. You'll find all you want *there*, you quivering, scheming little sissy!

ALBRECHT. When I first came to Vienna, it seemed like paradise, but now I do get a bit bored. Not here, of course, Baron. But you know what I mean. Same tired old exhibits. Nothing new ever seems to come in.

TSARINA (*now sitting on the* BARON's *knee shyly*). I remember the first time a man tickled the palm of my hand with his middle finger, when we shook hands, and then later he told me what he was. I was very religious then, and I thought he was wicked. I really did at the time.

KUNZ. Perhaps you were right.

LADY GODIVA. *I* went to our priest. He quoted Aquinas and said anything that was against nature was against God . . . He always kept an eye on me afterwards, always pulling me up and asking me questions.

STEINBAUER. *My* priest said: you *can't* be like that. You're a soldier, a man of courage and honour and virtue. Your uniform itself embodies the glory of the Empire and the Church. I worshipped Radetzky at the time, and he knew it. So he said do you think someone like Radetzky could have ever been like that? I didn't know about Julius Caesar and Alexander then.

FIGARO (*to* REDL, *who is like a frozen ox*). I hate these screamers, don't you?

LADY GODIVA. I used to go to the priest after I'd confessed I was in love with Fritz. Then I used to lie like crazy about it, and say nothing was happening, although we were having sex regularly. And he'd give me absolution and say, 'It may not take on immediately—'

Laughter.

If Fritz just moved his little finger at me, I'd go back. Then he went with a girl suddenly and got married. When she was pregnant, we had beers together, and he pinched my arm and kissed me. Then he laughed and said: You know what you are, find someone else the same . . . But he laughed . . .

FERDY. I should think so, you soppy little thing.

FERDY *is bored with all this and wants attention.*

I only went to a doctor once and he just said take more exercise, dear. So I did.

He executes a skilful entrechat to general amusement till REDL *strikes him hard across the face, knocking him down right into the other guests. The boy is stunned by the force of it. Silence.*

REDL. Baron – forgive me.

He clicks his heels and goes, followed presently by STEFAN *in silence. Then the* BARON *booms out over a few 'Wells!', etc.*

BARON. Someone pick up poor Ferdy. You silly boy! I knew you shouldn't have flirted with Colonel Redl. He's a dangerous man. Are you better? There now! Come along, everybody, that quite's enough melodrama. On with the ball – I suppose –

They reassemble. Lights lower. And they hear the spirit of Mozart as FERDY *sings, not without some sweetness, 'Vedrai Carino' or 'Batti, Batti'. Or something similar which is tolerably within his range.*

Fade.

SCENE TWO

Lecture Room. Rostrum. A glass of water. DR. SCHOEPFER *is speaking.*

SCHOEPFER. The *evasion*, naturally, of responsibility . . . For instance in enjoying the physical sensations of the body without any reference to the responsibilities involved in the relationship. Or, indeed, to society or any beliefs, such as a belief in God. They can never, in their ignorance, some men say folly, in their infirmity, never attain that complete love, the love that only is possible between men and women, whose shared interests . . .

There is a suppressed giggle.

. . . whose shared interests include the blessed gift of children and grandchildren which alone, I think, most people would agree even today, which alone gives a grand and enduring purpose to sexual congress.

He drinks from the glass of water.

Now, gentlemen: these traits are caused by regression to the phallic stage of libido development, and can be traced to what is in fact a flight from incest . . .

Fade.

SCENE THREE

A hill clearing outside Dresden, surrounded by fir trees. Cold winter. OBLENSKY *is warmly wrapped up in his greatcoat, sitting on a tree trunk smoking a cigarette.* STANITSIN *stands beside him.*

STANITSIN. Here he comes.

OBLENSKEY. To the minute. As you'd expect. You'd better give me the file. Oh, just a minute, have you got the parcel I asked for?

STANITSIN *nods.*

It wasn't easy this week getting in. The boy Kovacs is staying there while he's commanding this exercise.

REDL *enters, smoking a cigar. He looks cool and sure of himself.*

REDL. Mr. Smith?

OBLENSKY. Yes, indeed. Rather *this* is Mr. Smith.

REDL. Look, I haven't time to waste fooling about—

OBLENSKY. Quite. You got our message, and, blessedly, you are here, Colonel Redl.

REDL. And who the devil are you?

OBLENSKY. Colonel Oblensky.

REDL. Oblensky . . .

OBLENSKY *waits for the effect to take, and goes on.*

OBLENSKY. It won't take you long, Colonel. I know your regiment is waiting for you . . . loosely speaking. I have a file here, which I would like to acquaint you with briefly. Would you care to sit down?

REDL *doesn't move.*

Just a matter of minutes. I have no anxiety about you reaching for your revolver to shoot either of us. I know you will realize that all this file is duplicated both in Warsaw *and* St. Petersburg. What I do beg of you is to pause before you think of turning it on yourself. I think we can find a satisfactory, and probably long-term arrangement which will work out quite well for all of us, and no trouble.

REDL (*recovering, coldly*). May I see?

OBLENSKY. Naturally, oh, this is Lieutenant Stanitsin.

STANITSIN *bows.*

REDL. Mr. Smith?

STANITSIN. My pen name, sir.

REDL *puts out his hand impatiently for the file.* OBLENSKY *hands him the contents in batches. They watch* REDL *flip through, stone faced.*

REDL. Mess bills in Lemberg! Eighteen eighty-nine! Tailors' bills, jeweller's, stables, coachbuilders, tobacconists. What *is* all this? They're just bills.

OBLENSKY. Rather unusual bills for a young officer of no independent means.

REDL. I have an uncle –

OBLENSKY. You have no uncle, Colonel. Two bothers only. Both happily married – and penniless.

Hands him another bill.

Cartiers. One gold cigarette case inscribed 'to dearest Stefan with love, Alfred'.

REDL. My nephew.

OBLENSKY *hasn't the heart to smile at this.* REDL's *immediate humiliation is so evident.*

OBLENSKY. Your bank statements from the Austro-Hungarian Bank in both Vienna and Prague for the month of February.

REDL *hardly looks at them. Pause.*

REDL. Well?

OBLENSKY. I'm sorry, Colonel. We'll soon get this over. One letter, date, February 17th 1901. 'My darling, don't be angry. When I make no sign, you know or should know, that I love you. Please see me again. All I long for is to lie beside you, nothing else. I don't know what to do to kill the time before I see you again, and watch you, how I can do something to pass the time.'

REDL. It's no crime to write a love letter, Colonel, even if it isn't in the style of Pushkin.

OBLENSKY. The style's tolerable enough for a man in love . . . But this letter is not addressed to a woman.

REDL. There's no name on it.

OBLENSKY. There is on the envelope.

REDL. *Not* very convincing, Colonel.

OBLENSKY. Very well. Those – if you'd just glance through them quickly – are signed affidavits from –

REDL *won't look at them. He has mustered himself wonderfully. He feels the chance of a small hope.*

(*Politely, casually.*) The page at the Grand Hotel, a musician at the Volksgarten – this is only the last six weeks, you understand – a waiter at Sacher's, a Corporal in the Seventh Corps in Prague, a boatman in Vienna, a pastry cook, a compositor on the 'Deutsches Volksblatt' and a *reporter* on the 'Neue Freie Press'. (*Pause.*) One right-wing paper, one liberal, eh?

REDL *puffs on his cigar.*

REDL (*slowly*). Whores. Bribed, perjuring whores.

OBLENSKY. Yes. Against the word of a distinguished officer in the Royal Imperial Army . . . Oh, dear . . . Stanitsin. Photographs . . .

STANITSIN *hands a bundle of large photographs to* REDL *who looks at the first four or five. Then he hands them back. Pause. He sits on another trunk and slowly puts his face in his hands.*

STANITSIN *offers him a flask, which he drinks from.*

I think *I'll* have some, Stanitsin. Now that's all over, let us all have some. Forgive me, Colonel. Now: time is short for us. What you decide to do is up to you. There are three courses open to you. One we have mentioned. The second is to leave the army. The third is to remain in the army and continue with your brilliant career. Do you know what Russia spent on espionage last year. Colonel? Nine million roubles. Nine. This year it will be even more. What do your people spend? Half? No, I've watched you for more than ten years, and you'd be surprised probably, or perhaps I'm wrong, about how much I know about the kind of man you are. What can you do? Change your way of life? It's getting desperate already, isn't it? You don't know which way to turn, you're up to your eye-balls in debts. What could you do? Get thrown out, exposed for everything you are, or what the world would say you are. Would you, do you think, *could* you change your way of life, what else do you want after all these years, what would you do at your age, go back to base and become a waiter or a washer up, sit all alone in cafés again constantly *watching*? What are you fit for?

His tone relaxes.

The same as me, my dear friend, the same as me, and very good indeed you are at it, soldiering, war and treachery, or the treachery that leads to wars. The game. It's a fine one. And no one's better at it in Europe than me – at the moment. (*Smiles.*) Heavy turnover sometimes. Tell me, do none of your brother officers know or suspect?

REDL. Kovacs, Kupfer, Steinbauer . . . No.

OBLENSKY. And Kunz? Kunz's only real indiscretion is the Baron's annual ball, and he could always say he went as a relation or even as a tourist even though it's hardly respectable. We've never caught him out in all these years, have we, Stanitsin? He does . . . doesn't he . . . ?

REDL. I assume so.

OBLENSKY. The other two, Steinbauer and Kupfer, well, they seem to have left wormcasts all over Europe, so they're no threat to you. And Kovacs, he's only – been – with *you*, hasn't he?

REDL. Yes.

OBLENSKY. Sure?

REDL (*wryly*). Colonel Oblensky, I may find myself here before you, in this position, but I remind you that I *am* an officer in the Austrian Chief of Staff's Counter Espionage Department. *I* know how to interrogate myself. The answer's yes.

OBLENSKY *smiles.*

OBLENSKY. Oh, I'm the last to underestimate you, Colonel. Last report from General Staff Headquarters January 5th: 'supremely capable, learned, intuitive and precise in command, tactful, excellent manners.' And now your handling of the corps exercise on Monday: 'He is uncommonly striking. Both as a battalion and regimental commander.' And there's your Regiment, the 77th Infantry. Didn't the Emperor call it 'my beautiful Seventy Seventh'. Oh, you certainly chose the right career, Colonel. Cigarette?

I think the really interesting thing about you, Redl, is that you yourself are really properly aware of your own distinction – as you should be. If you ever do feel any shame for what you are, you don't accept it like a simpleton, you heave it off, like a horse that's fallen on you. And the result is, I suppose what they mean by that splendid Viennese style. Ah, the time, yes, we must be going. Give the Colonel his package.

STANITSIN *does so*.

REDL. Is that all?

OBLENSKY. You must be returning to the regiment, Colonel.

REDL. What's this?

OBLENSKY. Mr. Smith will contact you when you've had a few days to rest and recover generally. The package contains seven thousand kronen in notes . . . Far more than *you* pay, Colonel.

REDL *puts it in his pocket slowly, collects himself, and bows*.

Goodbye, Colonel. I don't suppose we shall ever meet again for a long time – if ever . . . It *is* a little risky, even for you, isn't it?

He laughs, full of good humour.

Oh, Stanitsin, the parcel.

He hands a paper bag to REDL, *who, puzzled, takes from it an Etonian straw boater*.

Perhaps you should return it to the British Ambassador.

He laughs heartily.

Forgive me, Colonel, but I do have a very clumsy, clumsy sense of humour sometimes. No, always!

STANITSIN *smiles and goes out. The two men watch him. Presently they hear his laughter floating back through the woods.*

Curtain.

Act Three

SCENE ONE

REDL's *apartment in Vienna. Baroque, luxurious. It is late afternoon, the curtains are drawn, the light comes through them and two figures can just be seen in bed. One is* REDL *who appears to be asleep. The other, the figure of a* YOUNG MAN, *is getting up very quietly, almost stealthily, and dressing. There is a rattle of coins and jewellery.*

REDL. Don't take my cigarette case, will you? *Or* my watch.

The boy hesitates.

There's plenty of change. Take that. Go on. Now you'd better . . . hurry back.

The boy slips out quickly, expertly, REDL *sits up and lights a cigar. He gets up and puts on a beautiful dressing gown. Presently* KUPFER *comes in.*

Who's that? Oh, you? Why don't you knock?

KUPFER. I knew you were alone.

REDL. What's the time?

KUPFER. Four. Shall I open the shutters?

He does so. REDL *shrinks a little.*

REDL. That's enough.

KUPFER. The sun's quite hot.

He sits in an armchair by the window.

I waited. Till your little friend left.

REDL. Very courteous. Well?

KUPFER. I've news.

REDL. Bad, no doubt.

KUPFER. Afraid so.

REDL. Out with it.

KUPFER. Stefan was married secretly this morning. (*Pause.*) To the Countess Delyanoff.

Pause.

REDL. Naturally. The bitch . . . Does she want to see me?

KUPFER. Why, yes – she's waiting.

REDL. Well, go and get her. And then go away.

KUPFER *turns.*

No. Wait outside.

KUPFER *goes and* REDL *smokes his cigar, looking out of the window. Soon the* COUNTESS *enters.*

COUNTESS. Alfred?

REDL. So: you pulled it off.

COUNTESS. Alfred. We've endured all of that. Can't we –

REDL. No. What's he doing, marrying you?

COUNTESS. He loves me. No more . . .

REDL. I suppose you're calving.

COUNTESS. I'm having his child, Alfred.

REDL. I knew it! Knew it!

COUNTESS. He *would* have married me. He was disgusted by your behaviour.

REDL. Oh?

COUNTESS. You must admit, Alfred, telling him I was Jewish wasn't very subtle – for *you.*

REDL. Well, you are, aren't you? And I don't believe you'd told him.

COUNTESS. No, I hadn't. But my *not* telling him was cowardly, not vulgar, like yours *was.* You surprise me, Alfred.

REDL. And he'll have to resign his commission as he's no means?

COUNTESS. He wants to go into journalism.

REDL. And become a politician.

COUNTESS. Alfred, we had such feeling for each other once.

REDL. I didn't, you Jewish prig, you whited sepulchre, does he know what you really are, apart from a whore, a whoring spy?

COUNTESS. No. He doesn't. No one knows. Except you. It's extraordinary you should have kept it a secret, but I don't expect you to behave differently now.

REDL. Don't count on it . . . You little Jewish spy—

COUNTESS. I'm not, not now, Alfred, you know . . . it was my husband, when he was alive—

REDL. Don't snivel. You took *me* in.

COUNTESS. I didn't. I loved you . . .

REDL. Well, I didn't love you. I love Stefan. *We* just fooled one another. Oh, I tried to hoax myself too, but not really often. So: tonight's your wedding night. (*Pause.*) I tell you this: you'll never know that body like I know it. The lines beneath his eyes. Do you know how many there are, do you know one has less than the other? And the scar behind his ear, and the hairs in his nostrils, which has the most, what colour are they in what light? The mole on where? Where, Sophia? I know the place here, between the eyes, the dark patches like slate – like blue when he's tired, really tired, the place for a blow or a kiss or a bullet. You'll never know like I know, you can't. The backs of his knees, the pattern on the soles of his feet. Which trouble him, and so I used to wash them and bathe them for hours. His thick waist, and how long are his thighs, compared to his calves, you've not looked at him, you never will.

COUNTESS. Stop it!

Pause.

REDL. You don't know what to do with that. And now *you've* got it.

COUNTESS. God, I'm weary of your self-righteousness and all your superior railing and your glib cant about friendship and the army and the way you all roll out your little parade:

Michelangelo and Socrates, and Alexander and Leonardo. God, you're like a guild of housewives pointing out Catherine the Great.

REDL. So: you'll turn Stefan into another portly middle-aged father with – what did you say once – snotty little longings under their watch chains and glances at big, unruptured bottoms.

COUNTESS. Alfred: every one of *you* ends up, as you well know, with a bottom quite different, much plumper and far wider than any ordinary man.

REDL. You think, people like you, you've got a formula for me. You think I'm hobbled, as you say. But I'm free of you, anyway. You, what about you. I can resist you!

COUNTESS. Do you know, remember, what you once said to me: I can never blame you. You are my heart.

REDL. I do blame you. I was lying. And Stefan is my heart.

Pause.

COUNTESS. He said you told him I was Jewish. And what I looked like, what I *would* look like, drooping hairy skin and flab, and so on –

REDL. And now you're going to be a mother. You think you're a river or something, I suppose.

COUNTESS. That's right, Alfred. A sewer. Your old temple built over a sewer.

REDL. Sophia, why don't we . . . ?

COUNTESS. No, Alfred. I'm in your grip. But I'll make no bargains. Do as you wish.

REDL. I bought him a beautiful new gelding last week.

COUNTESS. It should be back in your stables by now. And your groom's got all the other –

REDL. Get out.

COUNTESS. I'm going, Alfred. Do as you wish. You may think a trick was played on you once, but you've repaid and re-played it a thousand times over. I pity you: really –

REDL. Don't then. I'm really doing quite well.

She goes out. KUPFER *comes in.*

KUPFER. Well?

REDL. Well? Nothing . . . I suppose you think you're moving in?

KUPFER. Do you want me to draw up a full report on your file on the Countess?

REDL. That file is *my* property. And *you'll* do as you're told. I'm going to sleep. Close the shutters.

KUPFER *does so.* REDL *falls asleep almost immediately on the bed. Soon little moaning voices are heard from him.* KUPFER *smokes a cigarette in the early evening light.*

Fade.

SCENE TWO

The Red Lounge of the Sacher Hotel, Vienna. A string orchestra plays. REDL *and* KUPFER *are drinking together.* KUPFER *is in a sour, watching mood.* REDL *is even cooler than usual and is smoking and appraising the other occupants of the lounge. He hails a* WAITER.

REDL (*to* KUPFER). Another?

KUPFER. No. I'm going.

REDL (*to the* WAITER). Just one then. So soon?

Pause.

KUPFER. Why St. Petersburg, for heaven's sake?

REDL. Because I've signed the order, and General Staff is not equipped to countermand orders. It works on the sweet Viennese roundabout method. Anyway, there's no one else.

KUPFER. But a whole year. I don't even speak Russian. It's nonsense.

REDL. Not to the Bureau. And now you *can* learn Russian, as I did. You should pick it up in half that time. It's the vowels that'll bring *you* down.

KUPFER. Thank you.

REDL. I'll get you back before the year's out. Don't worry.

KUPFER. You *are* sure of yourself, aren't you?

REDL. I have to be, don't I? And why not?

He takes his drink from WAITER.

No one is interested in doubts. This is an age of iron certainties, that's what they want to know about, run by money makers, large armies, munitions men, money makers for money makers. *You* were born with a silver sabre up your whatnot.

Lifts his glass.

St. Petersburg! I'll give you some names and addresses.

KUPFER. If only you'd at least admit it's because of Mischa. Why can't you be honest?

REDL. Because honesty is no use to you. People who don't want it are always yelling the place down for it like some grizzling kid. When they get it they're always miserable . . . Besides, Mischa is getting married, as you know.

KUPFER. I thought you'd put the stopper on that.

REDL. I didn't think we should tie him to a girl in a confectionery shop, a broad-faced, big-hipped little housefrau who can hardly read and write, and, what's more, doesn't care, all chocolates and childbirth. Still, if he wants that, he shall have it. It's a poor reward. Sad, too . . .

KUPFER. You do pick them, don't you?

REDL. Yes . . . But that is the nature of it. Marriage has never occurred to *you* for instance, has it?

Pause.

Since Stefan I've let them go their own ways. If that's all, if that's the sum, of it, if that's what they want . . .

KUPFER. At least be honest with your*self*. The girl came round again last night.

REDL. Did she then? I told Max to throw her out. Next time he'll throw her down the stairs.

KUPFER. Then *she'll* end up in hospital as well.

REDL. Damn it, he's only got a nervous breakdown, or whatever they call it nowadays.

KUPFER. She says he's off his head.

REDL. Nonsense. He's always been over-strung. Maybe a bit unbalanced. He'll recover. And then he can marry her.

KUPFER. And he calls *me* cruel?

REDL. *You* were born like it. All your sort of people are. It's expected of you.

KUPFER. And what about *your* sort of peole then?

REDL. Sometimes it's inescapable. I'm still nicer than you, Kupfer.

KUPFER. Why do you hate me, Alfred?

Pause.

Why then?

REDL. I've said often enough no one, and not you, is to call me Alfred in public . . . (*Hesitates.*)

KUPFER. Then why do you let me live with you?

REDL. You don't. I allow you a room in my apartment.

KUPFER. Exactly. You know, better than anyone, about jealousy.

REDL. It's a discipline, like Russian. You master it, or you don't. It's up to you, isn't it? Ah, here's Hötzendorf and Möhl.

KUPFER. Who's the boy?

REDL. Try and restrain your curiosity a little.

They rise and greet GENERAL HÖTZENDORF, GENERAL MÖHL *and* SUB-LIEUTENANT VIKTOR JERZABEK. *All salute stiffly, aware of their own presence in the lounge.*

HÖTZENDORF. Ah, Colonel, the Lieutenant tells me that great automobile and chauffeur outside belong to you.

REDL. Yes, sir. New toy, I'm afraid.

HÖTZENDORF. Expensive toy. Don't see many like that. Thought it must belong to some fat Jew.

REDL *is discomfited*.

Oh, don't misunderstand me, the vehicle itself is in impecctable taste, Redl, like everything to do with you.

REDL. Will you join us, sir?

HÖTZENDORF. Just having a quick dinner. Brought some work with us, then back to the office.

MÖHL. The lieutenant is the only one who seems able to take down the General's notes fast enough.

HÖTZENDORF. Well, quickly then. I wanted a word with you.

REDL. Waiter! I was just celebrating some good fortune. My uncle in Galicia has just left me a legacy.

Chairs are feverishly placed round the table for the arrivals. Everyone sits and orders.

HÖTZENDORF. Well done. Good. Yes, very good taste. Though I still prefer a good pair of horses, can't run an army with automobiles. No, but you know it's not that the Jews themselves are specially rotten. It's what they represent. For instance, no belief in service, and how can the Empire survive without the idea of service? Look at the Jews in Galicia, you must know, Redl, getting them into the army – quite impossible.

REDL. Indeed. *And* the high percentage of desertion.

MÖHL. Really? I didn't know that.

REDL. Nineteen per cent.

HÖTZENDORF. There you are. They're outsiders, they feel outsiders, so their whole creed of life must be based on duplicity – by necessity.

REDL. I agree, sir. Even their religion seems to be little more than a series of rather pious fads.

HÖTZENDORF. Quite. We're all Germans, all of us, and that's the way of it. At least: Jews when they get on, remind us of it.

REDL. Which I suppose is a useful function.

HÖTZENDORF. Talking of that, Redl, I want to congratulate you on your handling of that Cracow spy affair. Everyone, absolutely everyone's most impressed and highly delighted, including the Emperor himself.

REDL. I'm deeply honoured, sir.

HÖTZENDORF. Well. You do honour to us. I see you already have the order of the Iron Crown Second Class. Möhl here is recommending you for the Military Service Medal.

REDL. I don't know what –

HÖTZENDORF. You know your stuff, Redl. You've an extraordinary understanding and intuition as far as the criminal intelligence is concerned. And, there it is, spies are criminals like any other. We all just use them like any thief or murderer.

MÖHL. That's right, he's right.

HÖTZENDORF. Cracow is our first bastion against Russia. If war breaks out, it's imperative those fortresses don't crack. They'll go for them first. If that little ring you rounded up had succeeded, we could have lost a war the day it started. From April I am proposing that you take over the Prague Bureau. Rumpler will direct Vienna.

REDL. I'm overwhelmed, sir.

MÖHL. To be confirmed of course.

REDL. Of course.

HÖTZENDORF *raises his glass.*

HÖTZENDORF. Congratulations, Colonel. To your continued success in Prague.

They drink the toast. The three arrivals rise at a signal.

Well, gentlemen. Goodbye, Redl. Oh, this young man tells me he's your nephew.

REDL. That's right, sir.

HÖTZENDORF. Good. Well, the General Staff can do with all the Redls there are around.

Salute. They pass through the lounge. REDL *sits.* KUPFER *is dumbfounded.*

REDL. Rumpler *would* stay in Vienna, naturally, with his coat of arms. Still, Prague . . .

KUPFER. Nephew!

REDL. Not yet. But I can't let an unknown Lieutenant from nowhere ride about Vienna in my new Austro-Daimler Phaeton. And I promised him faithfully the other day he could drive it himself sometime. He's quite clever mechanically.

KUPFER *turns on his heel, and goes out.* REDL *lights a cigar and nods to the* HEAD WAITER.

Send me the waiter over. I want the bill.

WAITER. Yes, sir.

REDL. No, not him. The young one.

Fade.

SCENE THREE

Hospital Ward. High, bare and chill. In an iron bed, sitting up, is a young man, MISCHA LIPSCHUTZ. *Beside him is a girl,* MITZI HEIGEL. *The sound of boots striking smartly on the cold floor of a hospital corridor.* REDL *enters briskly. In greatcoat, gloves, carrying cane. An* ORDERLY *comes up to him respectfully.*

ORDERLY. Colonel, sir.

REDL. Colonel von Redl. To see Mischa Lipschutz.

ORDERLY. At once, Colonel, sir.

He leads him to MISCHA'S *bed.* MISCHA *hardly takes him in.* MITZI *looks up, then down again, as if she has become numbed by sitting in the same cold position so long.*

ORDERLY. Shall I tell the young lady to go?

REDL. No. Mischa. How are you? I've brought you a hamper.

No response. He hands it to the ORDERLY.

See that he gets all of it. Are you feeling any better? When do you think you'll be out then, eh? You look quite well, you know. . . . Perhaps you're still not rested enough. . . . Mischa . . . (*To* ORDERLY.) Can't he hear me? He looks all right.

ORDERLY. Perhaps your voice sounds strange, just a fraction sir? Mischa: Colonel Redl is here.

MISCHA. Mischa.

ORDERLY. How are you, the Colonel's asking?

MISCHA. I've been here quite a long time. I don't quite know how long, because we're absorbed into the air at night, and then, of course they can do anything they like with you at will. But that's why I keep rather quiet.

REDL. Who, Mischa?

MISCHA. They do it with rays, I believe, and atoms and they can send them from anywhere, right across the world, and fill you up with them and germs and all sorts of things.

REDL. Mischa, do you know where they are?

MISCHA. On a star, sir, on a star. Just like you. I expect you were sent to Vienna too, sir, because you are the same kind of element as me. The same dual body functioning.

REDL *stands back. The* ORDERLY *shrugs, the* GIRL *doesn't look up.* REDL *walks out quickly.*

Fade.

SCENE FOUR

An hotel room near the Polish border in Galicia. It is cheap, filled with smoke but quite cosy. OBLENSKY is sprawled on a low sofa, his tunic open, relaxed, hot with much vodka. REDL is slightly drunk too, though less cheerful.

OBLENSKY. Come here, over here, have some more. Where are you, Redl, you're always disappearing? Why are you so restless always? All the time limping home with scars, and now you've got a bitten lip, I see. Tell me now, about this new boy, what's it – Viktor –

REDL. He's not new.

OBLENSKY. I thought it was last February.

REDL. December.

OBLENSKY. Five months! Oh, I suppose that is a long time for you.

REDL. How often are you unfaithful to your wife?

OBLENSKY. When I'm not working too hard, and if I can arrange it, daily.

REDL. You seem to arrange most things.

OBLENSKY. Don't say it in that tone of voice. I was looking it up the other day. You've had eighty thousand kronen out of me over the years.

REDL. Out of Mother Russia.

OBLENSKY. Quite so. And she can ill afford your way of life.

REDL. She's had her money's worth.

OBLENSKY. Not over Cracow.

REDL. Oh, not again.

OBLENSKY. Well, later. Tell me about what's it, Viktor? Is he handsome?

OBLENSKY. Yes, but how handsome, in what way?

REDL. Tall, fair, eyes pale . . .

OBLENSKY. Is that what you like? Watery?

REDL. Tell me what *you* like.

OBLENSKY. My dear friend, ha!

He roars with laughter.

Nothing has the enduring, unremitting crudity of what I like. And *no* interest. I like nothing exotic. Now, the Countess, you know, Delyanoff, you used to write those strained love letters to, I could have had her at any time, naturally. But, nothing, no interest, here, whatsoever.

He crosses himself.

Too exotic. And I suppose intelligent. I can understand *you* trying her out very well. All I want is a lump, a rump, a big, jolly roaring and boring, let us have no illusion, heaving lovely, wet and friendly, large and breasty lump!

He roars, jumps up laughing, and fills their glasses.

What I wouldn't do for one now! Yes, with you here too, Redl! Would that disgust you?

REDL. No.

OBLENSKY. Flicker of interest?

REDL. Very little I *have* watched.

OBLENSKY. Oh, dear. You make me feel cruder than ever. Tears of Christ! I'd make her jump and giggle and give her fun. All girls like fun. Even if they're educated. Do you give fun? Much?

REDL. Some, I imagine. Perhaps not too much. If I liked anyone it was because they were beautiful, to me, anyway.

OBLENSKY. Yes, I see. That's quite different. I don't see very much beauty. I mean I don't need it. You're a romantic. You lust after the indescribable, describe it, to yourself at least, and it becomes unspeakable.

REDL. You sound like a drunken Russian Oscar Wilde.

OBLENSKY. Me? Oscar Wilde!

He splutters with pleasure, and pours them out more vodka.

Perhaps there's a cosy chambermaid here, if they have such a thing in this hole. I'll ask Stanitsin. Do you get afraid very often?

REDL. Yes.

OBLENSKY (*switching*). I'll tell you some things that stick in my throat about you people. Do you mind?

REDL. If you wish.

OBLENSKY. Well, one: you all assume you're the only ones who can understand anything about yourselves.

REDL (*politely*). Yes?

OBLENSKY. Well, two: frankly you go on about beauty and lyricize away about naked bodies as if we were all gods.

REDL. Some of us.

OBLENSKY. Or else you carry on like – rutting pigs.

They both address each other in a friendly way across the barrier they both recognize immediately.

It isn't any fun having no clear idea of the future, is it? And you can't re-make your past. And then when one of you writes a book about yourselves, you pretend it's something else, that it's about married people and not two men together . . . That is not honest, Alfred.

REDL. Don't be maudlin, Colonel.

OBLENSKY. Redl; you are one of those depressing people whom you always know you are bound to disappoint. And yet one tries. (*He looks quite jolly all the same.*) Well, you must be used to dancing at two weddings by this time. You've been doing it long enough.

REDL. You do enjoy despising me, don't you? Can we finish now?

OBLENSKY. Not till Cracow is settled. I don't despise you at all. Why should I? I don't care. I'm only curious.

REDL. My confessions are almost as entertaining as the Cracow fortifications.

OBLENSKY. You're quite wrong, quite, quite . . . I listen to you, I enjoy your company, see how much vodka we've drunk together, I don't drink with many people, Alfred. May I? I don't know anyone quite like you. It's taken a long time, hasn't it? You're giving nothing away this time.

REDL. What about Cracow?

OBLENSKY. Well, my dear friend, it was most embarrassing. Suddenly, my whole organization pounced on – *poum*! And who did it! You!

REDL. It was unavoidable. I felt there were suspicions . . .

OBLENSKY. But no warnings . . .

REDL. I tried, but it had to be.

OBLENSKY. Hauser was about my best agent.

REDL. I'm sorry. But you might have lost *me* otherwise.

OBLENSKY. Maybe. But if *I* don't turn up with something, something *new*, I'll be roasted. You've got to *give* me someone. And someone significant I can parade at a big trial, like your affair. Well?

Pause.

REDL. Very well. I have someone.

OBLENSKY. Who?

REDL. Kupfer.

OBLENSKY. Isn't he on your staff? St. Petersburg?

REDL. Yes.

OBLENSKY. Governments don't usually pounce on the diplomatic or military missions of other governments.

REDL. If it were outrageous enough.

OBLENSKY. Well, if you can fix it, and it's really scandalous.

REDL. I can.

OBLENSKY. Very well then, fix it, Redl.

He hurls his glass into the fireplace where it smashes.

Fix it. Now: We've hardly started yet.

FADE

SCENE FIVE

REDL's *apartment in Prague. A beautiful baroque room, dominated by a huge porcelain fireplace and double Central European windows.* VIKTOR *is in bed, naked from the waist up.* REDL *is staring out of the window angrily. Pause.*

VIKTOR. I think *I'll* get up . . .

REDL. Why do you make such disgusting scenes with me? If you had the insight to imagine what you look like.

VIKTOR. Oh, don't. (*He flings his blond head across the pillow.*)

REDL. Oh, stop screaming, you stupid little queen! You don't want to get married, you whore, you urchin! You just want to bleed me to death. You want more. Dear God, if ever there was a ludicrous threat, you don't want the girl or any girl, you couldn't. I've seen her too, remember. *I* could, mark you, and *have*. But not you. When I think . . . How do you imagine you would ever have got a commission in a cavalry regiment, you, who would have bought you three full-blooded horses, and paid your groom and mess bills, *and* taught you to shoot like a gentleman, to behave properly as a Fire leader and be a dammed piss-elegant horseman in the field? You couldn't open your mouth and make an acceptable noise of any sort at all.

VIKTOR *weeps softly*.

You're so stupid you thought you could catch me with a shoddy ruse like that. You'll get no bills paid, nor your automobile, that's the bottom of it, you're so avaricious, you'll get nothing. You're so worthless you can't even recognise the shred of petty virtues in others, some of which I have still. Which is why you have nothing but contempt for anyone, like me, who admires you, or loves you, or wants and misses you and has to beg for you at least one day a fortnight.

Yesterday, yesterday, I spent two excruciating hours at the most boring party at Möhl's I've ever been to, talking to endless people, couldn't see or hear, hoping you – God knows where you were – that you'd possibly, if I was lucky, might turn up. Just hoping you might look in, so I could light your cigarette, and watch you talking and even touch your hand briefly out of sight.

VIKTOR. I *do* love you.

REDL. In your way, yes. Like a squalling, ravenous, raging child. You want my style, my box at the opera instead of standing with the other officers. You're incapable of initiating anything yourself. If the world depended on the Viktors, on people like you, there would be no first moves made, no inexpedient overtures, no serving, no invention, no spontaneity, no stirring whatsoever in you that doesn't come from elsewhere . . . Dear Mother of God, you're like a woman!

VIKTOR *howls.* REDL *pulls him out of bed by the leg and he falls heavily to the ground with a thump.*

You've no memory, no grace, you keep nothing.

REDL *bends over him.*

You are thick, thick, a sponge, soaking up. No recall, no fear. You're a few blots . . . All you are is young. There's no soft fat up here in the shoulder and belly and buttocks yet. But it will. Nobody loves an old, squeezed, wrinkled pip of a boy who was gay once. Least of all people like me or yourself. You'll be a vulgar fake, someone even toothless housewives in the market place can bait.

Grabs his hair and drags him.

You little painted toy, you puppet, you poor duffer, you'll be, with your disease and paunch and silliness and curlers and dyed wispy hair and long legs and varicose veins like bunches of grapes and prostate and thick waist and rolling thighs and big bottom, that's where we all go.

Slaps his own.

In the bottom, that's where we all go and you can't mistake it. Everyone'll see it.

He pauses, exhausted. His dressing gown has flown open. VIKTOR *is sobbing very softly and genuinely.* REDL *stands breathless, then takes the boy's head in his arms. He rocks him. And whispers:*

It's not true. Not true. You *are* beautiful . . . You always will be . . . There, baby, there . . . Baby . . . It won't last . . . All over, baby . . .

Fade.

SCENE SIX

Office of GENERAL VON MÖHL, TAUSSIG *is handing papers to the dazed* GENERAL.

TAUSSIG. This is the envelope, sir. As you see, it's addressed to Nicolai Strach, c/o General Postal Delivery, Vienna. It lay there for several weeks before it was opened by the Secret Police, who found it contained five thousand kronen and the names of two well-known espionage cut-outs, one in Dresden and another in Paris. The letter was re-sealed. Rumpler was informed immediately and we waited.

MÖHL. And?

TAUSSIG. Redl took three days' leave and motored in his automobile to Vienna where he picked up the letter. On Thursday evening.

Pause.

MÖHL. Redl?

He might almost have burst into tears.

TAUSSIG. Sir. Then. His account at the Austro-Hungarian Bank, unpaid bills for stabling, furniture, tailoring, *objects d'art* and so on. Automobile maintenance, totalling some fifty thousand crowns. Assets: a little over five, plus valuable personal properties as yet unvalued. Some securities worth perhaps eight thousand kronen. His servant Max is owed a year's wages, but doesn't seem to mind. A trunk full of photographs, women's clothes, underwear, etc., love letters to various identified and unidentified men, a signed oath from Lieutenant Jerzabek, swearing not to marry during Redl's lifetime and only afterwards by way of certain complicated financial losses in Redl's will. Redl's will . . .

MÖHL. All right. General Von Hötzendorf must be informed at once. No: I must do it. He'll go out of his mind. Redl! How people will enjoy this, they'll enjoy this. The *élite* caught out! Right at the centre of the Empire. You know what they'll say, of course? About the *élite*.

TAUSSIG. Perhaps it can be kept a secret, sir. Do you think? It's still possible.

MÖHL. Yes. We must do it now. Where is Redl?

TAUSSIG. The Hotel Klomser.

MÖHL. We'll see Hötzendorf, get his permission, and then we'll go there, together, you and I. We'll need a legal officer, Kunz I'd say. But he *must* be sworn to outright secrecy. Those damned newspapers . . .

TAUSSIG. Kunz is the man for that, sir.

MÖHL. Very well. Let's break the news to General Hötzendorf.

Fade.

SCENE SEVEN

REDL's *bedroom at the Hotel Klomser. Above his bed the black,*

double-headed eagle of Austria and a portrait of Francis Joseph.
REDL *is seated at a bureau. In front of him stand* MÖHL, TAUSSIG
and KUNZ. REDL *signs a document, gives it to* KUNZ, *who examines
it, then puts it into his briefcase which he straps up briskly.*

KUNZ. That's all, General Möhl . . .

REDL. You know, General, I know you'll be offended if I say this
because I know you're a deeply religious man, and I . . . well,
I've always felt there was a nasty, bad smell about the Church.
Worse than the Jews, certainly. As you know, I'm a Catholic
myself. Who isn't? Born, I mean.

He takes the champagne bottle out of the bucket and pours a glass.

Born. But I think I hate the Spaniards most of all. Perhaps
that's the flaw . . . of my character . . . they *are* Catholics.
Those damned Spaniards were the worst marriage bargain the
Habsburgs ever made. Inventing bridal lace to line coffins
with. They really are the worst. They stink of death, I mean.
It's in their clothes and their armpits, quite stained with it,
and the worst is they're so proud of it, insufferably. Like
people with stinking breath always puff and blow and bellow
an inch away from your face. No, the Spaniards are, you must
admit, a musty lot, the entire nation from top to bottom smells
of old clothes in the bottom of trunks.

MÖHL *motions to* TAUSSIG, *who hands him a revolver.* MÖHL
places it on the bureau in front of REDL. *Pause.*

TAUSSIG. Are you acquainted with the Browning pistol, Redl?

REDL. No. I am not.

TAUSSIG *takes out the Browning Manual and hands it to* REDL.

Thank you, Taussig. Gentlemen . . .

They salute and go out. REDL *pours another glass of champagne
and settles down to read the manual.*

Fade.

SCENE EIGHT

A street outside the Klomser Hotel. Early morning. MÖHL, TAUSSIG *and* KUNZ *wait in the cold.* REDL'S *light is visible.*

TAUSSIG (*looks at watch*). Five hours, General. Should we go up?

MÖHL. No.

KUNZ. Forgive me, gentlemen. I'm going home. My wife is waiting for me. My work seems to be done.

MÖHL. Of course.

KUNZ. Good night.

A shot rings out. They stare. KUNZ *moves off.*

MÖHL. Well . . .

They light a cigarette.

Fade.

SCENE NINE

A Chamber of Deputies. Vienna. Deputies. In the background blow-ups of The Times *for May 30th 1913, headed* 'SUICIDE OF AN AUSTRIAN OFFICER (FROM A CORRESPONDENT) VIENNA. MAY 29.' (*Facsimiles available from British Museum Newspaper Library.*)

DEPUTY. The autopsy showed the bullet had penetrated the oral cavity, passing obliquely through the brain from left to right. Death must have been practically instantaneous due to haemorrhage. The question is, not who gave this officer the manual, but who allowed him to be given a revolver for this purpose at all?

MINISTER. There will be no concealment of any irregularities.

DEPUTY. Is it not true that this officer was exposed by reason of his official contracts with certain confidential elements in the military-political sphere for a period of some years, with special duties in connection with the frontier protection and the order of armament?

DEPUTY. Was not this same officer in the confidence of Von Moltke the Chief of the Imperial German High Command?

DEPUTY. Surely someone must have been around with the wit or perception to have suspected something . . .

DEPUTY. Are we all asleep or what!

Roar.

DEPUTY. *What's become of us?*

Roars.

DEPUTY. Is it not true that he was, in fact, the son of one Marthe Stein, a Galician Jewess?

Uproar.

Why was this fact not taken note of?

MINISTER. The high treason which General Staff Colonel Redl was able to practise with impunity for a period of many years is an occasion of the gravest possible public disquiet, which is far from being allayed, if not actually increasing. This is due not only to the abominable crime committed by this officer – but more by the way in which the case has been managed by the authorities of the Royal and Imperial Army.

DEPUTY. Yes, but what do you *do* about it? What do you *do*?

MINISTER. We must not alarm the public more than is necessary. It is true that the crime committed by Colonel Redl against his country and the uniform he wore is felt in the most sensitive way by the whole population. However, the only adequate protection of the honour of officers lies in rigid standards, and if individuals act against the honour of that class, the only helpful thing is the expulsion from it of those individuals by all the forms prescribed by law . . .

Fade.

SCENE TEN

OBLENSKY's *office. Lights dimmed.* STANITSIN *working the magic lantern.*

OBLENSKY. Next!

A photograph is snapped on to the screen.

STANITSIN. Schoepfer. Julius Gerhard. M.D., Ph.D., F.R.C.S., Member Institute Neuro Pathology, Vienna. Member Vienna Institute. Hon. Fellow of the Royal Society of London. Born Prague March 25th 1871. Family Jewish. Distinguished patients. List follows. Political and Military. In 1897, at the age of twenty-five he delivered a brilliant lecture on the origins of nervous diseases . . .

Fade.

Edward Bond

Edward Bond is a major poet of the theatre, a radical humanist whose plays unsettle audiences by challenging their moral and political uncertainties. He first alarmed London audiences with *Saved*, which set of storms of controversy when it opened in 1965 at the Royal Court Theatre. Since then Bond has written a dozen more plays, each marking a new phase in his maturing as a dramatic thinker intensely focused on the connections between politics and moral decision, between the social order and the quality of individual lives. For Bond, an avowed socialist, there is no moral conduct without political responsibility, no chance of happiness under capitalism, which forces us to play assigned roles in a social masquerade that distorts our humanness and precludes the humane-ness which is our best hope for averting the ultimate violent action that cannot be called back.

The job of the writer, according to Bond, is to change the world by telling the truth about society, by showing that people think and behave according to motives dictated by class, not merit or choice. Traditional character-rooted notions of good and evil are irrelevant. Money and power, not genes or psychology, determine what happens to people and how it happens. So Bond places his characters' lives firmly in the social context. There's a political way to cut bread, wear shoes, see sunsets, and know things. We must grasp that connection as a fact of life in order to struggle towards a more humane world.

Born in 1934 of working-class parents in Holloway in North London, Bond has personally felt the dehumanizing effects of life in 'urban, crowded, regimented groups, working like machines (mostly for the benefit of other men)', a capitalist exploitation, according to Bond, which breeds the aggression and violence that threaten human survival. What he reports he got as a schoolboy from seeing Shakespeare's *Macbeth* suffuses his own plays: 'A sense of human dignity, of the value of human beings.'

Bond strikes a distinctive note among the dramatists in the postwar theatre renaissance by the passion of his concern for the suvival of the planet. Time is running out. Global violence may outstrip our best efforts to save ourselves. Society must be changed. 'Art must be the equivalent of hooliganism in the streets. It has to be disruptive and questioning' to show the fallacies our society is based on. 'If it isn't changed rationally, it must be changed by force.'

Predictably, the hooliganism of *Saved* outraged the British Establishment when it was staged at the Royal Court in 1965. The controversy it stirred hastened the end of censorship, however, which came in 1968. To celebrate, the Court staged a whole season of Bond plays and, ironically, *Saved* and *Narrow Road to the Deep North* soon after toured Europe under British Council auspices!

One critic confessed he hadn't begun to understand *Saved* until he had seen several other Bond plays. His response is not surprising, since Bond's intention is ethically and humanly complex. Each play is part of a comprehensive social vision unfolding gradually over the body of his work. In the dynamic of human history, Bond traces a hopeful pattern of evolutionary growth in consciousness. Each of his plays focuses on a particular stage in the sensitizing of the human mind to suffering and to the social roots of injustice and violence. Each play is organically related to the others.

Although *Saved* was at first howled down as a 'blockishly naturalistic' exhibition of disgusting cruelty, the notorious baby-stoning scene has come to be seen not as violence for its own sake, but as an expression of the cultural poverty for which society is more responsible than the individual. Later plays reach back to earlier historical periods, earlier instances of the social routes of violence, each with its own perspective. But no matter where Bond's plays are set, whether in the north London of the sixties as in *Saved*, ancient Troy as in *The Woman*, 18th-century England as in *Restoration*, or a Victorian never-never land in *Early Morning*, the society depicted is ours, the time is now or a flash-back to the time when the choices that led us here were made.

In *Restoration* an innocent man goes meekly to the gallows for his guilty master, presumably because the stability of the social order demands exculpation for the aristocrat. The servant Bob learns too late what he needs to know to save himself. Literacy alone might have sprung him from the trap, but Bob can't read. Nor can his mother. One of the stunning images that are powerful metaphors in Bond shows Bob's mother admiring the pretty seal on her son's pardon, put into her hands by Lord Are in cruel contempt for her illiteracy. Unable to make out the words, she uses the precious document to light his lordship's fire. Spectators at the play gasp audibly when she puts a match to it. In an earlier scene, Bob's own complicity in his dreadful fate is underscored when he shows his wife that the shackles on his legs are only for show. The irony of the image is that Bob's credulous stupidity, the ingrained habit of servitude, doom him far more certainly than his chains. He will not escape even though he can.

Violence abounds in Bond's plays. He physicalizes his subversive view in a theatre of shocking images and brazen analogies. 'I write about violence as naturally as Jane Austen wrote about manners. Violence shapes and obsesses our society, and if we do not stop being violent we have no future. People who do not want writers to write about violence want them to stop writing about us and our time,' Bond himself explained. In *The Pope's Wedding* (1962), a helpless old recluse is murdered. Cannibalism is a dominant image in *Early Morning* (1968). In *We Come to the River* (1976), old women and young widows scavenge for food on the battlefield among the wounded and dead. Soldiers under orders shoot them in cold blood. In *The Woman* (1978) Hecuba is impaled on a fence, her tits sticking up like knives. In *Saved* an infant sleeping in a pram is stoned to death by street toughs, among them the infant's own father. In *Summer* (1982), a victim, saved from the Nazis, spits on her benefactor. In *The Fool* peasants strip a clergyman naked and tear at his flesh. Such unsparing images struck audiences as offensive exaggerations at first. But such things happen, Bond argues, they are part of the reality we shrink from, the reality that conventional theatre and the establishment conspire to hide from us.

In each of Bond's plays at least one character struggles to a level of awareness that inspires constructive action to change things. Sometimes, as in *Saved*, that action is rudimentary. In *Restoration*, Bob's wife comes to understand that 'man is what he knows'. Although she cannot prevail against the obtuseness of her husband and his mother, she may escape herself into a better life. In *Lear*, Bond's reinterpretation of Shakespeare's masterpiece, Lear dies trying to tear down a wall he himself erected against his enemies, one of the hostile acts in a violent series that devastates his land and his subjects. Lear's action, however inadequate and belated, is a political action, which affirms important tenets of Bond's world view: that people can learn that their individual acts affect history, that action is quintessentially human and preferable to stoic resignation in the face of suffering, Shakespeare's Lear notwithstanding. Bond's Lear loses his life in a heroic gesture that is not futile because other and younger men see it and may be inspired by it.

Bond shows that violence arises out of the unequal distribution of power and opportunity. To make that idea material, he uses every theatrical resource, including explicit language and sexual frankness. He rudely deflates public icons. The evangelist Georgina and the British commodore in *Narrow Road to the Deep North* are more savagely ruthless than the 17th-century tyrant Shogo they overcome because they pervert religion and morality into tools of oppression.

Bond gives centre stage to peasants and the urban poor. He makes their ordinary inarticulacy eloquent by infusing dialect speech with poetic resonance and powerful rhythms. He ransacks the theatrical bag of tricks, and mixes genres and styles. Farce, burlesque, grotesquerie and fantasy erupt into stingingly realistic scenes. He pursues truth relentlessly until it becomes nightmare. His surreal effects transmute local history into universal metaphor.

One of Bond's most moving studies of an awakening into moral courage is the opera *We Come to the River*. The music was composed by the East German Hans Werner Henze, 'music's most noticeable political moralist,' who argues that music must help the oppressed in their struggle for world revolution. In Bond's text a General, gloating over the bloody rout of his enemies, visits a battlefield where the wounded cry out among the dead bodies of their comrades. He coldly orders off a young widow digging desperately for her husband's body. She accuses him of no longer knowing the difference between the quick and the dead, so many has he killed. The general resorts to the obscuring distortions relied on by those who run wars to protect themselves from truth: 'She's mad . . . I killed no one. They are war dead. They gave their lives.'

Like Lear, however, the general, having inflicted violence, suffers horrifying violence himself, when he is blinded like Shakespeare's Gloucester by cold-blooded assailants. Deprived of physical sight, he 'sees'. He begs for sanity before he dies. For Bond, of course, sanity means the rekindling in the human spirit of the justice and compassion natural to it.

In the general's self-deception and the grief of the young

woman, Bond shows his conviction that we are caught between two worlds: the daily world of rationalization and myth that supports the power structure in its repression and violence, and the raw and painful human world whose truth would energize us into rebellion if we saw it clearly.

Saved followed by only three years Bond's first professionally produced play, *The Pope's Wedding*. Less than ten years earlier, Osborne's *Look Back in Anger* had seemed revolutionary. But Jimmy Porter's literate diatribes on the futility of his life, did not prepare audiences for the self-demeaning gutter talk, the broken idioms of poverty and deprivation of the South London youths in *Saved*. The stuntedness of their speech reveals the stuntedness of their lives and imaginings. Their violence is less repugnant than the injustices institutionalized in the system. Society is at fault for the cultural impoverishment afflicting the underclass. Their frustrations boil over into acts of mindless savagery because they lack language and opportunity to conceive alternatives.

Denied even the concept of love or compassion, Pam feels no love or compassion for her unwanted baby. The young men in the park, including Fred, the baby's father, who stone the infant to death, are casually criminal, by reason of an accelerating bravado that is the only human value they have absorbed from the dehumanizing society they live in, a society that neither feeds nor educates them.

Len alone grasps some notion of kindness and loyalty. He doggedly clings to Pam in spite of her bristling hostility. He moves in with her family, buffering her from her parents and offering a kind of friendship to her father, who is the victim in a continual warfare with his unfaithful wife in a household rife with smouldering angers. Starved for elementary affection, Len dumbly attaches himself to Pam's baby, enduring with obtuse stoicism Pam's virulent efforts to oust him from her life.

Almost any scene in the play can illustrate the arresting, implicative power of Bond's images and the compressed eloquence of his dialogue. Len, Pam and her mother watch television while Pam's baby cries in another room. 'It goes on crying without a break until the end of the scene,' Bond's stage directions indicate, while Pam indifferently puts on her makeup and wrangles with Len. Her hopeless cynicism and Len's emotional hunger suffuse the scene.

PAM: It's bad enough bein' stuck with a kid without 'avin' you 'angin' roun' me neck. The 'ole street's laughin' be'ind yer back.

LEN: I ain' leavin' that kid.

PAM: Take it.

LEN: With me?

PAM: How else?

(PAM's *mother interrupts*).

MARY: 'E can't look after a kid.

PAM: Put it on the council.

MARY: They wouldn't 'ave it if they've got any sense.

(*The baby cries.*)

PAM: Well.

LEN: Kids need proper 'omes.

PAM: Yer see?

(*He goes out.*)

MARY: Wouldn't yer miss it?

PAM: That racket?

Their exchange has the amplitude of poetry in its emotional compression.

The *Saved* of the title refers to the final image of the play: Len mending a chair for the family. He has stayed on through the baby's death, Fred's trial and release, Pam's desperate flailings. His act is a kind of 'numb poetry,' a metaphor for an early stage of that awakening of human consciousness to which Bond attaches his hopes for moral regeneration. As Ronald Bryden perceived in his review of the play, *Saved* is accurate and honest, 'presenting its violence not as some neo-Gothic testimony to the cruel absurdity of the universe and human nature, but as a social deformity crying for correction.'

Major Plays

Saved, Royal Court Theatre, 1965

Narrow Road to the Deep North, Belgrade Theatre, Coventry, 1968

Lear, Royal Court Theatre, 1971

The Fool, Royal Court Theatre, 1975

We Came to the River, Royal Opera House, Covent Garden, 1976

The Woman, National Theatre, 1978
Restoration, Royal Court Theatre, 1981
The War Plays, RSC at the Barbican Pit, 1985.

Selected Bibliography

Bond, Edward. See prefaces and essays published with major plays.
— 'The Romans and the Establishment Fig Leaf,' *Theatre* (Spring 1981), pp. 39-42.
Coult, Tony. *The Plays of Edward Bond*. London and New York: Methuen, 2nd ed., 1979.
Hay, Malcolm and Philip Roberts. *Bond: A Study of His Plays*. London and New York: Eyre Methuen, 1980.
Innes, Christopher. 'The Political Spectrum of Edward Bond: From Rationalism to Rhapsody,' *Modern Drama* (June 1982), pp. 189-206.
Jones, Daniel R. 'Edward Bond's Rational Theatre,' *Theatre Journal* (December 1980), pp. 505-517.
Nadelman, Perry, 'Beyond Politics in Bond's *Lear*,' *Modern Drama* (September 1980), pp. 269-276.
Rademacher, Frances. 'Violence and the Comic in the Plays of Edward Bond,' *Modern Drama* (September, 1980), pp. 258-268.
Roberts, Philip (ed). Bond on File. London and New York: Methuen, 1985.
Scharine, Richard. *The Plays of Edward Bond*. Lewisburg, Pa.: Bucknell University Press; London: Associated University Presses, 1976.
Spencer, Jenny S. *Structure and Politics in the Plays of Edward Bond*. PhD dissertation in English, University of Iowa, 1982.
Tener, Robert L. 'Edward Bond's Dialectic: Irony and Dramatic Metaphor,' *Modern Drama* (September 1982), pp. 423-434.
Trussler, Simon. *Edward Bond*. Harlow: Longman, 1976.
Worth, Katherine J. *Revolutions in Modern English Drama*. London: G. Bell, 1973.

EDWARD BOND

Saved

AUTHOR'S NOTE

Saved is almost irresponsibly optimistic. Len, the chief character, is naturally good, in spite of his upbringing and
environment, and he remains good in spite of the pressures
of the play. But he is not wholly good or easily good because
then his goodness would be meaningless, at least for himself.
His faults are partly brought home to him by his ambivalence
at the death of the baby and his morbid fascination with it
afterwards.

It is true that at the end of the play Len does not know what
he will do next, but he never has done. On the other hand, he
has created the chance of a friendship with the father, and
he has been chastened but he has not lost his resilience (he
mends the chair). The play ends in a silent social stalemate,
but if the spectator thinks this is pessimistic that is because
he has not learned to clutch at straws. Clutching at straws is
the only realistic thing to do. The alternative, apart from the
self-indulgence of pessimism, is a fatuous optimism based
on superficiality of both feeling and observation. The gesture
of turning the other cheek is often the gesture of refusing to
look facts in the face – but this is not true of Len. He lives
with people at their worst and most hopeless (that is the point
of the final scene) and does not turn away from them. I cannot
imagine an optimism more tenacious, disciplined or honest
than his.

Curiously, most theatre critics would say that for the play
to be optimistic Len should have run away. Fifty years ago
when, the same critics would probably say, moral standards
were higher, they would have praised him for the loyalty and
devotion with which he stuck to his post.

By not playing his traditional role in the tragic Oedipus

pattern of the play, Len turns it into what is formally a comedy. The first scene is built on the young man's sexual insecurity – he either invents interruptions himself or is interrupted by the old man. Len has to challenge him, and get him out of the house, before he can continue. Later he helps the old man's wife, and this is given a sexual interpretation by the onlookers. Later still the old man finds him with his wife in a more obviously sexual situation. The Oedipus outcome should be a row and death. There *is* a row, and even a struggle with a knife – but Len persists in trying to help. The next scene starts with him stretched on the floor with a knife in his hand, and the old man comes in dressed as a ghost – but neither of them is dead. They talk, and for once in the play someone apart from Len is as honest and friendly as it is possible for him to be. The old man can only give a widow's mite, but in the context it is a victory – and a *shared* victory. It is trivial to talk of defeat in this context. The only sensible object in defeating an enemy is to make him your friend. That happens in this play, although in fact most social and personal problems are solved by alienation or killing.

I also shut out Len from the relation between Pam and Fred because (among other things) this let me explore the Oedipus atmosphere at other stages. In particular, the murder of the baby shows the Oedipus, atavistic fury fully unleashed. The scene is typical of what some people do when they act without restraint, and is not true just of these particular people and this particular occasion. Everyone knows of worse happenings. This sort of fury is what is kept under painful control by other people in the play, and that partly accounts for the corruption of their lives.

Clearly the stoning to death of a baby in a London park is a typical English understatement. Compared to the 'strategic' bombing of German towns it is a negligible atrocity, compared to the cultural and emotional deprivation of most of our children its consequences are insignificant.

Like most people I am a pessimist by experience, but an optimist by nature, and I have no doubt that I shall go on being true to my nature. Experience is depressing, and it would be a mistake to be willing to learn from it.

I did not write the play only as an Oedipus comedy. Other things in it – such as the social comment – are more important, but I have not described them in detail here because they are more obvious.

There is, however, a final matter. If we are to improve people's behaviour we must first increase their moral understanding, and this means teaching morality to children in a way that they find convincing. Although I suppose that most English people do not consciously disbelieve in the existence of God, not more than a few hundred of them fully believe in his existence. Yet almost all the morality taught to our children is grounded in religion. This in itself makes children morally bewildered – religion has nothing to do with their parents' personal lives, or our economic, industrial and political life, and is contrary to the science and rationalism they are taught at other times. For them religion discredits the morality it is meant to support.

Their problems in studying science and art are those of understanding – but in a religious morality it is one of believing. Most children, as they grow older, cannot believe in religion. We no longer believe in it ourselves, and it is therefore foolish to teach children to do so. The result is that they grow up morally illiterate, and cannot understand, because they have not been properly taught, the nature of a moral consideration or the value of disinterested morals at all.

This is not always noticed because we use words that still have moral connotations, but these are being lost and soon we could well be morally bankrupt. The prevalent morality can be described as opportunist prudentialism, and it is usually expressed with a nauseous sentimentality that I have avoided in this play because it sounds like parody.

There will always be some people sophisticated enough to do the mental gymnastics needed to reconcile science and religion. But the mass of people will never be able to do this, and as we live in an industrial society they will be educated in the scientific tradition. This means that in future religion will never be more than the opium of the intellectuals.

For several reasons morals cannot be slapped on superficially as a social lubricant. They must share a common basis with social organization and be consistent with accepted knowledge. You cannot, that is, 'have the fruit without the root'. Most people, when they think about this, ask only what *they* believe, or perhaps what has been revealed to them. But if they are interested in the welfare of others they should ask 'what is it possible for most people to believe?' And that means teaching, oddly enough, moral scepticism and analysis, and not faith.

SAVED was first presented by the English Stage Company at the Royal Court Theatre, London, on 3rd November, 1965, with the following cast:

LEN, twenty-one. Tall, slim, firm, bony. Big hands. High, sharp cheekbones. Pleasant pale complexion – not ashen. Blue eyes, thick fair hair a bit oily, brushed sideways from a parting. Prominent feet.

John Castle

FRED, twenty-one. Blond, very curly hair. Medium height. Well-shaped, steady, powerful body. Light tenor voice.

Tony Selby

HARRY, sixty-eight. Tall. Long thin arms. Long hands. Heavy, bony head with large eye-sockets and small eyes. Loose chin. Grey.

Richard Butler

PETE, twenty-five. Tallish. Well-built, red-faced. Makes very few gestures. Soft hair that tends to stick up lightly.

Ronald Pickup

COLIN, shortish. A bit thin. Loose (but not big) mouth. Shiny ears, curved featureless face. A few spots. Shouts to make himself heard. Eighteen.

Dennis Waterman

MIKE, tall. Well-built. Strong, easy, emphatic movements. Pleasant. Dark hair. Twenty.

John Bull

BARRY, twenty. A little below medium height. Fat.

William Stewart

PAM, twenty-three. Thin, sharp-busted. Heavy, nodal hips. Dark hair. Long narrow face. Pale eyes. Small mouth. Looks tall from a distance, but is shorter than she looks.

Barbara Ferris

MARY, fifty-three. Shortish. Round heavy shoulders. Big buttocks. Bulky breasts, lifeless but still high. Big thighs and little ankles. Curled grey hair that looks as if it is in a hair-net. Homely.

Gwen Nelson

LIZ, exactly as she sounds.   *Alison Frazer*

Directed by William Gaskill
Assistant to Director Jane Howell
Designed by John Gunter
Stage Manager Juliet Alliston
Assistant to Stage Manager Allison Rockley

Scene one	Living-room	Scene eight	Living-room
Scene two	Park	Scene nine	Living-room
Scene three	Park	Scene ten	Café
Scene four	Living-room	Scene eleven	Living-room
Scene five	Bedroom	Scene twelve	Bedroom
Scene six	Park	Scene thirteen	Living-room
Scene seven	Cell		

The area of the play is South London

The stage is as bare as possible – sometimes completely bare.

There should be an interval after Scene Seven.

SCENE ONE

The living-room. The front and the two side walls make a triangle that slopes to a door back centre.

Furniture: table down right, sofa left, TV set left front, armchair up right centre, two chairs close to the table.

Empty.

The door opens. Len comes in. He goes straight out again.

PAM (*off*). In there.

LEN *comes in. He goes down to the sofa. He stares at it.*

All right?

Pause. PAM *comes in.*

LEN. This ain' the bedroom.
PAM. Bed ain' made.
LEN. Oo's bothered?
PAM. It's awful. 'Ere's nice.
LEN. Suit yourself. Yer don't mind if I take me shoes off? (*He kicks them off.*) No one 'ome?
PAM. No.
LEN. Live on yer tod?
PAM. No.
LEN. O.

Pause. He sits back on the couch.

Yer all right? Come over 'ere.
PAM. In a minit.
LEN. Wass yer name?
PAM. Yer ain' arf nosey.

LEN. Somethin' up?

PAM. Can't I blow me nose?

She puts her hanky back in her bag and puts it on the table.
  Better.

She sits on the couch.

LEN. Wass yer name?

PAM. Wass yourn?

LEN. Len.

PAM. Pam.

LEN. O. (*He feels the couch behind with his hand.*) This big
  enough?

PAM. What yer want? Bligh!

LEN. Don't wan' a push yer off. Shove that cushion up.

PAM. 'Ang on.

LEN. 'Ow often yer done this?

PAM. Don't be nosey.

LEN. Take yer shoes off.

PAM. In a minit.

LEN. Can yer move yer – thass better.

PAM. Yer d'narf fidget.

LEN. I'm okay now.

PAM. Ow!

LEN. D'yer 'ave the light on?

PAM. Suit yerself.

LEN. I ain' fussy.

PAM. Ow!

LEN. Can yer shut them curtains?

PAM *goes left to the curtains.*

  Yer got a fair ol'arse.

PAM. Like your mug.

LEN. Know somethin'? – I ain' touched a tart for weeks.

PAM. Don't know what yer missin'.

LEN. Don't I?

PAM *sits on the couch, on the edge.* LEN *pulls her closer and takes off her shoes.*

  Lucky.

PAM. What?

LEN. Bumpin' in t'you.

PAM. Yeh.

LEN. Yer don't mind me?

PAM. No.

LEN. Sure?

PAM. Yer wan'a get on with it.

LEN. Give us a shout if I do somethin' yer don't reckon.

PAM. Bligh! Yer ain' better 'ave.

LEN. I could go for you. Know that?

Pause.

  This is the life.

PAM. Ow!

LEN. Sh! Keep quiet now.

PAM. Oi!

LEN. Sh!

PAM. Yer told me t'shout!

The door opens. HARRY *comes in. He goes straight out again.*

LEN (*lifts his head*). 'Ere!

PAM. What?

LEN. Oo's that?

PAM. Ol' man.

LEN (*sits*). Whass 'e want?

PAM. That cushion's stickin' in me back.

LEN. I thought yer reckon yer was on yer tod?

PAM. 'E's late for work.

LEN. O. Why?

PAM. Why?

LEN. Yeh.
PAM. I don't know.
LEN. Reckon 'e saw?
PAM. Shouldn't be surprised.
LEN. Will 'e be long?
PAM. Don't arst me.
LEN. O. Well.

They lie down again. Slight pause. LEN *lifts his head.*

'Ear that?
PAM. No.
LEN. I 'eard somethin'.

He goes to the door. He listens. He goes back to the couch and sits on the end.

PAM. Well?
LEN. Better 'ang on.
PAM. Why?
LEN. Better 'ad.
PAM. Think yer'll last?
LEN. Not if yer lie around like that.
PAM. Like what?
LEN. Sit up.
PAM. I juss got right.
LEN. More'n I 'ave. Chriss. (*He feels in his pocket.*) You smoke?
PAM. In me bag.
LEN. Where's yer bag?

PAM *nods at the table. He goes to the bag and takes out a cigarette. He lights it. He starts putting the cigarettes back.*

Oh, sorry.

He holds the packet out to her.

PAM. No thanks.
LEN (*he puts the cigarettes away. He sits on the edge of the*

couch. Pause. He taps his foot three or four times).   Wass
'is caper?

PAM. Wan'a cup 'a tea?

LEN. After.

PAM. 'E won't be long.

LEN. 'Adn't better. 'Ave a puff?

PAM. No.

LEN. Do yer dress up.

PAM. Sorry.

LEN. Yer never know 'oo's poppin' in.

He goes to the door and opens it.

PAM. You off?

LEN. I could'a swore I 'eard 'eavy breathin'.

PAM. Thass you.

LEN. 'Oo else yer got knockin' about? Yer ain't stuffed yer
grannie under the sofa?

PAM. She's dead.

LEN. 'Ard luck. – Wass 'is caper?

He sits on a chair.

My blinkin' luck.

He stands and walks.

'E'll be late, won't 'e! I 'ope they dock 'is bloody packet.

He listens by the door.

Not a twitter.

PAM. 'E ain' bin out the back yet.

LEN. The ol' twit.

PAM *laughs.*

Wass the joke?

PAM. You.

LEN (*amused*). Yeh. Me. Ha! 'E's a right ol' twit, ain' 'e!
'Ere, can I stay the night?

PAM. Ain' yer got nowhere?

LEN. Yeh! – Well?

PAM. No.

LEN. Yer're the loser. – Sure's 'e's goin'? – Why can't I?

PAM. Bligh! I only juss met yer.

LEN. Suppose 'e's stoppin' 'ome? Got a cold or somethin'.
I'd do me nut! – Yer'd enjoy it.

PAM. Big 'ead.

LEN. 'Ow many blokes yer 'ad this week?

PAM. We ain't finished Monday yet!

LEN. We'll take that into consideration.

PAM. Saucy bugger!

They laugh.

'Ow many times yer 'ad it this week?

LEN. I told yer once! 'Ow many blokes yer 'ad all told?

They laugh.

PAM. What about you an' girls?

LEN. Can't count over sixty.

They laugh.

PAM. Sh!

LEN. 'E'll 'ear. – Oi, tell us!

PAM. 'Ow many times yer done it in one night?

They laugh.

LEN. Why did the woman with three tits shoot 'erself?

PAM. Eh?

LEN. She only 'ad two nipples.

They laugh.

PAM. I don't get it. (*She laughs.*) What did the midwife say
to the nun?

LEN. Don' know.

She whispers in his ear. They laugh.

You're great! What about the woman with three tits 'oo
'ad quads?

PAM. Eh?
LEN. That'll teach 'er t'sleep with siamese twins!

They laugh. He whispers in her ear.

PAM. Yer ought a be locked up!
LEN. That's a feedin' problem!
PAM. Sh – thass the back door. 'E's bin out the lav.
LEN. Less give 'im a thrill.

He jumps noisily on the couch.

Cor – blimey!
PAM. You're terrible!

He takes some sweets from her bag.

They're my sweets.
LEN. Less 'ave a choose. (*Loudly.*) 'Ow's that for size?
PAM. What yer shoutin?
LEN (*he puts a sweet in her mouth*). Go easy! Yer wanna make
it last!

She laughs. He bites a sweet in half and looks at it.

Oo, yer got a lovely little soft centre.
(*Aside to* PAM). First time I seen choclit round it!

He jumps on the sofa.

PAM (*shrill*). Yer awful!
LEN. That still 'ard?

PAM (*laughs*). Leave off!

LEN. Come on, there's plenty more where that come from.

He puts a sweet in her mouth.

PAM (*splutters*). Can't take no more!

LEN. Yeh – open it. Yer can do a bit more!

PAM. Ow!

LEN. Oorr lovely!

He tickles her. She chokes.

This'll put 'airs on yer chest!

They try to laugh quietly. The door opens. HARRY *puts his head in. He goes out. He shuts the door.* LEN *calls:*

'Ave a toffee!

PAM. Oo-oo 'ave a toffee!

LEN. Tried that mint with the 'ole in it?

PAM. 'Ave a toffee!

LEN. What about the ol' dolly mixture? – Will 'e give yer a ruckin'?

PAM. Ain' got the nerve.

LEN (*calls*). Nosey ol' gander!

They laugh.

See 'is tongue 'angin' out?

PAM. 'E's fetchin' 'is dinner-box out the kitchen.

LEN (*calls*). Don't work too 'ard, mate!

PAM. Lay off, or 'e'll stay in out a spite.

LEN (*calls*). Take a toffee for tea break, Dad! – I'd like'a sleep round 'ere. Yer'd be lovely an' warm in the mornin'.

PAM. Yer're juss greedy!

LEN. I give yer 'alf the sweets!

PAM. I paid. Anyway, Mum'll be back.

LEN. O. That the front door?

PAM. Yeh.

She goes to the curtains.

  'E's off.

LEN. Didn't take long.

PAM. I tol' yer.

LEN. Better be worth waitin' for.

PAM. Up to you, ain' it!

LEN. Thass all right then.

She comes to the sofa and starts to undo his belt.

  This is the life.

SCENE TWO

Park.

PAM *and* LEN *in a rowing boat. Otherwise stage bare.*

LEN. Cold?

PAM. No.

LEN. Still pecky?

PAM. Yeh.

LEN. There's a bit'a choclit left. 'Ere.

PAM. No.

LEN. Go on.

PAM. Ta.

LEN. Thass yer lot.

PAM. Why?

LEN. No more.

Silence.

  I still ain' paid me rent this week.

PAM. Me mum won't reckon that.

LEN. Ain' got round to it.

PAM. Surprised she ain' said.

Slight pause.

LEN. She ever let on?

PAM. 'Bout us?

LEN. Yeh.

PAM. No.

LEN. She don't mind?

PAM. Don't 'ave to. Your money comes in 'andy.

Silence.

LEN. She reckon me, yer reckon?

PAM. Never arst.

LEN. Thought she might'a said.

PAM. Never listen.

LEN. O.

PAM. Yer ain't spent it?

LEN. 'Er rent?

PAM. Yeh.

LEN. Nah!

PAM. Juss wondered.

LEN. Don' yer truss me?

PAM. I'm goin' a knit yer a jumper.

LEN. For me?

PAM. I ain' very quick.

LEN. Can't say I noticed.

PAM. Yer'll 'ave t'buy the wool.

LEN. Knew there'd be a catch.

PAM. I got a smashin' pattern.

LEN. You worried about that rent?

PAM. I 'ad it give us.

LEN. Yer 'adn't better be one of them naggers.

PAM. What colour's best?

LEN. Thass about one thing your ol' girl *don't* do.

PAM. What?

LEN. Nag 'er ol' man.

PAM. What's yer best colour?

LEN. They all suit me.
PAM. I like a red. Or a blue.
LEN. Anythin' bright.

Slight pause.

PAM. I 'ave t' 'ave an easy pattern.
LEN. Will it be ready for the 'oneymoon?
PAM. We ain' 'avin' 'oneymoon.
LEN. 'Oo's payin'?
PAM. You.
LEN. I can see I'll 'ave t' watch out.

Pause.

PAM. Whass the time?
LEN. Don't know.
PAM. Gettin' on.
LEN. Shouldn't wonder.
PAM. Where's the choclit?
LEN. Yer 'ad it all.
PAM. O.
LEN. Sorry.
PAM. There weren't much.
LEN. I'll get some when we go in.
PAM. I 'ad a blinkin' great dinner.
LEN. I reckon yer got a kid on the way.
PAM. I ain'.
LEN. Never know yer luck.
PAM. Yer'll 'ave t' get up early in the mornin' t' catch me.
LEN. Done me best.
PAM. Yer got a dirty mind.

Slight pause.

LEN. I'm 'andy with me 'ands. Yer know, fix up the ol'
decoratin' lark and knock up a few things. Yeh. We'll 'ave
a fair little place. I ain' livin' in no blinkin' sty.

PAM. Sounds all right.

LEN. Easy t' kep swep' out an' that. Yer'll be all right.

PAM. I'd better.

He puts his head in her lap. There is a slight pause.

LEN. 'S great 'ere.

Pause.

Pam.

PAM. What?

LEN. Why did yer pick me up like that?

PAM. Why?

LEN. Yeh.

PAM. Sorry then?

LEN. Tell us.

PAM. 'Ow many girls you 'ad?

LEN. No, I tol' yer my life.

PAM. 'Old on.

LEN. What?

PAM. Yer got a spot.

LEN. Where?

PAM. 'Old still.

LEN. Is it big?

PAM. 'Old still.

LEN. Go easy!

PAM. Got it!

LEN. Ow!

She bursts a spot on his neck.

PAM. Give us yer 'anky.

LEN. Yer got it?

PAM. Yeh.

LEN. Ow! It d'narf 'urt.

He gives her his handkerchief. She dips her hand in the water and dries it on the handkerchief. She gives it back to him.

PAM. Yer wan'a wash sometimes.

LEN. Cheeky cow. (*Slight pause. They are both lying down.*)
  Yer wouldn't go back with any ol' sod?

PAM. You are rotten.

LEN. I'm sorry. Pam?

PAM. You're 'urtin' me leg.

LEN. I'm sorry.

PAM. No.

LEN. When yer goin' a start me jumper?

PAM (*still annoyed*). Why d'yer 'ave t' say that?

LEN. Tell us about me jumper.

PAM. Ain' got no wool.

LEN. I'll get it t'morra. An' we'll start lookin' for a place
  t'morra.

PAM. No places round 'ere.

LEN. Move out a bit. It's better out.

PAM. Yer'll be lucky.

LEN. Bin lucky with you. (*His head is in her lap. He twists so
  that he can put his arms round her.*) Ain' I bin lucky with you?

PAM. Yer don't deserve it.

LEN. I said I'm sorry – I won't arst no more. It's me good
  looks done it.

PAM. It *was* you. It weren't no one else.

LEN. Less go t'bed early t'night.

PAM. If yer go t' bed much earlier it won't be worth gettin' up.

LEN. Lovely. 'Ow about a sing-song.

PAM. No.

LEN (*sings*).

> Be kind to'yer four-footed friends
> That duck may be somebody's brother
> Yer may think that this is the end
> Well it is.

Slight pause.

  They must a' forgot us. We bin 'ere 'ours.

PAM. Do the rest.

LEN. Some mothers!

Pause.

Livin' like that must 'a got yer down.

PAM. Used to it.

LEN. They ought to be shot.

PAM: Why?

LEN. Don't it every worry yer?

PAM. Ow?

LEN. Supposed you turned out like that?

PAM. No.

LEN. 'Ow'd it start?

PAM. Never arst.

LEN. No one said?

PAM. Never listen. It's their life.

LEN. But –

PAM. Yer can't do nothin', yer know. No one'll thank yer.

LEN. 'Ow long's it bin goin' on?

PAM. Longer'n I know.

Pause. He sits and leans towards her.

LEN. Must a' bin bloody rotten when yer was a kid.

PAM. Never know'd no difference. They 'ad a boy in the war.

LEN. Theirs?

PAM. Yeh.

LEN. I ain't seen 'im.

PAM. Dead.

LEN. O.

PAM. A bomb in a park.

LEN. That what made 'em go funny?

PAM. No. I come after.

LEN. What a life.

PAM. I 'ad me moments.

LEN. I won't turn out like that. I wouldn't arst yer if I didn't
know better 'n that. That sort of carry-on ain' fair.

PAM. I know.

LEN. We'll get on all right. I wonder it never sent yer off yer nut.

PAM. Yer don't notice.

LEN. It won't be long now. Why don't yer blow up an' knock their 'eads t'gether?

PAM (*shrugs*). I 'ope I never see 'em again. Thass all.

Slight pause. LEN *looks round.*

LEN. I ain' got a decent jumper.

Pause.

'Ow'd they manage?

PAM. When?

LEN. They writes notes or somethin'?

PAM. No.

LEN. 'Ow's that?

PAM. No need.

LEN. They must.

PAM. No.

LEN. Why?

PAM. Nothin' t' say. 'E puts 'er money over the fire every Friday, an' thass all there is. Talk about somethin' else.

LEN. Whass she say about 'im?

PAM. Nothin'.

LEN. But –

PAM. She never mentions 'im an' 'e never mentions 'er. I don' wanna talk about it.

LEN. They never mention each other?

PAM. I never 'eard 'em.

LEN. Not once?

PAM. *No!*

LEN. It's wet down 'ere.

Pause.

I ain' livin' with me in-laws, thass a fact.

FRED (*off*). Four!

LEN. I never got yer placed till I saw yer ol' people.

PAM. I never chose 'em!

LEN. I never meant that! –

PAM. Don't know why yer wan'a keep on about 'em!

LEN. – I never try an' get at yer!

FRED *comes on down right. His back to the audience.*

FRED. Number-four-bang-on-the-door!

PAM. Thass us.

FRED. Less 'ave yer!

LEN. Less stay out!

PAM. Why?

FRED. Oi!

PAM (*to* LEN). Come on.

LEN. We're a pirate ship.

FRED (*taking the micky*). You devil!

PAM. Yer'll 'ave t' pay.

LEN. Come an' get us!

FRED. Wass up darlin'? 'As 'e got 'is rudder stuck?

PAM (*to* LEN). I'm 'ungry.

LEN. Why didn't yer say?

LEN *starts to pull in.* FRED *moves towards them as the boat comes in.*

FRED. Lovely. 'Elp 'im darlin'. Thass lovely. She 'andles that like a duchess 'andles a navvy's pick.

LEN. All right?

FRED. Lovely.

He leans out and jerks the boat in. PAM *stands awkwardly.*

LEN. Steady.

FRED. 'Old tight, darlin'.

He lifts her out.

Yer wanna watch Captain Blood there. Very nice.

LEN. Okay?

PAM. Ta.

FRED. Very 'ow's yer father.

LEN (*stepping out*). Muddy.

PAM (*to* LEN). I enjoyed that.

FRED. Same 'ere.

LEN. We'll do it again.

FRED. Any time.

PAM (*to* LEN). Got everythin'?

FRED (*to* PAM). You 'ave.

LEN (*clowning*). Watch it!

FRED. 'Oo's bin' 'aving a bash on me duckboards?

PAM (*to* LEN). Less 'ave me bag.

FRED. Bashin's extra.

PAM. Yer wanna get yerself a job.

FRED. I got one.

PAM. 'Irin' out boats!

FRED. I'd rather 'ire you out, darlin'.

LEN (*joking*). Watch it!

PAM (*to* LEN). Ready?

LEN. Yeh.

LEN *and* PAM *start to go right.*

FRED. Why, you got a job for us? I wouldn't mind a bit a
grind for you.

PAM. Yer'll 'ave t' join the union.

FRED. I'm in, love. Paid up.

LEN (*joking*). Yer'll be in the splash in a minute.

LEN *and* PAM *go out left.*

FRED (*to himself*). Right up. Like you, darlin'.

SCENE THREE

Park. Bare stage.

PETE, BARRY, MIKE, COLIN. PETE *wears a brown suit and
suede shoes. The jacket is short in the seat and tight on the
shoulders. His tie is black. The others wear jeans and shirts.*

MIKE. What time they bury the bugger?

PETE. Couldn't tell yer.

COLIN. Don' yer wan'a go?

PETE. Leave off! 'Oo's goin' a make me time up?

COLIN. Why yer goin' then?

PETE. The ol' lady'll ruck if I don't.

MIKE. Yeh, they reckon anythin' like this.

COLIN. Blinkin' morbid.

MIKE. Looks lovely in a black tie don' 'e!

They laugh.

PETE. What a carry on! 'E come runnin' round be'ind the bus. Only a nipper. Like a flash I thought right yer nasty bastard. Only ten or twelve. I jumps right down on me revver an' bang I got 'im on me off-side an' 'e shoots right out under this lorry comin' straight on.

MIKE. Crunch.

COLIN. Blood all over the shop.

MIKE. The Fall a the Roman Empire.

PETE. This lorry was doin' a ton in a built-up street.

BARRY. Garn! Yer never seen 'im.

PETE. No?

BARRY. 'It 'im before yer knew 'e was comin'.

PETE (*lighting his pipe*). Think I can't drive?

COLIN. What a giggle, though.

MIKE. Accidents is legal.

COLIN. Can't touch yer.

PETE. This coroner-twit says 'e's sorry for troublin' me.

MIKE. The law thanks 'im for 'is 'elp.

PETE. They paid me for comin'.

MIKE. An' the nip's mother reckons 'e ain' got a blame 'isself.

COLIN. She'll turn up at the funeral.

PETE. Rraammmmmmmmmm!

COLIN. Bad for the body work.

MIKE. Can't yer claim insurance?

PETE. No.

MIKE. Choked!

COLIN. Ruined 'is paint work.

BARRY. 'E's 'avin' yer on!

MIKE. Yer creep.

COLIN. Yer big creep.

PETE. Let 'im alone. 'E don't know no better.

COLIN. 'E don't know nothin'.

MIKE. Big stingy creep.

COLIN. Yer wouldn't 'ave the guts.

BARRY. No guts?

MIKE. Yeh.

BARRY. Me?

COLIN. Not yer grannie.

BARRY. I done blokes in.

MIKE. 'Ere we go.

BARRY. More'n you 'ad 'ot dinners. In the jungle. Shootin'
up the yeller-niggers. An' cut 'em up after with the ol'
pig-sticker. Yeh.

MIKE (*hoots*).

COLIN. Do leave off!

BARRY. You lot wouldn't know a stiff if it sat up and shook
'ands with yer!

MIKE. Aa! Shootin' up the yeller-nigs!

COLIN. Sounds like brothers a your'n.

BARRY. Get stuffed!

PETE (*to them all*). Chuck it, eh?

COLIN. Yeller-niggers! My life! What yer scratchin'?

MIKE. 'E's got a dose.

PETE. Ain' surprisin'.

COLIN. Ain' it dropped off yet?

MIKE. Tied on with a ol' johnny.

COLIN. It's 'is girl.

MIKE. 'Is what?

PETE. Gunged-up ol' boot.

COLIN. 'E knocked it off in the back a 'is car last night –

MIKE. 'Is what?

PETE. Pile a ol' scrap.

MIKE. Ought a be put off the road.

COLIN. 'E was knockin' it off in the back an' –

MIKE. I 'eard.

PETE. What?

MIKE. The back-bumper fell off.

PETE. Yeh?

COLIN. I's a fact!

PETE. My life!

MIKE. An' what she say?

COLIN. Yer juss drop somethin'.

BARRY. Bollocks!

He laughs at himself.

MIKE. Yeh!

COLIN. 'Aving trouble with yer 'orn?

BARRY. It weren't no bumper! Me fog lamp come off.

MIKE. 'Is fog lamp!

They roar with laughter.

COLIN. I knew somethin' come off!

MIKE. Flippin' fog lamp!

PETE. Thass what she calls it!

COLIN. Wonder it weren't 'is engine come out.

BARRY. Better'n nothin'.

MIKE. Yer couldn't knock someone down with that!

PETE. It'd come t' a stop.

MIKE. Shootin' up the yeller-niggers!

BARRY. Yeh, yer ain' lived!

LEN comes on down right.

PETE. Me mum's got a dirty great wreath.

MIKE. Yeh!

COLIN. Give somethin' for it?

PETE. I ain' a 'ippocrit.

COLIN. Oi – whass-yer-name!

LEN. Eh?

COLIN. It's – Lenny, ain' it?

LEN. Yeh. – O! 'Ow's it goin', admiral?

COLIN. 'Ow's yerself?

LEN. Not so dodgy. Long time.

COLIN. Me and 'im was t'school t'gether.

MIKE. Yeh?

COLIN. What yer bin doin'?

BARRY. Reform school?

MIKE. Don't 'e show yer up!

COLIN. Take no notice. Creep! – Workin'?

LEN. Worse luck.

COLIN. I couldn't place yer for a minute. (*Slight pause.*) Yeh.

LEN. Yer ain' changed much.

BARRY. What yer doin' now?

LEN. Waitin'.

MIKE. I – I!

COLIN. It was in the park, yer 'onour!

MIKE. This girl come up t'me.

COLIN. An' drags me in the bushes.

BARRY. Yer 'onour.

He laughs.

COLIN. I knew she was thirteen.

MIKE. But she twisted me arm.

COLIN. An' 'er ol' dad 'd bin bashin' it off for years.

BARRY. Yer 'onour.

He laughs.

COLIN. Twisted yer what?

MIKE. Never know yer luck!

COLIN. Married?

LEN. Gettin' ready.

BARRY. 'Oo with?

LEN. We're waitin' –

COLIN. Pull the other one!

MIKE. What for?

PETE. Till she drops 'er nipper.

COLIN. Else it looks bad goin' up the aisle.

MIKE. She can 'ide it be'ind 'er flowers.

BARRY. Is that what they carry 'em for?

COLIN. We live an' learn.

MIKE. Takes all sorts.

MARY *comes on up right.*

LEN. Thass us.

COLIN. *That?*

LEN *goes to* MARY.

PETE. One man's meat.

MIKE. More like scrag-end.

BARRY. Bit past it, ain' she?

PETE. She's still got the regulation 'oles.

MIKE. Experience 'elps. Yer get a surprise sometimes.

LEN (*to* MARY). Less give yer a 'and.

MARY. Whew! Ta.

She gives him the shopping bags.

LEN. Okay?

MARY. I was juss goin' ter drop 'em.

MIKE. 'Ear that.

BARRY. Goin' a drop 'em!

COLIN. In the park?

MIKE. At 'alf-past twelve?

PETE (*laughing*). The dirty ol' scrubber.

LEN *and* MARY *start to cross left.*

BARRY (*to* COLIN). That what they taught yer at school?

COLIN *whistles*.

LEN (*amused*). Put a sock in it.

BARRY. What yer got at the top a your legs? What time 's breakfast?

MARY. That your mates?

LEN. They're juss 'avin' a laugh.

MARY. You all right with them bags?

LEN. Yeh.

COLIN. Roger the lodger 'ad a bad cough.

MIKE. 'E sneezed so 'ard.

COLIN. 'Is door knob fell off.

BARRY. 'Is landlady said we'll soon 'ave yer well.

COLIN. So she pulled off 'er drawers.

MIKE. An' polished 'is bell!

MARY. Lot a roughs.

LEN *and* MARY *go out left*.

PETE. Makes yer think.

COLIN. What?

PETE. Never know what yer missin'.

MIKE. True.

PETE. I knew a bloke once reckoned 'e knocked off 'is grannie.

COLIN. Yeh?

PETE. All a mistake.

COLIN. 'Ow's that?

PETE. There was a power cut at the time an' –

BARRY. – 'E thought it was 'is sister.

PETE. Ain' yer clever!

MIKE. Trust the unions!

COLIN. Makes yer think, though.

BARRY *blows a raspberry*.

PETE (*smoking his pipe*). Never know 'alf what goes on.

MIKE. That age she must be 'angin' out for it.
PETE. Stuffin' it all in before it's too late.
COLIN. Yeh.

There is a slight pause.

PETE. Ooorrr! I'll 'ave t' fix up a little bird t'night. 'Ere, wass
  the time?
COLIN. Time we're back t' work.

They groan.

MIKE (*to* PETE). Time yer're round the church they'll 'ave
  'im down the 'ole or up the chimney or wherever 'e's goin'.
PETE. I reckon they wanna put 'im down the 'ole an' pull
  the chain.

SCENE FOUR

The living room. Dark.
  The door opens. MARY *comes in. She puts on the light.* HARRY
is sitting in the armchair. He is partly asleep. MARY *puts sauce,*
salt and pepper on the table and goes out. HARRY *gets up. He goes*
to the door and puts the light out. He goes back to the armchair.
  Pause.
  The door opens. MARY *comes in. She puts on the light. She*
takes knife, fork, spoon and table napkin to the table. She lays the
napkin as a small table cloth. The door opens. PAM *comes in.*
She wears a slip and carries a hair brush and cosmetics. She
switches on the TV set. MARY *goes out. Without waiting to*
adjust the set PAM *goes to the couch and sits. She makes up her*
face. The door opens. MARY *comes in with a plate of food.*

MARY (*calls*). It's on the table.

She walks towards the table. To PAM.

I told you not to walk round like that.

MARY *puts the food on the table and goes out.* PAM *goes to the TV set and adjusts it. She goes back to the couch and sits. She makes up her face.* MARY *comes in.*

(*At the door*). It's on the table! That's the second time!

She goes to the TV set.

I don't know 'ow they 'ave the nerve to put it on.

She switches to another channel. She steps back to look at the picture. She steps forward to adjust it. She steps back.

Hm.

She steps forward and adjusts it again.

If yer put it in the oven it goes 'ard as nails.

She steps back and looks at the set. She goes to the couch, sits and watches TV. Pause.

PAM. More like one a them daft mirrors at a circus.
MARY. The man'll 'ave to come an' fix it.

She goes to the set and adjusts it.

You don't know 'ow to switch it on. It goes all right when I do it.

LEN *comes in.*

LEN. Smells great.
MARY. You've let it ruin.
LEN. Nah.
MARY. Cold as Christmas.
LEN. Do me.

He sits at the table and eats.

MARY (*goes to the set and re-adjusts it*). I don't know. – Did yer put the light out in the scullery?
LEN. Yeh.

MARY. We need a new one. That's what's wrong with it.

She goes back to the couch and sits. She watches silently. Pause.

PAM. Looks like one a them black an' white minstrels.
MARY. Well you do it, an' don't sit there pokin' 'oles.
PAM. I ain' watchin'.
MARY. Sounds like it.

LEN *eats.* MARY *watches.* PAM *makes up.* HARRY *is still. The TV is fairly loud. A very long pause.*
   Slowly a baby starts to cry. It goes on crying without a break until the end of the scene. Nothing happens until it has cried a long while. Then MARY *speaks.*

   Can yer see?
LEN. Yeh.
MARY. Move yer seat.
LEN. I can see.

Pause.

   Yer a fair ol' cook.
MARY. It's ruined. Yer get no encouragement t' try.

Pause. The baby screams with rage. After a while MARY *lifts her head in the direction of the screams.*

   Pam-laa!

Slight pause. PAM *stands and puts her cosmetics in a little bag. She goes to the TV set. She turns up the volume. She goes back to the couch and sits.*

   There's plenty of left-overs.
LEN. Full up.
MARY. An' there's rhubarb and custard.
LEN: O.

Pause. The baby chokes.

PAM. Too lazy t' get up an' fetch it.

MARY. Don't start. Let's 'ave a bit a peace for one night.

Pause.

PAM. 'Is last servant died a over-work.

LEN. I ain' finished this, nosey.

MARY. Why don't yer shut that kid up.

PAM. I can't.

MARY. Yer don't try.

PAM. Juss cries louder when I go near it.

MARY (*watching TV*). I ain' goin' up for yer. (*Still watching TV.*) High time it 'ad a father. (*To* LEN). There's plenty a tea in the pot.

LEN (*watching TV*). Yeh.

MARY (*watching TV*). That's what it needs. No wonder it cries. (*Pause. To* LEN.) Busy?

LEN. Murder.

MARY (*watching TV*). Weather don't 'elp.

LEN (*still watching TV*). Eh? (*The baby whimpers pitifully. Pause. Still watching TV.*) Ha!

Pause. PAM *picks up her things and goes out.*

MARY. About time.

LEN. Wan'a cup?

MARY. No. There's milk in that custard. It'll only get thrown out.

LEN (*stands*). I'll bust.

He goes out.

MARY (*calls*). On the top shelf.

LEN (*off*). What?

MARY. It's on the top shelf!

Pause. LEN *comes in. He carries a plate to the table.*

Did yer get it?

LEN. Yeh.

He sits.

MARY. Shut that door, Len. Me 'ead's playin' me up again.
LEN. Take some a yer anadins.
MARY. I've 'ad too many t'day. Thass what makes it worse.

LEN *goes back to the door and shuts it. He goes to the table and eats.*

Did yer put the oven out?
LEN. An' the light.
MARY. I ain' made a money, y'know.

Suddenly the baby cries much louder.

Put some sugar on it.

LEN *sprinkles the sugar from a teaspoon.*

People'll send the police round 'ere next.
LEN. It'll cry itself t'sleep.

PAM *comes in. She wears a dress.*

MARY. It's still cryin'.
PAM. I thought the cat was stuck up the chimney.

She sits on the couch and pulls up her stockings.

'Ad a good look? – I'm tired a 'im watchin' me all the time.
MARY. I told yer t' get dressed in the scullery like anybody else.
PAM. I can dress where I like in me own 'ome.
LEN (*to himself*). O no.
PAM. You say somethin'?
LEN (*calmly*). Yeh – shut up.
PAM. I suppose that's your idea a good manners.

Pause.

When yer leavin' us? I'm sick an' tired a arstin'.

MARY. I don't wanna 'ear all this again t'night.

PAM. 'E gets on me nerves.

LEN. I ain' leavin' that kid.

PAM. Why?

LEN. With you?

PAM. It ain' your kid.

LEN. No?

PAM. Yer'll 'ave t' take my word for it.

LEN. Yer don't even know when you're lyin'.

Pause. The baby cries.

PAM. I don't understan' yer. Yer ain' got no self respect.

LEN. You 'ave like.

PAM. No one with any self respect wouldn't wanna stay.

LEN *pours tea for himself.*

Yer'll 'ave t'go sometime. Yer can't juss 'ang on till yer
rot.

MARY. Pack it up! No wonder that kid cries!

PAM. Why don't you tell 'im t' go? It's your job. 'E's gettin'
on me nerves every night. If it goes on much longer I'll
be ill.

MARY. That'll teach yer t'bring fellas back.

PAM (*to* HARRY). Why don't you tell im? It's your 'ouse.
There's bin nothin' but rows an' arguments ever since 'e
got 'ere. I've 'ad all I can stand! (*Slight pause.*) Dad!

HARRY. I ain' gettin' involved. Bound t'be wrong.

PAM (*to* LEN). I don't understan' yer. Yer can't enjoy stayin'
'ere.

LEN *drinks his tea.*

It's bad enough bein' stuck with a kid without 'avin' you
'anging roun' me neck. The 'ole street's laughin' be'ind
yer back.

LEN. I ain' leavin' that kid.

PAM. Take it.

LEN. With me?

PAM. 'Ow else?

MARY. 'Ow can 'e?

PAM. Thass 'is worry.

MARY. 'E can't look after a kid.

PAM. Put it on the council.

MARY (*shrugs*). They wouldn't 'ave it if they've got any sense.

The baby cries.

PAM. Well?

LEN. Kids need proper 'omes.

PAM. Yer see!

LEN (*looks in the teapot*). Out a' water.

He goes out.

MARY. Wouldn't yer miss it?

PAM. That racket?

The baby whimpers. There is a ring. PAM *goes out.* MARY *quickly tidies the couch.* LEN *comes back with the teapot.*

MARY. Did the door go?

LEN (*nods*). Juss then.

FRED (*off*). All right, all right. I said I'm sorry, ain' I?

PAM *is heard indistinctly.*

Well let's say 'allo first!

FRED *comes in.*

'Evenin'. 'Evenin', ma.

MARY. We're just watchin' telly.

FRED. Anythin' interestin'?

MARY. Come in.

FRED. 'Lo, Len. 'Ow's life?

LEN. Usual. 'Ow's the job?

FRED. Don't talk about it.

PAM *comes in.*

PAM. I still don't see 'ow that makes yer all this late.

FRED. Give it a rest, Pam.

PAM. The same last time.

MARY. Take yer coat off.

PAM. Yer oughta let me know if yer're goin'a be late.

FRED. 'Ow could I? Sorry love. We'll juss 'ave t' make it later in future.

PAM (*to* MARY). Can I put the kid in your room?

MARY. No wonder it can't sleep. Pushed around like some ol' door mat.

PAM. Can I or can't I? I ain' sittin' there with that row goin' on.

MARY. Do what yer like.

FRED (*to* PAM). Got plenty a fags?

MARY. Yer will anyway.

PAM (*to* FRED). Ready?

FRED. See yer, Lenny boy.

LEN. Yeh.

PAM. It's all the same if I was meetin' yer outside in the street. I'd be left standin' in the cold.

FRED (*following* PAM *to the door*). Got any fags? I left mine be'ind.

PAM *and* FRED *go out.* LEN *stacks the things on the table and takes some of them out. The baby's crying suddenly gets louder.* LEN *comes in again. He picks up the sauce and the table napkin and goes out.* MARY *turns off the TV set and goes out.* HARRY *goes to the table and pours himself tea.* LEN *comes back.*

LEN. O.

HARRY. Finished.

LEN. Ta.

Pause.

Wish t'God I could take that kid out a this.

HARRY (*drinks*). Better.

LEN. No life growin' up 'ere.

HARRY (*wipes his mouth on the back of his hand*). Ah.

LEN. Wish t' God I 'ad some place.

HARRY. Yer wan'a keep yer door shut.

LEN. What?

HARRY. T'night.

LEN. Me door?

HARRY. Yer always keep yer door open when 'e's sleepin' with 'er.

LEN. I listen out for the kid. They ain' bothered.

MARY (*off*). Night, Len.

LEN (*calls*). Night. (*To* HARRY.) More?

HARRY. No.

LEN. Plenty in the pot.

HARRY (*wipes his mouth on the back of his hand*). Yer'll catch cold with it open.

LEN (*holding the teapot*). Night, then.

He goes to the door.

HARRY (*sitting in the armchair*). Put that light out.

LEN *puts the light out and goes. The crying sobs away to silence.*

SCENE FIVE

LEN's *bedroom. It is shaped like the living-room. Furniture: a single bed up right, a wooden chair close to it.* PAM *is in bed.* LEN *stands centre, away from her.*

LEN. Did yer take yer medicine?

Pause.

Feelin' better?

PAM. I'm movin' down t' me own room t'morra. Yer'll 'ave
t' move back up 'ere.

LEN. Quieter up 'ere.

PAM. Like a blinkin' grave.

LEN. Why don't yer 'ave the telly up?

PAM. No.

LEN. Easy fix a plug.

PAM. Did yer see Fred?

LEN. Yer never took yer medicine. (*He pours her medicine and
gives it to her.*) 'Ere. (PAM *takes it.*) Say ta. (*She drinks it
and gives a small genuine* 'Ugh!') Read yer magazines?

PAM. Did Fred say anythin'?

MARY (*off*). Pam-laa! She gettin' up, Len?

PAM (*to herself*). O God.

MARY (*off*). The doctor says there's nothin' t' stop yer gettin'
up. Yer're as well as I am.

LEN *closes the door but the voice is still heard.*

Pam-laa! The dinner's on the table.

LEN. Yer better off up 'ere out a 'er way.

PAM. The cow.

LEN *straightens the bed.*

Leave that.

LEN. You're comin' undone.

PAM. Leave it.

LEN. It's all –

PAM. I said leave it!

LEN (*continuing*). Someone's got a give yer a 'and.

PAM. I won't 'ave yer pullin' me about.

LEN (*walking away*). Why don't yer sit in a chair for 'alf 'our?

PAM. Mind yer own business.

LEN. Yer ain't doin' yerself no good lyin' there.

MARY (*off*). She gettin' up?

LEN. I'm only tryin' a 'elp.

PAM. Don't want yer 'elp.

LEN. Yer got bugger all idea 'ow to look after yerself.

PAM. Go away.

LEN. Some one –

PAM. For Chrissake!

LEN. Someone's got a stick up for yer. (*Slight pause.*) Yer treated me like dirt. But I ain't goin' a carry on like that.

MARY (*off*). Pamm-laa!

PAM (*calls*). Shut up! I'm sick a' the lot of yer! (*Slight pause.*) Shut up!

LEN *goes out.*

PAM. Thank Chriss for that.

MARY (*off*). She up yet?

LEN *answers indistinctly.* Pause. PAM *pulls out the blankets that* LEN *tucked in.* LEN *comes back with the baby.*

LEN (*to baby*). 'Ello then! 'Ello then!

PAM. O no.

LEN. Look-ee that. 'Oo that mummy-there?

PAM. She's got the grub out on the table.

LEN. It'll keep.

PAM. She ain' better row me out for it.

LEN. Take it.

PAM. Put it back.

LEN. Yer ought a take it.

PAM. Don't keep tellin' me what I ought a do.

LEN. Yer ain' even looked at it for weeks.

PAM. Ain' going to.

LEN. Yer'd feel better.

Pause.

'Ello then.

PAM. Did yer give 'im what I wrote?

LEN. 'E's busy, 'e reckons. It's 'is busy time.

PAM. Ha!

LEN. 'Avin' yourn on a tray?

PAM. If yer like.

LEN. It knows yer voice.

PAM. Put it away before it starts.

LEN. Good for its lungs.

PAM. Yer d'narf annoy me, Len.

LEN. I know.

PAM. Yer're always pesterin' me.

LEN. Someone's got a look after yer.

PAM. There yer are! Thass another annoyin' thing t' say. (*She sits.*) This dump gives me the 'ump. Put that away.

LEN. Yer can't let it lie on its back all day. Someone's got a pick it up.

PAM (*sitting back*). Why should I worry? Its father don't give a damn. I could be dyin' an' 'e can't find ten minutes.

LEN. I'm blowed if I'm goin' a put meself out if yer can't co-operate.

He tries to put the baby in her arms.

PAM. I tol' yer take it back! Get off a me! Yer bloody lunatic! Bleedin' cheek! (*Calls.*) Mum!

LEN. You 'ave it for a change!

He puts the baby on the bed.

PAM. Yer goin' mad! It's fallin'. Catch it!

LEN *puts the baby so that it is safe.*

LEN. I ain' your paid nurse!

PAM (*calls*). Mum! – I know why Fred ain' come – yer bin tearin' up me letters.

LEN. 'E did!

PAM. Yer little liar! (*She turns away from the baby.*) I ain' touchin' it.

LEN. It'll stay there all night!

PAM. Thass what yer call 'elpin' me.

Pause. LEN *picks up the baby.*

See!

LEN. Can't give it a cold juss because we're rowin'.

He goes towards the door. He stops.

'E said 'e'd look in.

PAM (*she turns round*). When? (*She turns back to the wall.*)
What did 'e say?

LEN. I said yer wanted to see 'im. 'E goes 'e's up to 'is eyes
in it. So I said I got a couple of tickets for Crystal Palace.
'E's knockin' off early.

PAM. Saturday?

LEN. T'night.

PAM (*turns*). Yer got 'im downstairs!

LEN. No.

PAM (*calls*). Mum – is Fred there? Fred? – 'E might be early.

LEN. There's a good 'alf 'our yet.

PAM (*excited*). I 'ope 'is lot wins.

LEN. 'E might be late.

PAM. Not for football. Yer can say she's upstairs if yer wan'
a go. Put it like that.

LEN (*looks at child*). 'E's well away.

PAM. I ain' cut me nails all the time I bin in bed.

MARY (*off*). Lennie!

LEN. Shall I get the scissors?

PAM. She won't shut up till yer go down. I got me own.

MARY (*off*). Leonard! I keep callin' yer. (*Outside the door.*)
'Ow many more times. (*She comes in.*) I bin callin' the last
'alf 'our. Dinner won't be fit t'eat.

LEN. Juss puttin' the nipper back.

MARY. That's the last time I cook a 'ot meal in this 'ouse.
I mean it this time. (*To* PAM.) Yer can make yer own bed

t'morra, you. (*To* LEN.) I ain' sweatin' over a 'ot stove.
No one offers t'buy me a new one. (*To* PAM.) I can't afford
t' keep yer on yer national 'ealth no longer. I'm the one 'oo
ought to be in bed.

MARY *goes out.*

PAM. I got all patches under me eyes.
LEN. No.
PAM. I feel awful.
LEN. Yer look nice.
PAM. I'll 'ave t' 'ave a wash.
LEN. Yeh.

SCENE SIX

The Park. A bare stage. FRED *holds a fishing-rod out over the
stalls. He wears jeans and an old dull leather jacket.* LEN *sits
beside him on a small tin box. On the ground there are a bait
box, odds and ends box, float box, milk bottle, sugar bottle, flask
and net.*

LEN. Round our place t'night?
FRED. No.
LEN. It's Saturday.
FRED. O yeh.
LEN. She won't like it.
FRED. No.

Pause.

Yer wan' a get yerself a good rod.
LEN. Can't afford it.

FRED. Suit yerself.

LEN. Lend us yourn.

FRED. Get knotted.

Slight pause.

LEN. I in yer way then?

FRED. Eh?

LEN. Sittin' 'ere.

FRED. Free country.

LEN. Yer'd never think it.

FRED. Nippy.

LEN. Lend us yer jacket.

FRED. Jump in.

LEN. 'Ow much yer give for that?

FRED. Yer get 'em on h.p.

LEN. Fair bit a work.

FRED (*runs his hand along the rod*). Comes in 'andy.

Pause.

LEN. She said yer was comin' round for the telly.

FRED. News t' me.

LEN. Don't know whass on.

FRED. Don't care.

LEN. Never looked. (*Slight pause.*) Never bothers me. Easy find out from the paper if yer –

FRED. Don't keep on about it.

LEN. Eh?

FRED. Don't bloody well keep on about it.

LEN. Suits me. (*Slight pause.*) I was agreein' with yer. I thought like –

FRED. Oi – Len, I come out for the fishin'. I don't wanna 'ear all your ol' crap.

Slight pause. LEN *turns his head right and stares at the river.*

'Onest, Len – yer d'narf go on.

LEN. I only said I was agreein' with yer. Blimey, if yer can't ...

He stops. Pause.

FRED. Sod!
LEN. Whass up?
FRED. Bait's gone.
LEN. Gone? They've 'ad it away.
FRED. Never.
LEN. Must 'ave.
FRED. More like wriggled off.
LEN. I mounted it 'ow yer said.
FRED (*winds in*). Come 'ere. Look.

He takes a worm from the worm box.

Right, yer take yer worm. Yer roll it in yer 'and t' knock it out. Thass first. Then yer break a bit off. Cop 'old o' that.

He gives part of the worm to LEN.

LEN. Ta.
FRED. Now yer thread yer 'ook through this bit. Push it up on yer gut. Leave it. – Give us that bit. Ta. Yer thread yer other bit on the 'ook, but yer leave a fair bit 'angin' off like that, why, t'wriggle in the water. Then yer push yer top bit down off the gut and camer-flarge yer shank. Got it?
LEN. Thass 'ow I done it.
FRED. Yeh. Main thing, keep it neat.

He casts. The line hums.

Lovely.

A long silence.

The life.

Silence.

LEN. Down the labour Monday.

FRED *grunts*.

Start somethin'.

Silence.

No life, broke.

FRED. True.

Silence. LEN *pokes in the worm box with a stick.*

Feed 'em on milk.

LEN. Fact?

Silence.

I'll tell 'er yer ain' comin'.

FRED. Len!

LEN. Well yer got a let 'er know.

FRED. 'Oo says?

LEN. Yer can't juss –

FRED. Well?

LEN. Shut up a minute.

FRED. Listen, mate, shut yer trap an' give us a snout.

LEN. No.

FRED. Yer're loaded.

LEN. Scroungin' git! Smoke yer own. – She'll be up 'alf the
night. That'll be great. – I reckon yer got a bloody nerve
takin' my fags, yer know I'm broke. – Yer believe in keepin'
em waitin' for it.

Slight pause.

FRED. Yer used to knock 'er off, that right?

LEN. Once.

FRED. There yer are then.

LEN. What?

FRED. It's all yourn.

LEN. She don't wan'a know.

FRED. 'Ow's that?

LEN. Since you 'ad 'er.

FRED. What d'yer expect? No – they're like that. Once they go off, they go right off.

LEN. Don't even get a feel.

FRED. 'Appens all the time. Give us a snout.

LEN. No.

FRED. Tight arse.

Slight pause.

LEN. Skip?

FRED. Yeh?

LEN. What yer reckon on 'er?

FRED. For a lay?

LEN. Yeh.

FRED. Fair. Depends on the bloke.

LEN. Well?

FRED. No – get that any time.

Silence.

LEN. Gettin' dark.

Silence.

FRED. Call it a day.

LEN. In a minute.

FRED. Never know why yer stick that dump.

LEN. Seen worse.

FRED. I ain'.

Slight pause.

LEN. Skip?

FRED. Whass up now?

LEN. Why's she go for you?

FRED. They all do mate.

LEN. No, why's she – ill over it?

FRED. Come off it, she 'ad a drop a the ol' flu.

LEN. Yeh. But why's she like that?

FRED. It ain' me money.

LEN. They all want the same thing, I reckon. So you must 'ave more a it.

FRED. Thass true! Oi!

LEN. What?

FRED. Still.

Pause.

Thought I 'ad a touch.

Pause.

Nah.

They ease off. FRED *looks up at the sky.*

Jack it in.

LEN. Anyway, thass what they reckon.

FRED. Eh?

LEN. They all want the same thing.

FRED. O.

LEN. I reckon yer're 'avin' me on.

FRED. Me?

LEN. Like the fish that got away.

FRED. I ain' with yer.

He shakes his head.

LEN. That big! (*He holds his hands eighteen inches apart.*)

FRED (*laughs*). More like that! (*He holds his hands three feet apart.*)

LEN. Ha! Thass why she's sick.

FRED. Now give us a fag.

LEN. No.

FRED (*spits*). 'Ave t' light one a me own.

He takes one of his own cigarettes from a packet in his breast pocket. He does not take the packet from the pocket.

LEN. Mind the moths.

FRED. Yer ever 'ad worms up yer nose, in yer ears, an' down yer throat?

LEN. Not lately.

FRED. Yer will in a minute.

LEN. Well give us a snout then.

FRED. Slimey ponce!

He gives LEN *a cigarette.* LEN *gives* FRED *a light.*

LEN. I used a 'ear, know that?

FRED. 'Ear what? – 'E's like a flippin' riddle.

LEN. You an' 'er.

FRED. Me an' 'oo?

LEN. On the bash.

FRED. Do what?

LEN. Straight up.

FRED. Chriss.

LEN. Yeh.

FRED. Yer kiddin'.

LEN. On my life. Kep me up 'alf the night. Yer must a bin trying for the cup.

FRED (*draws his cigarette*). Why didn't yer let on?

LEN. No, it's all a giggle, ain't it?

FRED (*shrugs*). Yeh? Makes yer feel a right charlie.

He drops his cigarette on the floor and treads on it.

Chriss. Thass one good reason for jackin' 'er in.

LEN. Don't start blamin' me.

FRED. An' you was listenin'?

LEN. Couldn't 'elp it.

FRED. O.

He lays his rod on the ground and crouches to pack his things.

Yer didn't mind me goin' round 'er's.

LEN. Same if I did.

FRED. I didn't know like.

LEN. Yer never ruddy thought. Any'ow, I don't mind.

FRED. I thought she was goin' spare.

LEN. Wan'a 'and?

FRED. No. Give us that tin.

He packs in silence.

I reckon it was up t' you t' say. Yer got a tongue in yer
'ead.

Silence. MIKE *comes in. He has a haversack slung from one
shoulder and carries a rod. He wears a small, flashy hat.*

FRED. No luck?

MIKE. Wouldn't feed a cat.

LEN. Waste a time.

MIKE. Same 'ere.

FRED. Got a breeze up.

MIKE. What yer doin'?

FRED. Now?

MIKE. Yeh, t'night.

FRED. Reckon anythin'?

MIKE. Bit a fun.

FRED. Suits me.

MIKE. You're on.

FRED. Up the other end?

MIKE. 'Ow's the cash?

FRED. Broke. You?

MIKE. I'll touch up the ol' lady.

FRED. Get a couple for me.

LEN. That'll pay the fares.

MIKE. Pick yer up roun' your place.

FRED. Not too early. 'Ave a bath first.

MIKE. Never know 'oo yer'll be sleepin' with.

FRED. After eight.

MIKE. I feel juss right for it.

LEN. What?

MIKE. Out on the 'unt.

FRED (*imitates a bullet*). Tschewwwwww!

MIKE. 'E picks 'em up at a 'undred yards.

FRED. It's me magnetic cobblers.

PAM *comes in. She pushes the pram. The hood is up. A long blue sausage balloon floats from a corner of the hood.*

PAM. 'Ello.

FRED. Whass up?

PAM. Out for a walk.

MIKE (*nods at pram*). Bit late for that, ain' it?

PAM (*to* FRED). What yer got?

FRED. Nothin'.

PAM (*tries to look*). Less 'ave a look.

FRED. Nothin' for you!

PAM. Keep yer shirt on.

MIKE. Yer nearly missed us.

PAM (*to* FRED). Don't get so 'airy-ated.

MIKE. We was juss off.

FRED. What yer cartin' that about for?

PAM. Felt like a walk.

FRED. Bit late.

PAM. Why?

FRED. That ought a be in bed.

PAM. Fresh air won't kill it.

FRED. Should a done it earlier.

PAM. Never 'ad time. Why didn't you?

FRED. You know best.

PAM. When yer comin' round?

FRED. I'll look in.

PAM. When?

FRED. I don't know.

PAM. When about?

FRED. Later on.

PAM. Shall I get somethin' to eat?

FRED. No.

PAM. No bother.

FRED. The ol' lady'll 'ave it all set up.

PAM. I got two nice chops.

FRED. Shame.

PAM. Well see 'ow yer feel. There's no one in now. I got rid a 'em.

FRED. Pity yer didn't say.

PAM. What time then?

FRED. I'll be there.

PAM. Sure?

FRED. Yeh.

PAM. Say so if yer ain'.

FRED. I'll be there.

PAM. That means yer won't.

FRED. Up t'you.

PAM. Why don't yer say so?

FRED (*picks up his gear. To* MIKE). Thass the lot.

PAM. It ain' no fun waitin' in all night for nothin'.

MIKE. Ready?

FRED (*takes a look round*). Yeh.

PAM. Why can't yer tell the truth for once?

FRED. Fair enough. I ain' comin'.

LEN. Pam –

PAM. Yer 'ad no intention a comin'.

LEN. Yer left the brake off again.

MIKE (*to* FRED). Okay?

PAM (*to* LEN). Put it on, clever.

FRED (*to* MIKE). Yeh.

PAM (*to* FRED). I knew all along.

FRED. Come on, Pam. Go 'ome.

PAM. Fred.

FRED. I know.

PAM. I didn't mean t' go off. I was goin' a be nice, I still ain' better.

FRED. Go 'ome an' get in the warm. It's late.

LEN (*putting on the brake*). Yer wan' a be more careful.

PAM (*to* FRED). It's my fault. I never stop t'think.

FRED. Yer wan' a stop thinkin' about yerself, I know that.

PAM. It's them pills they give me.

MIKE (*to* FRED). You comin' or ain' yer.

FRED. Yeh.

PAM. No.

FRED. I'll come round one night next week.

PAM. No.

FRED. Monday night. Ow's that?

PAM. Yer'll change yer mind.

FRED. Straight from work.

PAM. Yer said that before.

FRED. It's the best I can offer.

PAM. I can't go back there now.

FRED. Yer'll be okay.

PAM. If I sit on me own in that room another night I'll go round the bend.

FRED. Yer got the kid.

PAM. Juss t'night. I couldn't stand it on me own no more. I 'ad a come out. I don't know what I'm doin'. That kid ought a be in bed. Less take it 'ome, Fred. It's 'ad newmoanier once.

FRED. You take it 'ome.

PAM. Juss this last time? I won't arst no more. I'll get mum t' stay in with me.

FRED. It's no use.

PAM. Yer ain' seen it in a long time, 'ave yer?

She turns the pram round.

It's puttin' on weight.

FRED. Eh?

PAM. It don't cry like it used to. Not all the time.

MIKE. Past carin'.

PAM. Doo-dee-doo-dee. Say da-daa.

FRED. Yeh, lovely.

He looks away.

LEN (*looking at the baby*). Blind.

PAM (*to* LEN). Like a top.

FRED. What yer give it?

PAM. Asprins.

FRED. That all right?

PAM. Won't wake up till t'morra. It won't disturb yer. What time'll I see yer?

FRED. I'll look in. I ain' sayin' definite.

PAM. I don't mind. Long as I know yer're comin'.

FRED. All right.

PAM. Pity t' waste the chops. I think I'll do 'em in case –

FRED. Yeh, right. It's all accordin'.

PAM. I'll wait up.

FRED. It'll be late, see.

PAM. Thass all right.

FRED. Pam.

PAM. I'll treat meself t' box a choclits.

FRED. There's plenty a blokes knockin' about. Why don't yer pick on someone else.

PAM. No.

MIKE. Yer can 'ave me, darlin'. But yer'll 'ave t' learn a bit more respect.

PAM. 'Ow can I get out with that 'angin' round me neck? 'Oo's goin' a look at me?

FRED. Yer ol' girl'll take it off yer 'ands.

MIKE. Drop 'er a few bob.

FRED. Yer don't try.

PAM. I can't!

FRED. Yer'll 'ave to.

PAM. I can't! I ain' goin' to!

FRED. I ain' goin' a see yer no more.

PAM. No.

FRED. We got a sort this out some time.

PAM. Yer promised!

FRED. It's a waste a time!

PAM. *They* 'eard!

FRED. No.

MIKE. Come on, mate.

FRED. It's finished.

MIKE. Thank Chriss. Less shift!

PAM. Juss t'night. I don't care if yer bin with yer girls. Come 'ome after. Juss once. I won't bother yer. I'll let yer sleep. Please.

FRED. Chriss.

PAM. O what d'you care? I was flat on me back three bloody weeks! 'Oo lifted a finger? I could a bin dyin'! No one!

She starts pushing the pram.

MIKE. Good riddance!

PAM (*stops*). You're that kid's father! Yeh! Yer ain't wrigglin' out a that!

FRED. Prove it.

PAM. I *know*!

FRED. You *know*?

MIKE. Chriss.

FRED. 'Alf the bloody manor's bin through you.

PAM. Rotten liar!

FRED. Yeh?

   To MIKE. Ain' you 'ad 'er?

MIKE. Not yet.

FRED. Yer'll be next.

Points to LEN.

   What about 'im?

To LEN. Eh?

To MIKE. Your's must be the only stiff outside the churchyard she ain' knocked off.

PAM. I 'ate you!

FRED. Now we're gettin' somewhere.

PAM. Pig!

FRED. Thass better. Now piss off!

PAM. I will.

MIKE. Ta-ta!

PAM. An' yer can take yer bloody bastard round yer tart's!
Tell 'er it's a present from me!

PAM *goes out. She leaves the pram.*

MIKE. Lovely start t' the evenin's entertainment.

FRED (*calls*). I ain' takin' it! It'll bloody stay 'ere!

MIKE. What yer wan'a let 'er get away with –

FRED. Don't you start! I 'ad enough with 'er!

LEN. I'd better go after 'er.

FRED. Send 'er back.

LEN. See 'ow she is.

LEN *goes out after* PAM.

FRED (*calls*). Don't leave 'er kid. Take it with yer.

MIKE *whistles after her.* FRED *throws his gear down.*
Lumbered!

MIKE. 'E'll send 'er back.

FRED. 'E ain' got the gumption. We'll drop it in on the way
back.

MIKE. Leave it 'ere. Won't be worth goin' time we're ready.

FRED. Give it five minutes.

MIKE. Yer won't see 'er again.

FRED. That won't be the worst thing in me life.

MIKE. Can't yer arst your Liz t' look after it?

FRED. She'd tear me eyes out.

Pause. They sit.

MIKE. They opened that new church on the corner.

FRED. What?

MIKE. They got a club.

FRED. O yeh.

MIKE. We'll 'ave a quick little case round.

FRED. T'night?

MIKE. Yeh.

FRED. Get stuffed.

MIKE. Straight up.

FRED. Pull the other one.

MIKE. Best place out for'n easy pick up.

FRED. Since when?

MIKE. I done it before. There's little pieces all over the shop, nothin' a do.

FRED. Fact?

MIKE. The ol' bleeder shuts 'is eyes for prayers an' they're touchin' 'em up all over the place. Then the law raided this one an' they 'ad it shut down.

FRED. Do leave off.

PETE *and* COLIN *come in right.*

PETE. 'Ow's it then?

MIKE. Buggered up.

COLIN. Like your arse.

MIKE. Like your flippin' ear in a minute.

PETE. I – I!

COLIN. Wass on t'night?

MIKE. Laugh.

BARRY *comes in after* PETE *and* COLIN.

BARRY. Fishin'?

FRED. 'Angin' the Chrissmas decorations.

BARRY. 'Oo's bin chuckin' big dog ends?

MIKE. Where?

BARRY. 'Ardly bin lit.

PETE. 'E's juss waitin' for us t'shift an' 'e'll be on it.

FRED (*holds it out*). On the 'ouse.

MIKE. 'As 'e got a little tin?

COLIN. Like'n ol' tramp?

BARRY. O yeh – 'oo's mindin' the baby?

COLIN (*seeing pram*). Wass that for?

MIKE. Pushin' the spuds in.

FRED (*flicks the dog end to* BARRY). Catch!

COLIN. 'Oo left it 'ere?

BARRY. 'E's takin' it for a walk.

PETE. Nice.

FRED. Piss off.

BARRY. We don't wan' the little nipper t'ear that! Oi, come 'ere.

COLIN *and* PETE *go to the pram.*

Oo's 'e look like?

They laugh.

MIKE. Don't stick your ugly mug in its face!

PETE. It'll crap itself t' death.

BARRY. Dad'll change its nappies.

COLIN (*amused*). Bloody nutter!

FRED. You wake it up an' yer can put it t'sleep.

COLIN *and* PETE *laugh.*

BARRY. Put it t'sleep?

COLIN. 'E'll put it t'sleep for good.

PETE. With a brick.

MIKE. 'E don't care if it's awake all night.

BARRY. 'Oo don't? I'm like a bloody uncle t' the kids round our way. (*He pushes the pram.*) Doo-dee-doo-dee-doo-dee

MIKE (*to* FRED). Jack it in eh?

FRED. Give 'er another minute.

MIKE. We should a made Len stay with it.

FRED. Slipped up. 'E dodged off bloody sharpish.

MIKE. Sly bleeder.

FRED. I don't know – bloody women!

MIKE. Know a better way?

FRED *and* MIKE *are sitting down left.* PETE *and* COLIN *are right.* BARRY *pushes the pram.*

BARRY.

> Rock a bye baby on a tree top
> When the wind blows the cradle will rock
> When the bough breaks the cradle will fall
> And down will come baby and cradle and tree
>> an' bash its little brains out an' dad'll scoop
>> 'em up and use 'em for bait.

They laugh.

FRED. Save money.

BARRY *takes the balloon. He poses with it.*

COLIN. Thought they was pink now.

BARRY (*pokes at* COLIN's *head*). Come t' the pictures t'night darlin'? (*He bends it.*) It's got a bend in it.

MIKE. Don't take after its dad.

BARRY (*blows it up*). Ow's that then?

COLIN. Go easy.

BARRY (*blows again*). Thass more like it. (*Blows again.*)

COLIN. Do leave off.

MIKE. That reminds me I said I'd meet the girl t'night.

BARRY *blows. The balloon bursts.*

COLIN. Got me!

He falls dead. BARRY *pushes the pram over him.*

Get off! I'll 'ave a new suit out a you.

BARRY (*pushing the pram round*). Off the same barrer?

PETE. Ain' seen you 'ere before, darlin'.

BARRY. 'Op it!

PETE. 'Ow about poppin' in the bushes?

COLIN. Two's up.

BARRY. What about the nipper?

PETE. Too young for me.

He 'touches' BARRY.

BARRY. 'Ere! Dirty bastard!

He projects the pram viciously after COLIN. It hits PETE.

PETE. Bastard!

PETE and BARRY look at each other. PETE gets ready to push the pram back – but plays at keeping BARRY guessing. MIKE and FRED are heard talking in their corner.

MIKE. If there's nothin' in the church, know what?

FRED. No.

MIKE. Do the all-night laundries.

FRED. Yer got a 'and it to yer for tryin'.

MIKE. Yer get all them little 'ousewives there.

FRED. Bit past it though.

MIKE. Yeh, but all right.

PETE pushes the pram violently at BARRY. He catches it straight on the flat of his boot and sends it back with the utmost ferocity. PETE sidesteps. COLIN stops it.

PETE. Stupid git!

COLIN. Wass up with 'im?

BARRY. Keep yer dirty 'ands off me!

PETE. 'E'll 'ave the little perisher out!

BARRY. O yeh? An' 'oo reckoned they run a kid down?

PETE. Thass different.

BARRY. Yeh – no one t' see yer.

PETE pulls the pram from COLIN, spins it round and pushes it violently at BARRY. BARRY sidesteps and catches it by the handle ιs it goes past.

BARRY. Oi – oi!

He looks in the pram.

COLIN. Wass up?

COLIN *and* PETE *come over.*

   It can't open its eyes.
BARRY. Yer woke it.
PETE. Look at its fists.
COLIN. Yeh.
PETE. It's tryin' a clout 'im.
COLIN. Don't blame it.
PETE. Goin' a be a boxer.
BARRY. Is it a girl?
PETE. Yer wouldn't know the difference.
BARRY. 'Ow d'yer get 'em t'sleep?
PETE. Pull their 'air.
COLIN. Eh?
PETE. Like that.

He pulls its hair.

COLIN. That 'urt.

They laugh.

MIKE. Wass 'e doin'?
COLIN. Pullin' its 'air.
FRED. 'E'll 'ave its ol' woman after 'im.
MIKE. Poor sod.
BARRY. 'E's showin' off.
COLIN. 'E wants the coroner's medal.
MIKE (*comes to the pram*). Less see yer do it.

PETE *pulls its hair.*

   O yeh.
BARRY. It don't say nothin'.
COLIN. Little bleeder's 'alf dead a fright.

MIKE. Still awake.
PETE. Ain' co-operatin'.
BARRY. Try a pinch.
MIKE. That ought a work.
BARRY. Like this.

He pinches the baby.

COLIN. Look at that mouth.
BARRY. Flippin' yawn.
PETE. Least it's tryin'.
MIKE. Pull its drawers off.
COLIN. Yeh!
MIKE. Less case its ol' crutch.
PETE. Ha!
BARRY. Yeh!

He throws the nappy in the air.

   Yippee!
COLIN. Look at that!

They laugh.

MIKE. Look at its little legs goin'.
COLIN. Ain' they ugly!
BARRY. Ugh!
MIKE. Can't keep 'em still!
PETE. 'Avin' a fit.
BARRY. It's dirty.

They groan.

COLIN. 'Old its nose.
MIKE. Thass for 'iccups.
BARRY. Gob its crutch.

He spits.

MIKE. Yeh!
COLIN. Ha!

He spits.

MIKE. Got it!

PETE. Give it a punch.

MIKE. Yeh less!

COLIN. There's no one about!

PETE *punches it.*

   Ugh! Mind yer don't 'urt it.

MIKE. Yer can't.

BARRY. Not at that age.

MIKE. Course yer can't, no feelin's.

PETE. Like animals.

MIKE. 'It it again.

COLIN. I can't see!

BARRY. 'Arder.

PETE. Yeh.

BARRY. Like that!

He hits it.

COLIN. An' that!

He also hits it.

MIKE. What a giggle!

PETE. Cloutin's good for 'em. I read it.

BARRY (*to* FRED). Why don't you clout it?

FRED. It ain' mine.

PETE. Sherker. Yer got a do yer duty.

FRED. Ain' my worry. Serves 'er right.

BARRY. 'Ere, can I piss on it?

COLIN. Gungy bastard!

MIKE. Got any matches?

They laugh.

PETE. Couldn't yer break them little fingers easy though?

COLIN. Snap!

PETE. Know what they used a do?

MIKE. Yeh.

PETE. Smother 'em.

BARRY. Yeh. That'd be somethin'.

COLIN. Looks like a yeller-nigger.

BARRY. 'Onk like a yid.

FRED. Leave it alone.

PETE. Why?

FRED. Yer don't wan' a row.

PETE. What row?

MIKE. What kid?

COLIN. I ain' seen no kid.

BARRY. Not me!

PETE. Yer wouldn't grass on yer muckers?

FRED. Grow up.

BARRY. D'narf look ill. Stupid bastard.

He jerks the pram violently.

PETE. Thass 'ow they 'ang yer – give yer a jerk.

MIKE. Reckon it'll grow up an idiot.

PETE. Or deformed.

BARRY. Look where it come from.

PETE. Little bleeder.

He jerks the pram violently.

  That knocked the grin off its face.

MIKE. Look! Ugh!

BARRY. Look!

COLIN. What?

They all groan.

PETE. Rub the little bastard's face in it!

BARRY. Yeh!

PETE. Less 'ave it!

He rubs the baby. They all groan.

BARRY. Less 'ave a go! I always wan'ed a do that!

PETE. Ain' yer done it before?

BARRY *does it. He laughs.*

COLIN. It's all in its eyes.

Silence.

FRED. There'll be a row.
MIKE. It can't talk.
PETE. 'Oo cares?
FRED. I tol' yer.
COLIN. Shut up.
BARRY. I noticed 'e ain' touched it.
COLIN. Too bloody windy.
FRED. Yeh?
PETE. Less see yer.
BARRY. Yeh.
PETE. 'Fraid she'll ruck yer.
FRED. Ha!

He looks in the pram.

    Chriss.
PETE. Less see yer chuck that.

PETE *throws a stone to* FRED. FRED *doesn't try to catch it. It falls on the ground.* COLIN *picks it up and gives it to* FRED.

MIKE (*quietly*). Reckon it's all right?
COLIN (*quietly*). No one around.
PETE (*quietly*). They don't know it's us.
MIKE (*quietly*). She left it.
BARRY. It's done now.
PETE (*quietly*). Yer can do what yer like.
BARRY. Might as well enjoy ourselves.
PETE (*quietly*). Yer don't get a chance like this everyday.

FRED *throws the stone.*

COLIN. Missed.
PETE. That ain't'!

He throws a stone.

BARRY. Or that!

He throws a stone.

MIKE. Yeh!
COLIN (*running round*). Where's all the stones?
MIKE (*also running round*). Stick it up the fair!
PETE. Liven 'Ampstead 'eath! Three throws a quid! Make a
    packet.
MIKE (*throws a stone*). Ouch!
COLIN. 'Ear that?
BARRY. Give us some.

He takes stones from COLIN.

COLIN (*throws a stone*). Right in the lug 'ole.

FRED *looks for a stone.*

PETE. Get its 'ooter.
BARRY. An' its slasher!
FRED (*picks up a stone, spits on it*). For luck, the sod.

He throws.

BARRY. Yyooowwww!
MIKE. 'Ear it plonk!

A bell rings.

MIKE. 'Oo's got the matches?

He finds some in his pocket.

BARRY. What yer doin'?
COLIN. Wan'a buck up!
MIKE. Keep a look out.

He starts to throw burning matches in the pram. BARRY *throws a stone. It just misses* MIKE.

    Look out, yer bleedin' git!

COLIN. Guy Fawkes!

PETE. Bloody nutter! Put that out!

MIKE. No! You 'ad what you want!

PETE. Yer'll 'ave the ol' bloody park 'ere!

A bell rings.

BARRY. Piss on it! Piss on it!

COLIN. Gungy slasher.

MIKE. Call the R.S.P.C.A.

A bell rings.

FRED. They'll shut the gates.

PETE (*going*). There's an 'ole in the railin's.

BARRY. 'Old on.

He looks for a stone.

PETE. Leave it!

BARRY. Juss this one!

He throws a stone as PETE *pushes him over. It goes wide.*

    Bastard!

To PETE. Yer put me off!

PETE. I'll throttle yer!

BARRY. I got a get it once more!

The others have gone up left. He takes a stone from the pram and throws it at point blank range. Hits.

    Yar!

COLIN. Where's this 'ole!

MIKE. Yer bleedin' gear!

FRED. Chriss.

He runs down to the rod and boxes. He picks them up.

BARRY. Bleedin' little sod!

He hacks into the pram. He goes up left.

PETE. Come on!

A bell rings. FRED *has difficulty with the boxes and rod. He throws a box away.*

FRED. 'Ang on!

He goes up left.
They go off up left, making a curious buzzing. A long pause.
PAM *comes in down left.*

PAM. I might a know'd they'd a left yer. Lucky yer got
someone t' look after yer. Muggins 'ere.

She starts to push the pram. She does not look into it. She speaks in a sing-song voice, loudly but to herself.

'Oo's 'ad yer balloon. Thass a present from grannie. Goin'
a keep me up 'alf the night? Go t' sleepies. Soon be 'ome.
Nice an' warm, then. No one else wants yer. Nice an' warm.
Soon be 'omies.

SCENE SEVEN

A cell. Left centre a box to sit on. Otherwise, the stage is bare.
*   A steel door bangs.* FRED *comes in from the left. He has a mack over his head. He sits on the case. After a slight pause he takes off the mack.*

Silence. A steel door bangs. PAM *comes in left.*

PAM. What 'appened?
FRED. Didn't yer see 'em?
PAM. I 'eard.

FRED. Bloody 'eathens. Thumpin' and kickin' the van.

PAM. Oo?

FRED. Bloody 'ousewives! 'Oo else? Ought a be stood up an' shot!

PAM. You all right?

FRED. No. I tol' this copper don't open the door. He goes we're 'ere, the thick bastard, an' lets 'em in. Kickin' an' punchin'.

He holds up the mack.

Look at it! Gob all over.

He throws it away from him.

'Course I ain' all right!
Mimicking her. 'Are yer all right?'

PAM. They said I shouldn't be 'ere. But 'e was ever so nice. Said five minutes wouldn't matter.

FRED. Right bloody mess.

PAM. They can't get in 'ere.

FRED. I can't get out there!

PAM. I ain't blamin' yer.

FRED. Blamin' me? Yer got bugger all t'blame me for, mate! Yer ruined my life, thass all!

PAM. I never meant –

FRED. Why the bloody 'ell bring the little perisher out that time a night?

PAM (*fingers at her mouth*). I wanted a –

FRED. Yer got no right chasin' after me with a pram! Drop me right in it!

PAM. I was scared t' stay –

FRED. Never know why yer 'ad the little bleeder in the first place! Yer don't know what yer doin'! Yer're a bloody menace!

PAM. Wass it like?

FRED. They wan' a put you in, then yer'll find out. Bring any burn?

PAM. No.

FRED. Yer don't think a nothin'! Ain' yer got juss one?

PAM. No.

FRED. Yer're bloody useless.

PAM. What'll 'appen!

FRED. 'Ow do I know? I'll be the last one a know. The 'ole thing was an accident. Lot a roughs. Never seen 'em before. Don't arst me. Blokes like that anywhere. I tried to chase 'em off.

PAM. Will they believe that?

FRED. No. If I was ten years older I'd get a medal. With a crowd like our'n they got a knock someone. (*He goes right.*) Right bloody mess.

PAM. Yer never bin in trouble before. Juss one or two woundin's an' that.

FRED. 'Alf murdered with a lot a 'and bags!

PAM. Yer wan' a arst t' see the doctor.

FRED. Doctor! They shouldn't let him touch a sick rat with a barge pole. (*He walks a few steps.*) It's supposed a be grub. A starvin' cat 'ld walk away. (*He walks a few more steps.*) Wass bin 'appening?

PAM. Don't know.

FRED. On yer own?

PAM. What about them others?

FRED. What about 'em?

PAM. I could say I saw 'em.

FRED. That'd make it worse. Don't worry. I'm thinkin' it all out. This way they don't know what 'appened. Not definite. Why couldn't I bin tryin' a 'elp the kid? I got no cause t' 'arm it.

He sits on the box.

PAM. I tol' 'em.

FRED (*he puts his arms round her waist and leans his head against her*). Yer'll 'ave t' send us letters.

PAM. I'm buyin' a pad on me way 'ome.

FRED. Pam. I don't know what'll 'appen. There's bloody gangs like that roamin' everywhere. The bloody police don't do their job.

PAM. I'll kill meself if they touch yer.

A steel door bangs. LEN *comes in left.*

I tol' yer t' wait outside.

LEN. I got 'im some fags. (*To* FRED.) I 'ad a drop 'em 'alf.

PAM. 'E still won't leave me alone, Fred.

LEN. I only got a minute. They're arstin' for a remand.

FRED. Chriss. That bloody mob still outside?

LEN. They've 'emmed 'em off over the road.

FRED. Bit bloody late.

PAM. Tell 'im t' go.

LEN. We both got a go. That inspector wants you.

FRED. Where's the snout?

LEN. Put it in yer pocket.

FRED (*to* PAM). See yer after.

She puts her arms round him before he can take the cigarettes.

PAM. I'll wait for yer.

FRED (*pats her back*). Yeh, yeh. God 'elp us.

LEN (*to* PAM). Yer'll get 'im into trouble if yer don't go.

FRED *nods at* PAM. *She goes out crying.*

FRED. 'Ow many yer got?

LEN. Sixty. I 'ad a drop 'em 'alf.

FRED. Will it be all right?

LEN. Give 'em a few like, an' don't flash 'em around.

FRED. She never 'ad none. I'll do the same for you sometime.

LEN. Put 'em in yer pocket.

FRED. I don't know what I'll get.

LEN. Manslaughter. (*Shrugs.*) Anythin'.

FRED. It was only a kid.

LEN. I saw.

FRED. What?

LEN. I come back when I couldn't find 'er.

FRED. Yer ain't grassed?

LEN. No.

FRED. O.

LEN. I was in the trees. I saw the pram.

FRED. Yeh.

LEN. I saw the lot.

FRED. Yeh.

LEN. I didn't know what t'do. Well, I should a stopped yer.

FRED. Too late now.

LEN. I juss saw.

FRED. Yer saw! Yer saw! Wass the good a that? That don't 'elp me. I'll be out in that bloody dock in a minute!

LEN. Nothin'. They got the pram in court.

FRED. Okay, okay. Reckon there's time for a quick burn?

LEN. About.

He gives FRED *a light.*

INTERVAL

SCENE EIGHT

The living-room.

HARRY *irons,* LEN *sits.*

LEN. Yer make a fair ol' job a that.

Pause.

Don't yer get choked off?

HARRY. What?

LEN. That every Friday night.
HARRY. Got a keep clean.
LEN. Suppose so.

Pause.

Yer get used t' it.
HARRY. Trained to it in the army.
LEN. O.
HARRY. Makes a man a yer.

MARY *comes in. She looks around.*

MARY *to* LEN. I wish yer wouldn't sit around in yer ol' work-
clothes an' shoes. Yer got some nice slippers.

MARY *goes out.*

LEN. She won't let Pam.
HARRY. Eh?
LEN. She won't let Pam do that for yer.
HARRY. Don't take me long.

Long pause.

LEN. Yer could stop 'er money.

Slight pause.

Then she couldn't interfere.
HARRY. Don't take long. Once yer get started.
LEN. Why don't yer try that?
HARRY. That Pam can't iron. She'd ruin 'em.
LEN. Ever thought a movin' on?
HARRY. This stuff gets dry easy.
LEN. Yer ought a think about it.
HARRY. Yer don't know what yer talking about, lad.
LEN. No. I don't.
HARRY. It's like everthin' else.
LEN. 'Ow long yer bin 'ere?

HARRY. Don't know. (*He stretches his back. He irons again.*) Yer mate's comin' out.

LEN. Yeh. Why?

HARRY. Pam's mate. (*He spits on the iron.*) None a it ain' simple.

LEN. Yer lost a little boy eh?

HARRY. Next week, ain't it?

LEN. I got a shirt yer can do. (*Laughs.*) Any offers?

HARRY. She meet 'im?

LEN. Ain' arst.

HARRY. You?

LEN (*shrugs*). I'd 'ave t' get time off.

HARRY. O.

LEN. 'Ow d'yer get on at work?

HARRY (*looks up*). It's a job.

LEN. I meant with the blokes?

HARRY (*irons*). They're all right.

LEN. Funny, nightwork.

PAM *comes in. She has her hair in a towel. She carries a portable radio. Someone is talking. She sits on the couch and finds a pop programme. She tunes in badly. She interrupts this from time to time to rub her hair.*

LEN (*to* HARRY). 'Ow about doin' my shirt?

He laughs. PAM *finishes tuning. She looks round.*

PAM. 'Oo's got my *Radio Times*? You 'ad it?

HARRY *doesn't answer. She turns to* LEN.

You?

LEN (*mumbles*). Not again.

PAM. You speakin' t' me?

LEN. I'm sick t' death a yer bloody *Radio Times*.

PAM. Someone's 'ad it. (*She rubs her hair vigorously.*) I ain' goin' a get it no more. Not after last week. I'll cancel it. It's the last time I bring it in this 'ouse. I don't see why I 'ave t' go on paying for it. Yer must think I'm made a money. It's never 'ere when I wan'a see it. Not once. It's always the same. (*She rubs her hair.*) I notice no one else offers t' pay for it. Always Charlie. It's 'appened once too often this time.

LEN. Every bloody week the same!

PAM (*to* HARRY). Sure yer ain' got it?

HARRY. I bought this shirt over eight years ago.

PAM. That cost me sixpence a week. You reckon that up over a year. Yer must think I was born yesterday.

Pause. She rubs her hair.

Wasn't 'ere last week. Never 'ere. Got legs.

She goes to the door and shouts.

Mum! She 'eard all right.

She goes back to the couch and sits. She rubs her hair.

Someone's got it. I shouldn't think the people next door come in an' took it. Everyone 'as the benefit a it 'cept me. It's always the same. I'll know what t' do in future. Two can play at that game. I ain' blinkin' daft. (*She rubs her hair.*) I never begrudge no one borrowin' it, but yer'd think they'd have enough manners t' put it back.

Pause.

She rubs her hair.

Juss walk all over yer. Well it ain' goin' a 'appen again. They treat you like a door mat. All take and no give. Touch somethin' a their'n an' they go through the bloody ceilin'. It's bin the same ever since –

LEN. I tol' yer t' keep it in yer room!

PAM. Now yer got a lock things up in yer own 'ouse.

LEN. Why should we put up with this week after week juss because yer too –

PAM. Yer know what yer can do.

LEN. Thass yer answer t' everythin'.

PAM. Got a better one?

HARRY. They was a pair first off. Set me back a quid each.
Up the market. One's gone 'ome, went at the cuffs. Worth
a quid.

LEN. Chriss.

Pause.

PAM. I mean it this time. I'm goin' in that shop first thing
Saturday mornin' an' tell 'im t' cancel it. I ain' throwin'
my money down the drain juss to –

LEN. Wrap up!

PAM. Don't tell me what t' do!

LEN. Wrap up!

PAM. Thass typical a you.
She goes to the door and calls. Mum!
To LEN. I ain' stupid. I know 'oo's got it.
Calls. Mum! – She can 'ear.

HARRY. Ain' worth readin' any'ow.

LEN. Don't start 'er off again.

PAM (*to* LEN). You ain' sittin' on it, a course!

LEN. No.

PAM. Yer ain' looked.

LEN. Ain' goin' to.

PAM. 'Ow d'yer know yer ain' sittin' on it?

LEN. I ain' sittin' on it.

PAM (*to* HARRY). Tell 'im t' get up!

HARRY. Waste a good money.

PAM (*to* LEN). Yer'll be sorry for this.

LEN. I'll be sorry for a lot a things.

HARRY. Cuffs goin' on this one.

PAM (*by* LEN's *chair*). I ain' goin' till yer move.

HARRY. Lot a lies an' pictures a nancies.

PAM. Yer dead spiteful when yer wan'a be.

LEN. Thass right.

PAM (*goes to the couch, rubbing her hair*). 'E'oo laughs last. Fred's coming 'ome next week.

LEN. 'Ome?

PAM. 'Is ol' lady won't 'ave 'im in the 'ouse.

LEN. Where's 'e goin'?

PAM. Yer'll see.

LEN. 'E ain' 'avin' my room.

PAM. 'Oo said?

LEN. She won't let yer.

PAM. We'll see.

LEN. Yer ain' even arst 'er.

PAM. O no?

LEN. No.

PAM (*rubs her hair*). We'll see.

LEN. I'll 'ave one or two things t' say. Yer too fond a pushin' people about.

PAM. Must take after you.

LEN. I thought 'e'd be sharin' your room.

PAM. I ain' rowin' about it. 'E'll 'ave t' 'ave somewhere t' come out to. Chriss knows what it's like shut up in them places. It'll be nice an' clean 'ere for 'im when yer're gone.

LEN. 'Ave yer arst 'im yet?

PAM. I ain' rowin' about it. If 'e goes wanderin' off 'e'll only end up in trouble again. I ain' goin' a be messed around over this! We ain' gettin' any younger. 'E's bound a be different. (*She rubs her hair.*) Yer can't say anythin' in letters. Yer can't expect 'im to.

LEN. 'Ave yer arst 'im.

PAM. I don' wan' a talk about it.

LEN. You meetin' 'im?

PAM. Why? – You ain' comin'!

LEN. 'Oo said?

PAM. 'E don't want you there!

LEN. 'Ow d'yer know?

PAM. O let me alone!

LEN. 'E's my mate, ain' 'e?

PAM. I'm sick t' death a you under me feet all the time! Ain' yer got no friends t' go to! What about yer people? Won't they take yer in either?

LEN. Yer arst some stupid questions at times.

PAM. Yer can't 'ave no pride. Yer wouldn't catch me 'angin' round where I ain' wanted.

LEN. 'Oo ain' wanted?

PAM. I don't want yer! They don't want yer! It's only common sense! I don't know why yer can't see it. It's nothin' but rows an' arguments.

LEN. 'Oo's fault's that?

PAM. Anybody else wouldn't stay if yer paid 'em! Yer caused all the trouble last time.

LEN. I knew that was comin'.

PAM. None a that 'ld a 'appened if yer ain' bin 'ere. Yer never give 'im a chance.

LEN. Yeh, yeh.

PAM. Yer live on trouble!

LEN. That ain' what 'e told everyone.

PAM. Same ol' lies.

LEN. Listen 'oo's talkin'!

PAM. Yer start off gettin' 'im put away –

LEN. Don't be bloody stupid!

PAM. Jealous! An' now 'e's comin' out yer still can't let 'im alone!

LEN. *You* can't leave 'im alone yer mean!

PAM. Yer laughed yer 'ead off when they took 'im away.

LEN. Bloody stupid! You arst 'im!

PAM. Comin' 'ere an' workin' me up!

LEN. Yer wan'a listen t' yerself!

PAM. So do you.

LEN. Shoutin'.

PAM. 'Oo's shoutin'?

LEN. You are!

PAM. Yer 'ave t' shout with you!

LEN. Thass right!

PAM. Yer so bloody dense!

LEN. Go on!

PAM. Yer 'ave t' shout!

LEN. Yer silly bloody cow!

PAM. Shoutin' 'e says! 'Ark at 'im! 'Ark at 'im!

LEN. Shut up!

PAM. We ain' carryin' on like this! Yer got a stop upsettin' me night after night!

LEN. You start it!

PAM. It's got a stop! It ain' worth it! Juss round an' round.

A very long silence.

Yer can't say it's the kid keepin' yer.

A long silence.

It certainly ain' me. Thass well past.

Silence.

Yer sit there in yer dirty ol' work clothes. (*To* HARRY.) Why don't yer turn 'im out? Dad.

HARRY. 'E pays 'is rent.

PAM. Fred'll pay.

HARRY. 'As 'e got a job?

PAM. 'E'll get one.

HARRY. Will 'e keep it?

PAM. Thass right!

LEN. Now 'oo's startin' it?

PAM. You are.

LEN. I ain' said a word.

PAM. No – but yer sat there!

LEN. I got some rights yer know!

PAM. Yer're juss like a kid.

LEN. I'm glad I ain' yourn.

PAM. I wouldn't like t' 'ave your spiteful nature.

LEN. I certainly wouldn't like yourn!

PAM. Thass right! I know why yer sittin' there!

LEN. Yer know a sight bloody too much!

PAM. I know where my *Radio Times* is!

LEN. Stick yer bloody *Radio Times*!

PAM. I know why yer sittin' there!

LEN. That bloody paper!

PAM. Why don't yer stand up?

LEN. Yer don't even want the bloody paper!

PAM. As long as yer causin' trouble –

LEN. Yer juss wan' a row!

PAM. – then yer're 'appy!

LEN. If yer found it yer'd lose somethin' else!

PAM (*goes to* LEN's *chair*). Stand up then!

LEN. No!

PAM. Can't it a got there accidentally?

LEN. No!

PAM. Yer see!

LEN. I ain' bein' pushed around.

PAM. Yer see!

LEN. Yer come too much a it!

PAM. No yer'd rather stay stuck!

LEN. A sight bloody too much!

PAM. An' row!

LEN. Shut up!

PAM. Thass right!

LEN. I tol' yer t' shut up!

PAM. Go on!

LEN. Or I'll bloody well shut yer up!

PAM. O yeh!

LEN. Yer need a bloody good beltin'.

PAM. Touch me!

LEN. You started this!

PAM. Go on!

LEN (*he turns away*). Yer make me sick!

PAM. Yeh – yer see. Yer make me sick!

She goes to the door.

    I ain' lettin' a bloody little weed like you push me around!
Calls. Mum.

She comes back.

    I wish I 'ad a record a when yer first come 'ere. Butter
wouldn't melt in yer mouth.

Calls. Mum!

HARRY (*finishing ironing*). Thass that, thank Chriss.

PAM (*calls*). Mum! – She can' 'ear.

Calls. You 'eard?

HARRY. Put the wood in the 'ole.

LEN. I'd like t' 'ear what they're sayin' next door.

PAM. Let 'em say!

LEN. 'Ole bloody neighbour'ood must know!

PAM. Good – let 'em know what yer're like!

LEN. 'Oo wen' on about pride?

PAM (*calls through door*). I know yer can' ear.

MARY (*off*). You callin' Pam?

PAM (*to* LEN). One thing, anythin' else goes wrong I'll know
'oo t' blame.

MARY (*off*). Pam!

PAM. Let 'er wait.

MARY (*off.*) Pam!

LEN (*calls*). It's all right! One a 'er fits!

PAM (*calls*). 'E's sittin' on the chair.

MARY (*off*). What?

PAM (*calls*). 'E's got my paper!

MARY (*off*). What chair?

PAM (*calls*). 'E 'as!

MARY (*off*). I ain' got yer paper!

PAM (*calls*). It don't matter!

MARY (*off*). What paper's that?

PAM (*calls*). It don't matter! You bloody deaf?

LEN. Now start on 'er!

HARRY (*piling his clothes neatly*). Didn't take long.

PAM (*to* LEN). Yer're so bloody clever!

LEN. If I upset yer like this why don't *you* go?

PAM. Thass what you want!

LEN (*shrugs*). You want *me* t' go!

PAM. I ain' bein' pushed out on no streets.

LEN. I'm tryin' t' 'elp.

PAM. Yer wouldn't 'elp a cryin' baby.

LEN. Yer're the last one a bring that up!

PAM. 'Elp? – after the way yer carried on t'night.

LEN. I lost me job stayin' out a 'elp you when yer was sick!

PAM. Sacked for bein' bloody lazy!

LEN (*stands*). Satisfied?

PAM (*without looking at the chair*). Yer torn it up or burnt it!
   Wouldn't put that pass yer!

PAM *goes out. Silence.* HARRY *finishes folding his clothes.*

MARY (*off*). Found it yet?

Pause.

HARRY. Wan'a use it?

LEN. No.

HARRY *folds the board.*

SCENE NINE

The living-room.
LEN *has spread a paper on the floor. He cleans his shoes on it.*
MARY *comes in. She is in her slip. She walks about getting ready.*

MARY. 'Ope yer don't mind me like this.

LEN. You kiddin'?

MARY. It's such a rush. I don't really wan'a go.

LEN. Don't then.

MARY. I said I would now.

LEN. Say yer don't feel up to it.

MARY. Yes. (*She goes on getting ready*.) Makes a change I suppose.

LEN. Never know, it might be a laugh.

MARY. Yer got a do somethin' t' entertain yerself.

Pause.

I 'ope yer ain' usin' 'er *Radio Times*.

LEN. Ha!

MARY. She's got no patience. It'll land 'er in trouble one a these days. Look at that pram. I told 'er t'wait. She should a got two 'undred for that.

LEN. Easy.

MARY (*looks at her shoes*). This ain' nice. No, she 'as t' let it go for fifty quid, the first time she's arst. Can't be told. Yer couldn't give these a little touch up for me?

LEN. Sling 'em over.

MARY. Ta, dear.

LEN. What yer put on these?

MARY. That white stuff.

LEN *polishes her shoes in silence*.

Thinkin'?

LEN. No.

MARY. Whass worryin' yer?

LEN. Nothin'.

MARY. I expect yer're like me. Yer enjoy the quiet. I don't enjoy all this noise yer get.

LEN. She said somethin' about my room?

MARY (*amused*). Why?

LEN. What she say?

MARY. That worried yer?

LEN. I ain' worried.

MARY. She's not tellin' me 'ow t' run my 'ouse.

She pulls on her stockings.

LEN. O. (*Holds up her shoes.*) Do yer?

MARY. Very nice. Juss go over the backs dear. I like t' feel nice be'ind. I tol' 'er there's enough t' put up with without lookin' for trouble.

LEN. Better?

MARY. Yes. I 'ad enough a that pair last time.

She steps into one shoe.

We're only goin' for the big film. She can do what she likes outside.

LEN (*gives her the other shoe*). Thass yer lot.

MARY. 'E wants lockin' up for life. Ta, dear. I don't expect yer t' understand at your age, but things don't turn out too bad. There's always someone worse off in the world.

LEN (*clearing up the polishing things*). Yer can always be that one.

MARY. She's my own flesh an' blood, but she don't take after me. Not a thought in 'er 'ead. She's 'ad a rough time a it. I feel sorry for 'er about the kid –

LEN. One a them things. Yer can't make too much a it.

MARY. Never 'ave 'appened if she'd a look after it right. Yer done a lovely job on these. What yer doin' t'night?

LEN (*sews a button on his shirt*). Gettin' ready for work.

MARY. Yer don't go out so much.

LEN. I was out Tuesday.

MARY. Yer ought a be out every night.

LEN. Can't afford it.

MARY. There's plenty a nice girls round 'ere.

LEN. I ain' got the energy these days. They want – somethin' flash.

MARY. Yer can't tell me what they want. I was the same that age.

LEN. I ain' got time for 'alf a 'em. They don't know what they got it for.

MARY. I thought that's what you men were after.

LEN. 'Alf a 'em, it ain' worth the bother a gettin' there. Thass a fact.

MARY. What about the other 'alf?

LEN. Hm!

MARY (*having trouble with her suspender*). Yer 'ave t' go about it the right way. Yer can't stand a girl in a puddle down the back a some ol' alley an' think yer doin' 'er a favour. Yer got yer own room upstairs. That's a nice room. Surprised yer don't use that. I don't mind what goes on, yer know that. As long as yer keep the noise down.

LEN. Ta.

MARY. It's in every man. It 'as t' come out.

Pause.

We didn't carry on like that when I was your age.

LEN. Pull the other one.

MARY. Not till yer was in church. Anyway, yer 'ad t' be engaged. I think it's nicer in the open. I do.

LEN. I bet yer bin up a few alleys.

MARY. You enjoy yerself. I know what I'd be doin' if I was you.

LEN. You meetin' a fella?

MARY. No! I'm goin' out with Mrs Lee.

LEN. Waste.

MARY. Don't be cheeky.

LEN. Yer look fair when yer all done up.

MARY. What you after? Bin spendin' me rent money?

LEN. Wass on?

MARY. Don't know. Somethin' daft.

LEN. Shall I look it up?

MARY. They're all the same. Sex. Girls 'angin' out a their dresses an' men bendin' over 'em.

LEN. It's one of them nudes. 'Eard the fellas talkin'.

MARY. Shan't go in.

LEN. Don't know what yer missin'.

MARY. Different for men.

LEN. Always full a tarts when I bin.

MARY. Thass where yer spend yer money.

LEN. Very nice. Big ol' tits bouncin' about in sinner-scope.

MARY. Don't think Mrs Lee'd fancy that.

LEN. I'll 'ave t' take yer one a these nights.

MARY. I'd rather see Tarzan.

LEN. Thass easy, come up next time I 'ave a bath.

MARY. Count the 'airs on yer chest?

LEN. For a start.

MARY. Sounds like a 'orror film.

LEN. I enjoy a good scrub. On me back.

MARY. Thass the regular carry-on in China.

LEN. No 'arm in it.

MARY. No.

Slight pause.

Pam's very easy goin' for a nice girl. I suppose yer miss that.

LEN. Takes a bit a gettin' used to.

MARY. 'Ow'd yer manage?

LEN. Any suggestions?

Slight pause.

MARY. Bugger!

LEN. Eh?

MARY. Thass tore it!

LEN. Wass up?

MARY. O blast! I caught me stockin'.

LEN. O.

MARY. That would 'ave to 'appen.

LEN. 'Ow'd yer do it?

MARY. Juss when I'm late. Bugger it.

She looks in the table drawer.

'Ardly worth goin' in a minute. Excuse my language. Never find anythin' when yer want it in this place.

LEN. What yer lost?

MARY. It's the only decent pair I got.

LEN. Thass a shame.

MARY. It'll run.

LEN. Less 'ave a shufties.

MARY. Caught on that blasted chair. It's bin like that for ages.

LEN. Yeh. Thass a big one.

MARY. Pam's got 'er nail-varnish all over the place except when yer wan'a find it.

LEN (*offers her the needle*). 'Ave a loan of this.

MARY. It'll run, y'see.

LEN. Less do the cotton.

MARY. I certainly can't afford new ones this week.

LEN (*threading the needle*). Not t' worry.

MARY. I'm no good at that.

LEN. Well, 'ave a bash.

MARY. It'll make it worse.

LEN. No it won't.

MARY (*puts her foot on the chair seat*). You do it.

LEN. Me?

MARY. I never could use a needle. I should a bin there by now.

LEN. I don't know if I –

MARY. Get on. It's only doin' me a good turn.

LEN. It ain' that. I –

MARY. Mrs Lee's waitin'. I can't take 'em off. I'm in ever such a 'urry. They'll run.

LEN. Yeh. It's dodgy. I don't wan'a prick –

MARY. Yer got steady 'ands your age.

LEN (*kneels in front of her and starts darning*). Yeh. (*He drops the needle*). O.

MARY. All right?

LEN. It's dropped.

MARY. What?

LEN. Me needle.

MARY. Yer're 'oldin' me up.

LEN (*on his hands and knees*). 'Ang on.

MARY. That it?

LEN. No.

MARY (*she helps him to look*). Can't a got far.

LEN. It's gone.

MARY. What's that?

LEN. Where?

MARY. That's it. There.

LEN. O. Ta.

MARY (*puts her foot back on the chair*). I ain' got all night.

LEN. I'll 'ave t' get me 'and inside.

MARY. You watch where yer go. Yer ain' on yer 'oneymoon yet. Yer 'and's cold!

LEN. Keep still, or it'll jab yer.

MARY. You watch yerself.

LEN. I'll juss give it a little stretch.

MARY. All right?

LEN. Yer got lovely legs.

MARY. You get on with it.

LEN. Lovely an' smooth.

MARY. Never mind my legs.

LEN. It's a fact.

MARY. Some people'd 'ave a fit if they 'eard that. Yer know what they're like.

LEN. Frustrated.

MARY. I'm old enough t' be yer mother.

HARRY *comes in. He goes straight to the table.*

To LEN. Go steady!

LEN. Sorry.

MARY. You watch where yer pokin'. That 'urt.

LEN. I tol' yer t' keep still.

MARY. Yer'll make it bigger, not smaller.

HARRY *takes ink and a Pools coupon from the table drawer. He puts them on the table.*

LEN. That'll see yer through t'night.

He ties a knot in the thread.

MARY. Wass up now?

LEN. Scissors.

MARY. Eh?

LEN. I 'ad 'em juss now.

MARY. Bite it.

LEN. Eh?

MARY. Go on.

LEN (*leans forward*). Keep still.

MARY. I can't wait all night.

LEN *bites the thread off*. HARRY *goes out.*

Took yer time.

LEN (*stands*). Ow! I'm stiff.

MARY (*looks*). Ta, very nice.

LEN. Ain' worth goin' now.

MARY. 'Ave I got me cigarettes?

LEN. Might be somethin' on telly.

MARY. I can't disappoint Mrs Lee.

LEN. I 'ad a feelin' 'e'd come in.

MARY. Yer'll be in bed time I get back.

LEN. She won't wait this long.

MARY. I'll say good night. Thanks for 'elpin'.

LEN. Stay in an' put yer feet up. I'll make us a cup of tea.

MARY. Can't let yer friends down. Cheerio.

LEN. Okay.

MARY *goes.* LEN *takes a handkerchief from his pocket. He switches the light off and goes to the couch.*

SCENE TEN

A café.

Furniture: chairs and three tables, one up right, one right and one down left. Apart from this the stage is bare.

LEN *and* PAM *sit at the table up right.*

LEN (*drinks tea*). Warms yer up.

Pause.

These early mornin's knock me out. 'Nother cup?

Pause.

PAM. Wass the time?
LEN. Quarter past.
PAM. Why ain't they got a clock?

Pause.

LEN. 'Ave another one.
PAM. Thass the fourth time yer keep arstin.
LEN. Warm yer up.
PAM. Go an' sit on yer own table.

Pause.

LEN. Sure yer wrote the name right?
PAM. We'll look bloody daft when 'e finds you 'ere. Wass 'e goin' to say?
LEN. 'Ello.

Pause.

Let me go an' find 'im.
PAM. No.
LEN. There's no use –

PAM. No!

LEN. Suit yerself.

PAM. Do I 'ave t' say everythin' twice?

LEN. There's no need t' shout.

PAM. I ain' shoutin'.

LEN. They can 'ear yer 'alf way t' –

PAM. I don't wan'a know.

LEN. Yer never do.

Silence.

PAM. Len. I don't want a keep on at yer. I don't know what's the matter with me. They wan'a put the 'eat on. It's like death. Yer'd get on a lot better with someone else.

LEN. Per'aps 'e ain' comin'.

PAM. They must 'ave all the winders open. It's no life for a fella. Yer ain' a bad sort.

LEN. Yeh. I'm goin' a be late in.

PAM. Don't go.

LEN. You make me money up?

PAM (*after a slight pause*). Why can't yer go somewhere?

LEN. Where?

PAM. There's lots a places.

LEN. 'Easy t' say.

PAM. I'll find yer somewhere.

LEN. I ain' scuttlin' off juss t' make room for you t' shag in.

PAM. Yer're a stubborn sod! Don't blame me what 'appens t' yer! Yer ain' messin' me about again.

LEN. I knew that wouldn't last long!

PAM. I'm sick t' death a yer. Clear off!

She goes to the table down left and sits. LEN *goes out left. Pause. He comes back with a cup of tea. He puts it on the table in front of* PAM. *He stands near the table.*

LEN. It'll get cold.

Pause.

Did 'e say 'e'd come?

Pause.

Did 'e answer any a your letters?

She re-acts.

I juss wondered!
PAM. I tol' yer before!
LEN. Thass all right then.

Pause.

PAM. It's like winter in 'ere.

There are voices off right. Someone shouts. A door bangs open.
MIKE, COLIN, PETE, BARRY, FRED *and* LIZ *come in.*

COLIN. 'Ere we are again.
BARRY. Wipe yer boots.
MIKE. On you!
BARRY. Where we sittin'?
MIKE. On yer 'ead.
BARRY. On me arse!
LIZ. Don't know 'ow 'e tells the difference.

She laughs.

FRED. This'll do.
PETE. All right?
LIZ. Can I sit 'ere?
MIKE. Sit where yer like, dear.
BARRY. What we 'avin'?
PETE (*to* FRED). What yer fancy?
FRED. What they got?
PETE (*looks left*). Double egg, bacon, 'am, bangers, double
    bangers, sper-gety –
BARRY. Chips.
FRED. Juss bring the lot.

PETE. Oi, ease off.

FRED. An' four cups a tea.

PETE. I'm standin' yer for this!

FRED. Make that twice.

BARRY. An' me!

PETE (*to* LIZ). Wass yourn, darlin'?

FRED. Now or later?

PETE. Now, t' start with.

BARRY. Tea and crumpet.

LIZ. Could I 'ave a coffee?

FRED. 'Ave what yer like, darlin'.

BARRY. Cup a tea do me!

COLIN. Wass she 'avin' later!

LIZ. Dinner.

MIKE. Teas all round then.

BARRY. Right.

MIKE (*to* FRED). Sit down, we'll fix it.

PETE, MIKE *and* COLIN *go off left.*

FRED. Where's all the burn?

LIZ. I only got one left.

FRED (*calls*). Get us some snout.

MIKE. Five or ten?

FRED *makes a rude gesture.* LIZ *offers him her cigarette.*

FRED. Keep it, darlin'. I'm okay.

He turns to LEN *and* PAM. Oi, 'ello then. 'Ow's it goin'?

He stands and goes down to their table. LEN *has already sat.*

PAM. 'Ello.

FRED. Thass right, yer said yer'd be 'ere. (*Calls.*) That grub ready? (*To* PAM.) Yeh.

BARRY (*to* FRED). Big gut!

COLIN (*off*). Give us a chance!

PETE (*off*). They didn't teach yer no manners inside.

FRED. Yer're arstin' for trouble. I don't wan'a go back juss yet.

PAM. You all right?

FRED. Yeh. You look all right.

LIZ. Don't yer reckon 'e looks thin?

PAM. I can't –

LIZ. Like a rake. I tol' yer, didn't I? Yer wan'a get some meat on yer.

FRED. I will when that grub turns up.

BARRY *and* LIZ *are sitting at the table up right.* BARRY *bangs the table.*

BARRY. Grub!

COLIN (*off*). Ease up, louse!

BARRY (*calls*). Make that two coffees. (*He puts on an accent.*) I feel like a cup.

LIZ. Ain' what yer sound like.

PETE (*off*). Shut 'im up!

BARRY *makes a gesture.*

FRED. Why did the policewoman marry the 'angman?

LIZ. Eh?

FRED. They both liked necking.

They laugh.

PETE (*off*). Why was the undertaker buried alive?

LIZ. 'Is job got on top a 'im.

They laugh.

BARRY. Why did the woman with three tits 'ave quads?

MIKE. We 'eard it!

The rest groan.

COLIN (*off*). What about the sailor 'oo drowned in 'is bath?

FRED. 'Is brother was the fireman 'oo went up in smoke.

They laugh.

PETE (*off*). Didn't know they let yer 'ave jokes inside.

LIZ. Wass it like?

FRED. In there?

LIZ. Yeh.

FRED (*shrugs. To* LEN). 'Ow's the job?

LEN. Stinks.

FRED. It don't change. (*He sits at their table.*) Long time.

LIZ. Got a light?

FRED (*to* PAM). I got yer letters didn't I.

PAM. Yeh.

FRED. I ain' good at writin'.

PETE, COLIN *and* MIKE *shout and laugh, off*.

PAM. Where yer goin'?

FRED. I'm goin' to 'ave the biggest nosh-up a me life.

BARRY (*to* FRED). Did yer be'ave yerself inside?

PAM (*to* FRED). No, after that.

FRED. O yer know.

PAM. Yer fixed up?

FRED. 'Ow?

PAM. I'll take yer roun' our place.

FRED. O –

LEN. Yer can muck in with me a couple a nights. Give yerself
time t' get straight.

FRED. Ta, I don't wan' a put –

LEN. Yer won't be in the way for a couple of days.

PAM. Mum'll shut up. It'll be nice and quiet. Thass what
yer need.

FRED. Yer must be kidding!

BARRY (*to* LIZ). Arst 'im if 'e be'aved isself.

LIZ (*to* FRED). 'Ear that?

FRED. Yer know me.

BARRY. Not 'arf.

FRED. One day.

LIZ. Yeh.

FRED. This padre 'as me in.

BARRY. O yeh.

FRED. Wants t' chat me up. 'E says nothin that comes out a
a man can be all bad.

BARRY. Whass that?

FRED. Then 'e 'ops out an' I 'as a little slash in 'is tea.

LIZ *and* BARRY *laugh* – LIZ *very loudly*.

LIZ. What 'appened?

FRED. 'E reckoned they ain' put the sugar in.

They laugh.

Another bloke –

LIZ. Yeh.

FRED. Stares at me. Keeps starin' at me. All day. It's 'is first
day, see.

BARRY. Go on.

FRED. So I gets 'im on the landin' an' clobbers 'im.

BARRY. Bang!

FRED. An' it only turns out 'e'd got a squint!

They laugh.

LIZ. Wass it like inside?

FRED. I got chokey for the clobberin'. Bread and water!

BARRY. On yer jack.

FRED. Only good thing there's no one t' scrounge yer grub.

BARRY. Yer d'narf tell 'em.

FRED. Ain' my sort a life. Glad I done it once, but thass their
lot. Ain' pinnin' nothin' on me next time.

LIZ. Wass it like?

FRED. In there?

LIZ. Yeh.

FRED. Cold.

LIZ. Eh?

FRED. Cold.

Silence. MIKE *comes in a few paces from the left.*

MIKE. Won't be 'alf a jik.

FRED. 'Bout time.

COLIN (*off*). 'E still moanin'?

COLIN *comes on and stands with* MIKE.

FRED. Eh?

COLIN. Bet yer couldn't carry-on in there.

FRED. Lot I couldn't do in there, if yer like t' look at it.

MIKE. We ain' got a treat yer everyday.

FRED. I'll pay for this if you like. (*To* LIZ.) Lend us ten bob.

PETE *comes in*.

PETE. 'Oo arst yer t' pay?

FRED. I reckon it's worth one lousy meal.

PETE. Yer made yer own decisions, didn't yer?

BARRY (*comes down*). Wass up?

PETE. We ain' got a crawl up yer arse.

COLIN. Grub smell all right, don't –

PETE. 'Ang on a minute, Col.

MIKE (*to* PETE). Nah, it's 'is first day out, Pete. Let 'im settle down.

COLIN. Come on.

He starts to go left.

PETE. 'E ain' swingin' that one on me.

PETE *and* COLIN *go out left*.

MIKE (*to* FRED). 'E got out the wrong bed this mornin'.

MIKE *follows them off. Slight pause.*

FRED (*laughs*). It's the ol' lag comin' out a me! (*Shouts.*) Whoopee!

BARRY. Ha-ha! Whoopee!

FRED.
> She was only a goalkeeper's daughter
> She married a player called Jack

It was great when 'e played centre forward
But 'e liked to slip round to the back.

(*He laughs.*) I used a lie in me pit thinkin' a that.

COLIN (*off*): What?

FRED: Nosh.

LIZ. That all?

FRED. An' tryin' a remember whass up your legs.

LIZ. I'll draw yer a picture. Give us a light.

FRED (*to* PAM). Give 'er a light.

He gives her a box of matches. She takes them to LIZ. *To*

LEN. Wass 'er game?

LEN. I don't wan'a get involved, mate.

FRED. Yeh? Yer should a read them crummy letters she
keeps sendin'. She ain' goin' a catch me round 'er place.

LEN. No. What was it like?

FRED. No, talk about somethin' else.

LEN. No, *before*.

FRED. Yer 'eard the trial.

PAM *comes back to the table.*

Go away, Pam.

PAM. I wan' a finish me tea.

LEN. Thass cold.

FRED. Can't yer take a 'int? Take yer tea over there.

PAM. Wass goin' on?

LEN. Nothin'!

FRED. No one's talkin' about you.

PAM (*going to sit down at the table*). I'd rather –

FRED. O Pam!

She goes to the unoccupied table and watches them.

'Er ol' people still alive? If yer can call it that.

LEN. Yeh.

FRED. Yer ain' still livin' there?

LEN. I'm goin' soon.

FRED. Yer're as bad as them. She won't get me there in a
  month a Sundays.

LEN. What was it like?

FRED. I tol' yer.

LEN. No, before.

FRED. Before what?

LEN. In the park.

FRED. Yer saw.

LEN. Wass it feel like?

FRED. Don't know.

LEN. When yer was killin' it.

FRED. Do what?

LEN. Wass it feel like when yer killed it?

BARRY (*to* LIZ). Fancy a record?

LIZ. Wouldn't mind.

BARRY. Give us a tanner then.

LIZ. Yer're as tight as a flea's arse'ole.

BARRY. An 'alf as 'andsome. I know. – Out a change.

LIZ *gives him sixpence. He goes off down right.* MIKE *brings on
two cups.*

MIKE. Comin' up.

FRED. Very 'andy.

BARRY (*off*). 'Ow about 'I Broke my 'Eart'?

LIZ. Yeh. Thass great.

BARRY (*off*). Well they ain' got it.

LIZ. Funny! What about 'My 'Eart is Broken'?

MIKE (*to* LIZ). One coffee.

BARRY (*off*). They got that.

LIZ (*to* MIKE). The sugar in it?

MIKE. Taste it.

MIKE *goes off left.*

LEN. Whass it like, Fred?

FRED (*drinks*). It ain' like this in there.

LEN. Fred.

FRED. I tol' yer.

LEN. No yer ain'.

FRED. I forget.

LEN. I thought yer'd a bin full a it. I was –

FRED. Len!

LEN. – curious, thass all, 'ow it feels t' –

FRED. No!

He slams his fist on the table.

LEN. Okay.

FRED. It's finished.

LEN. Yeh.

FRED (*stands*). What yer wan' a do?

The juke box starts.

LEN. Nothin'.

FRED. Wass 'e gettin' at?

LEN. It's finished.

PETE, MIKE, COLIN *and* BARRY *come on.* PAM *stands.* LIZ *still sits.*

FRED. I were'n the only one.

LEN. I ain' gettin' at yer, skip.

PETE. Wass up?

FRED. Nothin' a do with you.

PAM. 'E was rowin'.

FRED. It's nothin'. Where's that grub?

PAM. I knew 'e'd start somethin'.

FRED. Forget it.

PAM. I tol' 'im not t' come.

FRED. Where's that flippin' grub? Move.

COLIN *and* MIKE *go off left.*

PAM. 'E won't let me alone.

FRED. I'm starvin' I know that.

PAM. 'E follers me everywhere.

FRED. Ain' you lucky.

PAM. Tell 'im for me! 'It 'im! 'It 'im!

FRED. It's nothin' a do with me!

PAM. It is! It is!

BARRY. She's started.

FRED. 'Ere we go!

He sits and puts his head in his hands.

PAM (*to* LEN). See what yer done?

FRED. Didn't take 'er long.

PAM. It's your place t' stick up for me, love. I went through all that trouble for you! Somebody's got a save me from 'im.

FRED. Thanks. Thanks very much. I'll remember this.

He stands and starts back to his own table.

LIZ (*starting to click her fingers*). I can't 'ear the music!

PAM (*to* LEN). Don't bloody sit there! Yer done enough 'arm!

PETE 'Oo brought 'er 'ere?

FRED. Chriss knows!

PAM (*pointing to* LEN). 'E started this!

FRED. I don't care what bleedin' wet started it. You can stop it!

PAM (*to* LEN). I 'ate yer for this!

FRED. BELT UP!

PAM (*goes to* FRED, *who sits at his table*). I'm sorry. Fred, 'e's goin' now. It'll be all right when 'e's gone.

LEN *does not move.*

FRED. All right.

PAM (*looks round*). Where's 'is grub? 'E's starvin' 'ere. (*She goes to touch his arm.*) I get so worked up when 'e –

FRED. Keep yer 'ands off me! So 'elp me I'll land yer so bloody 'ard they'll put me back for life!

PETE (*moving in*). Right. Less get ourselves sorted out.

COLIN *comes on left.*

PAM. It don't matter. I juss got excited. (*Calls.*) Where's 'is breakfast? It'll be time for –

FRED. Breakfast? I couldn't eat in this bloody place if they served it through a rubber tube.

PETE. Come on! (*Calls.*) Mike!

FRED. All I done for 'er an' she 'as the bloody nerve t' start this!

PETE. Come on, less move.

BARRY. She wants throttlin'.

MIKE *comes on left.* COLIN *and* FRED *go out right. The door bangs.*

LIZ. I ain' drunk me coffee.

PETE. I said move!

MIKE. Flippin' mad'ouse.

MIKE *goes out right. The door bangs.*

LIZ. We paid for it!

PETE. Move!

LIZ *and* BARRY *go out right. The door bangs.*

You come near 'im again an' I'll settle yer for good. Lay off.

PETE *goes out right. The door bangs.* LEN *still sits.* PAM *stands. Pause.*

LEN. I'll see yer 'ome. I'm late for work already. I know I'm in the way. Yer can't go round the streets when yer're like that. (*He hesitates.*) They ain' done 'im no good. 'Es gone back like a kid. Yer well out a it. (*He stands.*) I knew the little bleeder 'ld do a bunk! Can't we try an' get on like before? (*He looks round.*) There's no one else. Yer only live once.

SCENE ELEVEN

The living-room.

On the table: bread, butter, breadknife, cup and saucer and milk.

MARY *sits on the couch.*

HARRY *comes in with a pot of tea. He goes to the table. He cuts and butters bread. Pause while he works.*

MARY *goes out.* HARRY *goes on working.* MARY *comes back with a cup and saucer. She pours herself tea. She takes it to the couch and sits. She sips.*

HARRY *moves so that his back is to her. He puts his cup upright in his saucer. He puts milk in the cup. He reaches to pick up the teapot.*

MARY *stands, goes to the table, and moves the teapot out of his reach. She goes back to the couch. Sits. Sips.*

MARY. My teapot.

Sips. Pause.

HARRY. My tea.

He pours tea into his cup. MARY *stands and goes to the table. She empties his cup on the floor.*

HARRY. Our'n. Weddin' present.
MARY (*goes to the couch and sits*). From *my* mother.
HARRY. That was joint.
MARY. Don't you dare talk to me!

HARRY *goes out.*

MARY (*loudly*). Some minds want boilin' in carbolic. Soap's too good for 'em. (*Slight pause.*) Dirty filth! Worse! Ha! (*She goes to the door and calls*). Don't you dare talk to me!

She goes to the couch and sits. HARRY *comes in.*

HARRY. I'll juss say one word. I saw yer with yer skirt up. Yer call me filth?

HARRY *goes out. Slight pause.* MARY *goes to the table and empties his slices of bread on to the floor. She goes back to the couch and drinks her tea.*

MARY. Mind out of a drain! I wouldn't let a kid like that touch me if 'e paid for it!

HARRY *comes in. He goes straight to the table.*

HARRY. I don't want to listen.
MARY. Filth!
HARRY. There's bin enough trouble in this 'ouse. Now yer wan'a cause trouble with 'im!
MARY. Don't talk t' me! You!
HARRY (*sees his bread on the floor*). Yer juss wan'a start trouble like there was before! (*He stoops and picks up the bread.*) Middle-age woman – goin' with 'er own daughter's leftovers – 'alf 'er age – makin' 'erself a spectacle – look at this! – No self control.
MARY. Filth!
HARRY. Like a child – I pity the lad – must want 'is 'ead tested.
MARY. There'll be some changes in this 'ouse. I ain' puttin' up with this after t'day. Yer can leave my things alone for a start. All this stuff come out a my pocket. I worked for it! I ain' 'avin' you dirtyin' me kitchin. Yer can get yerself some new towels for a start! An' plates! An' knives! An' cups! Yer'll soon find a difference!
HARRY. Don't threaten me –
MARY. An' my cooker! An' my curtains! An' my sheets!
HARRY. Yer'll say somethin' yer'll be sorry for!

He comes towards her. There is a chair in the way. He trips over it. The leg comes off.

MARY. Don't you touch me!

HARRY. Two can play at your game! Yeh! I can stop your money t'morra!

MARY. Don't yer raise yer 'and t' me!

HARRY *goes back to the table. He starts cutting bread. Pause.*

I knew yer was stood outside when 'e was there. I 'eard yer through the door. I'd a bet my life you'd come in!

HARRY. Old enough t' be 'is mother. Yer must be 'ard up!

MARY. I seen you stuck 'ere long enough! You couldn't pick an' choose!

HARRY. One was enough.

MARY. No one else would a put up with yer!

HARRY. I can do without! Yer ain' worth it!

MARY. Ha! I saw yer face when yer come through that door. I bin watchin' yer all the week. I know you of old, Harry!

HARRY. Yer'll go out a yer mind one day!

MARY. Filth!

HARRY. I 'ad enough a you in the past! I ain' puttin' up with your lark again. I'm too old. I wan' a bit a peace an' quiet.

MARY. Then why did yer come in?

HARRY. Me pools was in that table.

MARY. Yer was spyin'! Yer bin sniffin' round ever since! I ain' puttin' up with your dirt! (*She picks up the teapot.*) Yer can bloody well stay in yer room!

PAM *comes in.*

PAM. Chriss. (*Calls.*) It's them!

HARRY (*cutting bread*). I ain' sunk so low I'll bother *you*!

MARY. Yer jealous ol' swine!

HARRY. Of a bag like you?

MARY. 'E don't think so! I could a gone t'bed, an' I will next time 'e arsts me!

HARRY. Now 'e's caught a sniff a yer 'e'll be off with 'is tail between 'is legs?

She hits him with the teapot. The water pours over him. PAM *is too frightened to move.*

Ah!

MARY. 'Ope yer die!

HARRY. Blood!

MARY. Use words t' me!

HARRY. Blood!

PAM. Mum!

HARRY. Ah!

LEN (*off*). Whass up?

HARRY. Doctor.

MARY. Cracked me weddin' present. 'Im.

LEN *comes in.*

LEN. Blimey!

HARRY. Scalded!

PAM. Whass 'appenin'?

HARRY. She tried t' murder me!

MARY. Yer little liar!

PAM. Are yer all right?

HARRY. Yer saw 'er.

MARY. 'E went mad.

LEN. It's only a scratch.

PAM (*to* MARY). Why?

MARY. 'Effin an' blindin'.

LEN. Yer'll live.

HARRY. Blood.

PAM (*to* MARY). Whass 'e done?

LEN. 'E's all wet.

MARY. Swore at me!

PAM. Why?

HARRY. Doctor.

MARY. There's nothin' wrong with 'im.

HARRY. Scalded.

MARY. I 'ardly touched 'im. 'E needs a good thrashin'!

LEN (*to* PAM). Get a towel.

HARRY. I ain' allowed t' touch the towels.

MARY. I kep' this twenty-three years. Look what 'e's done to it!

PAM. *What 'appened?*

LEN. Nothin'. They 'ad a row.

PAM. 'E called 'er a bag.

LEN. It's nothin'. I'd better be off t' work. They'll give us me cards. We juss seen Fred. 'E looks all right, well 'e don't look bad. It ain' Butlins. (*To* PAM.) Get 'im up t' bed. Put the kettle on. Yer could all do with a cup a tea.

PAM (*to* MARY). What made yer start talkin'?

MARY. Yer 'eard 'im call me a bag. (*To* LEN.) 'E went mad over catchin' you last week.

LEN (*looking at* HARRY's *head*). Yer'll 'ave t' wash that cut. It's got tealeaves in it.

HARRY *dabs at it with the tail of his shirt.*

PAM. Caught 'oo last week?

MARY (*pointing to* HARRY). 'Is filth. (*Points to* LEN.) Arst 'im!

PAM (*to* LEN). What 'appened?

LEN. Nothin'.

HARRY. I was cuttin' bread. (*He picks up the knife.*) She flew at me!

PAM (*to* LEN). I knew it was you! (*To* HARRY.) Whass 'e done?

LEN. Nothin'.

MARY. Filth!

HARRY. I found 'em both.

He points with the knife to the spot.

LEN (*pulling at* HARRY). No!

HARRY. She'll 'ave t' 'ear.

LEN (*he pulls at him*). No!

HARRY. She 'ad 'er clothes up.

PAM. No!

LEN. Yer bloody fool! Yer bloody, bloody fool!

LEN *shakes* HARRY. *The knife waves through the air.*

HARRY. Ah!

PAM. That knife!

MARY. Filth!

PAM. 'E'll kill 'im!

LEN. Bloody fool.

PAM (*screams*). Oh! No! – Whass 'appenin' to us?

She sits on the couch and cries. Pause.

HARRY. 'Im an' 'er.

PAM (*crying*). Why don't 'e go? Why don't 'e go away? All my friends gone. Baby's gone. Nothin' left but rows. Day in, day out. Fightin' with knives.

HARRY. I'm shakin'.

PAM (*crying*). They'll kill each other soon.

LEN (*to* PAM). Yer can't blame them on me!

PAM (*crying*). Why can't 'e go away!

HARRY (*removes his shirt*). Wet.

PAM (*crying*). Look at me. I can't sleep with worry.

MARY. Breakin' me 'ome.

PAM (*crying*). 'E's killed me baby. Taken me friends. Broken me 'ome.

HARRY. More blood.

MARY. I ain' clearin' up after 'im. 'E can clear 'is own mess.

PAM (*crying*). I can't go on like this.

LEN (*to* PAM). There was nothin' in it!

PAM (*crying*). I'll throw myself somewhere. It's the only way.

HARRY. Cold.

LEN *goes to* HARRY.

PAM (*sitting and crying*). Stop 'im! They'll kill each other!

LEN (*stops*). I was goin' a 'elp 'im.

PAM (*crying*). Take that knife. The baby's dead. They're all gone. It's the only way. I can't go on.

MARY. Next time 'e won't be so lucky.

PAM (*crying*). Yer can't call it livin'. 'E's pullin' me t' pieces. Nothin' but trouble.

LEN. I'm tryin' t' 'elp! 'Oo else'll 'elp? If I go will they come back? Will the baby come back? Will 'e come back? I'm the only one that's stayed an' yer wan'a get rid a me!

PAM (*crying*). I can't stand any more. Baby dead. No friends.

LEN. I'll go.

PAM (*crying*). No one listens. Why don't 'e go? Why don't they make 'im go?

MARY. 'E can stay in 'is own room after t'day.

LEN. I'll find somewhere dinnertime.

HARRY. Me neck's throbbin'.

PAM (*crying*). No 'ome. No friends. Baby dead. Gone. Fred gone.

SCENE TWELVE

LEN's *bedroom*.

LEN *lies face down on the floor. The side of his face is flat against the floorboards. He holds a knife. There is an open suitcase on the bed. In it are a few things. Pause.*

The door opens. HARRY *comes in. He wears long white combinations. He wears pale socks. No shoes. His head is in a skull cap of bandages. He comes up behind* LEN. LEN *sees him slowly.*

HARRY. Evenin'.

LEN. Evenin'.

HARRY. Get up. Yer'll catch cold down there.

LEN. 'Ow's yer 'ead?

HARRY (*touches it*). Don't know.

LEN. Thass a good sign.

HARRY. All right now?

LEN. I was listenin'.

He draws the knife between two boards.

Clears the crack. Yer can 'ear better.

HARRY. Thass a good knife.

LEN. She's got someone with 'er.

HARRY. Thought yer might like someone t' say good night.

LEN. Yer can 'ear 'er voice.

HARRY. No.

LEN. She's picked someone up. I couldn't get anywhere with me packin'.

HARRY. No, I saw 'er come in.

LEN. Could a swore I 'eard someone.

HARRY. Not with 'er!

LEN. She's still good lookin'.

HARRY. 'Er sort's two a penny. Lads don't 'ave t' put up with 'er carry-on.

LEN. I used t' 'ear Fred an' her down there.

HARRY. No more.

LEN. Kep' me awake.

HARRY (*sits on the bed*). Tired. Nice 'ere.

LEN. Seen worse.

HARRY. Quiet.

LEN. Sometimes.

Pause.

HARRY. She's cryin'.

LEN. O.

HARRY. In bed. I passed 'er door.

LEN. I knew I 'eard somethin'.

HARRY. Thass what yer 'eard.

LEN *puts a pair of socks in the case.*

Won't be the last time.

LEN. Eh?

HARRY. 'Owlin in bed.

LEN. O.

HARRY. She'll pay for it.

LEN. What?

HARRY. 'Er ways. Yer'll get yer own back.

LEN. I lost me case keys.

HARRY. Yer'll see.

LEN. Long time since I used it.

HARRY. Where yer goin'?

LEN. 'Ad enough.

HARRY. No different any other place.

LEN. I've heard it all before.

Pause.

HARRY. Thought yer'd like t' say good night.

LEN. Yeh. Ta.

HARRY. They're all in bed.

LEN. I get in the way, don't I?

HARRY. Take no notice.

LEN. Sick a rows.

HARRY. They've 'ad their say. They'll keep quiet now.

LEN. I upset every –

HARRY. No different if yer go. They won't let yer drop.

LEN. Different for me.

He puts a shirt in the case.

   I never put a finger on your ol' woman. I juss give 'er a 'and.

HARRY. I known 'er longer'n you.

LEN. She reckoned she was late.

HARRY. Ain' my worry.

LEN. But yer 'ad a row.

HARRY. She 'ad a row.

LEN. You shouted.

HARRY. It ain' like that.

LEN. I 'eard yer.

HARRY. It clears the air. Sometimes. It's finished. – You
   shouted.

Pause.

LEN. I'll 'ave t' look for that key.

HARRY. I left 'er once.

LEN. You?

HARRY. I come back.

LEN. Why?

HARRY. I worked it out. Why should I soil me 'ands washin' an' cookin'? Let 'er do it. She'll find out.

LEN. Yer do yer own washin'.

HARRY. Eh?

LEN. An' cookin'.

HARRY. Ah, *now.*

Pause.

LEN. I can do without the key. I ain' goin' far.

HARRY. Bin in the army?

LEN. No.

HARRY. Yer can see that. Know where yer goin'?

LEN. Someplace 'andy. For work.

HARRY. Round Fred?

LEN. No.

HARRY. She won't see 'im again.

LEN. Best thing, too. Yer ain' seen what it done t' 'im. 'E's like a kid. 'E'll finished up like some ol' lag, or an' ol' soak. Bound to. An' soon. Yer'll see.

He moves the case along the bed.

That'll keep till t'morrow.

HARRY. It's a shame.

LEN. Too tired t'night. Wass a shame?

HARRY. Yer stood all the rows. Now it'll settle down an' yer –

LEN. I 'ad my last row, I know that.

HARRY. Sit 'ere.

LEN (*sits on the bed*). It's bin a 'ard day.

HARRY. Finished now.

A long pause.

LEN. I'd like t' get up t'morrow mornin' and clear right out.
    There's nothin' t' keep me 'ere. What do I get out a it?
    Jack it in. Emigrate.

HARRY. Yer're too young t' emigrate. Do that when yer past
    fifty.

LEN. I don't give a damn if they don't talk, but they don't even
    listen t' yer. Why the 'ell should I bother about 'er?

HARRY. It's juss a rough patch. We 'ad t' sort ourselves out
    when you joined us. But yer fit in now. It'll settle down.

LEN. No one tells yer anything really.

Slight pause.

  Was she all right?

HARRY. Eh?

LEN. In bed.

HARRY. Yer know.

LEN. No.

HARRY. Up t' the man.

LEN. Yeh?

HARRY. I 'ad the best.

LEN. Go on.

HARRY (*quietly*). I 'ad 'er squealing like a pig.

LEN. Yeh.

HARRY. There was a little boy first.

LEN. In the war.

HARRY. Then the girl.

LEN. On leave.

HARRY. An' back t' the front.

LEN. Go on.

HARRY. I saw the lot.

LEN. What was it like?

HARRY. War?

Slight pause.

Most I remember the peace an' quiet. Once or twice the 'ole lot blew up. Not more. Then it went quiet. Everythin' still. Yer don't get it that quiet now.

LEN. Not 'ere.

HARRY. Nowhere.

LEN. Kill anyone?

HARRY. Must 'ave. Yer never saw the bleeders, 'ceptin' prisoners or dead. Well, I did once. I was in a room. Some bloke stood up in the door. Lost, I expect. I shot 'im. 'E fell down. Like a coat fallin' off a 'anger, I always say. Not a word.

Pause.

Yer never killed yer man. Yer missed that. Gives yer a sense a perspective. I was one a the lucky ones.

Pause.

LEN. 'Oo tied your 'ead?

HARRY. I managed. I never arst them.

LEN. I'm good at that.

HARRY. No need.

Pause.

Nigh on midnight.

LEN. Gone.

He takes off his shoes and stands. He drops his trousers.

HARRY. Yer don't wan'a go.

LEN. Eh?

HARRY. Don't go. No point.

LEN (*his trousers round his ankles*). Why?

HARRY. Yer'd come back.

LEN. No use sayin' anythin' t'night –

HARRY. Don't let 'em push yer out.

LEN. Depends 'ow I feel in the mornin'.

He sits on the bed and pulls off his trousers.

HARRY. Choose yer own time. Not when it suits them.

LEN. I don't know anythin' t'night.

HARRY. I'd like yer t' stay. If yer can see yer way to.

LEN. Why?

HARRY (*after a slight pause*). I ain' stayin'.

LEN. What?

HARRY. Not always.

LEN. O, yeh.

He puts the case on the floor.

HARRY. Yer'll see. If I was t' go now she'd be laughin'. She'd soon 'ave someone in my bed. She knows 'ow t' be'ave when she likes. An' cook.

LEN. Yeh, yeh.

He slides the case under the bed and sits on the bed.

HARRY. I'll go when I'm ready. When she's on 'er pension. She won't get no one after 'er then. I'll be *out*. Then see 'ow she copes.

LEN. Ain' worth it, pop.

HARRY. It's only right. When someone carries on like 'er, they 'ave t' pay for it. People can't get away with murder. What 'd 'appen then?

LEN. Don't arst me.

HARRY. She thinks she's on top. I'll 'ave t' fall back a bit – buy a few things an' stay in me room more. I can wait.

LEN. 'Ead still 'urt?

HARRY. She'll find out.

LEN. I can let yer 'ave some aspirins.

HARRY. Eh?

LEN. Can yer move up.

Harry stands.

No, I didn't mean that.

HARRY. Yer should be in bed. We don't wan'a waste the light.

LEN. I won't let on what yer said.

HARRY. Eh?

LEN. You leavin'.

HARRY. She knows.

LEN. Yer told 'er?

HARRY. We don't 'ave secrets. They make trouble.

He goes to the door.

Don't speak to 'em at all. It saves a lot a misunderstandin'.

LEN. O.

HARRY. Yer'll be all right in the mornin'.

LEN. No work t'night?

HARRY. Saturday.

LEN. I forgot.

HARRY. Night.

LEN. Funny we never talked before.

HARRY. They listen all the time.

LEN. Will yer come up next Saturday night?

HARRY. No, no. Cause trouble. They won't stand for it.

LEN. I'd like t' tell 'er t' jump off once more.

HARRY. Sometime. Don't upset 'er. It ain' fair. Thass best all round.

LEN (*looks round*). It's like that.

HARRY. Listen!

LEN. What?

HARRY *holds up his hand. Silence.*

Still cryin'?

HARRY. She's gone quiet.

Silence.

There – she's movin'.

Silence.

LEN. She's 'eard us.

HARRY. Best keep away, yer see. Good night.
LEN. But –
HARRY. Sh!

He holds up his hand again. They listen. Silence. Pause.

HARRY. Good night.
LEN. 'Night.

HARRY *goes.*

SCENE THIRTEEN

The living-room.

PAM *sits on the couch. She reads the* Radio Times.

MARY *takes things from the table and goes out. Pause. She comes back. She goes to the table. She collects the plates. She goes out.*

Pause. The door opens. HARRY *comes in. He goes to the table and opens the drawer. He searches in it.*

PAM *turns a page.*

MARY *comes in. She goes to the table and picks up the last things on it. She goes out.*

HARRY'*s jacket is draped on the back of the chair by the table. He searches in the pockets.*

PAM *turns a page.*

There is a loud bang (off).

Silence.

HARRY *turns to the table and searches in the drawer.*

MARY *comes in. She wipes the table top with a damp cloth.*

There is a loud bang (off).

MARY *goes out.*

HARRY *takes ink and envelope out of the drawer. He puts them on the table. He sits on the chair. He feels behind him and takes a pen from the inside pocket of his jacket. He starts to fill in his football coupon.*

A short silence.

PAM *quickly turns over two pages.*

Immediately the door opens and LEN *comes in. He carries the chair that* HARRY *tripped over and broke. He takes it down right and sets it on the floor. He crouches. His head is below the level of the seat. He looks under the chair. He turns it upside down. He fiddles with the loose leg.*

MARY *comes in. She straightens the couch. She takes off her apron and folds it neatly. She sits on the couch and pushes the apron down the side of the couch.*

Silence.

Stop.

LEN *turns the chair upright. He still crouches. He rests his left wrist high on the chair back and his right elbow on the chair seat. His right hand hangs in space. His back is to the audience. His head is sunk into his shoulders. He thinks for a moment.*

PAM *stands and goes to the door.*

LEN. Fetch me 'ammer.

PAM *goes out.* HARRY *writes.* MARY *sits.* LEN *presses his hand on the seat and the chair wobbles.* MARY *takes up the* Radio Times *and glances at the back page.* HARRY *takes a small leather folder out of the inside pocket of his jacket. He places the folder on the table.*

PAM *comes in and sits on the couch.*

LEN *turns the chair upside down and looks at it.*

MARY *puts the* Radio Times *back on the couch. She pats the pillow.* PAM *picks up the* Radio Times. *In one connected movement* LEN *turns the chair upright and stands to his full height. He has grasped the seat at diagonally opposite corners, so that the diagonal is parallel with the front of his body. He brings the chair sharply down so that the foot furthest from him strikes the floor first. It makes a loud bang. Still standing upright he turns the chair upside down and looks at the leg. He turns the chair upright and sets it down. He crouches. He places the flat of his palm on the seat. The chair still has a little wobble.*

PAM *folds the* Radio Times *and puts it down.*

HARRY *takes a stamp from the folder.* LEN *sits on the chair and faces front. He puts his head between his knees to peer under the chair.* HARRY *licks the stamp and silently stamps the envelope. He reaches behind him and puts the folder and the spare coupon in the inside pocket of his jacket.*

LEN *gets off the chair and crouches beside it. His back is to the audience. He bends over the chair so that his stomach or chest rests on the seat. He reaches down with his left hand and pulls the loose rear leg up into the socket.*

HARRY *reaches behind him and puts his pen into the breast pocket of his jacket. He puts the ink in the table drawer.*

LEN *slips his left arm round the back of the chair. His chest rests against the side edge of the seat. The fingers of his right hand touch the floor. His head lies sideways on the seat.*

MARY *sits.* PAM *sits.*

HARRY *licks the flap on the envelope and closes it quietly.*

The curtain falls quickly.

Joe Orton

Joe Orton, 'the Oscar Wilde of Welfare State gentility,' had been a playwright for only three years when his lover, Kenneth Halliwell, battered out his brains with a hammer and took his own life with an overdose of the barbiturate, Nembutal. Some decades before, the original Oscar Wilde had amused himself by announcing in 'The Decay of Lying' the paradox that 'Life imitates Art far more than Art imitates life'. Though Wilde himself pointed out that such paradoxes are dangerous, the temptation is great to describe Joe Orton's life as an imitation of his art. Just two months before he was murdered, two of Orton's short plays, *The Ruffian on the Stair* and *The Erpingham Camp*, opened at the Royal Court under the collective title *Crimes of Passion*. The former play climaxes with a jealous murder; the latter ends with the fatal beating of the title character. Writing in his diary a month before *Crimes of Passion* opened, Orton recorded that Halliwell was predicting disaster for the production and warning that, if it did not fail, 'disaster more intolerable' was bound to happen. Though he may not have admitted it, Halliwell, who had once been Orton's mentor and was now watching his former protégé zoom toward the stars while his own career languished, was consumed by the mean jealously well known to failed artists. When the prayed-for-failure did not materialize and his jealously became intolerable, Halliwell committed his own crime of passion.

While the leaving of his life was as violent as his plays, the living of it was as unsavoury. 'I'm from the gutter,' Orton quotes himself in his diary, 'and don't you ever forget it because I won't.' Born in Leicester in 1933 to a gardener father and a machinist mother, Orton was a sickly child, suffering from asthma. Inadequately educated, he was, by some accounts, semi-literate, although the diary, which he was keeping at the age of sixteen, expressed his thoughts clearly in spite of his bad spelling. His one love was the theatre, and, after a series of dull jobs, dully filled, he won acceptance to the Royal Academy of Dramatic Arts, having first worked to eliminate a lisp and a strong regional accent. Receiving a Leicester Council grant, he went to London in 1951 where, after beginning his studies at the Royal Academy of Dramatic Arts, he met Halliwell, the fellow student who would become his murderer. They quickly formed an intimate relationship.

Seven years older than Orton and better educated, Halliwell had already begun to write. After RADA and Orton's brief attempt at an acting career, Halliwell and Orton moved in together to pursue writing careers. Living austerely on Halliwell's small inheritance and the earnings from temporary jobs, they collaborated on a series of failed novels.

By 1957 Orton was writing independently, but no more successfully. A 'connoisseur of chaos' and 'an enemy of order', as John Lahr describes him, Orton was given to anti-social pranks. He and Halliwell thumbed their noses at society by vandalizing library books, for example. The walls of their claustrophobic flat were decorated with photographic plates, ripped out of art books. They wrote suggestive captions and blurbs and constructed startling collages before returning the library books to the shelves. Charged with malicious damage, they were sent to jail for six months. The experience changed Orton. 'Being in the nick brought detachment to my writing,' he said. 'I wasn't involved anymore and it suddenly worked.' He mailed *The Ruffian on the Stair* to the BBC radio in a prison envelope; and his writing career took off.

His jail term also sharpened Orton's contempt for society. 'Before, I had been vaguely conscious of something rotting somewhere; prison crystallized this. The old whore society really lifted up her skirts and the stench was pretty foul.' A confirmed anti-social rebel now, and a natural outcast as a homosexual, Orton began to use his new-found success to outrage society publicly as he had attacked it covertly in the Islington Library.

He had nothing to lose anymore, he thought, in a society he regarded as run by fools. High on his list were the police and members of the Catholic church, both satirized in *Loot*. However, like his model, Oscar Wilde, he put the average respectable Englishman, whose style he found obnoxious, at the very top. To Giles Gordon he remarked, 'I think the English have the worst taste of any people in the world.'

He delighted in nettling the public by flaunting his sexual licence. John Lahr quotes him as saying, 'Sex is the only way to infuriate them.' He larded his plays with sexual innuendoes and improprieties, especially of the homosexual variety, thereby advancing the banner of his own minority, as if to say, 'I'm gay and I'm proud.' But he by no means sentimentalizes homosexuality in his plays. It was more important to shock conservative audiences than to plead a cause. 'I'm to be at King's Cross station at eleven,' Mike says in *The Ruffian on the Stair*. 'I'm meeting a man in the toilet.'

His efforts to offend his fellow-Englishmen grew more outrageous. Howard Brenton in *The Churchill Play* was to attack the most sacrosanct of modern British heroes by depicting Winston Churchill as an effeminate twister of the truth. But Orton outdid him seven years earlier by introducing a replica of the Churchillian penis taken from a 'larger than life-sized bronze statue' into *What the Butler Saw*. In performance, however, the penis became a cigar for the play's 1960 premiere and remained so until the 1975 Royal Court revival.

As if venting his spleen against society in his plays was not enough, Orton tried another prankish tactic both theatrical and faintly decadent, since it verged on trans-sexuality. He invented a kind of alter ego in the person of a prudish, clean-skirted Englishwoman, one Mrs. Edna Welthorpe, in whose name he wrote indignant letters to the press excoriating the 'mental and physical perversion' of Orton's plays. He was behaving like the dandy of Albert Camus' *The Rebel*, who takes narcissistic pleasure in admiring an image of himself as a defiant social rebel.

Orton's continuing social vandalism did not impede his career. He rapidly became a commercially successful playwright. *Ruffian on the Stair*, which the BBC Radio aired in 1964, premiered on the stage in 1966. Orton followed it up quickly with *Entertaining Mr. Sloane*, his first full-length play, which opened at the small New Arts Theatre even before *Ruffian* was broadcast. When *Sloane* transferred to the West End, Orton became a hit playwright.

Numerous critics have labelled the two plays Pinteresque, citing the atmosphere of uncertainty and vague terror that pervades them. (Actually, Orton admitted stealing a scene from Pinter's *The Birthday Party* for the first scene of *Ruffian*, but he removed it before the Royal Court opening of the play.) In both Orton plays, a mysterious young man, amoral, sexually ambiguous, vaguely criminal, intrudes on a marginal household, a familiar opening situation in Pinter plays. In *Sloane* the young man actually rents a room; in *Ruffian* he claims to be seeking lodging, but actually only seeks entrance in order to terrorize the young woman in the house with physical violence (he breaks her window) and verbal threats expressed as casual conversation: 'Do you know I could murder you? Easy as that. (*He snaps his fingers.*) That's how these assaults on lonely women are all committed.' Both plays are replete with half-explained allusions to crimes and both make sex a treacherous battleground.

Although Orton admitted admiring Pinter as, aside from Beckett, the only dramatist worthy of respect, he was 'much more concerned than Pinter with the elaboration of plot, obsessively detailed and precise plot,' as John Russell Taylor noted. Certainly the plot of *Entertaining Mr. Sloane* is complexly elaborate. Eighteen-year-old Sloane takes a room with Kath, a stupid, middle-aged woman, whose father recognizes Sloane as the perpetrator of a murder he had witnessed. Kath's mysteriously prosperous brother Ed engages Sloane as a chauffeur and tries to draw him into a homosexual relationship. In the meantime Kath becomes pregnant by him. When her father reveals his knowledge of Sloane's crime, the young man beats him senseless. Ed cynically uses the consequent death of his father to blackmail Sloane into sexual servitude. In fact, Kath and Ed agree to share Sloane's sexual favours, a typical Orton stroke.

Unlike most of Pinter's plays, Orton's plays move beyond implications and threats to explicitly violent action. In *Ruffian*, the mysterious youth, Wilson, by pretending to have sex with Mike's woman, goads Mike into shooting him. His motive is the hope that Mike will have to pay for his crime.

Since major crimes are seen to be committed in Orton's plays and since the criminals then get off, Orton can demonstrate one of the more cynical aspects of his social view, namely, that criminals have nothing to fear from formal justice. The substratum of the criminal proletariat is beyond the reach of social authority.

Orton's next play, *Loot*, was a failure in its 1965 Cambridge premiere, a result Orton ascribed to its being played overtly for laughs. Outrageous scenes like the one in which Hal and his accomplice dump Hal's mother out of her coffin so they can hide their stolen loot in it can only achieve their comic effect and their essential meaning if they are played with deadpan seriousness. Dejected by the play's failure, Orton threatened to give up the stage to write for television. However, in September 1966, the Charles Marowitz production of *Loot* opened in London, became a big hit, and won the *Evening Standard* and the *Plays and Players* awards.

It was at this point that Orton's life began to imitate his art in earnest. His mother died during the run of *Loot*. While the cast was travestying a mother's funeral nightly on stage, Orton found a way to travesty his real-life mother's funeral. He carried his dead mother's false teeth to the theatre and thrust them into the hands of cast members, as if to vindicate the chattering teeth gag in the play. 'What, you find that gag coarse and vulgar? Here, try the reality.'

Orton's last play, *What the Butler Saw*, which John Lahr calls his masterpiece, was not produced until two years after Orton's death. Set in a psychiatric clinic, it combines the stylish wit of comedy of manners with the frenetic complications of French farce. Characters dash on and off the stage in hilarious attempts to conceal their own sexual peccadilloes, while they're busily trying to expose the furtive sexual fumblings of others. They hide behind screens, don and discard their clothing, seduce and are seduced in most of the conceivable sexual pairings, including incestuous ones. Orton ends the play when Sergeant Match descends to the stage by a rope ladder dropped through a skylight, for all the world like a Euripidean *deus ex machina*. That the resemblance is not accidental is clear. Match is dressed in a bloody, leopard-spotted dress, so that he looks like a grotesque mockery of Agave in the dreadful final scene of *The Bacchae*. In Lahr's phrase, it was 'an act of literary aggression which Orton carried to its logical extreme'.

Orton's reputation got a mighty posthumous boost when the Royal Court Theatre produced its Orton Festival, mounting the three full-length plays, two of which – *Entertaining Mr. Sloane* and *What the Butler saw* – were then transferred to the West End. Orton's reputation is still commercially and critically high. During 1984 *Loot* was again revived successfully in the West End and, in a single summer, all of Orton's major plays were staged in summer stock in the United States.

Loot is a good illustration of three characteristics important in Orton's work: his emulation of Oscar Wilde, his great gift of irony, and his frightening vision of the human personality.

Orton freely acknowledged his debt to Wilde. He listed Wilde among his most admired models, though he claimed – surely with tongue in cheek, considering his own life style – to abhor Wilde's life. One of Orton's declared ambitions was to produce a contemporary counterpart to *The Importance of Being Earnest*. Certainly *Loot*, though it concerns itself with a different level of society, nevertheless echoes *Earnest* in the kind and quality of its wit. When Hal says 'Every luxury was lavished on you – atheism, breastfeeding, circumcision,' we hear a vulgarized Lady Bracknell: 'Ignorance is like a delicate, exotic fruit; touch it and the bloom is gone.' Orton catches both the rock-ribbed insouciance and the total disregard for conventional sentiments typical of Wildean aphorism. In *Loot*, Fay sets the stage for McLeavy's proposal so: 'Go ahead. Ask me to marry you. I've no intention of refusing. On your knees. I'm a great believer in traditional positions.' This is intriguingly close to Gwendolen's handling of Jack's proposal to her in *Earnest*: 'And to spare you any possible disappointment, Mr. Worthing, I think it only fair to tell you quite frankly beforehand that I am fully determined to accept you.' However, while admitting the similarity between Orton's wit and Wilde's, we must acknowledge a crucial difference – Wilde's characters are harmless butterflies; Orton's are murderous sociopaths.

Irony is the basis of much of Orton's comedy. The ironic juxtaposition of act and word is an essential feature of Orton's ability to make us laugh. 'The happenings may be as outrageous as you like . . . but the primness and propriety of what is said hardly ever breaks down,' explains Taylor. We howl when Orton's dirty-handed characters speak like altar boys. 'Bury her naked. My own mum?' agonizes Hal in the midst of dumping her body out of her coffin to make room for his loot. The mismatch of behaviour, crudely self-centred and ruthless, and expression, full of piety and platitude, forces us to experience the hypocrisy that Orton wants to point up.

He extracts the richest comic irony from perversions of virtue. 'Where's the money?' demands Truscott of Hal. 'In church,' Hal answers truthfully. His reward is a brutal kick from Truscott, who is incapable of recognizing truth. The action is a reversal of the more common irony in which the listening character is deceived by a lie. Here Truscott is deceived by truth and we laugh at him for being so stupid and at the same time we laugh at Hal for bringing the kick upon himself. An additional level of irony arises from the fact that Hal really wants to lie and can't. Perversely, he gets the kick a lie would deserve in a moral context.

Another of *Loot*'s ironies lies in Orton's treatment of McLeavy. The only character in the play who commits no crime is the only one punished. McLeavy takes society at its word – crime must be reported to the authorities, truth must be told. When he acts on his virtuous assumptions, he finds himself hauled off to prison. In Orton's world only a fool believes that society is clean under her skirts.

Finally, *Loot* shows very clearly the frightening image of the human personality found throughout Orton's plays. His people are marked by an amoral flatness of character. They are affectless, without any inclination to introspection. Except for McLeavy, they never examine moral questions or show emotion about what they do. Fay bears no emotional freight from her history of murder. Hal shows no qualms at the probability that his father will have to be murdered to protect him and his accomplices. Fay, Hal, and the others act exclusively out of their immediate desires, usually for money or sex. Like Punch or the Big Bad Wolf or Jarry's Ubu, they grab for whatever makes them salivate. Their reflexive, unthinking behaviour makes Orton characters comic – like marionettes or cartoon animals. But it also makes them frightening because we recognize that such people exist, people who, because they are incapable of emotional response, are capable of the most horrendous acts. When Orton offers such flamboyant caricatures, such perversions of human-kind who know neither guilt nor pity, he is a realist.

Orton's realism mingles the cold wit of Wildean aphorism, the sharp irony of gross actions clothed in hypocritical words, and the absolute ruthlessness of the creature who acts without compunction, and he makes of those elements a world that is comic and terrifying. It is comic as long as we let ourselves think it is not real. It is terrifying when we realise it *is* real. As he makes us laugh, he also makes us shudder.

Major Plays

Entertaining Mr. Sloane, New Arts Theatre, then Wyndham's Theatre, 1964.

Loot, Arts Theatre, Cambridge, 1965, revised for Jeanetta Cochrane Theatre, 1966.

The Ruffian on the Stair, Royal Court Theatre, 'production without decor', 1966, revised 1967.

What the Butler Saw, Queen's Theatre, 1969.

Selected Bibliography

Bigsby, C. W. E. *Joe Orton*. London and New York: Methuen, 1982.

Charney, Maurice. *Joe Orton*. New York: Grove Press, 1984.

Dean, Joan. 'Joe Orton and the Redefinition of Farce,' *Theatre Journal* XXXIV, 4 (December 1982) 481–492.

Fox, James. 'The Life and Death of Joe Orton,' *Sunday Times Magazine*, 22 November 1970, 49.

Gordon, Giles. Interview with Joe Orton, *Transatlantic Review* 24, (Spring 1967) 93–100. (This is the source of many Orton quotations.)

Lahr, John. *Prick Up Your Ears: The Biography of Joe Orton*. London: Allen Lane; New York: Knopf, 1978.

Orton Joe. *The Complete Plays*, introduction by John Lahr. London: Eyre Methuen; New York: Grove Press, 1976.

—. Interview in *Plays and Players* 11 (August 1964) 16.

Taylor, John Russell. *The Second Wave: New British Drama for the Seventies*. London: Methuen; New York: Hill and Wang, 1971.

JOE ORTON

Loot

To Peggy

LORD SUMMERHAYS.	Anarchism is a game at which the Police can beat you. What have you to say to that?
GUNNER.	What have I to say to it! Well I call it scandalous: that's what I have to say to it.
LORD SUMMERHAYS.	Precisely: that's all anybody has to say to it, except the British Public, which pretends not to believe it.

Misalliance George Bernard Shaw

The first London production of LOOT *was given at the Jeanetta Cochrane Theatre by the London Traverse Theatre Company on 29 September 1966, with the following cast:*

MCLEAVY	Gerry Duggan
FAY	Sheila Ballantine
HAL	Kenneth Cranham
DENNIS	Simon Ward
TRUSCOTT	Michael Bates
MEADOWS	David Redmond

Directed by Charles Marowitz

Designed by Tony Carruthers

Act One

A room in MCLEAVY'S *house. Afternoon.*

Door left with glass panel. Door right. A coffin stands on trestles. MCLEAVY, *in mourning, sits beside an electric fan.*

FAY, *in a nurse's uniform, enters from the left.*

FAY. Wake up. Stop dreaming. The cars will be here soon. (*She sits.*) I've bought you a flower.

MCLEAVY. That's a nice thought. (*Taking the flower from her.*)

FAY. I'm a nice person. One in a million.

She removes her slippers, puts on a pair of shoes.

MCLEAVY. Are those Mrs McLeavy's slippers?

FAY. Yes. She wouldn't mind my having them.

MCLEAVY. Is the fur genuine?

FAY. It's fluff, not fur.

MCLEAVY. It looks like fur.

FAY. (*standing to her feet*). No. It's a form of fluff. They manufacture it in Leeds.

She picks up the slippers and takes them to the wardrobe. She tries to open the wardrobe. It is locked. She puts the slippers down.

You realize, of course, that the death of a patient terminates my contract?

MCLEAVY. Yes.

FAY. When do you wish me to leave?

MCLEAVY. Stay for a few hours. I've grown used to your company.

FAY. Impossible. I'm needed at other sickbeds. Complain to the Society if you disagree with the rules.

She picks up his coat, holds it out for him to put on.

You've been a widower for three days. Have you considered a second marriage yet?

MCLEAVY (*struggling into his coat*). No.

FAY. Why not?

MCLEAVY. I've been so busy with the funeral.

FAY. You must find someone to take Mrs McLeavy's place. She wasn't perfect.

MCLEAVY. A second wife would be a physical impossibility.

FAY. I'll hear none of that. My last husband at sixty came through with flying colours. Three days after our wedding he was performing extraordinary feats.

She takes the coathanger to the wardrobe. She tries to open the wardrobe door, frowns, puts the coathanger beside her slippers.

You must marry a girl with youth and vitality. Someone with a consistent attitude towards religion. That's most important. With her dying breath Mrs McLeavy cast doubt upon the authenticity of the Gospels. What kind of wife is that for you? The leading Catholic layman within a radius of forty miles. Where did you meet such a woman?

MCLEAVY. At an informal get-together run by a Benedictine monk.

FAY takes the flower from his hand and pins it on to his coat.

FAY. Was she posing as a Catholic?

MCLEAVY. Yes.

FAY. She had a deceitful nature. That much is clear. We mustn't let it happen again. I'll sort out some well-meaning young woman. Bring her here. Introduce you. I can visualize her – medium height, slim, fair hair. A regular visitor to some place of worship. And an ex-member of the League of Mary.

MCLEAVY. Someone like yourself?

FAY. Exactly. (*She takes a clothes brush and brushes him down.*) Realize your potential. Marry at once.

MCLEAVY. St Kilda's would be in uproar.

FAY. The Fraternity of the Little Sisters is on my side. Mother Agnes-Mary feels you're a challenge. She's treating it as a specifically Catholic problem.

MCLEAVY. She treats washing her feet as a Catholic problem.

FAY. She has every right to do so.

MCLEAVY. Don't Protestants have feet then?

FAY. The Holy Father hasn't given a ruling on the subject and so, as far as I'm concerned, they haven't. Really, I sometimes wonder whether living with that woman hasn't made a free thinker of you. You must marry again after a decent interval of mourning.

MCLEAVY. What's a decent interval?

FAY. A fortnight would be long enough to indicate your grief. We must keep abreast of the times.

She takes the brush to the wardrobe and tries to open it.

(*Turning, with a frown.*) Who has the key to this cupboard?

MCLEAVY. Harold.

FAY. Why is it locked?

MCLEAVY. He refused to give a reason.

MCLEAVY *shakes the wardrobe door.*

FAY. Your son is a thorn in my flesh. The contents of his dressing-table are in indictment of his way of life. Not only firearms, but family-planning equipment. A Papal dispensation is needed to dust his room.

She goes out left. MCLEAVY *follows her. She can be heard calling:*

(*Off.*) Harold! (*Farther off.*) Harold!

> HAL *enters right. He goes to the wardrobe, unlocks it, looks in, and locks the wardrobe again. He stands beside the coffin and crosses himself.* FAY *and* MCLEAVY *re-enter left.*

FAY (*pause, with a smile*). Why is the wardrobe locked?

HAL. I've personal property in there.

MCLEAVY. Open the door. There's enough mystery in the universe without adding to it.

HAL. I can't. You wouldn't wish to see. It's a present for your anniversary.

MCLEAVY. What anniversary?

HAL. Your being made a knight of the Order of St Gregory.

MCLEAVY. I'm not convinced. Open the wardrobe.

HAL. No.

FAY (*to* MCLEAVY). You see how far things have progressed? Your son won't obey you. (*To* HAL.) Are you still refusing to attend your mother's funeral?

HAL. Yes.

FAY. What excuse do you give?

HAL. It would upset me.

FAY. That's exactly what a funeral is meant to do.

MCLEAVY. He prefers to mourn in private.

FAY. I'm not in favour of private grief. Show your emotions in public or not at all.

HAL (*to* MCLEAVY). Another wreath has arrived.

MCLEAVY. Is it roses?

HAL. Roses and fern.

MCLEAVY. I must look.

> *He goes out left.*

FAY. I sometimes think your father has a sentimental attachment to roses.

HAL. Do you know what his only comment was on my mother's death?

FAY. Something suitable, I'm sure.

She takes the mattress cover from the mattress and folds it.

HAL. He said he was glad she'd died at the right season for roses. He's been up half the night cataloguing the varieties on the crosses. You should've seen him when that harp arrived. Sniffing the petals, checking, arguing with the man who brought it. They almost came to blows over the pronunciation.

FAY *hangs the folded mattress cover over the screen.*

If she'd played her cards right, my mother could've cited the Rose Growers' Annual as co-respondent.

FAY. The Vatican would never grant an annulment. Not unless he'd produced a hybrid.

HAL (*at the coffin, looking in*). Why was she embalmed?

FAY. She asked to be scientifically preserved after her last attack.

HAL *stares into the coffin, deep in thought.* FAY *joins him.*

You couldn't wish her life. She was in agony since Easter.

HAL. Yes, the egg I presented to her went untouched.

FAY. On doctor's orders, I can tell you in confidence.

Pause.

Sit down, Harold. I want a word with you. Your father can't be expected to help at the moment.

HAL *sits.* FAY *sits opposite him.*

(*Folding her hands in her lap.*) The priest at St Kilda's has asked me to speak to you. He's very worried. He says you spend your time thieving from slot machines and deflowering the daughters of better men than yourself. Is this a fact?

HAL. Yes.

FAY. And even the sex you were born into isn't safe from your marauding. Father Mac is popular for the remission of sins, as you know. But clearing up after you is a full-time job. He simply cannot be in the confessional twenty-four hours a day. That's reasonable, isn't it? You do see his point?

HAL. Yes.

FAY. What are you going to do about this dreadful state of affairs?

HAL. I'm going abroad.

FAY. That will please the Fathers. Who are you going with?

HAL. A mate of mine. Dennis. A very luxurious type of lad. At present employed by an undertaker. And doing well in the profession.

FAY. Have you known him long?

HAL. We shared the same cradle.

FAY. Was that economy or malpractice?

HAL. We were too young then to practise, and economics still defeat us.

FAY. You've confirmed my worst fears. You have no job. No prospects. And now you're about to elope to the Continent with a casual acquaintance and not even a baby as justification. Where will you end? Not respected by the world at large like your father. Most people of any influence will ignore you. You'll be forced to associate with young men like yourself. Does that prospect please you?

HAL. I'm not sure.

FAY. Well, hesitation is something to be going on with. We can build on that. What will you do when you're old?

HAL. I shall die.

FAY. I see you're determined to run the gamut of all experience. That can bring you nothing but unhappiness. You've had every chance to lead a decent life and rejected them. I've no further interest in your career. (*She rises to her feet.*) Call your father. He's surely had enough of the company of plants for the present.

HAL *goes to the door left.*

HAL (*calling*). Eh, Dad!

FAY. Shhh! This is a house of mourning.

HAL *returns and sits.*

The priest that came to pay his condolences had such quiet tones that at first I thought they'd sent along a mute.

MCLEAVY *enters carrying a large wreath marked off into numbered squares.*

MCLEAVY. The Friends of Bingo have sent a wreath. The blooms are breathtaking.

He puts the wreath down. Sits. Takes out a newspaper. FAY, *standing beside the coffin, looking into it, silently moves her lips in prayer, a rosary between her fingers.*

(*With a loud exclamation.*) Another catastrophe has hit the district! Bank robbers have got away with a fortune.

FAY (*looking up*). Which bank?

MCLEAVY. Next door to the undertakers. They burrowed through. Filled over twenty coffins with rubble.

FAY. Rubble?

MCLEAVY. From the wall. Demolished the wall, they did.

FAY. People are so unbalanced these days. The man sitting next to you on the bus could be insane.

MCLEAVY. Where the money has gone is still occupying the police. It's one of the big gangs, I expect.

HAL. What do you known of the big gangs? It's a small gang. Minute.

FAY. Do you know the men concerned?

HAL. If I had that money, I wouldn't be here. I'd go away.

FAY. You're going away.

HAL. I'd go away quicker.

FAY. Where would you go?

HAL. Spain. The playground of international crime.

FAY. Where are you going?

HAL. Portugal.

Pause.

You'll have to get up early in the morning to catch me.

Door chimes. HAL *goes to the window, draws back the curtains and looks out.*

Dennis is here with the cars.

FAY. Is he driving?

HAL. Yes. He looks impressive. Close proximity to death obviously agrees with him.

He goes out left.

MCLEAVY (*putting away the newspaper*). What's the plan for the afternoon?

FAY. The funeral will occupy you for an hour or so. Afterwards a stroll to the house of a man of God, a few words of wisdom and a glance through the Catholic Truth Society's most recent publication should set your adrenalin flowing. Then a rest. I don't want you overstrained.

MCLEAVY. When did you say you were leaving? I don't wish to cause you any inconvenience.

FAY. I'll decide when you've inconvenienced me long enough.

MCLEAVY. You're very good to me.

FAY. As long as you appreciate my desire to help. My own life has been unhappy. I want yours to be different.

MCLEAVY. You've had an unhappy life?

FAY. Yes. My husbands died. I've had seven altogether. One a year on average since I was sixteen. I'm extravagant you see. And then I lived under stress near Penzance for some time. I've had trouble with institutions. Lack of funds. A court case with my hairdresser. I've been reduced to asking people for money before now.

MCLEAVY. Did they give it to you?

FAY. Not willingly. They had to be persuaded. (*With a bright smile.*) I shall accompany you to your lawyers. After the reading of your wife's will you may need skilled medical assistance.

MCLEAVY (*with a laugh*). I don't think there are any surprises in store. After a few minor bequests the bulk of Mrs McLeavy's fortune comes to me.

FAY. I've also arranged for your doctor to be at your side. You've a weak heart.

DENNIS *enters left.*

DENNIS. Good afternoon. I don't want to be too formal on this sad occasion, but would you like to view the deceased for the last time?

FAY *takes out a handkerchief.*
HAL *enters.*

(*To* HAL.) Give us a hand into the car with the floral tributes.

HAL *takes out several wreaths,* DENNIS *picks up the rest.*

(*To* FAY.) We'll need help with the coffin. (*Nods to* MC-LEAVY.) He's too near the grave himself to do much lifting.

FAY. Harold can carry his mother to the car.

DENNIS. A charming suggestion. (*To* MCLEAVY.) If you'll be making your last good-byes while I give them a hand?

Takes the wreaths to the door. HAL *enters left.*

(*Passing* HAL *in the doorway.*) I want a word with you.

DENNIS *goes out left.* HAL *is about to follow him.*

FAY (*calling*). Come and see your mother, Harold. You'll never see her again.

MCLEAVY, HAL and FAY *stand beside the coffin, looking in.*

She looks a treat in her W.V.S uniform. Though I'd not care to spend Eternity in it myself.

HAL. She's minus her vital organs, isn't she?

FAY. It's a necessary part of the process.

MCLEAVY. Where are they?

FAY. In the little casket in the hall. Such tranquillity she has. Looks as though she might speak.

MCLEAVY (*taking out a handkerchief, dabbing his nose*). God rest the poor soul. I shall miss her.

FAY. Death can be very tragic for those who are left.

They bow their heads in silence.

HAL. Here, her eyes are blue. Mum's eyes were brown. That's a bit silly, isn't it?

FAY. I expect they ran out of materials.

MCLEAVY. Are her eyes not natural, then?

FAY. No. (*With a smile, to* HAL.) He's such an innocent, isn't he? Not familiar with the ways of the world.

MCLEAVY. I thought they were her own. That surprises me. Not her own eyes.

DENNIS *enters with a screwdriver.*

DENNIS. The large harp we've placed on top of the motor. On the coffin we thought just the spray of heather from her homeland.

MCLEAVY. It's going to take me a long time to believe she's dead. She was such an active sort of person.

FAY (*to* DENNIS). You're going abroad, I hear?

DENNIS. Yes.

FAY. Where did you get the money?

DENNIS. My life insurance has matured.

MCLEAVY (*to* DENNIS). Tragic news about your premises. Was the damage extensive?

DENNIS. The repair bill will be steep. We're insured, of course.

MCLEAVY. Was your Chapel of Rest defiled?

DENNIS. No.

MCLEAVY. Human remains weren't outraged?

DENNIS. No.

MCLEAVY. Thank God for that. There are some things which deter even criminals.

DENNIS. I'm concerned with the actual furnishings damaged – I mean, the inside of the average casket is a work of art – time and labour, oh, it makes you weep.

MCLEAVY. The bodies laid out. Waiting for burial. It's terrible thoughts that come to me.

DENNIS. It broke my heart. Dust and rubble.

MCLEAVY. What a terrible thing to contemplate. The young men, thinking only of the money, burrowing from the undertakers to the bank. The smell of corruption and the instruments of death behind them, the riches before them. They'd do anything for money. They'd risk damnation in this world and the next for it. And me, a good man by any lights, moving among such people. They'll have it on their conscience. Even if they aren't caught, they'll suffer.

DENNIS. How?

MCLEAVY. I don't know. But such people never benefit from their crimes. It's people like myself who have the easy time. Asleep at nights. Despite appearances to the contrary, criminals are poor sleepers.

FAY. How do you sleep, Harold?

HAL. Alone.

DENNIS. We'll be leaving in a short time, Mr McLeavy. I'd like to satisfy myself that everything is as it should be. We pride ourselves on the service.

MCLEAVY. What clothes would they wear, d'you suppose? Dust is easily identified. They'd surely not work in the nude? God have mercy on them if they did. Even to avoid the hangman I'd not put up with precautions of that nature.

FAY. They'd wear old clothes. Burn them after.

MCLEAVY. If you could get a glance between their toes you'd find the evidence. But to order a man to remove his clothes isn't within the power of the police. More's the pity, I say. I'd like to see them given wider powers. They're hamstrung by red tape. They're a fine body of men. Doing their job under impossible conditions.

HAL. The police are a lot of idle buffoons, Dad. As you well know.

MCLEAVY. If you ever possess their kindness, courtesy and devotion to duty, I'll lift my hat to you.

DENNIS. I'm going to batten down the hatches now.

MCLEAVY (*glancing into the coffin*). Treat her gently. She was very precious to me.

He goes out left.

FAY (*following* MCLEAVY, *turning in the doorway*). I'll be consoling your father if I'm needed. Be careful what you talk about in front of the dead.

She goes out left.
DENNIS *opens a packet of chewing-gum, puts a piece in his mouth, takes off his hat.*

DENNIS. Lock the door.

HAL. It won't lock.

DENNIS. Put a chair under the handle. We're in trouble

HAL *wedges a chair under the handle.*

We've had the law round our house.

HAL. When?

DENNIS. This morning. Knocked us up they did. Turning over every bleeding thing.

HAL. Was my name mentioned?

DENNIS. They asked me who my associate was. I swore blind

I never knew what they were on about. 'Course, it's only a matter of time before they're round here.

HAL. How long?

DENNIS. Might be on their way now. (*He begins to screw down the lid of the coffin.*) Don't want a last squint, do you? No? Where's the money?

HAL *taps the wardrobe.*

In there? All of it? We've got to get it away. I'll lose faith in us if we get nicked again. What was it last time?

HAL. Ladies' overcoats.

DENNIS. See? Painful. Oh, painful. We were a laughing-stock in criminal circles. Banned from that club with the spade dancer.

HAL. Don't go on, baby. I remember the humiliating circumstances of failure.

DENNIS. We wouldn't have been nicked if you'd kept your mouth shut. Making us look ridiculous by telling the truth. Why can't you lie like a normal man?

HAL. I can't, baby. It's against my nature.

He stares at the coffin as DENNIS *screws the lid down.*

Has anybody ever hidden money in a coffin?

DENNIS *looks up. Pause.*

DENNIS. Not when it was in use.

HAL. Why not?

DENNIS. It's never crossed anybody's mind.

HAL. It's crossed mine.

He takes the screwdriver from DENNIS, *and begins to unscrew the coffin lid.*

It's the comics I read. Sure of it.

DENNIS (*wiping his forehead with the back of his hand*). Think of your mum. Your lovely old mum. She gave you birth.

HAL. I should thank anybody for that?

DENNIS. Cared for you. Washed your nappies. You'd be some kind of monster.

HAL takes the lid off the coffin.

HAL. Think what's at stake.

He goes to wardrobe and unlocks it.

Money.

He brings out the money. DENNIS *picks up a bundle of notes, looks into the coffin.*

DENNIS. Won't she rot it? The body juices? I can't believe it's possible.

HAL. She's embalmed. Good for centuries.

DENNIS puts a bundle of notes into the coffin. Pause. He looks at HAL.

DENNIS. There's no room.

HAL lifts the corpse's arm.

HAL (*pause, frowns*). Remove the corpse. Plenty of room then.

DENNIS. Seems a shame really. The embalmers have done a lovely job.

They lift the coffin from the trestles.

There's no name for this, is there?

HAL. We're creating a precedent. Into the cupboard. Come on.

They tip the coffin on end and shake the corpse into the wardrobe. They put the coffin on the floor, lock the wardrobe and begin to pack the money into the coffin.

DENNIS. What will we do with the body?

HAL. Bury it. In a mineshaft. Out in the country. Or in the marshes. Weigh the corpse with rock.

DENNIS. We'll have to get rid of that uniform.

HAL (*pause*). Take her clothes off?

DENNIS. In order to avoid detection should her remains be discovered.

HAL. Bury her naked? My own mum?

He goes to the mirror and combs his hair.

It's a Freudian nightmare.

DENNIS (*putting lid upon coffin*). I won't disagree.

HAL. Aren't we committing some kind of unforgivable sin?

DENNIS. Only if you're a Catholic.

HAL (*turning from the mirror*). I am a Catholic. (*Putting his comb away.*) I can't undress her. She's a relative. I can go to Hell for it.

DENNIS. I'll undress her then. I don't believe in Hell.

He begins to screw down the coffin lid.

HAL. That's typical of your upbringing, baby. Every luxury was lavished on you – atheism, breast-feeding, circumcision. I had to make my own way.

DENNIS. We'll do it after the funeral. Your dad'll be with the priest.

HAL. O.K. And afterwards we'll go to a smashing brothel I've just discovered. Run by a woman who was connected with the Royal Family one time. Very ugly bird. Part Polish. Her eyes look that way. Nice line in crumpet she has. (*He sits astride the coffin.*)

DENNIS. I can't go to a brothel.

HAL. Why not?

DENNIS. I'm on the wagon. I'm trying to get up sufficient head of steam to marry.

HAL. Have you anyone in mind?

DENNIS. Your mum's nurse.

HAL. She's older than you.

DENNIS. An experienced woman is the finest thing that can happen to a lad. My dad swears by them.

HAL. She's three parts Papal nuncio. She'd only do it at set times.

DENNIS. Oh, no. She does it at any time. A typical member of the medical profession she is.

HAL. You've had her? (DENNIS *grins*.) Knocked it off? Really?

DENNIS. Under that picture of the Sacred Heart. You've seen it?

HAL. In her room. Often.

DENNIS. On Wednesday nights while you're training at St Edmund's gymnasium.

They lift the coffin back on to the trestles.

I'd like to get married. It's the one thing I haven't tried.

HAL. I don't like your living for kicks, baby. Put these neurotic ideas out of your mind and concentrate on the problems of everyday life. We must get the corpse buried before tonight. Be in a tricky position else. And another stretch will be death to my ambitions. I put my not getting on in life down to them persistently sending me to Borstal. I might go permanently bent if this falls through. It's not a pleasant prospect, is it?

The coffin is back upon the trestles.
DENNIS *takes the chewing-gum from his mouth and sticks it under the coffin. He puts on his hat.* HAL *sits.*

Was it Truscott searched your house?

DENNIS. Yes. And he had me down the station for questioning. Gave me a rabbit punch. No, I'm a liar. A rabbit-type punch. Winded me. Took me by the cobblers. Oh, 'strewth, it made me bad.

HAL. Yes, he has a nice line in corporal punishment. Last time he was here he kicked my old lady's cat and he smiled while he did it. How did he get into your house?

DENNIS. He said he was from the sanitary people. My dad let him in. 'Course, I recognized him at once.

HAL. Did you tell him?

DENNIS. Yes.

HAL. What did he say?

DENNIS. Nothing. He kept on about testing the water supply. I asked him if he had a warrant. He said the water board didn't issue warrants.

HAL. You should've phoned the police. Asked for protection.

DENNIS. I did.

HAL. What did they say?

DENNIS. They said that one of their men called Truscott was at our house and why didn't we complain to him?

HAL. What did Truscott say?

DENNIS. He said he was from the water board. My nerves were in shreds by the end of it.

FAY approaches the door left. Her shadow is cast on the glass panel.

FAY (*off*). What are you doing, Harold?

HAL goes to the coffin and kneels in prayer.

HAL. That brothel I mentioned has swing doors. (*He bows his head.*) You don't often see that, do you?

DENNIS takes the chair from under the door handle and opens the door quietly.

DENNIS. We're ready now.

FAY enters in mourning with a veil over her hair. She carries an embroidered text. Her dress is unzipped at the back. She goes to the wardrobe and tries to open the door. She sees in the mirror that her dress is unzipped, comes to the coffin and bows her head over it. HAL, still kneeling, zips her dress up. MCLEAVY enters blowing his nose, a sorrowful expression upon his face.

MCLEAVY (*to* DENNIS). Forgive me being so overwrought, but it's my first bereavement.

DENNIS. The exit of a loved one is always a painful experience.

FAY, *the dress zipped, straightens up.*

FAY. Here – (*she puts the embroidered text on to the coffin.*) – the Ten Commandments. She was a great believer in some of them.

HAL *and* DENNIS *lift the coffin.*

MCLEAVY (*greatly moved, placing a hand on the coffin*). Good-bye, old girl. You've had a lot of suffering. I shall miss you.

HAL *and* DENNIS *go out with the coffin.* FAY *throws back her veil.*

FAY. She's gone. I could feel her presence leaving us. Funny how you know, isn't it?

MCLEAVY. That dress is attractive. Suits you. Black.

FAY. It's another piece of your late wife's finery. Some people would censure me for wearing it. (*She puts a hand on his arm, smiles.*) Are you feeling calmer now?

MCLEAVY. Yes. I've a resilient nature, but death upsets me. I'd rather witness a birth than a death any day. Though the risks involved are greater.

TRUSCOTT *enters left.*

TRUSCOTT. Good afternoon.

FAY. Good afternoon. Who are you?

TRUSCOTT. I am attached to the metropolitan water board. I'm on a fact-finding tour of the area. I'd like to inspect your mains supply.

MCLEAVY. It's outside.

TRUSCOTT. Is it?

Pause, ruminates.

I wonder how it came to be put out there. Most ingenious. You're sure there isn't a tap in this cupboard?

He tries the wardrobe door and smiles.

MCLEAVY. It's in the garden.

TRUSCOTT. Where?

MCLEAVY. I don't know.

TRUSCOTT. I suggest, then, that you find it, sir. Any property belonging to the council must be available on demand. The law is clear on that point.

MCLEAVY. I'll find it at once, sir. I wouldn't wish to place myself outside the law.

He goes off right.

TRUSCOTT (*turning to* FAY). Who has the key to this cupboard?

FAY. The son of the house.

TRUSCOTT. Would he be willing to open it? I'd make it worth his while.

FAY. I've already asked for it to be opened. He refused point-blank.

TRUSCOTT. I see. (*Chews his lip.*) Most significant. You'll be out of the house for some considerable time this afternoon?

FAY. Yes. I'm attending the funeral of my late employer.

TRUSCOTT. Thank you, miss. You've been a great help. (*He smiles, goes to window.*) Who sent the large wreath that has been chosen to decorate the motor?

FAY. The licensee of the King of Denmark. I don't think a publican's tribute should be given pride of place.

TRUSCOTT. You wouldn't, miss. You had a strict upbringing.

FAY. How do you know?

TRUSCOTT. You have a crucifix.

FAY'S *hand goes to the crucifix on her breast.*

It has a dent to one side and engraved on the back the

words: 'St Mary's Convent. Gentiles Only.' It's not difficult
to guess at your background from such tell-tale clues.

FAY. You're quite correct. It was a prize for good conduct. The
dent was an accident.

TRUSCOTT. Your first husband damaged it.

FAY. During a quarrel.

TRUSCOTT. At the end of which you shot him.

FAY (*taken aback*). You must have access to private information.

TRUSCOTT. Not at all. Guesswork mostly. I won't bore you
with the details. The incident happened at the Hermitage
Private Hotel. Right?

FAY (*a little alarmed*). This is uncanny.

TRUSCOTT. My methods of deduction can be learned by anyone with a keen eye and a quick brain. When I shook your
hand I felt a roughness on one of your wedding rings. A
roughness I associate with powder burns and salt. The two
together spell a gun and sea air. When found on a wedding
ring only one solution is possible.

FAY. How did you know it happened at the Hermitage Private
Hotel?

TRUSCOTT. That particular hotel is notorious for tragedies of
this kind. I took a chance which paid off.

He takes out his pipe and chews on it.

Has it never occurred to you to wonder why all your husbands met with violent deaths?

FAY. They didn't!

TRUSCOTT. Your first was shot. Your second collapsed whilst
celebrating the anniversary of the Battle of Mons. Your
third fell from a moving vehicle. Your fourth took an overdose on the eve of his retirement from Sadler's Wells. Your
fifth and sixth husbands disappeared. Presumed dead. Your
last partner suffered a seizure three nights after marrying
you. From what cause?

FAY (*coldly*). I refuse to discuss my private life with you.

TRUSCOTT. For ten years death has been persistently associated with your name.

FAY. You could say the same of an even moderately successful undertaker.

TRUSCOTT. Undertakers have to mix with the dead. It's their duty. You have not that excuse. Seven husbands in less than a decade. There's something seriously wrong with your approach to marriage. I find it frightening that, undeterred by past experience, you're contemplating an eighth engagement.

FAY. How do you know?

TRUSCOTT. You wear another woman's dress as though you were born to it.

FAY (*wide-eyed with wonder*). You amaze me. This dress did belong to Mrs McLeavy.

TRUSCOTT. Elementary detection. The zip is of a type worn by elderly women.

FAY. You should be a detective.

TRUSCOTT. I'm often mistaken for one. Most embarrassing. My wife is frequently pestered by people who are under the impression that she is a policeman's wife. She upbraids me for getting her into such scrapes. (*He laughs.*) You recognize the daily bread of married life, I'm sure. (*He chews on his pipe for a moment.*) When do you intend to propose to Mr McLeavy?

FAY. At once. Delay would be fatal.

TRUSCOTT. Anything taken in combination with yourself usually results in death.

FAY. How dare you speak to me like this! Who are you?

TRUSCOTT *takes out his notebook and pencil.*

TRUSCOTT (*pleasantly*). I'm a council employee who has let his imagination wander. Please forgive me if I've upset you.

He tears a page from the notebook and hands it to FAY.

Sign this chit.

FAY (*looking at it*). It's blank.

TRUSCOTT. That's quite in order. I want you to help me blindly without asking questions.

FAY. I can't sign a blank sheet of paper. Someone might forge my name on a cheque.

TRUSCOTT. Sign my name, then.

FAY. I don't know your name.

TRUSCOTT. Good gracious, what a suspicious mind you have. Sign yourself Queen Victoria. No one would tamper with her account.

FAY *signs the paper and gives it back to* TRUSCOTT.

I think that's all I want from you, miss.

FAY. Will you do one thing for me?

TRUSCOTT. What?

FAY. Let me see you without your hat.

TRUSCOTT (*alarmed*). No. I couldn't possibly. I never take my hat off in front of a lady. It would be discourteous.

MCLEAVY *enters right*.

Have you been successful in your search, sir?

MCLEAVY. Yes. Next to my greenhouse you'll find an iron plaque. Under it is a tap.

TRUSCOTT. Thank you, sir. I shall mention your co-operation in my next report. (*He touches his hat.*) Good afternoon.

He goes off right.

MCLEAVY. I hope he finds what he's looking for. I like to be of assistance to authority.

FAY. We must watch that he doesn't abuse his trust. He showed no credentials.

MCLEAVY. Oh, we can rely on public servants to behave themselves. We must give this man every opportunity to do his duty. As a good citizen I ignore the stories which bring officialdom into disrepute.

   HAL *enters left.*

HAL. There's a delay in starting the car. A flat tyre. (*Taking off his coat.*) We're changing the wheel.
MCLEAVY. I hardly think it proper for a mourner to mend the puncture. Is your mother safe?
HAL. Dennis is guarding the coffin.
MCLEAVY. Be as quick as you can. Your mother hated to miss an appointment.
HAL. The contents of that coffin are very precious to me. I'm determined to see they get to the graveyard without mishap.

   He goes off left.

MCLEAVY (*with a smile, shaking his head*). It's unusual for him to show affection. I'm touched by it.
FAY. Mrs McLeavy was a good mother. She has a right to respect.
MCLEAVY. Yes. I've ordered four hundred rose trees to help keep her memory green. On a site, only a stone's throw from the church, I intend to found the 'Mrs Mary McLeavy Memorial Rose Garden'. It will put Paradise to shame.
FAY. Have you ever seen Paradise?
MCLEAVY. Only in photographs.
FAY. Who took them?
MCLEAVY. Father Jellicoe. He's a widely travelled man.
FAY. You mustn't run yourself into debt.
MCLEAVY. Oh, Mrs McLeavy will pay for the memorial herself. The will is as good as proven.

   FAY *sits beside him, takes his hand.*

FAY. I don't know whether you can be trusted with a secret, but it would be wrong of me to keep you in the dark a moment longer. Your wife changed her will shortly before she died. She left all her money to me.

MCLEAVY. What! (*Almost fainting.*) Is it legal?

FAY. Perfectly.

MCLEAVY. She must've been drunk. What about me and the boy?

FAY. I'm surprised at you taking this attitude. Have you no sense of decency?

MCLEAVY. Oh, it's God's judgement on me for marrying a Protestant. How much has she left you?

FAY. Nineteen thousand pounds including her bonds and her jewels.

MCLEAVY. Her jewels as well?

FAY. Except her diamond ring. It's too large and unfashionable for a woman to wear. She's left that to Harold.

MCLEAVY. Employing you has cost me a fortune. You must be the most expensive nurse in history.

FAY. You don't imagine that I want the money for myself, do you.

MCLEAVY. Yes.

FAY. That's unworthy of you. I'm most embarrassed by Mrs McLeavy's generosity.

MCLEAVY. You'll destroy the will?

FAY. I wish I could.

MCLEAVY. Why can't you?

FAY. It's a legal document. I could be sued.

MCLEAVY. By whom?

FAY. The beneficiary.

MCLEAVY. That's you. You'd never sue yourself.

FAY. I might. If I was pushed too far. We must find some way of conveying the money into your bank account.

MCLEAVY. Couldn't you just give it to me?

FAY. Think of the scandal.

MCLEAVY. What do you suggest then?

FAY. We must have a joint bank account.

MCLEAVY. Wouldn't that cause an even bigger scandal?

FAY. Not if we were married.

MCLEAVY. Married? But then you'd have my money as well as Mrs McLeavy's.

FAY. That is one way of looking at it.

MCLEAVY. No. I'm too old. My health wouldn't stand up to a young wife.

FAY. I'm a qualified nurse.

MCLEAVY. You'd have to give up your career.

FAY. I'd do it for you.

MCLEAVY. I can give you nothing in return.

FAY. I ask for nothing. I'm a woman. Only half the human race can say that without fear of contradiction. (*She kisses him.*) Go ahead. Ask me to marry you. I've no intention of refusing. On your knees. I'm a great believer in traditional positions.

MCLEAVY. The pains in my legs.

FAY. Exercise is good for them. (MCLEAVY *kneels.*) Use any form of proposal you like. Try to avoid abstract nouns.

HAL *enters left.*

HAL. We're ready. The leader of the Mother's Union has given the signal for tears. (*He picks up his coat.*) We must ride the tide of emotion while it lasts.

FAY. They'll have to wait. Your father is about to propose to me. I think you may stay.

MCLEAVY (*struggling to his feet*). I'm giving no exhibition. Not in front of my son.

HAL. I'm surprised he should wish to marry again. He couldn't do justice to his last wife.

Car horn. DENNIS *enters left.*

DENNIS. Would everybody like to get into the car? We'll have the priest effing and blinding if we're late.

MCLEAVY (*to* FAY). This is so undignified. My wife isn't in her grave.

FAY. And she never will be if you insist on prolonging the proceedings beyond their natural length.

MCLEAVY. I'll propose to you on the way to the cemetery, Nurse McMahon. Will that satisfy you?

DENNIS (*to* FAY). You can't marry him. You know the way I feel about you.

FAY. I couldn't marry you. You're not a Catholic.

DENNIS. You could convert me.

FAY. I'm not prepared to be both wife and missionary.

HAL (*putting an arm round* DENNIS). He's richer than my dad, you know.

FAY. Has he his bank statement on him?

DENNIS. I came out without it.

Car horn.

MCLEAVY. Mrs McLeavy is keeping her Maker waiting. I'll pay my addresses to you after the interment.

Prolonged car horn.

Come on! We'll have a damaged motor horn to pay for next!

FAY. I've decided not to attend. I shall wave. Show my respects from afar.

MCLEAVY. The number of people staying away from the poor woman's funeral is heartbreaking. And I hired a de luxe model car because they're roomier. I could've saved myself the expense.

He goes off left.

DENNIS (*to* FAY). I'd slave for you.

FAY (*pulling on her gloves*). I can't marry boys.

HAL. He'd grow a moustache.

FAY. It really doesn't concern me what he grows. Grow two if it pleases him.

HAL. Would it please you? That's the point.

FAY. The income from fairgrounds might interest me. Otherwise a man with two has no more fascination than a man with one.

DENNIS. A fully productive life isn't possible with a man of Mr McLeavy's age.

FAY. We shall prove you wrong. He'll start a second family under my guidance.

HAL. You're wasting your time. He couldn't propagate a row of tomatoes.

Car horn.

FAY (*to* DENNIS). Get in the car! I've no intention of marrying you.

DENNIS (*to* HAL, *in tears*). She's turned me down. She's broken my heart.

HAL. She doesn't know what she's missing, baby.

DENNIS. But she does! That's what's so humiliating. (*He wipes his eyes with the back of his hand.*) Well, the funeral is off as far as I'm concerned.

HAL. You're driving the car. People will notice your absence.

FAY *is at the wardrobe.*

FAY (*pause*). Where did you get your money?

DENNIS. My auntie left it to me.

FAY. Is that true, Harold?

HAL (*after an inner struggle*). No.

DENNIS. I mean my uncle.

FAY (*to* HAL). Is that true?

HAL (*desperate, looking at* DENNIS). No.

DENNIS. You make our life together impossible. Lie, can't you?

HAL. I can't, baby. It's my upbringing.

Car horn.

DENNIS. Try to control yourself. If I come back and find you've been telling the truth all afternoon – we're through!

He goes off left. FAY *takes two black-edged handkerchiefs from her handbag, shakes them out, gives one to* HAL.

FAY. Blow your nose. People expect it.

She lowers her veil. They both go to the window. They wave. Sound of a car receding. Pause. FAY *turns from the window. She goes to the wardrobe. She throws off her veil.*

Come here. Open this cupboard.

HAL *puts his handkerchief into his pocket.*

Don't hesitate to obey me. Open this cupboard.

HAL. Why are you so interested?

FAY. I've a coatee in there.

HAL. Really?

FAY. I bought it three days ago. I must change. Mourning gets so grubby if you hang around in it for long.

She looks at HAL *in silence.*

I've got a key. I could see in. Quite easy.

HAL. I've got something in there.

FAY. What?

HAL. A corpse.

FAY. You've added murder to the list of insults heaped upon your family?

HAL. One doesn't have to murder to acquire a corpse.

FAY. You're running a private mortuary, then?

Pause.

Where are you concealing the money?

HAL. In my mother's coffin.

FAY. That'd be an unusual hiding-place.

Pause.

Where is it now? Answer at once. I shan't repeat my question.

HAL. The money is putting on incorruption. The flesh is still waiting.

FAY. Where is it waiting?

HAL. In that cupboard.

FAY. Open it.

HAL. You have a key.

FAY. I haven't.

HAL. You were lying?

FAY. Yes.

HAL gives her the key. She opens the wardrobe, looks in, closes the door and screams.

This is unforgivable. I shall speak to your father.

Pause.

She's standing on her head.

HAL. I concealed nothing from you.

FAY. Your explanation had the ring of truth. Naturally I disbelieved every word.

HAL. I want her buried. Are you prepared to help me?

FAY. Oh, no! I couldn't. This is a case for the authorities.

HAL. You'll never make it to the altar without my help.

FAY. I need no help from you to get a man to bed.

HAL. My father holds it as a cherished belief that a whore is no fit companion for a man.

FAY. As a creed it has more to offer than most.

HAL. My mate Dennis has done you. He speaks of it with relish.

FAY. Young men pepper their conversation with tales of rape. It creates a good impression.

HAL. You never had the blessing of a rape. I was with him at his only ravishment. A bird called Pauline Ching. Broke a tooth in the struggle, she did. It was legal with you. While Jesus pointed to his Sacred Heart, you pointed to yours.

FAY. I never point. It's rude.

HAL. If I tell my father, he'll never marry you.

FAY. I haven't decided whether I wish to marry your father. Your friend is a more interesting proposition.

HAL. He won't be if you grass to the police.

FAY (*pause*). Blackmail? So early in the game.

> HAL *takes out a comb and goes to the mirror. He combs his hair.*

HAL. I want the body stripped. All I ask is an hour or two of Burke and Hare. It isn't a thing someone of the opposite sex can do. And I'm a relative, which complicates the issue.

FAY. You intend a country burial?

HAL. Yes.

FAY. Suppose a dog were to discover her? When they were out hunting for foxes. Do you set no store by the average foxhound?

HAL. Perfectly preserved body of a woman. No sign of foul play. The uniform we'll burn. The underwear you can keep.

FAY. Your mother's underclothes?

HAL. All good stuff.

FAY. I couldn't. Our sizes vary.

HAL. For the bonfire then. Her teeth can go in the river.

FAY. We're nowhere near the river.

HAL. We can borrow your car.

FAY. Provided you pay for the petrol.

HAL. Right.

FAY. Where will she be?

HAL. In the back seat. (*He puts the comb away.*) She always was a back-seat driver.

He opens the wardrobe and wheels the bed to the wardrobe door.

FAY. What about payment?

HAL. Twenty per cent.

FAY. Thirty-three and a third.

HAL. You can keep her wedding ring.

FAY. Is it valuable?

HAL. Very.

FAY. I'll add it to my collection. I already have seven by right of conquest.

HAL pulls the screen round the bed.

Thirty-three and a third and the wedding ring.

HAL. Twenty per cent, the wedding ring and I pay for the petrol?

FAY. Thirty-three and a third, the wedding ring and you pay for the petrol.

HAL. You drive a hard bargain.

FAY. I never bargain.

HAL. Done.

He throws the mattress cover to her.

Put her in that.

FAY goes behind the screen.

FAY. I need help to get her out of the cupboard.

HAL goes behind the screen.

I'm not taking the head end.

HAL. She won't bite. You have your gloves on.

They lift the corpse from the wardrobe and lay it on the bed. Something drops from it and rolls away.

FAY. What's that?

HAL (*appearing from behind the screen, searching*). Nothing, nothing.

FAY (*poking her head over the screen*). A screw from the coffin, perhaps?

HAL. Was it the wedding ring?

FAY (*looking*). No. Nothing important.

HAL. I'm inclined to agree.

> FAY *goes behind the screen.* HAL *takes a sheet from off the screen and spreads it on the floor.*

FAY (*from behind the screen*). Lovely-shaped feet your mother had. For a woman of her age.

> *She hands a pair of shoes across the screen.* HAL *places them in the centre of the sheet.*

What will you do with the money?

> *She hands a pair of stockings over the screen.*

HAL. I'd like to run a brothel. (*He pushes the stockings into the shoes.*) I'd run a two-star brothel. And if I prospered I'd graduate to a three-star brothel. I'd advertise 'By Appointment'. Like jam.

> FAY *hands a* W.V.S. *uniform across the screen.* HAL *folds it up and puts it into the sheet.*

I'd have a spade bird. I don't agree with the colour bar. And a Finnish bird. I'd make them kip together. To bring out the contrast.

> FAY *hands a slip across the screen.* HAL *puts it into the pile.*

I'd have two Irish birds. A decent Catholic. And a Protestant. I'd make the Protestant take Catholics. And the Catholic take Protestants. Teach them how the other half lives. I'd have a blonde bird who'd dyed her hair dark. And a dark bird who'd dyed her hair blonde. I'd have a midget. And a tall bird with big tits.

FAY *hands across the screen in quick succession, a pair of corsets, a brassiere and a pair of knickers.* HAL *puts them into the pile.*

FAY. Are you committed to having her teeth removed?
HAL. Yes.

Pause.

I'd have a French bird, a Dutch bird, a Belgian bird, an Italian bird—

FAY *hands a pair of false teeth across the screen.*

—and a bird that spoke fluent Spanish and performed the dances of her native country to perfection. (*He clicks the teeth like castanets.*) I'd call it the Consummatum Est. And it'd be the most famous house of ill-fame in the whole of England.

FAY *appears from behind the screen.* HAL *holds up the teeth.*

These are good teeth. Are they the National Health?
FAY. No. She bought them out of her winnings. She had some good evenings at the table last year.

FAY *folds up the screen. The corpse is lying on the bed, wrapped in the mattress cover, tied with bandages.*

HAL (*approaching the bed, bowing his head*). She was a great lady. Nothing was too good for her. Which is why she had to go.
FAY (*taking a key from her handbag, gives it to* HAL). Fetch the car. Pay cash. It's not to be charged to my account.

TRUSCOTT *approaches the door left. His shadow is cast upon the glass panel. He knocks on the door.* HAL *picks up the sheet with the clothes in it. He looks for somewhere to put them.* FAY *opens the door.* TRUSCOTT *stands outside, smiling.*

TRUSCOTT (*touching his hat*). I'm back again, miss.

> FAY *slams the door.* HAL *stuffs the sheet and clothes into the bedpan attached to the invalid chair.* FAY *pulls the screen round the bed.*

(*Calling.*) Might I have a word with you.

> HAL *closes the lid of the bedpan, concealing the clothes.*

FAY (*calling, answering* TRUSCOTT). Yes.

TRUSCOTT. Let me in, then, I can't hold a conversation through a keyhole. I'm a council employee. I might lose my pension.

> HAL *sits in the invalid chair.* FAY *opens the door.* TRUSCOTT *enters.*

What's going on in this house?

HAL. Nothing.

TRUSCOTT. You admit it? You must be very sure of yourself. Why aren't you both at the funeral? I thought you were mourners.

FAY. We decided not to go. We were afraid we might break down.

TRUSCOTT. That's a selfish attitude to take. The dead can't bury themselves, you know.

> *He takes his pipe from his pocket and plugs it with tobacco.*

FAY. What are you doing here?

TRUSCOTT (*smiling*). I've been having a look round your charming house. Poking and prying.

HAL. Have you a search warrant?

TRUSCOTT. What for?

HAL. To search the house.

TRUSCOTT. But I've already searched the house. I don't want to do it again.

FAY. It's common knowledge what police procedure is. They must have a search warrant.

TRUSCOTT. I'm sure the police must, but as I've already informed you, I am from the water board. And our procedure is different.

He puts the pipe into his mouth, lights it, draws on it.

(*Chewing on his pipe.*) Now, I was sent on a fool's errand a few minutes ago. Unless I'm much mistaken, the object of my search is in that cupboard.

Pause.

Open it for me.

HAL. It isn't locked.

TRUSCOTT. I can't take your word for it, lad.

> HAL *opens the wardrobe door.* TRUSCOTT *puts on a pair of spectacles, and stares in. He shakes his head. He takes off his spectacles.*

This puts an entirely different complexion on the matter.

FAY. It's empty.

TRUSCOTT. Exactly. There's still a lot of routine work to be done, I can see that. Would you mind waiting outside, miss? I'd like a word with this lad alone. I'll let you know when you're wanted.

> FAY *and* HAL *exchange bewildered glances.* FAY *goes off left.*

(*Laughing pleasantly.*) I always have difficulties with the ladies. They can't accept a *fait accompli.*

Pause. He takes the pipe from his mouth and stares speculatively at HAL.

What do you know of a lad called Dennis?

HAL. He's a mate of mine.

TRUSCOTT. You don't want to spend your time with a youth like him. He's not your type. He's got five pregnancies to his credit.

HAL. Anyone can make a mistake.

TRUSCOTT. Maybe. But he's obviously getting into the habit of making mistakes. Where does he engender these unwanted children? There are no open spaces. The police patrol regularly. It should be next to impossible to commit the smallest act of indecency, let alone beget a child. Where does he do it?

HAL. On crowded dance floors during the rhumba.

    FAY *enters left.*

TRUSCOTT (*removing his pipe, patiently*). I'm a busy man, miss. Do as you're told and wait outside.

FAY. What's your name?

TRUSCOTT. I prefer to remain anonymous for the present.

FAY. Your Christian name.

TRUSCOTT. I'm not a practising Christian.

FAY. Is it Jim?

TRUSCOTT. No.

FAY. A man at the door says it is.

TRUSCOTT. I'd like to help him, but I'm not prepared to admit to any name other than my own.

FAY. He says his name is Meadows.

TRUSCOTT (*pause, nods his head sagely*). One of my names is Jim. Clearly this fellow is in possession of the fact and wishes to air his knowledge. I shall speak to him.

    TRUSCOTT *goes off left.*

FAY (*closing the door, whispers*). There's a uniformed police-man at the door! They're on to us.

HAL. It's bluff.

FAY. No. God works for them. They have Him in their pockets like we've always been taught.

HAL. We've got to get rid of him. He'll find the body next.

He opens the wardrobe door and puts FAY'S *shoes and the coathanger inside. He closes the door quickly and turns to* FAY.

Remember when we were wrapping her up?

FAY. It's not something I care to reminisce about.

HAL. Something dropped out? We couldn't find it?

FAY. Yes.

HAL. I know what it was.

FAY. What?

HAL. One of her eyes!

> *They drop to their knees. They search.* TRUSCOTT *enters. They stand.*

TRUSCOTT (*smiling*). Just a bobby making a nuisance of himself.

> *He goes to the screen and glances behind it. Pause. He takes the pipe from his mouth.*

The theft of a Pharaoh is something which hadn't crossed my mind.

> *He folds the screen revealing the corpse, swathed in the mattress cover and tied with bandages.*

Whose mummy is this?

HAL. Mine.

TRUSCOTT. Whose was it before?

HAL. I'm an only child.

TRUSCOTT. A word of warning. Don't take the mickey. You'll make me angry. (*He smiles.*) O.K.?

FAY. It's not a mummy. It's a dummy. I used to sew my dresses on it.

TRUSCOTT. What sex is it?

FAY. I call it 'she' because of my sewing. The garments were female and because I'm literal-minded I chose to believe I was making them on a lady.

TRUSCOTT. Splendid. Excellently put.

HAL. No actual evidence of sex can be given. It's contrary to English law.

TRUSCOTT. Yes, a tailor's dummy provided with evidence of sex would fill the mind of the average magistrate with misgiving. Why is it wrapped?

HAL. We were taking it in the car.

FAY. To a carnival. She's part of a display.

TRUSCOTT. What part?

FAY. A sewing-class. Prewar. The difference in technique is to be demonstrated.

TRUSCOTT. Is this dummy a frequent visitor to exhibitions?

FAY. Yes.

TRUSCOTT. When is the object's outing to take place?

FAY. It isn't going now.

TRUSCOTT. The treat has been cancelled?

FAY. Yes.

TRUSCOTT. Why?

HAL. My mate Dennis was to have arranged transport. He let us down.

TRUSCOTT. I can believe that. From all I've heard of your friend I'd say he was quite capable of disappointing a tailor's dummy.

He puts his pipe into the corner of his mouth. He takes out his notebook and makes notes.

You claim this object is awaiting transport to a carnival where it will be used to demonstrate the continuity of British needlework?

FAY. Yes.

TRUSCOTT. Sounds a reasonable explanation. Quite reasonable.

He puts the notebook away and chews on his pipe. He observes HAL *narrowly.*

What were you doing on Saturday night?

Pause as HAL *tries to avoid telling the truth. He stares at* FAY *in an agony.*

HAL (*at last*). I was in bed.

> FAY *breathes a sigh of relief.*

TRUSCOTT. Can you confirm that, miss?

FAY. Certainly not.

TRUSCOTT (*to* HAL). What were you doing in bed?

HAL. Sleeping.

TRUSCOTT. Do you seriously expect me to believe that? A man of your age behaving like a child? What was your mate doing on Saturday night?

HAL. He was in bed as well.

TRUSCOTT. You'll tell me next he was sleeping.

HAL. I expect he was.

TRUSCOTT (*to* FAY). What a coincidence, miss. Don't you agree? Two young men who know each other very well, spend their nights in separate beds. Asleep. It sounds highly unlikely to me. (*To* HAL.) What is your excuse for knowing him?

HAL. He's clever. I'm stupid, see.

TRUSCOTT. Why do you make such stupid remarks?

HAL. I'm a stupid person. That's what I'm trying to say.

TRUSCOTT. What proof have I that you're stupid. Give me an example of your stupidity.

HAL. I can't.

TRUSCOTT. Why not? I don't believe you're stupid at all.

HAL. I am. I had a hand in the bank job.

> FAY *draws a sharp breath.* HAL *sits frozen.* TRUSCOTT *takes his pipe from his mouth.*

(*With a nervous laugh.*) There, that's stupid, isn't it? Telling you that.

TRUSCOTT (*also laughing*). You must be stupid if you expect me to believe you. Why, if you had a hand in the bank job, you wouldn't tell me.

FAY. Not unless he was stupid.

TRUSCOTT. But he is stupid. He's just admitted it. He must be the stupidest criminal in England. Unless – (*He regards* HAL *with mounting suspicion.*) – unless he's the cleverest. What was your motive in confessing to the bank job?

HAL. To prove I'm stupid.

TRUSCOTT. But you've proved the opposite.

HAL. Yes.

TRUSCOTT (*baffled, gnawing his lip*). There's more to this than meets the eye. I'm tempted to believe that you did have a hand in the bank job. Yes. I shall inform my superior officer. He will take whatever steps he thinks fit. I may be required to make an arrest.

FAY. The water board can't arrest people.

TRUSCOTT. They can in certain circumstances.

FAY. What circumstances?

TRUSCOTT. I'm not prepared to reveal the inner secrets of the water board to a member of the general public. (*To* HAL.) Where's the money?

HAL (*closing his eyes, taking a deep breath*). It's being buried.

TRUSCOTT. Who's burying it?

HAL. Father Jellicoe, S.J.

TRUSCOTT. Come here! Come here!

HAL *goes over, his hands trembling as they button up his coat.*

I'm going to ask you a question or two. I want sensible answers. None of your piss-taking. Is that understood? Do I make myself plain? I'm talking English. Do you understand?

HAL. Yes.

TRUSCOTT. All right then. As long as we know.

A pause, in which he studies HAL.

Now, be sensible. Where's the money?

HAL *looks at his watch.*

HAL. By now I'd say it was half-way up the aisle of the Church of St Barnabas and St Jude.

He half turns away. TRUSCOTT *brings his fist down on the back of* HAL'S *neck.* HAL *cries out in pain and collapses on to the floor rubbing his shoulder.*

FAY (*indignant*). How dare you! He's only a boy.

TRUSCOTT. I'm not impressed by his sex, miss. (*To* HAL.) I asked for the truth.

HAL. I'm telling the truth.

TRUSCOTT. Understand this, lad. You can't get away with cheek. Kids nowadays treat any kind of authority as a challenge. We'll challenge you. If you oppose me in my duty, I'll kick those teeth through the back of your head. Is that clear?

HAL. Yes.

Door chimes.

FAY. Would you excuse me, Inspector?

TRUSCOTT (*wiping his brow*). You're at liberty to answer your own doorbell, miss. That is how we tell whether or not we live in a free country.

FAY *goes off left.*

(*Standing over* HAL.) Where's the money?

HAL. In church.

TRUSCOTT *kicks* HAL *violently.* HAL *cries out in terror and pain.*

TRUSCOTT. Don't lie to me!

HAL. I'm not lying! It's in church!

TRUSCOTT (*shouting, knocking* HAL *to the floor*). Under any other political system I'd have you on the floor in tears!

HAL (*crying*). You've got me on the floor in tears.

TRUSCOTT. Where's the money?

HAL. I've told you. In church. They're quoting St Paul over it.

TRUSCOTT. I don't care if they're quoting the Highway Code over it. One more chance. Where is it?

HAL (*desperate, trying to protect himself*). In church! In church. My dad's watching the last rites of a hundred and four thousand quid!

> TRUSCOTT *jerks* HAL *from the floor, beating and kicking and punching him.* HAL *screams with pain.*

TRUSCOTT. I'll hose you down! I'll chlorinate you!

> HAL *tries to defend himself, his nose is bleeding.*

You'll be laughing on the other side of your bloody face.

> FAY *enters left, supporting* MCLEAVY, *who is heavily bandaged.*

FAY. They've had an accident!

> TRUSCOTT *leaves* HAL, *pulls the bed from the wall and shoves it to* MCLEAVY, *who faints on to it, just missing the corpse.* HAL *drags the corpse from the bed and shoves it behind the screen.*

TRUSCOTT (*to* MCLEAVY). Have you reported the accident?

> MCLEAVY *opens his mouth. He is too overcome by emotion to speak.*

FAY. It's the shock. Taken away his power of speech, it has.

TRUSCOTT. Has this happened before?

FAY. Yes. Six or seven times.

TRUSCOTT. If he's going to make a habit of it he ought to learn a sign language. (*To* MCLEAVY.) Do you understand me, sir?

> MCLEAVY *closes his eyes, shudders.* TRUSCOTT *straightens up.*

I've known people communicate with the dead in half this time.

MCLEAVY (*moaning*). Oh . . . Oh . . .

TRUSCOTT. What has happened, sir?

MCLEAVY. I've had an accident.

TRUSCOTT. I shall have to make a full report.

He takes out his note-book.

MCLEAVY. Are you qualified?

TRUSCOTT. That needn't concern you at present, sir. I shall let you know later. Now give me a full statement.

MCLEAVY passes a hand across his brow and clears his throat.

MCLEAVY. We set off in high spirits. The weather was humid, a heat mist covered the sky. The road to the graveyard lay uphill. It was a sad occasion for me. In spite of this I kept a tight hold on my emotions, refusing to show the extent of my loss. Along the route perfect strangers had the courtesy to raise their hats. We got admiring glances for the flowers and sympathetic nods for me.

Pause.

The dignity of the event was unsurpassed.

He bows his head, everyone waits. TRUSCOTT *taps sharply on the bedrail with his pencil.*

Then, as the solemn procession was half-way up the hill, a lorry, clearly out of control, came hurtling down on top of us. It struck the first car, holding the remains, and killed the undertaker—

HAL. Not Dennis!

MCLEAVY. No. Mr Walter Tracey. The hearse was a wreck within seconds. Meanwhile the second part of the cortège crashed into the smoking wreckage. I was flung to one side, hitting my head on the bodywork of the vehicle. The next thing I knew I was being helped out by passers-by. The road looked like a battlefield. Strewn with the injured and dying. Blood, glass.

He chokes. Pause.

Several fires were started.

HAL. Was the actual fabric of the coffin damaged?

MCLEAVY. No. Your mother is quite safe.

HAL. No dents? No holes?

MCLEAVY. No. People remarked on the extreme durability of the lid. I was about to give the undertaker a recommendation. Then I remembered that he wasn't capable of receiving one.

TRUSCOTT. Surely he understood when he took on the job that he couldn't make capital out of his own death?

FAY. Where is the coffin?

MCLEAVY. Outside.

FAY (*to* TRUSCOTT). Can it be brought in?

TRUSCOTT. By all means. We mustn't keep a lady waiting.

HAL *goes off.* TRUSCOTT *turns to* MCLEAVY.

Why are you bandaged? Is that a result of the accident?

MCLEAVY. Indirectly. My wounds stem from a fear-crazed Afghan hound that was being exercised at the time. I was bitten about the face and hands. In my nervous state I was an easy target.

TRUSCOTT. Did you take the owner's name?

MCLEAVY. No.

TRUSCOTT. It all seems highly irregular. The dog will have to be destroyed.

MCLEAVY. I don't hold it responsible for its actions. It was frightened.

TRUSCOTT. I've been frightened myself on occasions. I've never bitten anyone. These people should learn to control their pets.

MCLEAVY. The woman who owned the dog had fainted.

TRUSCOTT. She sounds an unstable kind of person to me.

> HAL *and* DENNIS *enter with the coffin. It is charred, blackened and smoking.*

FAY. Who'd think she'd be back so soon?

MCLEAVY. She could never make up her mind in life. Death hasn't changed her.

DENNIS. Your wreaths have been blown to buggery, Mr McLeavy. We might manage a repair job on that big harp.

HAL. What are we going to do for the replay?

MCLEAVY. Buy fresh ones, I suppose. Always some new expense.

> *The coffin is set down. The side falls away, revealing the banknotes inside.* DENNIS *stands in front of the coffin, shielding the contents from* TRUSCOTT *and* MCLEAVY. MCLEAVY *holds out a hand and tries to shake* DENNIS'S *hand.*

(*To* TRUSCOTT.) You must congratulate this boy. He rescued the coffin from the blazing car at considerable personal risk.

TRUSCOTT (*dryly*). If he behaves with such consideration to a dead woman, what might we not expect with a live one?

HAL. We need a finishing touch. Know what it is? A holy image. Centre. Between candles.

FAY. I have a Madonna.

HAL. What could be better? Make a gesture. She knew what disappointment was, didn't she? Same as us. A little imagination. What wonders can't it accomplish.

DENNIS. Oh, yes. We've found in the trade that an impression can be created with quite humble materials: a candle, half a yard of velvet and a bunch of anemones and the effect is of a lying in state.

MCLEAVY. My photo of His Holiness would enhance the scene, only it's three Popes out of date.

FAY. Mrs McLeavy won't mind. She wasn't a woman who followed the fashions. Go and get it.

> MCLEAVY *stands, moves to the door.* TRUSCOTT *bars his path.*

TRUSCOTT. I must ask you to remain where you are. No one is to leave without my permission.

MCLEAVY. Why?

TRUSCOTT. When you disobey my orders, sir, you make my job doubly difficult.

MCLEAVY. On what authority do you give orders?

TRUSCOTT. You'd be considerably happier if you allowed me to do my duty without asking questions.

MCLEAVY. Who are you?

TRUSCOTT. I'm an official of the Metropolitan Water Board, sir, as I've already told you.

MCLEAVY. But the water board has no power to keep law-abiding citizens confined to their rooms.

TRUSCOTT. Not if the citizens are law abiding.

MCLEAVY. Whether they're law abiding or not the water board has no power.

TRUSCOTT. I don't propose to argue hypothetical cases with you, sir. Remain where you are till further notice.

MCLEAVY. I shall take legal advice.

TRUSCOTT. That is as may be. I've no power to prevent you.

MCLEAVY. I want to telephone my lawyer.

TRUSCOTT. I can't allow you to do that. It would be contrary to regulations. We've no case against you.

> TRUSCOTT *chews on his pipe.* MCLEAVY *stares in fury.*

FAY. Can't he fetch the Pope's photo?

TRUSCOTT. Only if some responsible person accompanies him.

HAL. You're a responsible person. You could accompany him.

TRUSCOTT. What proof have I that I'm a responsible person?

DENNIS. If you weren't responsible you wouldn't be given the power to behave as you do.

TRUSCOTT *removes his pipe, considers.*

TRUSCOTT. That is perfectly correct. In which case I shall accompany you, sir. Come with me.

TRUSCOTT *and* MCLEAVY *go off left.*

HAL (*closing the door*). We must return the remains to the coffin and the money to the cupboard.

DENNIS. Why?

FAY. Mr McLeavy may ask for the coffin to be opened. Formaldehyde and three morticians have increased his wife's allure.

DENNIS. But a corpse is only attractive to another corpse.

HAL. We can't rely on him having heard that.

DENNIS *begins to unscrew the coffin lid.* FAY *and* HAL *drag the corpse from behind the screen.*

DENNIS (*looking up*). What's that!

FAY. Mrs McLeavy.

DENNIS (*to* HAL). How much have you told her?

HAL. Everything.

DENNIS. We've never involved a woman in anything unsavoury before.

He takes the lid off the coffin. FAY *piles money into his arms.* HAL *does the same.*

(*To* FAY.) Half of this money is mine. Will you marry me?

HAL. We're splitting the money three ways now, baby. You'll have thirty-four thousand.

DENNIS (*to* FAY). Is that enough?

FAY. You've a slight lead on Mr McLeavy at the moment.

She kisses him. DENNIS *trembles and drops the money back into the coffin.*

HAL (*angry*). Hurry up! What's the matter with you?

DENNIS. My hands are trembling. It's excitement at the prospect of becoming engaged.

HAL. You're too easily aroused. That's your trouble.

MCLEAVY'S *shadow appears on the glass panel.* DENNIS *tips the money into the coffin.*

MCLEAVY (*off*). I'll complain to my M.P. I'll have you reported.

HAL *shoves the lid on to the coffin.* MCLEAVY *enters.*

He's turned the water off. I've just been trying to use the toilet—

FAY (*standing in front of him, preventing him seeing the corpse*). Oh, please! You don't have to explain.

HAL *tries to drag the corpse away.* DENNIS *opens the wardrobe.*

MCLEAVY. I don't believe he's anything to do with the water board. I was handcuffed out there. D'you know that? Handcuffed.

He sees the corpse. He gives a shriek of horror.

What in Heaven's name is that!

FAY. It's my appliance.

MCLEAVY. I've never seen it before.

FAY. I kept it in my room. It was personal.

MCLEAVY. What is it doing down here?

FAY. I'm going to do some work. For charity.

MCLEAVY. What kind of work?

FAY. I'm making the vestments for Our Lady's festival. I was commissioned. My altar cloth at Easter brought me to the attention of the Committee.

MCLEAVY. My congratulations. You'll want plenty of room to work. (*To* DENNIS.) Take Nurse McMahon's applicance to my study.

FAY (*anxious, with a smile*). It's most kind of you, Mr McLeavy, but I'd prefer to work down here. Mrs McLeavy's presence will bring me inspiration.

MCLEAVY. Very well, you have my permission to work down here. I look forward to seeing the finished results.

TRUSCOTT *enters.*

TRUSCOTT (*To* MCLEAVY). Do you still want your padre's photograph, sir?

MCLEAVY. Yes.

TRUSCOTT. You'll find a policeman outside. He will accompany you. Off you go.

MCLEAVY. I resent your manner of speaking! I'm the householder. I can't be ordered about like this.

TRUSCOTT (*shoving him to the door*). Don't make my job any more tiring than it is, sir. Fetch the photograph in question and wait outside until I call.

MCLEAVY *goes off left.*

(*To* DENNIS.) I want a word with you. (*To* HAL *and* FAY.) The rest of you outside!

HAL. Can't I stay with him? He's the nervous type.

TRUSCOTT. I'm nervous as well. I'll be company for him—

FAY. It'd be better if I was present. He's more relaxed in the company of women.

TRUSCOTT. He'll have to come to terms with his psychological peculiarity. Out you go!

FAY *and* HAL *go off left.*

(TRUSCOTT *faces* DENNIS, *the corpse between them.*) Now then, I'm going to ask a few questions. I want sensible answers. I've had enough fooling about for one day. (*He observes* DENNIS *narrowly.*) Have you ever been in prison?

DENNIS. Yes.

TRUSCOTT. What for?

DENNIS. Stealing overcoats and biting a policeman.

TRUSCOTT. The theft of an article of clothing is excusable. But policemen, like red squirrels, must be protected. You were rightly convicted. What do you know of paternity orders?

DENNIS. Is that when birds say you've put them in the club?

TRUSCOTT. Don't try to evade the issue. How many women have you made pregnant?

DENNIS. Five.

TRUSCOTT. You scatter your seed along the pavements without regard to age or sex. (*He taps the corpse.*) What are you doing with this? Have you taken up sewing?

DENNIS. I was putting it in the cupboard.

TRUSCOTT. Why?

DENNIS. To keep it hidden.

TRUSCOTT. Don't try to pull the wool over my eyes. I've been told the whole pathetic story. You ought to be ashamed of yourself.

DENNIS (*pause, with resignation*). Am I under arrest, then?

TRUSCOTT. I wish you were. Unfortunately what you've done isn't illegal.

DENNIS (*pause, with surprise*). When did they change the law?

TRUSCOTT. There never was any law.

DENNIS. Has it all been a leg-pull? My uncle did two years.

TRUSCOTT. What for?

DENNIS. Armed robbery.

TRUSCOTT. That is against the law.

DENNIS. It used to be.

TRUSCOTT. It still is.

DENNIS. I thought the law had been changed.

TRUSCOTT. Who told you that?

DENNIS. You did.

TRUSCOTT. When?

DENNIS. Just now. I thought there'd been a reappraisal of society's responsibilities towards the criminal.

TRUSCOTT. You talk like a judge.

DENNIS. I've met so many.

TRUSCOTT. I'm not impressed by your fine friends.

He chews on his pipe and watches DENNIS *closely.*

Where's the money from the bank job?

DENNIS. What bank job?

TRUSCOTT. Where's it buried?

DENNIS. Buried?

TRUSCOTT. Your mate says it's been buried.

DENNIS (*indignant*). He's a liar!

TRUSCOTT. A very intelligent reply. You're an honest lad. (*He smiles and puts an arm around* DENNIS'S *shoulders.*) Are you prepared to co-operate with me? I'll see you're all right.

DENNIS *edges away.*

I'll put a good word in for you.

DENNIS (*nervous, laughing to hid his embarrassment*). Can't we stand away from the window? I don't want anybody to see me talking to a policeman.

TRUSCOTT. I'm not a policeman.

DENNIS. Aren't you?

TRUSCOTT. No. I'm from the Metropolitan Water Board.

DENNIS. You're the law! You gave me a kicking down the station.

TRUSCOTT. I don't remember doing so.

DENNIS. Well, it's all in the day's work to you, isn't it?

TRUSCOTT. What were you doing down the station?

DENNIS. I was on sus.

TRUSCOTT. What were you suspected of?

DENNIS. The bank job.

TRUSCOTT. And you complain you were beaten?

DENNIS. Yes.

TRUSCOTT. Did you tell anyone?

DENNIS. Yes.

TRUSCOTT. Who?

DENNIS. The officer in charge.

TRUSCOTT. What did he say?

DENNIS. Nothing.

TRUSCOTT. Why not?

DENNIS. He was out of breath with kicking.

TRUSCOTT. I hope you're prepared to substantiate these accusations, lad. What evidence have you?

DENNIS. My bruises.

TRUSCOTT. What is the official version of those?

DENNIS. Resisting arrest.

TRUSCOTT. I can see nothing unreasonable in that. You want to watch yourself. Making unfounded allegations. You'll find yourself in serious trouble.

He takes DENNIS *by the collar and shakes him.*

If I ever hear you accuse the police of using violence on a prisoner in custody again, I'll take you down to the station and beat the eyes out of your head.

He shoves DENNIS *away.*

Now, get out!

DENNIS *is about to leave the corpse.*

And take that thing with you. I don't want to see it in here again.

DENNIS *goes off left with the corpse.*
TRUSCOTT *closes the door and, as he does so, sees something on the floor. He puts his pipe into the corner of his mouth and picks up the glass eye. He holds it to the light in order to get a better view. Puzzled. He sniffs at it. He holds it close to his ear. He rattles it. He takes out a pocket magnifying-glass and stares hard at it. He gives a brief exclamation of horror and surprise.*

Curtain

Act Two

TRUSCOTT, *by the window, is examining the eye under a pocket magnifying-glass.*

MCLEAVY *enters carrying a photograph of Pope Pius XII.* FAY *follows him.*

MCLEAVY. Is it possible to use the toilet, sir?

TRUSCOTT (*putting the eye into his pocket*). The water is off.

FAY. Who turned it off?

TRUSCOTT. My men did.

MCLEAVY (*handing the photograph to* FAY). I'm getting on the phone. I'll have your particulars filed.

TRUSCOTT. I've disconnected the telephone.

MCLEAVY. Why?

TRUSCOTT. You always begin your sentences with 'Why?' Did they teach you to at school?

MCLEAVY. Now, look here – I've a right to know – are you from the sanitary people? I never knew they had power over the post office. Aren't they separate entities? (*To* FAY.) The water board and the post office? Or have they had a merger? (*To* TRUSCOTT.) They'd never connect up the water board and the post office, would they?

TRUSCOTT. I'm not in a position to say, sir.

MCLEAVY. Produce your warrant and you're justified. If not, get out of my house. Even a Government department should take account of death.

TRUSCOTT. Less of that. I must ask you to respect my cloth.

MCLEAVY (*to* FAY). Is he a priest?

FAY. If he is he's an unfrocked one.

MCLEAVY (*stares at* TRUSCOTT, *goes closer to him, wonderingly*). Who are you?

TRUSCOTT. My name is Truscott.

MCLEAVY. What in Hell kind of a name is that? Is it an anagram? You're not bloody human, that's for sure. We're being made the victims of some kind of interplanetary rag. (*To* FAY.) He's probably luminous in the dark. (*To* TRUS-COTT.) Come on, I don't care what infernal power you represent. I want a straight answer.

> TRUSCOTT *regards* MCLEAVY *calmly and in silence.*

I'll go next door – they're Dubliners. If you're the Angel of the Lord Himself, they'll mix it with you.

TRUSCOTT. I've warned you already about leaving this room. Do as you're told or take the consequences.

MCLEAVY. I'll take the consequences.

TRUSCOTT. I can't allow you to do that.

MCLEAVY. You've no power to stop me.

TRUSCOTT. I must disagree. I'm acting under orders.

MCLEAVY. Whose?

TRUSCOTT. My superior officer's.

MCLEAVY. I don't believe he exists!

TRUSCOTT. If you don't control yourself, I shall have to caution you.

MCLEAVY. I know we're living in a country whose respect for the law is proverbial: who'd give power of arrest to the traffic lights if three women magistrates and a Liberal M.P. would only suggest it; but I've never heard of an employee of the water board nicking a kid for stealing apples, let alone a grown man for doubting whether he had any right to be on the planet.

> *Silence.* TRUSCOTT *removes his pipe from his mouth slowly, weighing his words before he speaks.*

TRUSCOTT. If you'll give me your undivided attention for a few

moments, sir, I promise you we'll have this whole case
sorted out. It isn't a game we're playing. It's my duty, and
I must do it to the best of my ability.

The door right is flung open, DENNIS *and* HAL *burst in with
the corpse.* TRUSCOTT *looks steadily and searchingly at them.
He points to the corpse with his pipe.*

What are you doing with that thing?

DENNIS. We were taking it outside.

TRUSCOTT. Why? Did it need the air?

HAL. We were putting it in the garage.

TRUSCOTT. This isn't the garage. What do you mean by
bringing it back into this room?

HAL. A police sergeant was in the garage.

TRUSCOTT. I'm sure he has no particular aversion to sharing a
garage with a tailor's dummy.

HAL. He wanted to undress it.

TRUSCOTT. What possible objection could there be to an
officer undressing a dummy?

DENNIS. It isn't decent.

HAL. It's a Catholic.

TRUSCOTT (*with contempt*). The things you say are quite
ludicrous, lad. (*He laughs mirthlessly.*) Ho, ho ho. Take it to
the garage. The bobby won't interfere with it. He's a married
man with children.

No one moves. TRUSCOTT *chews on his pipe; he takes pipe
from his mouth.*

Go on! Do as I say.

FAY. No! I'd rather it didn't go. I want it here.

TRUSCOTT. Why?

FAY. It's valuable.

TRUSCOTT. Has its value increased during the last few minutes?

FAY. No.

TRUSCOTT. If it's your usual custom to encourage young men to run up and down garden paths with tailor's dummies, you must be stopped from exercising such arbitrary power.

FAY. I did want it in the garage, but after what has been said I feel I can't allow her out of my sight.

TRUSCOTT. Really, miss, your relationship with that object verges on the criminal. Has no one in this house any normal feelings? I've never come across such people. If there's any more of it, I shall arrest the lot of you.

MCLEAVY. How does the water board go about making an arrest?

TRUSCOTT. You must have realized by now, sir, that I am not from the water board?

MCLEAVY. I have. Your behaviour was causing me grave concern.

TRUSCOTT. Any deception I practised was never intended to deceive you, sir. You are – if I may say so – an intelligent man. (*He laughs to himself.*) You saw through my disguise at once. It was merely a ruse to give me time to review the situation. To get my bearings on a very tricky assignment. Or two tricky assignments. As you will shortly realize. (*He smiles and bows to* MCLEAVY.) You have before you a man who is quite a personage in his way – Truscott of the Yard. Have you never heard of Truscott? The man who tracked down the limbless girl killer? Or was that sensation before your time?

HAL. Who would kill a limbless girl?

TRUSCOTT. She was the killer.

HAL. How did she do it if she was limbless?

TRUSCOTT. I'm not prepared to answer that question to any-one outside the profession. We don't want a carbon-copy murder on our hands. (*To* MCLEAVY.) Do you realize what I'm doing here?

MCLEAVY. No. Your every action has been a mystery to me.

TRUSCOTT. That is as it should be. The process by which the

police arrive at the solution to a mystery is, in itself, a
mystery. We've reason to believe that a number of crimes
have been committed under your roof. There was no legal
excuse for a warrant. We had no proof. However, the water
board doesn't need a warrant to enter private houses. And
so I availed myself of this loophole in the law. It's for your
own good that Authority behaves in this seemingly alarming
way. (*With a smile.*) Does my explanation satisfy you?

MCLEAVY. Oh, yes, Inspector. You've a duty to do. My
personal freedom must be sacrificed. I have no further
questions.

TRUSCOTT. Good. I shall proceed to bring the crimes to light.
Beginning with the least important.

HAL. What is that?

TRUSCOTT. Murder.

FAY (*anxiously*). Murder?

TRUSCOTT. Yes, murder. (*To* MCLEAVY.) Your wife passed
away three days ago? What did she die of?

FAY. The death certificate is perfectly legible.

TRUSCOTT. Reading isn't an occupation we encourage among
police officers. We try to keep the paper work down to a
minimum. (*To* MCLEAVY.) Have you no grumble at the
way your wife died?

MCLEAVY. None.

TRUSCOTT. You're easily satisfied, I see. I am not.

FAY. Mrs McLeavy's doctor signed the death certificate.

TRUSCOTT. So I understand. But he'd just come from diagnos-
ing a most unusual pregnancy. His mind was so occupied by
the nature of the case that he omitted to take all factors into
consideration and signed in a fuzz of scientific disbelief. Has
anyone seen Mrs McLeavy since she died?

HAL. How could we?

TRUSCOTT. Can all of you swear you've had no commerce with
the dead?

DENNIS. We're not mediums.

TRUSCOTT. That's a pity. It would have considerably simplified my task if you had been.

FAY. I wasn't going to mention it, but I had a psychic experience last night. Three parts of Mrs McLeavy materialized to me as I was brushing my hair.

TRUSCOTT. Was her fate discussed?

FAY. Yes. In great detail.

MCLEAVY. I never knew you had visions.

TRUSCOTT (*to* FAY). Mrs McLeavy and I are perhaps the two people most closely involved in her death. I'd be interested to hear her on the subject.

FAY. She accused her husband of murder.

Sensation.

MCLEAVY. Me? Are you sure she accused me?

FAY. Yes.

MCLEAVY. Complete extinction has done nothing to silence her slanderous tongue.

TRUSCOTT. Was anyone with her at the end? (*To* HAL.) Were you?

HAL. Yes.

TRUSCOTT. Was she uneasy? Did she leave no last message?

HAL. No.

TRUSCOTT. Was this her usual custom?

HAL. She hadn't died before.

TRUSCOTT. Not to the best of your knowledge. Though I've no doubt our information isn't as up to date as we supposed. Did she whisper no last words? As you bent to kiss her cheek before she expired?

HAL. She spoke of a book.

TRUSCOTT. Which?

HAL. A broken binding recurred.

TRUSCOTT. Was it a metaphor?

HAL. I took it to be so.

TRUSCOTT *goes to the bookcase. He takes down a book.*

TRUSCOTT. Apart from Bibles, which are notorious for broken bindings, there is this – The Trial of Phyllis McMahon. Nurse accused of murdering her patient.

He fixes FAY *with a steely look; she turns pale.*

One of my own cases.

He turns over pages, staring hard and with recognition at the photograph.

Look at this photograph.

HAL. It's you.

TRUSCOTT. Yes, most unflattering, isn't it? They always choose the worst. I cannot get them to print a decent picture.

He tears the photograph from the book, screws it into a ball and stuffs it into his pocket.

DENNIS. Is there a photo of the nurse?

TRUSCOTT. Unfortunately not. Someone has torn every picture of the nurse from the book.

Once again he turns his piercing gaze upon FAY; *she looks uncomfortable.*

However, we have something equally damning – the hand-writing of the accused.

He opens the book at a page of handwriting.

And here – (*Triumphantly he takes a sheet of paper from his pocket.*) – the evidence on which I propose to convict: a recent specimen of the handwriting of your late wife's nurse. Identical in every respect.

MCLEAVY (*staring at the sheet of paper*). But this is signed Queen Victoria.

TRUSCOTT. One of her many aliases.

MCLEAVY *stares in amazement at the evidence.*

HAL. If it was one of your own cases, how is it she didn't recognize you?

TRUSCOTT. Two very simple reasons. I conduct my cases under an assumed voice and I am a master of disguise. (*He takes off his hat.*) You see – a complete transformation. (*To* MCLEAVY.) You've had a lucky escape, sir. You'd've been the victim of a murder bid inside a month. We've had the tabs on her for years. Thirteen fatal accidents, two cases of suspected fish poisoning. One unexplained disappearance. She's practised her own form of genocide for a decade and called it nursing.

FAY (*staring at him, agitatedly*). I never killed anyone.

TRUSCOTT. At the George V hospital in Holyhead eighty-seven people died within a week. How do you explain that?

FAY. It was the geriatric ward. They were old.

TRUSCOTT. They had a right to live, same as anybody else.

FAY. I was in the children's ward.

TRUSCOTT. How many innocents did you massacre – Phyllis?

FAY. None.

TRUSCOTT. I fail to see why you choose to cloak the episode in mystery. You can't escape.

FAY. Mrs McLeavy accused her husband.

TRUSCOTT. We can't accept the evidence of a ghost. The problems posed would be insuperable.

FAY. You must prove me guilty. That is the law.

TRUSCOTT. You know nothing of the law. I know nothing of the law. That makes us equal in the sight of the law.

FAY. I'm innocent till I'm proved guilty. This is a free country. The law is impartial.

TRUSCOTT. Who's been filling your head with that rubbish?

FAY. I can't be had for anything. You've no proof.

TRUSCOTT. When I make out my report I shall say that you've

given me a confession. It could prejudice your case if I have to forge one.

FAY. I shall deny that I've confessed.

TRUSCOTT. Perjury is a serious crime.

FAY. Have you no respect for the truth?

TRUSCOTT. We have a saying under the blue lamp 'Waste time on the truth and you'll be pounding the beat until the day you retire.'

FAY (*breaking down*). The British police force used to be run by men of integrity.

TRUSCOTT. That is a mistake which has been rectified. Come along now. I can't stand here all day.

FAY (*drying her eyes*). My name is Phyllis Jean McMahon alias Fay Jean McMahon. I am twenty-eight years of age and a nurse by profession. On the third of December last I advertised in the trade papers for a situation. Mr McLeavy answered my request. He wished me to nurse his wife back to health: a task I found impossible to perform. Mrs McLeavy was dying. Had euthanasia not been against my religion I would have practised it. Instead I decided to murder her. I administered poison during the night of June the twenty-second. In the morning I found her dead and notified the authorities. I have had nothing but heartache ever since. I am sorry for my dreadful crime. (*She weeps.*)

TRUSCOTT (*looking up from his notebook*). Very good. Your style is simple and direct. It's a theme which less skilfully handled could've given offence. (*He puts away his notebook.*) One of the most accomplished confessions I've heard in some time.

He gives MCLEAVY *a police whistle.*

I'll just arrange transport. Blow that if she should attempt to escape. My men will come to your aid immediately. The sooner we get a spoonful of Mrs McLeavy on a slide the sooner McMahon faces that murder rap.

He goes off left.

MCLEAVY (*to* FAY). How could you rob me of my only support?

FAY. I intended to provide a replacement.

MCLEAVY. I never knew such wickedness was possible.

FAY. You were aware of my character when you employed me. My references were signed by people of repute.

MCLEAVY. You murdered most of them.

FAY. That doesn't invalidate their signatures.

MCLEAVY. Pack your bags! You're not being arrested from my house.

FAY *dabs at her eyes with a handkerchief.*

DENNIS. I've never seen you in adversity. It's an unforgettable experience. I love you. I'll wait for you for ever.

FAY. No, you'll tire of waiting and marry someone else.

HAL. He won't be able to. (*He runs his hand along the coffin lid.*) Not when the Inspector asks to see mum's remains. He'll have us by the short hairs, baby.

TRUSCOTT *re-enters left with* MEADOWS.

TRUSCOTT. We're ready when you are, McMahon.

FAY *holds out her hand to* HAL. HAL *shakes it and kisses her.*

HAL (*kissing* FAY'S *hand*). Good-bye. I count a mother well lost to have met you.

DENNIS *kisses* FAY'S *hand.*

DENNIS. I shall write to you. We're allowed one letter a week.

FAY. How sweet you are. I'd like to take you both to prison with me.

TRUSCOTT. They'd certainly do more good in Holloway than you will. Take her away, Meadows.

MEADOWS *approaches* FAY *with the handcuffs. She holds out her hands.* MEADOWS *hesitates, bends swiftly and kisses* FAY'S *hand.*

Meadows!

MEADOWS *handcuffs* FAY, *and leads her out*.

Nothing but a miracle can save her now.

MEADOWS *goes off with* FAY.

(*To* MCLEAVY). I understand your wife is embalmed, sir?

MCLEAVY. Yes.

TRUSCOTT. It's a delicate subject, sir, but for the post-mortem we shall want Mrs McLeavy's stomach. Where are you keeping it?

MCLEAVY. In the little casket.

TRUSCOTT. Where is it?

HAL. In the hall.

TRUSCOTT. Fetch it, will you?

HAL *goes off left*.

DENNIS. I have something to say which will be a shock to you, Inspector.

TRUSCOTT (*nodding, taking out his pipe*). What is it? Tell it to your uncle (*He smiles*.)

DENNIS. After I'd reached the coffin I went back for the little casket. As I reached it a violent explosion occurred. The lid of the casket was forced open and the contents dispersed.

HAL *enters left. He carries the casket. He turns it upside down. The hinged lid swings free*.

It's well known in the trade that the viscera, when heated, is an unstable element.

HAL. The contents of my mother's stomach have been destroyed.

TRUSCOTT *shakes his head, bowled over*.

TRUSCOTT. What an amazing woman McMahon is. She's got away with it again. She must have influence with Heaven.

HAL. God is a gentleman. He prefers blondes.

TRUSCOTT. Call her back! Look sharp! She'll sue us for wrongful arrest.

HAL *and* DENNIS *go off left.*

MCLEAVY (*to* TRUSCOTT). I'm sorry, sir, but I'm rather confused as to what has been said and in answer to whom.

TRUSCOTT. Briefly, sir, without your wife's stomach we have no evidence on which to convict.

MCLEAVY. Can't you do a reconstruction job on my wife's insides.

TRUSCOTT. Even God can't work miracles, sir.

MCLEAVY. Is the world mad? Tell me it's not.

TRUSCOTT. I'm not paid to quarrel with accepted facts.

FAY *enters with* HAL *and* DENNIS.

Well, McMahon, you've had another twelfth-hour escape?

FAY. Yes. I shall spend a quiet hour with my rosary after tea.

MCLEAVY (*to* FAY). I know one thing, you'll be black-listed. I'll see you never get another nursing job.

TRUSCOTT. There's no need to be vindictive. Show a little tolerance.

MCLEAVY. Is she going to get away with murder?

TRUSCOTT. I'm afraid so, sir. However, I've an ace up my sleeve. The situation for law and order, though difficult, is by no means hopeless. There's still a chance, albeit a slim one, that I can get McMahon as accessory to another crime. And one which the law regards as far more serious than the taking of human life.

MCLEAVY. What's more serious than mass murder?

TRUSCOTT. Stealing public money. And that is just what your son and his accomplices have done.

MCLEAVY. Harold would never do a thing like that. He belongs to the Sons of Divine Providence.

TRUSCOTT. That may make a difference to Divine Providence, but it cuts no ice with me.

He takes the eye from his pocket.

During the course of my investigations I came across this object. Could you explain to me what it is?

He hands the eye to MCLEAVY.

MCLEAVY (*examining it*). It's a marble.

TRUSCOTT. No. Not a marble. (*He regards* MCLEAVY *calmly.*) It looks suspiciously to me like an eye. The question I'd like answered is – to whom does it legally belong?

MCLEAVY. I'm not sure that it is an eye. I think it's a marble which has been trod on.

TRUSCOTT. It's an eye, sir. (*He takes the eye from* MCLEAVY.) The makers' name is clearly marked: J. & S. Frazer, Eye-makers to the Profession.

FAY. It's mine. My father left it to me in his will.

TRUSCOTT. That's a strange bequest for a father to make.

FAY. I always admired it. It's said to have belonged originally to a well-loved figure of the concert platform.

TRUSCOTT. You're a clever woman, McMahon. Unfortunately you're not quite clever enough. I'm no fool.

FAY. Your secret is safe with me.

TRUSCOTT. I've a shrewd suspicion where this eye came from. (*He smiles.*) You know too, don't you?

FAY. No.

TRUSCOTT. Don't lie to me! It's from your sewing dummy, isn't it?

FAY (*laughing*). It's no good, Inspector. You're too clever by half.

TRUSCOTT. I'm glad you've decided to tell the truth at last. We must return the eye to its rightful owner. Unwrap the dummy.

FAY. No, no! You can't undress her in front of four men. I must do it in private.

MCLEAVY. One moment. (*To* TRUSCOTT.) Let me see that eye.

>   TRUSCOTT *gives it to him.*

(*To* FAY.) Who gave you this?

FAY. It's from my dummy. Didn't you hear the Inspector?

MCLEAVY (*to* TRUSCOTT). Is it likely they'd fit eyes to a sewing machine? Does that convince you?

TRUSCOTT. Nothing ever convinces me. I choose the least unlikely explanation and file it in our records.

MCLEAVY (*to* FAY). Who gave you this? Come on now!

DENNIS. I gave it to her. A woman gave it to me as a souvenir.

MCLEAVY. Of what?

DENNIS. A special occasion.

MCLEAVY. It must've been a very special occasion if she gave you her eye to mark it. Come along, I'm not the police. I want a sensible answer. Who gave it to you?

HAL. I did.

MCLEAVY (*shrieks*). You! Oh, Sacred Heaven, no!

TRUSCOTT. We're open to serious discussion, sir, but not bad language.

MCLEAVY. This is stolen property. This eye belongs to my wife.

TRUSCOTT. On what do you base your assumption?

MCLEAVY. My wife had glass eyes.

TRUSCOTT. A remarkable woman, sir. How many were in her possession at the time of her death?

MCLEAVY. None.

TRUSCOTT. I see.

MCLEAVY. These were fitted after death. Her own were taken away.

TRUSCOTT. Where to?

MCLEAVY. I don't know.

TRUSCOTT. Did you never think to inquire?

MCLEAVY. No.

TRUSCOTT. You act in a singularly heartless manner for someone who claims to have been happily married.

MCLEAVY. Oh, Inspector – (*Brokenly*) – my son, you heard him confess it, has stolen the eyes from the dead; a practice unknown outside of medical science. I have reared a ghoul at my own expense.

Silence. TRUSCOTT *considers.*

TRUSCOTT. What do you wish me to do, sir?

MCLEAVY. Fetch a screwdriver. The coffin must be opened. I want to know what else thievery stoops to. Her head may have gone as well.

DENNIS. Might I advise caution, Mr McLeavy? From a professional point of view? The coffin took a pasting, you know.

FAY. She may be in pieces.

MCLEAVY. Fetch a screwdriver.

HAL. Couldn't we bury the eye separately?

MCLEAVY. I can't ask the priest to hold the burial service over an eye. Fetch a screwdriver.

Nobody moves. TRUSCOTT *draws a deep breath.*

TRUSCOTT. What good will it do, sir?

MCLEAVY. I'm not interested in doing good. There are organizations devoted to that purpose. Fetch a screwdriver! Do I have to repeat it like the muezzin?

DENNIS *gives* MCLEAVY *a screwdriver.* MCLEAVY *hands the eye to* TRUSCOTT *and begins to unscrew the coffin lid.*

TRUSCOTT. This is unwarranted interference with the rights of the dead. As a policeman I must ask you to consider your actions most carefully.

MCLEAVY. She's my wife. I can do what I like with her. Anything is legal with a corpse.

TRUSCOTT. Indeed it is not. Conjugal rights should stop with the last heartbeat. I thought you knew that.

MCLEAVY *begins to unscrew the second side of the coffin.*

I must say, sir, I'm aghast at this behaviour. Equivalent to tomb robbing it is. What do you hope to gain by it? An eyeless approach to Heaven is as likely to succeed as any. Your priest will confirm what I say.

MCLEAVY *bows his head, continues his work.*

You strike me, sir – I have to say this – as a thoroughly irresponsible individual. Always creating unnecessary trouble.

HAL. We'll have the house full of the law. Half our fittings will be missing. That's why they have such big pockets on their uniforms.

TRUSCOTT. Your son seems to have a more balanced idea of the world in which we live than you do, sir.

MCLEAVY. My duty is clear.

TRUSCOTT. Only the authorities can decide when your duty is clear. Wild guesses by persons like yourself can only cause confusion.

MCLEAVY *lifts the coffin lid.*

HAL. He's going to be shocked. See him preparing for it. His generation takes a delight in being outraged.

MCLEAVY *looks into the coffin, gives a grunt of disbelief, staggers back, incredulous.*

DENNIS. Catch him! He's going to faint.

He and FAY *support* MCLEAVY *and help him to the bed.* MCLEAVY *sinks beside the corpse in a state of shock.*

MCLEAVY. Where? (*Bewildered.*) Where? (*He follows* HAL'S *glance to the corpse and recoils in horror.*) Oh, the end of the world is near when such crimes are committed.

TRUSCOTT. The opening of a coffin couldn't possibly herald Armageddon. Pull yourself together, sir.

FAY (*to* TRUSCOTT). The condition of the corpse has deteriorated due to the accident. Do you wish to verify the fact?

TRUSCOTT (*shuddering*). No, thank you, miss. I receive enough shocks in the line of duty without going about looking for them.

FAY (*to* DENNIS). Replace the lid on the coffin.

DENNIS *does so*.

MCLEAVY (*to* HAL). I shall disown you. I'll publish it abroad that I was cuckolded.

FAY (*to* TRUSCOTT). It's been a harrowing experience for him.

TRUSCOTT. He was warned in advance of the consequences of his action.

HAL (*kneeling to* MCLEAVY). I'm in a bit of a spot, Dad. I don't mind confessing. Don't get stroppy with me, eh?

MCLEAVY. I'm sorry I ever got you. I'd've withheld myself at the conception if I'd known.

TRUSCOTT. Such idle fantasies ill become you, sir.

MCLEAVY *chokes back his sobs*.

Fathers have discovered greater iniquities in their sons than the theft of an eye. The episode isn't without instruction.

MCLEAVY. Where did I go wrong? His upbringing was faultless. (*To* DENNIS.) Did you lead him astray?

DENNIS. I was innocent till I met him.

HAL. You met me when you were three days old.

MCLEAVY (*to* HAL). Where are your tears? She was your mother.

HAL. It's dust, Dad.

MCLEAVY *shakes his head in despair*.

A little dust.

MCLEAVY. I loved her.

HAL. You had her filleted without a qualm. Who could have affection for a half-empty woman?

MCLEAVY (*groaning*). Oh, Jesus, Mary, Joseph, guide me to the end of my wits and have done with it.

HAL. You've lost nothing. You began the day with a dead wife. You end it with a dead wife.

MCLEAVY. Oh, wicked, wicked. (*Wildly.*) These hairs – (*Points.*) – they're grey. You made them so. I'd be a redhead today had you been an accountant.

TRUSCOTT (*removing his pipe from his mouth*). We really can't accept such unlikely explanation for the colour of your hair, sir.

> MCLEAVY *wails aloud in anguish.*

Your behaviour indicates a growing lack of control. It's disgraceful in a man of your age and background. I'm half inclined to book you for disturbing the peace.

> FAY *hands* MCLEAVY *a handkerchief. He blows his nose. He draws himself up to his full height.*

MCLEAVY. I'm sorry, Inspector. My behaviour must seem strange to you. I'll endeavour to explain it. You can then do as you think fit.

FAY. Consider the consequences of telling the truth. It will kill Father Jellicoe.

DENNIS. My pigeons will die if I'm nicked. There'll be nobody to feed them.

> *Silence.* TRUSCOTT *opens his notebook and looks at* MC-LEAVY.

MCLEAVY. I wish to prefer charges.

HAL (*desperate*). If my Aunt Bridie hears of this, she'll leave her money to an orphanage. You know how selfish she is.

TRUSCOTT. Whom do you wish to charge, sir?

MCLEAVY (*pause, struggles with his conscience, at last*). Myself.

TRUSCOTT (*looking up from his notebook*). What crime have you committed?

MCLEAVY. I— I— (*Sweating.*) I've given misleading information to the police.

TRUSCOTT. What information?

MCLEAVY. I told you that the eye belonged to my wife. It doesn't. (*Conscience stricken.*) Oh, God forgive me for what I'm doing.

TRUSCOTT. If the eye doesn't belong to your wife, to whom does it belong?

> MCLEAVY *is unable to answer; he stares about him, perplexed.*

FAY (*with a smile*). It belongs to my sewing dummy, Inspector. Your original deduction was quite correct.

> TRUSCOTT *slowly puts away his notebook and pencil.*

TRUSCOTT. I ought to have my head examined, getting mixed up in a case of this kind. (*To* MCLEAVY.) Your conduct is scandalous, sir. With you for a father this lad never stood a chance. No wonder he took to robbing banks.

MCLEAVY (*in shame*). What are you going to do?

TRUSCOTT. Do? I'm going to leave this house at once. I've never come across such people. You behave as though you're affiliated to Bedlam.

MCLEAVY. But – the bank robbery – is the case closed?

TRUSCOTT. No, sir, it's not closed. We don't give up as easily as that. I'm going to have this place turned upside down.

MCLEAVY. Oh, dear, what a nuisance. And in a house of mourning, too.

TRUSCOTT. Your wife won't be here, sir. I shall take possession of the remains.

FAY. Why do you need the remains? You can't prove Mrs McLeavy was murdered.

TRUSCOTT. There's no cause for alarm. It's a mere formality.

You're quite safe. (*He smiles. To* MCLEAVY.) There's no one more touchy than your hardened criminal. (*He puts his pipe away.*) I'll be back in ten minutes. And then, I'm afraid, a lot of damage will be done to your property. You'll be paying repair bills for months to come. One unfortunate suspect recently had the roof taken off his house.

MCLEAVY. Isn't there anything I can do to prevent this appalling assault upon my privacy?

TRUSCOTT. Well, sir, if you can suggest a possible hiding-place for the money?

MCLEAVY *hangs his head.*

MCLEAVY (*almost in a whisper*). I can't, Inspector.

TRUSCOTT. Very well. You must take the consequences of ignorance. (*He tips his hat.*) I'll be back soon.

He goes off left.

MCLEAVY. Oh, what a terrible thing I've done. I've obstructed an officer in the course of his duty.

HAL (*hugging him*). I'm proud of you. I'll never feel ashamed of bringing my friends home now.

MCLEAVY. I shan't be able to face my reflection in the mirror.

FAY. Go to confession. Book an hour with Father Mac.

HAL. Oh, not him! Three brandies and he's away. The barmaid at the King of Denmark is blackmailing half the district.

MCLEAVY. I'll say nothing of what I've discovered if you return the money to the bank. You're not to keep a penny of it. Do you understand?

HAL. Yes, Dad. (*He winks at* DENNIS.)

MCLEAVY. I'll go and ring Father Jellicoe. My soul is in torment.

MCLEAVY *goes off left.*

HAL (*closing the door, to* FAY). Unwrap the body. Once we've got it back into the coffin we're home and dry.

FAY *pulls the screen round the bed. She goes behind the screen to unwrap the corpse.*

DENNIS. What are we going to do with the money?
HAL. Put in into the casket.
DENNIS. Won't he want that?
HAL. He knows it's empty.

DENNIS *takes the lid from the coffin.*

DENNIS. Why didn't we put it in there in the first place?
HAL. My mum's guts were in there. The damp would've got at the notes.

HAL *opens the casket.*

Got a hanky?

DENNIS *throws a handkerchief over.* HAL *wipes the inside of the casket.*

DENNIS. Oh, you've gone too far! Using my handkerchief for that. It was a birthday present.

HAL *throws him the handkerchief back.*

HAL. Relax, baby. You'll have other birthdays.

DENNIS *throws the bundles of notes to* HAL. HAL *packs them into the casket.*

I shall accompany my father to Confession this evening. In order to purge my soul of this afternoon's events.
DENNIS. It's at times like this that I regret not being a Catholic.
HAL. Afterwards I'll take you to a remarkable brothel I've found. Really remarkable. Run by three Pakistanis aged between ten and·fifteen. They do it for sweets. Part of their religion. Meet me at seven. Stock up with Mars bars.

FAY *appears from behind the screen, folding the mattress cover.*

FAY. Don't look behind there, Harold.

HAL. Why not?

FAY. Your mother is naked.

> *She hangs the folded cover over the screen.*
> HAL *packs the last bundle of notes into the casket.*

HAL. We're safe.

> *He bangs down the lid.*

Nobody will ever look in there.

> TRUSCOTT *enters left.*

TRUSCOTT. I've fixed everything to my satisfaction. My men will be here shortly. They're perfectly capable of causing damage unsupervised, and so I shall take my leave of you. (*He bows, smiles.*)

FAY (*shaking hands*). Good-bye, Inspector. It's been nice meeting you again.

TRUSCOTT. Good-bye. (*He nods to* HAL *and* DENNIS.) I'd better take the little casket with me.

HAL. It's empty!

TRUSCOTT. I must have it certified empty before I close my report.

FAY. We're having it de-sanctified. Mr McLeavy is on the phone to the priest about it.

TRUSCOTT. Our lads in forensic aren't interested in sanctity. Give me that casket!

> MCLEAVY *enters left. He sees* TRUSCOTT *and cowers back.*

MCLEAVY. You're back already? Have you decided to arrest me after all?

TRUSCOTT. I wouldn't arrest you if you were the last man on earth. (*To* HAL.) Give me that casket! (*He takes the casket from* HAL. *To* MCLEAVY.) I'll give you a receipt, sir.

*He looks for somewhere to rest the casket, sees the empty
coffin puts the casket down.*

Where is Mrs McLeavy?

FAY. She's behind the screen.

TRUSCOTT *looks behind the screen and raises his eyebrows.*

TRUSCOTT. Did she ask to be buried like that?

MCLEAVY. Yes.

TRUSCOTT. She was a believer in that sort of thing?

MCLEAVY. Yes.

TRUSCOTT. Are you, sir?

MCLEAVY. Well no. I'm not a member myself.

TRUSCOTT. A member? She belonged to a group, then?

MCLEAVY. Oh, yes. They met a couple of times a week. They
do a lot of good for the country. Raising money for charities,
holding fetes. The old folk would be lost without them.

TRUSCOTT. I've heard many excuses for nudists, sir, but never
that one.

MCLEAVY (*pause*). Nudists?

TRUSCOTT. Your wife was a nudist, you say?

MCLEAVY. My wife never took her clothes off in public in her
life.

TRUSCOTT. Yet she asked to be buried in that condition?

MCLEAVY. What condition?

TRUSCOTT. In the nude.

MCLEAVY (*with dignity*). You'd better leave my house, Inspector. I can't allow you to insult the memory of my late wife.

TRUSCOTT (*tearing a sheet of paper from his notebook*). You give
me a lot of aggravation, sir. Really you do. (*He hands the
paper to* MCLEAVY.) You'll get your property back in due
course.

*He lifts casket, the lid swings away and the bundles of bank-
notes fall to the floor.* TRUSCOTT *stares at the notes scattered
at his feet in silence.*

Who is responsible for this disgraceful state of affairs?

HAL. I am.

TRUSCOTT (*stoops and picks up a bundle of notes*). Would you have stood by and allowed this money to be buried in holy ground?

HAL. Yes.

TRUSCOTT. How dare you involve me in a situation for which no memo has been issued. (*He turns the notes over.*) In all my experience I've never come across a case like it. Every one of these fivers bears a portrait of the Queen. It's dreadful to contemplate the issues raised. Twenty thousand tiaras and twenty thousand smiles buried alive! She's a constitutional monarch, you know. She can't answer back.

DENNIS. Will she send us a telegram?

TRUSCOTT. I'm sure she will.

He picks up another bundle and stares at them.

MCLEAVY. Well, Inspector, you've found the money and unmasked the criminals. You must do your duty and arrest them. I shall do mine and appear as witness for the prosecution.

HAL. Are you married, Inspector?

TRUSCOTT. Yes.

HAL. Does your wife never yearn for excitement?

TRUSCOTT. She did once express a wish to see the windmills and tulip fields of Holland.

HAL. With such an intelligent wife you need a larger income.

TRUSCOTT. I never said my wife was intelligent.

HAL. Then she's unintelligent? Is that it?

TRUSCOTT. My wife is a woman. Intelligence doesn't really enter into the matter.

HAL. If, as you claim, your wife is a woman, you certainly need a larger income.

TRUSCOTT takes his pipe from his pocket and sticks it into the corner of his mouth.

TRUSCOTT. Where is this Jesuitical twittering leading us?

HAL. I'm about to suggest bribery.

> TRUSCOTT *removes his pipe, no one speaks.*

TRUSCOTT. How much?

HAL. Twenty per cent.

TRUSCOTT. Twenty-five per cent. Or a full report of this case appears on my superior officer's desk in the morning.

HAL. Twenty-five it is.

TRUSCOTT (*shaking hands*). Done.

DENNIS (*to* TRUSCOTT). May I help you to replace the money in the casket?

TRUSCOTT. Thank you, lad. Most kind of you.

> DENNIS *packs the money into the casket.* FAY *takes* MRS MCLEAVY'S *clothes from the bedpan on the invalid chair and goes behind the screen.* TRUSCOTT *chews on his pipe.* HAL *and* DENNIS *take the coffin behind the screen.*

MCLEAVY. Has no one considered my feelings in all this?

TRUSCOTT. What percentage do you want?

MCLEAVY. I don't want money. I'm an honest man.

TRUSCOTT. You'll have to mend your ways then.

MCLEAVY. I shall denounce the lot of you!

TRUSCOTT. Now then, sir, be reasonable. What has just taken place is perfectly scandalous and had better go no farther than these three walls. It's not expedient for the general public to have its confidence in the police force undermined. You'd be doing the community a grave disservice by revealing the full frightening facts of this case.

MCLEAVY. What kind of talk is that? You don't make sense.

TRUSCOTT. Who does?

MCLEAVY. I'll go to the priest. He makes sense. He makes sense to me.

TRUSCOTT. Does he make sense to himself? That is much more important.

MCLEAVY. If I can't trust the police, I can still rely on the Fathers. They'll advise me what to do!

He goes off left. HAL *appears from behind the screen.*

HAL. You'll be glad to know that my mother is back in her last resting-place.

TRUSCOTT. Good. You've carried out the operation with speed and efficiency. I congratulate you.

DENNIS *appears from behind the screen.*

DENNIS. We're ready for the eye now. If you'd like to assist us.

TRUSCOTT (*taking the eye from his pocket*). You do it, lad. You're more experienced in these matters than me.

He hands DENNIS *the eye.*

HAL. You'd better have these as well.

He hands DENNIS *the teeth.*
DENNIS *takes the eye and teeth behind the screen.*

TRUSCOTT. Your sense of detachment is terrifying, lad. Most people would at least flinch upon seeing their mother's eyes and teeth handed around like nuts at Christmas.

FAY *appears from behind the screen.*

FAY. Have you given a thought to the priest?

TRUSCOTT. We can't have him in on it, miss. Our percentage wouldn't be worth having.

FAY. Mr McLeavy has threatened to expose us.

TRUSCOTT. I've been exposed before.

FAY. What happened?

TRUSCOTT. I arrested the man. He's doing twelve years.

HAL. If you wish to arrest my dad, you'll find me an exemplary witness.

TRUSCOTT. What a bright idea. We've vacancies in the force for lads of your calibre. (*To* FAY.) Are you with us, McMahon?

FAY. Yes, it seems the best solution for all of us.

DENNIS folds up the screen. The coffin is lying on the bed.

TRUSCOTT (*to* DENNIS). And you?

DENNIS. I've never seen the view from the witness box. It'll be a new experience.

The door left bursts open. MCLEAVY *enters with* MEADOWS.

MCLEAVY (*pointing to* TRUSCOTT). This is the man. Arrest him.

TRUSCOTT. Good afternoon, Meadows. Why have you left your post?

MEADOWS. I was accosted by this man, sir. He insisted that I accompany him to the Catholic church.

TRUSCOTT. What did you say?

MEADOWS. I refused.

TRUSCOTT. Quite rightly. You're a Methodist. Proceed with the statement.

MEADOWS. The man became offensive, sir. He made a number of derogatory remarks about the force in general and yourself in particular. I called for assistance.

TRUSCOTT. Excellent, Meadows. I shall see H.Q. hear of this. You have apprehended, in full flight, a most dangerous criminal. As you know, we've had our eye upon this house for some time. I was about to unmask the chief offender when this man left the room on some excuse and disappeared.

MEADOWS. He was making a bolt for it, sir.

TRUSCOTT. You have the matter in a nutshell, Meadows. Put the cuffs on him.

MEADOWS handcuffs MCLEAVY.

You're fucking nicked, my old beauty. You've found to your cost that the standards of the British police force are as high as ever.

MCLEAVY. What am I charged with?

TRUSCOTT. That needn't concern you for the moment. We'll fill in the details later.

MCLEAVY. You can't do this. I've always been a law-abiding citizen. The police are for the protection of ordinary people.

TRUSCOTT. I don't know where you pick up these slogans, sir. You must read them on hoardings.

MCLEAVY. I want to see someone in authority.

TRUSCOTT. I am in authority. You can see me.

MCLEAVY. Someone higher.

TRUSCOTT. You can see whoever you like, providing you convince me first that you're justified in seeing them.

MCLEAVY. You're mad!

TRUSCOTT. Nonsense. I had a check-up only yesterday. Our medical officer assured me that I was quite sane.

MCLEAVY. I'm innocent. (*A little unsure of himself, the beginnings of panic.*) Doesn't that mean anything to you?

TRUSCOTT. You know the drill, Meadows. Empty his pockets and book him.

MCLEAVY *is dragged away by* MEADOWS.

MCLEAVY. I'm innocent! I'm innocent! (*At the door, pause, a last wail.*) Oh, what a terrible thing to happen to a man who's been kissed by the Pope.

MEADOWS *goes off with* MCLEAVY.

DENNIS. What will you charge him with, Inspector?

TRUSCOTT. Oh, anything will do.

FAY. Can an accidental death be arranged?

TRUSCOTT. Anything can be arranged in prison.

HAL. Except pregnancy.

TRUSCOTT. Well, of course, the chaperon system defeats us there.

He picks up the casket.

The safest place for this is in my locker at the station. It's a maxim of the force: 'Never search your own backyard – you may find what you're looking for.' (*He turns in the doorway, the casket under his arm.*) Give me a ring this evening. I should have news for you of McLeavy by then. (*He hands a card to* FAY.) This is my home address. I'm well known there.

> *He nods, smiles, and goes off left. Sound of front door slamming. Pause.*

HAL (*with a sigh*). He's a nice man. Self-effacing in his way.
DENNIS. He has an open mind. In direct contrast to the usual run of civil servant.

> HAL *and* DENNIS *lift the coffin from the bed and place it on the trestles.*

HAL. It's comforting to know that the police can still be relied upon when we're in trouble.

> *They stand beside the coffin,* FAY *in the middle.*

FAY. We'll bury your father with your mother. That will be nice for him, won't it?

> *She lifts her rosary and bows her head in prayer.*

HAL (*pause, to* DENNIS). You can kip here, baby. Plenty of room now. Bring your bags over tonight.

> FAY *looks up.*

FAY (*sharply*). When Dennis and I are married we'd have to move out.
HAL. Why?
FAY. People would talk. We must keep up appearances.

> *She returns to her prayers, her lips move silently.* DENNIS *and* HAL *at either side of the coffin.*

> *Curtain*

Author's Note

to the first edition of the play in 1967

The Lord Chamberlain grants a licence to the play subject to the following conditions:

(i) The corpse is inanimate and not played by an actress.

(ii) On page 79 the casket is wiped with a handkerchief. The Lord Chamberlain is particularly anxious that no stain shall appear on the handkerchief.

The following alterations to the text are required:

Act One: Page 21 'Run by a woman who was connected with the Royal Family one time.' For 'Royal Family' substitute 'Empire Loyalists'.

Page 22 'Under that picture of the Sacred Heart.' For 'Sacred Heart' substitute 'Infant Samuel'.

Page 36 'While Jesus pointed to his Sacred Heart, you pointed to yours. I never point. It's rude' must be cut.

Page 39 For 'Consummatum Est' substitute 'Kingdom Come'.

Page 51 For 'buggery' substitute 'beggary'.

Act Two: Page 79 'Run by three Pakistanis aged between ten and fifteen. They do it for sweets. Part of their religion.' For 'Pakistanis' substitute 'kids'. 'Part of their religion' must be cut.

Page 85 For 'fucking' substitute 'bleeding'.

Peter Barnes

'Encountering Barnes is somewhat like fencing in a Noël Coward drawing-room while seething with the stomach pit anger of the early John Osborne and then leaving the room for a short session in the late Joe Orton's black-comic vomitorium,' T. E. Kalem wrote in a review of the 1971 American premiere of *The Ruling Class*. His remarks suggest that mélange of styles and effects that give Barnes's plays the wild anarchic exuberance that is his dramatic signature. Like other new wave dramatists, he rejects naturalism as a reactionary artistic form, 'a side road on the great march of drama'. He wants to get back to the days of the Elizabethans and Jacobeans when audiences went to the theatre not for a slice of life, but for something more. 'My motto is more, more, more – of everything. Not less, less, less,' he declared in a recent interview.

Influenced by Brecht in his searing social passion and his antipathy for the upper classes and by Artaud in his outrageous theatricality, he parodies the techniques of both. His admirers rank him with Beckett and Pinter; his detractors, whom he insists outnumber his admirers, dismiss him as shallow or charlatan. For most of his career critical attention has been sharply divided. He trains a mordantly savage wit on the most inherently tragic human situations – what happened at Auschwitz, for example – and evokes laughter that leaves a bitter taste in the mouth. He cracks jokes about Christ and then makes us feel guilty for laughing at them.

Perhaps his manipulation of laughter is his most singular contribution to dramatic form. Implicit in his uses of comic techniques is a message that counters traditional views of the function of laughter as liberating. We shouldn't be laughing, Barnes says. The universe is absurd, blind chance rules the world, and we are in peril of the apocalypse. The comic attitude shores up society's rottenness by diverting our attention. It is reassuring in a time when we need to be disturbed into vigilance. 'It is too feeble a weapon against the barbarities of life,' Barnes holds, 'an excuse to change nothing, for nothing needs changing when it's all a joke.' In *The Bewitched* the professional clown Morra and his apprentice-son Rafael debate the possibility of changing the world with comedy:

> RAFAEL: I believe I can do more and mix a little purpose wi' my wit.
> MORRA: Fatal. I've survived two reigns by having no purpose 'cept to please. If thou has a message, send 't by messenger.

Critics and audiences are often irritated by what seems to be a paradox (not only in Barnes, but in early Howard Brenton, Edward Bond, and David Hare, as well), what John Russell Taylor labels 'the dark fantastic':

> Again and again these dramatists are attracted to such subjects as child murder, sex murder, rape, homosexuality . . . Their characteristic tone is outrageous comedy . . . even in the most overtly serious treatment of this kind of subject. . . .

Barnes compounds the paradox by admitting that he dug into the holocaust 'to see if there was comedy in it'. In the Epilogue to *Laughter*, which is itself composed of the two one-acts, *Tsar* and *Auschwitz*, two Jewish comics in baggy pants tell bad jokes as they are being gassed. *Laughter* is an experiment to demonstrate how dangerously likely it is that laughter will inure us to reality. However, the risk of misunderstanding is so great that the Royal Shakespeare Company refused to produce the play. Peter Hall said it would close down the National if he staged it.

Unlike Arnold Wesker and others of the new wave playwrights, Barnes insists he is a non-autobiographical writer. Born in London's East End, he boasts he is an authentic Cockney. The family moved to the seaside where they ran an amusement stall on the pier until the war, which shifted his father into factory work and sent Barnes to the country with thousands of other evacuated children. What Barnes remembers about the war is being 'mad on movies,' an interest that led to his becoming a movie reviewer for the Greater London Council house organ. Later, after working as a story editor for Warwick Films, he turned to writing for the camera, reaching the television screen in 1960 with a mystery, *The Man with a Feather in his Hat*. Like his coeval, Peter Nichols, however, he found the television medium too constricting and, in the early sixties, he began to write for the stage.

Though Barnes left school at seventeen, he is among the most scholarly of dramatists. An auto-didact, he made a home for himself in the Reading Room of the British Museum, which he uses as a free office from which to undermine the society that provides it, as Karl Marx did before him. Working there from nine to five, Barnes pores over the books he depends on for the massive research he does for all his plays. The details of historical events are painstakingly accurate. In *Auschwitz*, for example, the catalogues of concentration camp horrors recited by Gottleb are reproduced from Nazi documents. They are harrowing to hear in the theatre, as they must have been harrowing for Barnes to read. Their unmistakable authenticity predictably offends audiences and arouses critical hostility. For, as Barnes implies, we are like the civil servants in the play. We don't want to know the truth. Gottleb bluntly tells them, 'You know extermination facilities were established in Auschwitz in June for the liquidation of all Jews in Europe,' but they respond, 'Who knows that? We don't know that.' Gottleb relentlessly answers, 'You don't know that only knowing enough to know you don't want to know that.' In all of his plays, Barnes insists that we must come to know.

Barnes' first two plays did not attract much attention. *The Ruling Class*, which opened at Nottingham Playhouse in 1968, was his artistic breakthrough and began what critic Bernard Dukore calls 'the Barnes controversey,' that is the sharply divided critical opinion about his work. Set in contemporary England, it is built on images of Jack the Ripper, the archaic rituals of the House of Lords, and the ossified habits of the landed gentry. A savage attack on the ruling class, the play has an aristocratic protagonist who thinks he's God, exchanging that delusion for another when he becomes Jack the Ripper. In Act I the dotty Earl plays God as if he were a good-natured amateur clown, dancing the Varsity Drag, blessing W. C. Fields and speaking in puns. As long as he remains a clown, the gentle J. C., he is an object of contempt, victimized by the machinations of his family. But in Act II, transformed into the malevolent and murderous Jack the Ripper, he gradually takes control, ruling with ruthlessly absolute authority. While he insisted the world was based on principles of love, everyone thought he was mad. As a sadistic autocrat, he is regarded as a perfectly normal member of society. He takes his seat in the mummified House of Lords and his subjects prostrate themselves before him.

That easily-triggered instinct of servility before the show of power is one of humankind's most self-destructive qualities, according to Barnes, and accounts in part for the persistence of an unjust and dangerous class system. In *The Ruling Class*, even the would-be revolutionary, Dan Tucker, can't give up abasing himself in service to the Gurney family despite the £20,000 inheritance that should set him free. His habit of servility leads to his conviction for a murder his master commits, a motif repeated a few years later in Edward Bond's *Restoration*.

In *The Bewitched*, a huge play of thirty scenes and some forty characters, the fate of seventeenth-century Europe is cast on the marriage bed of the stuttering, mis-shapen cretin, King Carlos of Spain, who is barely potent. His courtiers battle for the privilege of carrying his footstool or placing a stick between his teeth during his epileptic fits.

Barnes' plays have been called *baroque* and *Jacobean*, terms which link them to the late Renaissance from which he draws inspiration and models. They suggest his lush extravagance of language and emotion, his macabre violence, his grim view of life and the frequent grotesqueness of his verbal and visual images. And Barnes is a master of the grotesque. J. C.'s rebirth in *The Ruling Class* is a good example. When, seized with labour pains, the Earl crashes against the recorder, an incongruous eight-foot beast in morning coat and top hat bursts through the french windows and pummels him in a series of vicious wrestling holds to bring off the monstrous birth transforming the gentle J. C. to Jack the Ripper.

There are similar grotesqueries in *The Bewitched*. Out of a widening crack, which seems full of dark, glutinous liquid, a shapeless body, completely wrapped in a pale pink membrane, emerges. Fully grown, it hauls itself feebly out of the sack to flop onto the floor, where it lies curled in the foetal position. The climax of the second act is the impaling of Ana on the tip of an eight foot phallus.

Barnes' language is as dizzily inventive, 'varying incessantly and vertiginously from the sheerly magnificent and poetic to the deliberately banal and colloquial,' as Harold Hobson wrote. While Barnes exploited contemporary English from gutter slang and the doggeral of pop song lyrics to formal rhetoric in *The Ruling Class*, he invented an archaic language that incorporates modern colloquialisms for *Leonardo's Last Supper* and *Noonday Demons* rather as Anthony Burgess did for the futuristic *A Clockwork Orange*.

The dialogue in a Barnes play challenges actors to go beyond the ordinary limits of their verbal skills. In *The Ruling Class* the psychotic McKyle, the AC/DC God, zaps the Earl of Gurney with a vocal electric charge, 'Zzzzzzzzzz,' and roars his claim to higher status than the Earl in a half-English, half-Scottish dialect, 'I'm the High Voltage Man, nearer to God than you sentimental clishmac laverer.'

Readers of *The Ruling Class* should pay close attention to the McKyle episode, Act One, Scene Sixteen. Not only is it a spectacular act climax, but it is the structural fulcrum of the play. Determined to cure J. C. of his unnatural celebration of life – which he expresses by such antic exhortations as 'bless the weasel, bless the mighty cockroach, bless me' – the family hires the psychiatrist Herder. In Scene Sixteen, Herder confronts the Earl with another self-proclaimed Messiah, the demented McKyle. The encounter is like an electro-shock treatment for the Earl. McKyle claims to be able to exert his will on others by means of electrical charges. When he whips off his glove and points his finger, the suggestible Earl doubles over in pain. But he is more profoundly affected by Dr. Herder's devastating assault on his claim to be the God of Love. 'No God of Love made this world,' says Herder. 'I've seen a girl of four's nails had been torn out by her father. I've seen the mountains of gold teeth and hair and the millions boiled down for soap.' These holocaust images break the Earl's composure; he blinds himself with a sticking plaster and begins to stutter, 'S-S-sometimes G-G-God turn his back on his p-p-people . . . .' The doctor rips away the plaster, McKyle breaks the Earl's staff. His defences gone, the Earl collapses.

As he writhes in agony, the part of the Earl that is the gentle J. C., God the Son, dies. He screams, 'I'm splitting. I tear. Torn.' In J. C.'s place is born the new Earl as lord of the manor. 'Crowned. Coming out crowned. BORN . . . I AM THE FATHER.' In a clap of thunder, amidst what appears to be primal chaos, the Earl announces his new identity, 'Jack. I'm Jack. I'm Jack.' The spectacular scene is as vivid and compelling as James Frazer's descriptions in *The Golden Bough* of the killing of the old god-king and the bringing forth of the new. But there is a key difference. In the ancient primitive cultures that created them, the ritual called forth the new god in the service of life. The ritual in

The Ruling Class calls forth the opposite, a god-king who mocks and destroys life. He is at once the Earl's father, the hanging judge; God the father who can look on at the world's atrocities without covering His eyes or lifting a finger; and Jack, the self-appointed Ripper, who serves God by the imposition of bloody punishment. The rest of the play, which traces the triumph of this life-hating trinity, expresses Barnes' main accusation against all classes in society – that they, which is to say we, prefer Jack to J. C.

Barnes' assiduous self-education made him not only an unusually literate dramatist, whose plays are full of literary allusions and classical references, but an accomplished editor and adaptor of the work of other dramatists whom he admires. Since 1970 when he combined Wedekind's *Earth Spirit* and *Pandora's Box* into the single play *Lulu*, he has adapted other plays by Wedekind as well as plays by Feydeau, Brecht, and a variety of Jacobeans. (See the reference to Chapman's *Bussy d'Ambois* in *The Ruling Class*.) He is particularly drawn to Ben Jonson and has done modern versions of *Volpone* and *The Alchemist*, among others.

Barnes and Jonson have much in common. Both create hugely voracious characters; both are linguistically extravagant, especially in invective. Barnes praises Jonson for a quality that sets Barnes himself apart from most of his contemporaries, 'The meaning of Jonson isn't between the lines, it's in the lines.' In *Laughter*, when the Tsar's impaled victim hideously screams, 'Arrrarrrhh', and the Tsar answers, 'T'is easy f'you t'say that', there is no subtext. The bitterly comic words mean exactly what they say, and as in Jonson, that is sufficient. Barnes praises Jonson's 'farty vulgarity', a quality ripely abundant in any Barnes play.

In *Leonardo's Last Supper* and *Noonday Demons*, Barnes' first pair of one-acts, Jonsonian-sized avarice climaxes in comic murder. In *Leonardo's Last Supper*, set in a French charnel house, a family of greedy undertakers murder Da Vinci for the burial commission. In *Noonday Demons*, Egyptian cave-dweller St. Eusebius, greedy for God's favour, murders his saintly rival St. Pior. Both plays use excremental imagery and dazzling flights of vituperation.

Red Noses, a complex treatment of medieval Christendom during the height of the Plague, was staged by the Royal Shakespeare Company in 1985. Dukore, author of the only full-length study of Barnes' plays, calls it his greatest work. 'When I write a play,' Barnes said, 'I'm literally trying to change the world.'

Whether he succeeds at that or not, it is likely that his plays will 'prove a turning point in the drama of the second half of the twentieth century,' as Hobson predicted.

Major Plays

The Ruling Class, Nottingham Playhouse, 1968.
Leonardo's Last Supper & *Noonday Demons*, Open Space Theatre, 1969.
The Bewitched, RSC at the Aldwych Theatre, 1974.
Laughter, Royal Court Theatre, 1978.
Red Noses, RSC at the Barbican Theatre, 1985.

Selected Bibliography

Barnes, Peter (with T. Hands, I. Wardle, C. Blakely, J. Hammond). 'Ben Jonson and the Modern Stage,' *Gambit* 6 (1972), pp. 5–30.

—. 'Liberating Laughter,' *Plays and Players* 25 (March 1978), pp. 14–17.

Dukore, Bernard F. *The Theatre of Peter Barnes*. London: Heinemann, 1981.

Esslin, Martin. 'Green Room,' *Plays and Players*, 21 (August 1974), pp. 12–13.

Nightingale, Benedict. 'Green Room,' *Plays and Players*, 21 (July 1974), pp. 12–13.

Shafer, Yvonne. 'Peter Barnes and the Theatre of Disturbance,' *Theatre News*, December 1982, pp. 7–9. (Interview with Barnes.)

Taylor, John Russell. *The Second Wave*. London: Methuen; New York: Hill and Wang, 1971.

PETER BARNES

The Ruling Class

For Charlotte

Author's Note

When first presented at the Nottingham Playhouse and subsequently at the Piccadilly Theatre, the play was divided into three acts. Act One ended with the entrance of Marguerite, Scene Seven. The play is formally constructed into two acts but the physical demands of the leading role may make it necessary to split it into three.

The Ruling Class was first presented at Nottingham Playhouse on 6 November 1968 and was subsequently transferred to The Piccadilly Theatre, London, on 26 February 1969. The play was presented by Gene Persson and Richard Pilbrow with the following cast:

13TH EARL OF GURNEY	Peter Whitbread
TOASTMASTER	Robert Robertson
DANIEL TUCKER	Dudley Jones
BISHOP LAMPTON	Ronald Magill
SIR CHARLES GURNEY	David Dodimead
DINSDALE GURNEY	Jonathan Cecil
LADY CLAIRE GURNEY	Irene Hamilton
MATTHEW PEAKE	Brown Derby
14TH EARL OF GURNEY	Derek Godfrey
DR PAUL HERDER	David Neal
MRS. TREADWELL	Ann Heffernan
MRS. PIGGOT-JONES	Elizabeth Tyrrell
GRACE SHELLEY	Vivienne Martin
MCKYLE	Ken Hutchison
MCKYLE'S ASSISTANT	Terence Ratcliffe
KELSO TRUSCOTT, Q.C.	Laurence Harrington
GIRL	Vicky Clayton
DETECTIVE INSPECTOR BROCKETT	Peter Whitbread
DETECTIVE SERGEANT FRASER	Robert Robertson
FIRST LORD	C. Denier Warren
SECOND LORD	Brown Derby
THIRD LORD	Timothy Welsh

Directed by STUART BURGE
Designed by JOHN NAPIER
Lighting by ROBERT ORNBO

PROLOGUE

Three distinct raps. Curtain rises. Spot Down Stage Centre. The 13TH EARL OF GURNEY *stands in full evening dress and medals at a banqueting table. On it a silver coffee pot and a half-filled wine glass.*

A TOASTMASTER *in scarlet jacket and sash stands beside him; he has just rapped his gavel for silence.*

13TH EARL OF GURNEY. The aim of the Society of St. George
 Is to keep green the memory of England
 And what England means to her sons and daughters.
 I say the fabric holds, though families fly apart.
 Once the rulers of the greatest Empire
 The world has ever known,
 Ruled not by superior force or skill
 But by sheer presence. (*Raises glass in a toast.*)
 This teeming womb of privilege, this feudal state,
 Whose shores beat back the turbulent sea of foreign
   anarchy.
 This ancient fortress, still commanded by the noblest
 Of our royal blood; this ancient land of ritual.
 This precious stone set in a silver sea.
TOASTMASTER. My Lords, Ladies and Gentleman. The toast is
 – England. This precious stone set in a silver sea.
13TH EARL OF GURNEY AND VOICES. England. Set in a silver sea.

He drinks. The National Anthem plays over as his LORDSHIP *comes rigidly to attention, whilst behind him, the* TOASTMASTER *exits, and the table is taken off. The Anthem ends.*

 Lights up on his Lordship's bedroom. An ornate four-poster bed Stage Centre, and a wardrobe near a door Stage Left. Dressed in a traditional butler's uniform, DANIEL TUCKER, *his Lordship's aged manservant, creakingly lays out his master's dressing-gown on the bed, whilst his* LORDSHIP *undresses.*

TUCKER. How was your speech, sir?

13TH EARL OF GURNEY (*dropping jacket absently on floor*). Went well, Tuck. Englishmen like to hear the truth about themselves.

TUCKER *painfully picks up the jacket, whilst his* LORDSHIP *sits on the edge of the bed.*

The Guv'nor loved this bed.

TUCKER. Wouldn't sleep anywhere else, sir.

13TH EARL OF GURNEY. Took it all over the world, Delhi, Cairo, Hong Kong. Devilish great man, the Guv'nor. Superb shot.

TUCKER (*kneeling to take off his Lordship's shoes*). Did wonderful needlework too, sir 'Petit-Point'.

13TH EARL OF GURNEY (*undoing his trousers*). Tuck, I'm getting married again.

TUCKER. Yes, my lord.

13TH EARL OF GURNEY. Miss Grace Shelley. Charles is right. Sake of the family. Gurney name. Been putting it off. Only Jack left.

TUCKER. This house used to be full of mischief . . . mischief . . .

13TH EARL OF GURNEY. Four young devils. Thought I was safe enough.

TUCKER. Master Paul would have been the 14th Earl.

13TH EARL OF GURNEY. District Officer at twenty-one. Dead at twenty-three. Beri-beri. Picked it up off some scruffy fuzzy-wuzzy in a dressing-gown, shouldn't wonder.

TUCKER (*getting up slowly*). Young Richard used to play the xylophone.

13TH EARL OF GURNEY. And young Raymond killed in Malaya. Not one of 'em buried in England. Never seen their graves.

TUCKER (*crossing to the wardrobe with clothes*). You could do that on your honeymoon, your lordship.

13TH EARL OF GURNEY. There's still Jack. (*They look at each other.*) It's all based on land, Tuck. Can't have those knaves from Whitehall moving in. So it's Miss Grace Shelley.

TUCKER. Is she anyone, sir?

13TH EARL OF GURNEY. No one. But Charles recommends her as good breeding stock. Family foals well. Sires mostly. There's always room at the top for brains, money or a good pair of titties.

TUCKER. Miss Shelley seems well-endowed, sir.

TUCKER *comes back with a flat leather case from the wardrobe. He opens it for his* LORDSHIP, *who is deep in thought. Inside are four coils of rope, each eight feet long, made of silk, nylon, hemp and cord respectively.*

Your lordship?

13TH EARL OF GURNEY. What? Eh? (*Looking.*) Yes, I suppose so. Hard day. Need to relax.

TUCKER. May I suggest silk tonight, sir?

13TH EARL OF GURNEY. Good idea, Tuck. For St. George.

TUCKER *takes the silk rope and goes round to a pair of steps. He places them under a cross-beam at the corner of the bed and climbs up with the rope.*

13TH EARL OF GURNEY. Ah, Tuck, there's no end to duty. Every day's like climbing a mountain. How did Tiberius do it at his age?

TUCKER. Will-power, sir.

13TH EARL OF GURNEY. The Law's been my life, Tuck. And the reason is the soul of the Law. A judge can't be unreasonable. So how can he be a lover, eh? Ours is a damned dry world, Tuck.

TUCKER. A long life, and a grey one, your lordship.

13TH EARL OF GURNEY (*musing*). The power of life and death. No need of other vices. If you've once put on the black cap, everything else tastes like wax fruit.

TUCKER *ties the rope to a hook on the cross-beam. The rope hangs down in a noose. His* LORDSHIP *peers up.*

Noose a bit high, Tuck. Pull the knot down half an inch.

That's it.

TUCKER comes down.

TUCKER. Will that be all, your lordship?

13TH EARL OF GURNEY. Whisky and soda in about five minutes as usual. Oh, Tuck, tell Cook the trial ends tomorrow. She knows I don't like passing sentence on an empty stomach.

TUCKER. Very good, my Lord.

TUCKER exits Stage Left. Humming to himself, his LORDSHIP goes to the wardrobe and brings out a three-cornered cocked hat, a sword in a scabbard and a white tutu ballet skirt.

13TH EARL OF GURNEY. Nothing like a good English breakfast. Big meal of the day for the Guv'nor. Always sat at the head of the table. All the mail in front of him. He'd pass it out to the rest of us. Same with the newspapers. Always read *The Times* through first, in case there was anything too disturbing in it. Mother didn't know what the word 'Socialist' meant till she was past fifty. Remember standing at the foot of this bed here, tell him I wanted to be a painter. 'The Gurneys have never been slackers,' he said. 'Pulled their weight. Earned their privileges.' Great concession letting me study law. Not the Gurney tradition. Always the army. (*He puts the tutu on, delicately flouncing it out.*) The smell of cordite. The clash of steel. Feet, feet, feet, the boys are marching! A little more grape-shot Captain Bragg! Give 'em the cold steel boys.' (*He straps the sword to his side and puts on the three-cornered hat.*)

Now dressed in three-cornered hat, ballet skirt, long underwear and sword, the 13TH EARL OF GURNEY curtseys and moves towards the steps, trembling slightly in anticipation.

Close. I can feel her hot breath. Wonderful. One slip. The worms have the best of it. They dine off the tenderest joints. Juicy breasts, white thighs, red hair colour of rust . . . the worms have the best of it. (*He climbs up the steps, stands under the noose and comes to attention.*) It is a far, far better thing I do now, than I have ever done. (*He slips the noose over his head, trembling.*) No, sir. No bandage. Die my dear doctor? That's the last thing I shall do. Is that you, my love? Now, come darling . . . to me . . . ha! . . .

Stepping off the top of the steps, he dangles for a few seconds and begins to twitch and jump. He puts his feet back on the top of the steps. Gasping, he loosens the noose.

(*Trembling hoarsely.*) Touched him, saw her, towers of death and silence, angels of fire and ice. Saw Alexander covered with honey and beeswax in his tomb and felt the flowers growing over me. A man must have his visions. How else could an English judge and peer of the realm take moonlight trips to Marrakesh and Ponders End? See six vestel virgins smoking cigars? Moses in bedroom slippers? Naked bosoms floating past Formosa? Desperate diseases need desperate remedies. (*Glancing towards the door.*) Just time for a quick one. (*Reverently places noose over his head again.*) Be of good cheer, Master Ridley, and play the man. There's plenty of time to win this game, and thrash the Spaniards too. (*Excitedly draws his sword.*) Form squares men! Smash the Mahdi, and Binnie Barnes!

With a lustful gurgle he steps off. But this time he knocks over the steps. Dangling helpless for a second he drops the sword and tries to tear the noose free, gesturing frantically. Every muscle begins to tremble. His legs jack-knife up to his stomach; they jack-knife again and again with increasing speed and violence. The spasms reach a climax, then stop suddenly. The body goes limp and sways gently at the end of the rope. A discreet knock on door Stage Left.

TUCKER (*voice off*). Your lordship? Are you ready?

The door opens slightly. TUCKER *shuffles in carrying a tray with whisky and soda. He sees his* LORDSHIP.

Bleeding bloody hell!
Blackout.

Curtain.

Act One

SCENE ONE

A great church organ thunders out 'The Dead March from Saul'. The curtain parts enough to reveal the imposing figure of BISHOP BERTRAM LAMPTON, *magnificently dressed in red cope, surplice, embroidered stole and mitre.* FOUR PALL BEARERS *in top hats and morning-coats slowly cross Down Stage, bearing a coffin, draped with the Gurney banner.*

BISHOP LAMPTON (*chanting*). I am the Resurrection and the Life, saith the Lord; he that believeth in me though he were dead, yet shall he live; and whosoever liveth and believeth in me shall never die.

Gilead is mine, and Manasses is mine: Ephraim also is the strength of my head; Judah is my lawgiver,

Moab is my washpot; over Edom will I cast out my shoe:

Philistria, triumph thou because of me.

Who will lead me onto the strong city: who will bring me into Edom?

The PALL BEARERS *exit Right. The curtain opens behind the* BISHOP *to show his Lordship's relatives dressed in black, standing grouped in the drawing room of the Gurney country house.*

BISHOP LAMPTON and RELATIVES (*singing*). 'All things bright and beautiful. All creatures great and small. All things wise and wonderful, the Lord God made them all. The rich man in his castle, the poor man at his gate. God made them high and lowly, and ordered their estate . . .'

As they sing BISHOP LAMPTON *disrobes, handing his cope, surplice*

and mitre to TUCKER. *The* BISHOP *has shrunk to a small, bald-headed, asthmatic old man in dog-collar and gaiters. As the last note of the hymn dies away and* TUCKER *staggers off Wings Left with the robes, he smooths down his non-existent hair and waddles Up Stage to join the others.*

SCENE TWO

The large drawing room of Gurney Manor. It is seventeenth century, except for the high double french-windows, now heavily curtained, Stage Right. Running the length of the back wall Up Stage is a narrow gallery: small stairways, Up Stage Left and Right, lead up to it. On the wall above the gallery are portraits of past Earls. Up Stage Centre, below the gallery, is a wide double-doorway leading to the hall. Just above it the Gurney crest. Door, Down Stage Left, and alongside, a bell-rope. Sofa and chairs Centre Stage. Desk, chair and coffee table adjacent to the windows.

LADY CLAIRE GURNEY *is on the sofa: long black cigarette holder, long black velvet gloves.* SIR CHARLES GURNEY *stands ramrod stiff, his legs slightly apart, whilst* DINSDALE GURNEY *lounges on the arm of the sofa, elegantly picking his noise.* BISHOP LAMPTON *joins them.*

SIR CHARLES. Excellent service, Bertie. Created exactly the right impression.

DINSDALE. Damned if I could understand a word of it.

BISHOP LAMPTON (*asthmatically*). Hardly expected you to, young man. It was a Church service. A service, Charles, I might add, I could not have conducted for someone who may have lain violent hands upon himself. A disturbing rumour has reached my ears. Did Ralph commit suicide?

SIR CHARLES (*slightly exasperated*). Suicide? Tucker found Ralph hanging in the bedroom dressed in a cocked hat, underpants and a ballet skirt. Does that *sound* like suicide?

DINSDALE. I'm sure if Uncle Ralph had wanted to do anything foolish he'd have done it decently. Bullet through the head, always the Gurney way.

SIR CHARLES. No idea how these malicious rumours get started. The Coroner's verdict is clear enough. Accident brought on by the strain of overwork.

BISHOP LAMPTON (*smiling*). Had to be sure. He's buried in consecrated ground.

DINSDALE (*thoughtfully*). Still, you know, I must say it's odd, Uncle Ralph found hanging around like that in a ballet skirt.

CLAIRE (*maliciously*). Charles didn't you say Ralph always was rather artistic?

SIR CHARLES. He was wilful, stubborn, and this time he went too far. But he was my brother – well, half-brother. I won't have you calling him *artistic*.

BISHOP LAMPTON (*between gasps: puzzled*). Cocked hat? Why was he wearing a cocked hat?

SIR CHARLES. Trying it on for size obviously. I told him not to stay a widower. The Guv'nor didn't. Understood his duty to the family. Had to start breeding again. Not pleasant, I grant you, for a man of Ralph's age. But it was something he had to get on top of.

BISHOP LAMPTON. Underpants? Why was he in his underpants?

SIR CHARLES. Why not? Going to bed wasn't he? Thought our troubles were over when he took a fancy to young Grace Shelley. That would have solved everything.

CLAIRE. Yes, wouldn't it just.

DINSDALE. Frankly, I don't understand all the plother. Uncle Ralph has an heir – Jack, the 14th Earl of Gurney.

SIR CHARLES (*stroking his moustache*). Yes . . . It's going to be awkward. Damned awkward.

CLAIRE. Ralph was aware of the situation. I'm sure he's made proper arrangements. A matter of finding out who he's appointed guardian of the estate.

BISHOP LAMPTON (*sitting up*). But what was he doing in a *ballet-*

skirt? Answer me that!

TUCKER *enters Up Stage Centre.*

TUCKER. Mr Matthew Peake to see you, Sir Charles.

SIR CHARLES. Right. Show him in.

TUCKER *steps aside, and* MATTHEW PEAKE, *solicitor, enters and gives him his trilby. He is a dessicated, deferential man with round shoulders, winged collar and a briefcase.*

SIR CHARLES. I believe you know everyone here, Peake.

PEAKE. I have had that honour, Sir Charles.

SIR CHARLES. All right, Tucker, that'll be all. We're not to be disturbed.

PEAKE. Sir Charles, might I suggest Tucker stays. (*Taps briefcase significantly.*)

SIR CHARLES. What? Oh quite. Well, Tucker, seems you're going to hear something to your advantage.

TUCKER. Yes, sir.

He stands discreetly in the background, holding PEAKE'S *trilby.*

PEAKE. May I take this opportunity to express my condolensces.

CLAIRE. Tucker, *do* sit down.

TUCKER. Thank you, madam.

He sits on the edge of a chair, whilst PEAKE *crosses to the desk, and takes out some legal documents.*

PEAKE. Hmmm, may I say, Sir Charles, how refreshing it is to meet with such restraint. Usually I'm afraid these occasions are so . . . (*Purses lips in distaste.*) emotional.

SIR CHARLES. Do get on with it.

PEAKE. But, Sir Charles, shouldn't we wait? His Lordship's heir . . .

SIR CHARLES. Jack's been notified. Wasn't able to get away for the funeral. Not likely to come now.

PEAKE. Very well, Sir Charles. I'll inform him later.

All eyes now on PEAKE *as he puts on horn-rimmed spectacles, and reads in a dry monotone.*

(*Reading.*) 'I, Ralph, Douglas, Christopher, Alexander, Gurney, of Gurney House in the county of Bedfordshire, hereby revoke all former Wills and Codicils and declare this to be my last Will. I appoint Mr. Matthew Peake of 17 Brownlow Gardens, Bedfordshire, to be the sole executor of this my Will. I give and bequeath unto my manservant, Daniel Tucker, the sum of twenty thousand pounds free of duty.'

Murmours of surprise from the listeners. But no reaction from TUCKER *himself.*

There follow a number of bequests to various charities, which his Lordship was interested in. I'll run through them briefly. 'I bequeath the sum of five thousand pounds to the Tailwavers Registered National Charity. Three thousand pounds to the Bankers Beneficent Society Ltd.' . . .

TUCKER. Yippee! (*Shoots off the chair.*) *Twenty thousand! Twenty thousand smackers! Yawee!*

Jumping clumsily into the air, and clicking his heels together, he flicks PEAKE's *trilby on to his head and gleefully capers forward.* (*Singing in a croak.*) 'I'm Gilbert the Filbert the Knut with a "K".' (*Gives gouty high kick.*) The pride of Piccadilly, the blasé roué. Oh Hades! The Ladies (*Ogles* CLAIRE.) who leave their wooden huts, For Gilbert the Filbert, the Colonel of the Knuts.' Yah!

Flinging open the door Up Stage he leaps raggedly out, arms held high. There is a crash off as he hits something followed by a cackle of laughter. Silence in the room.

DINSDALE. Tucker seems het up.

BISHOP LAMPTON. 'So are the ways of everyone that is greedy of gain'. What about the Zambesi Mission, Peake? And the Overseas Bishoprics Fund?

SIR CHARLES. Never mind that, Bertie. What about the estate?

PEAKE (*continues reading*). 'I devise and bequeath all the remainder of my estate both real and personal whatsoever and wheresoever to which I might be entitled or over which I have any disposing at the time of my death, to my beloved son, Jack, Arnold, Alexander, Tancred, Gurney, the 14th Earl of Gurney, for his own use absolutely.'

SIR CHARLES (*repeating slowly*). 'For his own use absolutely.' But who's been appointed legal guardian?

PEAKE. No one.

BISHOP LAMPTON. 'By the rivers of Babylon there we sat down, yea, we wept when we remembered Zion.'

SIR CHARLES (*stunned*). You mean Jack is free to run the estate . . . and everything . . .?

CLAIRE. Think of Jack in the Royal Enclosure.

BISHOP LAMPTON. Jack in the Athenæum.

SIR CHARLES (*grimly*). It's obvious Ralph has let his personal feelings come before his duty to his family. We'll have to fight. Awkward. Scandal an' all. but we've no choice.

PEAKE (*diffidently reading*). 'If this my Will is contested, the whole of my estate, both real and personal, is bequeathed to the charities named herewith: The Earl Haig Fund, Lord Wharton's . . .'

The rest is drowned out as all start shouting angrily. They are too busy yelling to notice TUCKER *appear in the doorway Up Stage Centre smoking a cigar. He disappears for a second, re-appearing immediately carrying a large hall vase. Holding it up, he deliberately drops it on the floor. It smashes with a loud crash. The shouting stops. They all turn in astonishment.* TUCKER *takes the cigar out of his mouth and makes the announcement in his usual calm, respectful tone.*

TUCKER. Ladies and gentlemen. The Queen's Right Trusty and Well Beloved Cousin – Jack, Arnold, Alexander, Tancred, Gurney, the 14th Earl of Gurney.

Surprised gasps. TUCKER *steps to one side. The sound of*

approaching footsteps. All eyes on the door. BISHOP LAMPTON'S *asthma becomes painfully pronounced as the tension mounts. His breathing turns into a thin, high-pitched screech as the new* EARL OF GURNEY *finally appears in the doorway: a Franciscan monk of the Capuchin Order. His habit is a coarse, brown tunic, cord, girdle, pointed cowl, bare feet in sandals. Tall and ascetic, the* EARL *has a sensitive face, fair beard and a magnetic personality.*

EARL OF GURNEY (*gently*). Hello . . . (*Hands clasped in his large sleeves, he crosses Down Stage.*) I'm sorry I wasn't here before but I only received the news yesterday. I'm afraid our little community is somewhat cut off. I hope you'll forgive me. I know he would. My sorrow isn't less, or the pain. I've just been to his grave. Thank you, Uncle Charles, for making all the arrangements.

SIR CHARLES *looks uncomfortable.*

Aunt Claire, it's been so long. You haven't changed.

CLAIRE. Nor you.

EARL OF GURNEY. You must be Dinsdale?

DINSDALE. Er – yes, I must. How do you do, sir.

EARL OF GURNEY (*turning to* BISHOP LAMPTON). Are you still angry with me, Bishop?

But speechless with asthma, BISHOP LAMPTON *can only wave him away feebly.*

First let me put your minds at rest. The choice has been made. I've come back to take my proper place in the world. The monastic ideal isn't easy. I've had many broken nights. But I've come back refreshed. (*He smiles.*) Though hardly equipped for society. I shall need your help, Uncle Charles. We're all one family. Let's wash away the old sores. If the Bishop doesn't mind. I think we should pray.

SIR CHARLES. Pray?

EARL OF GURNEY. For love and understanding. Surely you pray for love and understanding?

CLAIRE (*looking at* SIR CHARLES). Every night. Without success.

PEAKE *moves silently towards the door.*

EARL OF GURNEY. You too, Mr. Peake.

PEAKE. I'm Methodist.

EARL OF GURNEY. I'm sure you're still a Christian. (*Gestures gently.*) Come, for me.

PEAKE. Yes, my lord.

Embarrassed, he begins awkwardly to kneel. CLAIRE *smiles slightly and joins* PEAKE *and* TUCKER *on her knees.* SIR CHARLES *is about to protest but then thinks better of it. Clenching his jaw he follows pulling* DINSDALE *down with him.* BISHOP LAMPTON *fights off a violent asthma attack with an inhaler whilst the others kneel round the* EARL. *The lights start to dim down to a Spot on them as he holds out his hand in blessing.*

EARL OF GURNEY. A prayer should rise up like incense. For you are acknowledging the power and goodness of God. It's an act of faith and a union. A prayer is not a request, but an appeal. To pray means to ask, to beg, to plead. A prayer is a message to Heaven. You are talking directly to God . . . express your desires freely, don't be afraid, I know them already. (*They all look up at him in horror.*) For I am the Creator and ruler of the Universe, Khoda, the One Supreme Being and Infinite Personal Being, Yaweh, Shangri-Ti and El, the First Immovable Mover, Yea, I am the Absolute Unknowable Righteous Eternal, the Lord of Hosts, the King of Kings, Lord of Lords, the Father, Son and Holy Ghost, the one True God, the God of Love, the Naz!

A strangled cry from BISHOOP LAMPTON *as he slips off his chair and thuds unconscious on to the floor in the darkness.*

SCENE THREE

A plain white backing lowered immediately Down Stage Centre into the spot, cutting the EARL OF GURNEY *from view.* SIR CHARLES *and* DR PAUL HERDER, *a thin man with a cold manner, enter from Wings Left and stand in front of it.*

DR HERDER. His lordship is a paranoid-schizophrenic.

SIR CHARLES. But he's a Gurney.

DR HERDER. Then he's a paranoid-schizophrenic-Gurney who believes he's God.

SIR CHARLES. But we've always been Church of England.

DR HERDER. In paranoid-schizophrenia the patient's relationship with reality is disturbed. His idea of the world we live in is determined solely by his feelings. What he feels *is* *– is*.

SIR CHARLES. If my nephew's bonkers, why the blazes did you let him out?

DR HERDER. He's a voluntary patient in a private clinic, free to leave when he chooses. His father insisted on no official certification. If you want him permanently detained here, bring him before the Board of Control or get the Master in Lunacy to sign an order.

SIR CHARLES (*quickly*). Er – later, when we've got a few things settled.

DR HERDER. From the medical point of view a plunge into the waking world won't do the Earl any harm.

SIR CHARLES. Won't do him any harm. What about the rest of us?

DR HERDER. He's not dangerous. Provided he's left relatively secluded it shouldn't be too difficult. It'll be a very interesting experiment. A harsh dose of reality can sometimes help towards a cure.

SIR CHARLES. Cure! You've had him here for seven years already, and look at him. What've you been doing?

DR HERDER. Exercising patience and understanding. Something

he'll need from his family.

SIR CHARLES (*testily*). Yes, yes, but why haven't you used the knife?

DR HERDER. Because labotomy is irrelevant and dangerous in this case. He showed classic schizophrenic symptoms by withdrawing from his environment. Then, of course, he never forgot being brutally rejected by his mother and father at the age of eleven. They sent him away, alone, into a primitive community of licensed bullies and pederasts.

SIR CHARLES. You mean he went to Public School.

HERDER *nods and they begin to walk slowly to the Wings Left, Spot follows them, whilst another Spot remains on the white backing, which is taken up to show the* EARL OF GURNEY *standing in exactly the same place as before, Centre Stage.*

DR HERDER. You must realize the Earl's strange position. It's what makes him such an interesting case. Remember, he's suffering from delusions of *grandeur*. In reality he's an Earl, an English aristocrat, a peer of the realm, a member of the ruling class. Naturally, he's come to believe there's only one person grander than that – the Lord God Almighty Himself.

SIR CHARLES (*suspiciously*). Are you English?

DR HERDER. No.

SIR CHARLES. Ahhh . . .

They exit.

SCENE FOUR

Spot on the EARL, *Stage Centre, remains.*

EARL OF GURNEY (*looking after them*). Q.E.D. If I saw a man eating grass I'd say he was hungry. They'd have him certified. They claim snow is only precipitation and not candied dew and the single heart-beat only the contraction and dilation of the central organ of the vascular system. *Whroom.* (*He makes a circular motion with his right hand.*) I'm always thinking so fast. Could a rooster forget he was a rooster and lay an egg? *Whroom.* Space and time only exist within the walls of my brain. What I'm trying to say is, if the words sound queer or funny to your ear, a little bit jumbled and jivy, sing mares eat oats and does eat oats and little lambs eat ivy. Ivy? Who's Ivy? ...I...

Lights come up to show CLAIRE *listening attentively on sofa.*

I am that Lord Jesus come again in my body to save the sick, the troubled, the ignorant. I am He that liveth and behold I am alive for everyone. (*Opens his arms mimicking American nightclub entertainer Ted Lewis.*) Is everybody happy? Now hear this, I came to proclaim the new Dispensation. The Gospel Dispensation promised only salvation for the soul, my new Dispensation of Love gives it to the *body* as well. J. Christ Mark 1 suffered to redeem the spirit and left the body separated from God, so Satan found a place in man, and formed in him a false consciousness, a false love, a love of self. EXPLODE only FEEL, LOVE, and sin no more. Most everything you see, touch and FEEL glorifies my love. (*Mimes putting on a hat.*) The top hat is my mitre and the walking stick my rod. (*Twirls imaginary stick.*) I'm sorry. I really must apologize. Once I get started I find it damnable difficult to stop. They diagnose it as arbitrary discharge from the speech centre. Diarrhoea of the mouth. Nobody else gets much of a look-in.

CLAIRE. It's fascinating.

EARL OF GURNEY. If there's anything you'd like me to explain, fire away.

CLAIRE. How do you know you're ... God?

EARL OF GURNEY. Simple. When I pray to Him I find I'm talking to myself.

CLAIRE. I see. How did it happen? How did you come to be in this state . . . of grace?

EARL OF GURNEY. Like every prophet I saw visions, heard voices. I ran but the voices of St Francis, Socrates, General Gordon, and Tim O'Leary the Jewish Buddha all told me I was God. Pretty reliable witnesses – agreed? It was Sunday August 25th at 3.32 standard British Summer Time. I heard with my outward ear a terrible thunder clap and I saw a great body of light like the light from the sun, and red as fire, in the form of a drum. I clapped my hands and cried Amen! Hallelujah! Hallelujah! Amen! I cried out, Lord what will you do! But the light vanished . . . a blackness of darkness until a great brush dipped in light swept across the sky. And I saw the distinction, diversity, variety, all clearly rolled up into the unity of Universal Love.

CLAIRE. Where did all this happen?

EARL OF GURNEY. East Acton. Outside the public urinal.

CLAIRE. What does it feel like to be God?

EARL OF GURNEY. Like a river flowing over everything. I pick up a newspaper and I'm everywhere, conducting a Summit Conference, dying of hunger in a Peruvian gutter, accepting the Nobel Prize for Literature, raping a nun in Sumatra.

CLAIRE. You don't look any different.

EARL OF GURNEY (*starts taking off his monk's habit*). When a parasite called the Sacculina attacks the common shore crab, it bores a tiny hole through the crab's protective outer shell. Once in the body it spreads like a root devouring the tissues and turning the flesh to pulp. It's no longer crab's flesh but Sacculina. The crab is transformed, even its sex changes. The outer shell remains unaltered, but inside is a new creature. (*He is dressed underneath in a loose-fitting white tropical suit and Eton tie: his hair cascades over his shoulder.*) I was devoured by the Divine Sacculina, it hollowed me out. Under this protective shell I'm God-filled.

TUCKER *stands in the doorway Up Stage Centre.* SIR CHARLES, *with a briefcase under his arm, comes in behind him.*

TUCKER. Your lordship, sir . . .

As SIR CHARLES *impatiently brushes past,* TUCKER *grabs the bottom of his jacket and jerks him back.*

SIR CHARLES. What in . . . ?

TUCKER. I *haven't* finished yet, Sir Charles. (*Continuing unruffled.*) Your lordship, Sir Charles Gurney.

TUCKER *steps aside, lets the furious* SIR CHARLES *into the room, then exits.*

SIR CHARLES. Insolent clown!

TUCKER (*reappearing*). I *heard* that, sir.

He disappears again.

SIR CHARLES. The world's gone mad. He'll have to go.

CLAIRE. Hadn't we better wait till things get sorted out? Someone new might not understand the situation.

SIR CHARLES (*opening his briefcase on desk*). How come he's still here anyway, with twenty thousand in the bank? Why's he hanging on?

EARL OF GURNEY. Out of love. He knows he's needed.

SIR CHARLES (*taking out a document*). Love? Tucker? Rot. Now, m'boy, certain matters concerning the estate need clearing up. Nothing important. Just needs your signature. Gives me power to handle odd things.

EARL OF GURNEY. Of course, Uncle. (*Crosses to him, putting on glasses.*)

SIR CHARLES (*hastily*). You don't have to read it. Just take my word.

EARL OF GURNEY. I take your word. I put on my glasses because I feel cold. Need one of Dr Jaegers' Sanitary Woollens to keep my soul-duft in. Where do I sign?

SIR CHARLES. Just there.

The EARL *signs with a flourish.* SIR CHARLES *glances triumpantly at* CLAIRE.

Excellent. Excellent. Easily done, eh? (*Reads.*) 'I the undersigned . . . Mycroft *Holmes*? Who's Mycroft Holmes?

TUCKER (*entering carrying robes and coronet*). Brother of Sherlock Holmes, illiterate oaf!

SIR CHARLES. But your name's Jack!

EARL OF GURNEY (*fiercely*). Never call me that! (*Strokes forehead.*) Jack's a word I reject absolutely. It's a word I put into my galvanized pressure-cooker, whrr . . .

CLAIRE. Your pressure-cooker?

EARL OF GURNEY. I don't mince words, I prefer them parboiled fried or scrambled. Jack's dead! It's my old shell-name – a sham name.

CLAIRE. All right, what should we call you then?

EARL OF GURNEY. Any of the nine billion names of God. My lordship will do, or J.C., Eric, Bert, Barney Entwistle. I don't need to cling to one name. I know exactly who I am.

TUCKER (*indicating robes*). You asked for these, my lord.

EARL OF GURNEY. Burn 'em, Mr Tucker. Burn 'em.

SIR CHARLES. What? Great Scott, man, these are your coronation robes! Marks of our elevation.

TUCKER. Lot of tradition here, your lordship.

EARL OF GURNEY. The axe must be laid to the root. Pomp and riches, pride and property will have to be lopped off. All men are brothers. Love makes all equal. The mighty must bow down before the pricks of the louse-ridden rogues. (*Suddenly warmly embraces* SIR CHARLES.) I love you dearly, Uncle Charles. (*Gestures to robes.*) Keep them if you feel so lost. But soon you will abandon everything to follow me. Come, Mr Tucker, join me in a constitutional before lunch.

TUCKER *dumps the robes and they move to french-windows Stage Right.*

Enjoy yourself whilst I'm gone. Relax. Have sex.

He exits with TUCKER. CLAIRE *and* SIR CHARLES *look after him.*

SIR CHARLES (*exploding*). My God!

EARL OF GURNEY (*popping his head back*). Yes?

CLAIRE. No, no. Nothing.

The EARL *exits again.*

Well, you heard what he said, Charles.

SIR CHARLES (*trembling with rage*). I did . . . bowing before rogues
. . . destroying property . . . all men equal . . . (*Pointing after*
EARL.) My God, Claire, he's not only *mad*, he's *Bolshie!*

Lights down.

SCENE FIVE

*Spot up immediately on a metal sun lowered from Flies, Down Stage
Centre, Footlights up as* TUCKER *and the* EARL OF GURNEY *enter
Wings Right.*

EARL OF GURNEY. Just smell that soul-duft from the lawns and
hedgerows. What a beautiful day I've made. Look – Soft
Thistle and Nigella. (*Crouches down.*) My sweet poetics. (*Ear
to imaginary flower.*) What? No water in days. I can't be
expected to think of everything. I'll see to it. Remember the
Sunday picnics here, Mr Tucker, in my old shell-days? The
world was all top hats and white lace.

TUCKER (*taking out a hip-flask*). And the best heavy silverware.
A snort, your lordship?

EARL OF GURNEY. Not during Yom Kippur.

TUCKER. You mind if I partake?

EARL OF GURNEY. Go ahead. I'm God-intoxicated. If only I knew
then who I was now. (*Stretching out hand.*) Ah, Mr

Grasshopper, of course I bless you, my chirrup, along with General de Gaulle.

TUCKER (*drinking*). First chance I've had of speaking to you alone, your lordship. Be on guard, sir.

EARL OF GURNEY (*straightening up*). Mr Tucker, I'm puzzled.

TUCKER. The family. I've seen 'em at work a'fore. They got the power and they made the rules. They're back there plotting against you like mad.

EARL OF GURNEY. Love cannot doubt nor faith the mustard seed, no more plotting, Mr Tucker, please. It's negativism. Plotting's a word I put into my pressure-cooker, whrrr. It's gone. Feeling persecuted's one of the signs of paranoid schizophrenia. Many poor wretches in Dr Herder's Dancing Academy suffered from same. But I am being watched they said. Everybody is against me they cried. (*Shakes himself vigorously.*) You've set up profound negative disturbances with your Kremlin plots, Mr Tucker, I'm going in. (*Turns abruptly and walks Upstage Centre.*) Resist it, Mr Tucker, that way madness lies.

He disappears into the darkness. TUCKER *looks after him, swaying slightly.*

TUCKER. That's the thanks you get. He's the same as all the rest, what he doesn't want to be so just *isn't* so. Tried to help, you stupid old fool. No skin off my nose. My twenty thousand's safe – and I deserve every last penny of it, and more, more, more! Why should I worry – villa in the South of France, and a bit o' golden crumpet every day, breast and buttocks done to a turn. (*He cackles.*) Just pack a tooth-brush and a French letter and you're away Daniel Tucker. What's keeping you then, Dan? You've got the scratch. (*Drinks, gloomily.*) Fear. Be honest now, Daniel. Fear and habit. You get into the habit of serving. Born a servant, see, son of a servant. Family of servants. From a nation of servants. Very first thing an Englishman does, straight from his mother's womb is touch his forelock. That's how they can tell the wrinkled little bastard's English. *Me*, this tired old creeping servant, I'm the real England, not beef-eating Johnny Bullshit. I know my history. Masters and servants, that's the way of it. Didn't think I was like that, eh? A lot yer don't know about Daniel Tucker. Just old faithful Tucker. Give doggy boney. Just 'ere for comic relief. Know who I really am? (*Beckons confidentially.*) Alexei Kronstadt. Number 243. Anarchist – Trotskyist – Communist – Revolutionary. I'm a cell! All these years I've been working for the Revolution, spitting in the hot soup, peeing on the Wedgwood dinner plates. (*Coming to attention and singing.*) 'Then raise the scarlet standard high! Within its shade we'll live or die; Tho' cowards flinch and traitors sneer, We'll keep the red flag flying here.'

Spot out. He exits.

SCENE SIX

Lights up to show EARL OF GURNEY *crucified on a wooden cross, leaning against the far wall to the right of the centre doorway. The cross-beam is above the gallery.* TUCKER *is still heard singing faintly off. Lights up to show* CLAIRE, *by the sofa, smoking nervously and staring up at the* EARL *on the cross.*

CLAIRE. J.C.? . . . Bert? . . . my Lord? . . . Barney Entwistle?

Still no response from the EARL. TUCKER *comes in Up Stage, pushing a tea-trolley. He crosses to* CLAIRE, *wincing at every sound, obviously suffering from a bad hangover.*

TUCKER. Tea, madam?

CLAIRE. Oh, yes. What was that you were singing just now, Tucker?

TUCKER. An old German hymn, madam – Tannenbaum. Lemon

or milk, madam?

CLAIRE. Lemon.

He pours shakily as a flustered DINSDALE *enters Up Stage.*

DINSDALE. I say, where's the Guv'nor? Is that tea? Just the job, Tucker.

CLAIRE. Your father's in town. Another meeting with Sir Humphrey Spens trying to find a way round this mess.

DINSDALE. When's he back?

CLAIRE. Any time now if he doesn't drop in on his mistress first.

DINSDALE *shoots a sidelong glance at* TUCKER, *who is too busy pouring and shuddering with nausea, to react.*

DINSDALE. Ah, hmm. Hope he gets things settled soon. It's already getting awkward. They're used to us Gurneys being in everything. Mrs Piggot-Jones and Mrs Treadwell and the other old girls thought it'd be a splendid idea for the new Earl to open the Fête, Sunday week.

CLAIRE. Naturally you told them it was impossible.

TUCKER. Milk or lemon, sir?

DINSDALE. Lemon, Tucker. But dammit I am prospective Parliamentary candidate for the division. Had to watch my step with 'em. Couldn't say he was 'non-compis'.

CLAIRE. If you're going to be a successful Conservative politician, you'll have to learn to make convincing excuses.

DINSDALE. Where is he now?

TUCKER *hands him his tea.*

CLAIRE (*gesturing behind him*). Up there.

DINSDALE (*turning*). Oh . . . Ah!

He gives an involuntary cry of fright at his first sight of the EARL *on the cross and spills some tea.*

TUCKER (*tetchily.*) Now look what you've done. (*Wipes carpet with foot.*) Never get tea-stains out. Show some consideration.

DINSDALE. Is it Yogi or something?

TUCKER has walked Up Stage to the cross.

TUCKER. Tea, my lord?

CLAIRE. It's no good, Tucker, I've tried. He's asleep; dead to the world.

EARL OF GURNEY. His Body sleeps but his Divinity is always watching. Yes, Mr Tucker. Milk please. Any toasted muffins?

TUCKER. Yes, sir. Shall I bring them up?

EARL OF GURNEY. No thanks. I'll be right down.

The EARL twists round, and clambers off the cross.

DINSDALE. It's Yogi, isn't it? A form of Yogi?

CLAIRE. Don't give me another headache, Dinsdale.

EARL OF GURNEY (*puts his hands together, Indian style*). Welcome, Dinsdale.

DINSDALE. Oh, ah, yes. How are you?

EARL OF GURNEY. Sometimes my spirit sinks below the high watermark in Palestine, but I'm adjusting gradually.

TUCKER uncovers a dish of muffins and sways slightly.

Mr Tucker, you look ill. Bed, Mr Tucker. Right now.

TUCKER. Thank you, my lord.

EARL OF GURNEY. Take a cup of Dr Langley's Root and Herb Bitters. It acts directly on the bowels and blood, eradicates all liver disorders, dyspepsia, dizziness, heartburn . . .

TUCKER (*exiting*). Yes, sir.

EARL OF GURNEY (*calling*). . . . . foul stomach and *piles*.

TUCKER is heard muttering agreement off.

For what I am about to receive may I make myself truly thankful. (*Eats muffin.*) I must soon be moving on. Sail to Wigan, Wrexham, Port Said and Crewe.

CLAIRE and DINSDALE exchange uneasy glances.

First I shall command the Pope to consecrate a planeload of

light-weight contraceptives for the priest-ridden Irish. (*Mimes blessing.*) 'Pax et benedícto . . . adjutorium nostrum. Dóminus vobíscum'. (*Chanting.*) Arise, shine for my light is come and the glory of the Lord is risen upon thee . . . (*Singing with actions.*) 'Here is the Drag, See how it goes; Down on the heels; Up on the toes. That's the way to the Varsity Drag.' (*He dances round in exuberant ragtime.*) 'Hotter than hot, Newer than new! Meaner than mean, Bluer than blue. Gets as much applause as waving the flag!'

TUCKER *appears in doorway Up Stage Centre with two solid, middle-aged* WOMEN *in grotesque hats.* CLAIRE *glares angrily at a horrified* DINSDALE.

TUCKER. Mrs Piggot-Jones – Mrs Treadwell.

EARL OF GURNEY (*singing at newcomers*). . . . 'You can pass many a class whether you're dumb or wise. If you all answer the call, when your professor cries . . .'

Suddenly, despite themselves, MRS PIGGOT-JONES, MRS TREADWELL *and* TUCKER *sweep irresistably Down Stage with the Earl, in an all-singing, all-dancing chorus line.*

EARL OF GURNEY, TWO WOMEN and TUCKER (*singing*). 'Everybody down on the heels, up on the toes, stay after school, learn how it goes: Everybody do the Varsity . . . Everybody do the Varsity . . . Everbody do the Varsity Drag!'

They finish in line Down Stage, arms outstretched to the audience, puzzled.

EARL OF GURNEY (*without pause*). Welcome, ladies. I'm the new Lord.

MRS TREADWELL, *a dumpy woman in straw hat decorated with wax fruit, gives a dazed smile, whilst the boney* MRS PIGGOT-JONES, *in tweed and trilby, lets out a bewildered grunt. Clutching his head,* TUCKER *weaves his way out.*

You know Lady Claire and my cousin Dinsdale?

DINSDALE. This is a surprise. Delightful though, delightful.

MRS TREADWELL (*recovering her natural obsequiousness*). Dear Mr Dinsdale, do forgive us, but we've come to try and persuade his lordship to open our little Church Fête. Do say yes, my lord.

EARL OF GURNEY. I always say yes, yes, whatever the question.

MRS TREADWELL (*delighted*). Your lordship.

MRS PIGGOT-JONES. Splendid!

CLAIRE. Now ladies, if you'll excuse us, we have a lot to do.

EARL OF GURNEY. Stay for tea. (*To* MRS TREADWELL.) You be mother.

Gurgles of delight from the two women. Whilst MRS TREADWELL *pours,* DINSDALE *looks uncertain, and* CLAIRE *watches with increasing tension.*

CLAIRE (*low*). Dinsdale, see if your father's come back.

DINSDALE *hurries out.*

EARL OF GURNEY. Now ladies, tell me my part in this gala opening. Do I charm bracelets, swing lead, break wind, pass water?

MRS TREADWELL. No, you make a speech.

EARL OF GURNEY. On what text, Mother Superior?

MRS PIGGOT-JONES. We leave that to the speaker. It can be any topic of general interest. Hanging, Immigration, the Stranglehold of the Unions. Anything . . .

MRS TREADWELL. So long as it isn't political.

EARL OF GURNEY. Nat-ur-ally.

MRS PIGGOT-JONES. As the Fête *is* in aid of the British Legion I've always felt the speeches should be something about Britain and our way of life.

EARL OF GURNEY (*off-handed*). Britain is an imaginary island off the continent of Europe, covering 93,982 square miles, with a population of over 52 million, lying in a westerly wind belt. A fly-blown speck in the North Sea, a country of cosmic unimportance in my sight. (*Sadly at them.*) You can't kick the natives in the back streets of Calcutta any more.

MRS TREADWELL (*giggling*). He's joking again. Aren't you, my lord?

MRS PIGGOT-JONES. I am not laughing, Pamela. I'm afraid we can't stay here, Lady Claire.

CLAIRE. Then for Christ's sake, go!

EARL OF GURNEY. Please don't go for my sake. (*Casually takes a bunch of imitation wax grapes from* MRS TREADWELL'S *hat and starts eating them.*) Hmm, delicious. Home-grown?

MRS TREADWELL. No, I bought them, I mean . . .

EARL OF GURNEY. I've decided to begin my second ministry at your gathering. Last time I preached the Word in Holy Galilee I spoke in parables. MISTAKE. Now I must speak plain. (*Crosses hand on chest.*) God is love.

MRS TREADWELL (*frightened*). Love?

EARL OF GURNEY. God is love as water is wet as jade is green as bread is life so God is love.

MRS TREADWELL *and* MRS PIGGOT-JONES *begin to back towards the door Up Stage Centre.* DINSDALE *is heard calling off beyond the french windows.*

EARL OF GURNEY (*advancing after them*). Mrs Pamela Treadwell, can you love? Can your blood bubble, flesh melt, thighs twitch, heart burst for love?

MRS TREADWELL. Your lordship, I'm a married woman.

EARL OF GURNEY. Sexual perversion is no sin.

DINSDALE (*voice off*). I say, have you seen my father?

EARL OF GURNEY (*advancing*). Remember the commandment I gave you, love one another as I loved you.

MRS PIGGOT-JONES (*retreating*). Stay back! My husband is a Master of Hounds!

EARL OF GURNEY. Fill your hearts, let your eyes sparkle, your soul dance. Be *bird-happy*!

MRS PIGGOT-JONES }
MRS TREADWELL   } Ahh!

Their nerve breaks. They turn and plunge for the door, but are frozen in mid-flight as they see the cross for the first time.

MRS PIGGOT-JONES. What is it?

EARL OF GURNEY. A Watusi walking-stick! Big people the Watusis. Listen, ladies.

But with cries of fear the two women rush Up Stage Centre. SIR CHARLES *appears in the doorway and is flattened by them as they charge out into the passage, followed by the* EARL, *who is heard calling:*

(*Voice off.*) Don't be frightened. Hear the word of the Lord.

SIR CHARLES (*picking himself up*). Treadwell . . . Piggot . . . What the blazes are they doing here? Great Scott, who's the idiot responsible?

DINSDALE (*voice off*). I say, I say, have you seen my father?

CLAIRE *gestures expressively*.

SIR CHARLES. Oh. Dinsdale.

CLAIRE. You'll have to do something about that boy.

SIR CHARLES. He'll soon be off our hands. Old Barrington-Cochran's on his last legs. That means a by-election.

CLAIRE. Dinsdale's such a fool.

SIR CHARLES. One time thought of bringing him into the business, but it's too risky. Can't have Dinsdale messing about with money. He's proved disappointing.

DINSDALE *re-enters*.

DINSDALE. Oh, there you are.

CLAIRE. What did Sir Humphrey say?

SIR CHARLES. Gave me a lot o' expensive legal fal-de-roll. As it stands, there's no chance of breaking the Will. Only one possible solution. A male heir.

CLAIRE. A what?

SIR CHARLES. If Jack had a son, Sir Humphrey says we could have him certified quietly, because everything could then pass to the heir. We'd administer the estate till the boy came of age. That way everything'd remain in the family.

CLAIRE (*sarcastically*). Oh, brilliant. A small point, but before he can have an heir, our lunatic nephew has to be married.

SIR CHARLES. Exactly. And the sooner the better!

The EARL *enters Up Stage Centre playing a flute.*

EARL OF GURNEY. Married?

SIR CHARLES. Yes, J.C., you should take a wife.

EARL OF GURNEY. Who from?

CLAIRE. I'm sure we'll be able to find you a suitable young goddess.

SIR CHARLES. Most appropriate, eh-eh?

They chuckle to themselves.

EARL OF GURNEY. But I can't marry a second time.

They immediately stop chuckling.

SIR CHARLES. A *second* . . .

CLAIRE (*sceptically*). Second wife? You believe you're already married?

EARL OF GURNEY. On August 28th in the year of me, 1961.

SIR CHARLES *looks across doubtfully at* CLAIRE *who shakes her head.*

Somerset House records will confirm. Father wanted it kept secret for some reason.

He walks away to Wings Right playing the 'Drinking Song' from 'La Traviata' on the flute.

SIR CHARLES. This wife of yours? What's her name?

EARL OF GURNEY. Marguerite Gautier.

SIR CHARLES. French.

DINSDALE (*slowly*). Marguerite Gautier? . . . Gautier? . . . I say, isn't that the 'Lady of the Camelias'?

EARL OF GURNEY. You know her too? Wonderful!

He exits playing the aria. DINSDALE *and* SIR CHARLES *exchange looks and rush after him. Blackout.*

SCENE SEVEN

Spot up on white screen lowered Down Stage Left to show CLAIRE *and* DR HERDER *talking.*

DR HERDER. Of course there's no question of marriage. He has no wife, but he believes he has, which is the same thing.

CLAIRE. Why did he pick on Marguerite Gautier?

DR HERDER. Another martyr for love. His delusions are of a piece. Marguerite is the only person he trusts.

CLAIRE. Why does he keep on about love?

DR HERDER. Because he hasn't had any. Or wasn't shown any, which is just as bad. He wants us all to love goodness. To love goodness is to love God, to love God is to love the 14th Earl of Gurney.

CLAIRE. That's very clever. Is it the truth?

DR HERDER. Lady Claire, don't come to me for the truth, only explanations.

CLAIRE. Does any of his talk mean anything?

DR HERDER. To him, yes. Your nephew suffers from the delusion that the world we live in is based on the fact that God is love.

CLAIRE. Can't he see what the world's really like?

DR HERDER. No. But he will, when he's cured.

CLAIRE. Can I ask one more question?

DR HERDER. If it's as revealing as the others.

CLAIRE. Why does he hate being called Jack?

DR HERDER. Because it's his real name. Naturally he rejects it violently. If he ever answers to the name of Jack, he'll be on the road to sanity.

CLAIRE. How are my questions revealing?

DR HERDER. The first one you asked me was about love.

White screen taken up and lights up as they move into the drawing-room of Gurney Manor where TUCKER *is pouring drinks.*

CLAIRE. This is our own Tucker, Dr Herder. He's been with the family for over forty years.

TUCKER. Man and snivelling boy, sir.

DR HERDER. Really. How do you find the new Earl, Tucker?

TUCKER. By sniffing. He's a Gurney, sir. A real Gurney.

DR HERDER (*puzzled*). You don't find him odd?

TUCKER. Odd? Soda, sir?

DR HERDER. Please. Yes, odd. Peculiar.

TUCKER. Oh, you mean *nutty*. Yes, he's a nut-case all right, but then so are most of these titled flea-bags. Rich nobs and privileged arse-holes can afford to be bonkers. Living in a dream world, aren't they, sir? Don't know what time o' day it is. Life's made too easy for 'em. Don't have to earn a living so they can do just what they want to. Most of us'd look pretty cracked if we went round doing just what we wanted to, eh, sir?

DR HERDER (*bewildered*). Yes, I suppose . . .

CLAIRE (*smiling*). The late Earl left Tucker twenty thousand pounds. Since then he's been very outspoken.

TUCKER *hands a drink to* DR HERDER *and another to* CLAIRE.

CLAIRE. Not for me, Tucker.

TUCKER. Waste not want not. (*He drinks.*) Doctor, you might take a look at my back. The ol' lumbago's acting up again.

SIR CHARLES *and* DINSDALE *enter arguing with the* EARL OF GURNEY.

DINSDALE (*gesturing with the book*). But I've shown you it's in here. *The Lady of the Camelias* by Alexandre Dumas. *Camille.*

The opera by Verdi *La Traviata*. Same woman. A figure of romance.

EARL OF GURNEY. My dear chap, you prove my point ipso facto, a divine figure of romance. Paul, what a pleasant surprise.

DR HERDER. How are you?

EARL OF GURNEY. In the middle of a debate on the existence of my wife Marguerite. With passions roused and intellects sharpened, pray continue, Dinsdale Gurney.

SIR CHARLES. I give up. You did say it'd be impossible to convince him, doctor.

DR HERDER. Impossible. But you can try.

CLAIRE *takes the book from* DINSDALE, *opens it and shows it to the* EARL.

CLAIRE. Look. it's a play, *The Lady of the Camelias*. Fiction.

EARL OF GURNEY (*taking book*). Ah, yes, a biography of my Marguerite – affectionately known as La Dame Aux Camelias. (*Sternly*.) Dinsdale, this book looks tired from over-reading. You should let it out more.

CLAIRE. You aren't married. The woman doesn't exist.

EARL OF GURNEY. Come, come, you exaggerate unduly. (*Makes circular movement with right hand*.) You'll be saying I'm not God, Jesus, and the Holy Ghost next.

CLAIRE. You're not! God wouldn't be so ridiculous waving his arms like a maniac dressed in a white suit and carnation.

EARL OF GURNEY. The prophet Ezekiel lay three hundred days on his left side and forty days on his right. He cut his hair and divided it into three parts. The first part he burnt, the second he chopped into pieces, the third he scattered into the wind. Ridiculous, mad, certifiable. It was all merely a sign of something more important. God teaches by signs as well as words.

DR HERDER (*with satisfaction*). He can defend his beliefs with great skill.

DINSDALE. All right, if you're God, reveal your Godhead.

The EARL *immediately starts to unzip his flies.*

No, no. A miracle. Show us a miracle.

EARL OF GURNEY. A miracle. (*Holds out his hand.*) Here's a miracle.

DINSDALE. Where?

EARL OF GURNEY. This hand. This city network of tissues, nerves, muscles, ligaments, carpals, metacarpals and phalanges. And what about the hairy-nosed wombat?

DINSDALE. Not that sort. A miracle like the making of loaves and fishes.

EARL OF GURNEY. Oh, those. You see ten billion million miracles a day, yet you want your conjuring tricks, your pretty flim-flams, from the incense burners. I can't raise Lazarus again, he's decomposed, so bring me that table.

CLAIRE. What are you going to do?

EARL OF GURNEY. A grade-one Galilee miracle.

CLAIRE *starts to say something but* DR HERDER *gestures. He nods to* DINSDALE, *who drags the coffee table to Stage Centre, and steps back uncertainly. They are all roughly grouped behind it.*

EARL OF GURNEY. Instead of raising Laz, I'll raise yon table.

SIR CHARLES. That table?

EARL OF GURNEY. Ten feet. Not by mirrors or crippled midgets behind black curtains, but by the power of love.

CLAIRE. Just love?

EARL OF GURNEY. It moves mountains, and makes the puny weed split the rock. Look.

All eyes now sceptically on the table. The EARL *stretches out his hands, palms upwards. As he slowly starts to raise them, lights imperceptibly begin to dim.*

Believe in me, in love, in loving goodness, raise yourself up . . . Rise, up, up. See, see . . . slowly, slowly. One foot, two feet, three, four . . . slowly up . . . five, six, seven . . . rise, rise up . . . Eight, nine, ten. (*His arms are now above his head.*)

There! The table floats ten feet in space.

TUCKER (*pointing up excitedly*). Ahhh! Look, I see it! Up there! (*He lurches forward, grasping a half-empty whisky decanter.*) Sh-miracle, sh-miracle, halleluja sh-miracle. Praise the Lord and pass t' ammunition.

SIR CHARLES. Drunken lout!

TUCKER *collapses in a stupor in a chair. The spell is broken.* CLAIRE *crosses angrily to the table.*

CLAIRE. It didn't rise. (*Raps it.*) Here it is.

EARL OF GURNEY (*making circle with hand*). Tucker saw, believed, yeees.

CLAIRE. Did you see it, doctor?

DR HERDER. No.

SIR CHARLES. 'Course not. Damned rot.

EARL OF GURNEY (*shakes his head*). Into any platinum pressure-cooker, grrh grrhh shurhh . . .

CLAIRE. There's no miracle. No wife. She doesn't exist. She's fiction. Part of a play. An opera. She's not flesh and blood. Not real.

EARL OF GURNEY (*flapping hands, disturbed*). Gross gree crull craaah . . .

DR HERDER. Shhh. Listen.

From the corridor beyond the darkened room comes the sound of a woman singing. 'Go diam fie – ga-ca-e-ra-pi-do – e il gan dio dell 'a-mo-re . . .' It grows louder. We can hear the rustle of crinoline. They turn towards the doorway. Up Stage Centre: The Lady of the Camelias stands there, in a Spot, carrying a camellia and singing the 'Drinking Song' from 'La Traviata'.

LA DAME AUX CAMELIAS (*singing*). 'Eun fior che na – sce e muo – re, ne, piu si puv go-der – Go-diam, c-In-vi-ta, c'in-vi-taun, fervi do-ae-cen-to-la-sin-gheer . . .'

EARL OF GURNEY. Marguerite!

Blackout.

SCENE EIGHT

Lights up on the Drawing Room of Gurney Manor where CLAIRE *and* SIR CHARLES *are arguing with measured ferocity.*

CLAIRE. How *dare* you bring that woman here?

SIR CHARLES. You should be grateful to Miss Shelley.

CLAIRE. Grace Shelley is your mistress. Hairs on the collar, stains on the sheets, I know you.

SIR CHARLES. And I know you. Miss Shelly's just a hard-working girl.

CLAIRE. Only on her back. First you try and palm her off on to your own brother.

SIR CHARLES. Ralph needed a wife. He took a fancy to Miss Shelley.

CLAIRE. That didn't work, so now you try her for the son. It's incestuous.

SIR CHARLES. Don't talk to me about incest. I remember young Jeremy Gore. You knew his father and I went to school together. But you went ahead and seduced his son. That's incest, madam.

CLAIRE (*wearily*). What's the use? It isn't worth raising one's voice. But why the devil didn't you warn us?

SIR CHARLES. No time. After what that 'Trick-Cyclist' chappie told me I knew we'd never convince Jack he wasn't married and this Marguerite filly didn't exist. So I 'phoned Grace and explained the position. She got dressed up in some theatrical togs and came down. Put me on a first-rate show, I thought.

CLAIRE. It had impact.

SIR CHARLES. Anyway, Jack believes she's Marguerite. All she has to do now is convince him he has to marry her again. Shouldn't be difficult.

CLAIRE. Dr Herder'll object.

SIR CHARLES. Object? He's got no right to object to anything, he's not family.

CLAIRE. He could make things difficult by having Jack declared insane before he's produced an heir for you.

SIR CHARLES. Damn kraut! You'd better keep an eye on him, my dear. I'll have my hands full getting Grace married and pregnant.

GRACE SHELLEY *comes in Up Stage Centre, a blonde, still dressed in a low-cut ball gown, she gestures with the camelia.*

GRACE. *What an entrance.* Beautiful, *but* beautiful. The look on your faces. I should have stuck to the classics. I was trained for it y'know – Mrs Phoebe Giavanno, 27A Brixton Hill. She sang with Caruso. Grand old lady. 'From the diaphragm dear, from the diaphragm.' Always said I had the voice. Let's face it, Bert Bacharach is great but he's not in the same class as Giuseppi Verdi. Phew, this dress's tight. How did they breathe? I feel constipated. (*Notices cross by the door for the first time.*) *Christy O'Connor,* what's that? Is the roof falling in or something?

CLAIRE. Any minute now. (*Moving Up Stage.*) Your flower's wilting, my dear.

GRACE. (*waving it cheerfully*). Can't be. It's wax.

CLAIRE. Careful your husband-to-be doesn't eat it for breakfast.

She exits.

GRACE. You're right, Charlie Boy. She's an ice-cold Biddy.

SIR CHARLES. Too clever by half, that woman. But I get things done my way. She doesn't know what she wants.

GRACE. But I do, Charlie Boy. Lady Grace, Lady Grace Gurney, the Countess of Gurney.

SIR CHARLES. Now look here, Grace, you mustn't call me Charlie Boy. We have to be careful.

GRACE. If that's what you want.

SIR CHARLES. It's not what I want. It's what has to be. I'm very fond of you, m'dear, you know that.

GRACE. You've a funny way of showing it. First you push me into the arms of your half-dead half-brother, and then on to his looney son.

SIR CHARLES. I'd make any sacrifice for the sake of the family. You sure you can handle the situation? Tricky an' all, marrying a man who thinks he's God.

GRACE. It happens all the time. (*Crossing to french windows.*) On certain nights. In front of the right audience. When the magic works. I've known what it's like to be a God too. (*Sees someone outside.*) Ah, there he is on the lawn. Let's get the show on the road. Damn, where's my lousy camelia. (SIR CHARLES *hands it to her, she hitches up her dress.*) I'll be glad to get out of this clobber. (*Pats bare bosom.*) No wonder she was dying of consumption. (*Coughs hoarsely.*)

SIR CHARLES. Careful now.

GRACE. Trust me, Charlie B . . . Charles. I've got too much at stake to blow it.

Holding the camelia modestly across her chest, and smiling wanly, she glides out. SIR CHARLES *looks at the audience.*

SIR CHARLES. Damned plucky filly.

DINSDALE *enters Up Stage Centre.*

DINSDALE. I say, Mother's just told me this Lady-of-the-Camelia-woman's a fake. I know J.C.'s as batty as a moor-hen, sir, but this isn't playing the game.

SIR CHARLES. Game? What game? It's no game, sir! This is real.

Blackout.

SCENE NINE

Footlights up immediately. A metal sun lowered from Flies. The
EARL *lying Down Stage Right, rouses himself as* GRACE *enters Wings*
Left.

EARL OF GURNEY. My dreams made flesh or a reasonable
facsimile thereforeto. (*Gets up, bows politely.*) Eh – bien,
comment allez-vous, madame?

GRACE. Sorry, I don't speak French.

EARL OF GURNEY. German? Italian? Albanian? Yiddish?

GRACE. No. English.

EARL OF GURNEY. English. Why didn't you say so before?
Nothing to be ashamed of, hard language to master. But we
can't play this love-scene with mere words, be they English,
Japanese or Serbo-Croat.

GRACE. Love scene? What now?

EARL OF GURNEY. Love isn't just for one season. (*Smiles, flapping
arms like a bird.*) Hweet, hweep.

GRACE. Hweet?

EARL OF GURNEY (*arms quivering*). Tsiff-tsiff-tsiff. (*Hopping.*)
Chiff-chaff-chaff-chaff.

GRACE (*laughing*). Oh, well. (*Flaps arms.*) Chiff-chaff.

They circle round each other with tiny bird movements; GRACE
bending forward and hopping, the EARL *bobbing his head and*
making low loping sweeps.

EARL OF GURNEY (*long drawn-out, high-pitched*). Pioo . . . pioo .
. . pioo.

GRACE. Cuckoo!

EARL OF GURNEY (*crescendo*). Pioo.

GRACE (*breathless*). I'll bet even Ludovic Koch wasn't made love
to with bird cries.

EARL OF GURNEY. What else would you like? The Grand Canyon?
A musical teacup? A hundred pre-sold holy wafers? A disused
banana factory? Absolution?

GRACE. A white wedding.

EARL OF GURNEY. Will next Tuesday suit you?

GRACE. You deserve a big kiss.

EARL OF GURNEY. Not here in the garden. Last time I was kissed in the garden – it turned out rather awkward.

GRACE. Ah, but Judas was a man.

EARL OF GURNEY (*nodding*). Hmm, yes, a strange business. (GRACE *laughs*.) Who are you?

GRACE. A woman.

EARL OF GURNEY. Descended from Eve.

GRACE. No, a doorstep. I'm an orphan.

EARL OF GURNEY. Then we'll be orphans together, Marguerite.

GRACE. Call me Grace, as I don't speak French.

EARL OF GURNEY. A good name. It means a gift of faith.

GRACE. Which is what I have in you. I'm holding you to that wedding.

EARL OF GURNEY. Hold hard. You'll be my Queen of Queens.

GRACE. I'll be satisfied with Lady Gurney.

EARL OF GURNEY (*takes her hands*). And I say unto you, thou shall love the Lord thy God with all thy heart and with all thy soul and with all thy mind.

GRACE. I do.

EARL OF GURNEY. I want to show you the bottom drawer of my soul. (*Suddenly joyful.*) Oh, but I'm happy, I'm the sunshine-man, the driver of the gravy-train, chu-chu-chu. (GRACE *laughs*.) It's all so simple, for me. Paradise is just a smiling face. What's it for you?

GRACE. Me? Paradise? Oh, a fireplace. A cosy room.

EARL OF GURNEY (*nodding*). A little nest . . .

Hand in hand they go into a dance routine to Wings Right.

GRACE (*singing*). 'That nestles where the roses bloom.'

EARL OF GURNEY (*singing; indicating partner*). 'Sweet Gracey and me . . .'

GRACE (*singing: looking at him*). 'And a baby makes three.'

GRACE (*singing*).
EARL OF GURNEY (*singing*). } 'We're going to our blue heaven.'

GRACE kisses him, exits Wings Right. The EARL *takes out a pocket telescope, opens it out and stares after her as* DINSDALE *enters sulkily.*

DINSDALE. What are you looking at?

EARL OF GURNEY (*handing him telescope*). Beauty in motion.

DINSDALE (*looking*). I can't see a thing.

EARL OF GURNEY. Because you're not looking with the eyes of love.

DINSDALE (*coming to a decision*). Hang it all, whatever else you are, you're still a Gurney. That Camelia woman's really Grace Shelley. Close friend of my father's. He's put her up to it.

The EARL *stops humming.*

Got her to dress like that. Absolutely ridiculous.

The EARL *shivers with cold.*

He wants you married off.

The EARL *puts his hand to his face; when he takes it away his features are covered with white make-up.*

Mother's in it too. Shouldn't be surprised if even old Tuck knew. Everbody but me.

EARL OF GURNEY (*shrinking miserably*). Stop! You're making me a crippled dwarf, a deformed midget, a crippled newt!

DINSDALE (*sees the* EARL *with bent knees, now half-size*). What're you doing?

Stage Lights Up.

EARL OF GURNEY. It's your negative insinuendo.

DINSDALE. Insinuendo?

EARL OF GURNEY (*making circle with right hand*). Insinuendo is insinuation towards innuendo, brought on by increased negativism out of a negative reaction to your father's positivism. (*Takes out glasses, breaks them, puts half frame over one eye, peers up at* DINSDALE.) Your negativism is fully charged. I see by the Habeas Corpus parchment round your neck.

DINSDALE. I don't know what the devil you're on about, but I resent your attitude. I only told you about Grace Shelley . . .

EARL OF GURNEY (*tearing off his jacket and shirt*). She's my Righteous-Ideal-Planned-Wife. Don't forget, besides being God, Christ and the Holy Ghost, I'm also a San D., B.F.C. and D.A.C. – Doctor of Sanitation, Bachelor of Family Life, and Doctor of Air Conditioning. Please remember that you're dealing with the Big One. I've told aged Tucker. Injecting me with his Kremlin-plot negative-microbes. I said verbatim. Feeling persecuted is paranoid schizophrenia-wretches. Dr H. suffered from it. But watched they said against me . . .one of the signs. Many poor 'erders' Dancing Academy. I *am* being EVERYBODY they CRIED . . . whrr! rr! . . . rrr! Krr-krr-krek!

He scuttles absurdly Up Stage and clambers on to the cross. On the back of his vest are painted the words 'God is Love'. DINSDALE *exits as the* EARL *clings to the cross, his painful, metallic cries growing louder and louder. The lights dim down. The cries stop abruptly.*

SCENE TEN

Lights Up as BISHOP LAMPTON *and* SIR CHARLES *enter Up Stage Centre glancing with distaste at the* EARL, *stretched out on the cross.*

BISHOP LAMPTON. I will not solemnize any marriage, even of my own nephew, during the period from Advent Sunday till eight days after Epiphany. So it must be on Tuesday the 12th. Eight a.m. Private Chapel. Ordinary Licence. But I have grave misgivings, Charles. Grave misgivings.

SIR CHARLES. Misgivings? About Jack?

BISHOP LAMPTON. No, about the bride, Miss Shelley. Who is she? What is she? I fear she may be using this marriage merely to advance her social position. I hear she's an 'entertainer'.

SIR CHARLES. I'll vouch for Grace Shelley.

BISHOP LAMPTON. No doubt. I hear she's a most handsome woman. I venture you've been dazzled by her charms. 'A woman whose heart is snares and nets.' I, however, due to my cloth – and age – can take a more dispassionate view of her character and motives.

SIR CHARLES. Dash it all, Bertie, you know the position. We can't be fussy. Grace – Miss Shelley – is the best we can come up with. This is a crisis.

BISHOP LAMPTON. Even so, we shouldn't be too hasty. God in his infinite wisdom has clouded our nephew's senses. But it can only be temporary. I take it as a sure sign of hope that his delusions are at least of a *religious* nature. Consider the consequences of this mis-mating, Charles. When he recovers, he'll find himself married to a woman who is frankly not suitable. And he *will* recover. God is merciful.

SIR CHARLES. Can't wait on God's mercy, Bertie, everything's going to pot. Dr Herder agrees.

BISHOP LAMPTON. Dr Herder? 'Herder'? Is he English?

SIR CHARLES. No.

BISHOP LAMPTON. Ahh . . .

SIR CHARLES. Mark my words, this'll be the making of Jack.

BISHOP LAMPTON (*sagely*). It's true, there's nothing like marriage to bring a fella' to his senses.

They exit Up Stage as Spot Up Down Stage Left on DR HERDER *and* CLAIRE *standing in front of a white backing lowered from the Flies. A couch to Left.*

CLAIRE. My husband's an idiot.

DR HERDER (*icily*). I've no idea what he's playing at, and it's not strictly my concern. The Earl's no longer under my care. But that charade with Miss Shelley made me feel an absolute fool, and I don't care to underestimate myself.

CLAIRE. I apologize. Charles has some idea Jack might accept her if she dressed up as the Lady of the Camelias.

DR HERDER. Sometimes it's very easy to forget that outside this comedy Sir Charles occupies a position of responsibility and power. I just learned he's on the Board of the Guggenheim Research Foundation. Extraordinary.

CLAIRE. Ah, yes, he mentioned you were asking for a grant. You won't have any trouble.

DR HERDER. It's only a nominal 130,000. For the study of paranoid schizophrenic rats.

CLAIRE (*sitting on couch*). Sounds fascinating.

DR HERDER. I should have said electrically controlled paranoid rats.

CLAIRE. Electrically?

DR HERDER. We insert very fine silver wires into the rat's midbrain. The rat's behaviour is controlled by the strength of the current passed through them. By pressing a button and stimulating one area in its mid-brain, the rat is made to feel threatened. It attacks any rat in sight. There's really no threat, but the mid-brain can't tell the difference. Roughly the same thing happens with a human paranoid. No silver wires, but an unknown area of his brain is stimulated, and he feels threatened without cause. Naturally, men aren't rats.

CLAIRE. Only a man would say so.

DR HERDER (*smiling*). I'm speaking bioloically. Eventually we'll have to conduct similar experiments on the human brain.

CLAIRE. Today rats. Tomorrow the world. Who will you wire for visions?

DR HERDER. First of all myself, naturally.

CLAIRE (*taking off glove*). I see. Then if I press a button, you'd limp for me, feel fear and love . . .

DR HERDER. Love? No. Desire, yes.

CLAIRE. By pressing a button? (*Raises finger and mimes pressing.*)

DR HERDER (*covers her hand*). Not too hard. I might get over-stimulated and lose control.

CLAIRE. You, lose control? Think of the risk, doctor.

DR HERDER. There's only one commandment a doctor need ever worry about. 'Thou shalt not advertise.'

DR HERDER *kisses* CLAIRE'S *hand. Spot out.*

SCENE ELEVEN

Lights Up. The EARL *stops jerking on the cross.*

EARL OF GURNEY. My heart rises with the sun. I'm purged of doubts and negative innuendos. Today I want to bless everything! Bless the crawfish that has a scuttling walk, bless the trout, the pilchard and periwinkle. Bless Ted Smoothey of 22 East Hackney Road – with a name like that he needs blessing. Bless the mealy-redpole, the black-gloved wallaby and W.C. Fields, who's dead but lives on. Bless the skunk, bless the red-bellied lemur, bless 'Judo' Al Hayes and Ski-Hi-Lee. Bless the snotty-nosed giraffe, bless the buffalo, bless the Piccadilly Match King, bless the pigmy hippo, bless the weasel, bless the mighty cockroach, bless me. Today's my wedding day!

Wedding bells peal out.

SCENE TWELVE

Screen lowered immediately Down Stage Centre, cutting out the cross from view. On it, a photo-collage of Society weddings. BISHOP LAMPTON *enters imposingly, Wings Right, in full regalia, followed by* CLAIRE *and* DINSDALE. TUCKER *hobbles in from Wings Left. They cross slowly Down Stage Centre. With* CLAIRE *and* DINSDALE *on his right, and* TUCKER *on his left.* LAMPTON *turns and faces the audience.*

The bells stop ringing. An organ plays 'The Wedding March' as GRACE *in a white wedding dress and an apprehensive* SIR CHARLES *enter Wings Right. They all wait for the groom. The* EARL *scampers in Wings Right in a cut-away jacket, no shirt and broken glasses and flute hanging from his chest.* BISHOP LAMPTON *shudders.*

BISHOP LAMPTON (*reading from prayer book*). 'Dearly beloved, we are gathered together here in the sight of God . . .'

The EARL *clasps his hands above his head and shakes them triumphantly.*

'. . . and in the face of this company to join together this man and this woman in Holy Matrimony, which is an honourable estate.'

EARL OF GURNEY. Instituted by me in the time of man's innocence.

GRACE *puts her fingers to his lips.*

BISHOP LAMPTON (*looking up warningly*). 'Therefore if anyone can show just cause why they may not be lawfully joined together, let him now speak, or else hereafter forever hold his peace.'

CLAIRE, DINSDALE *and* SIR CHARLES *stare deliberately at the audience. Silence.*

TUCKER. Load o' British jelly-meat whiskers! Stand up on your tea-soaked haunches and stop it. Piddling, half-dead helots.

SIR CHARLES. Quiet, man. Show some respect.

TUCKER (*indignantly*). I'm always respectful. S'what I'm paid for. No one can say I'm not respectful. (*Removes his false teeth.*) There.

SIR CHARLES. 'I require and charge you both that if either of you have an impediment why ye may not be lawfully joined together in matrimony ye do now confess it.'

EARL OF GURNEY (*quietly*). Yes, I'm afraid I do know an impediment.

His family glance anxiously at each other.

CLAIRE. It's only a rhetorical question, like all the others in the wedding service.

EARL OF GURNEY. 'Tis no good glossing o'er the facts. Certain R.C. knackers think I'm already married to the Virgin Mary.

SIR CHARLES. We're not concerned with what other people think.

BISHOP LAMPTON. Especially not Roman Catholics. 'Wilt thou have this woman to thy wedded wife, to live together after God's ordinance in the holy state of matrimony? Wilt thou love her . . .'

EARL OF GURNEY. From the bottom of my soul to the tip of my penis, like the sun in its brightness, the moon in its beauty, the heavens in their emptiness, streams in their gentleness, no breeze stirs that doesn't bear my love.

BISHOP LAMPTON. Blasphemous . . .!

GRACE. But will you love *me*?

EARL OF GURNEY. I will.

BISHOP LAMPTON (*quickly to* GRACE). 'Wilt thou have this man to thy wedded husband, to live together after God's ordinance.'

GRACE. I will.

BISHOP LAMPTON. Who gives this woman to this man?

SIR CHARLES. I do.

BISHOP LAMPTON (*to* EARL). Repeat after me, I, J.C., take thee Grace Shelley to my wedded wife . . .

EARL OF GURNEY. I, J.C. the Holy Flying Roller, the Morning Star, known to his intimates as the Naz, take thee Marguerite, called Grace Shelley because she doesn't speak French.

BISHOP LAMPTON *shudders and plunges on.*

BISHOP LAMPTON (*to* GRACE). Repeat after me.

GRACE. I know the lines. I, Grace Shelley, take thee J.C. to my wedded husband to have and to hold from this day forward, for better for worse, for richer for poorer, in sickness and in health, to love and to cherish till death do us part, according to God's holy ordinance and thereto I give thee my troth.

SIR CHARLES *steps foward with the ring and hurriedly puts it on* GRACE's *finger*.

BISHOP LAMPTON (*with increasing speed*). 'For as much as these two persons have consented together in holy wedlock, I pronounce that they be man and wife together. In-the-name-of-the-father-and-of-the-Son-and-of-the-Holy-Ghost-whom-God-hath-joined-together-let-no-man-put-asunder . . .' (*One last effort.*) Lord have mercy upon us!

ALL. Christ have mercy upon us.

BISHOP LAMPTON. Lord have mercy upon us!

BISHOP LAMPTON *sinks to the floor exhausted, but* DINSDALE *and* SIR CHARLES *jerk him up as the bells peal and the organ booms*.

SCENE THIRTEEN

Bells and organ fade down. The screen is taken up to show a small buffet has been laid out – drinks, sandwiches, and a wedding cake. The EARL *picks up* GRACE *and carries her laughing into the drawing-room.*

DINSDALE (*to* BISHOP LAMPTON). Frankly, I thought it was going to be a jolly sight worse.

BISHOP LAMPTON (*being helped out of his vestments by* TUCKER). Worse? How could it have been worse? When that woman entered in *white* I knew. (*Shudders.*) An actress, married in white, *white*.

GRACE. Hildegarde! This is a bit tatty. No reception, no guests, a few curled sandwiches and a deformed wedding cake. William Hickey won't give us a mention.

TUCKER. It's not my fault, your ladyship.

GRACE. 'Your ladyship.' (*Brightening.*) That's better. Now watch 'em creep and crawl at Harrods.

BISHOP LAMPTON *slumps down on a chair whilst the* EARL *hands* SIR CHARLES *and* DINSDALE *paper hats and coloured balloons. They put on the hats.*

SIR CHARLES (*to* GRACE). We thought you'd prefer a quiet affair.

GRACE. It's like a wet Monday in Warrington. What about a toast to the newly-weds or something? Let's try and keep it a bit trad.

SIR CHARLES. Oh, very well. Ladies and gentlemen – to the long life, prosperity and happiness of the bride and groom.

They drink.

EARL OF GURNEY (*picking up knife*). Thank you, ladies and gentlemen, in reply I name this ship 'Loving Kindness'. May I keep her and all who sail in her. (*Cuts wedding cake.*)

TUCKER. Ah, your ladyship, you should have seen the late Earl's wedding. Over five hundred guests. The créme de menthe. Wastrels all! Lords of conspicuous consumption.

SIR CHARLES *has taken* GRACE *aside.*

SIR CHARLES (*low*). Can't say I fancy the idea of you alone with him.

GRACE (*low, angry*). Everything's still yours, even if you've given it away.

EARL OF GURNEY. Good. Let's have a minute's silence.

CLAIRE. What for?

EARL OF GURNEY. For all the dead books of World War I. For Mr Moto, the Cisco Kid and Me. Muffle the drums, beat the retreat. Quiet, sshh, silence . . .

The sudden silence is physical. Even after only a few seconds the tension grows. The strain is too much. All burst out at once –

'Why the devil . . .' 'I say . . .' 'Hell . . .!'

(*Sadly.*) Terrible, isn't it? That's why I have to talk, sing, dance.

GRACE (*glancing at* SIR CHARLES). And make love?

TUCKER (*singing in hoarse croak*). 'Oh, how we danced on the night we were wed . . .'

While he cavorts around, GRACE *takes the* EARL'S *arm and they slip away Up Stage Centre.*

'We pledged our true love and a word wasn't said.' My mother loved that song. Mammy! Mammy! You weighed twenty stone but you were my little Mammy.

SIR CHARLES. Tucker!

TUCKER. I'm sorry, sir. I thought you might wish me to liven up this wake.

SIR CHARLES (*noticing bride and groom are missing*). Where have they gone?

CLAIRE. Upstairs.

DINSDALE. Must say I wouldn't much like to be in her shoes tonight.

TUCKER. Not her shoes he'll be in, Master Dinsdale, sir.

BISHOP LAMPTON (*shuddering*). White . . .

SIR CHARLES (*angrily*). You never stop talking, Bertie. All of you sneering, sniggering. (*Lights dim down.*) We've got to pull together in this. Families like ours set the tone. Doesn't help poking and prying into personal lives. The strength of the English people lies in their inhibitions. What are they doing up there? (*He now stands in Single Spot Down Stage Left, still wearing a paper hat with a tiny bell at the end.*) You go to any foreign country and see the difference. There's always some scruffy chappie on a street corner who wants to tell you all about his love life, and sell you a strip of dirty postcards. What are they doing up there? Sacrifices must be made. Nothing more to be said. (*Looks up.*) *What . . . are . . . they . . . doing*

. . . up . . . there?

Spot out.

SCENE FOURTEEN

Spot up immediately on the four-poster bed and a chair. GRACE *is stripping to music played softly over. Her movements are provocative, but utterly unselfconscious. Stepping out of her wedding dress,* GRACE *bends to pick it up. She drapes it over the chair.*

GRACE. I always get first night nerves. Any good performer does. You have to be keyed up to give a good show. I've done it all, from Stanislavski to Strip. Never think I once worked as a stripper, would you? It's true, as God is my witness – no, you weren't there, were you, J.C.? Greasy make-up towels, cracked mirrors, rhinestones and beads. What a world. (*Takes off stocking and throws is absently into audience.*) I sang 'This Can't Be Love'. Funny, I did the same act later at the 'Pigalle' for twice the money without removing a stitch. (*Proudly.*) Of course, some women can strip without taking their clothes off. (*She sits on a chair and takes off other stocking.*) Nobody could call me undersexed, but I could never get worked up watching some man strip down to his suspenders and jockstrap. Where's the fun? I suppose some people just enjoy the smell of a steak better than the steak itself. (*Throws stocking into audience.*) If my mother could see me now – it's what she always wanted for me – the Big Time. She never forgave Dad for being born in Clapham. Guess she found it hard to settle down to civilian life after being in a touring company of *Chu Chin Chow*. Nobody need worry about me fitting in. (*Walks momentarily into darkness, left.*) All I have to do is play it cool. (*Reappears into Spot, in black nightdress, miming drinking tea with finger cocked up.*) I can cock my little finger with the best. (*Calls Wings Right.*) What you doing in there, Honey?

She stares as the EARL *enters unsteadily from Wings Right, in white pyjamas and riding a one-wheel bicycle.*

It's ridiculous! It's not dignified!

EARL OF GURNEY (*wobbling*). Dignity has nothing to do with divinity.

GRACE (*sudden panic*). Not here! Not now! A *bike*? You're mad.

EARL OF GURNEY. Don't be frightened.

GRACE (*recovering*). I'm not frightened. But I didn't expect to see my husband riding a one-wheel bike on his wedding night.

EARL OF GURNEY. It's the only way to travel. (*Jumps off bike.*) Remember, God loves you, God wants you, God needs you. Let's to bed.

Spot fades out. Music swells up. From out of the darkness the beating of giant wings as a great bird hovers overhead, followed by the sound of rain falling heavily.

SCENE FIFTEEN

Lights up on dressing-room to show SIR CHARLES *standing by the french-windows staring out moodily at the rain.* GRACE *enters.*

GRACE. It was a damn long night. I'm starving.

SIR CHARLES. What happened?

GRACE. Happened?

SIR CHARLES (*impatiently*). Last night. What did he do?

GRACE. Rode around on a one-wheel bicycle.

SIR CHARLES. Filthy beast! . . . That must be the Guv'nor's old bike. The attic's full of his junk. So he just rode around all night, then?

GRACE. First the bike, then me.

SIR CHARLES. Oh.

GRACE. His mind may be wonky but there's nothing wrong with the rest of his anatomy.

SIR CHARLES (*gloomily*). We Gurneys have always been damnably virile.

GRACE. I thought you'd be delighted to find he's not impotent.

SIR CHARLES (*frowning*). I am. I am. Delighted.

> CLAIRE *enters briskly.* SIR CHARLES *quickly lets go of* GRACE'S *hand.*

CLAIRE. 'morning. Well, what happened last night? Was it successful?

GRACE. I should have sold tickets.

SIR CHARLES. Really, Claire, how can you ask a question like that?

CLAIRE. Why not? This is your idea, remember? If your nephew's incapable, then somebody else may have to step into the breach for him.

GRACE. Charles, tell her to keep her sharp tongue and low mind to herself.

CLAIRE. She has claws.

GRACE. This is my pad now. If you want to keep kibbitzing here, belt up on the snide remarks or you'll find yourself horizontal.

CLAIRE. Horizontal's more your position than mine, dear.

GRACE. Listen you Black Witch of the North.

> *There is the sound of a commotion from the corridor.* TUCKER *comes in arguing with* DR HERDER.

TUCKER. Why can't you look at my back? It's 'cause I'm on the National Health, isn't it? Damn money-grubbers, you and your Hypocrite's Oath . . . Your ladyship, Dr Paul Herder. Lunch is ready, Madam.

> TUCKER *shuffles out.* DR HERDER *faces* CLAIRE, GRACE *and* SIR CHARLES, *who instinctively unite against him, their internal quarrel forgotten.*

DR HERDER. I've come to offer my congratulations, if that's the right word.

SIR CHARLES. This is Dr Herder, Lady Gurney.

GRACE. How do you do, Doctor. So nice to meet you at last. You'll stay for lunch. I want to talk to you about my husband. I'm sorry you weren't told about the wedding, but it was done in such a rush we didn't have time to invite anybody except the close family. Besides, you would have tried to talk me out of it. It wouldn't have done any good . . . (*ironically*) you see, I love him!

She exits.

DR HERDER. You should have consulted me before you went ahead. It's madness.

SIR CHARLES. Come, come, Doctor. You said he needed a harsh dose of reality. You can't have a harsher dose of the stuff than marriage.

DR HERDER. It can't even be legal.

SIR CHARLES. It's legal. My brother-in-law conducted the service. He's a Bishop, and a Bishop would never do anything that wasn't legal.

He exits.

DR HERDER. And what do you say, Lady Claire.

CLAIRE. Congratulations.

DR HERDER. Congratulations?

CLAIRE. On getting your Guggenheim Grant.

DR HERDER. You made love to me to make sure I didn't cause any trouble.

CLAIRE. You seduced me to make sure of that 130,000 for your schizophrenic rats. Don't be tiresome.

DR HERDER. I don't like being made a fool of, Claire.

CLAIRE. You haven't been. Charles would have gone ahead with the marriage anyway. The Gurneys must have an heir. As soon as there is one Charles will have J.C. committed. The only way you would change the plot is by making the 14th Earl of Gurney like the rest of us. And you haven't got much time. Lady Grace Shelley isn't the type to survive the rabbit test for long.

DR HERDER (*quiet hate*). Verdammt. Verdammt. Verdammt.

Blackout.

SCENE SIXTEEN

A roll of thunder. Spot up on GRACE *framed in the doorway Up Stage Centre. She is nine months pregnant. Lights full up to show* DR HERDER, CLAIRE *and* SIR CHARLES *watching her waddle in. The* EARL *comes in behind her, with the same heavy tread, leaning on a shepherd's crook, as if he, too, is carrying.*

GRACE. Can you beat it, J.C.'s got labour pains too.

DR HERDER. It's called 'couvade'. Sympathetic illness. Psychosomatic. Not at all unusual.

SIR CHARLES. Hmm. I never felt a thing when Lady Claire here was pregnant.

CLAIRE. I'm sure you didn't.

EARL OF GURNEY (*helping* GRACE *into chair, she winces and the* EARL *clutches his stomach*). Ooh-ah, Mighty Mouse is roaring.

DR HERDER. What are you going to call the child?

SIR CHARLES. Vincent, after the Guv'nor.

EARL OF GURNEY (*firmly*). No shell name. We'll call the little beggar Bussay d'Ambois, the UNO Boy-Wonder. And if it's a girl, Capucine.

SIR CHARLES. Capucine? You can't call anyone Capucine?

TUCKER *enters.*

TUCKER. Dr Herder. Mr McKyle is here.

DR HERDER. Show them straight in.

TUCKER. Certainly, sir, I'll lay down on the doorstep and let 'em walk over me.

He exits.

CLAIRE. Do you need us?

DR HERDER. Yes. But whatever happens, please don't interfere or interrupt, unless I ask.

CLAIRE. What are you going to do?

DR HERDER (*picks up tape-recorder*). Prove it's impossible for two objects to occupy the same space at the same time. A colleague of mine, Dr Sackstead, has agreed to send me some help as a personal favour.

SIR CHARLES. All these damned experiments. Look at the last one with the lie-detector. You asked him if he was God, he grinned, said 'No' and the damn fool machine sayd he was lying.

DR HERDER. You've forced me to risk the unorthodox. (*Takes the EARL's arm.*) I'm going to show you the world in the hard light of Truth.

EARL OF GURNEY. I am the Light of Truth, the Light of the World.

DR HERDER (*into tape-recorder*). This is experiment fifteen.

SIR CHARLES. All these damned experiments.

TUCKER enters.

TUCKER. Dr Herder. Mr McKyle . . .

MCKYLE enters, brushing past him impatiently, followed by a burly ASSISTANT.

Oh, charming.

He exits.

MCKYLE (*gesturing*). Mae assistant, Mr Shape.

MCKYLE is a powerful gaunt man, with an iron-grey beard and brusque manner. He is still wearing gloves.

ASSISTANT. Dr Sackstead was held up. He hopes to be along later.

MCKYLE. Shall we gie on wi' it?

DR HERDER. Let me introduce you.

MCKYLE. No need. I'm sure they a' ken me here. (*The others look puzzled; he takes off right-hand glove, extends fingers.*) Ach, who else has electricity streaming fraw his fingers and eyeballs? I'm the High Voltage Messiah.

CLAIRE. The who?

MCKYLE. The Electric Christ, the AC/DC God. You look fused. Cannae y'see the wall plug in mae forehead? Here, here. The booster converter. Takes everything I eats and drinks and converts it into watts and kilowatts.

All stare except ASSISTANT *and* DR HERDER. SIR CHARLES *and* CLAIRE *are about to protest.* DR HERDER *gestures to them to keep quiet and flicks on the tape-recorder.*

DR HERDER. Are you saying you're God too?

MCKYLE. God 1, 2, 3, 4, 5, 6, 7, 8, 9, 10. AC/DC. Havenae' y' seen God a'fore?

EARL OF GURNEY (*quietly*). They have, sir. Your remarks are in extreme bad taste. I'm God.

MCKYLE (*focussing on him for the first time*). Yer' nae God. Yer' what mae snot-rag's made of. (*Plugs deaf-aid in ear.*) I've obliterated hundreds o' dupe-Messiahs in mae time.

EARL OF GURNEY (*begins to circle slowly clock-wise*). You think I'd go around saying I was God if I could help it? Mental hospitals are full of chaps saying they're God.

MCKYLE (*moving slowly around in opposite direction*). It's a bit much o' Sackstead sending me twenty million miles through Galactic space and the interplanetary dust piled two feet thick outside the windows, to bandy words wi' a poxy moon-looney who thinks he's me.

EARL OF GURNEY. I'm here. You're there.

MCKYLE. Ach, I'm here and I'm there too. (*Opposite each other again*.) Dinnae trifle wi' me. I'm Jehovah o' the Old Testament, the Vengeful God. Awae or you'll be *dropped*.

DR HERDER. You can't both be God.

MCKYLE. He's only a bleery-eyed blooster, an English pinhead, the hollowed out son o' a Cameronian brothel-keeper.

EARL OF GURNEY. That's because I'm not myself today. (*To* DR HERDER.) You're trying to split my mind with his tongue.

MCKYLE. Awae home, laddie, afore I burn you to a crispy noodle.

EARL OF GURNEY. You can't touch me. I'm the Rock. (*Becomes square, massive*.) And the Vine. (*Stretching arms up*.) The goat. (*Springs into chair, fingers as horns*.) The East Wind. (*Blows*.) The Sacred Bug. (*Jumps down, scuttles along*.) The Upright Testicle (*Jerks upright*.) The Bull.

As they watch him paw and bellow, fascinated, MCKYLE *picks up the empty brandy glass from the table and before the* ASSISTANT *can stop him takes a bite out of it. having recaptured their horrified attention, he continues talking with his mouth full of blood.*

MCKYLE. I saw mae son Jamie dei. He had cancer at the base of his spine and one in his head. They used the black spider treatment on him. It crawled all over, using its feelers, cracking the body vermin and germs wi' its nippers. (*Suddenly to* GRACE.) I can cure yer bursting. Fire a laser beam doon into yer eye, let a black spider crawl down to clear away the sick pus the sack o' pus, the white pus, the deid . . .

GRACE *rises, shaken.*

But first I'll deal wi' yon Irishman. (*Stands on one leg*.) I'm earthed. (*Whipping off glove he suddenly whirls round and stabs forefinger at the* EARL's *stomach*.) Zzzzzzzz . . .

The EARL *tries to protect himself with his hands but slowly doubles up, letting out a long groan which turns into a cry of pain as* GRACE, *who has staggered to her feet, collapses on the floor clutching her stomach.*

DR HERDER. Damn!

SIR CHARLES. Grace. Grace.

CLAIRE (*hurrying to the door*). Tucker!

SIR CHARLES (*to* DR HERDER *bending down to* GRACE). Your responsibility, sir. Damn you.

TUCKER *appears in doorway.*

DR HERDER. Tucker – Nurse Brice. And tell the midwife to be ready!

MCKYLE (*taking bulb out of standard lamp*). I'm *dead!* (*Sticks finger into the socket, shakes violently.*) Re-ch-a-r-ge!

DR HERDER. Get her upstairs.

SIR CHARLES (*picking* GRACE *up*). If we lose this child . . .

They move Up Stage to the door.

MCKYLE (*shaking*). B-B-Burn-n-n-n a f-f-f-eath-e-e-e-e-er o-o-o-n-d-d-er her n-n-nose!

DINSDALE *rushes in excitedly.*

DINSDALE. Super news! Old Barrington-Cochran's dying. It'll mean a by-election.

CLAIRE. Not now, Dinsdale!

EARL OF GURNEY. *Paul, Paul, why persecutest thou me?*

All look round and up to the EARL *who has, in the confusion, climbed up to the gallery and is now spread out on the cross.* SIR CHARLES *hurries out with* GRACE *in his arms.* CLAIRE *quickly follows as* TUCKER *reappears in the doorway.*

DR HERDER (*to* ASSISTANT). Don't let 'em leave!

He exits.

TUCKER. Don't worry, Doctor. I'm a Brown belt. Fifth Dan. (*Assumes Judo stance, with loud grunts.*) Ho – Ha!

DINSDALE. Will somebody please tell me what's going on?

TUCKER (*pouring drink*). Life, Master Dinsdale, sir. The right moth-eaten tapestry of life.

DR HERDER *re-enters with* CLAIRE.

DR HERDER. Mrs Grant's a fully qualified midwife. She'd resent me interfering professionally. Anyway, I'll be extremely busy down here.

CLAIRE. You're not going on with this?

DR HERDER. It's our last chance. Sackstead will never agree to let McKyle out again.

DINSDALE. Where's father?

CLAIRE. Pacing the corridor upstairs.

DR HERDER. Come, McKyle, get your finger out. (*Up at cross.*) Gentlemen, it's impotant to know which of you is telling the truth. If one of you is God, the other must be somebody else.

MCKYLE. Your Worship, Ladies and Gentlemen o' the Jury. I stand accused o' nae being who I am: to wit, the aforesaid, after-mentioned, hereafter-named, uncontested GOD. These are facts. I made the world in mae image. I'm a holy terror. Sae that accounts fer the bloody mess it's in. Gi' up y' windy wa's McNaughton and plead insanity.

EARL OF GURNEY. If it's facts you want, the Great Peacock is a Moth which only lives two days. With no mouth to eat or drink it flies miles to love, breed and die. Consider a life o' love without one selfish act, members of the Jury.

MCKYLE. Ach, and they put me awae for seventeen years. Only the sick wi' spiders webs round their brains clack o' about lo'e and goodness. I'm a braw God fer bashing bairns' head on rocks, a God for strong stomachs.

EARL OF GURNEY. You're one of the Fu Manchu gang. (*Gestures at audience.*) They're children of condensed sunlight.

MCKYLE. The children o' licht you ken, are faw awa'. This is Earth. An early failure o' mine. Earth is where I dump the excrement o' the Universe, the privy o' the Cosmos.

EARL OF GURNEY. I'm too full of Grace to listen. People care for love – love for everything that's necessary for the continuation of life.

TUCKER (*lurching forward*). We don't want love, we want a fat slice o' revenge. Kiss me arse!

DINSDALE (*indignantly*). Tucker, you're an unmitigated stinker.

DR HERDER. No God of *love* made this world. I've seen a girl of four's nails had been torn out by her father. I've seen the mountains of gold teeth and hair and the millions boiled down for soap.

EARL OF GURNEY (*he stumbles desperately off the cross, putting sticking plaster over his eyes*). S-S-some-times G-G-God turns his b-b-back on his p-p-people . . .

MCKYLE. And breaks wind and the stench clouds the globe! That's settled the verdict 'tween twa' poor Scottish loons. I'm the High Voltage Man, nearer to God than yon sentimental clishmac-laverer.

EARL OF GURNEY. There's a light of truth inside as well as a light of truth outside.

DR HERDER (*violently*). Here's the truth! (*Rips sticking plaster from the* EARL's *eyes.*) You're *Jack Gurney*, the 14th Earl of Gurney.

Roll of thunder.

MCKYLE. I'm Cock o' the North, mae boys. Oh. I'm Cock o' the North. (*Breaks* EARL's *staff across knee.*)

EARL OF GURNEY (*writhing as if in labour*). ELOI ELOI.

DR HERDER. Your loving family tricked you into marriage because they want an heir.

EARL OF GURNEY. Pater-Noster-Pater-Noster-Pater-Noster . . .

DR HERDER. If the baby turns out to be a boy they'll have you certified, committed, and in a strait-jacket before you can say another Pater-Noster.

EARL OF GURNEY (*in great pain*). I am the Father. Cherish the worm. Errsh . . . I'm splitting. I tear. Torn. (*Writhing.*) Crowned. Coming out crowned. BORN . . . I *AM* THE FATHER.

A clap of thunder. CLAIRE *jumps up.*

CLAIRE (*shouting, putting hands to head like horns*). You're the father of nothing! You're Jack – Jack the *Cuckold*!

MCKYLE (*firing with both hands at* EARL). Zzzzzzzzzz . . .

The EARL *lets out an extraordinary deep-throated cry, careering backwards, bucking and twisting from the force of the imaginary electrical charge. He crashes against the recorder on the table, starting it playing back at high speed. Simultaneously, there is a clap of thunder, the french-windows fly open and with a rush of cold wind a monstrous eight-feet beast bursts in. It walks upright like a man, covered with thick black hair swept out from each side of its face like a gigantic guinea-pig, and is dressed incongruously in high Victorian fashion: morning coat and top hat. None of the others see the beast, which grabs the* EARL *and shakes him violently, to the accompaniment of high-speed jabber from the tape-recorder, thunder-claps and* MCKYLE'S *harsh chants 'two million volts zzzzz three million zzzzzzzzzz'.*

The EARL *wrestles in an epileptic fit, saliva dribbling from his mouth.* CLAIRE *and* DINSDALE *watch with well-bred revulsion,* DR HERDER *and* ASSISTANT *with clinical interest while pushing the heavy furniture out of the way as the beast pummels his victim in a series of vicious wrestling holds. The* EARL'S *legs and arms are twisted, and his face forced back by a heavy paw. He struggles, but his strength soon leaves him. As the background noise reaches a crescendo, the beast slams him down across its knee, tosses him onto the floor and then looking down at the unconscious man, raises its hat, grunts and lurches out the way it came in.*

The EARL *lies still, Stage Centre, one leg twisted under his body.* MCKYLE *stops chanting, and* CLAIRE *switches off the tape-recorder, whilst* DINSDALE *and* TUCKER *close the french-windows. Silence. There is the distinct sound of a single slap and a baby begins to cry faintly. The* ASSISTANT *straightens the* EARL'S *leg whilst* DR HERDER *bends down and lifts his head. The* EARL'S *eyes open.*

EARL OF GURNEY (*feebly*). Jack.

DR HERDER. What?

EARL OF GURNEY. Jack. My name . . .

DR HERDER (*dawning realization*). Yes, Jack. That's right, your name's Jack. (*Looks up at others*.) It's worked!

MCKYLE. Cowl the Minnie! Hallelujah! Hallelujah!

DINSDALE. Oh, well done.

EARL OF GURNEY. Jack. My name's Jack . . .

SIR CHARLES *enters Up Stage, a bundle in his arms.*

SIR CHARLES (*holding up bundle triumphantly*). It's a *boy*!

EARL OF GURNEY. Jack. I'm Jack. I'm Jack. I'm Jack!

The baby starts to cry.

Curtain.

Act Two

SCENE ONE

'Oh for the Wings of a Dove' played over, then out of the darkness
BISHOP LAMPTON's *voice intones:*

BISHOP LAMPTON (*over*). Vincent, Henry, Edward, Ralph
Gurney, I baptize thee in the name of the Father and of the
Son and of the Holy Ghost.

*Baby cries. Photographer's flash momentarily lights a christening
group of* SIR CHARLES, CLAIRE, DINSDALE, DR HERDER, TUCKER
and BISHOP LAMPTON, *grouped around* GRACE *with the child.*

*Then lights up on the drawing-room, now containing pieces of
Victorian furniture and bric-a-brac. The cross has gone.* TUCKER
pulls off the BISHOP's *robes.*

GRACE. What a pair of lungs. The little devil up-staged
everybody. He's a trouper.

SIR CHARLES (*jovially, at baby*). Coochy-coochy. He's a splendid
fella, eh, Bertie?

BISHOP LAMPTON. A vessel newly filled with the Holy Spirit, but
I fear regrettably leaky.

GRACE. Leaky or not, he's saved you Gurneys from becoming
extinct.

She exits.

SIR CHARLES. Things are beginning to get back to normal.

DR HERDER. What are we going to do about his lordship?

SIR CHARLES. The family came to a decision some time ago, that
after certain matters had been cleared up he'd be put away.
Permanently this time. For his own good.

CLAIRE. That was before, Charles. The situation's changed.

BISHOP LAMPTON. I gather he's improved. But we can't be sure he won't sink back into darkness and shadow.

DINSDALE. Sometimes it's worse than when he was completely potty. I mean, we're all just waiting for him to go off again, tick-tick-tick-tick-*boom*. We've been darned lucky up to now but with a possible by-election in the offing, it's too risky.

SIR CHARLES. Can't say I'm the sensitive type, but the strain of the last few months is beginning to tell. I think it's best all round if Jack were put away. (*Notices* TUCKER *staggering off with the vestments.*) And he's not the only one we can say goodbye to.

TUCKER *scowls darkly at him, as* GRACE *comes back in.*

GRACE. Nothing like a couple of nursemaids to take the curse out of having kids.

CLAIRE. We were talking about Jack.

GRACE. He's a helluva problem. What do you say, Doctor?

DR HERDER (*drily*). Thank you for asking. You must realize that the battle between the God of Love and the Electric Messiah was a tremendous breakthrough.

GRACE. Is he cured?

DR HERDER. He's on the way to recovery. His behaviour is nearer the acceptable norm. I don't know whether it's permanent. I do know, you mustn't have him committed. I've got a full schedule of research lined up, but I'm taking valuable time out for this therapy. This case could become a classic of psychology – Freud's Anna O., now Herder's Earl of Gurney.

EARL OF GURNEY. Call me Jack.

The EARL *stands in the doorway Up Stage Centre with an ancient shotgun levelled at them. Before they can react he pulls the trigger and says 'click'; nothing happens. He has changed; no beard, his hair is short, and he wears an old-fashioned dark suit with waistcoat and stiff collar. His words and gestures are still slightly out of 'synch'.*

It's a pleasant name. (*Imitating bell.*) J-J-Jack, J-J-Jack, J-J-Jack.

Using his shotgun as a temporary crutch he crosses Stage Centre with a peculiar loping hop.

SIR CHARLES. And he's recovering? (*To the* EARL.) Why are you walking like that?

The EARL *pulls of his right shoe, feels inside, and takes out a large pebble. He shows it to* SIR CHARLES *by way of reply.*

(*Disappointed.*) Oh. A stone.

CLAIRE. Reasonable.

EARL OF GURNEY (*gesturing with gun*). I found it in the attic.

GRACE. Why aren't you resting?

EARL OF GURNEY. I wanted to apologize for not being at my own son's christening.

GRACE. The little devil stole the show.

EARL OF GURNEY. I must be sure before I make my first public appearance. Very important to leave the right impression. When I g-g- huitment, re-return dunt d-d- impression of overall superiority and volatile farts the shadow of it is sludged ghoul of a whore, whoredom's bloddy network. (*Struggles fiercely to regain control.*) Hold sir, hold hold hold hold sir. (*Recovering, to* DINSDALE.) A relative who said he was Christ could hardly be a political asset for you, Dinsdale.

DR HERDER. I don't know. The Tory Leader's the son of a carpenter, after all.

EARL OF GURNEY (*surprised*). Lord Salisbury's a carpenter's son. Really?

CLAIRE. How are you feeling?

EARL OF GURNEY. Lazarus felt like I feel. Odour of dung. Duat d' d' s'muss bed sores the executioners arrive for Nijinsky the liquid streets unstable my wooden leg needs morphine. (*Struggling, sweating.*) *Back, sir. Back, sir. Back.*

(*Controlled.*) Be patient, I'll learn the rules of the game.

DR HERDER. We know you will.

CLAIRE. You've changed already.

TUCKER *enters carrying a cape and deerstalker cap.*

TUCKER. You wished to take a constitutional at noon, my lord.

EARL OF GURNEY. Thank you, Tuck. Invaluable man, Tuck.

TUCKER. There's some 'ere who don't think so, your lordship. (*Darkly at* SIR CHARLES.) No names, no pack-drill. I know they're waiting to give me the boot.

EARL OF GURNEY (*sadly*). You and me both, Tuck. We must give 'em no cause, no cause.

GRACE (*helping him on with the cape*). Don't stay out too long, Jack.

EARL OF GURNEY. Just want to get the feel of terra firma. I must learn to keep my mouth shut, bowels open and never volunteer. Come, Tuck.

They exit through french-windows.

CLAIRE. Well? Has he changed or hasn't he? I agreed with you before, Charles, he was hopeless and the sooner we put him away the better. Now it'd be stupid. I know he'll recover.

GRACE. And if he does? Where does that leave us? He mightn't understand what we did.

DINSDALE. I say, aren't you all jumping the gun? Look at the way he suddenly goes off. 'Volatile farts a' a' duat.' What's all that then?

DR HERDER. Paralalia – speech disturbance. It would be simpler if a man was paranoid one moment and cured the next. Unfortunately, it takes time.

DINSDALE. There's all this Victorian bric-a-brac stuff he's got everywhere. And what about him thinking the leader of the Conservative Party was the Marquis of Salisbury?

DR HERDER. Sicilian peasants thought Churchill was a kind of tomato. Thousands of Indians have never heard of Gandhi.

Political ignorance is not a symptom of psychosis. It might even be considered a sign of mental health.

CLAIRE. Bertie, you haven't seen much of Jack lately. What's your opinion?

BISHOP LAMPTON. The acid test still is, would he pass muster in the Athenæum? Could he be introduced to members without raising eyebrows?

DR HERDER. In the end it's really her ladyship's decision.

GRACE. Oh, hell. Thanks a lot. I don't know. There's the baby . . . What if he suddenly . . .? Have I got to right now? Jeez, I can't make up my mind.

SIR CHARLES. You don't have to. It's done. I've already asked the Master in Lunacy to come down and certify Jack's insane.

A single shot, off Right, breaks the stunned silence. CLAIRE, DR HERDER *and* GRACE *look at each other, then rush out of the french-windows.*

SIR CHARLES (*hopefully, to* DINSDALE). Do you think Jack's done the decent thing at last?

BISHOP LAMPTON *crosses himself.*

Lights down.

SCENE TWO

Spot up on metal sun hanging Down Stage Centre: some white feathers float down. Footlights up to show the EARL *standing with* TUCKER, *Down Stage Right, looking blankly at his smoking shotgun, a dead dove at his feet. Voices are heard calling off.*

TUCKER (*shakily*). That's how accidents happen. That could have been me, your lordship. You've been waving that gun all over the place. (*Takes out hip-flask.*) Not that anyone'd have cared much. No one to weep for poor creeping Tucker.

(*Drinks.*) But I'm not ready for stoking the fiery furnace yet. I've got an awful lot of living to do. Girls by the hundreds to name only a few . . .

GRACE, CLAIRE *and* DR HERDER *rush anxiously on Wings Right.*

GRACE. What happened? You all right?

TUCKER. As rain, your ladyship. Just a little accident. The gun went off. But Ironside never flinched.

CLAIRE. You're not hurt, Jack?

EARL OF GURNEY (*indicating dove, takes off hat*). R.I.P.

GRACE. Where the devil were you, Jeeves?

CLAIRE. Guzzling! Your job's to look after his lordship, Tucker.

TUCKER. I know my job, Lady Claire, and my place. And that's indoors. It's f-f-freezing.

With the exception of the EARL *the others are already feeling cold. They shift from one foot to the other to keep warm during the rest of the scene.* SIR CHARLES *hurries on, Wings Right.*

SIR CHARLES (*sees* EARL). Oh. Still in one piece?

CLAIRE. Disappointed?

EARL OF GURNEY. I was trying to do what's expected. I recall it's a sign of normalcy in our circle to slaughter anything that moves. All I did was . . .

He aims the shotgun up at the Flies off Left, and pulls the trigger. To everyone's horror, the second barrel fires. There is a bellow of pain from the Flies, a cry 'Ahhjjj . . .' followed by a crash as someone hits the ground.

SIR CHARLES *rushes off with a reluctant* TUCKER. DINSDALE *can be heard calling 'I say, where is everybody? H-e-ll-ooo', as* CLAIRE, DR HERDER *and* GRACE *look suspiciously at the* EARL.

EARL OF GURNEY. I had a stone in my shoe and an accident with an old gun, so you still think I'm insane. I know a man who hated the sight of his wrinkled socks, so he wore his girl friend's girdle to keep 'em up. Now she's his wife. (*Fiercely.*)

I've got to stop talking. (*Takes* GRACE's *hand*.) Just give me time.

DR HERDER (*deliberately*). Sir Charles has asked the Master in Lunacy to come here to commit you to an institution.

EARL *lets go of* GRACE's *hand; he becomes rigid and sways*.

Naturally I'll oppose any commitment. But in the end it depends on how you act.

EARL OF GURNEY (*stops swaying*). Perhaps it's for the best. If I satisfy the Lunatic Master, I'll be officially sane, and I'll have a certificate to prove it. (*Quietly.*) But Charles has been unwise. (*All shiver.*) You'll catch your deaths out here. Odd expression.

DR HERDER. L-L-Let's go in then. We've got work to do.

EARL OF GURNEY. I'll stay a moment and compose myself.

DR HERDER *nods and exits briskly Wings Right, with* CLAIRE.

GRACE. What a family. Enough to drive anyone round the bend. Will you be all right, Jack?

EARL OF GURNEY (*arm around her*). The only sensible thing I've done in the last seven years was to marry you.

GRACE (*touched*). There now. There now. Don't stay out too long, Honey. (*Moves off, shivering.*) Charles is a bloody moron. I'll have his guts for garters.

As she exits Wings Left, the metal sun is taken up.

EARL OF GURNEY (*softly*). Soft. Softly. Down, down, down, oh, let me keep it down, pianissimo, damp down, damp down. Down. (*Voice rises despite himself.*) I'm a soft grub ununduuulating. They'll rip me open. (*Trembling.*) Nail my brain to my skull. Strom, strom, grunk, grok, *Crunk*. Fug. That means you. *Fug. Fug. Fug.* Silence when you speak S-i-l-e-n-c-e. Steady the Buffs, waiter, I say, waiter, there's a moustache in my soup. (*Violently.*) Kerr-un-crrr. KORKSHIST – KORKSHIST – KUK-KUK-KUK-KUK-KUK-KUK...

Unable to stop he takes out two strips of sticky-tape and sticks them across his mouth. Now he can't speak and his savage struggle to control himself can only be expressed in abrupt body movements. He starts leaping, spreading out his cape; higher and higher, till a last climatic leap, and he lands, crouching in a ball, Down Stage Centre. Dim Lights Up Stage Centre, to show a dark shadowy figure waiting in the drawing room behind him: it is the MASTER IN LUNACY.

SCENE THREE

Lights up on the MASTER, KELSO TRUSCOTT, Q.C., *in the drawing-room, which now contains more Victorian bric-a-brac: stuffed pheasants, wax fruit under glass, and a red-plush sofa. The* EARL *straightens up resolutely and is joined by* TUCKER. *The* EARL *hands him his hat and cape and* TUCKER *gives him* The Times *newspaper in return. The* EARL *puts it under his arm and sticks a briar pipe firmly in his mouth. Turning sharply on his heels, he squares his shoulders and marches purposefully Up Stage to join* TRUSCOTT, *a big hard-faced man who is looking through some documents.*

TRUSCOTT. Where did you spring from?

EARL OF GURNEY. You must be Truscott, the Lunatic fella.

TRUSCOTT (*frowning*). I'm the Master of the Court of Protection. The title 'Master in Lunacy' isn't used nowadays.

It is obvious TRUSCOTT *is scrutinizing the* EARL *closely.*

EARL OF GURNEY. How about a snifter? No? All right then, Tuck.

TUCKER. Very good, sir. Watch yourself now. He looks a fishy-eyed, light-fingered gent to me. (*Glaring at* TRUSCOTT.) I know the price of everything in this room. So if there's anything missing we shall know where to look.

He exits Up Stage Centre. TRUSCOTT *stares after him.*

EARL OF GURNEY. I'd better introduce myself first. Jack Gurney. (*With slightest emphasis.*) The Earl of Gurney. I believe Charles considers me incapable and you're here to commit me officially.

TRUSCOTT. Not exactly, my lord. I make a recommendation to a Nominated Judge and he does the actual committing. My main concern is property and its proper administration. This investigation, however, is rather informal. A favour to Charles. (*Takes out silver snuff box.*) Yours is a confusing case. (*Taps the snuff box three times and takes snuff.*) Two doctors recommend you to be put under care, but Dr Herder says you're nearly back to normal. Of course, he *is* a foreigner and his idea of normal may not be mine.

Despite himself the EARL's *hand trembles, as he fills his pipe.* TRUSCOTT *watches closely.*

EARL OF GURNEY. How do you find out?

TRUSCOTT. You talk. I listen.

EARL OF GURNEY (*sits on sofa*). Ah, yes, talk. Judas talk t-t-t-t-talk . . . (*Tails off miserably.*)

TRUSCOTT (*glances at file*). Do you still believe you're Christ, my lord? (*No reply.*) Are you God? (*No reply.*) Come, sir, are you the God of Love?

The EARL *stares into space, deep in thought, then slowly rises and points at him.*

EARL OF GURNEY. Harrow may be more clever.

TRUSCOTT (*incredulously*). What!?

EARL OF GURNEY (*singing*). 'Rugby may make more row. But we'll row, row for ever. Steady from stroke to bow. And nothing in life shall sever the chain that is round us now . . .'

TRUSCOTT *crosses grimly to the* EARL, *stares at him, and then, without warning joins in, in a barber-shop duet.*

TRUSCOTT and EARL OF GURNEY. 'Others will fill our places, dressed in the old light blue. We'll recollect our races. We'll to the flag be true.' (*They mime rowing.*) 'But we'll still swing together and swear by the best of schools. But we'll still swing together and swear by the best of schools!'

EARL OF GURNEY. I didn't realize – you're *Kelso* Truscott. *The* Kelso Truscott who scored that double century at Lords.

TRUSCOTT (*modestly*). A long time ago.

EARL OF GURNEY. Of course, I was pretty low down the school when you were in your glory, Truscott. They said when you got back after the Lords match dressed in a kilt, you debagged the Chaplain and hit the local constable over the head with an ebony shelalee.

TRUSCOTT (*chuckling*). Ah, schooldays, schooldays. It's all ahead of you then . . . You realize, your lordship, the fact that we're both Old Etonians can have no possible influence on my recommendation. (*Taps snuff box.*) Of course, I find it even harder to believe now. Etonians aren't exactly noted for their grey matter, but I've always found them perfectly adjusted to society. (*Sniffs.*) Now, are you the God of Love?

EARL OF GURNEY (*fiercely*). He no longer exists. I was wild with too much jubilating. I've been raving for seven years, Truscott. But everyone's entitled to one mistake.

TRUSCOTT. Seven years. That accounts for your not being at any of the Old Boys' Reunion Dinners.

EARL OF GURNEY (*bitterly*). I went around saying the Lord loooooves you LOOOOOVES. Tch. Grrk. (*Bites hard on pipe.*) Sorry there, Truscott. It's embarrassing for a fella to remember what a spectacle he's made of himself. Naturally I get tongue-tied. Bit shame-faced, don't y'know.

TRUSCOTT. You seem right enough to me, but these things are deceptive. Is there anything you feel strongly about, your lordship?

EARL OF GURNEY. My w-w-wasted years. I woke up the other day and I had grey hairs. Grey hairs and duty neglected. Our country's being destroyed before our e-e-eyes. You're MOCKED in the Strand if you speak of patriotism and the old Queen. Discipline's gone. They're sapping the foundations of our society with their adultery and fornication!

TRUSCOTT *crosses Down Stage Left and pulls bell-rope.*

The barbarians are waiting outside with their chaos, anarchy, homosexuality and worse!

SIR CHARLES, CLAIRE, GRACE *and* DR HERDER *hurry in Up Stage Centre.*

GRACE. Well?

TRUSCOTT (*putting papers into the briefcase*). Dr Herder you said you thought his lordship was on the road to recovery. I can't agree.

SIR CHARLES. *There.*

TRUSCOTT. You're too cautious. For my money he's recovered.

GRACE *kisses the* EARL *impulsively.*

GRACE. We're grateful to you, Mr Truscott.

TRUSCOTT. Thank you, your ladyship. (*To the* EARL.) We'll expect you at the next Reunion Dinner, my lord. Lady Claire, a pleasure. Dr Herder, congratulations. Splendid achievement. (*To* SIR CHARLES.) You're lucky this was only a friendly investigation, old boy. We take a dim view of frivolous complaints.

He exits.

SIR CHARLES. Truscott's a damn ass. Can't he see I'm right?

GRACE. Right? I've had enough of your right. You've stuck your aristocratic schnozzle into my affairs for the last time. Right? Jack's changed. Right? Everything's changed – you, me, us, them. It's a new deal all round. Right? You know what I mean. Right? *Right!*

She exits.

SIR CHARLES. Did what I thought best.

DR HERDER. The best you can do now is to leave Jack alone. He's made a spectacular breakthrough. We're in the process of making a new man.

CLAIRE. I'm always on the lookout for new men.

SIR CHARLES *exits.*

You did it, Jack. Wonderful.

DR HERDER. Leave him, he's been under a great strain. I didn't think he was ready for that blockhead Truscott.

CLAIRE. Blockhead or not, he brought in the right verdict.

DR HERDER. I suspect the Earl's behaviour just happened to coincide with his idea of sanity. Your nephew needs very delicate handling at this stage. And if possible, a little love.

CLAIRE. That shouldn't be too difficult.

DR HERDER. You helped Sir Charles crucify him.

CLAIRE. Jack's changed. He's strong now.

DR HERDER. What about us?

CLAIRE. We're too much alike. Ice on ice. I wanna' feel *alive.*

DR HERDER. And you think Jack'll perform that miracle?

CLAIRE. Oh, rats to you.

Lights dim to a Spot on the EARL *as they exit.*

SCENE FOUR

The EARL *hunches his right shoulder and drags his left leg.*

EARL OF GURNEY. Deformed, unfinished, sent before me time, those eminent doctors of Divinity, Professors McKyle and Herder cured me of paranoid delusions fantasy obsessions of love, that's where it ended, a solvental of inner and outer tensions. No more inter-stage friction. See how I marshal words. That's the secret of being normal. (*He pulls the words out of his mouth.*) 'I' – straighten up there. 'AM' – close up, close up with 'I' you 'orrible little word. 'GOD' . . . I AM GOD. Not the God of Love but God Almighty. God the Law-Giver, Chastiser and Judge. For I massacred the Amalekites and the Seven Nations of Canaan, I hacked Agag to pieces and blasted the barren fig-tree. I will tread them in mine anger and trample them in my fury, and their blood shall be sprinkled upon my garments. For the day of vengeance is in my heart! Hats off for the God of Justice, the God of Love is dead. Oh, you lunar jackass. *She betrayed you.* Lust muscles tighten over plexus. Guilty, guilty, guilty. The punishment is death. I've finally been processed into right-thinking power. They made me adjust to modern times. This is 1888 isn't it? I knew I was Jack. Hats off. I said Jack. I'm Jack, cunning Jack, quiet Jack, Jack's my name. (*Produces knife, flicks it open.*) Jack whose sword never sleeps. Hats off I'm Jack, not the Good Shepherd, not the Prince of Peace. I'm Red Jack, Springheeled Jack, Saucy Jack, Jack from Hell, trade-name Jack the Ripper! . . . Mary, Annie, Elizabeth, Catherine, Marie Kelly. (*Sings.*) 'Six little whores glad to be alive, one sidles up to Jack, then there were five.'

He exits Wings Left, slashing the air with his knife.

SCENE FIVE

Lights up to show GRACE *and* DINSDALE *talking in the drawing-room, now completely furnished in authentic Victorian style.*

DINSDALE. How could you have asked 'em? What about my career?

GRACE. Politics is no career for a healthy young chap. You should go out to work like the rest of us.

DINSDALE. But look what happened last time.

GRACE. That's why I got 'em to come again. When they see how Jack's changed they'll spread the word. Everybody'll know he's back to normal.

DINSDALE. I don't think he is.

GRACE. Your're just siding with your father. He won't admit Jack's cured because it doesn't suit him.

DINSDALE. I don't know how you persuaded 'em to come.

GRACE. I'm her ladyship. Sixty miles outside London an awful lot of cap tugging and forelock touching still goes on. You couldn't keep 'em away.

TUCKER *enters*.

TUCKER. Mrs Treadwell and Mrs Piggot-Jones, your ladyship.

Two heads, topped with absurd hats, peer round the door. MRS TREADWELL *and* MRS PIGGOT-JONES *edge their way apprehensively into the room. Though relieved to see the cross has gone they keep close together for protection.*

GRACE. Welcome, ladies. You can serve tea now, Jeeves.

TUCKER *crosses to the tea-trolley*.

MRS TREADWELL (*nervously*). Everything's changed.

GRACE. Yes his Nibs – Jack's just crazy about this Victorian stuff.

MRS PIGGOT-JONES. It's very hard-wearing.

GRACE. I hear the atmosphere was a trifle strained on your last visit.

MRS TREADWELL. Well, it was our first meeting with his lordship. Neither Mrs Piggot-Jones nor myself knew him personally. Though of course we knew his father.

GRACE. I never knew mine. But my mother knew Lloyd George.

DINSDALE. He wasn't himself, don't y'know. Bit unsettled. Didn't have a wife and family then.

MRS TREADWELL. How is the Right Honourable Lord Vincent,

your ladyship?

GRACE (*laughing*). 'The Honourable Lord Vince.' Oh, he's fine, just like his dad.

The two women look startled.

(*Quickly.*) I know Jack wants to explain about last time.

TUCKER *serves tea.*

MRS TREADWELL (*tentatively*). He asked me if I loved. Your manservant heard him.

TUCKER (*cupping right ear*). What's that? Speak, up, missus.

MRS TREADWELL. Why did he say God is love?

EARL OF GURNEY. Because he was mad. Mad with grief. His father had just died.

A sombrely dressed EARL OF GURNEY *enters smiling, with* CLAIRE. *He is quiet, self-possessed.* CLAIRE *sits on the sofa, fascinated.*

GRACE. Talk of the devil. Darling, you remember Mrs Piggot-Jones and Mrs Treadwell?

EARL OF GURNEY. Tucker, why are those table legs uncovered? Stark naked wooden legs in mixed company – it's not decent. Curved and fluted, too. Don't you agree, Mrs Treadwell?

MRS TREADWELL. Well, I do think young girls nowadays show too much. After all, the main purpose of legs isn't seduction.

EARL OF GURNEY. Cover 'em with calico or cotton, Tucker.

TUCKER. Yes, sir, no, sir, three bags full sir. I'm a 104-year-old Creep and I 'ave to do everything.

He exits, mumbling.

EARL OF GURNEY. Now ladies, when did we meet?

MRS TREADWELL. Remember you asked me if I loved?

EARL OF GURNEY. *Please*, not in front of women and children.

MRS PIGGOT-JONES. I've told Pamela not to brood about it.

EARL OF GURNEY. Let's have no talk of bestial orgasms, erotic tongueings. It burns small high-voltage holes in the brain. It's been proved in oscillographs.

GRACE. My husband hates anything suggestive.

MRS PIGGOT-JONES. So do I. I find the whole subject distressing. I can't understand why the Good Lord chose such a disgusting way of reproducing human beings.

EARL OF GURNEY. Anything more refined would be too good for producing such two-legged, front-facing Hairies.

CLAIRE. Who did you finally get as Guest Speaker for your Church Fête?

MRS TREADWELL. Sir Barrington-Cochran. That was just before he became ill.

MRS PIGGOT-JONES. Made a splendid speech, didn't he, Pamela, about the rise of crime and socialism.

DINSDALE. I intend to campaign actively, for the reintroduction of the death penalty.

EARL OF GURNEY (*trembling*). You mean there's no death penalty in England's green and pleasant?

MRS TREADWELL. Surely you knew, your lordship?

GRACE. We're a bit out of touch. My husband only reads *Punch*.

EARL OF GURNEY. Is nothing sacred? Why, the Hangman holds society together. He is the symbol of the Great Chastiser. He built this world on punishment and fear.

MRS TREADWELL *and* MRS PIGGOT-JONES *nod vigorously*.

Snuff out fear and see what discords follow. Sons strike their doddering dads, young girls show their bosoms and ankles and say rude things about the Queen. Anything goes and they do it openly in the streets and frighten the horses.

MRS PIGGOT-JONES. It's the times we live in. But what can one do?

EARL OF GURNEY. Bring back fear. In the old days the Executioner kept the forelock-touching ranks in order. When he stood on the gallows, stripped to the waist, tight breeches, black hood, you knew God was in his heaven, all's right with the world. The punishment for blaspheming was to be broken on the wheel. First the fibula. (*Mimes bringing down an iron bar*.) Cra-a-ack. Then the tibia, patella and femur. *Crack, crack, crack*. The corpus, ulna and radius, *crack*. 'Disconnect dem bones, dem dry bones, Disconnect dem bones dem dry bones. Now hear the word of the Lord.'

Irresistably the two women join in.

EARL OF GURNEY, MRS PIGGOT-JONES and MRS TREADWELL (*singing*). 'When your head bone's connected from your neck bone, your neck bone's connected from your shoulder bone, your shoulder bone's connected from your backbone. Now hear the word of the Lord. Dem bones dem bones dem dry bones. Now hear the word of the Lord . . .'

EARL OF GURNEY. We understand each other perfectly. But that's only to be expected. Breeding speaks to breeding.

MRS PIGGOT-JONES (*flushing with pleasure*). How splendid, your lordship.

MRS TREADWELL. I've always believed I'm descended from the Kings of Munster, even though my family originally came from Wimbledon.

MRS PIGGOT-JONES. Forgive me for saying, so, my lord, but this is so different from our last visit. Such an unfortunate misunderstanding.

EARL OF GURNEY. Don't give it another thought, madam. I don't hold it against you. I'm sure I forgot it the moment you left. (*Crosses to desk*.) Now forgive me, I have so much to do. (*To* GRACE.) My dear, why don't you show our guests round the estate?

GRACE. Fine. Give us a hand, Dinsdale.

EARL OF GURNEY. Don't forget to show these good ladies my coronation robes, the mantle of crimsom velvet lined with white taffeta, edged with miniver. Good day, ladies. You may withdraw.

He dismisses them with a regal wave of his hand. MRS PIGGOT-JONES *and* MRS TREADWELL *find themselves curtseying. The* EARL *turns away and picks up some letters from his desk.*

MRS PIGGOT-JONES (*low*). He's so impressive, your ladyship, such natural dignity.

GRACE. He's still a bit eccentric.

MRS PIGGOT-JONES. Runs in the family. But it's only on the surface. Deep down one knows he's sound.

They stop in the doorway and look back at the EARL *calmly slitting open a letter with a paper-knife.*

MRS TREADWELL. He's so like his father. He gets more like him every day, it's frightening.

As they exit DINSDALE *turns, gives a delighted thumbs-up sign and hurries after them.*

GRACE. Claire . . .

CLAIRE. I'll stay and keep Jack company.

GRACE. You seem to be doing a lot of company keeping lately. Don't put yourself to so much trouble.

CLAIRE. No trouble. It's a pleasure.

GRACE. We're going to miss you when you leave.

She exits. CLAIRE *watches the* EARL *deftly slitting open envelopes one after the other.*

SCENE SIX

The EARL *puts down the paper-knife and smiles. Throughout the scene the lights imperceptively fade down as dusk falls.*

CLAIRE. Good. That leaves the two of us.

EARL OF GURNEY. I'm still not word perfect. That talk of bestial orgasms, erotic tongueings – was very unfortunate.

CLAIRE. They didn't mind much what you said. Your manner won 'em over. Just the right blend of God-given arrogance and condescension.

EARL OF GURNEY. I stand outside watching myself watching myself. (*Pulls up the corners of his mouth.*) I smile, I smile, I smile.

CLAIRE. I like your smile. Before I was only sorry for you.

EARL OF GURNEY. Ah, before, madam. Before I was a mass of light. Mad, you see. Nothing was fast enough to match my inner speed. Now I'm sane. The world sweats into my brain, madam.

CLAIRE. Don't keep calling me madam.

EARL OF GURNEY. It's hard to look at people from down-wind. They smell, they stink, they stench of stale greens, wet nappies. It's terrible but it's the real thing.

CLAIRE. I've always wanted to find the real thing. Do you remember our first talk together after you came back?

EARL OF GURNEY. I remember nothing.

CLAIRE. Explode, only feel, you said. Poor Jack. You didn't know how impossible it was for our sort to feel.

EARL OF GURNEY. Why do you remember now what I said then, when I can't remember myself?

CLAIRE. Because you're so different. I keep thinking about something that happened at my last term at Roedean. There'd been reports of a prowler in the grounds, probably a Peeping Tom. Something woke me about 2 a.m. and I went to the window and looked out. There was a shadow in the shadows. Somebody was watching me. It was a hot night but I started shivering and shaking. It was *marvellous*.

EARL OF GURNEY. Yea, I say unto you, fear Him. I'm no shadow. I'm flesh and bloood. Touch.

CLAIRE (*touching his cheek*). Perhaps I'm not really dead, only sleeping. Wake me with a kiss.

EARL OF GURNEY (*takes her hand away*). Remember our common consanguinity.

CLAIRE. Don't be ridiculous. I'm married to your father's half-brother for my sins. That makes us practically strangers, bloodwise.

He attempts to move away. She steps in front of him.

EARL OF GURNEY (*smiling*). Are you accosting me?

CLAIRE (*playing up*). That's right, ducks. 'Ow's about it?

They come close in the half-light. She kisses him on the mouth. The Set begins to change to a nineteenth-century slum street in Whitechapel. A gauze lowered Up Stage, shows a dark huddle of filthy houses, broken doors, windows stuffed with paper. Beyond, an impression of dark alleys, low arches, row upon row of lodging houses. It is dark and foggy. Stage Left, a single flickering street lamp. Stage Right a filthy brick wall with the name of the street: 'Buck's Row'. Drunken singing and street cries can be heard off: 'Apple-a-pound-pears, whelks, they're lovely' and the clip-clop of a horse-drawn van over cobbles.

The overall effect is of a furnished room in the middle of a London street.

Moonlight shines through the french-windows as the EARL *and* CLAIRE *cross the street to the sofa.*

We'll be alone here. They're all out except Tucker and he's drunk. Listen . . .

They listen to a drunk singing in the distance.

You don't seem surprised this has happened to us, Jack?

EARL OF GURNEY. We were destined to meet.

CLAIRE. That sounds romantic. More please.

EARL OF GURNEY (*low, passionate*). Suuuuuck. GRAHHH. Spinnkk. The flesh lusteth against the spirit, against God. Labia, foreskin, testicles, scrotum.

CLAIRE. *That's* romantic?

EARL OF GURNEY. Orgasm, coitus, copulation, fornication. Gangrened shoulder of sex. If it offends. (*Softly into her ear.*) Tear. Tear. Spill the seed, gut-slime.

CLAIRE. I know some women like being stimulated with dirty words, filthy talk. I don't.

She starts taking off his jacket, waistcoat and shirt.

EARL OF GURNEY. You want maggots crawling through black grass.

CLAIRE. I want to hear you say you love me, even if it isn't true.

EARL OF GURNEY. I've seen three thousand houses collapse exposing their privees to the naked eye. *Oh, run, Mary, RUN.*

CLAIRE. You're talking nonsense again, Jack.

EARL OF GURNEY (*softly*). If thy eye offends thee pluck it out. You'll be nicked down to your bloody membrane, Mary.

CLAIRE. I want to hear how beautiful you think I am.

EARL OF GURNEY. You want two seconds of DRIPPING SIN to fertilize sodomized idiots.

CLAIRE. Say something soft and tender.

EARL OF GURNEY (*tenderly*). You want gullet and rack. Gugged SHAARK.

CLAIRE. Tell me I'm fairer than the evening star. Clad in the beauty of a thousand nights.

EARL OF GURNEY (*now stripped to the waist, she caresses him*). Cut-price lumps of flesh: three and six an hour. Calves paunches, tender tongue, ear-lobes, e-e-ar-lobe-sss, hearts, bladders, teats, nippelezzz.

CLAIRE (*shivering*). Lover.

EARL OF GURNEY. The sword of the Lord is filled with blood.

CLAIRE (*trembling violently*). Stop talking, Jack, and make me immortal with a kis.

Putting his left arm around her waist he pulls her close, forcing her head back with a kiss. Taking out his knife, he flicks it open, and plunges it into her stomach. Bucking and writhing with the great knife thrust, CLAIRE *can only let out a muffled cry as the* EARL's *mouth is still clamped over hers in a kiss. She writes, twists and moans under two more powerful stabs. He lets her go.*

AHHHRREEEE. I'M ALIVE. ALIVE.

She falls and dies. The EARL *stands listening for a second, puts his knife away, picks up his clothes and crosses Stage Right and leaves silently by the french-windows. Even as he does so, the Set begins to change back to the drawing-room interior, the gauze and street lamp are taken up as the noises off grow louder. Someone is heard yelling: 'Help! Police!' Sounds of men running. A police whistle blows shrilly, followed by a jumble of panic-stricken cries. These merge into a Newsboy shouting 'Read all about it 'Orrible Murder. Murder and Mutiliation in White-Chapel. Maniac claims another victim. Mary Ann Nichols found murdered in Buck's Row. Read all about it!' The drawing-room set is now completely restored. The hysterical hubbub dies down to a solitary drunk singing incoherently: 'Come Into the Garden Maud'. It grows louder as he comes closer.* TUCKER *enters swaying and singing.*

TUCKER. 'Come into the sh' garden Maudy.' Did you s' ring? (*Blinks, sees* CLAIRE *on the floor.*) S'Lady Claire . . . are you comfortable? Stoned, eh? (*Stumbles over.*) Can I be of . . . aeeeehh.

He gives a great rasping intake of breath at the sight and stands mumbling in shock. Then he shakes all over. But not from fear.

(*Gleefully.*) One less! One less! Praise the Lord. *Hallelujah.*

Convulsed with glee he capers creakingly round the corpse in a weird dance. He freezes in mid-gesture as voices are heard off. SIR CHARLES, DINSDALE *AND* DR HERDER *and* GRACE *come in.*

SIR CHARLES. No lights, Tucker?

DINSDALE *switches on the lights.*

DR HERDER. My God!

They rush over. GRACE *puts her hand to her mouth in horror. Appalled,* DR HERDER *bends to examine the corpse whilst* SIR CHARLES *stares in disbelief, unable to find words to express himself. Finally he turns and explodes indignantly at the audience:*

SIR CHARLES. All right, who's the impudent clown responsible for this?

Blackout.

SCENE SEVEN

A great church organ plays, and a choir sings the 'Dies Irae'. As the last note of the terrifying hymn dies away, lights up on the drawing-room to show DETECTIVE INSPECTOR BROCKETT, *a middle-aged man with tired face, feeling his stomach, whilst his assistant,* DETECTIVE SERGEANT FRASER, *checks through some notes. The carpet by the sofa has been pulled back and there is a cardboard outline of Claire's body on the floor.*

FRASER (*reads quickly*). 'Five-inch gash under right ear to centre of throat severing windpipe. Three stab wounds in lower abdomen. Two knife wounds, one veering to right slitting the groin and passing over the lower left hip, and the other straight up along the centre of the body to the breast-bone. Severe bruising round the mouth. The pathologist thinks the murderer must have had some medical knowledge.' Reminds me of the Drayhurst killing, sir.

BROCKETT. Not really. Martha Drayhurst was found all over the place. Arms and legs in Woolwich, trunk in Euston Station, and the rest of her turned up in Penge. Old Sam Drayhurst had a quirky sense of humour for a butcher. At least Lady Claire was all in one piece.

Footsteps outside.

They're back. Bishop Lampton'll be with 'em. How do you address a bishop?

FRASER. Bishop, sir.

BROCKETT. Bishop, Bishop.

BISHOP LAMPTON *enters supported by* SIR CHARLES *and* DINSDALE. *They have just come from the funeral.*

BISHOP LAMPTON. This house is doomed, Charles. I should never have allowed my poor sister to marry into this accursed family. It's another House of Usher.

Carefully avoiding the outline on the floor they half-carry him Down Stage Left and drop him into a chair, gasping.

SIR CHARLES. Don't talk rubbish, Bertie. Terrible business, but we mustn't lose our heads.

DINSDALE. How could anything like this happen to us? What was mother thinking of?

SIR CHARLES (*urgently*). Not in front of strangers, Dinsdale. Brockett, why aren't you running this animal to earth?

BROCKETT. Don't you worry, sir, we'll get him. But there's still a few points I'd like to clear up. We know the butler found the body just after the killer left by the french-windows. When you came in a moment later, whereabouts was he standing?

SIR CHARLES. Who, Tucker?

GRACE *enters.*

GRACE. The baby's asleep. What are you lot doing?

SIR CHARLES. Brockett, this is her ladyship. He wants to know how we found Tucker beside Claire's body.

GRACE. Oh, here.

She stands beside the outline, puts her left foot out and raises both her arms.

Like the Hokey-Cokey.

BROCKETT. Why would he be doing anything like the Hokey-Cokey?

DINSDALE. He was drunk and he had his teeth out.

BROCKETT. I'd better have another word with Tucker. Run a double check on him, Sergeant.

SIR CHARLES. Senile old fool should have been booted out years ago. not the only one you should re-check. What about my nephew?

GRACE (*deliberately*). You've been through a lot, Charles, but I warn you.

DINSDALE. That's rather disgraceful, Father.

BISHOP LAMPTON. Uncalled for, Jack's behaved splendidly.

SIR CHARLES. I'm not saying he's involved but . . .

GRACE. *But* I'll give you *but*.

BROCKETT. We have the medical reports on his lordship. But if you have something to add.

GRACE. Charles isn't doing this 'cause of what happened to Claire. He's jealous 'cause I love my husband. Charles and me were lovers! I was this randy old goat's mistress!

BISHOP LAMPTON (*wailing*). Aeeeh. Cleanse your hands, you sinner.

SIR CHARLES. Madam, you'll *never* be a Gurney.

GRACE. I'd rather be dead.

DINSDALE (*stricken*). Mother knew, she knew before she died. Father, I have to say this. You've proved a big disappointment to me.

SIR CHARLES. It's *mutual* sir.

BROCKETT. Does his lordship know about the relationship, Lady Grace?

GRACE. No, and he's not going to unless somebody blabs. (*Looks round at* BROCKETT.) Anyway, it's none of your business, Copper!

BISHOP LAMPTON. Private matters, sir. A gentleman would have left!

As the family are suddenly conscious again of the two policemen and start yelling at them, the EARL *enters, a commanding figure in black carrying a black silver-top cane.*

EARL OF GURNEY. Is this the way to act in the presence of death? (*They stop shouting.*) Remember where you are and what happened here.

He pauses by the outline on the floor. Embarrassed, the others clear their throats.

BISHOP LAMPTON. Forgive them, they know not what they do.

EARL OF GURNEY. Oh, Dinsdale, you should answer those messages of condolence. Even if you don't feel like it.

SIR CHARLES. Nonsense. Let 'em wait.

DINSDALE (*defiantly*). You're right, Jack. Create a good impression. It'll take my mind off things. Been a bad day for me what with one thing and another.

He exits Up Stage Centre. GRACE *moves round beside the* EARL.

BROCKETT. My lord, there are still a few details I'd like to clear up. On the night of the murder you talked with Lady Claire till 11.30. How was she when you left her?

EARL OF GURNEY. Unhappy.

BROCKETT. Why's that?

GRACE (*pointedly*). What with one thing and another, she had plenty of reasons, don't you think.

SIR CHARLES. Dammit, Brockett, what the devil does it matter how my wife was feeling.

BROCKETT (*sighing*). You went straight up to bed and heard nothing.

EARL OF GURNEY. Thought I heard Tucker singing.

BROCKETT. Hmm, but he said he didn't leave the kitchen till 12. Odd. Important question, my lord. Think hard now. Has anything unusual happened here recently; anything out of the ordinary?

The EARL *thinks, shakes his head.*

Bishop? Your ladyship?

They shake their heads.

Sir Charles?

TUCKER *is heard singing off.* BROCKETT *turns swiftly.*

Get him, Fraser!

FRASER *rushes out Up Stage Centre and reappears dragging* TUCKER *who is dressed in a striped jacket, bow-tie and straw hat; he carries a battered suitcase festooned with foreign labels.*

TUCKER. What's the idea? I got a plane to catch.

BROCKETT. You going somewhere, Tucker?

TUCKER. *Mr* Tucker, *Flatfoot*. Looks like it don't it. It's cockles and champagne for yours truly, gay Paree where all the girls say oui oui.

GRACE. Bit sudden isn't it?

TUCKER. I'm a creature o' impulse, your ladyship. (*Singing melodiously as he shuffles to exit with suitcase.*) 'Goodbye, I wish you all a last . . . g-o-o-d-b-y-e.'

As he gestures farewell FRASER *pulls him back into the room.*

BROCKETT. You're not going anywhere, Tucker, me lad. I've got questions I want answering.

TUCKER. I told you all I know.

BROCKETT. Have you? . . . Daniel Tucker alias Alexei Kronstadt Communist Party Member Number 243!

SIR CHARLES. Murdering swine!

TUCKER *gives a frightened cry and rushes for the exit Up Stage Centre, but the* EARL OF GURNEY *bars the way.*

TUCKER. Let me pass, let me pass!

As FRASER *pulls* TUCKER *back amid excited shouts,* DINSDALE *hurries in.*

DINSDALE. What's going on?

GRACE. They say old Jeeves is a Bolshie.

EARL OF GURNEY. T-U-C-K-E-R. Are you a low-life leveller? An East End agitator?

TUCKER. How can I be an agitator. I've got a weak chest. (*Suddenly defiant.*) What if I am? You don't know what it's like being a servant, picking up the droppings of these Titled Turds. Everybody has to have secrets. What's it to you how

I spend my leisure time, Flatfoot?

BROCKETT. You're a suspect in a murder case. You concealed certain facts about yourself. What else are you hiding, Tucker?

TUCKER (*agitated*). Suspect? Suspect? I don't *do* anything. I just pays me dues to the Party and they send me pamphlets, under plain covers. And every year I get a Christmas card from Mr Palme Dutt.

BROCKETT (*sticks out leg and raises arms*). Why were you standing like this beside the body? EH? EH? You told me you discovered her dead just before the others came back. But his lordship swears he heard you down here in this room, a *half-hour* earlier.

TUCKER (*frightened*). You got it wrong, my lord. I wasn't here. This is ol' Tuck, your lordship. (*Jigs up and down.*) All talk, no action. (*Sobbing.*) I couldn't do a crime even if I wanted. Not the type.

As he takes out a handkerchief to wipe his eyes, a half-dozen silver spoons fall out of his pocket with a clatter.

GRACE. Jeeves!

SIR CHARLES. You brainwashed thug!

BROCKETT *puts the silverware on to a chair and gestures impatiently for* TUCKER *to disgorge.*

TUCKER. Hope there's no misunderstanding. Just a few little keepsakes. (*Brings out a handful of knives and forks from a bulging pocket.*) Mementoes of my 107 happy years with the Gurney family. (*Produces complete silver cruet set.*) I took 'em for their sentimental value. They call me Mr Softee. (*Produces jewel-encrusted snuff box.*) A few worthless trinkets to help keep the memory green when I'm swanning on the Cote de Jour. (*Finally adds gold bowl from the back of his trousers.*)

BROCKETT. You forgotten something?

TUCKER. No, that's the lot. Oh, goodness me . . . (*Removes hat with feigned surprise and takes out a small silver dinner-plate hidden in the crown.*) Tell you what, your lordship, I'll keep these instead of the two weeks money you owe me in lieu of notice.

DINSDALE. I say, look here, Inspector.

He and FRASER *have opened* TUCKER'S *suitcase. All the others move over except the* EARL.

BROCKETT (*bringing out books*). Lenin's 'Complete Revolutionary'. Mao Tse-Tung's 'Selected Writings'.

FRASER (*discovering pile of photographs*). Look at these, sir.

BROCKETT (*looks at them slowly*). Dis-gus-ting . . .

Shocked gasp from SIR CHARLES *and* DINSDALE *as they glance over his shoulder.* GRACE *takes a photograph and turns it round and round.*

GRACE. How the devil did she get into that position.

BROCKETT. We'll keep this as evidence.

TUCKER *staggers over to the* EARL *who stands dark, impaccable.*

TUCKER. Your lordship, say something for me. You're the only one who can help. You always was my favourite, Master Jack. You always was my favourite. (*Sobbing.*) Before he died the old Earl, s'bless him, said look after that feeble-minded idiot Master Jack for me, Tuck. I could have gone but I stayed.

EARL OF GURNEY. If thy hand offends thee, cut it off. Tuck, Tuck, you rot the air with your sexual filth. And there's an innocent baby upstairs. It was you, spawned out of envy, hate, revenge. *You* killed her. *Oh, Dan, Dan, you dirty old man.* (*Lifts* TUCKER *up bodily by his armpits and drops him in front of* BROCKETT.) Take him away, Inspector.

BROCKETT. Daniel Tucker, I must ask you . . .

TUCKER (*at the* EARL). Judas Jack Iscariot! You've sold me down the sewer, hard-hearted, stony-hearted, like the rest. And I knows s'why. You did it. You and Sir Charles, standing there like a pickled walrus. You Gurneys don't draw the line at murder. (*Suddenly exploding with rage and fear*.) Upper-class excrement, you wanna' do me dirt 'cause I know too much. I know one percent of the population owns half the property in England. That vomity 'one per cent' needs kosher killing, hung up so the blue blood drains out slowly and easy. Aristocratic carcasses hung up like kosher beef *drip-drip-drip*.

FRASER *grabs him as he lurches forward. The* EARL *whispers to* DINSDALE *who helps* FRASER *pick* TUCKER *up. As they carry him out, stiff and horizontal Up Stage he starts bawling:*

'Then comrades come rally. And the last fight let us face. The International Army, Unites the human race.' (*Passing* GRACE *he tips his hat*.) 'I'm only a strolling vagabond, so good night, pretty maiden, *good night*.'

GRACE. What an exit.

BROCKETT. Sorry you heard all that, your ladyship, but I had to let him rave on. The more they talk, the more they convict themselves.

GRACE. At least, Inspector, this destroys any doubts anyone might have had about Jack.

BROCKETT. Of course, my lady.

SIR CHARLES. Good work, Inspector. Let me show you out.

BROCKETT (*to the* EARL). My lord, I'd just like to say what a pleasure it's been meeting you. It couldn't 'ave been easy. But you realized I was only doing my job. You've shown me what 'noblesse oblige' really means.

He gives a slight bow and exits, with SIR CHARLES.

BISHOP LAMPTON (*looking down at the outline*). She was beautiful as Tirzah, comely as Jerusalem, the darling of her mother, flawless to her that loved her. Dead now. Gone, down, down, down, down.

EARL OF GURNEY. Up, up, up, up, she flies. Her soul flies up. Surely you believe she's gone to another place to enjoy even greater privileges than she had on earth?

BISHOP LAMPTON. I have to. I'm a bishop. Forgive an old man's wavering. I remember her fondly, such a terrible death.

EARL OF GURNEY. Lean on me. Trust God's judgement.

BISHOP LAMPTON. You make an old man ashamed. You've become a great source of strength to me, Jack. (*Grasps his arm.*) I won't forget what you've done, Jack. You were the instrument that restored my faith. I feel reborn. I've found the way. Now let me walk humbly with my God.

The EARL *walks with him Up Stage, then hands him to* GRACE *and the two exit.*

SCENE EIGHT

The EARL *takes out a pair of binoculars from the desk as cries are heard off.*

TUCKER'S VOICE (*hysterical*). I done nothing! I want justice!

BROCKETT'S VOICE. Justice is what you're going to get, Tucker. If he gives you any trouble, Fraser, break his arm. Now, MARCH!

TUCKER'S VOICE. I'm another Dreyfus case!

The EARL *leans on his cane and looks out of the french-windows through the binoculars.*

EARL OF GURNEY. Left-right, left-right, left-right, left-right, left-right.

DR HERDER, *tired and sick, enters with the aid of walking stick. He stares at the* EARL, *crosses, and stops beside Claire's outline on the floor.*

DR HERDER. Mir ist es winterlich im Leibe. She was cut up like meat.

EARL OF GURNEY. Left-right, left-right, left-right.

DR HERDER (*looks across at* EARL). It's not possible. I cured you. You could never turn violent. It's not in your illness. If I'd failed I'd know it. You'd retreat back into delusion. You haven't. You've accepted the world on its own terms. You believe more or less what other people believe.

EARL OF GURNEY (*turns, raising cane in salute*). En guarde. Your job's done, Herr Doktor. I'm adjusted to my environment. I brush my teeth twice daily. And smile. You trepanned me, opened my brain, telephoned the truth direct into my skull, as it were.

DR HERDER. Let me be the judge of that.

EARL OF GURNEY. There's only one Judge here. (*Looks at him through the wrong end of the binoculars.*) You've shrunk to a teutonic midget.

DR HERDER. You call that being adjusted?

EARL OF GURNEY. Behaviour which would be considered insanity in a tradesman is looked on as mild eccentricity in a lord. I'm allowed a certain lat-i-tude. (*He lunges at* DR HERDER.)

DR HERDER (*involuntarily parrying stroke with his stick*). I want to know about Claire.

EARL OF GURNEY. An irreversible rearrangement of her structural molecules has taken place, Doctor. She's dead. One of the facts of life.

DR HERDER. I know that.

EARL OF GURNEY. She lies stinking. Algo mortis, rigor mortis, livor mortis. She's turning to slime, Doctor. She's puss. Doctor, stinking puss, Doctor!

DR HERDER. I don't wish to know that!

EARL OF GURNEY. Then kindly leave the stage. (*Lunges.*) These are scientific facts.

DR HERDER (*parrying*). You killed her.

EARL OF GURNEY. A touch.

DR HERDER. You killed heeeeeeeeer.

He leaps at the EARL, *flailing wildly with his stick.*

EARL OF GURNEY (*parrying the stroke*). Ha, a swordsman worthy of of me steel. Didn't we meet at Heidelberg?

DR HERDER. You killed her!

EARL OF GURNEY (*driving him back*). You were fornicating lovers. Sperm dancers.

DR HERDER. It's a lie. Lady Claire meant nothing to me.

EARL OF GURNEY. Cock-a-doodle-do!

DR HERDER (*lashes out*). *You* killed her.

EARL OF GURNEY (*beating off the attack*). I'm cured, Herr Doktor, M.D., Ph.D. You cured me. I was a pale lovesick straw-in-the-air moon-looney. You changed me into a murderer, is that what you're saying?

DR HERDER (*attacking wildly*). Yes. No. Yes. May God forgive me.

EARL OF GURNEY. *Never*. What proof have you?

DR HERDER. I don't need proof, I *know*.

EARL OF GURNEY (*parrying with contemptuous ease*). Physician heal thyself. Don't you recognize the symptoms? You suddenly *know* against all the evidence. you don't need proof from anybody or anything. This monstrous belief of yours that I'm guilty is a clear case of paranoia. I've heard of 'transference', Doctor, but this is ridiculous! . . . if they ask about me at the trial, tell them the truth.

DR HERDER. What truth?

EARL OF GURNEY. That I'm a hundred per cent normal. (*He lunges and hits* DR HERDER, *who sits with a bump.*) Touché, Herr Doktor.

Clicking his heels, he salutes with his cane and crosses Up Stage Right. DR HERDER *remains on the floor. The lights dim slightly as he punches the ground in frustration.*

DR HERDER. He's right. He is normal. It's only a feeling. (*Shudders.*) I can't rely on feelings. Everything he's done conforms to a classic recovery pattern. His occasional paralalia is normal. Even his trying to blackmail me into saying he's completely normal, is normal. Natural I should have doubts.

This is pioneer work. Claire's death, one of those terrible ironies – nothing to do with the case. Unpleasant as he is, the good lord's himself again . . . My head's splitting. I've had an abdomen full of the upper classes. Claire, Claire, I should have specialized in heart diseases. (*Suddenly trembling with rage.*) *Cock-a-doodle-do*. Scheisshund! He made me deny you. (*He picks up and clasps cardboard outline tenderly.*) *Cock-a-doodle-do. Cock-a-doodle-do. Cock-a-doodle-do.*

He exits crowing with the cardboard outline.

SCENE NINE

SIR CHARLES *and* GRACE *enter Up Stage Centre.*

SIR CHARLES. *There.* It's what I've always said. You simply can't give the working-class money.

GRACE (*to the* EARL). It must have been a terrible shock for you, Sweet. Someone like Jeeves – someone you've known all your life turning out to be a killer. I was proud of you.

SIR CHARLES. Yes, Jack, this time you behaved like a Gurney should.

GRACE. You might apologize for all the stinking things you've said about him.

SIR CHARLES. Jack understands. I did what I had to.

EARL OF GURNEY. I won't forget what you did, Charles. (*Arm round* GRACE's *shoulder.*) Or you, my dear.

GRACE (*eagerly*). Jack, let's take off. It's been hell here. We need a holiday.

EARL OF GURNEY. No. here I stand. Now our little local difficulty has been solved I must show myself. It'll be the perfect story-book ending.

DINSDALE *enters carrying the* EARL's *Parliamentary robes.*

I'm taking my seat in the House of Lords.

SIR CHARLES. What . . . ?

GRACE (*disturbed*). What, now? So soon after your illness? I mean, are you ready for them?

EARL OF GURNEY. Are *they* ready for me, madam?

DINSDALE. We're going to work as a team once I get elected. Jack in the Lords, me in the 'other place'. We think alike on lots of things.

DINSDALE *helps the* EARL *on with his Parliamentary robes.*

SIR CHARLES. It's asking for trouble. What happens if you have a relapse? Fine spectacle you'd make, gibbering in the Upper House.

GRACE. You're so bloody tactful, Charles. (*Helps* DINSDALE.) If Jack thinks he's ready, then he's ready and I'm with him all the way.

SIR CHARLES. It's out of the question.

EARL OF GURNEY. Who asked you a question, pray? Did anybody here ask him a question?

They shake their heads.

Nobody asked a question so I'll ask a question. Who's the legit head of the family Gurney-cum-Gurney?

SIR CHARLES. You are, Jack, but . . .

EARL OF GURNEY. Don't let me hear you answering unasked questions again.

DINSDALE. Don't make a complete ass of yourself, Father.

GRACE. From now on just keep quiet, Charles.

EARL OF GURNEY. Your days of hard manipulating are over. Your brain's silting, Charles!

SIR CHARLES (*starts to grow old, his limbs shake slightly*). Don't talk to me like that! After all I've done. (*Voice quavers.*) Where'd you be without me? No wife, no Gurney heir without me – answer me, sir! (*Passes hands over hair and moustache: they turn white.*) I'm giving you the benefit of my experience, years of . . .

DINSDALE *sniggers*.

SIR CHARLES (*petulantly*). What are you sniggering at, you young pup?

DINSDALE. I wasn't sniggering.

SIR CHARLES. You were sniggering too. I know sniggering when I hear it, I'm not deaf. You've got nothing to snigger about. It'll happen to you one day. You'll be standing there and then suddenly nobody's taking any notice. You start coughing and coughing. Skin goes dry and the veins show through. Everything turns watery. It dribbles away, bowels, eyes, ears, nose . . . hmm. The hard thing is you're still twenty-one inside, but outside your feet go *flop, flop, flop, flop*, nothing you can do, *flop, flop, flop* . . .

The EARL *points to* SIR CHARLES, DINSDALE *nods and lead him firmly Up Stage*.

DINSDALE. That's enough, Father. You've had a long innings. It's beddy-byes and milk-rusks for you now.

GRACE (*carefully adjusting the* EARL'S *robe*). He's getting tiresome, but I feel obligated. He did introduce us, Honey. Luckily Dinsdale can handle him. That boy's come on. He worships you, you know.

EARL OF GURNEY. Splendid fella', Dinsdale.

GRACE. Guess we've all changed. You're more than just cured, Jack. People look up to you now. You've got something extra. What we used to call star quality!

EARL OF GURNEY. Ek, ek, ek, ek. It's going to be a triumphant climax.

GRACE. Talking about climaxes, we must get together again. We were more loving when you were batty. (*Closer to him*.) Now it should be even better. Do you love me, Jack?

EARL OF GURNEY. Y'know, in Roman times it was always the women who turned down their thumbs when defeated gladiators asked for mercy, Annie.

GRACE (*laughing*). Annie? Why Annie?

EARL OF GURNEY. Mary, Annie, Elizabeth, Catherine, Marie Kelly – a name by any other name would smell as sweet.

GRACE (*anxiously*). Jack, you're not going off again?

EARL OF GURNEY. It's nothing m'dear. Don't forget I've a big day ahead of me. I'm speaking in the House of Lords.

GRACE (*relieved*). Oh, you've got first-night nerves. Don't worry, you'll kill 'em.

EARL OF GURNEY. In time. Perhaps.

GRACE. I know it. Then you'll get around to me, I hope. Promise?

The EARL *nods, smiling.*

Jack, Jack, you're so attractive when you smile like that. (*Kisses him.*) Jack, Jack . . .

EARL OF GURNEY. Must get my grunch thoughts in order, marshal my facts, prepare my argument, pro and contra.

GRACE. You don't have to worry. After all, you're one of 'em, only more so. Be your own sweet self and they'll adore you as I adore you, Jack. (*Kissing him again and moving Up Stage.*) I just love happy endings.

The lights dim. The 'Pomp and Circumstance March' is played softly over.

SCENE TEN

The image of the EARL *in his Parliamentary robes Down Stage Centre is menacing as he hunches his shoulder and drags his leg.*

EARL OF GURNEY (*softly*). Tash t'ur tshh t'aigh, s'sssh kkk? Freee 'eee u Me Me Me epeeeeee . . . tita a-a-a- grahhh scrk Khraht! (*Sounds now coming from back of throat, rising intensively.*) Grak

GRACK. Graaa gruuuuuuuaaKK ka-ka-ka-ka-ka. YU. OOOO. YU. (*Arm jerks out convulsively at audience, his leg twists under him.*) YU. Screee. Fuuuuuuth, CRUUUKK-aa-K. (*Grinds heel into ground, face contorted with rage.*) HRRRUUUR TRUGHUUUK. (*As if bringing up phlegm, the cries now come from the pit of the stomach.*) Ha-CH-U-UR-UR. URRR. GoooooaRCH. TROKK! EK-K-Y. Arri-Bra-K-Yi-Skiiii, Arrk-ar-rk ARR ARR K-K-K-K, YIT YIT TRUGHUUGH ARK KKK A-A-A-A-A-A-KRUTK! aaaaaaaaaaaAAA-ARRRRRR!

SCENE ELEVEN

Even as the scream dies away a backcloth with a blow-up photograph of Westminster captioned 'House of Lords' is lowered, Stage Centre. On either side of it massive purple drapes. The 'Pomp and Circumstance March' is loud now as two tiers of mouldering dummies dressed as Lords and covered with cobwebs are pushed on either side, Stage Right and Left. Smothered in age-old dust, three goitred LORDS *with bloated stomachs and skull-like faces crawl on stage groaning, to take their places beside the dummies and the* EARL OF GURNEY. *One of them drags a skeleton behind him. The music stops as the* FIRST LORD *hauls himself as upright as his twisted body allows.*

1ST LORD (*croaking*). My Lords, I wish to draw attention to the grave disquiet felt throughout the country at the increase in immorality.

2ND LORD (*wheezing*). I must support the noble lord. For thirteen years there has been no flogging, and there has been a steadily rising volume of crime, lawlessness and thuggery. I believe the cissy treatment of young thugs and hooligans is utterly wrong.

3RD LORD. My Lord, we must step up the penalties by making hanging and flogging the punishments for certain State crimes. In order to protect the public the criminal must be treated as an animal.

The EARL OF GURNEY *jerks up. All eyes on him.* DINSDALE *and* SIR CHARLES *hobbling on two walking sticks, enter Wings Left.*

EARL OF GURNEY. My Lords, I had doubts about speaking here but after what I've heard, I realize this is where I belong. My Lords, these are grave times, killing times. Stars collapse, universes shrink daily, but the natural order is still crime – guilt – punishment. Without pause. There is no love without fear. By His hand, sword, pike and grappling-hook, God, The Crowbar of the World, flays, stabs, bludgeons, mutilates. Just as I was – is – have been – flayed, bludgeoned . . . (*Recovering.*) You've forgotten how to punish, my noble lords. The strong MUST manipulate the weak. That's the first law of the Universe – was and ever shall be world without end. The weak would hand this planet back to the crabs and primeval slime. The Hard survive, the Soft quickly turn to corruption. (*Shuddering.*) *God the Son* wants nothing only to give freely in love and gentleness. It's loathsome, a foul perversion of life! And must be rooted out. *God the Father* demands, orders, controls, crushes. We must follow Him, my noble lords. This is a call to greatness . . . On, on you noblest English.
I see you stand like greyhounds in the slips
Straining upon the start. The game's afoot
Follow your spirit; and upon this charge
Cry, God for Jack, England and Saint George.

A pause, then all burst into spontaneous shouts of 'hear-hear', 'bravo', as the excited PEERS, *waving order-papers, stumble over to congratulate the* EARL.

DINSDALE. Bravo! Bravo! You see, Father, you see. He's capable of anything!

SIR CHARLES (*waving stick excitedly*). *He's one of us at last!*

They all exit except the EARL, *singing exultantly.*

ALL (*singing*). 'Let us now praise famous men
And our fathers that begat us.
Such as did there rule in their kingdoms
Men renowned for their power.'

EPILOGUE

The EARL *is alone amongst the dummies. The chorus fades down with the lights.* GRACE *enters Up Stage Centre singing, in a black night-dress.*

GRACE (*singing*). 'Along came Jack, not my type at all . . .
You'd meet him on the street and never notice him . . .
But his form and face, his manly grace. Makes me – *thrill* . . .
I love him . . .'

He stands smiling as she circles him sensually.

'I love him, because he's . . . wond-er-ful . . .'

She yields as he pulls her close.

'Because he's just my Jack.'

Faint street-cries are heard over and they kiss passionately. As the EARL *envelops her in his Parliamentary robes, his hand reaches for his pocket. The lights fade down slowly, then, out of the darkness, a single scream of fear and agony.*

Curtain.